Disabled Students in Education:

Technology, Transition, and Inclusivity

David Moore
Leeds Metropolitan University, UK

Andrea Gorra
Leeds Metropolitan University, UK

Mike Adams
Essex Coalition of Disabled People, UK

John Reaney
Leeds Metropolitan University, UK

Helen Smith
Leeds Metropolitan University, UK

Information Science
REFERENCE

Managing Director:	Lindsay Johnston
Senior Editorial Director:	Heather Probst
Book Production Manager:	Sean Woznicki
Development Manager:	Joel Gamon
Development Editor:	Michael Killian
Acquisitions Editor:	Erika Gallagher
Typesetters:	Jennifer Romanchak, Mackenzie Snader
Print Coordinator:	Jamie Snavely
Cover Design:	Nick Newcomer, Greg Snader

Published in the United States of America by
Information Science Reference (an imprint of IGI Global)
701 E. Chocolate Avenue
Hershey PA 17033
Tel: 717-533-8845
Fax: 717-533-8661
E-mail: cust@igi-global.com
Web site: http://www.igi-global.com

Library of Congress Cataloging-in-Publication Data

Disabled students in education: technology, transition, and inclusivity / David Moore ... [et al.].
. p. cm.
 Includes bibliographical references and index.
 Summary: "This book reports on research projects aimed at improving the educational prospects of disabled people, through its discussion of three main themes--technology, transition and inclusivity"--Provided by publisher.
  ISBN 978-1-61350-183-2 (hardcover) -- ISBN 978-1-61350-184-9 (ebook) -- ISBN 978-1-61350-185-6 (print & perpetual access) 1. People with disabilities--Education. 2. Inclusive education. 3. People with disabilities--Effect of technological innovations on. I. Moore, David, 1950-
 LC4015.D545 2012
 371.9'046--dc23
 2011020010

British Cataloguing in Publication Data
A Cataloguing in Publication record for this book is available from the British Library.

Table of Contents

Section 1
Technology

Section 2
Transition

Section 3
Inclusivity

Detailed Table of Contents

Section 1
Technology

Chapter 1

   Simon Ball, JISC TechDis, UK

This chapter describes some of the techniques and considerations that teachers can use to make their teaching more inclusive. The techniques are usable without requiring a high level of technological expertise or investment of time. The chapter highlights case studies where technology has been used successfully to develop aspects of inclusive practice.

Chapter 2

   J.A. Renshaw, Leeds Metropolitan University, UK
   B. Boullier, Hollybank Trust, UK
   S. Geddes, Hollybank Trust, UK
   A. Moore, Hollybank Trust, UK

This chapter describes research investigating the feasibility of using eye tracker technology as an aid to the teaching of symbol recognition to people with profound multiple learning difficulties (PMLD). An eye tracker can be used to provide accurate and relevant real-time information concerning where a student is looking as they search for frequently used symbols. It is argued that the system has the potential to provide a rich way of communicating and gives instantaneous feedback on symbol recognition performance, thus enabling teachers to change their teaching strategies if necessary.

Chapter 3

Damian Copeland, Leeds Metropolitan University, UK

This chapter argues that 'haptic' (touch-based) technologies can assist people with visual impairment in their every-day life. It provides a background to the technologies and identifies how they can be used in educational contexts. This is important not least because the use of haptics within formal education has been limited, particularly in post-primary education.

Chapter 4

John Gray, Leeds Metropolitan University, UK
Gill Harrison, Leeds Metropolitan University, UK
Andrea Gorra, Leeds Metropolitan University, UK
Jakki Sheridan-Ross, Leeds Metropolitan University, UK

This chapter discusses the use of software that simulates disabilities. The software has been used within a computer aided test, with a view to raising awareness of disability issues amongst university staff. The authors provide evidence that for most users their awareness of disability issues increased because of using the simulation software.

Chapter 5

David Moore, Leeds Metropolitan University, UK

This chapter reviews recent work concerning computer systems for people with autism. It argues that autism-specific systems may play a beneficial role in the education of students with autism. The chapter also outlines a number of apparent weaknesses that currently exist in this research area.

Chapter 6

Salima Y Awad Elzouki, Leeds Metropolitan University, UK
Bridget Cooper, Sunderland University, UK

This chapter reports on an extensive longitudinal study in a unit for children with severe autism and learning difficulties. The primary focus is on the potential use of computer technology to help with 'theory of mind' concepts. The authors argue that emotional understanding can potentially be enhanced through computer based activities but that this is uniquely different for each individual.

Section 2
Transition

This chapter argues for the importance of pro-actively engaging disabled learners in events and activities designed to encourage their participation in Higher Education. The barriers that might be faced by disabled learners are discussed. The chapter gives a detailed analysis of how a specific regional partnership in the UK has tackled these issues, with a view to making transition to University smoother.

The authors argue that far fewer people with autism are successful at gaining admission to University than should be the case. The authors also examine the difficulties likely to be faced by students with autism when they do get into University. A number of important recommendations to improve provision is offered.

This chapter contains a critical appraisal of the social model of disability. It is argued that, the hitherto valuable role of the social model of disability notwithstanding, the model has now been assimilated within dominant discourses, and has thus undermined the drive to change the life experiences of disabled people. Examples from psychiatry and mental health are used to support and illustrate this argument.

Section 3
Inclusivity

The authors discuss recent policy developments in the UK and the impact of these developments on the way institutions organise their support structures and strategies. It is argued that the current funding model adopted in the UK compels students to take on the identity of a disabled student. The chapter discusses the potentially problematic connotations associated with this.

Chapter 11

This chapter presents a case study of a major UK University and its work to ensure inclusivity for all students. A key aspect of this has been the establishment of a forum of staff and students to represent, campaign for and raise awareness of the needs of disabled people in the University. The author offers a series of recommendations for other organisations wishing to establish such a forum.

Chapter 12

This chapter examines the nature and level of support that might be expected to be provided by universities and colleges to their disabled students, in the specific case of Northern Ireland. It is argued that that much progress has been made in terms of physical accessibility, but that much work is still required to establish a strategic approach to the provision of a high quality service. The chapter offers important practical insights into the demanding challenge of inclusivity in a complex Further and Higher Education system.

Chapter 13

This chapter discusses a study that investigated the views of dyslexic university students and their learning support staff concerning the provision made for dyslexia support in Higher Education. The author suggests how the views of diverse stakeholders might be better used to improve learning support provision for dyslexic students. Implications for policy and practice are discussed.

Chapter 14

The focus in this chapter is on physical education and the 'lived experience' of this by young people with disabilities. The authors argue for the use of an 'inclusive research' approach when researching disabilities. They also advocate the use of 'narratives', ie stories based on research data, and demonstrate their use in a seminar designed to promote student thinking about the meaning and experiences of education for people with disabilities.

Chapter 15

Alan Hurst, National Bureau for Students with Disabilities, UK

This chapter provides compelling evidence of the need for more and better staff training. The author discusses important practical issues such as what staff development sessions should contain, how they should be presented and who should be involved. Examples of tasks that have been found to be valuable in disability education sessions are also offered.

Chapter 16

Michael Adams, Essex Coalition of Disabled People, UK
Sally Brown, Leeds Metropolitan University, UK

The chapter provides an overall summary of the progress made by Higher Education across the UK in making inclusive learning, teaching and assessment practices a reality. It discusses the advances, and the many inhibitors to advance, that have occurred in recent years. The authors argue for a 'narrative for the future' that has 'disabled people at the heart of solutions'.

Preface

This book contains chapters that report on 15 research projects aimed at improving the educational prospects of disabled people. Recent legislation (e g in the UK 'SENDA', the Special Educational Needs and Disability Act (2001)), has increasingly focused attention on the rights of disabled people. Much remains to be done to bring this to fruition, however. For example Adams, in the final chapter of this book, points out that official UK figures show that in 2005, 18 year old disabled people in the UK were only 40% as likely to go to university as their non-disabled peers. The inequity of such a position is exacerbated by the fact that it is widely believed that education is a primary means by which disabled people can lead a full and productive life. As Hurst (1996) has argued, when disabled people enter Higher Education they are taking an opportunity to increase their knowledge, to develop social skills, to obtain good qualifications, and to expose themselves to debate and discussion; all of which constitute an important experience for inclusion. It is hoped that this book will contribute to raising awareness of the current inequities, and more importantly, give practical advice on how this might be achieved.

Perhaps the stereotypical view of disability is that it involves a physical impairment such as not being able to walk. Brown and Adams (2006) argue that, at least as far as UK Higher Education is concerned, many of the needs of physically disabled people are successfully addressed. Brown and Adams also argue that the challenge now is to ensure that, having made the physical adjustments to enable disabled people to participate in Higher Education, their educational needs are met. It is this challenge with which the current volume is concerned. Given this, it is not surprising, perhaps, that most (but not all) of the chapters are concerned with what might be called "cognitive disabilities".

As the book title suggests, three overarching themes are discussed: technology, transition and inclusivity. There can be little doubt that the rapid technological developments that have characterised the decades since the middle of the nineteenth century have given great scope for improving the quality of life of disabled people. William Horwood's highly recommended novel *Skallagrig* (1987) gives a very moving if fictional account of the transformation in the life of its central character, brought about by developments in computing. More recently, Shneiderman and Plaisant (2010, p 49) argue that "the potential for benefit to people with disabilities is one of the gifts of computing".

For everyone, transition is an important, and often a very challenging, aspect of life in general and of educational life in particular. Key educational transitions are the initial transition from the home to an educational establishment and then, in the UK, from primary to secondary school (in the UK at around the age of 11 or 12), from secondary education to tertiary education or work (in the UK at around the age of 16), from tertiary to Higher Education or work (in the UK tertiary education typically ends at the age of around 18) and finally from Higher Education into work. Not all these transitions apply to everyone, of course, depending on the age at which they leave education and enter the workforce. What probably does apply to everyone is that each transition, as well as being, by definition, a state of change, tends to represent a particularly challenging period. For disabled people the challenge may be greatly magnified. A person with Asperger Syndrome, for example, may have struggled and worked hard to establish a relatively stable and comfortable life within the social context of their (typically small) primary school, only to have to face the daunting challenge of making sense of the much bigger and more complex social context at secondary school. It is for reasons like this that transition features heavily in this book.

Our final theme, inclusivity, is an important one in education for two main reasons. There has been, certainly in the UK, a debate about whether to integrate disabled people into 'mainstream' education or to maintain separate specialist institutions for disabled people. The debate remains a live one, with advocates of both positions much in evidence, but currently in the UK the tendency is for the former position – integration - to hold sway. The second reason for the importance of the theme is that there is a debate in education between an 'adjustment' model and an 'inclusivity' model. The former, which seems to be currently the predominant one in the UK involves, for example, setting an assignment or examination and then making adjustment for disabled students; a typical example is to give a dyslexic student 25% extra time on an examination, and perhaps a separate examination room and perhaps an amanuensis. Proponents of an inclusivity model, by contrast, argue that if assessments are designed appropriately in the first place, such that all student needs are catered for, there should be no need for adjustments.

These, then are our three themes. As one would expect, the themes interact with one another in interesting ways. Modern advances in educational technology, as discussed for example in Simon Ball's chapter, give an excellent example of how technology is being and can be used to assist the education of disabled and non-disabled students. But equally the technology can be used to increase inclusivity and ease transitions. Similarly, the chapter by John Gray et al discusses how simulation technology may make educators more aware of the difficulties they may inadvertently cause disabled students in the work they set. We have seen this chapter as part of the technology theme, but it could equally be part of the inclusivity theme, since an awareness of how coursework might be perceived by disabled students should lead to additional inclusivity being built into the work.

We turn now to give a brief précis of each of the chapters in the book, starting with the technology theme. Simon Ball's chapter, *The Art of the Possible*, in many ways sets the scene for the technology section of the book, by giving a very useful overview of the current state of the art of educational technologies that are designed to help disabled students. Ball argues that technology can be utilised in many circumstances in teaching to improve accessibility and inclusion. He presents a number of techniques that teachers can use to make their teaching more inclusive without requiring a high level of technological expertise or indeed a large investment of time input. The chapter also provides some very useful case studies of the successful use of technology in inclusive practice.

Difficulties in communicating can prevent those with profound multiple learning difficulties (PMLD) from fulfilling their needs and ambitions. Tony Renshaw, Brian Boullier, Stuart Geddes and Ailsa Moore describe, in their chapter, *An Assessment of Eye Tracking as an Educational Aid for People with Profound Multiple Learning Difficulties (PMLD)*, how a non-invasive eye tracking technology is used to provide those with PMLD, with a richer way of communicating. This eye tracking technology records information as to where a participant with profound multiple learning difficulties is actually looking, providing a more precise alternative to the traditional method of eye pointing at symbols. The authors argue that the eye tracking system gives immediate feedback on symbol recognition performance which not only enables teachers to adapt their teaching strategies but also facilitates a richer interactive experience between them and their student.

'Haptic' or touch-based technologies can assist people with visual impairment in their every-day life, as particularly those who are deaf-blind rely heavily on their sense of touch. While Braille is probably the technology most commonly associated with tactile feedback, the number of its users is falling. Only a small number of touch-based or haptic devices provide assistance to blind or severely visually impaired people. In his chapter *Haptics as an Assistive Technology*, Damian Copeland provides a fascinating background to haptic technologies and identifies how these can be used in educational contexts. This is important not least because the use of haptics within formal education has been limited, particularly in post-primary education. Despite usefully identifying some multimodal devices, Copeland concludes that further research is required to develop an affordable refreshable haptic graphic display.

John Gray, Gill Harrison, Andrea Gorra and Jakki Sheridan-Ross discuss in their chapter, *Using a Computer Aided Test to Raise Awareness of Disability Issues Amongst University Teaching Staff*, the use of a computer aided test that has been developed to help university staff to become aware of issues faced by students with disabilities. This software is designed to demonstrate some accessibility issues associated with a range of disabilities, such as visual, hearing, physical and cognitive impairments. In addition, the test provides advice on good practice and website links to further relevant information. The test has been used to train university staff in disability issues and has proved a successful staff development tool. Staff reactions to the test have been positive and feedback indicates that using the computer aided simulation has generated an increased awareness of disability issues and an understanding by staff of the need to make changes to their future practice to improve the educational experience of disabled students.

Technology in the form of computer-based learning systems can be helpful for people with autism. David Moore argues in his chapter *Computer Based Learning Systems for People with Autism* that there is considerable evidence that people with autism tend to enjoy working with computers, because, for example, they offer a relatively controlled environment where users can progress at their own pace. This chapter not only reviews recent work concerning computer systems for people with autism but most importantly makes a case for the use of autism-specific systems to play a beneficial role in the education of students with autism.

Furthermore, Moore introduces in his chapter software that has been developed as part of a research project and which addresses some shortcomings of existing computer-based learning systems. This system allows users to create their own individualised scenarios for social skills education for those with autism and can be requested free of charge from the author.

Moore argues that there are a number of weaknesses currently in the research concerning computer systems for people with autism. One of these weaknesses is that most work to date has investigated the technology for people with Asperger Syndrome (generally seen as a mild form of autism). Very little attention has been paid to the important issue of whether and how people with severe autism might benefit from the technology. The chapter by Salima Elzouki and Bridget Cooper, *Understanding and Enhancing Emotional Literacy in Children with Severe Autism Using Facial Recognition Software* reports research designed to begin to address this weakness. The research involved an extensive longitudinal study in a unit for children with severe autism and learning difficulties. The authors argue that emotional understanding can potentially be potentially enhanced through computer based activities but that this is uniquely different for each individual.

We turn now to the transition theme of the book. As argued earlier, disabled people remain disproportionately under-represented in Higher Education. One of the factors behind this is a view sometimes taken by young disabled people that Higher Education is "not for us". An important aspect, therefore, of transition into Higher Education is to encourage disabled people to apply in the first place. It is this issue that underpins the chapter by Helen Smith, *Let's Get Set for University!* Smith argues for the importance of pro-actively engaging disabled learners in events and activities designed to encourage their participation in Higher Education. The chapter discusses the barriers that might be faced by disabled learners and gives a detailed analysis of how a specific regional partnership in the UK has tackled these issues, with a view to making transition to university smoother.

The theme of barriers to entry is also picked up in the chapter by Salima Elzouki, Elizabeth Guest and Chris Adams, in their chapter *Students with Autism in Higher Education*. The authors argue that far fewer people with autism get into university than ought, ethically and pragmatically, to be the case. When students with autism do get to university, they may face many difficulties, and the authors movingly illustrate this through a narrative of two such students and through a case study of a further student as written by his social worker. The authors also provide a case study of how a specific university supports students with autism, and offer a number of important recommendations arising from their empirical work.

The way in which disabled people are treated in education and elsewhere is likely to be dependant, at least in part, on the view of disability taken by their educators and indeed by society as a whole. Until recently the medical model held sway, a model in which disability and impairment are seen as being the same thing and are seen as located in the individual, not in society and structures. In recent decades, however, this has tended to be displaced in favour of the social model of disability; in this model impairment is believed to lead to disability because societal processes and structures are arranged in such a way that some impaired people cannot participate; this is taken to include attitudes, not just physical barriers. Bill Penson, in his chapter *Reappraising the Social Model of Disability: A Foucauldian Reprise*, interrogates the social model of disability from the perspective of the work of the French philosopher Michel Foucault (1926–1984), in particular Foucault's idea of 'docile bodies'. Whilst acknowledging the hitherto valuable role of the social model of disability, Penson puts forward an argument that the social model has now been assimilated within dominant discourses, and that this has undermined the drive to change the life experiences of disabled people. He cites examples from psychiatry and mental health to support this and suggests, following Foucault, that the disabled body is positioned within medical and legal discourses which maintain the subjugation of that body. This is a thought-provoking chapter which questions our adherence to the social model of disability.

The book's final set of chapters addresses the issue of inclusivity. The potential dichotomy between striving to make the university experience inclusive for all students, when the existing funding model to support disabled students centres around making individual adjustments, is highlighted in the chapter, *Support for Disabled Students in Higher Education: A Move Towards Inclusion*, by John Reaney, Andrea Gorra and Hanim Hassan. Using Leeds Metropolitan University as a case study, Reaney, Gorra and Hassan discuss recent policy developments in the UK, particularly the introduction of Disabled Students' Allowances (DSA), and their subsequent impact on the way institutions have organised their support structures and strategies. Additionally, it raises the issue of how the current funding model compels students to take on the identity of a disabled student and discusses the potentially negative connotations associated with this whilst making suggestion for further research.

Ian Clarke, in his chapter *Disabled Students in Higher Education: Lessons from Establishing a Staff Disability Forum* presents a case study of a major UK university and its work to ensure inclusivity for all students. A key aspect of this has been the establishment of a forum of staff and students which works to represent, campaign for and raise awareness of the needs of disabled people in the university. Specifically, the forum has a remit of initiating and monitoring key actions such as reviewing disability education, running major consultation events and organising a Quality Enhancement Audit, which includes the important issue of seeking to avoid unwitting discrimination in policies or procedures. The chapter contains valuable lessons concerning inclusivity in Higher Education institutes, and the author offers a series of recommendations for other organisations wishing to establish such a forum.

The nature and level of support that might be expected to be provided by universities and colleges to their disabled students is examined in the specific case of Northern Ireland in Pauline Dowd's chapter, *Supporting Learning in Further and Higher Education in Northern Ireland*. Dowd argues that while much progress has been made across both Further and Higher Education sectors in Northern Ireland, in terms of physical accessibility, much work is still required particularly across the Further Education sector to establish a strategic approach to the provision of a high quality service which meets the requirements of the recent disability legislation in the UK. Dowd's chapter offers important practical insights into the demanding challenge of inclusivity in a complex Further and Higher Education system.

Dyslexia is the most prevalent disability in terms of student numbers in Higher Education in the UK. This makes the research study described in Tim Deignan's chapter *Modeling and Developing a Dyslexia Support System* particularly important. Deignan's exploratory study investigated the views of dyslexic university students and their learning support staff concerning the provision that is made for dyslexia support in Higher Education. He considers the implications of the study findings for policy and practice, and suggests how the views of diverse stakeholders might be better used to improve learning support provision for dyslexic students.

Hayley Fitzgerald, Anne Jobling and Annette Stride, in their chapter *Inclusivity and Research: Capturing the Lived Experience of Young People with Disabilities*, argue powerfully for the use of an 'inclusive research' approach in general, and in particular when researching disabilities. They also advocate the use of 'narratives', ie stories based on research data. They provide two very moving narratives in the chapter, and demonstrate their use in a seminar designed to promote student thinking about the meaning and experiences of education for people with disabilities. The focus in the chapter is on physical education and the 'lived experience' of this by young people with disabilities. However, the narrative-based approach is likely to be very powerful in other areas of education also.

A vitally important aspect of the success or otherwise of disabled students is the ability of their teaching staff to cater for their specific needs; as with all students, their day to day educational experience in the tutorial room or lecturer theatre is of paramount importance. This suggests that staff training may be crucial, a theme that is discussed in Alan Hurst's chapter *Reflections on Personal Experiences of Staff Training and Continuing Professional Development for Academic Staff in the Development of High Quality Support for Disabled Students in Higher Education*. Hurst provides compelling evidence of the need for more and better training, by examining students' issues, staff concerns, and aspects of institutional policies. He goes on to discuss important practical issues such as what staff development sessions should contain, how they should be presented and who should be involved. Hurst also gives some very useful examples of tasks that have been found to be valuable in disability education sessions.

Finally, Mike Adams and Sally Brown round off the book by discussing the advances, and the many inhibitors to advance, that have occurred in the years between this current volume and their earlier book in a similar area (Adams & Brown, 2006). Adams and Brown also argue for a 'narrative for the future' that has 'disabled people at the heart of solutions'.

These, then, are the chapters. As well as the unifying themes of technology, transition and inclusivity, discussed earlier, there are other themes common to several chapters. Much of the book is concerned with what are sometimes called 'hidden disabilities', in particular, in the current case, dyslexia (chapters by Deignan, and Gray et al) and autistic spectrum conditions (chapters by Moore, Elzouki & Cooper, and Elzouki et al). This emphasis on hidden disabilities is in part a response to a concern that such disabilities have been under-researched hitherto. Another common theme arises from a belief that the success or otherwise of disabled students depends in large measure on the educational practices of the educational institution that they attend. Thus several chapters are case studies of specific organisations, namely those of Smith, Reaney et al, Clarke, Dowd, and Hurst. An important corollary to such a case study approach is insights into the 'lived experiences' of the students themselves. Two of the chapters, by Haley et al and by Elzouki and Cooper, give illuminating and moving portraits of such lived experiences, in very different educational establishments. A final common theme to many of the chapters is that they give practical advice and recommendations to administrators, practitioners and students, in particular, perhaps, the chapters by Ball, Elzouki et al, and Hurst. Similarly, Moore's chapter discusses software that is available for readers to request, and Gray et al's chapter refers readers to a website that enables readers to use their simulations.

As Mike Adams and Sally Brown argue in the final chapter of the book, many challenges remain to be addressed before disabled students have the equality of educational opportunities that, in both a pragmatic and ethical sense, they should have. We hope that this book will play some part in starting to meet these challenges. We anticipate that the book will be of interest to disabled students, their parents and teachers, and the people who run, and set policies for, their educational providers, and would welcome feedback from any reader on any of the issues the book raises.

REFERENCES

Adams, M., & Brown, S. (Eds.). (2006). *Towards Inclusive Learning in Higher Education: developing curricula for disabled students. Abingdon*. Routledge.

Horwood, W. (1987). *Skallagrig*. London: Penguin Books Ltd.

Hurst, A. (1996). Reflecting on researching disability and Higher Education . In Barton, L. (Ed.), *Disability and Society: emerging issues and insights*. London: Longman.

Shneiderman, B., & Plaisant, C. (2010). *Designing the User Interface*. Boston: Addison-Wesley.

Acknowledgment

The editors would like to thank the many people who have contributed to the Disability Research Group conferences upon which this book is largely based. In particular we thank Rhiannon Thomas-Osborne and Louise Conyard for their tireless work in organising the conferences and ensuring their smooth running.

We would also like to thanks the many reviewers of the chapters in the book: Arabella Ashfield, Zillah Boriston, Hannah Buckland, Belinda Cooke, Barry Fearnley, Thomas Fletcher, Dave Hufton, Ko Koens, James McGrath, Jayne Mothersdale, Carol Potter, Steve Robertson, Stephen Sayers, Jenny Seavers, Sue Sherwin, Meg Soosay, Stan Timmins, Pip Trevorrow, Andreas Walmsley, Paul Wetherly.

David Moore
Leeds Metropolitan University, UK

Andrea Gorra
Leeds Metropolitan University, UK

Mike Adams
Essex Coalition of Disabled People, UK

John Reaney
Leeds Metropolitan University, UK

Helen Smith
Leeds Metropolitan University, UK

Section 1
Technology

Chapter 1
The Art of the Possible:
Using Technology to Make Teaching More Inclusive

Simon Ball
JISC TechDis, UK

ABSTRACT

Inclusive practice is both an ethical and legal requirement in UK higher education. Technology can be utilised in many circumstances in teaching to improve accessibility and inclusion. Some techniques are very simple to learn and can potentially have a significant impact upon students. This chapter describes some of the simple techniques and considerations that teachers can use to make their teaching more inclusive without requiring a high level of technological expertise or time input. It also highlights some case studies where technology has been used successfully to uncover or develop an aspect of inclusive practice.

INTRODUCTION

Technology, possibly more than any other development in teaching in recent years, has the potential to provide and liberate, but there exists also a responsibility on educators to ensure it does not prevent and restrict. In the case of disabled

DOI: 10.4018/978-1-61350-183-2.ch001

students, this responsibility is a legal requirement (UK Government, 1995).

There is a vast variety of types of technology that can be added to the educator's palette of tools, with many purposes and myriad audiences (Hart, 2010). Technology should never be the driver for pedagogy, but rather a means to facilitate it, and in particular a means to facilitate inclusive pedagogy (Ball, 2009). All learning, teaching and assessment must be created with inclusion in mind to some degree. Technology can aid that inclusivity in many cases, although there are bound to be some occasions where the use of technology is not the best solution, which is entirely appropriate as technology is merely one of a suite of potential solutions.

More than aiding inclusivity, technology can also aid productivity, both on the part of the learner and the teacher (Ball and McNaught, 2008). We are not suggesting, as some have done before, that moving to electronic marking of scripts, for example, will suddenly result in a greatly reduced time on task for teachers, although in some cases this may well be the case (McCormack and Jones, 1998; Ryan et al., 2000). The technologies that are described in this chapter, however, are more than merely 'assistive technologies' aimed at users with very specific needs, such as screen reading software or voice recognition systems. Many of the tools we will highlight can potentially aid the productivity of all teachers/learners if used appropriately.

The increasing pervasiveness of technology into the realm of the classroom, lecture theatre, laboratory, studio and field offers an opportunity for increased engagement with a wider variety of learners (Roschelle et al., 2007). In some instances the characteristics of these learners are known and can be directly catered for via 'reasonable adjustments' (UK Government, 1995), but in most cases educators are not aware of the full range of needs and learning styles that may be present within any given student cohort (even where the cohort is 'known' it is likely that undisclosed or even undiagnosed disabilities may be present, in particular dyslexia or mental health issues) (University of Exeter, undated). The range of potential characteristics and needs across an educator's audience is as large as within the general populace, and learning, teaching and assessment must be designed and delivered with this factor very much in mind. This chapter will highlight

the effects that good and poor practice can have on the learner's experience. It will also provide examples of where the techniques have been successfully put into practice.

'Design for All' and the 'Holistic Approach'

In brief, 'Design for All' (also known as 'Universal Design') proposes the creation of a resource that is accessible to, and usable by, every member of the community for whose use it is intended (European Commission, undated). However, this very definition is a contentious one. Some would argue that 'Design for All' simply means the creation of a single resource that can be accessed and effectively used by every person on the planet. Others would argue that the creation of a range of different resources, all of which are suitable for some users, and which reach all users when taken as a whole, also fits within the definition of 'Design for All' (Aslaksen et al., 1997). Then there are those who would argue that 'Design for All' is an inappropriate term, detracting from the real aim which is to create resources that are fit for purpose, and therefore which serve the users for whom they are intended. Other terms have been suggested that more accurately fit the intention, such as 'User-Centred Design' or better still 'User-Sensitive Design' (Newell & Gregor, 2000). For the mainstream educator this debate is a side issue. What is important is that when designing or creating materials for learning, teaching or assessment, the designer takes consideration of the full range of characteristics and needs the audience will exhibit (including technological and informational as well as traditional 'accessibility' needs) and caters for as many of them as possible accordingly.

Many educators find the matrix of potential learner needs and helpful technologies a challenge that they do not have the time or skill to address, and seek a checklist or set of guidelines they can use. While some education institutions provide such checklists for specific areas (for example checklists on how to make documents or presentations more accessible (University of Bradford, undated)), there is no way to provide a comprehensive checklist as the area is much too diverse. Some have tried to apply the Web Accessibility Initiative Web Content Accessibility Guidelines to the field of teaching and learning, but as Kelly et al. (2004) suggest these are much too narrow and restrictive to be of use to an educator aiming to provide more inclusive learning, teaching and assessment. Instead, Kelly et al. (2004) propose that educators take a 'Holistic Approach' to designing and delivering learning, looking at the range of media available to support or deliver each task and selecting the best fit for the learner cohort. This implies that the way a particular piece of learning is delivered to one cohort may not be appropriate for the next cohort, and this is entirely appropriate for a flexible educator. The one great saving grace for the use of technology in teaching, learning and assessment is that in many cases formats are interchangeable, or at least content can be transposed, and so the task of re-evaluating and if necessary changing the way in which learning is delivered is not as great as it might otherwise be. This concept is explored much further in a subsequent article by Kelly et al. (2007).

It is important to note that mainstream educators are not expected to be experts in assistive technology. Indeed, the scope and function of the technologies available are always changing and there are experts who can advise on the way they interact with learning resources. Rather, educators should be aware of the ways in which users interact with learning materials, and the ways in which technology can enhance the learning, teaching and assessment process, and this is what this chapter aims to achieve.

ESTABLISHING THE PARAMETERS

Establishing Purpose of a Teaching Resource

When designing or creating learning, teaching or assessment resources, it is best practice to work from the intended learning outcomes, as we can then work backwards to analyse a range of potential pathways to achieving them. Determining the learning outcomes will outline what the resource aims to achieve and what it will deliver to learners (supporting Biggs' (1996) 'constructive alignment' theory). There may need to be separate considerations made for short and long term usage (for example materials designed for this year's 'known' student cohort may also serve future 'unknown' cohorts). Referring back to the learning outcomes will also keep any subsequent reviews, modifications or 'reasonable adjustments' relevant and on track.

There are many types of learning resource with an array of different purposes. The Accessibility Passport (Ball & Sewell, 2008) may be of use in establishing the purpose of a resource in relation to inclusivity. This tool enables the specifier and designer of a resource to record, via a series of prompt questions, the academic level the resource is intended for, or the accessibility features that were or were not designed in. For example, during the development of a resource, it may be the case that no consideration was made for blind users because the 'known' current cohort did not contain any such students, but noting this fact in the Accessibility Passport means that if someone is reusing the resource with future cohorts this may need to be revisited. This is a pragmatic way of achieving the 'anticipatory' requirement of the legislation (UK Government, 1995) without creating an unnecessary workload. For further information on the Accessibility Passport see www.accessibilitypassport.org.

Establishing Access

Alongside establishing the purpose of a given resource, consideration also needs to be made as to how and where the resource will be accessed. Will it be delivered to students directly? Could it have a life beyond its immediate delivery? Will it be open-access, behind a firewall, on a learning platform, or require user registration or verification? How might the resource be accessed: via a PC or Mac, a mobile device or a user with low internet connection speed (or all of the above)? In some cases it may even be relevant to consider how the resource interacts with assistive technologies, particularly if the resource is delivered via a subject-specific or relatively uncommon medium (for example LaTeX, or CAD). These are also key questions when planning the extent of the 'Design for All' commitment. For example one's commitment to attempt to 'Design for All' may be greater for a resource to be delivered to 400 learners each year for 5 years than for a resource to be used only once with a small cohort of 'known' students.

There is a range of documents that may prove useful in establishing the access conditions of a learning, teaching or assessment resource. The online resource 'Upwardly Mobile: A Guide to Getting Started with Inclusive Mobile Learning' (JISC TechDis, undated a) guides educators on how to use mobile devices to deliver inclusive learning. Another document that clearly introduces key accessibility principles, albeit in relation to the designing or commissioning of a website is 'Publicly Available Specification 78: Guide to good practice in commissioning accessible websites' (Disability Rights Commission, 2006).

The Types of Users

Once you have determined the purpose of your resource and the physical access to it in terms of technology (or devices) and security, you can begin to assess the likely characteristics of the users and plan the design and delivery of the resource accordingly. If the audience is discrete and known, certain assumptions can be made regarding the likely user characteristics in terms of level of academic ability (such as if the resource will be accessed only by final year undergraduates), or the mode of access (such as if the resource will only be accessible during supervised sessions in particular computer suites). However, as indicated above, assumptions about the users' needs or impairments cannot be made, because not all such needs are evident to the observer. If the audience is much wider or public, then few assumptions can be made. The discussion of user needs that follows can be utilised as a general guide to creating an inclusive learning environment, regardless of which needs may or may not be visible or invisible among the student cohort.

USER NEEDS: HOW TECHNOLOGY CAN BE USED TO INCLUDE DIFFERENT TYPES OF USERS

The user needs that may be expressed by users of a resource are many and varied, as any educator will know. Many users may not be aware of some of their needs or characteristics, and many more may have several needs, some of which require apparently conflicting accommodations. However, in terms of designing and delivering learning, teaching and assessment, most can be generalised into the following groups (LSIS, undated):

Mobility and Dexterity Needs

This group of users includes people who cannot physically access a computer using the conventional input devices (i.e. a keyboard or mouse). It may be considered reasonable to assume that all users will be able to input to a computer using some device, but not to predict what that device might be (for example students might use voice recognition software, virtual or physical head pointing or screen reading and navigating software). In its simplest form this means that resources should be navigable and usable by using only the keyboard (for example 'tabbing' from item to item on forms or hotspot diagrams) and by using only a click-input device (for example any data entry boxes and drop-down lists should be operable via an on-screen keyboard).

Visual Needs

Some users of the resource will have no vision (needing, for example, alternative text provision for images and graphics); some will have low vision (needing clear and consistent layout with a high degree of contrast). Some will be able to see only part of the screen at one time (for example if requiring magnification–therefore graphics and especially graphics depicting text need to be checked for pixelation issues). Some will be unable to distinguish certain, or indeed any, colours (thereby making it essential that colour alone is not used to convey information–such as question numbers in an online assessment changing colour when the question has been completed, where changing from a red cross to a green tick would provide a shape indication as well as a colour indication). These are all issues to consider when putting together a learning resource, and usually easy to simulate to some degree to check whether resources are accessible or not (see, for example, www.vischeck.com).

Auditory Needs

Some users of the resource will be Deaf and others hard of hearing. This has implications not just for the use of sound in the resource (audio and video files and related subtitling or transcription issues, for example), but also in that many deaf users' first language will be British Sign Language (BSL). BSL has a different structure and syntax from written or spoken English (and is recognised as a language in its own right) and so the use of Plain English will be beneficial to this group, as well as to other users for whom English is not their first language (for further information on the Plain English Campaign visit www.plainenglish.co.uk).

Cognitive Needs/Learning Difficulties/Learning Disabilities/Dyslexia

A high proportion (15-20% (Disabled World, 2010)) of the population has some kind of cognitive need or learning difficulty, including a variety of conditions known collectively as dyslexia (according to Jacklin et al. (2007) dyslexic students accounted for half of all declared disabilities in UK higher education in 2006). Other needs manifest in a variety of ways, such as difficulties with numbers, time or information management, navigation and short term memory. Ensuring the resource exhibits clarity of purpose, layout and structure will aid these users. Many students with dyslexia have a particular difficulty with reading high contrast text (for example black text on a white background) and prefer a reduced contrast such as navy on white, or black on cream. This particular preference is in direct contrast to the preference of many learners with low vision, who prefer high contrast. If using electronic media it is usually a relatively simple task to put into the hands of the learner the ability to alter colours and contrast to suit their needs–certainly much easier than if using traditional print media.

Technological Needs

Some users will be accessing the resource via a mobile device with a small screen–therefore you should test your resource to see how it exhibits on these devices. This may be especially the case with revision materials or lecture synopses placed on the learning platform. Some users may be accessing the web via a slow internet connection–you will need to ensure that any graphics or bandwidth-heavy features are used appropriately and that there is alternative information for those who cannot or do not wish to wait for the material to download. Some users may not have the technical ability or confidence to access or download complex or multimedia content. All content should be appropriately signposted and explained, with complex content available in alternative formats. Users who are not campus-based may not be able to access all materials placed on the learning platform due to security requirements–this should be checked prior to uploading resources.

Other Needs

There are myriad other needs that the user group will feature to some extent. These include needs related to specific conditions such as epilepsy or autism (for example it is common for people with autism to find flashing displays or repetitive sounds especially distracting, or to experience difficulty in interpreting two-dimensional representations of three-dimensional objects–see www.jisctechdis. ac.uk/simdis for a simulation of this effect).

One important point to note is that all of the good practice techniques described in this chapter to benefit these various groups of users will in fact benefit a much larger proportion of users than simply the groups listed here. Good practice in the design and delivery of learning, teaching and assessment resources will benefit all users (which is why completely new resources should be road-tested by a diverse range of users wherever possible, both disabled and non-disabled), and that is why this chapter does not focus on disability per se but on good (inclusive) practice.

GETTING STARTED: PRACTICAL TIPS ON EVERYDAY INCLUSIVE TECHNIQUES

Producing inclusive learning experiences need not and should not be a specialist subject. The more small modifications we can make to everyday

practice to make it more inclusive, the less need there will be for larger scale adjustments for which specialist input is required. This section highlights just a small selection of easy-to-implement techniques using commonplace or free technologies that can make an enormous difference to the inclusivity of learning, teaching and assessment.

Everyday Inclusion with Text Documents

Basic Best Practice with Text Documents

The simplest modification to everyday practice that will result in the most widespread potential impact is to adopt a more inclusive approach to producing text documents.

- Ensure the text is sans serif for online reading (e.g. Arial), with a minimum font size of 12. Evidence in this area is inconclusive, with some studies indicating that serif fonts (e.g. Times New Roman) are more readable for printed text and sans serif for online text, some suggesting there is no overall difference for readers with typical vision, and yet others claiming that sans serif fonts are more readable for people with dyslexia or visual impairment. For a summary of the literature up to 2005, see Poole (2005). If the evidence is suggesting that there is little difference for most users, but that sans serif fonts benefit some people in some circumstances, then there is no justification for **not** using a sans serif font unless other factors apply in a particular context. Guiding learners on how to change the font may be the best approach.
- Ensure the text is left aligned, not justified as justified text leads to 'rivers of white' (Page, 2009) appearing between unevenly spaced words, which can be a significant distraction to many readers.

- Clear space can be just as useful as the text! Over cluttering and complicating the page reduces readability.
- Avoid excessive use of capitalised, underlined or italicised text, consider bold for emphasis. If denoting quotes, indenting will mark them out visually without adding the unnecessary complication of italicising them, which prevents readers from making out the shape of words.

Best Practice with Printed Text Documents (see JISC TechDis (2009) for Further Details)

- Ensure the colour of the background and colour of text show good contrast, but without the glare of black on white.
- Printing on pale pastel colour backgrounds can increase readability for a number of users as it reduces the glare of white paper.
- A paper with high gloss can cause glare when reading, a matt paper should reduce glare. Unbleached paper is not only better for the environment, but more accessible due to reduced glare.
- Ensure any background is a continuous single colour. A patterned background decreases readability.

If You Only Have Time to Make One Change Right Away....

If you only have time to make one change immediately as a result of reading this chapter (and we sincerely hope that over time you will do more!), the biggest difference you can make to the widest range of potential readers of your documents is to utilise Heading Styles in the most common form of text document: those created using word processing software such as Microsoft ® Word, Open Office etc.

Styles and Headings

One of the most important things to consider when creating a document is the appropriate use of Styles and Headings. Microsoft® Word and Open Office have an inbuilt structuring system which should be used when creating any document. Heading tags can be used to denote headings and sub-headings thus providing an intrinsic structure.

Using Heading Styles is merely a slight adaptation to the way most of us instinctively format headings in our documents. Usually, because most of us are self-taught, we put our top level heading into a large font size, and make it bold, and sometimes underline it, then we use decreasing versions thereof for lower level headings. The same principles still apply when using Heading Styles but in terms of accessibility there is a wide difference, with documents created using Heading Styles being accessible via the Document Map or other overview features, which can enable users to navigate an appropriately styled long document, providing an aid in terms of keeping track of which section the user is reading and where it sits in the broader document structure. This can be of particular assistance to learners with dyslexia or visual impairment. Commercial mind mapping software often integrates with word processing tools, allowing a long document to be exported to a mind map in seconds, providing it has been structured using heading styles.

Using Audio to Enhance Text Documents

It is also possible to greatly increase the usability of a text document by adding an audio file. This could be a spoken version of the text within the document, or it could be used to add supplementary information, or to provide a description of an image for those that cannot see it – this is often more useful than a transcript if lots of technical words or names are present, as screen reading technology does not always pronounce those accurately. Inserting audio may however significantly increase the file size - this may be an issue for learners accessing over a slow connection.

Everyday Inclusion with Presentations

Accessible Presentations

A major part of the learning experience of a student can centre on presentation and lecture scenarios, therefore ensuring a basic understanding in accessible presenting techniques can greatly enhance the learning experience for a large number of students exhibiting a wide range of needs.

Best Practice with Presentation Technique

When physically presenting a session there are a number of tips and techniques which should be used to ensure that you are able to engage as many members of the audience as possible. The right delivery will ensure listeners gain the most possible out of the presentation.

- Face forward at all times when speaking, you may not know whether there are any lip readers in the audience.
- If available use a microphone, it may be connected to an induction loop and your voice may not carry as far as you think it does!
- Ensure you vocalise all information present on the slides, a visually impaired learner (or one sitting at the back of a large auditorium) will not be able to access the material on the screen. Stating 'this slide explains the concept' is not acceptable. However, reading out slides verbatim is not necessary as this may not be helpful for those that can read effectively.

- When taking questions from the audience, repeat it from the front, enabling all participants to hear the question.

Using Presentation Software Accessibly

When creating a Microsoft® PowerPoint or Open Office Impress slide show, regardless of whether it will be used in a delivery format or distributed electronically, a number of slide content issues should be considered:

- Use short concise ideas and content, using bullet points and lists where appropriate.
- When using bullet points and lists ensure every point is ended with punctuation (e.g. a full stop, semi-colon or comma). Ensuring this will enable a screen reader user to distinguish between different ideas. Without the presence of punctuation different ideas will be read as a single sentence, without pausing between concepts.
- Ensure the text is a minimum size of 24 where possible – if the text won't fit, then there is too much information for a single slide.
- Use the inbuilt slide design options within the software wherever possible. The slide design options can be accessed from Format > Slide Layout. By using these slide layout options all text inserted will appear within the presentation outline and will thus be accessible when the document is exported.

Accessibility Considerations of the Presentation Environment

The environment in which the presentation is being delivered will also affect the readability of material. For example, if presenting in a light room, display dark coloured text on a light coloured background (e.g. navy on cream). Conversely, if presenting in a darkened room, ensure the background colour is dark and the text light (e.g. yellow on black). If using a dark background ensure the weight of text is increased (e.g. put all text into bold). Remember in a room with no raised seating, the bottom of your slide will not be visible to those seated further back.

Use of the Notes Field

The Notes Field is one of the most important features which should be utilised when creating a Microsoft ® PowerPoint presentation that is going to have a life beyond the live presentation (i.e. distribution electronically or housing in a learning platform, for example). It provides an ideal opportunity to clarify or illuminate content presented on the slides. It is also important that the Notes Field is used to exemplify the meaning of any visual content, or to repeat any text added in the form of Text Boxes. For example if a presentation contains an image of a graph, the Notes Field should be used to explain the content of the graph and its reason for insertion. The reason for this is that screen reading software cannot access the slide directly. It can, however, access any information present in Outline View (i.e. text entered directly onto the slide template, but not text entered into additional Text Boxes – see the point relating to Slide Layout above) and the Notes Field. So all text not displayed in the Outline View should be copied into the Notes Field, along with full descriptions of any graphical information and the reason for its inclusion (for example it is insufficient to say 'This slide shows a representation of the Solar System' as there is no rationale included. It would be much better practice to add whatever you would have said verbally in relation to that image when delivering the presentation, perhaps 'This slide shows a representation of the Solar System, highlighting that the distances between the orbits of the outer four planets are much greater than between those of the inner four planets'.

Using Audio to Enhance Presentations

Audio files can be added to presentation slides in a similar way to text documents and can greatly enhance the usability of a presentation file placed on the web or on a learning platform i.e. a presentation that is being 'distributed' rather than 'presented'. Audio clips can be used to explain diagrams or flow charts, or to further illustrate the point being made on the slide. For example in a discussion of the use of music in psychotherapy, including examples of the types of music being discussed might help to illuminate the concept.

Using Audio to Enhance Presentations. Case Study 1: Increasing Use of Sound and Images in PowerPoint (Part 1)

The JISC TechDis HEAT Scheme (JISC TechDis, undated b) supported staff in using technology to uncover or develop an aspect of inclusive practice. Errietta Bissa's HEAT3 project (Bissa, 2009) in the Classics department of the University of Wales, Lampeter, used lecture recordings to add audio to PowerPoint files being made available to students after the event. This received very positive feedback. Of the 57% of students who used the audio-supported PowerPoints, 96% rated them as useful or very useful. Staff were initially concerned that the availability of these files would adversely affect attendance but these concerns proved unfounded, with attendance remaining at normal levels. In addition as word spread amongst students and lecturers, additional courses not included in Bissa's study adopted the practices developed: "This aspect of the pilot project was also fundamental towards increasing the staff's receptivity towards blended learning techniques and greater use of technology". A further point to note from the Bissa study is that lecturing staff accepted the presence of a portable recording device (with the aim of providing lecture recordings to students) much more readily than they accepted a microphone connected to a PC for the same purpose, which they found intrusive.

Format of PowerPoint Presentations

There are two formats of PowerPoint presentations commonly used to mount presentations on the web or learning platforms. The PPT format gives the learner access to the slides, Notes Field, Outline View and all of the authoring controls within the software. They can therefore adjust colours and font sizes to suit their own preferences, and if they use a screen reader they can access the information held in the Outline View and Notes Field (see above). The PPS format presents to the learner only a slideshow, which is not modifiable at all and not accessible to screen readers. Despite its inaccessibility some institutions recommend the use of PPS files because they can be viewed in a web browser and the learner does not need an installation of PowerPoint on their machine, which they would need to access PPT files. However, there is a free tool 'Impress' within the Open Office suite that will open PPT files, and so we would recommend to maximise accessibility that the PPT format is used, and guidance is provided on how to download the free Open Office software for learners who may not have access to PowerPoint. An alternative solution may be to export the final PowerPoint to Word and have both files available for download.

Accessible PDFs

Checking and Customising PDFs for Accessibility

If the source document has been properly created using styles and headings (such as described above) these will be carried over when the document is converted to PDF format. However if you do not have access to the source document or it was not well structured, it is possible to clear the existing structure and add the appropriate tags. A well structured document will be of immense benefit to many users, including those with dyslexia or vision impairments, who can use the screen-reader accessible bookmarks as an overview of the document headings and a quick method of jumping to different sections.

If you have Adobe ® Acrobat Professional, you can clear any existing document structure and add a new structure. This software also has a built-in accessibility-checking function.

Be aware that if you overlay text on graphical images on the PDF you create two potential accessibility problems. Firstly, the text maybe more difficult to read for people with visual impairment. Secondly, magnification and reflow are usually compromised when text is grouped with an image.

Customising PDFs for Personal Benefit: Personalising PDFs

If you have Adobe ® Reader (a free download from www.adobe.com) there are a number of ways you can adjust PDFs to suit your own preferences, if the features have not been disabled by the document author.

- Changing font and background colour. Select Edit > Preferences and select the Accessibility tab.
- Enlarging the text size. Select View > Zoom > Zoom To and select the appropriate magnification from the dialogue box.
- Alternative views. One of the lesser known but most useful groups of options.
  - If your chosen text size is proving too large for the document to display in your given window size, and horizontal scrolling is necessary, you can use the Reflow function (View > Zoom > Reflow) and the text will be re-arranged to fit within the window, regardless of text size. This can also be useful if trying to read columns of text that extend beyond the length of

the window, necessitating much vertical scrolling.

- ○ If you want to scan or read a long PDF, you can select View > Automatically Scroll, which scrolls down the PDF at a speed you control with the Up and Down arrow keys. This means you can sit in a more comfortable position to read, without having to keep a hand on the mouse or keyboard.
- ○ If you want to listen to a PDF rather than, or in addition to, viewing the text, select View > Read Out Loud > Activate Read Out Loud. There are then options you can choose from relating to the parts of the document you wish to have read out, while voice preferences can be selected under Edit > Preferences > Reading.

Everyday Inclusion Using Images

Images can be a great way of illuminating or presenting concepts for a variety of learners. No images should ever be removed from learning materials on accessibility grounds. However, it is essential that images are used as inclusively as possible. The most important aspect of this is the provision of alternative text or audio to explain the concepts contained within the image. Alternative text reading 'Periodic table' is useless, alternative text reading 'Periodic table showing the different groups or families' is little better, if the point of the diagram is to illustrate a particular aspect of this. A description of why the image is included, rather than just a literal description of its contents, is much more useful, for example: 'Periodic table showing the different groups or families of elements, in particular highlighting the alkaline earth metals such as Beryllium, Calcium and Strontium, all of which appear in a single vertical column of the table due to each having a valency of 2'. Where well-written body text explains the purpose of the image, alternative text may not be needed.

Images that serve only as eye candy are best with the alternative text left blank.

There are other considerations to be made regarding the use of images, in addition to the provision of alternative text. Learners with visual impairment may use a magnifier on their computer–this has two consequences relating to images:

- Pixelation–when images are enlarged, particularly if the original resolution is low, they can become distorted and 'blocky'– images of text are particularly prone to this. There is a magnifier built in to all Windows and Mac operating systems and this can be used to check whether images still make sense under magnification.
- Loss of holistic view–users of screen magnifiers will necessarily only be able to see a portion of the screen real estate that other users would see. This means that although they may be able to access all parts of an image, they may lose an overall or holistic perspective. If the purpose of the image was to illustrate just such an overarching concept, this may need to be explained in a different way.

Everyday Inclusion in Images. Case Study 1: Increasing Use of Sound and Images in PowerPoint (Part 2)

Another aspect of Errietta Bissa's Lampeter project (Bissa, 2009) involved the digitisation of the department's slide collection, making it more widely available to students. The students previously would view images of classical architecture or mythological artworks, for example, only for a short time via a projector in the lecture. Digitizing the slides and including them in PowerPoint presentations allowed the students to revisit the images several times, providing the opportunity for them to view images from different angles and perspectives. The feedback on this element of the project has been extremely positive in terms of increased student satisfaction, and an unexpected effect is that staff have expressed a greater interest in using PowerPoint in their lectures in order to make best use of the images available, with some requesting training in order to do so. A further unexpected development was the "increased willingness of students to comment, criticise and offer suggestions regarding blended learning, alternative teaching methods and e-resources in general" (Bissa, 2009). The project has also been of benefit financially to the department in that the cost of photocopying has been greatly reduced, with few students now needing printed copies of the images.

Everyday Inclusion Using Sound

The use of audio in teaching, learning and assessment is becoming much more common. Creating audio files is extremely easy. Most laptop computers contain a built-in microphone, while plug-in microphone headsets are easily obtainable for very little money. A free software program called Audacity (which works on Windows and Mac OS) enables the easy creation and editing of audio files. Tutorials on how to get started with Audacity are readily available on the web, but at its simplest, all you need to do is press the Record icon, speak, press the Stop icon, and go to File > Save As MP3. This will provide you with a file that you can share with students or colleagues as a simple alternative to text. Of course there are far more possibilities than that – it is easy to click-and-drag to highlight sections of your audio file, and delete them (using the Backspace or Delete keys), so you can quickly tidy up an audio file that had pauses, coughs etc. You can use the many options under the Effects menu to distort your sound file, or to add in extra features. This tool is potentially powerful in pedagogic terms, but at its simplest is very straightforward to use.

Sound files can be used to increase the accessibility of Word or PowerPoint files as described

above, or can be used more creatively as lecture summaries, revision guides, research tutorials, or a feedback mechanism. Providing feedback in audio form will be of great benefit to learners who have difficulty reading handwritten comments, or who may have anxiety issues (a reassuring tone of voice can be more supportive than 'cold' words on a page).

Everyday Inclusion Using Sound. Case Study 2: Adding Audio Recordings to PowerPoint Presentations Online

Price et al. (2009) at Aberystwyth University, Wales, UK, gave voice recorders to lecturers, and made the audio recordings available to students of languages and those for whom English is a second language–both alongside the relevant Microsoft® PowerPoint presentation and as a standalone resource. The recordings proved popular with staff, who appreciated the ease with which the voice recorders could be used and the audio files subsequently uploaded, and with students who appreciated the opportunity to use them for revision and during 'dead time', for example when commuting. Students with specific needs were especially pleased with this practice, one visually impaired student commenting "I find the audio recordings very useful. Having these audio files could replace my notetaker [in some contexts]," and one student with a long commute to university remarking "Syncing your audio files to your mp3 [player] is good–I put a couple on my iPod because my laptop dies halfway through my journey." Overall in their study 51 out of 62 students agreed the 'experimental podcasts' were an effective learning aid (Price et al., 2009).

Automated Text to Speech Conversion Tools

If you don't have time to create your own voiced audio files, or if your voice is not suitable for some reason, you can create automated readouts of your text documents. One simple tool to use for this purpose is the free DSpeech application, which will run from a memory stick if you do not have installation rights on your PC or if you move around between machines. With DSpeech you simply paste your text into the main window of the tool, and select Speak to hear it read aloud by a computer-generated voice. You can pause, adjust the volume, speed, pitch and even the voice itself (DSpeech picks up any voices available on your computer, usually a minimum of 3 options but more if you have particular text-to-speech software installed). If you want to save the spoken version simple go to File and choose the 'Save MP3 as' option.

There are other tools online that do a similar job, www.readthewords.com being a good example with over a dozen different voices and accents to choose from, but perhaps the very simplest to use is RoboBraille. Robobraille is free to non-commercial users and presuming you are working in English (there are other facilities for, at the time of writing, Danish, French, German, Greek, Italian, Lithuanian, Polish, Portuguese and Slovenian) simply attach a structured Word document (see above for details on how to Structure a Word document using Heading Styles) to an email, add nothing to the subject line or the email body, and send to britspeech@robobraille.org. (You can use usspeech@robobraille.org if you prefer a US accent). Within a matter of minutes you will receive in return an email containing a URL ending in '.mp3'. Depending on the way your computer is set up, if you click on this link either a dialogue box will appear giving you the opportunity to Save the MP3 to your computer, or a browser window will open and the MP3 will begin playing (if this happens, go to File in your browser and Save from there). The voice that RoboBraille uses is extremely human-like, possibly the best quality computerised voice currently available for free. If the RoboBraille readouts are too slow or fast for you, you can acquire a slower or faster version simply be repeating the exercise

but by adding up to three minus or plus signs in the Subject line of your email.

The RoboBraille website (www.robobraille.org) will also help you to produce DAISY (Digital Accessible Information Systems) versions of your structured Word documents (it takes you through adding particular codes at various points in the document). DAISY is a means of creating digital talking books for people who wish to hear and navigate written material presented in an audible format. The DAISY talking book format allows the user to navigate in the content and to put in bookmarks. Take care that the use of audio does not replace one barrier (for dyslexic people) with another barrier (for deaf people). Depending on the nature of the audio, a transcript or summary of the key points should be provided.

Everyday Inclusion Using Screen Capture

Screen capture adds another dimension to the use of audio–combining the audio recording with showing what is happening on the screen at the same time. This is obviously ideal for demonstrating specific computer-based techniques (for example, the use of a VLE or library system) or for explaining a visual representation in detail. Free tools such as Camstudio, Jing and the web-based ScreenToaster.com all allow the user to capture sound and screen easily, with all allowing a choice of full-screen or defined portion of the screen. Again the tools are simple to use, with minimal complications arising from selecting Full Screen recording and capturing a short (10-20 second) clip.

Everyday Inclusion Using Video

A variety of tools will help you to produce video footage, from simple plug-and-play webcams to mobile devices to high specification handheld video recorders. These devices all output in a dazzling array of formats, while most video footage used in learning materials or on the web tends to be in a few key formats: MPEG, MP4, AVI, SWF, FLV and so on. It is usually not as complicated as it might seem to change the format of recorded video. Searching the web for a free converter and adding to the search the format of your original video and your preferred end format usually provides suitable solutions. You can then use tools such as Windows Movie Maker or services like YouTube to caption your video if you wish to make it more accessible.

Everyday Inclusion Using Video. Case Studies 3-7: Use of Video in Learning and Teaching

- Smedley (2009) at Newport Business School gave digital voice recorders and video cameras to staff from Economics and Law modules with which to record feedback on student assignments. The staff were enthusiastic about their use, preferring the video cameras to the voice recorders due to the usability of the equipment, and although one-to-one support was needed to familiarise them with the devices, it was reported that the project increased optimism and confidence among staff in using technology to enhance the student learning experience: "The staff involved participated willingly following initial experiences and were more confident to 'have a go' themselves with little support being required, save for problem solving" (Smedley, 2009). Students were positive about the recordings but did comment that they had expected higher production quality from the videos, which indicates a degree of expectation management should be exercised when experimenting with the use of video.
- Hejmadi et al. (2009) at the University of Bath used audio and video recording equipment to create resources for students who were about to undertake international

placements, which were then hosted on the institution's VLE. Following the project students reported that they were more confident about applying for placements, felt more able to make decisions during their placement and were happy with the online support. Staff reported that they felt better able to support students who are undertaking placements.
- McLean and Hagan (2009) at the University of Ulster asked students to record videos during practical classes which the lecturers then uploaded to a bespoke video sharing website, YouTestTube.com. Students were then able to view, rate and comment on their videos and those of their peers. Despite 86% of the student cohort involved expressing initial apprehension about making videos, 72% later reported having enjoyed the process. Students found this a useful way to review practicals and found it interesting to view colleagues' videos, though some noted that they thought it would have been good to see a video of the practical before they did it themselves. The social networking elements of the YouTestTube.com site were found to be a powerful aspect of the project.
- Fenwick (2009) at the University of Hull used video cameras and voice recorders to record archaeology field trips. These recordings were then hosted on the University's VLE to be accessed both by students who had taken part in the visit, as a memory aid, and those who had been unable to attend. Students were enthusiastic about making the recordings and found reviewing them useful, particularly those who had taken part in the visit, and those with dyslexia or other specific learning difficulties, for whom non-text revision aids are often disproportionately useful—the video resources proved to be particularly useful in helping to remember the order of

specific techniques they had observed on the field trip. One cohort comprising mature students learning at a distance from the university reported that "featuring in their own films engendered a sense of belonging to the institution which was an unexpected benefit of the exercise" (Fenwick, 2009).

- Kincaid (2009) at the University of Chichester developed two kinds of video-based resource for her dance students; an instructional DVD following a 'reference book' format and a 'Visual Scribe' resource, which contained whole dance classes for students to watch back and reflect upon. She commented that prior to this work, she would receive notification that a student with dyslexia was in her class, but would have no idea of the practical implications of this in dance, presuming it to be related only to reading and writing difficulties. With the video resources she "wanted to be able to offer the students with dyslexia the chance to view their classes back at their own pace" (Kincaid, 2009). In feedback questionnaires students reported widespread support for this medium and wanted it to be continued in all such classes. Because of the positive feedback the University is investigating installing fixed cameras into dance studios to make the recording task easier for staff.

QUESTIONS TO ASK WHEN DESIGNING OR DELIVERING INCLUSIVE TEACHING MATERIALS

In order to create learning materials that are fit for use by all of the potential learners that may wish to access them, a process must be undertaken that examines the audience, the intended outcomes, the potential barriers to achieving those outcomes, and the ways in which different approaches, including technology options, might achieve those outcomes in different, or possibly better ways. A checklist would be of limited value as they encourage people to adopt a tick-box approach to accessibility which often limits further consideration beyond the specific issues highlighted. It may be more helpful to consider an overview of the decision-making process in the form of a series of questions. These are the kind of questions you are prompted to answer when completing an Accessibility Passport (as described above) and so looking at the Passport principles may also be of great value in creating accessible resources.

- What is the purpose of the material? It could be to provide information, encourage practising of a skill, develop understanding, prompt further thought, encourage interaction or collaboration, and so on. It is important to be able to define the purposes (and there may be several) quite precisely, because only this can lead to effective considerations of alternative routes to achieving the desired outcomes.
- What is the breadth of the audience? Is it the general public or a defined group? If it is a defined group is it a known group? If it is a known group have the learners been given the opportunity to explore and express their preferred means and modes of learning?
- Where is the resource likely to be used or accessed? Is it likely that mobile devices will be used to access the resource? Is it likely that users with slow internet connections will need to access the resource? Is it likely that users will need to access the material in short chunks (for example nursing students on placement grabbing 10 minutes online during a break)?
- What needs are easily within your ability and resource to cater for? There is a wealth of tips in this chapter and indeed the whole book that highlight what a wide range of accessibility techniques are within your

reach and how easily a large proportion of learning resources could be made more inclusive.

- Where can you go for expert advice on accessibility features that are beyond your capability? Do you know what inclusion expertise lies within your technological support service? Do you know what technological support lies within your disability support unit? Do you know which freely available national services you could turn to for advice?

- What alternatives are available for your resource? Could you create or present more than one option? Could you select what you think would be the most inclusive option but be aware of other options if a student requires something different? Are you sufficiently confident with simple technologies to be able to provide an instant spoken version of a text document, or a PDF generated from a structured Word document?

- Who makes the final decision on resourcing? If more resources are required to make your learning resource accessible, is the decision maker aware of the legal responsibilities or the potential consequences of not making adjustments or of not providing an inclusive experience?

CONCLUSION

There is no definitive right and wrong answer when creating inclusive learning and teaching materials, and no checklist or benchmark that one can accurately and objectively judge accessibility against. However, if the designer or educator understands the purpose of the materials and the ways in which they need to exhibit sufficient flexibility to meet the needs of the full range of likely users, then an inclusive resource is likely to result. The point of this chapter is to show what

can be done achievably with technology where appropriate, in the wider context set by the other chapters. This chapter will hopefully serve as a reference tool to enable that process become better understood and more widespread.

REFERENCES

Aslaksen, F., Bergh, S., Bringa, O. R., & Heggem, E. K. (1997). *Universal Design: Planning and Design for All. The Norwegian State Council on Disability*. Retrieved from http://home.online.no/~bringa/universal.htm

Ball, S. (2009). 12 Steps Towards Embedding Inclusive Use of Technology as a Whole Institution Culture. *JISC TechDis*. Retrieved from www.jisctechdis.ac.uk/12steps

Ball, S., & McNaught, A. (2008). Round Peg, Square Hole: Supporting Via the Web Staff and Learners Who Do Not Fit into Traditional Learner-Teacher-Institution Scenarios. In *Proceedings of the International Conference on Computers Helping People with Special Needs. Lecture Notes in Computer Science, 5105*, 215–218. doi:10.1007/978-3-540-70540-6_31

Ball, S., & Sewell, J. (2008). Accessibility Standards are not always enough: the development of the Accessibility Passport. In *Proceedings of the International Conference on Computers Helping People With Special Needs. Lecture Notes in Computer Science, 5105*, 264–267. doi:10.1007/978-3-540-70540-6_39

Biggs, J. (1996). Enhancing teaching through constructive alignment. *Higher Education, 32*, 347–364. doi:10.1007/BF00138871

Bissa, E. (2009). Providing digital resources in Classics. *JISC TechDis HEAT Scheme*. Retrieved from http://www.jisctechdis.ac.uk/techdis/resources/detail/HEAT/HEAT_Round3_HCA301

Disability Rights Commission. (2006). *Publicly Available Specification 78: Guide to good practice in commissioning accessible websites.* Retrieved from http://www.equalityhumanrights.com/uploaded_files/pas78.pdf

Disabled World. (2010). *Cognitive Disabilities.* Retrieved from http://www.disabled-world.com/disability/types/cognitive/

European Commission. (n.d.)) Design for All. Europe's Information Society Thematic Portal. Retrieved from http://ec.europa.eu/information_society/activities/einclusion/policy/accessibility/dfa/index_en.htm

Fenwick, H. (2009). Virtual field trips for archaeology. *JISC TechDis HEAT Scheme.* Retrieved from http://www.jisctechdis.ac.uk/techdis/resources/detail/HEAT/HEAT_Round3_HCA304

Hart, J. (2010). *The emerging Top 100 Tools for Learning 2010.* Retrieved from http://www.c4lpt.co.uk/recommended/top100-2010.html

Hejmadi, M., Bullock, K., & Lock, G. (2009). Creating video resources for students on placement. *JISC TechDis HEAT Scheme.* Retrieved from http://www.jisctechdis.ac.uk/techdis/resources/detail/HEAT/HEAT_Round3_BIO303

Jacklin, A., Robinson, C., O'Meara, L., & Harris, A. (2007). *Improving the experiences of disabled students in higher education* (pp. 22–23). Higher Education Academy.

JISC TechDis. (n.d.) The HEAT Scheme. Retrieved from http://www.jisctechdis.ac.uk/heat Kelly, B., Phipps, L., & Swift, E. (2004). Developing a holistic approach for e-learning accessibility. *Canadian Journal of Learning and Technology 30*(3).

JISC TechDis. (2009) Accessibility Essentials: The Complete Series. Retrieved from http://www.jisctechdis.ac.uk/accessibilityessentials

JISC TechDis. (n.d.) Upwardly Mobile: A Guide to Getting Started with Inclusive Mobile Learning. Retrieved from http://www.jisctechdis.ac.uk/upwardlymobile

Kelly, B., Sloan, D., Brown, S., Seale, J., Petrie, H., Lauke, P., & Ball, S. (2007). Accessibility 2.0: People, Policies and Processes. ACM International Conference Proceeding Series; Vol. 225 In *Proceedings of the 2007 international cross-disciplinary conference on Web accessibility* (W4A).

Kincaid, N. (2009). The Visual Scribe: podcasting for dance students with dyslexia. *JISC TechDis HEAT Scheme.* Retrieved from http://www.jisctechdis.ac.uk/techdis/resources/detail/HEAT/HEAT_Round3_PAL301

LSIS. (n.d.). *Excellence Gateway: Accessibility In Learning.* Retrieved from http://www.excellencegateway.org.uk/page.aspx?o=jisctechdis

McCormack, C., & Jones, D. (1998). *Building a web-based education system.* New York, NY: Wiley.

McLean, S., & Hagan, P. (2009). Creating reflective videos during practical classes. *JISC TechDis HEAT Scheme* Retrieved from http://www.jisctechdis.ac.uk/techdis/resources/detail/HEAT/HEAT_Round3_BIO301

Newell, A., & Gregor, P. (2000). "User sensitive inclusive design" – in search of a new paradigm. ACM Conference on Universal Usability, In *Proceedings of the 2000 conference on Universal Usability*, pp39-44. Retrieved from http://portal.acm.org/citation.cfm?id=355470

Page, T. (2009). *Text justification – issues and techniques.* Retrieved from http://www.pws-ltd.com/sections/articles/2009/justified_text.html

Poole, A. (2005). *Which are more legible: serif or sans serif typefaces?* Retrieved from http://www.alexpoole.info/academic/literaturereview.html

Price, G., Upton, S., & Lewis, G. (2009). Providing lecture recordings for language students. *JISC TechDis HEAT Scheme*. Retrieved from http://www.jisctechdis.ac.uk/techdis/resources/detail/HEAT/HEAT_Round3_ABER301

Roschelle, J., Patton, C., & Tatar, D. (2007). Designing networked handheld devices to enhance school learning. In M. Zelkowitz (Ed.) *Advances in Computers, 70*, 1-60.

Ryan, S., Scott, B., Freeman, H., & Patel, D. (2000). *The Virtual University: The Internet and resource-based learning*. Philadelphia, PA: Kogan Page.

Smedley, J. (2009). Using podcasts and vodcasts in assessment and feedback practices in Law and Economics. *JISC TechDis HEAT Scheme*. Retrieved from http://www.jisctechdis.ac.uk/techdis/resources/detail/HEAT/HEAT_Round3_ECONLAW301

UK Government. (1995). *Disability Discrimination Act*. Retrieved from http://www.legislation.gov.uk/ukpga/1995/50/contents

University of Bradford. (n.d.). *IT Services Documentation*. Retrieved from http://www.brad.ac.uk/lss/documentation/

University of Exeter. (n.d.). *Personal Tutoring: Supporting Students with Disabilities*. Retrieved from http://as.exeter.ac.uk/support/staffdevelopment/aspectsofacademicpractice/personaltutoring/supportingstudentswithdisabilities/

KEY TERMS AND DEFINITIONS

Accessibility: Accessibility is a term used to describe the degree to which a product, device, service, or environment is accessible by as many people as possible. Accessibility is often used to focus on people with disabilities and their right of access to entities, often through use of assistive technology, but is in fact much broader than that and applies to the entire population.

Accessibility Passport: The Accessibility Passport is a way of encouraging people who commission or design learning objects or software to take accessibility into account, and to give them feedback on the effectiveness and inclusivity of their materials. It is free to use and can be found at www.accessibilitypassport.org.

Anticipatory Requirement/Duty: This is a part of the UK legislation on disability requiring bodies or organisations to anticipate the kinds of barriers that may be operating in their domain and to take steps to remove them before any particular individual encounters them.

Assistive Technologies: Technically this term applies to specialist technologies used by disabled people to access daily living tasks (e.g. 'talking' measuring jugs for blind people) or more often computing technology (e.g. on-screen keyboards for people unable to type conventionally). In practice there is no division between technologies to aid disabled people and technologies designed to 'assist' anyone else. For example some would view a mind mapping tool as an aid for dyslexic people, and it can be advantageous in some circumstances to take that view, but many non-dyslexic people also benefit from such technologies. For this reason the author prefers to refer to all computer access technologies, be they aimed at disabled users or not, as 'productivity tools', which is a more inclusive term and avoids having to negotiate the grey area between 'assistive technologies' and other tools.

Click Input Device: Any device by which a command can be made to a computer by a single action (e.g. a click of a button). This term usually does not encompass 'point and click' devices such as traditional mice, but refers to technologies specifically that offer a click input but not pointing, usually used by people who do not have the motor control to handle a pointing device such as a mouse. An example may be a switch device that someone with very limited mobility may use in combination with an on-screen keyboard in order to type. The on-screen keyboard would be set to rotate through letters, and the user would 'click' their device to select the one they need.

Constructive Alignment: Constructive alignment is a principle used for devising learning, teaching and assessment activities, that directly address the learning outcomes intended in a way not typically achieved in traditional lectures, tutorial classes and examinations. Constructive alignment was devised by Biggs (1996), and represents a marriage between a constructivist understanding of the nature of learning, and an aligned design for outcomes-based teaching education.

DAISY: DAISY (Digital Accessible Information System) format, a means of structuring and delivering text documents in audio format, assists people who, for various reasons, have challenges using regular printed media. DAISY digital talking books offer the benefits of regular audiobooks, but they are superior because DAISY includes navigation.

Design for All / Universal Design: 'Design for All' (also known as 'Universal Design') proposes the creation of a resource that is accessible to, and usable by, every member of the community for whose use it is intended. See body text for a fuller discussion.

Disability: The inability of an individual to accomplish an everyday task due to society not making adjustments for their impairment. A wheelchair user is not disabled until they try to enter a building that has steps but no ramp – it is the lack of ramp that turns their impairment into a disability. This reflects the social model of disability.

Firewall: A firewall is a part of a computer system or network that is designed to block unauthorized access while permitting authorized communications.

Head pointing software: A tool to aid computer access by people who cannot use a traditional mouse. Software installed on the PC uses a webcam to capture movements of the user's head,

which is then interpreted as a command to move the cursor on the screen.

Holistic Approach: The Holistic Approach to e-Learning Design (see body text above) eschews rigid guidelines and standards for accessibility in learning, and e-learning in particular, focussing on practitioners applying their knowledge of the context as a super-consideration that can override guidelines where they do not aid accessibility. The Holistic Approach sees nothing wrong with adding value to different people in different ways – if a resource is perfect for blind users but useless for deaf users it should not be discarded, as the net result is everyone is disabled. Instead the resource should be maintained, but a suitable alternative created for the deaf users in addition to the original resource.

Impairment: A physical, cognitive, sensory, emotional or developmental condition or trait that gives rise to a disability if the environment or society is not constructed appropriately to accommodate it. This reflects the social model of disability.

Inclusion: The process by which users with all or any impairments or any other potentially disabling factors (such as geographic location, fluency of language or access to technology, for example) are catered for within the course of everyday provision.

Learning Platform: A learning platform is an integrated set of interactive online services that provide teachers, learners, parents and others involved in education with information, tools and resources to support and enhance educational delivery and management. Common examples in UK education include Virtual Learning Environments (VLE) and Learning Management Systems (LMS**).**

PAS78: Publicly Available Specification 78 "Guide to good practice in commissioning accessible websites" is a document published in 2006 providing guidance to organisations on how to go about commissioning an accessible website from a designer.

Pixelation: In computer graphics, pixelation (not 'pixilation' which is the process of becoming a pixie) is an effect caused by displaying a graphic at such a large size that individual pixels, small single-colored square display elements that comprise the image, are visible to the eye. It is a particular problem encountered by users of screen magnifiers, and is more likely to occur when images of text have been used instead of actual typed text (word processing software renders text in such a manner that pixelation is unlikely to occur at magnifications commonly used by screen magnifier users).

Reasonable Adjustments: A phrase introduced into UK law by the Disability Discrimination Act 1995, reasonable adjustment is a change to a system, procedure or physical entity to accommodate impaired or disabled users. In UK education, the only potential adjustments unlikely to be deemed reasonable are those that compromise Health and Safety requirements, those that compromise academic standards or those which place an undue financial burden on the organisation.

Screen Reading Software: Software that reads aloud the content of a computer screen, including commands and menus, to enable a blind or visually impaired user to control the computer and receive information from it. Not to be confused with text-to-speech software which simply converts on-screen text (not menus, commands etc) into audio form and is usually used by sighted people, often those with low vision or dyslexia.

Usability: Usability, like accessibility is a term used to describe the degree to which a product, device, service, or environment is usable by as many people as possible. It is possible for something to be accessible but not usable (a resource teaching drivers how to negotiate roundabouts can be made accessible to blind users, but will it ever be usable?) – studies have shown that many websites that reach particular accessibility standards are still declared unusable by users (e.g. http://www.ukupa.org.uk/events/presentations/helenpetriecityuniversity.pdf).

Voice Recognition Software: Computer software that allows commands and text-entry by voice. Usually this software needs to be trained to the user's voice to work effectively. Most operating systems have some kind of rudimentary voice recognition tool inbuilt.

Web Content Accessibility Guidelines (WCAG): Web Content Accessibility Guidelines (WCAG) are part of a series of Web accessibility guidelines published by the W3C's Web Accessibility Initiative. They consist of a set of guidelines on making web content accessible, primarily for disabled users, but also for all user agents, including highly limited devices, such as mobile phones. The current version is 2.0. http://www.w3.org/TR/WCAG20/.

Chapter 2

An Assessment of Eye Tracking as an Educational Aid for People with Profound Multiple Learning Difficulties (PMLD)

J.A. Renshaw
Leeds Metropolitan University, UK

B. Boullier
Hollybank Trust, UK

S. Geddes
Hollybank Trust, UK

A. Moore
Hollybank Trust, UK

ABSTRACT

This chapter describes a series of trials designed to assess the feasibility of using an eye tracker as an aid to the teaching of symbol recognition to those with profound multiple learning difficulties (PMLD). The study was funded by the Esmee Fairbairn Foundation under their "Hard to Reach" programme and was a collaborative venture between Leeds Metropolitan University and the Holly Bank Trust. The chapter demonstrates how an eye tracker can be used to provide, in real time, accurate and relevant information as to where a participant diagnosed as having PMLD is looking as they search for frequently used symbols. The authors conclude that the system has the potential to provide teachers, carers and parents, with a richer way of communicating and gives instantaneous feedback on symbol recognition performance thereby enabling teachers to change their teaching strategies if required. The study also yielded quantitative evidence of performance improvement and the authors propose a methodology for the use of this data to assess a participant's performance against a proposed national standard.

DOI: 10.4018/978-1-61350-183-2.ch002

INTRODUCTION

Non-disabled people can use several channels through which to communicate their wants, express an opinion or describe an idea. They can communicate verbally, through facial expressions and/or with gestures and body language to convey to others at least the gist of what they want. The basic skills to do this are acquired during childhood and are honed with varying degrees of success throughout the rest of their lives. People diagnosed as having PMLD are prevented from achieving the same levels as non-disabled people because of their disabilities but their needs and ambitions may be very similar to those of their non-disabled counterparts (Mencap, (n.d.), United Nations, n.d.).

This chapter describes the use of eye tracking technology to facilitate the learning of symbols through the use of which the limitations imposed by disabilities can be at least partially ameliorated. The approach belongs to a group of techniques known as augmentative and alternative communication (AAC) (Augmentative Communication in Practice,1998). Eye pointing is the name given to the technique in which a person fixates on a particular area of interest or object to indicate its selection (Augmentative Communication in Practice,1998). Symbols, usually cards with representations of objects on them are commonly used as a way of exchanging thoughts, feelings, information and to indicate choice. Their use is usually accompanied by a simple verbal description of the symbol (Augmentative Communication in Practice,1998, Schlosser and Sigafoos, 2006).

The current methodology of assessment, as to how well a person with PMLD learns to use the eye pointing technique, is for the person to whom the communication is directed, to assess the direction of the gaze and guess the target. The assessor's skill in doing this varies and is subjective. Despite their closeness to the person, opinions on how well a learner is doing, may vary amongst those charged with the person's care. This subjectivity and the lack of objective, quantitative data may adversely impact upon the person's education and assessment and may lead to delays in their progression or lead to inappropriate decisions as to the next step in their education programme (Augmentative Communication in Practice,1998, A guide to communicating with people with PMLD, n.d.).

At the suggestion of the parents of a young girl with Rett syndrome (RS), researchers at Leeds Metropolitan University and the Hollybank Trust decided to explore the feasibility of using eye tracking technology as an assessment tool. The aim was to ascertain whether it could be used a means of providing information to carers as they taught children and young adults how to read and use symbols. The system had the potential to provide a convenient and readily accessible way to record a student's progression and could provide an objective record of achievement.

BACKGROUND: REVIEW OF RESEARCH AND WORK DONE TO DATE

Profound Multiple Learning Difficulties

People with PMLD have more than one disability, profound learning and communication difficulties; their medical and health requirements may be numerous and complex. They need help all their life (Mencap, n.d.). Whilst children are protected by the UN Convention on the Rights of the Child (Article 13) there is less overt protection for adults with PMLD but they too must have the same rights as non-disabled people to be heard and to be able to communicate.

Emerson (2009) estimates that in 2008 there were just under 15,000 children under the age of 18 years and 16,000 adults with PMLD and that these populations would grow at the rate of 1.8% on average in the period 2009-2026.

Mencap states that many people with PMLD do not use formal communication systems such as speech, symbols or signs. Many children and young people with PMLD go through their entire lives without the benefit of assessment and consequently without the appropriate support resource (Mencap,n.d.).

Augmentative and Alternative Communication (AAC)

A person diagnosed with PMLD can have difficulty in communicating using conventional means. Augmentative and alternative communication (AAC) is a technique that has been developed over several years to facilitate communication with and the education of people whose disabilities frustrate normal methods of achieving these two goals.

There is growing evidence that the earlier a person with PMLD is trained to use AAC the more benefits that person derives from it (Augmentative Communication in Practice,1998). There is no single medical condition for which AAC cannot be beneficial (Augmentative Communication in Practice, 1998). Advances in technology mean that there is the potential to put, within the grasp of many, improvements in their communications and learning skills and thereby improve their independence and quality of life (MacDonald,1994; McFadden, 1995, Augmentative Communication in Practice,1998, Bunning, K., Heath, B. and Minnion, A.(2009), Bunning, K., Heath, B. and Minnion, A.(2010).

Eye pointing and the use of symbols are examples of AAC. Eye pointing is the name given to the technique in which a person fixates on a particular area of interest or object to indicate its selection. Symbols, usually cards with representations of objects on them, are commonly used as a way to exchange thoughts, feelings, and information and to indicate choice. Their use is usually accompanied by a simple verbal description of the symbol.

The current methodology of assessment as to how well a student with PMLD learns to use these techniques is subjective; involving a teacher standing in front of the participant and visually trying to assess what is being looked at. Opinions as to how successfully the student has understood the symbols may vary between those charged with the student's care despite their closeness to the student. In 2003, Kerr et al. showed how carers could report findings significantly at variance from those recorded using the appropriate test and technology. This subjectivity and the lack of objective, quantitative data may adversely impact upon the student's education and assessment and may lead to delays in their progression or inappropriate decisions as to the next steps in their education programme.

As has been stated earlier the motivation for this study came as a result of a request from a parent whose child had (RS). Several of the participants in this study also had RS. Garrett (2004) states that eye gaze and eye pointing are AAC techniques that can be used successfully in these cases. Garrett (2004) also states that up to that date there has been no research into assessment procedures despite the belief that those with RS do develop beyond the "pre-intentional communication" level (Garrett, 2004) of linguistic development. The current research may provide an indication, at least, of a way forward through the use of eye tracking.

Eye Tracking

Eye trackers record and provide data on a subject's eye movements in real-time. The recorded eye movements give an insight, under normal circumstances, into areas of interest or difficulty and can be analysed to provide an insight into the cognitive processes and strategies used by the participant whose eyes are being tracked (Duchowski, 2007). The equipment used in this study is non-invasive and exposes the participant to no health risk. The eye tracker uses algorithms to determine when and where the fixations have taken place i.e. the eye has remained relatively still in approximately the same location for a specified period of time. These fixations are assumed to equate to what the participant is thinking about when undertaking a task (Just and Carpenter, 1976 cited in Webb and Renshaw, 2008) but, whilst one cannot truly know what is going on in a participant's mind, the objective measurements used in this study are based on this assumption and its implied inference.

The eye tracker used in this study has several advantages over other types of eye tracker: The tracker looks like a normal computer monitor save for a camera and two near infra red light sources at its base. It is totally non-invasive, robust and easy to operate in many light conditions. Images of the eye movements can be relayed instantaneously to a second monitor so that the teacher can see where the student is looking in real time. The camera picks up the reflections of the light sources from the surface of the eyes every 50th of a second and time stamps the location in pixels of the eye gaze coordinates for both eyes. It can function even if the data is momentarily lost for both or for one eye. The eye gaze coordinate data can be further processed into fixations and recorded for analysis or overlaid, in various formats, onto images of the stimulus thereby providing several options for the visualisation of the eye movements detected. A computer driven display permits the display of a variety of stimuli and enables the test supervisor to control the timing and duration of the chosen stimuli. Using a web cam enables simultaneous recording of the teacher's instructions and coaching techniques (Webb and Renshaw, 2008). Furthermore it enables the capture of data which can then be analysed quantitatively to provide objective records of achievement and progress of both the participant and the teacher (in terms of teaching techniques for example).

EYE TRACKING AS AN EDUCATIONAL AID FOR PEOPLE WITH PROFOUND MULTIPLE LEARNING DIFFICULTIES (PMLD)

Issues, Controversies, Problems

The Adoption of Eyetracking Technology to Supplement AAC

AAC can be facilitated by a wide range of devices incorporating minimal or low technology to those with high technological specifications (Beukelman and Mirenda, 2005). The use of eye tracking technology in the way described in this chapter was, at the time innovative in the context of AAC. An exhaustive search of the published literature revealed only one other study using a similar approach namely the work of Baptista, Mercadente, Macedo and Schwartzman (2006). Baptista et al. (2006) conducted a pilot study, using a non invasive eyetracker, to verify whether seven girls with Rett syndrome (RS) use their eye gaze intentionally. The girls were asked to look, for five seconds, at pictures of animals, people and various types of fruit whilst their eyes were tracked for a period of about an hour. The girls sat on their parent's lap whilst sudden head movements were avoided through the use of an ophthalmologist's table. Their results indicated that the participants did respond to limited cognitive and semantic tasks in a consistent way.

Currently several eye tracker manufacturers (for example Dynavox and Tobii) offer a range of equipment specialising in the facilitating of AAC. However, the current study is unique in so far as it is the only study which attempts to use the technology and its outputs to assess participants during and post a symbols learning session.

In a more recent study Najafi, Friday and Robertson, (2008) assessed eye tracking technology from the point of view of its usefulness as pointing devices. They concluded that eye trackers had potential as pointing devices but that their successful deployment was dependant on a careful matching of their capability with the requirements, skill and personality of the person who was going to use the technology to point. Their study did not attempt to analyse data quantitatively.

The Study's Objectives

The objectives of the current study are two fold. One is to assess whether eye tracking technology can be used as a way of addressing teacher-student communication problems during a symbol recognition session. The second is to explore whether the quantitative data collected by the eye tracker can be used in some way to provide quantitative evidence of performance changes in terms of symbol recognition.

The original proposal presented to Esmee Fairbairn stated the following:

The study's objectives:

- To determine whether the eye tracking equipment can be used to monitor and measure the accuracy with which students with PMLD locate and recognise symbols.
- To provide a baseline for each participant against which progress over a period of time can be objectively assessed. (Renshaw, 2006, p2)

Criteria for Success

- If the equipment can record or provide feedback on changes in patterns of eye movement made by a student that are consistent with the either the tasks set or instructions issued by the teacher then this would vindicate the use of the technique.
- Teachers currently assess progress based on a subjective assessment of performance, their knowledge of the child and their years of experience in assessing such information. The eye tracker, if success-

fully deployed, should enable the collection of quantitative data the analysis of which, when triangulated with information recorded on the participant's record over a period of time by the Trust's staff, should tell a consistent and credible story of the participant's progress.

Proposed Scheme of Work

The proposed scheme of work, used in this current study, was designed to simulate a normal learning environment for those with PMLD. Before conducting this research, planning sessions were held to minimise school disruption and to ensure the smooth running of the esessions. The participants' teachers were asked to conduct a symbol recognition session whilst eye tracking took place. They were asked to teach the participant as if it were a normal lesson. Their only additional responsibility was to detect and respond to any indications of fatigue or stress from the participant.

Several steps were involved in the process and these were:

- To secure the approval of the University's ethic committee and that of the equivalent in Hollybank School.
- To select the participants
- To secure the informed consent from parents or guardians
- The preparation of the symbols for display
- To rehearse the evaluation processes
- The scheduling and incorporation of the evaluations into the school's time table and lesson plans
- The securing of the necessary school resources (room, teacher cover etc.).
- The calibration of the equipment to the eyes of the participants.
- The conducting of a symbol learning lesson whilst the eyes are tracked.
- The recording, management and preparation of the recorded eye tracking data.

- The creation of a database of valid data for analysis.
- Analysis and review of the data.
- Preparation of presentations and papers for publication to the University and School authorities and other learned and educational bodies.
- The review and planning of further work on the basis of lessons learnt.

After several unforeseen difficulties, which will be described later, there was some slippage of time scales from the original plan. Time scales and responsibilities were allocated to each of the above steps and agreed by both the teachers and researchers involved.

Methodology

Both the University and Hollybank School authorities gave ethical approval prior to the commencement of the study. The Hollybank process involved securing the written approval of the participants' parents or guardians. Preliminary trials ensured the reduction of potential eye tracking problems by selecting only those participants able to orientate their head appropriately and control their head's movement in front of the eye tracker. Those finally chosen for the study had little or no visual impairment, had symbol work written into their current educational programme and had successfully completed the calibration process described next.

Under normal circumstances the calibration process is very important for success in eye tracking. In this process the system displays several objects such as circles of colour that appear one at a time at known positions on the screen. The participant is asked to focus attention on each object as it appears. The system registers how many of the gaze positions are consistently within a tolerable range of the object's known position. Failure to meet the systems acceptance criteria results in a calibration failure. The process can

be repeated by repositioning the participant or reminding him/her to concentrate on looking at the target and/or by removing obstructions to the camera's line of sight to the eye such as hair, spectacle frames.

In this study adults were asked to look at two targets (solid circles of colour) rather than the normal five and the children were asked to watch two "fun" objects (a clown or toy duck) whose jittering was accompanied by an appropriate sound effect. Although every effort was made to achieve a perfect calibration at the beginning of each session there were many occasions where less than perfect calibrations were accepted in order that the interest of the participant was maintained. Imperfect calibrations may result in inaccurate reporting of gaze locations but as absolute accuracy was of secondary importance in this study and because the targets were large (256 by 218 pixels, or approximately 8.5 x 7 cm) this strategy was considered to be a risk worth taking.

Stimuli Design

The original intention was to use specialist software to design and control the presentation of the stimuli but trials demonstrated that it was incompatible with the eye tracking software. However, the same trials established that images inserted onto individual worksheets within the Microsoft Excel spreadsheet application worked well, enabling quick and easy switching between stimuli types with a click of a mouse button. Hollybank teaching staff selected the stimuli in accordance with guidelines set out in their schemes of work and following the progression needed to move up the pre-National Curriculum P-level scale. The images were of objects that participants would have recognised from their normal symbol recognition sessions in class. The set of stimuli consisted of photo realistic images, stylised symbols, words and a set of standard social information signs.

Each stimuli type was shown on a separate worksheet and each worksheet was arranged

Figure 1. Examples of the stimuli shown to the participants: Photorealistic (ball), symbol (spoon), social sign (disability) and word. (© 1981-2010, by DynaVox Mayer-Johnson LLC. All Rights Reserved Worldwide]. Used with permission.).

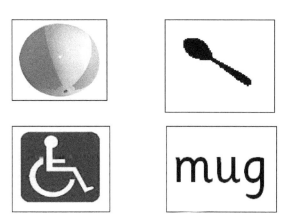

in order of the degree of difficulty as assessed by Hollybank staff i.e. coloured photo realistic images, coloured symbols, coloured social information signs and finally words. This hierarchy follows that outlined by Alison MacDonald (Augmentative Communication in Practice, 1998) and is based on the theory that as their mental development progresses individuals can perceive meaning from stimuli in progressively abstract terms. Four stimuli of known dimensions were evenly spaced horizontally and vertically on each worksheet; each stimulus was large enough (approximately 8.5 by 7 cms) to present a generous target to the participant and distributed over the screen so that their centres were approximately 13 cms apart. The "words" were written into the cells of a spread sheet using black letters on a white background in the Sassoon primary infant font, size 85. Examples of the stimuli are shown in Figure 1 and the complete set can be found in Appendix 2. The topics covered by each set of stimuli were the same: ball, TV, mug and spoon save for the social signs worksheet which showed the sign for an exit, wheelchair access, and the MacDonald and Coca-cola brand logos. The locations (in terms of X and Y coordinates in pixels) of the extremities of an imaginary box around each

object were determined. This information defined the parameters used to select the fixations counted in the data analysis described below.

Independent Assessment of Reading Levels

The process of reading is in part assisted by the use of symbol recognition. Hollybank School regularly assesses their pupils using a PIVATS system (Performance Indicators for Value Added Target Setting) of assessment, details of which are given in the Appendix 1.

PIVATS are used to show progress in small steps. There are two closely related assessment scoring schemes: (1) P Levels (1-8) used for pupils who are working below level 1 of the National Curriculum and (2) PIVATS, for which there are 5 levels a-e, giving more detailed information on progress up to level 2 of the National Curriculum. All the participants in this study were below the National Curriculum Level 1 level. The participants were assessed, by members of the Hollybank staff not involved in the eye tracking project, both at the start of this study and at its conclusion. The results of these assessments are shown in the next section that also gives details of the participants

Participant Details

Four female and eight male participants in total took part in the eye tracking sessions. They were split into two groups; seven children (under the age of 16) and five adults (16 +). All had given their consent via their parents or guardians; they had a range of disabilities as Table 1 shows.

The Eye Tracker

The images were displayed on a Tobii 1750 eye tracker which captures eye gaze coordinates every 50th of a second. The eye tracking data was collected on a Shuttle small form factor PC. The eye tracking software was configured such that eye positions were aggregated into fixations if they occurred within 40 pixels of each other within 100 ms and the stimulus type setting set to "screen" which enable the use of a standard excel spreadsheet as the stimuli presentation medium. Figure 2 shows, in diagrammatic form, the equipment configuration used in the experiment.

Equipment Setup

The participant sat in front of the eye tracking screen along side the teacher. The eye tracker was set up as a single processor, dual display system in accordance with the manufacturer's instructions (Tobii,2006). The dual screen configuration enabled the real time display of mobile eye movements as blue solid circles with a short tail, on a secondary screen visible only to the teacher (See Figure 2). The whole system was mounted on a height adjustable table under which the wheels of a wheel chair could be positioned. Wooden wedges placed under the eye tracker pedestal provided extra tilt when required i.e when the orientation of the eye tracker screen had to be adjusted to accommodate a participant's particular posture.

A conventional web cam recorded the participant's face and interactions between the participant and teacher. The eye tracker recorded the participant's eye movements over each worksheet and a mouse click enabled the teacher to switch between worksheets. The test supervisor controlled the eye tracking software via a keyboard connected to the PC.

Table 1. Details of participants showing their gender, age group, their PIVATS assessment at the beginning and end of the study and their disabilities

Participant Reference	Gender	Group A=Adult C= Child	PIVATS at the start of the study	Disabilities
f1	Female	C	3(i)	Rett syndrome, Epilepsy
f2	Female	C	2(ii)	Rett syndrome, Epilepsy
f3	Female	C	3(i)	Rett syndrome, Epilepsy
f4	Female	A	5	Rett syndrome, Epilepsy
m1	Male	C	4	Cerebral Palsy, Epilepsy
m2	Male	C	6	Cerebral Palsy, Epilepsy
m3	Male	A	5	Cerebral Palsy, Epilepsy
m4	Male	A	2	Accident induced brain damage
m5	Male	C	3(ii)	Cerebral Palsy, Autism
m6	Male	C	4	Global development delay, Chromosome deficiency, Epilepsy
m7	Male	A	8	Cerebral Palsy
m8	Male	A	6	Cerebral Palsy

Figure 2. Equipment Setup showing the plan view (top) and a side elevation (bottom)

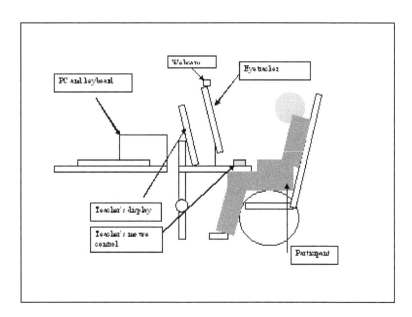

Participant Registration for an Eye Tracking Session

Hollybank support staff brought participants, one at a time, in their wheelchairs to the quiet room set aside for the evaluations. They were greeted by a teacher known to them and who would assist and coach them throughout the eye tracking session. They were also introduced to the researcher supervising the proceedings. A register was maintained of the participants' names, state of health, and any incidents earlier on that day that might adversely affect their performance. If there was a risk that the participant might be unduly stressed or fatigued by the session the session was terminated by the teacher.

A care assistant and/or teacher ensured they were comfortable and assisted in placing them and their wheelchair in such a position as to enable them to see the eye tracking screen and to enable the eye tracker to detect the participant's eyes so that calibration of the equipment could take place.

The Eye Tracking Session Process

No more than three calibrations per participant were attempted in any one session. Failure to calibrate terminated the session on that occasion and resulted in the participant being thanked and returned to his/her normal lessons.

Once calibration had been deemed a success the eye tracking session commenced immediately. The teacher sat alongside the participant and explained what was going on and what was expected of the participant. For the duration of the session a second screen enabled the teacher to see the eye movements, or lack of them, being registered by the system.

As each stimulus was presented the teacher would ask the participant to look at one of the objects on the screen changing the instruction should the secondary display indicate that the target image had been attained. These instructions were recorded by the eye tracking system via the web cam. The teacher had control of what was displayed continuously throughout the session and could decide what the next target was to be, give encouragement in cases of difficulty, or give words of congratulation on success. They were also asked to provide additional stimulus to the participant by giving verbal clues such as describing the object's colour, or what the participant might imagine they had done with the object the last time they had seen or used it at school or at home. The participants had to have attempted to look at each object on the worksheet before moving on to the next one in the sequence described earlier. Where it became apparent to the teacher that the participant had lost interest or was becoming stressed or uncomfortable the session was

terminated and the participant congratulated on a job well done and thanked for his/her efforts.

Data Preparation

The eye tracker records eye movements every 50th of a second. The software then aggregates the location of the gaze locations into fixations provided they meet certain criteria. The fixations and the scene to which they relate are also recorded in an avi (audio video interleave) file format which can be replayed at any time. The fixations and their location co-ordinates may also be exported into a spreadsheet for further analysis.

The analysis of data is based on a file listing a participant's fixation data annotated with the following information for each participant:

- the timing of key events (appearance of new stimuli, instructions from the teacher and termination of the session) which were ascertained from replaying the avi file and noting the timing of events recorded
- the participant's name, gender, group (adult or child) the date of the session,
- the timing of a stimuli's display, the timing of the first instance of a teacher's verbal instruction to look at a specific object
- and a code for the target being sought by the participant.

Consolidation of individual files into one enabled the extraction of data shown in a series of tables in the Data Analysis section.

Data Analysis

Anticipated Outcomes

The study's objectives call for a series of measures to be developed based on the data collected. The eye tracking data, was collected for each individual and placed in a database, enabling the computation of the following measures:-

Table 2. Analysis of the eyetracking sessions by group (adults/children) for each participant (reference). A 1 indicates the date upon which an eye tracking session.

	Adults							Children						
	Reference						Total Number of eye tracking sessions	Reference						Total Number of eye tracking sessions
recording date	f4	m3	m4	m5	m6	m7		f1	f2	f3	m1	m2	m8	
28/06/07				1			1	1		1		1		3
24/09/07	1	1	1			1	4	1	1	1	1	1		5
25/09/07				1			1			1				1
15/10/07	1	1		1	1	1	5		1	1			1	3
20/11/07					1	1	2	1		1		1		3
26/11/07	1	1	1			1	4						1	1
10/12/07					1		1	2	1	1	1			5
19/12/07	1	1	1			1	4						1	1
Totals	4	4	3	4	3	4	22	5	3	4	4	3	3	22

- The time taken to locate the correct symbol
- The proportion of times the correct symbol was selected

A third measure which would have computed the proportion of time the eye gaze was maintained on the correct symbol was contemplated but nor pursued as it might have resulted in asking the participants to do something which they would not do normally in the course of symbol use.

This data was to be collected at monthly intervals for a period of 6 months. However, participant illness and staff scheduling problems resulted in this plan not being fully implemented. The dates of visits actually achieved is shown in Table 2. It shows the date of each visit to the school, the participant seen on that day and the total number of eye tracking session conducted.

Discussion of the Results and Observations

The original objectives were:

- To determine whether the eye tracking equipment can be used to monitor eye movements during a symbol recognition session.
- Measure the accuracy with which students with PMLD locate and recognise symbols.
- To provide a baseline for each participant against which progress over a period of time can be objectively assessed.

Review of the Results

The equipment was successfully set up and did record the eye movements of several of the participants. During the symbol recognition sessions the teachers were able to monitor the eye movements on the second screen and adjust their interaction with their student appropriately; encouraging further effort should the target not quite be achieved or congratulating the student should the target be achieved. Rather than guessing where the participant might be looking, as would be the case under unassisted sessions without the eye tracker, this interaction was informed by knowledge of where the participant was actually fixating so had relevance and was timely.

Table 3 shows a summary of the results obtained over the period of the study. The table summarises

Table 3. Summary of the results obtained during the project for each of the participants showing: gender, age group, the days gap between the first data set (start) and the last data set analysed, the PIVATS scores, the number of images appropriately fixated upon (targets) and the average time (in seconds) taken to first fixate on the correct target after a verbal prompt

Participant	Gender	group A=Adult C=Child	Gap between assessments (Days)	Pivats score start	Pivats score end	Targets achieved: start	Targets achieved: last	Mean access times: start	Mean access times: last
f4	Female	A	86.0	5	6	11	11	1.5	2.3
m3	Male	A	81.0	5	6	6	6	4.0	2.2
m4	Male	A	86.0	2	3	7	5	6.4	6.7
m7	Male	A	86.0	8	8	14	21	1.1	1.0
m8	Male	A	65.0	6	8	3	7	7.6	8.5
Means			82.7			8.2	8.2	4.1	4.1
f1	Female	C	57.0	3(i)	5	3	5	61.9	91.9
f2	Female	C	21.0	2(ii)	5	2		26.9	
f3	Female	C	56.0	3(i)	6	4	3	9.8	22.2
m1	Male	C	21.0	4	6		3		91.9
m2	Male	C	57.0	6	8	2	3	35.0	31.0
m5	Male	C	56.0	3(ii)	6	3	5	112.5	5.9
m6	Male	C	36.0	4	6	2	2	66.0	36.6
Means		C	49.5			2.7	3.5	52.0	46.6

data from the records kept by the Hollybank Trust in terms of the participants' details, dates of visits and PIVATS scores at the beginning and end of the study. The number of fixations made on the targets shown to the participants at both the beginning and end of the study are shown in the table in conjunction with the mean time in seconds taken by each participant to achieve the target.

Observations conducted during the course of the eye tracked symbol recognition sessions showed that it took some time for the participants to fixate on the correct target and that this time seemed to differ between children and adults. Children seemed to take longer to access the targets, than their adult counterparts. Table 3 shows that for adults the time taken to access the targets was on average 4.1 seconds and did not vary from the start of the study to the last study session. However for children the mean access times do change. For those children that succeeded in the

task both at the start of the study and at the end the mean access time was 57.0 seconds (s) (at the beginning of the study) and 37.5 (s) (in their last session). An apparent improvement. However, a Student's paired sample t - test failed to establish significance due to the variability in both sets of data. No other significant differences were found either between groups (adults/children).

These results are to be expected. Intuitively adults on the whole would have more experience and practice at not only recognising the target but perhaps also in aiming their glances. So they would be quicker at accessing more targets than the children.

When participants were asked to locate a target and look at it they sometimes made mistakes. This aspect of their performance motivated the introduction of the next measure. The number of targets found are shown analysed by group (Adult/Child) and over time (first /last attempt) in Table 4. This shows that the mean number of targets achieved by adults at 8.2 per adult exceed that achieved by the child group whose mean is between 2 and 3. The child group shows a marginal increase in the number of targets achieved by the time of the later assessment from a mean of 2.3 to a mean of 3. The Adults remained unaltered over time at 8.2. In one respect these results are encouraging because it indicates that although it might take children longer to achieve a target they appear to achieve more targets as they gain experience. On the other hand the adult data seems to indicate that individuals meet their ceiling as they become adult. However, this is only one interpretation. Adults may have found the tasks too easy, they may have been bored or both. Further work is needed to determine the nature of this observed ceiling of achievement in this study.

The original intention was to collect data on the proportion of time individuals dwelt on a target. This data has not been collected because upon reflection it was not clear what it would establish apart from perhaps the ability of the participant to maintain his/her hold on a target. However why should participants want to do this? The stimuli used are not complex structures requiring cognitive effort to unravel their meaning which would be the normal reason for participants to dwell on a target. The symbols would be readily understood by the participants in this study; to ask participants to dwell on an image for no obvious reason other than to test their ability to control the movement of their eye is not natural and is outside the remit of this study.

Another aim of the study was to measure changes in performance over time. The data from the two adopted measures seems to indicate a relationship: in comparing differences between children's data and the adults' data it would appear that access time decreases and accuracy increases. Figure 3, based on the data in Table 4, shows this relationship between the two measures (targets fixated upon and access time) over the project's duration. The graph shows the data for the two

groups of participants (adults and children) at both the start and the end of the study. For both groups superimposed trend lines show a gradual improvement in skills. Adults are shown as having a consistently higher skill level than children however; the trend line (dashed line) for second set of child data shows a movement towards the adult position. Note: the adult "end of study" trend line is virtually identical to the "start" trend line and is not therefore plotted.

SOLUTIONS AND RECOMMENDATIONS

Overall Conclusions Drawn From the Data

This study uses two metrics; one is a count of the number of targets correctly fixated upon by the participants and the mean earliest time taken (mean access time) to achieve the properly fixated target. Differences between the performances of children and adults have been observed and for children at any rate there are some indications that even over the short duration of this study there were improvements in performance.

A National Standard Scale of Performance Measurement

These observed trends indicate that, if more data were collected, it would be possible to derive some standard performance curves or scales which could in turn be used as a means of assessing the performance of an individual on a national scale. It is envisaged that the two metrics, access time and accuracy, could be measured for an individual and compared with some national performance scales based on the same measures.

Although a level of statistical analysis has been attempted it would be wrong to place too much emphasis on the generalisations made based on

Figure 3. Showing the relationship between the count of appropriate fixations and the mean time to access the target in seconds by group of participants at both the start and end of the study

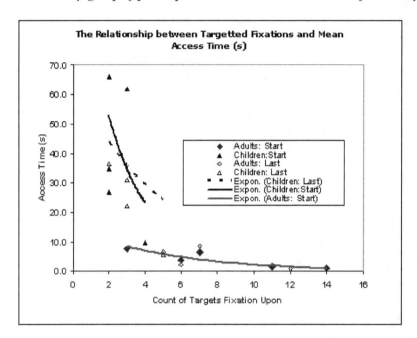

the outcomes; the data sample is very small and there are wide variations within each group.

Relationship of Eye Tracking Data and PIVATS

From the results obtained the relationship between the PIVATS scores and the two eye tracking metrics used in this study is not clear, again more data is required. However, even then it may be that the relationship may be tenuous. The PIVATS scores are broad in scope and, whilst respecting the level of skill and experience required to reach a PIVATS rating, they are determined subjectively whereas the eye tracking data is based on an objective measurement.

On balance, the study has demonstrated a possible way in which eye tracking may complement the existing measures of performance measurement but much more data is required to establish the validity of the approach.

Critique of the Study

In this section, the original objectives of the study are re-visited and their successful fulfilment assessed in the light of the study's actual achievements. The successful completion of the four aims would indicate the meeting of the study's objectives. One aim was to conduct a pilot study to assess whether the eye tracking technology could be used to assist carers with the task of teaching people symbols. A series of sessions using the eye tracker has been conducted for both children and adults. The methodology was not as simple to implement as first envisaged. A major difficulty was in arranging the equipment so that the camera element of the eyetracker could capture the reflections of light from the eyes of the participants. All the participants were in wheelchairs and in some cases their heads, were barely above the level of their knees making it difficult to position them at the required angle in relation to the light diodes and the eye tracker camera. A balance had to be struck between the height of the eye tracker support and

Table 4. The number of targets appropriately fixated upon and the mean time taken to first fixate on a target in seconds

First data set (start)						Second data set (end)					
ADULTS			CHILDREN			ADULTS			CHILDREN		
Participants	Number of Targets Hit	Mean access time	Participants	Number of Targets Hit	Mean access time	Participants	Number of Targets Hit	Mean access time	Participants	Number of Targets Hit	Mean access time
f4	11	1.5	f1	3	61.9	f4	11	2.3	f1	5	91.9
m3	6	4.0	f2	2	26.9	m3	6	2.2	f2		
m4	7	6.4	f3	4	9.8	m4	5	6.7	f3	3	22.2
m7	14	1.1	m1			m7	12	1.0	m1	3	91.9
m8	3	7.6	m2	2	35.0	m8	7	8.5	m2	3	31.0
			m5	3	112.5				m5	5	5.9
			m6	2	66.0				m6	2	36.6

the participants' proximity to the screen. Some participants could not orientate their head to face the screen and their heads had to be supported by their teacher so that they faced the screen. Some participants were not motivated to do their best (as assessed by the staff) on the day at the time of the test, some could not attend because they were too ill or exhausted by prior events in the day or were doing other things at their scheduled time. In some cases staff thought that the participants could not see the benefit of learning to use the symbol recognition strategy to meet their objectives as they already had developed other quite satisfactory alternative strategies.

However, our experience has shown that the technique does work and can help carers see where the participant is looking and enables them to give appropriate encouragement and support. It has also shown us that the greater control of head movement and the easier it is to position the participant directly in front of the screen the more successful the technique. One of the possible areas of research would be to develop a system whose positioning around the participant can cater for the presence of a wheel chair and/or a foreshortened participant torso.

Staff involved with the conducting of the eye tracker based symbol teaching sessions commented on how useful they found the information on where the participant was looking. The visualisation of the participant's fixations informed their advice, guidance and words of encouragement during the session. It enabled the lesson to progress once the participants' fixations were on target. However, this success was conditional on a reasonable calibration of the eyetracker to the participants' eyes and on some occasions, it was not always possible to assess whether an accurate calibration had actually been achieved because of the criteria set by the manufactures in terms of calibration. This should not be taken as a criticism but merely a reflection of the environment within which this study was taking place. On some occasions imperfect calibrations were accepted. The eye tracker is designed to give accurate readings of eye gaze coordinates within an accuracy of less than 0.5 degrees of visual angle. This is ideal for normal uses of the apparatus with non impaired participants. However, this is not the case in the current study. The boundaries within which fixations were allocated to targets were larger than normal to make allowance for the less than precise calibrations.

One of the current work's aims was to determine whether the eye tracking data can be used to monitor and measure the accuracy with which students with PMLD locate and recognise symbols in order to establish a baseline for each participant against which progress over a period of time can be objectively assessed. Eye tracking equipment has been used for such purposes but calibration can be difficult in some cases and calibrations with some errors may have to be accepted. Generally the following limitations hold true:

1. The eye tracker calibration process must be more or less satisfactorily completed.
2. The participant must be able to sit in front of the eye tracker with his/her face in line and parallel to the plane of the eyetracker screen for the duration of the symbol recognition session.

The study enabled the computation of the following statistics over a period of several months both on an individual and group basis:

*   The time taken to locate the correct symbol
*   The proportion of times the correct symbol was selected
*   The proportion of time the eye gaze was maintained on the correct symbol

Difficulties with equipment calibration meant that on some occasions data was not collected. However, there were a sufficient number of occasions where data was collected to make a start on providing quantitative data on a participant's

capabilities and to demonstrate trends related to age and experience.

Experiences gained from the study showed:

*   Despite a prior assessment validation process, in which likely candidates for this assessment were screened to see if their eyes could be captured, some calibrations remained problematic on the day because the correct orientation of the participant to the equipment was not achievable due to physical constraints emanating from the stance of the some of the wheel chaired participants.
*   The capturing of video and sound during the symbol recognition session was of fundamental importance in order to capture the coaching being given to the participant and to give an over view of what sessions were successful and those that were not. The first few evaluations did not have the sound recorded because the significance of the recordings was not appreciated.
*   Occasionally not all the participants were well enough or not free to take part in the sessions. There were delays in getting access to the participants compounded by then having to co-ordinate the diaries of Hollybank and University staff. These factors reduced the time interval between tests in some cases.

However, in terms of the stated objectives the project did demonstrate that the eye tracker could be used to assist the teacher in process of a symbol recognition session and that the feed back afforded by the technology as to where the participant was actually looking informed their interaction with him/her. Two measures seemed to be relevant to studies in this area 1) time to access the correct symbol and 2) the number of correct symbols fixated upon. There were indications that for children performance improved over the course of the study but that of adults remained relatively static. It is suggested that a national scale of performance be set up, based on the two eye tracker based metrics, which could then be used as a basis for indicating where on the scale an individual's performance lay.

The Teachers' View

In a post evaluation meeting the teachers were asked to comment on the study and the impact it had had on their teaching and learning strategies. They said that they had learnt how important it was that the participants knew the teachers taking part and that the teachers knew the participants their disabilities and the medication they were under as the latter could lead to significant variations in a participant's performance from day to day. The teachers also need to feel comfortable about operating the eye tracking equipment and can do it effectively and efficiently; for prolonged session may lead to participants experiencing discomfort because of their position in their wheel chair. Whilst every effort was made to orientate the eye tracker and modify the session's processes to accommodate individual participant's needs not all the physical constraints imposed by the design of the eyetracker were totally countered. These factors are very important and must be specifically addressed in any further research in this area.

On a positive note, the technology resulted in a series of snapshots demonstrating whether people maintained or developed their skills. Given that the nature of the learners in this study is such that they are trapped in their bodies, communication skills are very difficult to identify with real clarity and the snapshots of eye movement were extremely useful things to have. What this tool did was to give the teaching staff the opportunity to explore a range of communication styles that were needs-lead. This enabled them to say afterwards, quite categorically, those people who could recognise photographs, symbols, social signs, and words and those who could not. The fact that students have

the ability to demonstrate what they can do or what they know at that moment of time is important.

The teachers felt the study was a great starting point for more in depth research but that the tool should not be used in isolation. It has to be part of a tailor made package because the students' needs are so complex. The calibration problems experienced probably indicated a lack of understanding, at the time, of the circumstances and needs of some of the participants and may severely limit the wider applicability of the results. The problems may also originate from the fact that the equipment was designed for non-disabled people. However, since the study concluded the Dynavox company have introduced a product called the Eyemax, designed specifically for use by disabled people. The equipment is robust and can be more conveniently positioned by means of an adjustable arm than the pedestal mounted equipment used in this study.

Despite all these limitations however, the results did change the teaching strategies in respect of a one of the participants with Rett syndrome. The study showed that she could recognise more symbols than had been previously thought. This resulted in the participant's learning plan being revised by the teaching staff; this one case alone illustrates the potential of eye tracking as a means of assisting teachers with the tailoring of their teaching to an individual's needs. This one instance lead to the teaching staff expressing the view that any future research should focus on those people with RS.

FUTURE RESEARCH DIRECTIONS

The original intention was to provide some meaningful objective assessment of abilities rather than be reliant on subjective opinions of carers. The paper describes some quantitative measures and suggests that it would be possible to develop these into a national measure of assessment of reading performance. The school's staff are sceptical about this pointing out that there is such a wide number of variables affecting each individual's performance that such an aim might be overly ambitious. They also make the point that even if such a set of measures were developed they would only describe part of the story of that person's talents. What is required is a much broader set of inclusive measures incorporating well being and self esteem more along the lines of natural progression as opposed to the current emphasis, placed by funding bodies, on vertical progression even for those who cannot achieve the P5 level of scholastic attainment (Tomlinson, 2004).

The ultimate objective of this programme is to develop a series of educational assessment tools for students with PMLD for use by carers and teachers. These tools will use relevant computing and movement sensing technologies and where relevant incorporate custom-built software programmes. The aim is to use the most appropriate technologies to facilitate, monitor and record the effectiveness of training methodologies and progress in learning of students who are hard to reach by virtue of their PMLD.

This study is the first in the envisaged series. It is envisaged that this work may take several years to complete and it is therefore proposed to explore the opportunities in this area through a series of pilot tests assessing each technology for its appropriateness. A host of questions remain: Does gender have an impact? Does the nature of the stimuli impact upon performance? Do coaching techniques have to change to match the motivational needs of the participants? Further studies could establish how the results correlate to PIVATS scores and how performance changes with age.

CONCLUSION

This study shows it is feasible to use an eye tracker as an aid to symbol teaching. Other workers in this field come to the same conclusion; Boraston and Blakemore (2007) state that eye tracking technologies have the potential to offer insights into user performance. This study has confirmed that the fewer physical impairments a participant has to being seated in front of a screen and being able to keep their head up, the easier the technique is to use because calibration is more accurate and the system's ability to keep track of the eyes is much better.

Teachers found the real time display of the eye gazes during teaching sessions, an invaluable aid. It facilitated a richer experience for their pupil and themselves as it enabled instructions to specific, timely and relevant to the observed student's re-action to the task in hand. Most importantly, as a direct result of using this technology to monitor the performance of those with RS, the teaching staff saw with their own eyes an individual's performance and changed the teaching strategies for that individual.

Two measures, both generated by data collected via the eye tracker, were used to analyse the participants' performance. These were 1) a count of the number of successful fixations on a range of targets, and 2) a measure of the amount of time that elapsed between the teacher's verbal instruction and the correct target being fixated upon by the participant. The results seem to show that age and experience enabled more targets to be recognised faster. The authors suggest the eye tracking data collected could potentially be used as the basis for an objective assessment of any student's progress once sufficient data has been collected from a wider nationwide study.

ACKNOWLEDGMENT

We would very much like to express our gratitude to all the participants who took part, for their patience and determination to see things through to the end. To Esmee Fairbairn who were gracious enough to provide the project funding. To the staff at Hollybank who tolerated interruptions to their teaching sessions, to the management of both

Leeds Metropolitan University and Hollybank school without whose support none of this would have been possible.

REFERENCES

A guide to communicating with people with PMLD (n.d). *A guide to communicating with people with PMLD*. Retrieved May 1, 2010, from http://www.mencap.org.uk/guides.asp?id=459

Augmentative Communication in Practice. An Introduction. (1998). *Augmentative Communication in Practice: An Introduction.* Retrieved May 1, 2010, from http://callcentre.education.ed.ac.uk/SCN/Intro_SCA/IntroIN_SCB/introin_scb.html

Baptista, P. M., Mercadante, M. T., Macedo, E. C., & Schwartzman, J. S. (2006). Cognitive performance in Rett syndrome girls: a pilot study using eyetracking technology. *Journal of Intellectual Disability Research, 50*(2), 662–666. doi:10.1111/j.1365-2788.2006.00818.x

Beukelman, D., & Mirenda, P. (2005). *Augmentative and alternative communication: Supporting children and adults with complex communication needs* (3rd ed.). Baltimore: Paul H. Brookes.

Boraston, Z., & Blakemore, S. (2007). The application of eye-tracking technology in the study of autism. Topical Review. *The Journal of Physiology, 581*(3), 893–898. doi:10.1113/jphysiol.2007.133587

Bunning, K., Heath, B., & Minnion, A. (2009, Jul). Communication and Empowerment: A Place for Rich and Multiple Media? *Journal of Applied Research in Intellectual Disabilities, 22*(4), 370–379. doi:10.1111/j.1468-3148.2008.00472.x

Bunning, K., Heath, B., & Minnion, A. (2010). Interaction between teachers and students with intellectual disability during computer-based activities: The role of human mediation. *Technology and Disability, 22*(1/2), 61–71.

Department of Health. Valuing People: a new strategy for learning disability for the 21st Century. (2001). Retrieved May 1, 2010, from http://valuingpeople.gov.uk/dynamic/valuingpeople4.jsp

Duchowski, A. (2007). *Eye Tracking Methodology Theory and Practice* (2nd ed.). London: Springer-Verlag.

DynaVox Mayer-Johnson EyeMax - Eye Gaze & Eye Tracking Augmentative & Alternative Communication Device (n.d.) Retrieved May 1, 2010, from http://uk.dynavoxtech.com/products/eyemax/

Garrett, S. A. (2004). *Speech and Language Therapy in Rett syndrome.* Rett Syndrome Association UK.

Johnson, S., Hennessy, E., Smith, R., Trikic, R., Wolke, D., & Marlow, N. N.(2005). Academic attainment and special educational needs in extremely preterm children at 11years of age: The EPICure Study. *Archives of Disease Fetal neonatal Edition* 2009; 94, 283-289.

Kerr, A. M., McCulloch, D., Oliver, K., McLean, B., Coleman, E., & Law, T. (2003). Assessment of medical needs. *Journal of Intellectual Disability Research,* 134. doi:10.1046/j.1365-2788.2003.00453.x

Macdonald, A. (1994). Symbol Systems. In S.Millar and A.Wilson (Eds.), *Augmentative Communication in Practice: An Introduction* (pp 19-26). CALL Centre: University of Edinburgh.

McFadden, D. (1995) AAC in the community - A Personal Viewpoint, In S.Millar and A.Wilson (Eds.), *Augmentative Communication in Practice: An Introduction* (pp 90-91). CALL Centre: University of Edinburgh.

Najafi, L., Friday, M., & Robertson, Z. (2008). Two case studies describing assessment and provision of eye gaze technology for people with servere physical disabilities. *Journal of Assistive Technologies, 2*(2), 6–12. doi:10.1108/17549450200800013

Renshaw, J. A. (2006). *Educational Assessment of Children and Adults with Profound Multiple Learning Difficulties using Eye Tracking Technology*. Private communication.

Report, T. 14-19 Curriculum and Qualifications Reform (2004). *DfES Publications*. Retrieved May 1, 2010, from http://www.dcsf.gov.uk/14-19/documents/Final%20Report.pdf

Schlosser, R. W., & Sigafoos, J. (2006). Augmentative and alternative communication interventions for persons with developmental disabilities: Narrative review of comparative single-subject experimental studies. *Research in Developmental Disabilities, 27*, 1–29. doi:10.1016/j.ridd.2004.04.004

Tobii: Assistive Technology, Communication Solutions, Eye Control.(n.d.) Retrieved May 1, 2010, from http://www.tobii.com/assistive_technology.aspx.

United Nations Article 13 (n.d.) Retrieved May 1, 2010, from http://www.unicef.org/cbsc/files/Articles12-13-17.pdf

Webb, N., & Renshaw, J. A. (2008). Eyetracking in HCI. In Cains, P., & Cox, A. L. (Eds.), *Research Methods for human-computer interaction* (pp. 35–69). Cambridge, UK: Cambridge University Press.

ADDITIONAL READING

A guide to communicating with people with PMLD. (n.d.). Available from: http://www.mencap.org.uk/guides.asp?id=459

A Guide to Communicating with people with profound and multiple learning disabilities (PMLD). (n.d.). Available from: http://www.mencap.org.uk/guides.asp?id=459.[3]

Augmentative Communication. (n.d.). Available from: http://en.wikipedia.org/wiki/Main_Page. [6]

Augmentative Communication in Practice. *An Introduction*.(n.d.). Available from: http://callcentre.education.ed.ac.uk/SCN/Intro_SCA/IntroIN_SCB /introin_scb.html[4]

Bates, R. Donegan, M., Istance, H.O., Hansen, J.P. & Raiha, K.J. (n.d.). *Introducing COGAIN Communication by Gaze Interaction*. Retrieved from http://www.cse.dmu.ac.uk/~rbates/Bates15.pdf[1]

British Institute of Learning Disabilities – Journals. (n.d.). Available from: http://www.bild.org.uk/03journals.htm#BritishJournalLearningDisabilities

Department of Health, Valuing People: a new strategy for learning disability for the 21st Century. (n.d.). Available from: http://valuingpeople.gov.uk/dynamic/valuingpeople4.jsp[2]

DynaVox Mayer-Johnson | EyeMax - Eye Gaze & Eye Tracking Augmentative & Alternative Communication Device. (n.d.). Available from: http://uk.dynavoxtech.com/products/eyemax/

FE Works has been created by the Further Education Reputation Strategy Group (FERSG) to enhance the reputation of the FE sector on a national level.(n.d.). Available from: http://www.feworks.org/search/node/disabilities

(n.d.). *International Journal of Language & Communication Disorders*. Available from http://www.informaworld.com /smpp/title~content=t713393930.

Journal of Applied Research in Intellectual Disabilities - Journal Information. (n.d.). Available from: http://www.wiley.com/bw/journal.asp?ref=1360-2322

NHS Evidence - Learning Disabilities - Search Results - Profound & Multiple Disabilities. (n.d.). Available from: http://www.library.nhs.uk/learningdisabilities/SearchResults.aspx?catID=5024&tabID=289&

People with profound and multiple learning disabilities: A review of research about their lives. (n.d.). Available from: www.mencap.org.uk/displaypagedoc.asp?id=2362.

Playing With a Facial Mouse: Follow Your Nose. (n.d.). Available from: http://www.ablegamers.com/hardware-news/playing-with-a-facial-mouse-follow-your-nose.html

PMLD Network. (n.d.). Available from: http://www.pmldnetwork.org/resources/index.htm. [5]

Report, T. 14-19 Curriculum and Qualifications Reform (2004*). DfES Publications.* Available from:http://www.dcsf.gov.uk/14-19/documents/Final%20Report.pdf.

Resources - from the PMLD Network. (n.d.). Available from: http://www.pmldnetwork.org/resources/index.htm#seven

Royal College of Speech and Language Therapists. (n.d.). Available from: http://www.rcslt.org/[7]

Statistics on learning disabilities, information from the Foundation for People with Learning Disabilities. (n.d.). Available from: http://www.learningdisabilities.org.uk/information/learning-disabilities-statistics/

The PMLD Network. (n.d.). Available from: http://www.pmldnetwork.org/

Tobii: Assistive Technology, Communication Solutions, Eye Control (n.d.). Available from: http://www.tobii.com/assistive_technology.aspx

Wiley InterScience. (n.d.). JOURNALS. *Journal of Applied Research in Intellectual Disabilities.* Available from http://www3.interscience.wiley.com/journal/123330246/grouphome/home.html.

KEY TERMS AND DEFINITIONS

Eye Gaze Coordinates: Are the coordinates, measured in pixels, of the area of the screen at which the eye is pointing at the time of data capture. The equipment used in this study captured such data every 50th of a second. If certain parameters are met these coordinates are aggregated into fixations.

Fixations: A category of eye movement which stabilise the retina of the eye over an object of interest for a period of time usually around 250 milliseconds.

Eye Gaze: Is a term used in the context of this study to describe where a person looks: it may be formed from a series fixations.

Symbols: usually cards with representations of objects on them are commonly used as a way to exchange thoughts, feelings, information and to indicate choice. The representation of the objects can range from photo realistic images to the abstract.

PIVATS: Performance Indicators for Value Added Target Setting of assessment. A system to inform target setting for pupils of all ages whose performance is outside national expectations.

ENDNOTES

[1] This work available from the internet describes a European wide initiative to provide the disabled with access and control of computers and computer applications though eye gaze.

[2] *If you need statistics this offers a comprehensive source of data.*

[3] Does what it says on the can. It is a web page with numerous useful links for those working with PMLD.

[4] Well worth a read. It is some 90 pages long but is authoritative, readable and written by experts in their field.

[5] A web site teaming with information and useful links: a must for those impacted by or working with PMLD.

6   A thorough explanation of AAC in its various forms and some useful references; covers symbols and their use as well.

7   The RCSLT is the professional body for speech and language therapists and support workers. They set, promote and maintain high standards in education, clinical practice and ethical conduct. Their national campaigning work aims to improve services for people with speech, language, communication and swallowing needs and influence health, education and social care policies.

APPENDICES

Appendix 1: PIVATS Scales

Performance Indicators for Value Added Target Setting (PIVATS) is based up on the revised performance criteria published by DfES and QCA (2001) in "Supporting the Target Setting Process-Guidance for Effective Target Setting for Pupils with Special Educational Needs" and the QCA guidelines for planning, teaching and assessing the curriculum for pupils with learning difficulties which were again revised in 2004.The performance criteria have become known as the P Scales.

PIVATS scales is an assessment system to inform target setting for pupils of all ages whose performance is outside national expectations. It is an approach that may be used annually, as a baseline assessment or as a yearly measurement of added value. It is also a tool to support curriculum development, school improvement and self-evaluation and provides a common structure and language for schools and services to judge pupil performance. **PIVATS** is based upon attainment within the stated range but it is not disability specific, age-specific or linked to any type of provision.

Adapted from...
http://www.lancashire.gov.uk/corporate/web/view.asp?siteid=3899&pageid=14588&e=e. Last accessed June 2008.

The P levels are indicators as described below

P1: (i) Pupils encounter activities and experiences. They may be passive or resistant. They may show simple reflex responses, for example, startling at sudden noises or movements. Any participation is fully prompted.

P2: (i) Pupils begin to respond consistently to familiar people, events and objects. They react to new activities and experiences, for example, withholding their attention. They begin to show interest in people, events and objects, for example, smiling at familiar people. They accept and engage in coactive exploration, for example, focusing their attention on sensory aspects of stories or rhymes when prompted.

P3: (i) Pupils begin to communicate intentionally. They seek attention through eye contact, gesture or action. They request events or activities, for example, pointing to key objects or people. They participate in shared activities with less support. They sustain concentration for short periods. They explore materials in increasingly complex ways, for example, reaching out and feeling for objects as tactile cues to events. They observe the results of their own actions with interest, for example, listening to their own vocalisations. They remember learned responses over more extended periods, for example, following the sequence of a familiar daily routine and responding appropriately

P4: Pupils listen and respond to familiar rhymes and stories. They show some understanding of how books work, for example, turning pages, holding the book the right way up.Photos

P5: Pupils select a few words, signs or symbols with which they are particularly familiar and derive some meaning from text, symbols or signs presented in a way familiar to them. They show curiosity about content at a simple level, for example, they may answer basic two key-word questions about the story. They match objects to pictures and symbols.

P6: Pupils select and recognise or read a small number of words or symbols linked to a familiar vocabulary, for example, name, people, objects or actions. They match letters and short words. Social sight vocabulary

P7: Pupils show an interest in the activity of reading. They predict words, signs or symbols in narrative, for example, when the adult stops reading, pupils fill in the missing word. They distinguish between print or symbols and pictures in texts. They understand the conventions of reading, for example, following text left to right, top to bottom and page following page. They recognise some letters of the alphabet. Word recognition

P8: Pupils understand that words, signs, symbols and pictures convey meaning. They recognise or read a growing repertoire of familiar words or symbols, including their own names. They recognise the letters of the alphabet by shapes, names and sound. They begin to associate sounds with patterns in rhymes, with syllables, and with words, signs, symbols and letters.

Source: Private correspondence with Hollybank. Dated May 2008.

Appendix 2: Stimuli (Figure 4)

Figure 4. Images, not to scale, of the stimuli used in the study. The top row are photorealistic, the second row symbolic, the third row are social signs and the bottom row words(© 1981-2010, by DynaVox Mayer-Johnson LLC. All Rights Reserved Worldwide. Used with permission.).

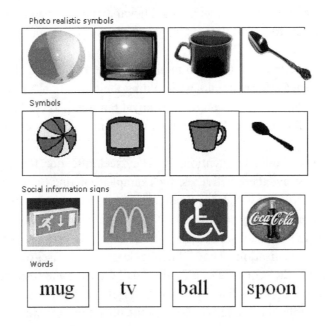

Chapter 3
Haptics as an Assistive Technology

Damian Copeland
Leeds Metropolitan University, UK

ABSTRACT

While visual and audible cues are used within the majority of educational environments, these can leave people with visual impairments, and especially deaf-blind people, at a severe disadvantage. People with visual disabilities often have a greater reliance on their sense of touch, and while touch-based, or haptic, technologies exist, the application of these within education is limited. This chapter discusses the background to haptic technologies, examines the available haptic technologies and identifies how and where these can be used within an educational context. It concludes by identifying that multimodal devices can go some way towards offering a practical assistive technology, but that further research is required to develop an affordable refreshable haptic graphic display.

INTRODUCTION

Blind and severely visually impaired people rely heavily on their sense of touch and there is a whole industry dedicated to the production of touch-based, or haptic, devices to assist them in going about their every-day lives. These include Braille books, monitors and writers, textured pavements and rotating knobs on pelican crossings, the

DOI: 10.4018/978-1-61350-183-2.ch003

raised dot on the 5-key on mobile phones and cash machines, to name but a few. Whilst for sighted people touch might be considered an augmentative sense for conveying additional information to things we see or hear, for blind (and to a greater extent deaf-blind) people it can be their main means of exploring the world around them. The use of haptics within formal education is still in its relative infancy compared to other modes of assistive technology and because of this there are no strict guidelines on how to educate blind and visually-impaired students using available haptic technologies. The focus of this chapter is on providing readers with enough information to enable them to identify relevant methods and approaches for their own individual circumstances.

BACKGROUND

Oakley, McGee, et al. (2000) state that haptics is an umbrella term covering how various types of feedback are perceived through the sense of touch. They identify these as being:

- **Proprioceptive:** Relating to sensory information about the state of the body (including kinaesthetic, cutaneous and vestibular sensations)
- **Vestibular:** Pertaining to the perception of head position, acceleration and deceleration
- **Kinaesthetic:** Meaning the feeling of motion. Relating to sensations originating in muscles, tendons and joints
- **Cutaneous:** Pertaining to the skin itself, or the skin as a sense organ. Includes sensation of pressure, temperature and pain
- **Tactile:** Pertaining to the cutaneous sense, but more specifically the sensation of pressure, rather than temperature or pain
- **Force Feedback:** Relating to the mechanical production of information sensed by the human kinaesthetic system

When the term "haptics" is referred to within this chapter it may relate to any of the feedback styles listed above. In order to understand how to select an appropriate haptic device, be it for education or use of an assistive technology, it is useful to understand why there is some disparity between the various types of feedback afforded by such devices.

Some of the earliest investigations into cutaneous stimulation and its perception by humans was conducted in the 19th century by Weber and Fechner (Lockhead, 2004) who developed formulae based on logarithms that linked stimuli to sensation in an attempt to prove that it was possible to determine the level of sensation experienced by a human in response to a known level of stimulation. This work was later expanded by Stevens in his 1957 paper On the Psychophysical Law (Stevens, 1957). Although these works may now be out of date, they are important because they were some of the earliest to put forward the argument that it is possible to determine a human response based on a known stimulus.

Bauer (1952) developed a series of experiments to determine whether texture could be used in the identification of controls within a low-light military environment. The results suggested that active feedback was far superior to passive feedback when working with textures. In this context, active refers to the user making physical movements to explore the device, whereas passive refers to the user remaining stationary while feedback is imparted by moving parts built into the device. This research was supported by Lederman, et al. (1999) who investigated the differences between active and passive touch when applied to the perception of roughness. This more recent research also investigated the difference in perception when using bare fingers, and having access to cutaneous feedback, when compared to using a hand-held probe, such as a stylus, and led the authors to comment on the "reduced effects" of "stick-like probes relative to the bare finger".

Despite these early findings, a large amount of research, if not the majority, has since been conducted in the development of devices that employ passive feedback. Perhaps more importantly, there are a number of commercially successful devices on the market today, such as SensAble Technologies PHANToM range of haptic devices (SensAble Technologies, 2010), which are normally used with attachments that do not support cutaneous feedback.

Scheibert et al. (2004) explain that touch is so difficult to understand with any completeness because it involves the study of extremely complex fields, including bio-mechanics and neuroscience. It is only by conducting experiments and recording the observations that we can truly begin to understand how the sense of touch really works. The following section discusses some of the research into this area and illustrates why much of the haptic research that has been performed is in contradiction to the findings of researchers such as Lederman, Bauer and Stevens.

Perception of Texture

Tuceryan and Jain (1998) have researched extensively into the nature and definition of texture, but concede that a true definition is elusive. They point out that "This difficulty is demonstrated by the number of different texture definitions attempted by vision researchers."

Rather than discussing texture, it may be more appropriate to reduce the scope slightly and to concentrate on the properties of roughness. It is in this specific area of tactile psychophysics and haptic perception that Lederman has contributed more than most since the 1970s. Much of Lederman's work has involved the use of flat metal plates containing regular grooves between raised surface peaks, or gratings (Lederman and Taylor, 1972). One might expect the nature of the gratings, their width or irregularity in spacing, to contribute most to the perception of roughness of the gratings. In fact, the results of Lederman's experiments suggest that the two factors that provided the greatest perception of a difference in the roughness of the surface were the alteration of the width of the spaces between the gratings and an increase in the downward finger pressure.

Penn, et al. (2001) have taken Lederman's work into a virtual environment, and have discovered that there are significant differences in the perception of roughness when compared to using "real-world" apparatus. Performing experiments using the SensAble PHANToM and Immersion Corporation IE3000 devices, they have found that not only do the limitations of the hardware preclude a direct translation of Lederman's work, but also that the relationship between the perceived roughness of the virtual textures and the geometry of those textures was the opposite of that found for the real textures used by Lederman, suggesting, then, that roughness perception may not translate well into a virtual environment.

Research into texture perception within virtual environments continues, however, and has, in the main, involved the use of hand-held probes, with few researchers having carried out experiments using devices that interact with the bare finger. Of those that have, the most documented have used an array of pins attached to a simple vibrating device, in an attempt to provide active feedback as to the roughness of the virtual object (Ikei, et al., 1997, Benali-Khoudja & Hefez, 2004). As Asamura (1999) points out, however, "if we vibrate the pins in order to give such dynamic signals, it induces vibratory sensation different from usual touch feeling". The reason for the high concentration of research in this area may have more to do with the relative simplicity of creating virtual environments that deliver vibrating passive feedback compared to those that allow active exploration, than with the belief that passive feedback is the most appropriate method of delivering information about texture.

Until Lederman's work comparing the visual and tactual exploration of textures, most researchers had taken it for granted that the perception of a texture would be different when felt rather than viewed. Lederman and Abbot (1981) found that this was not the case, and that there was correlation between a person's perceptions of texture when explored using the two modes. This may be the reason that multimodal exploration of texture, employing both sight and touch provides a much more consistent understanding of texture between subjects when compared to either sense employed alone (Klatzky & Lederman, 1987).

Perception of Shape

The above discussion on perception of texture provides only a brief insight into what constitutes extensive research into this area. Prior research with regard to perception of shape, however, is not so easy to find.

According to Biederman (1987), a single object can be represented in an infinite number of ways on the retina, in terms of orientation, colour, movement, whether all of the object can be seen, or whether parts of it are occluded, and so on. He goes on to demonstrate that, regardless of the nature of that presentation, the brain parses the information provided by the object in terms of a number of simple geometric shapes recalled from memory, and provides example shapes as cones, blocks and cylinders. According to Biederman's theory of recognition by components, or RBC, by abstracting an object into these shapes, we then recognise the object using stored images in memory. It is this abstraction process that allows the object to be viewed from different angles, for the image to be degraded or for parts to be occluded and yet still allows us to recognise the object.

If Biederman's RBC theory is correct, then it would seem reasonable to suggest that if tactual shape recognition were to follow a similar process then recognition of two-dimensional shapes using tactual interaction should be relatively easy; surely we have the capacity to recognise simple geometric shapes using touch? While this may be the case for sighted or late-blind people, for congenitally blind or early blind people, there is no visual reference point. How could blind people be expected to parse object imagery based on remembered shapes when the manner of confining those shapes to memory, namely sight, is missing?

Cameron (1897), who became blind at the age of five, provided a definite and touching insight into his memory and recognition of shapes. He stated that he considered size in terms of lengths of paper strips, and so it was difficult for him to conceptualise the notion of minuteness or infinity.

He had no experience of a polygon with more than six sides, and so when considering shapes with more than six sides, he abstracted them into shapes comprised of fewer sides and created a mental image of them being joined. This is interesting for two reasons; this abstraction into recognisable shapes shares some similarities to Biederman's RBC theory, but it also suggests that recognition can only be based on prior knowledge.

In some areas of tactual shape recognition, congenitally blind subjects have been seen to outperform sighted subjects. Davidson's research into pattern matching using tactile stimuli representing curved lines found that memory of curvature among the blind subjects was significantly greater than that of sighted subjects (Davidson, 1974). Davidson also found that subjects performed better when allowed free roam of the shapes compared to when their exploration method was constrained. Further experiments conducted by Copeland and Finlay (2008) seem to contradict Davidson's findings, however, and suggest that there is little difference in users' ability to identify shapes whether allowed free-roam or constrained. While a number of devices that only allow constrained exploration have been developed in an attempt to mitigate the technical and cost complications associated with haptic devices, these are not commercially available. The findings of Copeland and Finlay's study are important because they suggest that the production of a commercially viable refreshable device is a possibility.

It is difficult to determine with any degree of certainty how the traditionally visual cues of colour and shapes are interpreted in the minds of blind people. Zimler and Keenan (1983) conducted a series of experiments aimed at identifying whether descriptions based on these cues put blind people at a disadvantage. The experiments, conducted with groups of sighted and blind subjects, included a range of tasks including recall of spoken colours and imagery, the subjects being asked to develop an image in their minds of a described scene, on which questions were then asked. The results showed no significant difference between the two groups, leading the author to conclude that blind people's understanding of visual imagery is equally as strong as that of sighted people and suggesting that audio commentary of such concepts within an educational context should be understandable equally by sighted and visually impaired students.

Further, Zimler and Keenan highlight blind people's "remarkable ability" to process information usually considered visual. This may be due to the way that the brain processes visual information. Research by Sedato, et al. (1996) suggests that processing of tactile images in the blind happens in the primary visual cortex, the part of the brain that was previously thought only to process visual images. Sedato, et al. used positron emission tomography (PET) equipment to measure brain activity during a task involving sighted and blind participants. Participants were asked to run their fingers over a series of static tactile patterns representing Braille characters, as well as grooves representing angles and matching-width patterns. When the blind subjects ran their fingers over the tactile stimuli representing widths and angles, the primary visual cortex was activated. When they ran their fingers over the Braille characters, however, it was not. In the sighted subjects, activation of the primary visual cortex was suppressed when exploring the tactile stimuli, suggesting that attention was drawn away from the visual recognition part of the brain for those subjects and that the operation of the brain differs between sighted and blind people when processing tactile images.

These findings are of interest in an educational context as they suggest that it may be possible to present blind students with tactile artifacts for concepts where their only prior knowledge is via auditory means. This is supported by Kennedy et al (1992) who discovered that children can recognise simple shapes of which they have no haptic experience, but have had the shape previously described to them; in experiments the authors discovered that children were able to successfully identify shapes such as a moon, a rocket and an aeroplane.

Thompson, et al. (2006) cite a number of experiments conducted by Heller which confirm that blind people can effectively interpret two-dimensional images using tactual interaction, although it is recognised that congenitally blind people, in particular, have some difficulty in identifying represented images for which they have a lack of visual experience. Thompson states that while Heller's work suggests that this might be improved by offering training to the congenitally blind in order to assist them in performing the recognition tasks, it may be possible to improve the way that images are presented in order to provide more information. Thompson states that it is simply not good enough to flatten an object in order to represent it in a two-dimensional form without including information about its three-dimensional form. In order to do this, Thompson has developed a system called TexyForm. Using microcapsule swell paper, which swells to convey a tactile image when printed on using an ink-jet printer, TexyForm adds textures to two-dimensional images to suggest information about three-dimensional shape. Examples of some of the TexyForm textures along with descriptions are shown in Figures 1 and 2.

Examples of how Thompson applied these textures to images of everyday objects, after first flattening them into two-dimensional shapes are shown in Figure 3.

Thompson conducted a number of experiments to back up this theory, which were conducted with three groups: early blind, late blind and sighted blindfolded subjects. The results demonstrated a significant difference across all groups in favour of the TexyForm images, although the blindfolded sighted group stated that they did not feel like they were any easier to recognise, and in fact, there was less difference between treatments within the blindfolded sighted group compared with the other two groups.

Figure 1. Textures used to indicate vertically, horizontally oriented pieces and rounded surfaces

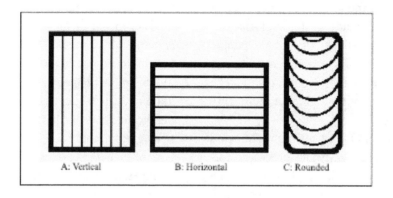

Figure 2. Other textures used to denote object solidity and protruding parts

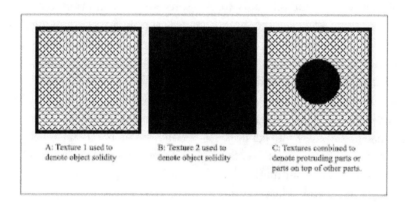

Thompson concludes by stating that it is possible for blind people to recognise images on a two-dimensional plane as long as three-dimensional information is also provided.

This is an interesting concept, but it is based on the assumption that blind people have no concept of two-dimensional images, and it is a natural assumption to make; as discussed earlier, sighted people abstract what they see into simple shapes, and so two-dimensional imagery naturally makes sense to them. Blind people, of course, have no such ability, and so would need to be taught how objects are represented in two dimensions, just as Thompson suggests. It appears, however, that this teaching often happens in infancy; there are many products on the market for blind children

aimed at giving them the skills to identify three-dimensional objects in a two-dimensional space, from games and puzzles to books. These are given further consideration later in this chapter when we start to examine the different possible uses of haptic devices.

The above research helps us understand how humans interact with their surrounding environment, whether it is via sight or touch, and it suggests, on the whole, that blind people have a similar understanding of shape and texture as sighted people. Furthermore, it highlights how we still know relatively little about these areas. While a number of researchers have concentrated on achieving a better understanding of some of the complexity of the tactual process with regard

Figure 3. Everyday shapes with TexyForm textures applied

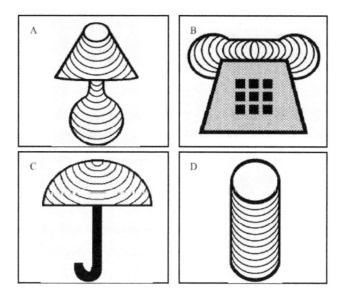

to perception of shape and texture, there has been little impact on the lives of ordinary blind people compared to the impact of the development of alternative reading methods.

The following section examines some of the advances that have been made with regard to haptic access to textual and graphical information.

HAPTICS TO EDUCATE AND INFORM

Issues, Controversies, Problems

Access to Textual Information

Braille is surely one of the most recognised uses of touch by blind and visually impaired people in everyday life. It is also closely related to access to graphics, and it is perfectly plausible that the two might be used in parallel, just as text and imagery are within visual media.

Prior to Louis Braille's invention of the Braille system in France in 1929, very few blind children were taught to read (International Braille Research Centre, 2010). Whilst none were taught to write, those that did learn to read were taught using raised

letters embossed onto paper by pressing copper wire into the back of the page. The resulting text was difficult to decipher, because it was hard to tell the letters apart. Having been taught using this system himself, Braille adapted an alternative system, which had been developed by the army for passing letters along trenches at night, to produce his system of reading using a code based on six raised dots. In addition to the alphabet, which includes letters, capitalisation, signed numbers and dates, Braille also developed codes for music and maths (RNIB, 2010). The standard Braille alphabet is shown in Figure 4.

There is no standard way to read Braille, some readers using one hand, and others using two, in a left hand → both hands → right hand pattern, left to right across a line of text. The majority of readers use either one or both index fingers, but combinations including middle fingers are not unheard of (Bertelson et al., 1984). The majority of sighted Braille readers read using vision (RNIB, 2010). According to Bertelson, the usual manner of reading is by the soft pad at the end of the finger, the very tip of the finger being less sensitive.

Figure 4. Standard Braille alphabet

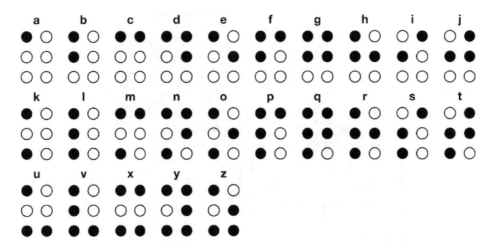

The exact arrangement of dots in a standard Braille "cell" differs slightly depending on country and whether the Braille characters are electronic or paper-based.

Braille is not necessarily accessible by the whole of the blind community; type 2 diabetes related retinopathy is the most common cause of blindness in adults under the age of 65 in the UK (NHS, 2010), and is also a major contributor to neuropathy, or long-term damage to nerve fibres. In real terms, this means that there is the likelihood that, if blindness is caused by diabetes, the associated neuropathy may seriously impair sufferers' ability to read Braille. According to Stevens (1996), even a typical 40-year old without diabetic neuropathy will have a two-point threshold (the distance between two points of pressure on the skin at which a person is able to discern them as two separate points) that is greater than that required for reading standard Braille. Stevens agrees with prior research that there seems to be heightened sensitivity in the preferred Braille reading finger(s), but this is only a benefit for people who were accomplished Braille readers prior to the onset of neuropathy.

Even where blind people without neuropathy are concerned, the use of Braille is limited. In the UK, for example, only about 3% of blind and visually impaired people are proficient enough in Braille to read a magazine or a book (Bruce, 1991) and only about 26% of blind students are Braille readers (Yu, et al., 2000).

Despite the reducing numbers of Braille readers, there is a vast array of Braille devices available, including keyboards for input, monitors for refreshable output and embossers for producing hard-copy.

A less-known alphabet aimed at blind people is Moon (Moon Literacy, 2006). This is similar to Braille in that it uses a raised coded alphabet, but it can offer benefits to people with a loss of sensitivity due to its use of lines and curves rather than dots. An example of the Moon alphabet is shown in Figure 5.

The main disadvantage of Moon is that it is rarely used outside the UK, and so resources can be difficult to acquire. There is a benefit in the existence of Moon in relation to haptic graphics in that it provides an example of lines and curves, some of the building blocks of images, being recognisable in circumstances where reduced sensitivity may be a problem.

There are a limited number of Moon educational devices available, and these tend to be dedicated to learning Moon rather than using Moon to learn other subjects.

Figure 5. Moon alphabet

Haptic Graphics

Despite the lack of research into user requirements for a haptic graphic display, a number of haptic devices have become commercially available, some with more success than others.

The PHANToM range of products, developed by SensAble Technologies in the early 1990s are devices that allow users to feel virtual objects in 3-dimensional space with up to 6, or even 7, degrees of freedom (DOF). The devices comprise moveable arm that can deliver resistance to enabling the user to sense varying degrees of free motion, stiffness or inertia. The arm can support a number of interface options, including a thimble, stylus, handle, scissors or grip, and so the device offers a wide range of possible uses, from 3-dimensional design to palpation simulation for medical training. PHANToM's success must be due in part to the wide range of supporting software applications that are available. Despite its undoubted success over the past 14 years, Kirkpatrick and Douglas (2001) found that when performing shape recognition tasks with the PHANToM, the most striking result was the difficulty of the task, although in a similar study, Jansson (2001) found that in the majority

of cases, practice with the device demonstrated an increase in performance. A whole range of information, including examples of successful applications can be found at SensAble's website (www.sensable.com).

One of the earliest successful haptic devices was the Optacon developed in the 1970s by the Telesensory Corporation (AFB, 2005). The device was produced for the daughter of John Linvill, a member of Stanford University's electrical engineering department and a founder of the company. The Optacon consisted of a handheld camera and a touch-pad comprising a tactile array of 144 vibrating pins. As the user moved the camera over printed text, the pins formed a vibrating representation of the text that imparted passive feedback to the user. Telesensory went on to develop the VersaBraille which displayed text held on cassette tape onto a 20-cell Braille display. They then designed a range of devices for people with low vision, but the lack of focus saw the company in decline. Failure to sell the company ended in bankruptcy in March 2005.

One of the current market leaders in the world of Braille display manufacture is KGS (KGS America LLC, 2010). Originally a solenoid manufacturer, KGS has been creating and marketing Braille cells and displays since the 1980s. In 2003, KGS developed their first haptic graphic display, the Dot View DV1, based on Braille cell technology. This was joined in 2004 by the DV2. The higher resolution, but smaller DV2 has a workspace of 3 x 4.5 inches comprising a pin-matrix of 32 x 48 taxels at a resolution of 10 taxels per inch. It has an impressive refresh rate of 20 frames per second, so is capable of displaying haptic movies, although this is of dubious practicability, and is controlled via a USB interface and comes with a PC software application that converts on-screen images to haptic graphics. The DV2 is a portable device, measuring just 6 x 8 inches and weighing 1.5kg. Portable it may be, but the DV2 is not cheap; at the time of writing, the recommended retail price was in excess of $16,000 USD.

In terms of success, Immersion Corporation must be the envy of most organisations looking to market haptic technologies. The company is the global market leader in haptics, with a mission to deliver the sense of touch to every "office, home, automobile, classroom and hospital" (Immersion Corporation, 2007). Founded in 1993, Immersion has built its business on force-feedback technology, now licensing it to such companies as Microsoft, Logitech, Sony, Siemens, Apple and Volkswagen. Some of the areas they are involved in include medical endoscopy simulators, programmable haptic controls for realistic driver training, video game controllers and 3D mice for 3-dimensional design, tactile ATM (cash machine) and kiosk touch screens with components such as haptic buttons that deliver feedback to act and feel like real buttons and scroll bars that deliver a stop sensation when reaching the first and last item, and devices aimed at university research such as the CyberGlove data glove.

Haptics within Education

In the UK, the number of registered blind children of compulsory education age is growing year on year (RNIB, 2010), although it is not clear whether the number of blind children is growing, or simply the percentage of blind children who go through the process of registration. In 2008 the number stood at almost 4,000, just over twice the number registered in 1991.

It was intended that this section should start with a discussion about how educating children such as these is main driver for further haptic research.

A large proportion of existing documented research into haptic presentation seems to commence with such comments as "recent research … has recognised the need for a more realistic tactile display" (Asamura et al., 1998), "micro-manufacturing Technologies [have] opened new possibilities for the production of actuators which are suitable for meeting the requirements of a high-resolution graphic tactile display." (Brenner, et al., 2001) "Virual reality and tele-existence have become attractive research topics" (Ino et al., 2003), "The goal of a haptic interface is to realistically stimulate the user" (Moy et al., 2000). Most of the other research referenced starts in a similar vein with very little information regarding the anticipated end purpose of the research in terms of users, environment or benefits.

Among the few researchers who do provide such a rationale are Yu and Brewster (2002), who identify the main application for their own research as access to maps and graphs in an educational environment for visually impaired people. They identify that this is normally addressed using swell paper which has the ability to display raised images and is relatively cheap and easy to use.

Cathy Mack, a former teacher of children with special needs agrees that the main use of haptic technologies is within an educational environment (Mack, 1994). She offers a very practical reason why it is necessary to involve blind children in technology, including computer controlled haptics, from an early age. She states that this is because an inability to interpret an image displayed on a haptic display may preclude today's school children from getting a job on leaving school. Mack suggests that unless blind children are taught to work with haptic graphics, then they are unlikely to pick this skill up; although one might imagine it to be a skill that comes naturally, Mack has discovered that the use of haptic graphics is more akin to an academic principle that requires instruction rather than a skill that can be self taught. While this may be the case, other types of haptic devices are in use for a range of different applications, and it is of interest to examine some of these and how they are used.

As mentioned previously, we still understand little about the sense of touch, a fact that Minoque and Jones (2006) believe contributes to a situation where "to date, very little empirical research has systematically investigated the value of adding haptic feedback to the complex process of teaching and learning".

While little empirical research may have been performed, Minogue and Jones (ibid) do not suggest that education is devoid of all haptic interaction. In fact there are many examples of the use of haptic devices within education. These tend, however, to be aimed at specific educational applications which require haptic feedback, rather than any association with students with disabilities. A particularly interesting example is that of the Haptic Cow (Balllle, et al., 2009). The Haptic Cow represents a successful application of haptics within the field of education. It employs the use of a PHANToM to convey realistic feeling to veterinary students learning to perform bovine rectal examinations. Figure 6 shows the Haptic Cow in use.

A relatively small amount of research has been performed into the use of haptics alongside more traditional teaching methods. A range of projects was presented at the First International Workshop on Haptic HCI (2000): Van Scoy et al demon-

strated a system that allows blind students draw mathematical functions for exploration using the PHANToM and Yu, et al. (2000) investigated the option of developing a system that allow graphs to be explored using haptic and audible feedback over the Internet, and Wies, et al discussed the possibilities of a web-based haptic display for teaching science.

While there may be a lack of computer-controlled haptic graphic displays on the market, there is a whole host of haptic graphics available which are produced using alternative technologies.

The Royal National Institute for the Blind (RNIB) runs a centre in the UK called the National Centre for Tactile Diagrams (NCTD, 2008), and provides a tactual image production service, creating diagrams, maps and graphics using a variety of processes and materials. These include the following:

- etched and moulded plastics
- models

Figure 6. Haptic Cow in a Teaching Environment

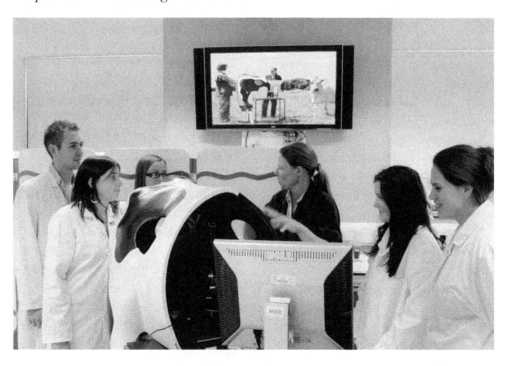

- smelly vision (the use of different odours impregnated into coloured paper sheets to represent colours, e.g. a strawberry odour for red)
- embossed graphics, created on paper from dots using a Braille printer
- heat pens, marker pens and print for use with swell-paper that swells in areas that come into contact with heat
- tactile graphics for use with touch-pads (see information on the Nomad below)
- vacuum forming, a process involving making a master image using various materials to raise an image above card then covering it in a sheet of thermoform, which once a vacuum is applied to it will mould itself to the master in order to make a tactile copy.

Of the services offered by NCTD, mapping has become a popular use for haptic technology; universities are producing tactile maps for blind students to help them find their way around campuses (E.g. University of York, 2005) and a book of tactile maps is available for London Underground stations Old Street, Westminster and Earls Court (RNIB, 2010).

In addition to its development of a tactile campus map, the University of York's Centre for Tactile Images (2007) has, until recently, advised on and developed tactile images for a number of institutions, including tactile images of paintings for the Royal Academy of Arts, tactile images of trains for the National Railway Museum, tactile images of Viking dress and paraphernalia for the Jorvik Viking Centre in York and, most recently, tactile floor plans and images of detail from stained glass windows and objects within Selby Abbey. Unfortunately, the Centre has recently closed due to a lack of financial support (University of York, 2010).

While accessibility to British visitor attractions for blind and visually impaired people is a noble quest, the range of materials and methods for developing tactile images described above

suggests that there must be myriad uses for such technology. The NCTD offers guidelines in this area and indicates that tactile graphics are useful in the following circumstances:

- Where the user is print-impaired and has some tactual ability
- To represent novel concepts not easily described in words
- Where the real object is unavailable for touching
- When the shape / form / pattern is important
- To illustrate scale & relationships: biology, maps, technology
- As a reference: once or as reminder
- To enhance educational experience by offering variety.

The NCTD suggests that this is a finite list and that tactile graphics should not be seen as a panacea for blind or visually impaired people. The Centre's website discusses a number of constraints on use of tactile images, stating, in particular, that tactile images should not attempt to display an exact replica of the original graphical information and that they are poor for representing fine detail or extremely large objects. It also suggests that training and support materials are of paramount importance.

Solutions and Recommendations

Guidelines for the Design of Haptic Graphics

In addition to the rules listed above, the NCTD also produces comprehensive guidelines on the use of tactile graphics. These make interesting reading and suggest, for instance, that a raised version of a printed picture will often not make sense to a blind person and that images should be simplified. They also state that representing part of the subject rather than the whole often makes more sense to a blind person, examples given being the outline of a leaf to represent a tree or a curly tail to represent a pig. On the whole, the guidelines state that it is of paramount importance to represent images in a way that make tactual rather than visual sense, an example being to represent a sunny day via a haptic image of a sun hat rather than of the sun; a blind child would have experience of the sun in terms of heat rather than as a ball in the sky. Images should be shown without perspective; a table has four legs, so although all four legs would not be seen when looking side on a table, they should all be shown. An example is given in Figure 7.

The guidelines summarise that tactile graphics should comprise simple and complete shapes, use clear spacing and discrimination between elements, only include details that are easy to comprehend, use meaningful references based on a blind person's understanding of the world and use simple two-dimensional viewpoints, at the same time avoiding linear outlines of shapes, too much detail, representations based on visual knowledge, stylised images, overlapping shapes, a confused layout and images with perspective.

Further guidelines for tactile design have been identified by Challis and Edwards (2000) during their design of the Weasel musical notation system. These are as follows:

1. A consistency of mapping should be maintained such that descriptions of actions remain valid in both the visual and non-visual representations
2. The tactile representation within an interface should focus on data that is static: it is difficult for users to identify where changes to an image have taken place using haptic interaction.
3. Height should be used as a filtering mechanism: the user should be able to home in on certain information types using height as a discriminating feature.
4. Avoid an excess of empty space as this is a significant source of confusion
5. A simple visual to tactile mapping is likely to produce many problems and is therefore unlikely to be the most efficient design strat-

Figure 7. Representation of a table for use with tactile images

egy: this is linked to the RNIB's guideline that images should be simplified.

6. Good design practice should, whenever possible, encourage a specific strategy for the exploration of a particular display: this is linked to the RNIB guideline that users should use a methodical approach to explore images.

7. Double clicking is an inappropriate form of interaction within static displays: double clicking does not deliver haptic feedback to the user.

8. A display should be sized and oriented such that users are not expected to overreach to discover the full extent of the display

9. Tactile objects should be simple.

The above guidelines can be interpreted to suggest that simplification of images into a blind person's perspective aids cognition. It is likely that this also aids *recognition*; there is a wide range of tactile toys and learning materials that are available specifically for blind and low vision children and, if these make sense to children, they may be remembered in later life. A range of these are available from the Royal National Institute for the Blind (RNIB, 2010). Examples include a shapes book shown above allows children to use simple geometric shapes to create two-dimensional representations of everyday objects, a counting panel toy that helps to teach blind children to count and also helps them "recognise pictorial representations of animals" (RNIB, 2010), and a "Shapes Feely Bag" toy that allows blind children to discover what simple two-dimensional shapes feel like. These are just a few examples and there are many similar children's learning aids available, so it may be reasonable to suggest that future blind adults will have a good understanding of two-dimensional representation of everyday objects.

The RNIB also offers a number of products aimed specifically at more traditional education, including a range of maths and science learning aids and even a tactile compass.

It should be noted that swell paper imaging services as well as learning aids for blind and visually impaired children and adults are offered by a number of organisations in addition to the RNIB. The RNIB has been chosen to illustrate the number of available products due to its independent status as the UK's national charity for blind people.

Haptics and MultiModality

It is important to remember that blind people exploring haptic graphics will not necessarily understand the context of the image without support via either a tactile or audible description, and any class facilitator using haptic graphics must be aware of this.

A number of researchers have developed their haptic devices by adding audible feedback to the tactile presentation. These include Van Scoy, et al (2005) and Yu, et al (2003) who were mentioned previously in this chapter.

While interactive haptic graphics represent a real breakthrough, Mack (1994) sums up the limitations of 2-dimensional educational tactile feedback materials by stating tactile images, regardless of whether being used with children or adults, should always be used in an informative manner rather than as a guessing game. The difficulty is in perspective and scale; it is unrealistic to present an image of a cat on an A4 workspace and ask the user to identify it and then to replace the image with a building, for example, and expect the user to be able to make sense of this. Mack uses the example of a church and states that it is better to guide the user, stating that the image represents a church, and explaining that one of the defining factors is the steeple at the top of the image. This is sound advice; surely it would be wrong to place a visually impaired child in a position of stress by asking him or her to guess as the nature of an image that makes little sense in the child's mind. As Kennedy et al. (1992) discovered, however, the cognitive load and associated stress may be mitigated if the child has prior knowledge of the subject by means other than haptic.

The Nomad, developed by Parkes (1988) of the University of Newcastle, New South Wales has had some success with regard to adding auditory cues to haptic graphics. Images are produced using a proprietary computer drawing package known as CAD (Can't Anyone Draw) and placed on a touch screen called the Nomad. Users can then explore the image by touching areas of it and as they explore it, a synthesised voice will describe the area being explored.

A more recent multimodal addition to the haptic graphic market, and specifically aimed at education is the Talking Tactile Tablet or T3 (TouchGraphics, 2010). The T3 connects to a computer using a USB interface and has a range of learning software available. The user places swell paper images on the face of the tablet and the tablet informs the software as areas of the images are touched by the user. Integrated audible feedback can be used to augment the tactile information. In addition, there is an authoring system available to allow teachers to produce their own training materials. At the time of writing, the cost of the basic T3 package is around $700 USD. Figure 8 shows the T3 in use.

Case Studies

Ideally this chapter would include summaries of a small number of real-life case studies to illustrate how haptic technologies are currently being used to assist blind and visually impaired students in an academic context. Unfortunately, case studies of this type are few, and those that have been documented have tended to concentrate on a single participant. A description of one worthwhile case study is provided below.

Figure 8. Blind Child using a Talking Tactile Tablet

Graham et al. (2007) conducted a study aimed at improving interaction when teaching visually impaired students. The study consisted of interviews with members of the RNIB and a late visually impaired student expert from the University of Ulster. Basing their case study on the teaching of electronic circuit diagrams and Unified Modeling Language (UML), they identified the main issue as being the ability for students with impaired sight to draw and understand diagrams. The authors considered the T3 for this task, but suggest that the device is not ideal for two reasons: the NCTD guidelines state that tactile images should not be used where fine detail is required, and the number of diagrams used for teaching these areas would require a significant amount of preparation compared to a solution that could display images dynamically. An interesting alternative explored was the use of Duplo® blocks which were found to be useful for identifying symbols. The authors suggest that preparing tactile handouts of lecture slides, using swell paper, would enhance the experience of lectures for visually impaired students. After the lecture, the handouts could be used in conjunction with a tablet device similar the T3 to allow the descriptions of tactile images to be read out as the student interacted with them. In addition, they suggest that providing audio handouts of the lecture in MP3 format would be of benefit to all students.

FUTURE RESEARCH DIRECTIONS

While Braille monitors and devices such as the PHANToM and T3 offer an invaluable opportunity for students in all levels of education, there is still no widely available, affordable refreshable device for the display of haptic graphics. Until there is, teaching many subjects to blind and visually impaired students will remain a challenge. This is particularly true with maths based subjects which rely on the ability to create and identify shapes and patterns.

The majority of research into the area of refreshable haptic graphic displays has concentrated on existing Braille technology, which according to recent studies (Copeland and Finlay, 2008) may be suitable candidate for the commercial development of these devices, although at the present time, haptic graphic displays based on Braille technology must be considered prohibitively expensive for home use and the majority of educational environments.

Until a suitable technology can be identified that makes these devices affordable, it is likely that blind and visually impaired students will remain disadvantaged within a significant number of educational subjects.

CONCLUSION

Despite half a century of research into the psychophysical aspects of touch, it remains our least understood sense. This directly impacts our ability to develop assistive technologies for people, and especially learners, with severe visual impairments.

It is likely that the majority of people who consider tactile feedback in association with visually impaired people will immediately think of Braille, but the number of Braille users compared to the number of people with visual impairments, certainly in the UK and USA, is falling. A major contributor to this fact is that the main reason for blindness in the western world is type II diabetes, which, not only has a tendency to affect the older generation, who are traditionally associated with a slower take-up of new technology, but it is also indicated with neuropathy, resulting in a reduction in tactual acuity. This has a direct impact on one's ability to sense the small number of closely positioned individual dots that make up Braille characters. Research suggests that while this is still an issue with regard to haptic graphics, the problem may be reduced somewhat by the number of dots that are used to form an image.

There is a wide range of learning materials available for children with visual impairments to allow them to explore the world around them, but this is much reduced when it comes to more formal education and certainly in post-primary education. There are a small number of devices on the market that go some way towards filling this gap, including the T3, but while they represent valuable progress, they are restricted in their inability to display information that can be refreshed in real-time. This relies on careful planning of lessons and could significantly increase the workload of those planning the lessons.

There would be tangible benefits to the availability of a refreshable haptic-graphic display in order for ad-hoc learning or for the ability to teach maths or science-based subjects that rely heavily on graphical representation. While a small number of such devices are commercially available, they have such a high cost associated with them that makes them impractical for use in the majority of situations.

Further research is required in order to identify a suitable technology for the development of an affordable refreshable haptic graphic display, and until one becomes commercially available, blind and visually impaired learners will remain at a disadvantage when compared to their fully-sighted counterparts.

ACKNOWLEDGMENT

The author would like to thank the following people for their kind permission to reproduce the images used in this chapter:

Figures 1-3: Dr. Leanne Thompson of Lancaster University, UK

Figure 6: Dr. Sarah Baillie of the Royal Veterinary College, London, UK Photographer: Peter Nunn

Figure 8: Steven Landau of Touch Graphics Inc, New York, USA

REFERENCES

AFB AccessWorld. (2005). From Optacon to Oblivion. Vol 6 (4). Retrieved 19th November, 2010, from http://www.afb.org/afbpress/pub.asp?DocID=aw060403

Asamura, N., Tomori, N., & Shinoda, H. (1998). Selectively stimulating skin receptors for tactile display. *Computer Graphics and Applications, 18*(6), 32–37. doi:10.1109/38.734977

Asamura, N., Yokoyama, N., & Shinoda, H. (1999). *A Method of Selective Stimulation to Epidermal Skin Receptors for Realistic Touch Feedback*. Paper presented at the IEEE Virtual Reality '99 Conference.

Baillie, S., Shore, H., Gill, D., & May, S. (2009). Introducing Peer Assisted Learning into a Veterinary Curriculum: A Trial with a Simulator. *Journal of Veterinary Medical Education, 36*(2), 174–179. doi:10.3138/jvme.36.2.174

Bauer, H. J. (1952). Discrimination of tactual stimuli. *Journal of Experimental Psychology, 44*(6), 455–459. doi:10.1037/h0056532

Benali-Khoudja, M., & Hafez, M. (2004). *VITAL: A Vibrotactile Interface with Thermal Feedback*. Paper presented at the IRCICA International Scientific Workshop.

Bertelson, P. (1984). *A Study of Braille Reading: 2. Patterns of Hand Activity in One-Handed and Two-Handed Reading*. Université libre de Bruxelles, Brussels, Belgium.

Biederman, I. (1987). Recognition-by-components: A theory of human image understanding. *Psychological Review, 94*(2), 115–117. doi:10.1037/0033-295X.94.2.115

Brenner, W., Mitic, S., Vujanic, A., & Popovic, G. (2001). *Micro-actuation Principles for High-resolution Graphic Tactile Displays*. Paper presented at the Eurohaptics 2001, Birmingham, UK.

Bruce, I., McKennell, A., & Walker, E. (1991). *Blind and partially-sighted adults in Britain: the RNIB survey*. London.

Cameron, A. (1897). The Imagery of One Early Made Blind. *Psychological Review, 4*(4), 391–392. doi:10.1037/h0063985

Challis, B. P., & Edwards, A. D. N. (2000). *Design principles for tactile interaction*. Paper presented at the Workshop on Haptic Human-Computer Interaction.

Copeland, D., & Finlay, J. E. (2008). *A Specification for a Haptic Graphic Display*. Paper presented at the Third International IASTED Conference on Human-Computer Interaction, Innsbruck, Austria.

Davidson, P. W., & Whitson, T. T. (1974). Haptic Equivalence Matching of Curvature by Blind and Sighted Humans. *Journal of Experimental Psychology, 102*(4), 687–690. doi:10.1037/h0036245

Graham, D., Benest, I., & Nicholl, P. (2007). *Interaction design for teaching visually impaired students*. Paper presented at the IASK International Conference on E-Activity and Leading Technologies.

Ikei, Y., Wakamatsu, K., & Fukuda, S. (1997). *Texture Display for Tactile Sensation*. Paper presented at the 7th International Conference on Human-Computer Interaction.

Immersion Corporation. (2007). *Engaging the Sense of Touch*. Retrieved 19th November, 2010, from http://www.immersion.com/

Ino, S., Shimizu, S., Odagawa, T., Sato, M., Takahashi, M., Izumi, T., & Ifukube, T. (1993). *A tactile display for presenting quality of materials by changing the temperature of skin surface*. Paper presented at the 2nd IEEE International Workshop on Robot and Human Communication.

Kennedy, J. M., Gabias, P., & Heller, M. A. (1992). Space, Haptics and the Blind. *Geoforum, 23*(2), 175–189. doi:10.1016/0016-7185(92)90015-V

KGS-America LLC. (2010). *KGS Corporation*. Retrieved 19th November, 2010, from http://www.kgs-america.com/

Kirkpatrick, A. E., & Douglas, S. A. (2001). *A Shape Recognition Benchmark for Evaluating Usability of a Haptic Environment*. Paper presented at the First International Workshop on Haptic Human-Computer Interaction.

Klatzky, R. L., Lederman, S. J., & Reed, C. (1987). There's More to Touch Than Meets the Eye: The Salience of Object Attributes for Haptics With and Without Vision. *Journal of Experimental Psychology. General, 116*(4), 356–369. doi:10.1037/0096-3445.116.4.356

Lederman, S. J., & Abbott, S. G. (1981). Texture Perception: Studies of Intersensory Organization Using a Discrepancy Paradigm, and Visual Versus Tactual Psychophysics. *Journal of Experimental Psychology, 7*(4), 902–915.

Lederman, S. J., & Taylor, M. M. (1972). Fingertip force, surface geometry and the perception of roughness by active touch. *Perception & Psychophysics, 5*(12), 401–408. doi:10.3758/BF03205850

Lockhead, G. R. (2004). Absolute Judgments Are Relative: A Reinterpretation of Some Psychophysical Ideas. *Review of General Psychology, 8*(4), 265–272. doi:10.1037/1089-2680.8.4.265

Mack, C. (1994). *Symposium on High-Resolution Tactile Graphics*. Retrieved 21st November, 2010, from http://www.trace.wisc.edu.

Minogue, J., & Jones, M. G. (2006). Haptics in Education: Exploring an Untapped Sensory Modality. *Review of Educational Research, 76*(3), 317–348. doi:10.3102/00346543076003317

Moon Literacy. (2006). *What is Moon?* Retrieved 21st November, 2010, from http://www.moonliteracy.org.uk/whatis.htm

Moy, G., Singh, U., Tan, E. & Fearing, R. S. (2000). Human psychophysics for teletaction system design. *The Electronic Journal of Haptics Research, 1*(3).

NHS. (2010). *Diabetic Retinopathy*. Retrieved 21st November, 2010, from http://www.cks.nhs.uk/patient_information_leaflet/diabetic_retinopathy#-461960

Oakley, I., McGee, M. R., Brewster, S., & Gray, P. (2000). *Putting the Feel in 'Look and Feel'*. Paper presented at the CHI 2000 Conference on Human Factors in Computing Systems, The Hague, Netherlands.

Parkes, D. (1988). *Nomad: an Audio-Tactile Tool for the Acquisition, Use and Management of Spatially Distributed Information by Partially Sighted and Blind Persons*. Paper presented at the Second International Symposium on Maps and Graphics for Visually Handicapped People, King's College, University of London.

Penn, P., Petrie, H., Colwell, C., Kornbrot, D., Furner, S. & Hardwick, A. (2001). *The Haptic Perception of Texture in Virtual Environments: An Investigation with Two Devices*. Paper presented at the First International Workshop on Haptic Human-Computer Interaction, Glasgow, UK.

RNIB. (2010). *National Centre for Tactile Diagrams*. Retrieved 21st November, 2010, from http://www.nctd.org.uk/

RNIB. (2010). *Prevalence Statistics*. Retrieved 3rd October, 2010, from http://www.rnib.org.uk/aboutus/Research/statistics/prevalence/Documents/2008_3_Revised-Prevalence_Stats_PDF.PDF

RNIB. (2010). *Reading Braille*. Retrieved 21st November, 2010, from http://www.rnib.org.uk/livingwithsightloss/readingwriting/braille/Pages/reading_braille.aspx

RNIB. (2010). *Supporting Tactile Graphics: Navigation*. Retrieved 21st November, 2010, from http://www.rnib.org.uk/professionals/accessibleinformation/accessibleformats/accessibleimages/tactilegraphics/supporting/Pages/navigation_strategies.aspx

SensAble Technologies. (2010). *PHANToM Haptic Devices*. Retrieved 30th March, 2010, from http://www.sensable.com/products-freeform-systems.htm

Stein, D. K. (2007). *Louis Braille: The Father of Literacy for the Blind*. Retrieved 19th November, 2010, from http://www.nfb.org/images/nfb/Publications/fr/fr28/fr280105.htm

Stevens, J. C. (1996). Tactile Acuity, Aging, and Braille Reading in Long Term Blindness. *Journal of Experimental Psychology. Applied, 2*(2), 91–106. doi:10.1037/1076-898X.2.2.91

Stevens, S. S. (1957). On the Psychophysical Law. *Psychological Review, 64*, 153–181. doi:10.1037/h0046162

Thompson, L. J., Chronicle, E. P., & Collins, A, F. (2006). Enhancing 2-D Tactile Picture Design from Knowledge of 3-D Haptic Object Recognition. *European Psychologist, 11*(2), 110–118. doi:10.1027/1016-9040.11.2.110

Touch Graphics. (2010). *Talking Tactile Tablet*. Retrieved 30th March, 2010, from http://touchgraphics.com/OnlineStore/index.php/featured-products/talking-tactile-tablet-2-ttt.html

Tuceryan, M., & Jain, A. K. (1998). *Texture Analysis. The* (2nd ed., pp. 207–248). Handbook of Pattern Recognition and Computer Vision.

University of York. (2005). *Touchy Feely Map Makes Life Easier on York Campus*. Retrieved 21st November, 2010, from http://www.york.ac.uk/admin/presspr/pressreleases/tactilemaps.htm

University of York. (2010). *Centre for Tactile Images*. Retrieved 21st November, 2010, from http://www.cs.york.ac.uk/tactileimages/

Van Scoy, F., Kawai, T., Darrah, M., & Rash, C. (2000). Haptic display of mathematical functions for teaching mathematics to students with vision disabilities: design and proof of concept. *Haptic Human-Computer Interaction, 2058*, 31–40. doi:10.1007/3-540-44589-7_4

Van Scoy, F., McLaughlin, D., & Fullmer, A. (2005). *Auditory Augmentation of Haptic Graphs: Developing a Graphic Tool for Teaching Precalculus Skill to Blind Students*. Paper presented at the Eleventh Meeting of the International Conference on Auditory Display (ICAD 05).

Wies E. F., G. J. A., Sile O'Modhrain M., Hasser C. J. & Bulatov V. L. (2001). Web-based Touch Display for Accessible Science Education. *Haptic Human-Computer Interaction*, 52-60.

Yu, W., & Brewster, S. A. (2002). *Multimodal Virtual Reality Versus Printed Medium in Visualization for Blind People*. ACM ASSETS.

Yu, W., & Kangas, K. (2003). *Web-based haptic applications for blind people to create virtual graphs*. Paper presented at the 11th Symposium on Haptic Interfaces for Virtual Environment and Teleoperator Systems, Los Angeles, California.

Yu, W., Ramloll, R., & Brewster, S. A. (2000). *Haptic graphs for blind computer users*. Paper presented at the First Workshop on Haptic Human-Computer Interaction.

Zimler, J., & Keenan, J. M. (1983). Imagery in the Congenitally Blind: How Visual are Visual Images? *Journal of Experimental Psychology. Learning, Memory, and Cognition, 9*(2), 269–282. doi:10.1037/0278-7393.9.2.269

ADDITIONAL READING

Altinsoy, E., Jekosch, U., & Brewster, S. A. (2009). *Haptic and Audio Interaction Design*. Fourth International Workshop (Vol. 5763). Berlin: Springer

Kahol, K., Hayward, V., & Brewster, S. A. (Eds.). (2009). *Ambient Haptic Systems* (Vol. 2(3)).

McGookin, D., & Brewster, S. A. (2006). *Haptic and Audio Interaction Design: First International Workshop* (Vol. 4129). Berlin: Springer

Oakley, I., & Brewster, S. A. (2007). *Haptic and Audio Interaction Design, Second International Workshop* (Vol. 4813). Berlin: Springer.

Pirhonen, A., & Brewster, S. A. (2008). *Haptic and Audio Interaction Design, Third International Workshop* (Vol. 5270). Berlin: Springer.

KEY TERMS AND DEFINITIONS

Afference: The process of a sensation being received by the body.

Cutaneous: Relating to the perception of shape, texture or temperature via sensations of the skin.

Degrees of Freedom (DOF): The various possible movement, rotations and tilts that are possible in 3-dimensional space.

Efference Copy: Memory of a physical sensation stored within the nervous system.

Force-Feedback: Relating to the mechanical production of information sensed by the human kinaesthetic system.

Haptic: Relating to the sense of touch.

Haptics: Umbrella term covering the perception of the various types of feedback that are perceived through the sense of touch.

Kinaesthetic: Relating to the feeling of motion via the muscles, tendons or joints.

MultiModal: Pertaining to a system that allow multiple modes of input or output, e.g. tactile and auditory feedback.

Proprioceptive: Relating to sensory information about the state of the body.

Tactile: Pertaining to the cutaneous sense, but more specifically the sensation of pressure, rather than temperature or pain.

Vestibular: Pertaining to the perception of head position, acceleration and deceleration.

Chapter 4

Using a Computer Aided Test to Raise Awareness of Disability Issues Amongst University Teaching Staff

John Gray
Leeds Metropolitan University, UK

Gill Harrison
Leeds Metropolitan University, UK

Andrea Gorra
Leeds Metropolitan University, UK

Jakki Sheridan-Ross
Leeds Metropolitan University, UK

ABSTRACT

This chapter reviews the use of simulating disabilities within a computer aided test to raise awareness of disability issues amongst university staff. It describes the reasons for creating the computer aided test, the choice of simulation as the basis for demonstrating some accessibility issues associated with a range of disabilities, the structure and content of the test, and the outcome of its presentation to several groups of participants. Feedback from staff that have used the test indicates that for most their awareness of disability issues has increased and that some plan to make changes to their future actions to improve the experience for students with some forms of disability.

INTRODUCTION

Universities in Europe and the United States have an increasing number of students with disabilities enrolling in them (HESA, 2008; U.S. Department of Education, 2006). For a variety of reasons,

including the association of computers with the provision of many kinds of aids to accessibility, Computer Science is a popular choice among these students (Francioni and Smith, 2005). The General Conference of the United Nations Educational, Scientific and Cultural Organization adopted the Convention against Discrimination in Education in 1960 (UNESCO, 1960). At present, European

DOI: 10.4018/978-1-61350-183-2.ch004

legislation against disability discrimination, with the exception of the UK, only exists in the employment field in the form of the Employment Directive 2000/78/EC, which aims to establish a general framework for equal treatment in employment and occupation (EDF, 2007). Even though this Directive addresses the vocational training of disabled citizens, there is no European legislation specifically addressing disability discrimination in the Higher Education section. In the UK and the United States, legislation such as the UK Disability Discrimination Act (HMSO, 1995), the UK Special Educational Needs and Disabilities act (HMSO, 2001), and the American Disabilities Act (ADA, 1990) lay upon universities the duty to consider and provide for the needs of disabled students in their teaching. Against this legislative background, staff teaching in Higher Education institutions need to be aware of the needs of disabled students and how best to accommodate them.

Leeds Metropolitan University (Leeds Met), like the vast majority of UK HE institutions, has a strong student facing Disability Services team that is highly successful in helping those students who identify themselves as requiring support due to their disabilities. The information made available to staff and students through this team is focused on explaining the form and nature of that support together with providing wider information and links that may prove helpful to disabled students. These include information about disability resource areas, alternative assessment arrangements, dyslexia tuition and IT support. This information is disseminated to the university staff through presentations and other staff development activities and information sessions; unfortunately, as is noted later, there is intense competition for the time and attention of academics and it is difficult to ensure that this information reaches them effectively.

The development of the computer aided assessment tool for disability awareness is one facet of the Leeds Met approach to raising the awareness of its staff in the field of supporting and developing all of its students. A key element of this tool is the inclusion of information and links to good practice regarding the range of impairments simulated together with links to wider information on the impairments and access to specific online tests that enable participants to evaluate their own status. Several participants have become aware of personal difficulties, for example colour blindness, through engaging with these tests. Initial trials of the test have indicated its usefulness and potential for the future. One important effect has been the increased interest and enthusiasm towards learning about disability issues, exemplified by the request for further specialised training sessions. There are plans to extend the range of impairments included in the simulations together with the addition of text to speech examples.

BACKGROUND

The computer aided test was created as a training tool to raise awareness of some common experiences faced by people with visual, motor, hearing and cognitive difficulties when using a computer. The test is primarily aimed at university academic staff and it has been used with support and technical staff, for example learning technologists, from across the university. For each impairment simulated, advice and guidance are offered through the test to help university teaching staff understand how they may best cater for the needs of students with such impairments. The primary intention of the test is to enable academic staff to experience some of the difficulties and frustrations met by people with a variety of visual, hearing, cognitive and motor impairments. The aim here is that this will help them to design online learning experiences with a view to minimising these difficulties. The guidance provides staff with advice, approaches and practice that others have found useful in designing inclusive activities. Much of this guidance promotes approaches whereby information is presented using multiple formats e.g. text and sound, images and text etc. and it is anticipated that one additional benefit from this will be enhancing the accessibility of the information across the wider student population. Presenting information in multiple formats is likely to accommodate a wider range of student learning preferences than solely using a single format.

The development of the computer aided test using simulations of disability arose from work done in 2003 where the impact of dyslexia on students studying computer programming was investigated (Powell et al, 2003). Talking to students and evaluating survey results for this work highlighted deficiencies in the authors' knowledge and understanding of the difficulties faced by students with disabilities. Though the research team had some awareness of several distinct disabilities (one member had specific experience of autism, another was partially deaf and yet another experienced motor problems arising from an illness) they were largely highly computer literate and in the main found it hard to appreciate the physical, social and psychological problems facing students with impairments.

At the same time there was a strong internal drive at Leeds Met to increase the use of online approaches for delivering learning materials. There was also a rising interest in using online approaches e.g. computer aided tests, for assessing students. To some extent this was a response to increasing staff work loads and the recognition that reusable automated assessment could have an impact on the work load associated with some aspects of assessment. It was also acknowledged that computer aided assessment could prove extremely helpful for formative assessments where students have opportunities to test their knowledge as they progress through their studies and gain feedback regarding their knowledge and understanding. One of the themes of the Leeds Met Assessment, Learning and Teaching strategy for the period 2005 – 2008 was:

"Rebalancing assessment practices to improve formative assessment and feedback to students."

This combination of increasing online delivery and rising interest in online assessment highlighted a need for some training activity or aid that would help academic and administrative staff appreciate the difficulties faced by the growing numbers of students with disabilities attending Leeds Met (currently some 1400 students in a population of some 50,000 students). In particular it was recognised that this training aid could be used by staff either as a group activity in an organised setting or as a stand alone activity (staff can interact with the test from their home or offices). In the discussions about which impairments might be simulated and how that might be accomplished it was agreed that a list based on ease and effectiveness of simulation be drawn up in order to build an early prototype.

The computing background of the staff involved enabled the development of an online tool and a small team led by John Gray developed a computer aided test for staff training (Harrison and Gray, 2006). Discussions early in the lifetime of the tool centred on what could be built and how it would be disseminated. In particular there was much debate about whether the work should be accessible and usable via the internet or whether it would be better to release it on a stand alone CD/DVD. One of the development issues that occupied much of these discussions related to the high level of interactivity envisaged for the tool and the known problems evident in the lack of compatibility among the potential range of internet browsers through which staff might access the tool. Ultimately an internet accessible version was agreed and a mix of technologies including CSS, XHTML and JavaScript were chosen as the development languages. The early prototypes were tailored to work with the then Leeds Met standard staff browser of Internet Explorer 6. Subsequently the tool was modified such that it would work with Internet Explorer 7 and 8, Opera 10.10, Firefox 3.6 and Safari 4.

The earlier work that reviewed dyslexic students and their success in computer programming (Powell et al., 2003) formed a major theme in Leeds Met's contribution to the collaborative UK HEFCE funded "Centre for Excellence in Teaching and Learning" (CETL) (HEFCE, 2005), in collaboration with the Universities of Durham, Newcastle and Leeds. The Centre is devoted to promoting "Active Learning in Computing" (ALiC) (Durham University, 2006; Leeds Metropolitan University, 2007) and is the only CETL within the Computer Science academic area. This CETL has a wide range of interests, including the consideration of students with disabilities studying computer science and how best to ensure their support, together with the issue of staff awareness of disability. The development of the computer aided test and the simulations it implements was funded by CETL ALiC.

RATIONALE

There is evidence that many members of teaching staff across academic disciplines are not sufficiently aware of the requirements of the legislation and its implications. Salzberg (2003) states that "while most faculty members are willing to cooperate, they are largely ignorant of the legal and programmatic issues that affect students with disabilities and have received little or no training in that regard". In Computer Science, for example, some academic staff will be expert in certain aspects of disability, and will incorporate it within their teaching. Examples of this would be the introduction of accessibility in a Java course via the Swing components (Cohen et al., 2005) or the design of websites accessible to blind users (Harrison, 2005). However, there remains a need for ensuring that training is made available for those staff members who do not necessarily specialise in the area.

There are many training initiatives, courses and informative websites about disability available for teaching staff of all academic disciplines including specialised training courses and materials relating to the use of computers by disabled students (TechDis, 2006c). These are delivered in many ways, for example as face to face workshops, or online (Pearson and Koppi, 2006), or as a website (UMUC, 2005). Similarly the JISC funded LexDis (LexDis, 2009) project aims to "..explore successful 'e-skills' and supporting strategies, including the use of assistive technologies, in a world of complex computer aided interactions introduced by e-learning and on-line social networks." However in relation to face to face training, there is evidence that short training sessions are needed. Salzburg et al. (2002) say that "[directors of disability service offices] note the difficulty in getting faculty members to attend, and....recommended that sessions be limited to one or two hours" (Salzberg, 2002). Similarly, a survey of professional development by Getzel et al. (2003, pg 63) found that "the competition for faculty members' time to participate in training or other activities was the greatest barrier".

This preference for short training sessions was one of the motivations behind the creation of the test described below. A further intention was the creation of an interactive experience that offered the user an element of fun and intrigue. The belief was that by allowing staff some opportunity to control and select aspects of the computer based questions, together with exposing them to something like the issues that those with a range of disabilities meet, they would engage with the experience more readily. Making the test available over the internet also means that staff can continue to explore and consider the implications of disability at their leisure. One feature that is promoted in organised sessions is the time and space to share and reflect on the experiences staff receive as a result of engaging in the test and to discuss how this might affect their teaching (and other) approaches to students.

HISTORY AND DEVELOPMENT OF THE COMPUTER AIDED TEST

In 2006, the development team devised an initial structure and suitable content for the test, to comply with its stated aims. In the succeeding period, the test has been presented to a variety of groups of users, and has been revised and improved in the light of feedback received. It has also been modified to ensure that it can be accessed successfully using a range of the most commonly used browsers (including Internet Explorer, Firefox, Opera and Safari).

HESA data (HESA 2008) for the last decade shows increasing numbers of students with disabilities enrolling on courses at UK HE institutions. Over the same period there has been a noticeable increase in the use of, and change to, online technologies used to support the student learning experience. In addition the changing legislation around disability (Disability Discrimination Act 2005, Special Educational Needs and Disability Act 2001) imposes increasing responsibilities on staff and HE institutions to ensure all students have appropriate access to learning materials and other documentation used to inform students about their studies. These changes give rise to the need for staff development to facilitate training for academic and administrative staff. The computer aided test was designed for use as a virtual training aid to simulate some experience of the frustrations met when using an online computer aided test as mediated through a range of impairments.

Issues, Controversies, Problems

Why Use Simulation?

Live simulations in which participants are constrained in ways that mimic a physical impairment have been used for many years; an example here might be placing an able bodied person into a wheelchair for a period of time, or blindfolding a person and setting them a specific task to complete. This approach has increasingly attracted criticism from a range of sources not least from disability groups. For many participants working from a wheelchair can be perceived as a piece of fun where they are able to play at being disabled without gaining a deep insight into what it means to be disabled. A particular criticism (Behler 1993) of them is that participants often focus on the immediate problems faced by being constrained in some way and ignore the wider medical and social models of disability. Briefly the medical model sees the person as the problem. Those with disabilities are seen as being dependent on others and that their particular impairments are symptoms that need to be cured. Here the disabled person is perceived as needing to adapt to the non-impaired world. The social model presents a world in which those with disabilities are excluded as a result of the ways in which the world is organised. This organisation places a range of constraints, including physical, cultural and attitudinal barriers, that prevent those with disabilities from engaging fully in society. This model has been developed by those with disabilities and has a clear aim of removing these barriers and offer the same opportunities and choices enjoyed by the wider society. Evidence of the impact of this model can be seen in the recent legislation aimed at reducing discrimination against those with disabilities.

Similarly in a recent post on the 'Barriers, Bridges and Books' blog titled 'Disability simulation exercises promote what?' the author makes this point very clearly:

"No simulation can give the true feelings of what it is like to have a disability"

According to Colella (2000) the use of participatory simulations in educational settings is increasing and one benefit is that they encourage interaction by the participants. Papadopoulos and Pearson (2007) state that "Simulations are potentially more valuable when learners can interact with the system, rather than simply observing the simulations in action". The decision to design and build an online interactive simulation to raise staff awareness of some of the difficulties and frustrations experienced by students with disabilities was motivated by the belief that after experiencing the simulations staff would make their own learning materials more accessible to all students. Careful design and selection of the interactions together with opportunities to share experiences of those interactions should help staff to appreciate some of the problems others face. Guidance on approaches to minimising some of these difficulties are intended to help staff to enhance the accessibility of their learning materials and teaching approaches.

It is important to ensure that any training or development involving able bodied people experiencing some form of disability on a temporary basis should not result in the participants feeling sorry for those who live with such disabilities. Perhaps more importantly they should not reinforce medical models of disability where those with disability are seen primarily in terms of their impairment(s). It is important that people involved in such training are offered opportunities to discuss and share what they have learned from the experience of being disabled and to articulate ways in which they can accommodate that learning among the student and staff populations.

In a seminal paper published in 2004 Burgstahler and Doe discussed the "positive and negative aspects of disability-related simulations; paradigm shifts regarding approaches to disability studies; implications for training educators and administrators, and examples of disability awareness activities that maximize positive outcomes." The Burgstahler paper offers some guidelines for creating effective simulations and the computer aided test is evaluated in a later part of this chapter (see 'Current State of the Test') using the original descriptions as presented in that paper.

Why Use a Computer Aided Test?

The benefits of using a computer aided test as context within to present the various simulations were partly, as indicated in the Rationale, that it would meet the perceived need for a relatively short training session. The development team considered that a desirable feature of any training session should be that it is interactive (whether for staff or students). A computer aided test using simulations of the experience of impairments was suited to these requirements. This approach was similar to that provided within the disability simulation area of the TechDis site (TechDis, 2006b). Another example of online simulation is the Screen reader simulation available at the WebAIM (WebAIMa) website. The Disability Rights Commission (2010) also took a similar approach where they offered a simulation of viewing a screen distorted to appear as though the viewer experienced cataracts.

Example simulations from the computer aided test include one in which the central area of a question is hidden behind a black blob, as though the person undergoing the test were experiencing deterioration of the eye caused by Age-Related Macular Degeneration, another presents a spoken question that is inaudible because of loud background noise, similar to that experienced by someone with tinnitus. This approach was designed to engender not only awareness of disability, but appreciation of the impact of disabilities for people working with computers.

Structure

The HESA statistics for 2007/08 show that the most commonly occurring disabilities among the student population are specific learning disabilities (such as dyslexia), vision and hearing impairments, mental health difficulties and mobility difficulties. These are consistent with the HESA statistics for the periods 2004 and 2007. Given that the test was to be delivered online and that it was to focus on the difficulties students with disabilities experienced it was recognised that the test should concentrate on simulations around visual impairment, hearing impairment, cognitive impairment and some aspects of mobility impairments i.e. impairments affecting the control of the PC peripherals rather than problems relating to wheelchair access. The idea was both to raise awareness of the difficulties experienced by students and to give useful information and advice on what could be done to minimise such.

The CETL ALiC team, consisting of a Site Coordinator, a Teacher Fellow and two Research Officers, generated and discussed ideas for questions. Since the questions were designed to simulate experiences of disabled people, many of them were likely to prove difficult to answer, this being inherent in the design if the questions were to be realistic. It was therefore decided to allow some alternative way of rendering the question in an "unimpaired" way, generally by clicking on a button, so that there might be some possibility of answering it. Instructions on how to activate this facility were shown on screen with each question (see Figure 1).

The content of most of the questions was relevant to their form, for example the question simulating Age-Related Macular Degeneration

(with a central blob) asked whether this particular condition caused deterioration of central, peripheral or all vision. When a respondent selected and submitted an answer to a question, the response indicated whether it was correct or not, together with a brief explanation of the reason why. This feedback was intended to reinforce the key learning points about the impairment.

Each question was accompanied by a series of links providing users with access to more detailed information concerning the particular impairment presented, good practice and guidance on how to minimise the impact of this impairment in online learning. In addition access to online diagnostics was added so that participants could check to see if they suffered from the impairment being simulated. This offered users a rich set of resources to investigate should they wish to do so.

Cycles of Feedback and Improvement

So far, the test has been experienced in face to face workshop sessions of between one and one and a half hours by six groups of up to 20 staff involved in Higher Education, the majority of them from the Computer Science area. It was presented at two face to face workshops inside

Figure 1. Question exemplifying the use of complex language

Instructions	Question Body	Useful Links
Click here with the mouse to see an alternative version [Simplified View]	Consider the following statement: The funnel-structured interview is best thought of as making use of a deductive approach whereby respondents will not initially feel threatened, as generalized open-ended questions are used at the beginning, before the interviewer progresses to closed questions. This structure may have the benefit that so much detailed information may be elicited early on that this eliminates the need for long sequences of closed questions and probes. Is the statement: ○ True. ○ False. [Submit]	**Good Practice** JISC-Techdis British Dyslexia Assoc Plain English Campaign Dyslexia Support Dyslexia in HE Comprehension Test

Leeds Met, the first in June 2006 and the second at the Staff Development Festival in September 2006, and later at another workshop at the Higher Academy Annual Conference in July 2007. The test has also been presented and demonstrated at various conferences (including the annual CAA conference and staff development sessions during 2008 and 2009. Further workshops were held in February 2010 when the test was presented to members of the Technology Enhanced Learning Network and subsequently to members of the Faculty of Business and Law. The workshops have been facilitated by members of the CETL ALiC team, and have catered for discussion as well as hands-on computer use. Extensive and valuable feedback has been obtained from them, and has shaped the further development and improvement of the test (Harrison and Gray, 2007).

The first presentation of the test took place in June 2006, and yielded a substantial number of comments. The overall reaction was overwhelmingly positive, participants stressing their appreciation of the empathetic aspect of the test. Several said that they had been reminded of or made newly aware of a wider range of types of disabilities than they had previously considered. They had enjoyed the interactive nature of the training experience, and thought the length of time allowed (an hour) was about right. Minor criticisms focused on the shortcomings of the interface and navigation, the small number and range of questions, and the lack of a page providing an introductory explanation of the test. The major criticism was that, although providing references to relevant material, it did not go far enough in giving detailed constructive advice on how to take forward what the participants had learned during the test, and how they might make use of it in their own future teaching. When asked how it would affect their future actions, those taking the test expressed their good intentions to incorporate accessibility ideas in future computer aided material and tests, but in a very vague fashion. This

relates to the criticism expressed above. Other suggestions made included:

- the involvement of disabled students in the evolution of the test
- the inclusion of other types of disability, e.g. mobility impairments
- wider dissemination of the test, for example via the internet
- some reference to or demonstration of the use of assistive technology, for example screen-readers.

In an attempt to address the major criticism arising from the first presentation and following careful consideration, a short page of practical advice was created and linked to each question. Improvements in layout and navigation were made, and the range of questions enlarged. The modification and enhancement of the test is seen as an ongoing process by the development team.

In subsequent presentations, feedback was similar (Harrison and Gray, 2007), though critical comments diminished as improvements had been made. The provision of more detailed sessions to follow up the original introductory one, specialising in for example hearing impairment or dyslexia, was suggested, and the important question of measuring the impact of the test on staff was raised. The existence of the short pages of practical advice led to a request that these should be easily downloadable and printable, either individually or as a combined document.

Standards and Guidelines

A great deal has been written about the use of standards and guidelines for the design and development of accessible web sites. This is acknowledged by the provision of support for both web designers and also content providers in the support pages associated with each of the simulations. Given that one aim in creating the test was to help staff increase the accessibility of their learning approaches and materials it seems apposite to say a little more about guidance for content providers. Probably the most focused of the existing guidelines currently available are the W3C Content Accessibility Guidelines 2.0. (WCAG) however, excellent as they are, it is clear that these guidelines contain elements that many staff would neither understand nor be able to control. According to the WAI-AGE (WAI_AGE) project "Initial results from our preliminary analysis shows that existing Web accessibility guidelines are not well known or understood by many of those writing accessibility guidelines and making recommendations for ageing or disability communities."

There are several facets of the WCAG that are helpful and these are utilised within the good practice links throughout the test. Examples here include:

- Don't use colour as the sole visual means of presenting information
- Use text and not images of text wherever possible
- Minimise the use of time constraints
- Ensure the website behaves as consistently as possible
- Have a consistent appearance/look-and-feel (e.g. all links and buttons should look and behave in the same way)
- Avoid using words in their non-literal sense (e.g. "it's raining cats and dogs")
- Provide clearly signposted, simplified summaries of the content of each page at the top of that page
- Provide an audio version of a site's content
- Break information into small, simple chunks and illustrate them visually wherever possible
- Always provide an obvious way for users to get back to simpler content if they find themselves on a page above their reading level.

A useful checklist for the WCAG guidelines has been created by WebAIM (Web Accessibility in Mind) (WebAIM 2010b) and this may prove helpful to some staff if used selectively.

One area that does not form part of the test is that of checking the compliance of web pages and sites against accessibility levels and it would seem that there would be some benefit here within the university for providing support and guidance for all staff to ensure that as far as possible teaching materials and related information comply with minimum accessibility standards.

CURRENT STATE OF THE TEST

Solutions and Recommendations

Structure

Presently the test has an explanatory entry page with links to the four areas referred to in the Background section. Each of the areas (visual, hearing, physical/motor and cognitive/learning impairment) contains a set of questions relating to and if possible simulating the experience of the particular type of impairment. Navigation through each set is facilitated using Next and Previous links.

Each individual question is displayed using three panels: the question body in the centre, instructions on how to proceed (for example how to render the question in an "unimpaired" way) on the left, and useful links on the right, including a link to the short page of practical advice designated the "Good Practice" page.

An example of a dyslexia-related question shown in Figure 1 illustrates the layout used. Figure 2 shows the effect on this question body of clicking the Simplified View button, and Figure 3 shows the Design Guidelines contained in the Good Practice page related to this question.

Figure 2. Simplified version of the question

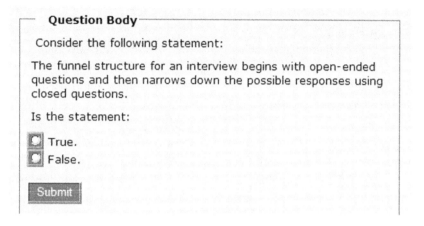

Figure 3. Guidelines available through the Good Practice link

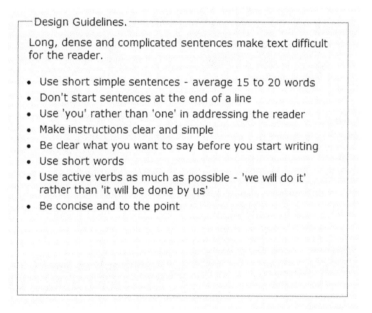

Topic Coverage of Questions

Questions in the visual impairment section simulated (as mentioned earlier) the effects of Age-Related Macular Degeneration, and also Tunnel Vision and "Floaters" within the eye. A question on colour-blindness showed text and background in a way that made them difficult to discriminate, and a further question illustrated the problems of using images containing text, which are non-

scalable, rather than text itself, which is. In the hearing impairment category, one question related to tinnitus, the experience of which was simulated by a question being spoken accompanied by a high level of background noise. Other questions illustrated the difficulties associated with the use of sign language and lip-reading for communication with deaf people. A video of poor practice for lip-reading involved a speaker turning away, putting a hand across his mouth, etc.

Questions on physical/motor impairment included some requiring accurate positioning of the mouse, with one question moving the answer box away whenever the mouse pointer approached it, making it impossible to select either of the answers. (This generally caused amusement in the test participants.) Use of the tab key, as a keyboard alternative to mouse usage, was also explored.

The cognitive/learning impairment section contained several questions on dyslexia, including one where the letters b and d were interchanged, and the letters p and q also. This was to illustrate one aspect of dyslexia, where perception of these different letters is confused. This led to statements such as "a qebal dike has the same numder of wheels as a puab dike" and "a droken tidia woulb repuire deb-rest anb qrodally a qob-cast", on which the participants had to comment as to whether they were true or false. A time-constrained question was also presented, with an impossibly short time limit.

Given the earlier discussion concerning the appropriateness of simulating disabilities it was deemed necessary to evaluate the computer aided test against the guidelines for using simulation provided by Burgstahler and Doe (2004). The Table 1 presents a comparison of these guidelines against brief comments of the degree to which the computer aided test complies with the various instructions embodied in the guidelines.

TECHNICAL ISSUES MET IN THE TEST

Having decided that the test should be web based and that there would be a variety of features used to support the simulations including mouse interaction, drag and drop, video clips, and audio clips this presented a series of development challenges. Perhaps the most troubling are the issues over differences in the way the most commonly used browser tools interpret some aspects of the languages used (typically XHTML, CSS and some

features of Javascript). In fact this is compounded by the different versions of individual browsers, most notably Internet Explorer and Firefox, and their continuing developments and improvements. As the test has been under development over several years the original versions of these browsers with which the test was compatible have indeed moved on and there are further changes to make in order to ensure the current version of the test runs smoothly under these new environments.

A difficulty frequently experienced by users has been the delay in loading the video and audio clips with a resulting frustration when interacting with some of the hearing impairment simulations.

FEEDBACK TO DATE

As stated previously the computer aided test has been presented and tested at a number of events and gained a variety of comments and suggestions for improvements from the participants. Following the incorporation of these improvements the test has been used with further groups of staff and formed the theme of a presentation at the Leeds Met Disability Research Conference in 2008. Feedback has been sought from all of these events and the outcomes are discussed below.

Feedback at the 2008 Disability Research Conference

When the test was presented at the 2008 Disability Research Conference there were several comments and suggestions from the audience. Two in particular were strongly aligned with proposed further work on the test.

There was a suggestion that the test would be enhanced if there was a short video introducing each of the categories where the speaker was a student living with a disability falling under that category. The aim here would be for the student to describe some of their experiences of studying and working online with that disability. This would

Table 1. Comparison of the Computer Aided Test with the Burgstahler and Doe Guidelines for using Simulations

Guideline	Description	How this is met by the Computer Aided Test
State Objectives Clearly	Make it clear to participants at the beginning of the activity what they will do and what they are expected to learn	As part of the original design it was recognised that users needed some instructions on how to interact with the simulations and these are placed on the introductory page for each of the categories.
Ensure Voluntary Participation	Allowing people to decline participation eliminates reluctant or resentful participation	Whenever the test has been used in public arenas all participants have chosen to engage in the simulations.
Illustrate Challenges and Solutions Related to both the System and the Individual	Avoid focusing exclusively on challenges imposed on individuals by a disability, and avoid comparing one disability experience to another. ... Use concrete examples to illustrate both barriers and strategies for overcoming barriers for people with disabilities	There is no explicit comparison of any one disability with another. Crucial elements of the simulations are both feedback to the answers submitted for the questions associated with the individual simulations and more importantly the items in the 'Useful Links' section shown to the right of each simulation. These links show known good practices to minimise the disadvantages experienced through the disability. They also offer the participant access to key support sites and possible online sites for self testing on disabilities. Users may also be directed to other helpful guides and advice for assisting people with the disability being simulated.
Demonstrate the Value of Universal Design	Simulations and debriefing discussions should examine the way in which a well-designed environment or activity can maximize access for everyone and minimize the need for individual accommodations	It is recognised that where accommodations to online materials are made to support particular disabilities there is the potential for all students accessing those materials to benefit also. Keeping the language of the learning materials simple will help both students with dyslexia and it will also assist other students studying the same materials. Feedback from the reviewers of some of the earlier papers also made this same point.
Include Consumers in Planning and, When Possible, Delivery of the Simulation	Consult people with disabilities when developing simulations and, when possible, involve them in the delivery, debriefing, and evaluation of simulation activities	From the beginning people with a variety of disabilities were consulted about their experiences. One member of the original team is partially deaf and provided specific input for the hearing simulations.
Support Positive Attitude Change	Participants should be encouraged to bring up personal beliefs or assumptions, even if negative, without fear of negative repercussions	Feedback questionnaires have been used to seek to identify participants' responses to both the simulations and also their awareness of disability issues. Providing opportunities for participants to share their experiences also allowed them to articulate prior beliefs and expectations of working with disabled students.
Debrief Thoroughly And Reflectively Acknowledge Discomfort	An important part of successful simulation activities is a full and meaningful debriefing to disengage participants from what is sometimes an emotional experience, as well as to sort out what was learned	Where there was an organised session participants were encouraged to discuss their experiences and to think about what they might mean for them in their work with students.

enable the test to embody student input explicitly and visibly much more effectively than inviting students to view the simulations and recording their responses.

A second comment focused on the problems surrounding the categorisation of disabilities into discrete and recognisable sets of symptoms. In itself this is in danger of reducing the aims of the test to a collection of symptoms that disregard the students behind the disabilities. Briefly the medical model sees the person as the problem and the solution is to change that person to fit in with the rest of the world. A more appropriate model is the social model in which the non-disabled world is regarded as excluding those with disabilities as a result of the ways in which it is organised. The solution here is to seek change in the non-disabled world to include those with disability. With regard to the computer-aided test the provision of advice and guidance that are aimed at helping a member of staff to modify their approaches to accommodate the needs of students with disability is strongly aligned with the social model of disability.

Feedback from other Workshops

The revised version of the test was offered as a self-taught resource to students on the Post Graduate Certificate of Higher Education course. More recently, Library staff (most concerned with supporting students with disabilities), Technology Enhanced Learning (TEL) Network staff and staff from the Faculty of Business and Law were asked to look at the test and evaluate it. The Library staff were asked to carry out this evaluation in a largely stand alone manner whereas the TEL Network and Business and Law staff were engaged in face to face sessions. These evaluations were accompanied by a questionnaire that sought to identify any impacts on staff that interacted with the test. A sample of the data collected from this is shown in Appendix A. Their evaluations are very much aligned to the earlier feedback and are strongly positive, though some technical problems such as difficulty in viewing video clips have been noted.

A large majority of those who took the test said that it had increased their awareness of disability and most staff took the time to indicate specific examples of this. These examples cover the full range of the simulations used. The comments staff provided indicate a high level of appreciation for the test. Staff were also asked to indicate how the test might influence their future actions and again responses for this are shown in Appendix A. Typically these responses demonstrate that staff focus on a particular facet of disability and plan to improve ways of minimising the impact of this by changing some way of working or approach to teaching. Perhaps the biggest area of focus here was on information presented textually;

staff highlighted the use of simpler language as something that could improve matters. An interesting observation here is that this is also highly likely to improve matters for all students, not just those with problems of dyslexia.

Feedback provided by one participant that was of particular interest:

"Overall, I realise that the test was trying to get some basic points across about some of the difficulties that people with disabilities face, but it served only to really annoy and irritate".

At one level this is exactly the type of response that the test is intended to create. If the participant, as an able bodied user, experienced frustration and annoyance at having to work with the simulations, how much greater are the frustrations of those living with disabilities in a world designed for the able bodied. One key aspect of the test that this response demonstrates is the need for participants to have an opportunity to discuss their learning and responses to the simulations and to share both discomfort and frustration with others.

A subsequent follow up interview with the staff who engaged in the test has been carried out with the aim of discovering what, if any, actual changes staff have made to their working practices, preparation of materials and/or teaching approaches. Responses to the question asking about any changes to their practices are shown in Appendix B. Overall most respondents had not revisited the simulations since the workshop though for most people this was largely due to pressures of time. Of the eleven respondents ten said that the simulations had affected their practice, attitude or values in some way and gave examples illustrating this. Most respondents indicated an increased awareness of issues around accessibility and offered some further example where their practice has changed. To some extent one can speculate that the examples offered by the respondents reflect the student populations they are working with and the approaches that they are currently using. So for example one respondent was "working with overseas student" and stated that the test had "changed my practice when working with anything screen based".

Wider Comments on the Test

The major feedback from staff indicates that the web-site used in a stand alone way, without the support of face to face workshop facilitators, is not as easy to navigate as they would like. Comments such as "Some of the 'cognitive' questions could be more obvious as to what the issue is" and complaints that the question about tinnitus could not be properly heard and the time-limited question went too fast (both deliberate features) also indicate that more work is needed to make the stand alone version of the test sufficiently self-explanatory in purpose and content as well as easier to navigate.

CURRENT IMPROVEMENTS TO THE TEST

Recognising that the test is likely to be used in both a stand alone as well as in organised group based activities the CETL ALiC team have looked at the responses gathered so far and revisited the Burgstahler guidelines with a view to enhancing the test. To date work on improving the navigation has been completed with the introduction of drop down menus available on all pages of the test. In addition the introduction and instruction elements of the simulations have also been revisited with a clear statement of the purpose for each test being added together with improved directions for engaging with the simulations.

Accepting the criticism over the delays in downloading the video and audio clips these have been moved onto YouTube and SoundBoard.

FUTURE RESEARCH DIRECTIONS

Clearly there is a continuing process of designing additional questions, collating further guidelines and enhancing the user interface and navigability of the test. Further analysis of user feedback will play a major role in this. The future delivery mode of the test is also under consideration, whether this should be as a stand alone Web resource, a face to face workshop of short duration, a component within a supported online course, or all of these. This range of delivery modes illustrates the flexibility of the tool. After being offered to academic staff in a limited number of disciplines within Leeds Met, it will be made available to new entrants to University teaching in all disciplines within the university. Dissemination to Computer Science departments in other universities will be facilitated by the ALiC Centre for Excellence in Teaching and Learning.

An online version of the test is available at the Leeds Met CETL ALiC website (2010). One possibility for the future could be to encourage the formation of a social network of users engaging in a dialogue of feedback around the test.

Evaluation of the impact on university teaching staff members has so far been limited. Immediate feedback on their reactions to the test has been obtained, and follow-up to assess any later effect on their actions has been undertaken with a limited number of staff. Though different models of evaluation of the effect of staff training exist, for example the Content/ Input/ Reaction/ Output model (Northumbria University, 2006); there is normally an "output" phase that attempts to assess the impact on staff. In the case of the test, this could include analysis of the number of staff who engage with the test as well as a more extensive and structured collection of feedback from users at some later time to analyse the effect of the test on their practice. The suggestion of involving disabled students in the evolution of the test has been pursued, and it is planned that this will happen using some existing focus groups in the near future. Follow-up sessions on specific impairments have not yet been created, but Leeds Met's Assessment, Learning and Teaching strategy (Leeds Metropolitan University, 2005) places considerable emphasis on the needs of disabled students, and the creators of the staff development programme have the requirements of disability training under consideration.

CONCLUSION

In conclusion, the computer aided test developed at Leeds Met to assist in Computer Science academic staff training in disability issues has proved a successful and useful tool. It provides a simulation of the experience of disabled students using a computer in their work or taking a computer aided test, and gives helpful advice to university teaching staff on how to approach their teaching and computer aided testing. Staff reactions to the test have been positive, and have indicated an increased interest in learning about disability through further sessions. There appears to be much potential for the future use of such a test.

REFERENCES

ADA. Americans With Disabilities Act (1990). Retrieved January 19, 2010, from http://www.usdoj.gov/crt/ada/adahom1.htm

Barriers, B., & Blog, B. (2010). Retrieved January 19, 2010, from http://bbandbohmy.blogspot.com/2010/01/disability-simulation-exercises-promote.html

Behler, G. T. (1993). Disability Simulations as a Teaching Tool: Some Ethical Implications and Issues. *Journal on Postsecondary Education and Disability, 10*(2), 1993.

Burgstahler, S., & Doe, T. (2004). Disability-related simulations: If, when, and how to use them. *Review of Disability Studies: An International Journal, 1*(2), 4-17. Retrieved January 19, 2010, from http://staff.washington.edu/sherylb/RDSissue022004.html

Cohen, R. F., Fairley, A. V., Gerry, D., & Lima, G. R. (2005). *Accessibility in Introductory Computer Science.* In Proceedings of the 36th SIGCSE Technical symposium on Computer science education, St. Louis, Missouri USA, February 23-27 (pp. 17-21). New York: ACM Press.

Colella, V. (2000). Participatory Simulations: Building Collaborative Understanding Through Immersive Dynamic Modeling. *Journal of the Learning Sciences, 9*(4), 471–500. doi:10.1207/S15327809JLS0904_4

Disability Rights Commission. (2010). *Accessibility Simulation.* Retrieved January 19, 2010, from www.drc-gb.org/employers_and_service_provider/services_and_transport/inaccessible_website_demo/start_page.aspx

Durham University. (2006). *Active Learning in Computing.* Retrieved January 19, 2010, from http://www.dur.ac.uk/alic/

EDF - European Disability Forum. (2007). *Promoting Equality and Combating Disability Discrimination: The Need for a Disability Specific Non-Discrimination Directive Going Beyond Employment.* Retrieved January 19, 2010, from http://cms.horus.be/files/99909 /MediaArchive/Top5Campaigns/Microsoft%20Word%20-%20The%20need%20for%20a%20Disability%20Specific%20Directive_October%202007_FINAL.pdf

Francioni, J. M., & Smith, A. C. (2005). *Computer Science Accessibility for Students with Visual Disabilities.* In Proceedings of the 36th SIGCSE Technical symposium on Computer science education, St. Louis, Missouri USA, February 23-27 (pp. 91-95). New York: ACM Press.

Getzel, E., Briel, L., & McManus, S. (2003). Strategies for Implementing Professional Development Activities on College Campuses: Findings from the OPE-Funded Project Sites (1999-2002). *Journal of Postsecondary Education and Disability*, *17*(1), 59–78.

Harrison, G., & Gray, J. (2006). *A Computer-Assisted test for Accessible Computer-assisted Assessment*. In Proceedings of the 10th CAA International Computer Assisted Assessment Conference, Loughborough, UK, July 4-5 (pp. 205-209). Loughborough: Professional Development Loughborough University.

Harrison, G., & Gray, J. (2007). *An Improved Computer-Assisted test for Accessible Computer-assisted Assessment*. In Proceedings of the 11th CAA International Computer Assisted Assessment Conference, Loughborough, UK, July 10-11 (pp. 253-265). Loughborough: Professional Development Loughborough University.

Harrison, S. M. (2005). *Opening the Eyes of Those Who Can See to the World of Those Who Can't: A Case Study*. In Proceedings of the 36th SIGCSE technical symposium on Computer science education, St. Louis, Missouri USA, February 23-27 (pp. 22-26). New York: ACM Press.

HEFCE. Higher Education Funding Council for England (2005). *Centres for Excellence in Teaching and Learning*. Retrieved January 19, 2010, from http://www.hefce.ac.uk/learning/TInits/cetl/

HESA. Higher Education Statistics Agency (2006). *First year UK domiciled HE students by qualification aim, mode of study, gender and disability 2005/06*. Retrieved January 19, 2010, from http://www.hesa.ac.uk/dox/dataTables/studentsAndQualifiers/download/disab0708.xls

HMSO. (1995). *Disability Discrimination Act 1995 (c. 50)*. Retrieved January 19, 2010, from http://www.opsi.gov.uk/acts/acts1995/1995050.htm

HMSO. (2001). *Special Educational Needs and Disability Act 2001*. Retrieved January 19, 2010, from http://www.opsi.gov.uk/acts/acts2001/20010010.htm

Leeds Metropolitan University. (2005). *Assessment, Learning and Teaching at Leeds Metropolitan University: an Education Strategy*. Retrieved January 19, 2010, from http://www.leedsmet.ac.uk/about/keydocuments/Version32AssesmentTeaching-LearningStrategy1.pdf

Leeds Metropolitan University. (2007). *Active Learning in Computing*. Retrieved January 19, 2010, from http://www.leedsmet.ac.uk/inn/alic

Leeds Metropolitan University. (2010). *Active Learning in Computing*. Retrieved January 19, 2010, from http://www.leedsmet.ac.uk/inn/alic/CAATest2010/

LexDis – Ideas for e-learning (2007). *JISC project 2007 – Feb 2009*. Retrieved Feb 1, 2010, from http://www.lexdis.org.uk/

Northumbria University. (2006). *Human Resources, Evaluation of Staff Training and Development: Guidance Notes*. Retrieved January 19, 2010, from http://northumbria.ac.uk/sd/central/hr/std/td_eval/

Papadopoulos, G., & Pearson, E., (2007). *Accessibility awareness raising and continuing professional development – The use of simulations as a motivational tool*. ALT online newsletter, Issue 7, January 2007.

Pearson, E. J., & Koppi, A. J. (2006). Supporting staff in developing inclusive online learning. In Adams, M., & Brown, S. (Eds.), *Towards Inclusive Learning in Higher Education* (pp. 56–66). London, New York: Routledge.

Powell, N., Moore, D., Gray, J., Finlay, J., & Reaney, J. (2003). *Dyslexia and Learning Computer Programming*. In Proceedings of the 4th Annual Conference of the LTSN Centre for Information and Computer Sciences, Galway, Ireland, August 26-28. (pp. 11-16). Newtownabbey: LTSN-ICS.

Salzberg, C. (2002). Opinions of disability service directors on faculty training: The need, content, issues, formats, media, and activities. *Journal of Postsecondary Education and Disability, 15*(2), 101–114.

Salzberg, C. (2003). *Preparing Higher Education Faculty for Students with Disabilities: It's right; it's smart; and it should be mandatory.* Retrieved January 19, 2010, from http://asd.usu.edu/resources/files/preparing_faculty.pdf

TechDis. (2006a). *TechDis.* Retrieved January 19, 2010, from http://www.techdis.ac.uk/

TechDis. (2006b). *Sim-dis: A view into the unknown.* Retrieved January 19, 2010, from http://www.techdis.ac.uk/resources/sites/2/simdis/index.htm

TechDis. (2006c). *TechDis Staff Packs.* Retrieved January 19, 2010, from http://www.techdis.ac.uk/index.php?p=3_3

UMUC. University of Maryland University College (2005). *Accessibility in Distance Education A Resource for Faculty in Online Teaching.* Retrieved January 19, 2010, from http://www.umuc.edu/ade/

UNESCO. The General Conference of the United Nations Educational Scientific and Cultural Organization (1960). *Convention against Discrimination in Education.* Retrieved January 19, 2010, from http://www.unhchr.ch/html/menu3/b/d_c_educ.htm

U.S. Department of Education, National Center for Education Statistics. (2006). *Question: What proportion of students enrolled in postsecondary education have a disability?* Retrieved January 19, 2010, from http://nces.ed.gov/fastfacts/display.asp?id=60

WAI-AGE Project. (2010). *European Commission IST Specific Support Action.* Apr 2007 – September 2010. Retrieved January 19, 2010, from http://www.w3.org/WAI/WAI-AGE/deliverables.html

WebAIM – Center for Disabled Persons, Utah University. (2010a). Retrieved February 10, 2010, from http://www.webaim.org

WebAIM – Center for Disabled Persons, Utah University. (2010b). Retrieved February 10, 2010, from http://www.webaim.org/standards/wcag/checklist

ADDITIONAL READING

Paciello, M. G. (2000). *WEB Accessibility for People with Disabilities.* Lawrence, KS: CMP Books.

This document is essential for those concerned with designing web pages and web content.

Though this text was published in 2000 and several areas are out of date it provides a very readable overview of many key issues surrounding web accessibility.

Web Accessibility Initiative - Essential Components of Web Accessibility. (2010). Retrieved February 10, 2010, from http://www.w3.org/WAI/intro/components.php.

KEY TERMS AND DEFINITIONS

CSS: CSS stands for Cascading Style Sheet. This is a document format which provides a set of style rules which can then be incorporated in an XHTML or HTML document. It is a means to separate web content from formatting and presentation information.

Browser: Short for *Web browser*, a software application used to locate and display Web pages.

FireFox: Firefox is a free, open source Web browser for Windows, Linux and Mac OS X.

Internet Explorer: The name of Microsoft's browser that enables you to view Web pages on the Internet using a graphical interface.

JavaScipt: Perhaps the most ubiquitous scripting language on the web, Javascript is a client side programming language which can be used with almost all user agents.

Opera: Opera is boasted as being the speediest and most standards-compliant of the current browsers in use.

Safari: The standard web browser provided with Apple Macintosh computers.

TechDis: JISC TechDis is the leading educational advisory service providing advice and guidance on technology and disability to promote an accessible and inclusive experience for students and staff. JISC TechDis is a JISC Advisory Service.

WebAIM: a non-profit organization based at Utah State University in Logan, Utah. WebAIM has provided web accessibility solutions since 1999. WebAIM's mission is to expand the potential of the web for people with disabilities by providing the knowledge, technical skills, tools, organizational leadership strategies, and vision that empower organizations to make their own content accessible to people with disabilities.

XHTML: XHTML (Extensible HyperText Markup Language) is a combination of XML and HTML which provides developers with a language which uses the HTML specifications within the constraints of the XML format.

Chapter 5
Computer–Based Learning Systems for People with Autism

David Moore
Leeds Metropolitan University, UK

ABSTRACT

This chapter reviews research and development work addressing computer-based learning systems (CBL) for people with autism. The chapter starts by considering the defining characteristics of autism. In the light of this understanding of autism, it is argued that CBL systems, in particular autism-specific systems, have the potential to play a beneficial role in the education of people with autism. Recent research and development work in the field is reviewed, and it is argued that there are several weaknesses currently. The author's research addresses some of these weaknesses; and the chapter concludes by briefly outlining this work, including the development of a simple computer-based "shell" system that readers may request from the author.

INTRODUCTION

This chapter overviews recent work concerning computer systems for people with autism. We begin by explaining what is meant by autism, then in the light of this understanding we make a case for using computer technology as an assistive technology for people with autism. We then briefly review work in the field, and argue that

DOI: 10.4018/978-1-61350-183-2.ch005

there are currently many weaknesses. One of these is that little if any research has looked at how the technology might help people with severe autism. In order to help to begin to address this, we have conducted a longitudinal study with some young people who are severely autistic. This study is discussed in the next chapter of this book (by Elzouki and Cooper).

The objectives of the current chapter therefore are (i) to make a case for the potential usefulness of computer technology for people with autism;

(ii) to suggest weakness with the current state of the art concerning computers and autism; (iii) to suggest ways in which the field might usefully move forward.

BACKGROUND

We start by outlining what we mean by "autism". This is not easy, because the literature contains different views about what exactly autism is. However, a commonly, if not universally, held view of the nature of autism is that it involves a "triad of impairments" (Wing, 1996; Jordan, 1991a) or a triad of "differences" (Hardy et al, 2002). There is a social difference: someone with autism may find it hard to relate to, and empathise with, other people. Secondly, there is a communication difference: someone with autism may find it hard to understand and use verbal and non-verbal communication. The third aspect of the triad is more controversial. Until recently, it was seen by the UK's National Autistic Society (NAS, 2005) as "Imagination (difficulty in the development of interpersonal play and imagination, for example having a limited range of imaginative activities, possibly copied and pursued rigidly and repetitively)" Currently, however, it is defined by the NAS (2010a) as a "difficulty with social imagination":

"Social imagination allows us to understand and predict other people's behaviour, make sense of abstract ideas, and to imagine situations outside our immediate daily routine. Difficulties with social imagination mean that people with autism find it hard to:

- understand and interpret other people's thoughts, feelings and actions
- predict what will happen next, or what could happen next

- understand the concept of danger, for example that running on to a busy road poses a threat to them
- engage in imaginative play and activities: children with autism may enjoy some imaginative play but prefer to act out the same scenes each time
- prepare for change and plan for the future
- cope in new or unfamiliar situations.

Difficulties with social imagination should not be confused with a lack of imagination. Many people with autism are very creative and may be, for example, accomplished artists, musicians or writers."

Much current thinking is that this triad of differences is at least partly underpinned by a "theory of mind" difference (eg Baron-Cohen, 2001)—people with autism may have a difficulty in understanding mental states and in ascribing them to themselves or to others.

The goal of, and the challenge for, those caring for people with autism may be seen as enabling them to lead a "happy and satisfying life" (Carlton, 1993) and to achieve what Brown (1993) refers to as "full age appropriate autonomy". Education is seen by many as key to achieving this goal (e.g. Aaron and Gittens, 1998; Oberleitner et al, 2006).

Autism is usually seen as a "spectrum condition": it varies in degree of severity, from severe autism, displaying the above triad to a large extent, to mild autism. The mild end of the spectrum is often referred to as "Asperger Syndrome" (eg Attwood, 2007). A commonly used expression is "autism spectrum disorder". Recently the less pejorative expression "autism spectrum condition" has come into vogue. It has the advantage of seeing autism as a condition rather than disorder, thus avoiding the pejorative connotations of the latter. Indeed a recent paper discusses the "autie advantage" (Wolman, 2010), highlighting what are seen there as "benefits" of being on the autism spectrum.

Estimates of the incidence of autism vary. According to at least one account (Safran, 2008), it appears to be increasing, having moved from 2 – 6 per 1,000 births in 2004, to 1/150 in the US in 2007 and 1/100 in the UK in 2007. This may however be partly an issue of increased identification and recognition of the condition.

Why Might Computer Systems Help People with Autism?

One answer to this question is that there is considerable evidence that people with autism may tend to enjoy working with computers:

- The UK National Autistic Society suggests "there is good evidence to suggest that children with autism can be motivated by well presented computer based activities" (NAS, 1995; cf. Cobb et al, 2010; Jordan, 1992b; Swettenham, 1996; Stokes, 2006a). In a study of children with autism using a computer to help their communication Hetzroni and Tannous (2004) found that "all participants preferred the computer interactive program". Murray (1997) suggests that use of computers may increase the self-esteem and optimism of users with autism and cause their most "world-excluding autistic behaviours" to occur less frequently. In a survey of Irish Primary Schools, Barry and Pitt (2006) found that teachers "agreed that technology is attractive to the learner with autism" (p 33).
- It has been suggested that children with autism may prefer a computer's "voice", since it is devoid of the subtle nuances that characterise human speech (Schlosser & Blischak, 2001; Nimmo, 1994).
- Similarly, it has been suggested that people with autism may find it hard to screen out unnecessary sensory information and that

"focusing on a computer screen where only necessary information is presented may minimise such difficulties" (Silver, 2000, p 36). In the same vein, the UK's National Autistic Society (NAS) suggest that "external events can be more easily ignored when focusing on a computer screen as the area of concentration is limited to the bounds of the screen. The small area of focus might explain why some people with autism can tolerate higher sensory input via a computer than they can apparently tolerate elsewhere" (NAS, 2010b).

Perhaps the main reason why people with autism might benefit from use of computer systems relates specifically to computer-based learning systems. In such a system the computer presents learning material to the individual student, giving them information, asking questions about it and offering additional information and exercises if necessary in the light of the student's response. Computer-based learning is often referred to as "computer-assisted instruction" (e.g. Pennington, 2010), "computer-assisted learning" or "computer-aided learning (e.g. Moore, McGrath, & Thorpe, 2000). Multimedia takes this a step further by using, in addition to text, some combination of sound, video, graphics and animation; multimedia systems therefore have a potentially large role to play in enhancing and enriching learning.

These systems may be seen as particularly important since as we saw earlier, many people believe that education is central to any attempts at helping people with autism. Simmonds, for example, argues that "the teacher will need to assume that the student will need to be taught *everything* that they need to learn" (Simmonds, 1993, emphasis added) and Attwood (1986) points out that children with autism have unique learning problems. Tantam (1993) claims that the style of teaching that a child with autism receives can influence behaviour for good or ill, and Powell and Jordan (1997): "good teaching can make a difference".

It can be argued that computer-based learning can make a useful contribution to such teaching. Computer-based learning systems are often seen as having several general advantages for the education of all students (whether or not they are deemed to be on the autism spectrum), in particular (Moore, 1998):

- Learning can progress at the pace of the individual student
- The student may feel free to experiment and interact without the fear of ridicule or embarrassment from his tutor or peers
- The computer has infinite patience
- Students can use the system at their own convenience
- Learning can to some extent be customised to the needs of the individual student.

These general advantages of CBL will apply, it can be argued, to the use of CBL systems by people with autism. In addition, it can be argued that further advantages may apply to the use of CBL by people with autism:

The computer presents a relatively controlled environment as a teaching tool and can eliminate many distractions of the normal classroom (Green, 1993; cf. Murray, 1997; Hetzroni and Tannous, 2004).

A further aspect of the controlled environment is the consistency and predictability (Swettenham, 1996; Stokes, 2006a; Jacklin and Farr; 2005; Herskowitz, 2009) which characterises CBL. The computer reacts the same way at all times, providing therefore a potentially reassuring environment. Stokes (2006a) argues "the computer does not send confusing social messages".

CBL may be able to help cater for the generic educational needs of children with autism, e.g. meeting targets in "small achievable steps" (Simmonds, 1993), working at their own pace, being able to correct "mistakes" (Jordan, 1992a),

simple, clear instructions (Marsden, 1993; Jordan, 1991a) and having things patiently explained, several times if necessary (cf. Nimmo, 1994). There is evidence (Higgins and Boone, 1996; Bernard-Opitz et al, 1990; Moore and Calvert, 2000) to suggest that use of CBL systems may lead to increased attention and rate of learning.

The computer-based learning exercises are repeatable and offer 'safe' experimentation with ideas.

They are to some extent adaptable in that, for example, text can be turned on and off depending on the perceived needs of the user

Computer-based learning can put the student in control of the learning, rather than being merely a passive receiver of information and instruction, and this may help encourage independent decision making (Silver, 2000).

Use of the computer keyboard may help with manual dexterity (Jordan, 1991b).

Similarly, the NAS (2010b) argue that the use of a computer keyboard may help create "an awareness of self", since the user may become aware that it is their touching of the keys that causes visible changes on the computer screen; the same argument would apply to the user making choices from a computer "menu".

If computers and/or the software can be taken home, this may help home-school liaison (cf. Anthony, 1992; Hagiwara and Myles, 1999) and may enable parents to "deliver instruction in the home setting" (Pennington, 2010, p 8).

Using computer-based learning systems (and indeed computer use in general) affords the opportunity for the students to become familiar with the technology and thus gain potentially marketable skills (Jordan, 1991b; Herskowitz, 2009). The NAS (2010b) claim that "for the same reason that computers can be useful learning tools for people with autism, many people at the high functioning end of the autistic spectrum find that they are extremely good at jobs which involve computers".

A further benefit concerns the individualised, one to one tutoring that may be made possible by CBL. Such a teaching mode is often seen as important for students with autism, e.g. Peeters (1995) talks of the "unbelievable luxury of individual attention", Higgins and Boone (1996) see individualisation as "key to appropriate instruction" for students with autism and Green suggests that it is useful to be able to "leave the child with the computer largely unattended" (Green, 1990; cf. Jordan, 1991a; Hetzroni and Tannous, 2004). Such individualised learning may be particularly appropriate for domain-specific education, e.g. Jordan (1992a) argues that learning of skills in mathematics should not depend on the acquisition of "other more difficult social skills".

In a specialist autism-dedicated school, such as those run by the NAS, the staff-student ratio is likely to be excellent. However, many children with autism will be taught in "special" schools with other children who have various forms of learning difficulties, or in special units in mainstream schools. Indeed, the choice of mainstream education might be seen as a good thing. Either way, the fact is that "pupils with autism are liable to be represented in all kinds of school" (Jordan, 1991a). As a result, there is a need for specialist knowledge and support within mainstream schools. It is, however, asking a lot for all schools to be able to provide the requisite support (Jordan and Powell, 1995) and CBL therefore has a potential role to play in contributing, in a small part at least, to such support. The argument in short is that to some extent the computer may make up for shortfalls in human provision in large classrooms.

Another part of the case for the use of CBL for people with autism concerns the added power and realism that can be achieved in CBL by the use of multimedia technology. An important use of multimedia is to give realistic interactive simulations of social situations, which are potentially very valuable to students with autism (Moore and Taylor, 2000). As Trehin (1996) says "the "multimedia" technology ought to enable

exercises to be offered which more closely match real (social) situations". Similarly, Hetzroni and Tannous (2004) suggest that multimedia systems can present controlled and structured simulated environments that provide children with autism with the chance to learn about and practise relevant skills. More generally, multimedia systems may be beneficial in that they can eliminate the need for reading in order to engage in CBL activities (Iacono and Miller, 1989). Conversely, Murray (1997) suggests that through computer use students with autism may become motivated to read.

In summary, there is much research to suggest that computers can have powerful benefits for learning. Moreover many of their affordances are those also associated with the highest quality traditional teaching which optimises learning for all students, but is essential for those who do not thrive in the current education system. Cooper (2004) argues that profoundly empathic teaching (usually found in one to one tutoring) offers many of these same affordances, patience and mutually respectful learning where students have more opportunity for participation and autonomy. Such personalised learning takes account of the learner's interests and ability levels and supports them with moment by moment contingent teaching, using multisensory activities and supports them without the pressure and anxiety caused by peers. Positive affect is central to effective learning.

Developments in neuroscience (Damasio, 1999, 2003) give weight to the emphasis on affect in learning previously articulated in the psychological literature of the sixties and seventies (Rogers, 1975; Purkey, 1970; Aspy, 1972). Damasio (1999) explains the significance of intense interaction and engagement in learning, where the senses are focussed on the object or person of interest. He emphasises the role of the human's own sense of body and self, in relation to the world they learn about. At each interaction a human being recreates an image of self (body and brain) in the mind. With each positive interaction, the sense of self is continually reinforced and updated and the person is encouraged to open up more, explore more and learn more. Negative interaction causes the brain and body to retract and protect itself. With positive multi-sensory interaction, the brain and body absorb the feedback, becoming increasingly engrossed and engaged, and better able to process and understand. This type of quality interaction seems to be stimulated by both personal tutoring and computer-based learning.

There is, then, a strong case to be made for CBL in the education of students with autism. In the light of such arguments as these, it is not, perhaps, surprising to find in the literature expressions of support for the use of CBL for pupils with autism. For example Oberleitner et al (2006) suggest that "computer technology is used more and more to augment the education of people with autism" (p 236) and Pennington (2010, p 8) argues that "recent innovations hint at the endless possibilities for the application of computer-based technologies … for students with ASD". And evidence, albeit much of it preliminary, is starting to accumulate to support the case for CBL for people with autism.

COMPUTERS AND AUTISM: CURRENT ISSUES

Issues, Controversies, Problems

"Collusion"

A major potential problem of the use of computers, particularly in an educational role, for people with autism, is that it may "collude with" the user's autism (eg Parsons and Mitchell, 2002). The concern is that because people with autism may spend time with the machine (the computer) rather than interacting with other people, this may in fact exacerbate any social difficulties they may have, by enabling them in effect to "hide away" from social interactions by concentrating on using the computer. Further, students with autism often have "obsessional interests" (e.g. Jordan and Pow-

ell, 1995) and there is a danger that the computer itself may become one such interest; all this could lead to less social interaction. Murray has argued along similar lines: "is there not a basic danger that the computer will be so appealing to autistic individuals that they will become more autistic in relating to it?" (Murray, 1997; cf. Peeters, 1995; Bernard-Opitz et al, 1990; Bishop, 2003; Jacklin and Farr, 2005).

One answer to this potential problem is to point out that the use of computers in general and CBL in particular is not being advocated as the *only* approach to education, hence any negative effects can be countered, in principle at least, by other educational approaches. Arguably, one should seek to use CBL only where appropriate and to integrate it into as coherent an educational experience as possible for individual students or groups of students. Educating students with autism may be difficult, there is unlikely to be a recipe for success (Powell and Jordan, 1997), and the challenge is to find the best use and combination of the various teaching possibilities. CBL will not necessarily be appropriate for all students and all circumstances, far from it; as Heimann et al (1995) put it: "a computer and a motivating multimedia program might be of help, but there is no absolute magic associated with the computer. For some children, other and different paths of learning must be explored and supported".

Neither of course does CBL use preclude other forms of tuition, e.g. in some organisations a student is asked to tell the class about the computer-based activity they have just completed (Anthony, 1992). Similarly, Iacono and Miller (1989) argue "the advantages [of CBL] for learners who are handicapped may lie in its use as an adjunct, rather than as an alternative to traditional instruction". A balance is therefore needed between CBL and other forms of tuition. An important issue, then, is how best to integrate CBL work with other forms of tuition and with the curriculum in general.

One answer to the concern that use of computers may collude with a user's autism, then, lies in the successful integration of computer-based work with other aspects of educational provision. A further argument is to point out that computer-based learning may well occur in a social situation, so that the concern with isolation need not arise. Murray (1997), for example, recommends that a tutor be present for at least part of the time during computer-based activity, and Higgins and Boone (1996) advocate the use of "computer buddies" although the quality of interaction may be very variable amongst school mates (Cooper and Brna, 2002). Similarly, Parsons and Mitchell (2002) argue for the adoption of collaborative working practices during computer-based work. Indeed designing well-thought out collaborative learning environments in which computer provision is embedded amongst natural human interaction in classrooms could improve positive interaction and learning generally (Cooper & Brna, 2002).

Further, there is some evidence that computer-based work can lead to more interaction with other people, for example better turn-taking (Chen and Bernard-Opitz, 1993; cf. Trehin, 1996; Jacklin and Farr, 2005; Heimann et al, 1995). The NAS (2005) argues that computer use gives "possibilities of non-verbal or verbal expression" and Murray argues that computers can facilitate communication, especially between the person with autism and their carers, providing a "sort of neutral interface through which communication can occur much more easily than is normal in autism" (Murray, 1997). Similarly, Hetzroni and Tannous (2004) found that some of the children in their study used more speech when they were working with the computer.

Access to the Technology

The problem here is that not all people with autism will necessarily have ready access to a computer. Murray (1997) suggests we ought to "make sure every class with an autistic child in it has at least one computer, preferably two. (Ideally every home - natural or residential - with an autistic individual

should also have at least one computer)", although for thirty children in a class this might be deemed woefully inadequate. Even this, though, is likely to be a very difficult aim to achieve, certainly in some parts of the world. In many developed countries there is much better access to ICT now but a lack of a detailed understanding in schools of why computers do support learning may inhibit their most effective deployment and use (Cooper & Brna 2002). It is worth noting that the multi-sensory nature of large interactive screens when used by young children had a powerful effect on engagement and learning (Cooper, 2003) suggesting that further research here with children with autism might prove valuable. The quality, robustness and adaptability of software and systems is also an issue in educational situations.

Autism-Specific and "General" Computer Systems

It can be argued that there are two main ways in which computer systems in general, and CBL systems in particular, can be used with people with autism. One is to use what might be called "generic" software. This is software which is not designed specifically for people with autism, but which nevertheless may be very useful for them.

A CBL system about a specific subject or topic (e.g. history) might be very useful, for instance. A possible characteristic of someone with Asperger Syndrome, for example, is an "intense interest in a particular subject" (Attwood, 1998), and a CBL system addressing that subject might promote and deepen the student's knowledge of it.

Further, in the UK context, at least, the National Curriculum will need to be taught to students with autism, as well as to their neuro-typical peers. Jordan (1991a; 1991b; 1992a; 1992b) has conducted an extensive study of the requirements of the National Curriculum and shown that it should be broadly available to students with autism. Jordan's study reveals a huge catalogue of potential difficulties within the National Curriculum for the student with autism. For example she points to an inability to derive meaning from text or make informed guesses about the meaning of words, over-rigid application of punctuation rules (Jordan, 1991b), difficulty in grasping scientific vocabulary (1992b) and difficulties with estimation (1992a; 1992b). CBL systems may well have a valuable role to play in addressing such difficulties. Anecdotal evidence suggests that a major current use of CBL in catering for such needs is to utilise generic "special needs" software. Such practice may well of course be educationally very valuable, not least because, as Jordan (1991b) points out "most pupils with autism will be outside of their appropriate key stage".

Another way in which computers might prove useful is what is sometimes called "autism-specific" systems (cf. Moore, 1998). These are computer systems, in particular CBL systems, specifically targeted at the core features of autism that we outlined earlier.

One argument for the importance of autism specific systems is that there is a lot of support for addressing autism-specific difficulties in the general education of people with autism (eg Batten et al, 2006), and that this should be reflected in computer systems (Moore et al, 2000; Cobb et al, 2010). Jordan, for example, claims: "of course, it will be a teaching priority to enable the pupil to improve interpersonal and communication skills and to help them participate appropriately in group situations" (Jordan, 1992a; cf. Yates, 1993; Powell and Jordan, 1997). The argument is that this emphasis on autism-specific issues should be reflected in computer systems (Moore et al, 2000)—ie autism-specific systems. Since each child is uniquely affected by their autism and by many other social and historical factors, any system, autism-specific or otherwise would still have to be highly adaptive, most especially for children with severe autism.

A second argument for the importance of autism specific systems is that if such systems are successful in making a contribution to helping in-

dividuals with autism address the autism-specific differences, this would enhance students' access to education in two ways. First, the systems would themselves form a part of the educational experience of the students with autism; this is important not least because as we suggested earlier, education is often seen as the chief way of alleviating the autism disability. Secondly, to the extent that the core impairments are addressed successfully, the ability of the students to benefit from education more generally will be enhanced, since a consequence of the impairments tends to be a difficulty in coping with educational interactions (Jordan, 1991 a). Yates (1993), for example, says "social and communicative problems... remain the main barriers to their achieving their full potential".

Access to good education, then, is a crucial issue for people with autism in the compound sense that autism can tend to be an impediment to quality education but is a condition that requires the highest quality education for its remediation. If autism specific computer systems are successful, they might improve the access of people with autism to education both directly, via their intrinsic educational benefits, and indirectly through the enhanced educational experiences that are likely to be a consequence of improvements to the triad of impairments (Moore and Taylor, 2000).

There is, then, much to be said for developing autism-specific computer systems. Despite this, however, the field remains relatively un-explored (Moore, 1998; Moore et al, 2005). Thus Beardon, Parsons, and Neale (2001) argue that "computerised learning for people with ASD is still in its infancy" (p 61), Hardy et al (2002, p 86) that "there is not much ASD specific software around", and Cobb et al (2010, p 4374) that "there are few adequate bespoke solutions on the market".

Autism-Specific Computer Systems: Some Recent Examples

Although there is little autism-specific software, there have been attempts recently to develop and

with Down's Syndrome and children with neither autism nor Downs Syndrome. The children were taught for two hours per day over five consecutive days. All 3 groups showed successful learning on the instructional task itself and were able to generalise to close transfer tasks. However, none of the children with autism was able to pass distant transfer tasks.

Systems to help with language development are also being built and studied (see Pennington (2010) for a review). Tjus, Heimann, and Lundalv (2003) have developed multimedia systems to enhance language and reading skills, and cite positive results of its use with young (mean age 11.4 years) children with autism (Tjus, Heimann, & Nelson, 2001; Tjus & Heimann, 2000). For example, they have built a program that enables a child to construct a sentence in text and receive "immediate multi-channel feedback" (p. 82); the authors found clear gains in literacy skills when the program was used in combination with appropriate teacher support strategies.

Similarly, positive results have been found when children with autism interacted with "Baldi", a computer-animated language tutor (Bosseler & Massaro, 2003). An experiment involving 8 children with autism, between 7 and 12 years of age, in which the students worked with the program a few times a week over a period of six months, showed that they all learned a significant number ($p < .001$) of new words and grammar, with 91% retention of new words after 30 days. A second experiment involving 6 of the children suggested that the vocabulary knowledge gained can transfer outside of the computer program, although there is as yet no evidence as to whether the children will use the vocabulary they have learned via Baldi, in spontaneous speech in social settings. Most of the children reportedly enjoyed working with Baldi.

Hetzroni and Tannous (2004) have developed a program ("I Can Word It Too") based on daily life activities in the areas of play, food and hygiene. They have conducted a study, involving 5 children with autism between the ages of 7 and

12, of the effects of using the program on the use of functional communication. They found that use of the program was effective in improving the communication of all participants, and that the participants were able to transfer the lessons learned to their natural setting in the classroom. The authors conclude that, "the simulated computer program appears to be a promising strategy for teaching pragmatics and generalising it to natural settings" (p. 111).

Computer-Based Learning and Autism: Current Weaknesses

Despite the increasing research in the field, as briefly reviewed above, there are many concerns with the area, which we will now discuss.

(i) Limited software

As suggested earlier, there is still relatively little software. Thus, for example, the UK NAS (1999, p 13) suggests "autism-specific software packages tend to be hard to come by". Software has tended to be developed for purposes of research rather than for the production of generally useful system development. A result is little autism-specific software for parents or teachers to use. The position is compounded by the fact that the software has been developed in different languages, e.g. Grynzspan's software is in French, Hetzroni's in Hebrew and Arabic. Most software uses English as its language, thus preventing non-English speakers from using it.

There is little commercially produced software. This is perhaps because the limited market for such software makes it commercially untenable to produce. There is some software that can be bought, in particular the Cambridge DVD mentioned earlier (the electronic encyclopaedia of emotions), Silver's "Emotion Trainer", "Gaining Face" and software from "Raising Horizons". It is not clear, though, how widely the software is actually used by people with autism. This is an empirical question, which would be well worth investigating. In the absence of firm evidence either way, one suspects that the software is little used in practice. Barry and Pitt (2006) have surveyed and interviewed teachers in Irish Primary Schools. They found a high level of use of special education software, but teachers reporting "significant shortcomings" from the point of view of the software's suitability for people with autism.

Such software development as there is tends to concentrate on single user applications. There are interesting exceptions to this, such as the work of Hanner et al (2003) and recent and planned work in collaborative virtual environments (eg Cobb et al, 2010; Cheng and Ye, 2010; Parsons et al, 2004). With these exceptions, though, the work primarily involves single user applications. Similarly, there has been relatively little work on the third component of the autism triad. Again there are exceptions to this, such as the work of Herrera and Vera (2005), which investigates virtual reality for "imagination training" (p 449), but generally the area is largely untouched.

More significantly, perhaps, there is a tendency for researchers to focus on the Asperger Syndrome end of the autism spectrum. In many ways this is understandable. A student seeking a PhD may well feel that they will get "better results" if they study computer systems with more able students. A consequence though is that the idea of using computer technology with the more severe end of the autism spectrum has seen very little research, not least because of the complexity of working with such students, especially for the novice researcher. Similarly, though perhaps for less understandable reasons, little software has been aimed at adults with autism; this perhaps reflects a general limitation in the autism literature, which tends to focus on young people. Golan and Baron-Cohen (2006) is an exception, investigating the use of an interactive guide to emotions, "Mind reading", for teaching emotional recognition to adults with autism.

A contributory factor, perhaps, to the dearth of software is the lack of accepted methodologies and *guidelines* for developing autism-specific software (Cobb et al, 2010; Grynszpan et al, 2005). Grynszpan does himself offer some guidelines, in particular "gradual introduction of new modalities", "support for executive functions" and "gradual display of steps in task execution" (Grynszpan, 2005 p 26-27). Higgins and Boone (1996) offer some 18 software design guidelines, although they "remain to be empirically validated" (Pennington, 2010, p 8). Current guidelines, however, tend to be very broad and sometimes contradictory, for example Higgins and Boone suggest using digitised rather than synthetic speech, whereas as we saw earlier it is also argued that suggested that children with autism prefer a computer's "voice", since it is devoid of the subtle nuances that characterise human speech. The current lack of guidelines may be a product of the youth of this area of study and is likely to improve over time. Indeed, Barry and Pitt (2006) are working on compiling guidelines for special education software design that is appropriate for people with autism. Importantly, the guidelines will seek to build on learner strengths as well as address difficulties. Barry and Pitt plan next to design and build software prototypes to test the validity of the guidelines in classroom settings.

For a variety or reasons, then, there is currently little software specifically designed for people with autism. A related concern is that limited research has been done to study how useful and effective the software is, and such research as there is tends to have small numbers in samples (Pennington, 2010). It is particularly important that there is little evidence concerning whether lessons learned on the computer generalise to everyday life, and what evidence there is tends not to look very promising; success on computer-based exercises tends not to be a predictor for analogous events in everyday life.

Further, the research literatures tend to be somewhat disparate. For example the paper by

Oberleitner et al (2006) does not cite any of the research projects mentioned earlier in this chapter, and visa-versa. There seem therefore to be pockets of isolated research to some extent unaware of each other's existence. This is likely to improve as time moves on and the very young area of study matures. Indeed this chapter may make a small contribution in this direction.

(ii) Black and White Questions

A fundamental concern with the use of computers to help teach people with autism, is what might be called the "black and white question" issue. Computers currently, and for the foreseeable future, can deal only with clear-cut, yes-no type questions. Social problems and situations however are rarely so clear cut. Let us consider an example from software that was developed by a former student of ours (the software is available by emailing the author of this chapter). The software concerned a school lunch hour and canteen, an aspect of everyday life found difficult by many people with autism (Cumine et al, 1998). The user is in charge of a character on the screen ("Johnny"). The user has to steer Johnny to an appropriate place in the queue for food. If the user moves Johnny to the front of the queue, he will see video on the screen in which he is told off by the dinner lady and asked to join the queue at the end. If the user tries to join the queue in the middle, he is told the error of his ways by one of the pupils and again asked to join the back of the queue. If he does join the back of the queue he successfully gets his food.

So far so good. The next stage of the software, however, involves choosing where to sit to eat the meal. The user has to choose between full, partially full and totally empty tables. Here the position is more tricky than the issue with the queue. Whilst everyone would probably agree that queues should be joined at the end, there are likely to be subtleties involved in the decision re whether to join people at a table or sit at an empty one. Do I know the people? Do they look like they're about

to leave? Do they look like they're discussing something important and don't want disturbing? Simulating such complexities in software is difficult. The computer cannot itself understand the complexities. This would require major advances in the field of artificial intelligence. Such advances are a long way off at the moment and may never happen. The only solution therefore is to program in the complexities. This involves a lot of work on the part of the programmer, thus potentially increasing the costs, and even then it may be very difficult to adequately capture all the subtleties that one is trying to portray.

(iii) User Variability

Another fundamentally important issue concerns user variability: how can software cater for student differences? There is a large range of academic ability within the population of people with autism (Aarons and Gittens, 1992), different people may have different likes and dislikes about for example a teaching package and may find different things distressing (Jordan, 1991b). It is important therefore that this is somehow taken account of in software systems. Presumably the ideal would be the flexibility to work with the student's strengths and compensate for the student's weaknesses (Jordan and Powell, 1995).

A further aspect of adaptability is to seek to adopt teaching matter which is relevant to the students' varying contexts of study. This will involve basing work where possible on the perceived interests of individual students, for example Jordan argues that it is best to base work with graphs on "topics of direct interest" to the student, and more generally that the curriculum for students with autism should be "tied to actual experiences" (Jordan, 1992a). This of course is well-recognised aspect of all high quality educational practice. Making learning meaningful, personal and relevant to everyday life is essential for motivation (Bruner, 1990).

There is, then, a need for software systems to be responsive to student differences (Trehin, 1996). This however is a complex technical challenge. Three lines of approach can be suggested: having the system dynamically change according to the perceived needs of the student, providing a generic system that can be altered for different students, providing a separate system for each student. Each of these three will briefly be discussed in turn.

Perhaps the most demanding approach from a technical point of view is to have the system dynamically adapt to the individual student. This is the approach taken by Davis (Davis et al, 2006). Ultimately one might hope that the system builds a "student model", ie learns about the student in the same way that a teacher does. However there are many complexities involved in maintaining a useful student model (Self, 1990) not least that it needs to account for affective as well as cognitive factors (Cooper, 2003). Further, many characteristics of a student with autism which one would want to record are very difficult to represent in a student model, for example possible distress they might be feeling. Thirdly, the classifications, for example, that a student with autism makes may be valid but "bizarre, eg bicycles and toilets belong together because you sit on them" (Sinclair and Green, 1995), and thus very difficult for a student model to cater for. The student modelling difficulties are great, therefore.

A second approach to the adaptability issue is to provide a generic system which can be configured according to individual student needs. This is a popular approach to adaptability in general Human Computer Interaction (HCI) work. In a special needs education context, Green et al (1995) advocate providing teachers with a "framework which can be adapted to a variety of uses" and Green (1993) argues for "an integrated set of adaptive programming support and learning management tools... an educational support environment". Further, much of the concern with producing material relevant to an individual student's interests can presumably be dealt with via generic material likely to be of interest to all students of a certain age, for example concerning dining room protocols, relationships with the opposite sex, football etc., which ultimately could be made available for tutor or student selection via a menu.

The third approach is to develop a separate system for each individual student. This is the approach that appears to be advocated by Higgins and Boone (1996). It has the advantage of allowing specific and precise tailoring, for example by incorporating into the system pictures of its user and the voice of the student's teacher. On the other hand one would intuitively imagine the task of writing separate programs to be too time consuming for tutors.

There are, then, possible means of addressing the adaptability issue. Further, any software system will of course be used at teacher discretion, and judgements about the appropriateness of given systems and student progress or lack of it with them can be made by the teacher.

Solutions and Recommendations

Our work at Leeds Metropolitan University is addressing four of the problems discussed above, namely the relative lack of work concerning adults with autism, the lack of work concerning computer systems for people with severe autism, the fact that most computer systems are for single users and the user variability issue. Our work relating to adults with autism is discussed in another chapter of this book (Guest and Elzouki). The next chapter of this book (Elzouki and Cooper) will discuss our work studying computer technology for young people with severe autism. Here we briefly consider firstly our work concerning collaborative virtual environments (CVE) for people with autism (Moore et al, 2005; Moore, 2009) and secondly our work on a "shell" system which carers of people with autism, or indeed people with autism themselves, can use to create practice scenarios relating to their specific interests and needs (Moore, 2009; Evans and Moore, 2007).

(i) Collaborative Virtual Environments

A CVE can be defined as a distributed computer-based virtual space (or set of spaces), in which people can meet and interact with others, via their "avatars". An avatar can be defined as a representation of the user's identity within the computer environment (Gerhard, Moore, & Hobbs, 2004). Users can typically select the nature of their avatar. The user "inhabits" their avatar and assumes the viewpoint of their avatar. Perhaps the most important current CVE is "Second Life" (Boulos et al, 2007).

We believe that CVE may have much potential, in three ways: as an assistive technology, as an educational tool and to help with any Theory of Mind (ToM) deficit. We will briefly look at each of these in turn. Concerning CVE as an assistive technology our argument is that people with autism may be able, via CVE, to communicate more fruitfully with other people, in that CVE permits meaningful and interesting communication and is simpler and less threatening than its face to face equivalent (cf. Cobb et al, 2010). CVE is a possible means, therefore, by which people with autism can communicate with others, and thus ameliorate their social and communication impairment and sense of isolation.

CVE may be useful as an educational tool in that the user's interlocutor in the CVE may be their "teacher", and the CVE could therefore be used for the purposes of practice and rehearsal of events in everyday life, for example a forthcoming school visit or wedding. Concerning the possible role of CVE in addressing any ToM issue, the user of a CVE can express their emotion via choice of an appropriate facial expression for their avatar (Fabri et al, 2004), in a similar way to using "emoticons" in chat room communication. And being able to express their own emotion, and being required to interpret the emotions displayed

by their interlocutors' avatars, may help address any ToM difficulties.

Given these potential advantages of the technology, we have conducted informal user studies involving the ability of young people with autism to recognise emotional expressions as depicted by an avatar (Moore et al, 2005) and to communicate with a tutor via a simulated CVE (Cheng, 2005).

(ii) A 'Shell' System

Turning to the 'shell' system, it may be apparent from earlier sections of this chapter, that a drawback with most CBL systems aimed at helping with social skills education is that they use a small selection of generic social scenarios. They are unlikely therefore to be in line with the different needs and interests of individual people with autism. It is this concern that led us to design and build a "shell" system designed to make it easy for parents and teachers to create their own individualised computerised materials for their children. Because of the widely varying nature of people with autism, and also the infinite number of different social situations children may find themselves in, we argue that children with autism may benefit from a program which may be individualised to their own particular needs. By providing a means for the child's parent or carer (or indeed the child himself) to design the materials themselves, via the "shell", they would be able to tailor the materials for the person in their care, using their own specialist knowledge of the child's abilities and needs.

The shell may be thought of as similar to a 'wizard' (such as is provided by some Microsoft applications), in that the shell guides the user through the necessary steps to build simple computer-based materials. The shell we believe enables the parents or teachers to demonstrate the subtle differences between seemingly similar social scenarios by perhaps writing a set of similar but different materials to cover the various eventualities. It also allows routines to be written which are specific to an individual child, and therefore absolutely appropriate for him or her. The shell has been built using Java and xml technologies, should run on any PC that uses Windows, and does not need an Internet connection. The shell is free to interested users.

The shell contains sample materials which can be used in their own right. People can use the shell to write their own materials based on the sample, or write new content from scratch, or edit content that they wrote earlier. When the material is complete the user will save it, and gradually therefore they will build up a bank of content. To use a specific example with their child, they can either run it on the computer or print it out.

The shell system has been evaluated at different stages of its development. An initial design was drawn up, based on literature concerning CBL for social skills education, in the shape of a series of storyboards. This design was evaluated by a teacher who works as the ICT coordinator in a special school (teaching a number of children with autism), a support group of parents of children with autism and a group of various clinicians who all have contact with children with autism. Feedback was used to inform the development of the first software prototype of the shell.

This prototype then underwent a usability evaluation, with 5 people performing the "heuristic evaluation" technique (Nielsen & Mack, 1994). The outcome from this informed amendments to the next prototype (the current version of the shell). This was then taken to a set of users, comprising parents and teachers of children with autism, for further evaluation, to assess the shell's usability and acceptability with the target audience.

The overall response to the system was very positive. Users seemed to find the shell easy and intuitive to use, even though some declared themselves "non-technical". The vast majority said they thought they would use the shell to write material for their children, and that it would enable them to write the sort of content they wanted. Most thought their children would want to use the

materials written with the shell. Participants in the evaluation suggested other uses for the shell, such as creating timetables or schedules. It was also suggested that children could use it to keep a diary, and one of the teachers proposed using it for literacy work at school, as a "writing framework".

The evaluations brought to light some additional features and enhancements that could usefully be made to the shell. One enhancement that might be particularly useful would be the addition of question pages, which would enable content to be written that presents children with choices and then shows the consequences of the choice they make. We hope to pursue such developments in the future.

The system is made freely available to interested parties and has thus far had about a thousand downloads. Details are discussed elsewhere (Moore, 2009; Evans and Moore, 2007), and a free copy of the software is available by emailing the author of this chapter.

FUTURE RESEARCH DIRECTIONS

In this chapter we have argued that although there is a good case for CBL for people with autism, and research and development is starting to occur in this area, many problems remain. An obvious area for further work, therefore, is to continue to address these problems. A particularly important aspect, perhaps, might concern the recent emergence of social software such as Facebook, and how this might work in the context of autism. Anecdotal evidence suggests these are being extensively used by people with autism, but relevant research literature is only just beginning to emerge (e.g. Bahiss et al, 2010). A potentially important, and hitherto largely unexplored aspect of this, and indeed of the use by people with autism of computer systems in general, is how the cultural background of the users might affect their computer use.

We also argue that research in the field of technology and people with autism might have

Cooper, B. (2004). Empathy, interaction and caring; teachers' roles in a constrained environment. *Pastoral Care in Education, 22*(3), 12–21. doi:10.1111/j.0264-3944.2004.00299.x

Cooper, B., & Brna, P. (2002). Supporting high quality interaction and motivation in the NIMIS in the classroom using ICT: the social and emotional learning in the NIMIS project. *Education Communication and Information, 2*(2/3), 109–138.

Cumine, V., Leach, J., & Stevenson, G. (1998). *Asperger Syndrome: A Practical Guide for Teachers*. London: David Fulton.

Damasio, A. (1999). *The feeling of what happens: body, emotion and the making of consciousness*. London: Heinemann.

Damasio, A. R. (2003). *Looking for Spinoza: Joy, sorrow and the feeling brain*. London: Heinemann.

Dautenhahn, K. (1999). Embodiment and Interaction in Socially Intelligent Life-Like Agents. In Nehaniv, C. L. (Ed.), *Computation for Metaphors, Analogy and Agents* (pp. 102–142). New York: Springer-Verlag. doi:10.1007/3-540-48834-0_7

Davis, M., Dautenhahn, K., Nehaniv, C., & Powell, S. (2006). Towards an interactive system eliciting narrative comprehension in children with autism: A longitudinal study. In Clarkson, J., Langdon, P., & Robinson, P. (Eds.), *Designing Accessible Technology* (pp. 101–114). London: Springer-Verlag. doi:10.1007/1-84628-365-5_11

Evans, R., & Moore, D. J. (2007) *A Computer-Based Story Builder Shell*. Internal paper, Leeds Metropolitan University. Available by email from d.moore@leedsmet.ac.uk.

Fabri, M., Moore, D. J., & Hobbs, D. J. (2004). Mediating the expression of emotion in educational collaborative virtual environments: an experimental study. *International Journal of Virtual Reality, 7*(2), 66–81. doi:10.1007/s10055-003-0116-7

Genessse, F. (1994). *Educating second language children: the whole child, the whole curriculum*. Cambridge, UK: Cambridge University Press.

Gerhard, M., Moore, D. J., & Hobbs, D. (2004). Embodiment and copresence in collaborative interfaces. *International Journal of Human-Computer Studies, 61*(4), 453–480. doi:10.1016/j.ijhcs.2003.12.014

Golan, O., & Baron-Cohen, S. (2006). Systemizing empathy: Teaching adults with Asperger Syndrome and High Functioning Autism to recognize complex emotions using interactive multimedia. *Development and Psychopathology, 18*(2), 589–615. doi:10.1017/S0954579406060305

Gray, C. (2000). *The new social story book: illustrated edition*. Arlington, TX: Future Horizons.

Green, S., Sinclair, F., & Pearson, E. (1995). From special needs to neural nets. In *Leadership for Creating Educational Change: Integrating the Power of Technology, Twelfth International Conference on Technology and Education* (Volume 2, pp. 740–2).

Green, S. J. (1990). *A Study of the Application of Microcomputers to Aid Language Development in Children with Autism and Related Communication Difficulties*. PhD Thesis, Sunderland Polytechnic.

Green, S. J. (1993). Computer-Based Simulations in the Education and Assessment of Autistic Children. In *Rethinking the Roles of Technology in Education, Tenth International Conference on Technology and Education*, (Volume 1 pp 334-336).

Grynszpan, O. (2005). *Multimedia human computer interfaces: designing educational applications adapted to high functioning autism*. PhD thesis, Paris XI University, Doctoral School of Computing, LIMSI-CNRS.

Grynszpan, O., Martin, J., & Nadel, J. (2005). Designing educational software dedicated to people with autism. In Pruski, A., & Knops, H. (Eds.), *Assistive Technology: From Virtuality to Reality, AAATE 2005, Assistive Technology Research Series 16* (pp. 456–460). Amsterdam: IOS Press.

Hagiwara, T., & Myles, B. (1999). A Multimedia Social Story Intervention: Teaching Skills to Children with Autism. *Focus on Autism and Other Developmental Disabilities, 14*(2), 82–95. doi:10.1177/108835769901400203

Hanner, S., Tomkinson, C., Byrne, J., Boadle, H., Lashley, N., & Stampone, S. (2003). Results after one year of facilitating autism friendly socialisation (FAFS) using laptops to network young people with autistic spectrum disorder. In *Lisboa 2003 – International-Autism-Europe Congress* (p. P31).

Hardy, C., Ogden, J., Newman, J., & Cooper, S. (2002). *Autism and ICT, A guide for teachers and parents*. London: David Fulton Books.

Heimann, M., Nelson, K., Tjus, T., & Gilberg, C. (1995). Increasing Reading and Communication Skills in Children with Autism Through an Interactive Multimedia Computer Program. *Journal of Autism and Developmental Disorders, 25*(5), 459–480. doi:10.1007/BF02178294

Herrera, G., & Vera, L. (2005). Abstract Concept and Imagination Teaching through Virtual Reality in People with Autism Spectrum Disorder. In Pruski, A., & Knops, H. (Eds.), *Assistive Technology: From Virtuality to Reality, AAATE 2005, Assistive Technology Research Series 16* (pp. 449–455). Amsterdam: IOS Press.

Herskowitz, V. (2009). *Autism and Computers: Maximizing Independence Through Technology*. Bloomington, IN: AuthorHouse.

Hetzroni, O. E., & Tannous, J. (2004). Effects of a Computer-Based Intervention Program on the Communicative Functions of Children with Autism. *Journal of Autism and Developmental Disorders, 34*(2), 95–113. doi:10.1023/B:JADD.0000022602.40506.bf

Higgins, K., & Boone, R. (1996). Creating Individualised Computer-Assisted Instruction for Students with Autism Using Multimedia Authoring Software. *Focus on Autism and Other Developmental Disabilities, 11*(2), 69–78. doi:10.1177/108835769601100202

Hill, E. L. (2004). Executive dysfunction in autism. *Trends in Cognitive Sciences, 8*(1), 26–32. doi:10.1016/j.tics.2003.11.003

Hobbs, D. J., & Moore, D. J. (1998). *Human Computer Interaction*. London: FTK Publishing.

Iacono, T. A., & Miller, J. F. (1989). Can Microcomputers be used to Teach Communication Skills to Students with Mental Retardation? *Education and Training of the Mentally Retarded, 22*(1), 32–44.

Jacklin, A., & Farr, W. (2005). The computer in the classroom: a medium for enhancing social interaction with young people with autistic spectrum disorders? *British Journal of Special Education, 32*(4), 202–210. doi:10.1111/j.1467-8578.2005.00398.x

Jordan, R. R. (1991a). *The National Curriculum: Access for Children with Autism. 1. The Special Educational Needs of Pupils with Autism*. Bristol, UK: The Inge Wakehurst Trust.

Jordan, R. R. (1991b). *The National Curriculum: Access for Children with Autism. 2. English*. Bristol, UK: The Inge Wakehurst Trust.

Jordan, R. R. (1992a). *The National Curriculum: Access for Children with Autism. 3. Mathematics*. Bristol, UK: The Inge Wakehurst Trust.

Jordan, R. R. (1992b). *The National Curriculum: Access for Children with Autism. 4. Science*. Bristol, UK: The Inge Wakehurst Trust.

Jordan, R. R., & Powell, S. (1995). Factors Affecting School Choice for Parents of a Child with Autism. *Communication*, Winter 1995, 5-9.

Mancil, G. R., Haydon, T., & Whitby, P. (2009). Differentiated Effects of Paper and Computer-Assisted Social Stories™ on Inappropriate Behavior in Children With Autism. *Focus on Autism and Other Developmental Disorders, 24*(4), 205–215. doi:10.1177/1088357609347324

Marsden, P. (1993). Asperger Syndrome: A Parent's View. In *Children with Asperger Syndrome, A Collection of Papers from Two Study Weekends run by the Inge Wakehurst Trust, 1992-1993*. London: The Inge Wakehurst Trust.

Moore, D., Cheng, Y., McGrath, P., & Powell, N. J. (2005). Collaborative virtual environment technology for people with autism. *Focus on Autism and Other Developmental Disorders, 20*, 231–243. doi:10.1177/10883576050200040501

Moore, D. J. (1998) Computers and People with Autism/Asperger Syndrome; *Communication*, Summer 1998, 20-21.

Moore, D. J. (2009). IT and Autism. Keynote speech, The 2009 *International Conference on the Current Trends in Information Technology*, December 15-16 2009, Dubai, United Arab Emirates.

Moore, D. J., McGrath, P., & Thorpe, J. (2000). Computer Aided Learning for people with autism - a framework for research and development. *Innovations in Education and Training International, 37*(3), 218–228. doi:10.1080/13558000050138452

Moore, D. J., & Taylor, J. (2000). Interactive multimedia systems for people with autism. *Journal of Educational Media, 25*(3), 169–177. doi:10.1080/1358165000250302

Moore, M., & Calvert, S. (2000). Brief report: vocabulary acquisition for children with autism: teacher or computer instruction. *Journal of Autism and Developmental Disorders, 30*(4), 359–362. doi:10.1023/A:1005535602064

Murray, D. K. C. (1997). Autism and information technology: therapy with computers. In Powell, S., & Jordan, R. (Eds.), *Autism and Learning: A Guide to Good Practice* (pp. 100–115). London: David Fulton.

Murray, S. (2007). *An interactive classroom timetable for children with high functioning autism: development and qualitative evaluation of a computer-based timetable*. PhD thesis, Queen Margaret University, Edinburgh, UK.

Murray, S., & Gillham, M. (2003). *Investigating the use of a computer-based, interactive timetable designed for primary school children with Asperger's Syndrome* (p. P9). Lisboa: International-Autism-Europe Congress.

NAS. (1995). *Fact Sheet – Computers and people with Autism*. London: National Autistic Society.

NAS (1999). Software for children with autism/Asperger Syndrome. *Communication*, Spring 1999, 13-16.

NAS. (2005). *What is autism?* Retrieved November 1, 2005 from http://www.nas.org.uk/nas/jsp/polopoly.jsp?d=211.

NAS. (2010a). *What is autism?* Retrieved September 13, 2010 from http://www.autism.org.uk/About-autism/Autism-and-Asperger-syndrome-an-introduction/What-is-autism.aspx.

NAS. (2010b). *Computers: applications for people with autism*. Retrieved June 22, 2010 from http://www.autism.org.uk/en-gb/working-with/education/educational-professionals-in-schools/resources-for-teachers/computers-applications-for-people-with-autism.aspx.

Nielsen, J., & Mack, R. L. (1994). *Usability Inspection methods*. New York: Wiley.

Nimmo, C. (1994). Autism and Computers. *Communication, 28*(2), 8–9.

Oberleitner, R., Ball, J., Gillette, D., Naseef, R., & Hudnall Stamm, B. (2006). Technologies to lessen the distress of autism. *Journal of Aggression, Maltreatment & Trauma, 12*(1/2), 221–242. doi:10.1300/J146v12n01_12

Parsons, S., & Mitchell, P. (2002). The potential of virtual reality in social skills training for people with autistic spectrum disorders. *Journal of Intellectual Disability Research, 46*(5), 430–443. doi:10.1046/j.1365-2788.2002.00425.x

Parsons, S., Mitchell, P., & Leonard, A. (2004). The use and understanding of virtual environments by adolescents with autistic spectrum disorders. *Journal of Autism and Developmental Disorders, 34*(4), 449–466. doi:10.1023/B:JADD.0000037421.98517.8d

Parsons, S., & Wallace, S. (2006, October). *Inclusive design and development of Virtual Environments for social understanding of children with Autistic Spectrum Disorders: the 'Your World' project*. Paper presented at the Technology and Autism Conference Coventry University, UK.

Peeters, T. (1995). The Best Treatment for Behaviour Problems is Prevention. *Communication,* Winter 1995 29-30.

Pennington R. C. (2010). *Computer-Assisted Instruction for Teaching Academic Skills to Students With Autism Spectrum Disorders: A Review of Literature*. In press for Focus on Autism and Other Developmental Disabilities.

Powell, S., & Jordan, R. (1997). Rationale for the approach. In Powell, S., & Jordan, R. (Eds.), *Autism and Learning - A Guide to Good Practice* (pp. 1–14). London: David Fulton.

Purkey, W. W. (1970). *Self-Concept and School Achievement*. New York: Prentice-Hall.

Quantock, P., Atlay, T., & Curtin, J. R. (2003). *work with me* (p. C54). Lisboa: International-Autism-Europe Congress.

Rajendran, G., & Mitchell, P. (2000). Computer mediated interaction in Asperger's syndrome: the Bubble Dialogue program. *Computers & Education, 35,* 187–207. doi:10.1016/S0360-1315(00)00031-2

Ranfelt, A. M., Wigram, T., & Øhrstrøm, P. (2009). Towards a Handy Interactive Persuasive Diary for Teenagers with a Diagnosis of Autism. In S. Chatterjee & P. Dev (Eds.) *Proceedings of the 4th International Conference on Persuasive Technology*. New York: ACM.

Robins, B., Dautenhahn, K., te Boekhorst, R., & Billard, A. (2004). Effects of repeated exposure to a humanoid robot on children with autism. In Keates, S., Clarkson, J., Langdon, P., & Robinson, P. (Eds.), *Designing a More Inclusive World* (pp. 225–236). London: Springer-Verlag. doi:10.1007/978-0-85729-372-5_23

Rogers, C. R. (1975). Empathic: An Unappreciated Way of Being. *The Counseling Psychologist, 5*(2), 2–10. doi:10.1177/001100007500500202

Safran, S. P. (2008). Why Youngsters With Autistic Spectrum Disorders Remain Underrepresented in Special Education. *Remedial and Special Education, 29*(2), 90–95. doi:10.1177/0741932507311637

Schlosser, R. W., & Blischak, D. M. (2001). Is there a role for speech output in interventions for persons with autism? *Focus on Autism and Other Developmental Disabilities, 16,* 170–178. doi:10.1177/108835760101600305

Self, J. (1990). Bypassing the Intractable Problem of Student Modelling. In Frasson, F., & Gauthier, G. (Eds.), *Intelligent Tutoring Systems - at the Crossroads of AI and Education* (pp. 107–123). Norwood, New Jersey: Ablex Publishing Corporation.

Silver, M. (2000) *Can people with autistic spectrum disorders be taught emotional understanding? The development and randomised controlled trial of a computer training package.* PhD thesis, University of Hull, UK.

Silver, M., & Oakes, P. (2001). Evaluation of a new computer intervention to teach people with autism or Asperger Syndrome to recognise and predict emotions in others. *Autism, 5*(3), 299–316. doi:10.1177/1362361301005003007

Simmonds, C. (1993). The Asperger Student in a Mainstream Setting. In *Children with Asperger Syndrome, A Collection of Papers from Two Study Weekends run by the Inge Wakehurst Trust, 1992-1993.* London: The Inge Wakehurst Trust.

Sinclair, F., & Green, S. J. (1995). Assessing Autism Using Neural Nets - Subdividing the Autistic Continuum Using neural network Technology. In *Leadership for Creating Educational Change: Integrating the Power of Technology, Twelfth International Conference on Technology and Education* (Volume 2 pp 743-745).

Stokes, E. (2006b). *Teaching and Research into Multimedia Games for Pupils on the Autistic Spectrum.* Proceedings of the Autism and Technology Conference, Coventry University, 6th October 2006.

Stokes, S. (2006a). *Assistive technology for children with autism.* Retrieved October 3, 2006, from http://www.cesa7.k12.wi.us/sped/autism/assist/asst10.htm

Swettenham, J. (1996). Can Children with Autism be Taught to Understand False Belief Using Computers? *Journal of Child Psychology and Psychiatry, and Allied Disciplines, 37*(2), 157–165. doi:10.1111/j.1469-7610.1996.tb01387.x

Tanaka, J. W., Wolf, J. M., Klaiman, C., Koening, K., Cockburn, J., & Herlihy, L. (2010). Using computerized games to teach face recognition skills to children with autism spectrum disorder: the Let's Face It! *Program. Journal of Child Psychology & Psychiatry, 51*(8), 944–952. doi:10.1111/j.1469-7610.2010.02258.x

Tantam, D. (1993). *A Mind of One's Own.* London: National Autistic Society.

Tjus, T., & Heimann, M. (2000). Language, multimedia and communication for children with autism– searching for the right combination. In Powell, S. (Ed.), *Helping children with autism to learn* (pp. 78–93). London: David Fulton publishers.

Tjus, T., Heimann, M., & Lundalv, M. (2003). *Multimedia enhancement of language and reading skills* (p. C14). Lisboa: International-Autism-Europe Congress.

Tjus, T., Heimann, M., & Nelson, K. E. (2001). Interaction patterns between children and their teachers when using a specific multimedia and communication strategy: observations from children with autism and mixed intellectual disabilities. *Autism, 5*(2), 175–187. doi:10.1177/1362361301005002007

Trehin, P. (1996) *Computer Technology and Autism.* Retrieved November 26, 2010 from http://www.autism-resources.com/papers/LINK.htm

Wing, L. (1996). *Autism Spectrum Disorders.* London: Constable.

Wolman, D. (2010). The autie advantage. *New Scientist, 1*(May), 33–35.

Yates, P. (1993). Social Skills Training. In *Children with Asperger Syndrome, A Collection of Papers from Two Study Weekends run by the Inge Wakehurst Trust, 1992-1993*. London: The Inge Wakehurst Trust.

KEY TERMS AND DEFINITIONS

Asperger Syndrome: Again, there is no universally agreed definition, but Asperger Syndrome is often regarded as a mild form of autism.

Autism: The literature contains different views about what exactly autism is, but a common view is that it involves a "triad of impairments" or a triad of "differences": (i) there is a social difference: someone with autism may find it hard to relate to, and empathise with, other people (ii) there is a communication difference: someone with autism may find it hard to understand and use verbal and non-verbal communication (iii) there is a possible difficulty with social imagination. Much current thinking is that this triad of differences is at least partly underpinned by a "theory of mind" differ-ence - people with autism may have a difficulty in understanding mental states and in ascribing them to themselves or to others.

Autism-Specific Systems: Computer systems, in particular CBL systems, specifically targeted at the core features of autism as outlined above.

Autism Spectrum Conditions: Autism is usually seen as a 'spectrum condition': it varies in degree of severity, from severe autism, displaying the above triad to a large extent, to mild autism. Because of this the expression 'autism spectrum condition' or 'autism spectrum disorder' is often used rather than just 'autism'.

Computer-Aided Instruction: Another name for computer-based learning systems.

Computer-Aided Learning: Another name for computer-based learning systems.

Computer-Based Learning Systems: Computer systems in which the computer presents learning material to the individual student, giving them information, asking questions about it and offering additional information and exercises if necessary in the light of the student's response.

Chapter 6
Understanding and Enhancing Emotional Literacy in Children with Severe Autism Using Facial Recognition Software

Salima Y Awad Elzouki
Leeds Metropolitan University, UK

Bridget Cooper
Sunderland University, UK

ABSTRACT

This chapter discusses some key aspects of a doctoral study which aimed to understand and enhance emotional literacy in children with severe autism using facial recognition software. Despite the considerable research carried out with young people with autism using technology, very few studies have considered those with severe autism and this study is significant precisely because of this. The methodology is discussed in detail because it had to be substantially adapted to meet the needs of these particular students. Eight children, in a special unit within a mainstream school in the UK, took part in the study over a thirteen month period, with varying degrees of engagement and progress. Each responded uniquely to various assessment studies and to a new teaching tool. The authors chose to examine the case of one student in depth in this chapter, to enable the reader to understand the whole process, and the complex issues involved.

DOI: 10.4018/978-1-61350-183-2.ch006

INTRODUCTION

This chapter will discuss a project which examines the use of computer technology and facial recognition software to enhance emotional literacy and is one of the few projects specifically designed for young people with severe autism. By studying severely challenging young people, this project begins to address one of the weaknesses in the area of computer-based learning (CBL) for people with autism, identified by Moore (2005 & 2009; cf. Moore's chapter in this book). The work also builds on previous studies outlined in Moore's chapter, of the use of computers with young people with autism in relation to theory of mind (ToM) (eg Silver, 2000; Silver and Oakes, 2001; Moore et al, 2005; Cheng 2005). Further, the success of Baldi (a computer-animated tutor) in increasing the vocabulary of children with autism (Bosseler & Massaro, 2003; Williams et. al., 2004) suggested the worth of investigating the use of a similar application to enhance the emotional literacy for young people with autism. Therefore, the aim of this study was to investigate how the use of animated characters might help young people with severe autism and learning difficulties to recognise facial expressions of emotions, in a safe environment.

The nature of the behaviour and interactions of young people with severe autism, inevitably affected the whole manner in which the study was conducted. For example, it was essential to carry out initial fieldwork to investigate their everyday school life before commencing the computer based studies. We begin therefore, with a detailed narrative about the complex and challenging context and daily routines of the school in which the research took place. Secondly we reflect on the methodology and the findings from an initial study. Next we look at the enhanced methodology for the subsequent study and consider in detail the process and some specific findings, through an extended case study of one young person. We are restricted to discussing only one of the eight cases

in detail in this chapter, with only brief mention of the other seven cases, which are discussed fully however, in the final doctoral thesis (Elzouki, 2010). Finally we discuss the lessons we learned from our research with conclusions and recommendations for future work.

BACKGROUND

Context of the Study

The entire longitudinal study was carried out over a period of 13 months, in a special educational unit of children with severe autism and learning difficulties which was located within a UK mainstream primary school. There were 11 children in the unit aged 5 to 11 years, divided into two classes, one Key Stage 1 (5-8 years) and the other Key Stage 2 (8-11 years). Of these, 8 children participated in our research, after gaining parental consent. The unit was staffed by a total of 6 people, including the head teacher of the unit. Four staff worked full time, two in each class. A fifth staff member worked part time to assist during lunch time.

Initially, it was important to observe the unit's daily sessions to gain insights into the children's life-world and to understand how the research could be conducted. This period of observation was extremely challenging for a novice researcher with limited real-world experience of children with autism, as the participants had particularly individual behaviours, for example, humming and singing, playing alone, flapping, spinning and rocking, screaming and crying, slapping and scratching either each other or members of staff and making incomprehensible voices. Most of the children seemed to inhabit their own world, or "agenda" as one teacher put it, and did not appear to empathise or sympathise with their teachers or peers. Their behaviours conformed with the common view of autism as involving a "triad of impairments" (Wing, 1996, Jordan, 1991) or a triad of "differences" (Hardy et al, 2002) and resonated with much theory of mind literature (Howlin et. al., 1999; Cohen, 2008). For example, Howlin et al. (1999) suggest that children with autism have a specific delay in the development of ToM as a consequence of difficulties in producing emotional expressions. This might explain their lower level of skills in reading and understanding facial expressions (Howlin et. al., 1999; Irish Society for Autism, 1995) and their limitations in understanding other people's mental states (Frith, 1989; Baron-Cohen, 2001).

However, some of the children in our study seemed to respond to one-to-one conversations, following an "intensive interaction" approach (Hewett & Nind, 1998), which most staff adopted. Finally, regarding their reactions to computers, some were interested while others had never used one and showed no interest in them, contrary to some of the evidence in the literature presented in Moore's earlier chapter. Detailed examples of the children's observed characteristics are described elsewhere (Elzouki et al, 2007). Below, we outline the nature of a typical day in this special unit, to help illuminate the context and challenges posed for both learning and research.

A Typical Day in the Unit

Usually in KS1 the staff commenced the day at nine o'clock by singing a greeting, to which each child was expected to reply in turn. KS2 children usually had their lessons during this time. After the greeting the KS1 pupils had a half-hour "choosing time", indicating their choice of activity to the staff via an appropriate symbol. The Picture Exchange Communication System (PECS) (Bondy, & Frost, 1994; Charlop-Christy, 2002) was used in the unit to facilitate communications with the children and to enable them to use the appropriate symbol. Each child had a folder with their name and picture which was used during their daily sessions. The folder contained symbols and photographs of different objects, for example a computer, a book, a TV and different games. Also it included different

kinds of fruits vegetables and colours. After the first activity from 10:00am-10:30am, they had a snack, also chosen using the PECS system, followed by morning break at 10:30am-11:00am.

The period 11:00am-11:45am was "work and activity time", during which the children usually had lessons such as painting or reading stories and some social activities. The staff tried to bring the children to sit around a big table in the middle of the classroom for these activities. However they were not always successful as some children did not respond and ran away from the table. In KS2 the staff tried more teaching activities with the children to prepare them for High School. However, not all children joined in and even if they did they often seemed disinterested in the activities. Nevertheless, students were usually offered maths lessons (including using the clock to learn about the time), writing lessons (including copying and tracing) and some science lessons. They also had a weekly computer lesson in the school ICT room, in addition to individual classroom-based computer activities. All activities were based on the child's learning ability, disposition and temper during the day, and each child was given a task that matched his learning ability and was supported by the staff.

At 11:45am-12:00 a brief social activity took place, as pupils were taken into lunch. This involved singing and the formation of a queue to go to the dining hall, no easy task with severely young people with autism. Lunch time itself, 12:00-12:30, was spent in the school's dining hall. Each group sat around one table and their teachers stood next to their table to help them. Later, between 12:30 and 13:00, the children would have a second play time. At this time most children gathered in the KS1 playground. At the beginning of the research a group of KS2 mainstream pupils came to join the unit's children. At a later stage, some of the KS2 children with autism began joining the mainstream children as part of inclusion programme. Our case study, Nabeel, was one of these children. The afternoons involved a second choosing time and a second work and activity time. The latter typically involved individual work on certain activities depending on abilities and interests, for example, writing, puzzles, building shapes and sorting out colours, shapes and numbers.

In summary, the staff tried to follow a specific schedule for the children every day in an attempt to keep them in a predictable environment. This strategy is well-articulated in the literature. For example Jordan (2001, p129) argues that the school "day should be structured". In fact, structured and predictable environments are needed by both young school children and also adults with autism who Cohen found "hate change" (Cohen, 1998, p. 23). More recently, some computer interventions started to try and address this issue. Murray (2007), for instance, studied the effect of using a computer-based interactive time table with a group of children with High Functioning Autism (HFA). Nevertheless, despite staff efforts, the behaviours of the children with autism in this special unit remained extremely unpredictable. This was the challenging context, then, in which our longitudinal study took place.

EMPIRICAL STUDIES

Study 1: Methodology

Initially a controlled experiment was planned, involving the children with autism as participants. The aim of the first part of the experiment was to establish the extent to which the participants could recognise facial expressions of emotions as a pre test. The pre test or as we call it, the 'recognition study', was conducted with the children in three stages, in which two types of faces were used; photographs of real people as displayed by Ekman (1975) and computer generated faces as created and validated by Fabri (2006). Since Fabri's faces were validated only by adults, prior to this research, a preliminary study had been conducted involving 49 neuro-typical (NT) children, the same age as our participants, in order to investi-

gate the authenticity of the facial representations for younger people. The overall percentage of correct identification was 95%. This was seen as sufficiently high to warrant the continued use of the avatar representations in the experiment with our participants with autism.

As mentioned above, this work was built on previous work in the area concerning ToM. It was unclear in previous studies, for example, Silver (2000) and Cheng (2005) whether participants received help from their parents and/or teachers when completing the computer based exercises. Therefore it was considered essential to study the actual interaction between the participants and the new system in order to address this limitation. For this reason, therefore, we adopted a methodological approach to develop familiarity with the students by non-participant observation. Given the nature of our participants, familiarity between the child and the observer was considered essential to avoid possible distress or upset during the computer intervention. Given this, "cooperative evaluation" (Dixon et. al., 2004) was chosen as theseensee most suitable technique to evaluate the new system with the participants. It was believed that, to apply cooperative evaluation with our group of severely challenged participants, the observer would require some knowledge of each child's needs. Initially therefore, non-participant observation (Robson, 1993; Fraenkel & Wallen, 2006) was seen as an appropriate means of gaining such knowledge. Hence, a period of non participant observation was undertaken, lasting six weeks, involving two half days a week, one for each class, supplemented by interviews with teachers about their understanding of the children.

A well known concern with observation is the danger of an observer effect, in which the person being observed may act differently precisely because they are being observed, thus threatening the validity of the results (Hobbs and Moore, 1998). However, Moore & Taylor (2000) argue that a paradoxical 'advantage' of the autism condition may be an absence of any experimenter effect,

necessitates "a coming-together of the insider's understanding with the outsider's puzzlement" (Rock, 2001, p33).

In practice, during the next six months data was collected using most of the methods above. Initially, observations were needed to collect additional details about the participants (cf. Rock, 2001). That was necessary before asking them any further questions about facial expressions or offering them any teaching sessions regarding possible new computer-based interventions. The time was spent observing and joining the children in their natural "world". This produced an in-depth understanding of the participants' interests, abilities and difficulties. Discovering and working with the child's own interest and capabilities was vital to make further studies realistic and reasonable, particularly for those who did not cooperate during the recognition study. In the light of increased knowledge about the participants, the researcher became an insider-outsider ethnographer (Atkinson et al. 2001), working with the children in their daily educational activities, under the auspices of staff members. Closer dialogue between the roles of 'insider' and 'outsider' was required and for a longer period of time, to develop better understanding and build trust. In fact, the insider participant observer role was needed more than non-participant observer at that time. This involved working alongside the participants in their daily educational activities to develop deeper understanding.

New computer systems were designed to meet the children's specific interests, initially to familiarise them with computers, particularly those who had never used computers before, then to facilitate further recognition studies. These further studies commenced with a recap of the initial recognition study, followed by different recognition studies based around the child's level of recognition and interests. A teaching tool was designed as in Figure 2 to teach those who were unable to recognise all (or indeed any) of the facial expressions. Prior to that storyboards were sketched and discussed with some technology specialists as well as the unit's head. The studies were conducted with each participant individually, as appropriate, depending on their perceived willingness to cooperate at that particular time.

Figure 2. Screenshot of the teaching tool

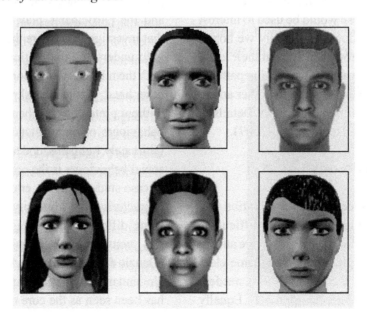

Finally, an assessment tool was designed to investigate what the children learned from the teaching tool as in Figure 3; this constituted the post test for the children. Next, following the Howlin et al approach (Howlin et al., 1999), those participants who were able to recognise all or some of the facial expressions were introduced to the Theory of Mind exercises that Howlin et al suggest.

In parallel with this, the teachers were observed as they worked with the children. Finally, to get feedback about the research conducted so far, letters were sent to staff and parents asking for their participation in two ways. Firstly, whether they would consent to a recorded interview, and secondly, whether they would consent to pictures of their faces being shown to the children, in a manner similar to that portrayed by the teaching tool. All teaching staff agreed to be interviewed;

in the event, only three of them were able to take part. Three parents agreed to be interviewed, although only two were able to take part. In total, five semi structured interviews (Robson, 2007) took place with the teaching staff and parents. They were asked whether they observed any improvements in the children's knowledge of facial expressions. Also, they had the chance to review the studies and the tools their children worked with. The interviews took place at the end of the research studies. All were audio recorded.

An empathic approach was adopted with the participants throughout, on the grounds that empathy has a major role in social interaction in general (Carr et. al., 2003) and in learning environments in particular (Cooper, 2006). In fact, empathy played an important role in creating positive relationships with the children in the unit. Importantly, being involved with the children in the way they liked

Figure 3. Screenshot of the assessment tool

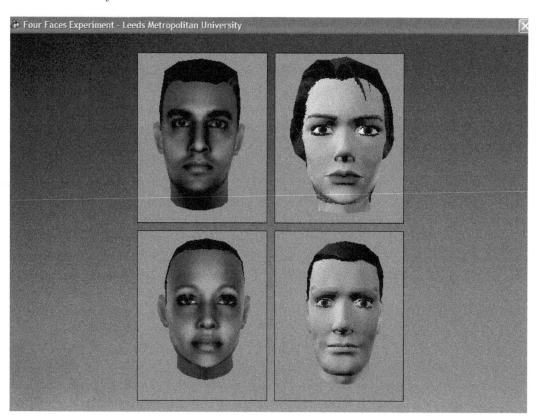

and using topics they were interested in, was seen as the key means of building a good relationship with them. This in turn was seen as a means of facilitating the introduction of new interventions and studies (cf. Sun Rise, 2006; Potter & Whittaker, 2001). In practice, the researcher's empathy with the participants engendered a degree of mutual trust and the researcher, in effect, became one of the adult team in the unit.

Given this new methodology, it is of course necessary to report results on a participant by participant basis. Space does not permit us to look at all the participants here. Rather, we report one case here as an example; remaining cases can be seen elsewhere (Elzouki, 2010). This case has been selected because the student was interested in computers and was therefore able to participate in all stages of the research, enabling the reader to follow them all. However all students were unique in their responses and while some progressed through al the studies, others only participated in more limited ways.

Study 2: Results – A Case Study

Our chosen case, Nabeel, as we will call him, was a 9 year old KS2 pupil at the time of our study. Nabeel has autism with moderate learning difficulties. He has good speaking abilities compared with some other children in the unit. Nabeel can construct full sentences to say what he wants very clearly and may address others by their names. However, he occasionally utters words and sounds that cannot be understood, and appears to be talking to some invisible person or object next to him. For example, sometimes he says, "Excuse me, excuse me" but then follows this with incomprehensible words or makes unknown sounds.

Nabeel is generally well behaved and friendly at school. Nevertheless, if he decides not to engage with an activity he tends to respond *"No, no"* or *"Ok, ok"* loudly, and continues with what he was already doing. Occasionally, Nabeel stays aloof from the others; he either lies down on the floor or sits in front of the classroom's window, appar-

ently talking to his reflection. Nabeel is interested in computers and often spends time sitting at the computer to play games. He uses the mouse and follows links in order to win a game or complete a task. At "choosing time", working with the computer tends to be his selected activity. Mostly he is interested in games involving 'Aliens and Mazes' which he prefers to play with the computer volume at its highest.

During the early part of our study, Nabeel had very little interaction with his peers during break times, but gradually formed some relationships with some peers in the mainstream part of the school. At meal times, in the dining hall, Nabeel knows where to queue and where to sit independently. At snack time, Nabeel is able to use the PECS system correctly to select his chosen snack items. During work time, KS2 children have activities, similar to the KS1 children, for example, they read stories and write numbers and letters. Nabeel generally takes part in these activities successfully, although when he is poorly or unhappy, he refuses to participate in any activity and prefers to lie down or remain alone.

However, when Nabeel is upset, his behaviour can change, even during computer sessions. For example, at one session he wanted to go on the internet, but he needed a password to log in. The teacher refused to give him the password because she wanted him to follow the session plan. Nabeel shouted and screamed, then he suddenly slapped the teacher. However, when he realised that his behaviour would not change the teacher's mind, he sat alone quietly for a few minutes then stood up and walked around the room. Finally, he came back to his chair and played with what was available.

Even with this extreme behaviour at times, Nabeel seemed the most sociable and friendly child in the unit during the period of our study. He enjoyed playing games on the computer and seemed happy and comfortable sitting next to the researcher. However, whenever he was asked a question about the computer game, he did not reply and continued playing, showing signs perhaps of an obsessive interest in the computer.

However he seemed to have some emotional awareness, for example, on one occasion, having done some work correctly, Nabeel turned his face towards the researcher, smiled and said "*Happy*". On the other hand, a common feature was that when he was poorly or unhappy he would lose interest in any activity. An example was when the children came back to school after the Christmas holiday, Nabeel cried most of the day. When he was asked, "*Why you are crying?*" he said, "*I want to go mummy*". He refused to answer any other question except, "*Are you sad Nabeel?*" to which he replied, "*No, I'm not happy*".

Once a background understanding of a participant, such as that for Nabeel just outlined, had been gained, it was possible to conduct some informal research orientated sessions with them. This followed essentially an action research approach (Noffke, 1997), with lessons from one research session informing the next. Here we give a brief overview of the sessions that involved Nabeel.

Session 1: Recap Study

The aim here was to investigate whether Nabeel's level of recognising facial expressions had changed in the period (approximately 6 months) of observation since the initial recognition study that was reported above. The recap study with Nabeel took place in the ICT classroom as suggested by the KS2 staff. It was carried out as if Nabeel and the researcher were playing a game, for example, "*Go back, now it's Nabeel's turn, ok!*", "*Ok, but look at these faces first*" and "*close your eyes*". When asked the specific questions of the study, Nabeel immediately pointed at the faces correctly, simultaneously saying, "*Happy, scared, grumpy and sad*", clearly and confidently. Since he pointed to all the faces correctly he was asked "*Which face did you like*" and he replied "*Happy one*".

For the faces in stages 2 and 3, Nabeel again answered all the questions correctly." When asked which faces he liked he said, "*She is grumpy, she is very angry, I don't like angry*". Then he con-

tinued "*I like happy*" and clicked on each slide of each stage while pointing to the happy face at each one of them.

Discussion

The empathic ethnographer role the researcher played with Nabeel before the recap study, engaging with him in different activities, may have helped in making this session informal and familiar, as in a previous games playing session. Indeed, play is recognised as significant to learning in general (Moyles, 2005; Broadhead, 2006) and to young people with autism in particular (Jordan, 2001; Cohen, 1998). As in the recognition study, Nabeel made interesting remarks about the computer faces (which were in black and white). In the recognition study he pointed at stage 2 faces and said, "*Its odd", its black and white*". Similarly, in the recap study, he described comparable faces as "*Empty*". Nabeel was able to point to all the study's faces correctly and therefore, following the approach of Howlin et al. (1999), no more teaching about facial expressions was required. Given his unpredictable social skills it was perhaps surprising that he recognised all the facial expressions and this may evidence the importance of entering the child's world to ascertain their real understanding (cf. Potter & Whittaker, 2001). In practice, the importance of the adult's role in entering the child's world and empathising with them was one of the practical outcomes of the interviews with the staff and parents, for example, one of Nabeel's teachers' stated that "*I think they trust you more when you have that bond and you can have a laugh with them*", by doing that "*You have more chance to step into their world*".

Session 2: Recognising Facial Expressions Based on Animal Pictures

The aim was to investigate whether Nabeel could recognise human facial expressions superimposed on animals. The rationale was partly to discover whether Nabeel could generalise beyond the initial exercise, and partly to evaluate the expressions' usefulness before using them with two other participants who seemed interested in a similar kind of animal. Nabeel was able to recognise all animal faces correctly and to identify them by their name and facial expression, for example, *"Simba happy"* and *"Errol grumpy"*.

Discussion

This session suggested a good ability on the part of Nabeel, in recognising facial expressions whatever representation they might have i.e. pictures of real people, computer generated faces or cartoon animal faces. Also, he showed a knowledge of the names of cartoon animal faces, which suggests he had remembered the film they were selected from i.e. *Lion King*. Finally, his identification of the frightened and angry facial expressions as *"scared" and "grumpy"* during session 1 and 2, might suggest previous knowledge of these faces. He might have learned these informal names from other environments apart from the unit, as there had been no specific lessons about facial expressions. It would be interesting indeed to conduct further research with children with autism, where expressions of emotions with alternative names might be investigated.

Session 3: Assessment Tool, Recognising Facial Expressions Represented by Animated Faces

The above sessions suggested Nabeel's ability in recognising all the faces he was presented with. His successful recognitions suggested that he had passed the pre test of the planned experiment and he was ready to have the post test. The post-test was based on recognising facial expressions of animated characters faces in a similar manner to the teaching tool. We called this the 'assessment tool' and we designed it following the approach suggested by Howlin (1999).

Once the assessment tool faces appeared on the screen as in Figure 3 above, Nabeel said *"Very nice four faces"*. When he was asked the recognition questions he pointed at the happy, sad and angry animated characters correctly, and said their names. He used *"grumpy"* when pointed to the angry face, similar to the previous sessions. However, Nabeel was unsuccessful in recognising the frightened face, when instead he pointed to the sad face.

Following Howlin's approach in teaching facial expressions to children with autism, a "prompt" was given to Nabeel about the frightened face. The assessment tool was designed to be used for this purpose. Consequently, the researcher increased the computer volume and clicked on the frightened face of the assessment tool. This caused the emotion to be pronounced and the frightened facial expression to be expressed by the character. After that, Nabeel was asked the recognition questions, and he was able to respond to all of them correctly.

Discussion

Initially, Nabeel successfully recognised the emotions displayed by the animated characters used in the assessment tool, apart from the frightened face. In fact, other children also found it difficult to recognise the frightened face. For example, the results of neuro-typical children in the recognition study mentioned above shows a lower percentage in recognising the frightened face compared to other faces.

However, designing the assessment tool to prompt children with the correct expression was useful in helping Nabeel to recognise the frightened face later. This result suggests that Nabeel was able to move to the second stage in understanding other people's feelings (Howlin et. al., 1999). This involves the recognition of schematic cartoon faces, as a precursor to contextualised Theory of Mind tests.

Session 4: Schematic Cartoons

This session aimed to study whether Nabeel could recognise the cartoon faces suggested by Howlin. Copies of the cartoon faces, on laminated card, were shown to Nabeel and he was asked to say which emotion was being depicted. He identified all the emotions correctly. He used "grumpy" for angry and "scared" for frightened, but these are taken as linguistic equivalents of the terms used by Howlin.

Discussion

Again Nabeel showed a good recognition of the schematic cartoon faces. His successful recognition of the cartoon representations suggested he was ready for the contextualised ToM tests.

Session 5: Contextualised Theory of Mind Tests

The approach advocated by Howlin et al (1999) suggests that if a child with autism is able to recognise the emotions depicted in the cartoon representations, teaching should move on to exercises involving cause and effect reasoning. The child will be shown a simple cartoon picture and asked to identify the likely emotion being felt by the person in the picture. For example, one picture shows a boy being bitten by a dog and the reader is asked to suggest the emotion felt by the boy. In our study we scanned a number of such pictures into a computer display. Nabeel was asked to work with 5 of these:

- A boy being bitten by a dog. Nabeel answered wrongly as he said "*Happy*"
- A boy in a room where a snake is creeping at the other side of the room. Nabeel answered correctly as he said "scary".
- A girl looking at a mouse coming into the room. Nabeel gave a wrong answer as he said "*Sad*". Then he said "*Shut up*". Then

he asked to do a different activity (to use 'Dazzle', a computer program for drawing and painting.

- A girl watching a spider creeping next to her. Nabeel said "*Scary spider*", the answer which Howlin et al (1999) deemed correct.
- A girl having a birthday party. Nabeel answered this correctly too as he said "*Happy*".

Discussion

Nabeel was able to identify three feelings correctly based on the five stories represented to him. Although that might be seen as a reasonably good score for a child with autism, Nabeel seemed bored and impatient within this session. This was revealed by his body language and his request to paint instead. Indeed it was clearly obvious that Nabeel was bored when he said "*Shut up*", a term he had never used during any computer session with the researcher before. However, being bored with the activities during this session did not affect Nabeel's usual good manners during computer sessions. When he was told that he would get to paint after he finished the task, he responded positively and asked to paint politely at the end of the session. Finally, although Nabeel responded to the activities, it could be questioned whether one should assume all children will be frightened of spiders or mice, as some might actually love to have them as pets. This might be a possible critique of Howlin's methodology and might be worthy of further investigation. Similarly it might be that the teaching tool (Figure 2) might be useful not just for comprehending facial expressions as below, but also for transferring these abilities to cause and effect reasoning.

Session 6: The Teaching Tool

The teaching tool is a simple computer system designed to help teach the children who were unable to recognise the faces in the recognition study. The storyboards and an earlier computer system (Cheng, 2005) were discussed with the unit head to identify which design for the new system might best suit the participant children, regarding the position of the faces, sound, text and colour. The design was based on six characters from which the child can choose, as shown in Figure 2 above. The character selected would appear at the left side of the screen with four buttons, each with one of the names of the universal facial expressions suggested by Ekman (1975), namely happy, sad, angry and frightened; an example is shown in Figure 4. Hovering the mouse over one of these buttons causes the emotion to be enunciated by the computer, and the facial expression to be expressed by the character. The sound used in the system was a child's voice, chosen out of five voices as the clearest, based on the views of four professional English adults. The user can play with one character at a time as long as he likes. The characters heads are animated and can move from one side to another.

Nabeel was introduced to this new tool first and he said, "*Very funny*". He appeared to like the way the faces changed. He started interacting with the faces himself and clicking on each button, then listening to the voice and repeating "*Very funny*" a few times.

Discussion

It was clear from Nabeel's response that the new tool was engaging, which was a good indicator, as engagement is a central requirement for effective learning (Cooper & Brna, 2002). While he was engaged playing with the tool Nabeel seemed happy, as he smiled and said "*Very funny*" each time the characters showed a different expression. This

Figure 4. A screenshot of one of the characters showing/expressing happy face

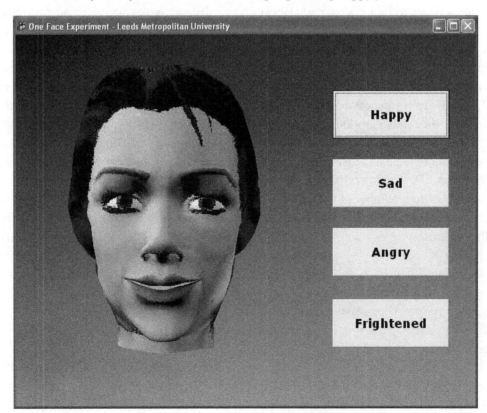

suggests that Nabeel liked and enjoyed playing with the tool, similar to the evidence suggested in Moore's chapter i.e. "people with autism may tend to enjoy working with computers". Additionally, Nabeel's response can be related to the argument suggested by the NAS (2010) which highlights the "awareness of self" that can be developed when using computers. Although Nabeel had showed a reasonable ability in recognising facial expressions since the first recognition study, one of his teachers during her interview at the end of the research stated that *"He is tuning in a lot more and, I think more than anybody"*. Then she continued *"He picks up on the facial expressions"* and *"It's nice that he can recognise facial expressions because nobody else in the class says you are happy or angry"*. Finally, she mentioned that *"it's important for all the children to learn these skills"* for her as a teacher and for their parents as well, to enable interaction.

As for the other participants in the study, those who had more opportunity to use the teaching tool such as Yazan, showed more progress in recognising facial expressions than those who had fewer opportunities such as Nasser, during the time span of the research. Additionally, the interview carried out with Jamal's parents at the end of the research highlighted the positive impact of using the teaching tool. His mother said that, *"He keeps saying smiley mouth all the time at home and now it comes to me why he said that"*; she thought that *"He understands facial expressions more now than in the past"* particularly the *"Happy and sad"*. Finally, she mentioned that Jamal became more able to recognise her face at home when she was happy or sad.

FINDINGS AND DISCUSSION

The extensive field work conducted during this research has yielded, we believe, a fascinating and intrinsically valuable and important insight into life in a unit for children with severe autism.

Much of the work tended to support existing views of the nature of autism. The common view of autism as involving a "triad of impairments" (Wing 1996, Jordan 1991) or a triad of "differences" (Hardy et al 2002) was observed clearly in the participants' behaviours during the non participant observation. The participants tended to be alone and aloof most of the time. Most had identified a corner that they seemed to regard as their own, and preferred to spend as much time as possible in their corner, rarely moving unless they needed something. On the other hand, if they did not get what they wanted they would tend to cry, scream or run around the class. Most of our participants found it hard to use verbal communication. There were two exceptions, who were able at least to ask for what they wanted in words. However, they were rarely able to form a full and comprehensible sentence, apart from when using the PECS system. On the whole, the children pointed to what they wanted.

Another social difficulty observed, particularly during the non-participant observation, was that the children did not appear to have empathy or sympathy with each other, again in line with much theory of mind literature (Howlin et. al., 1999; Cohen, 2008). For example, when one of KS2 staff left her post in the unit, the children did not demonstrate any symptoms of missing her, nor had they asked about her when she was crying most of the morning of her leaving day. However, the claim by Jordan (1992), that many students with autism will have "islets of ability" was borne out to a limited extent by our participants, in that one participant, for example, had excellent drawing skills.

Staff in the unit tended to adopt an approach very much akin to the "special teaching and guidance" approach advocated by Trevarthen et. al. (1998). Perhaps as a result of this, claims in the literature that "good teaching can make a difference" (Powell and Jordan, 1997; Tantam, 1993) were largely borne out by our fieldwork. The provision of supportive teaching did appear to make a difference to the children's behaviour and level of learning. In particular, the role of empathy in teaching and learning (Cooper, 2004) was observed clearly during the participant observation in the unit. The children were given excellent empathetic support by their tutors, who often showed great happiness when describing what might seem like small steps achieved by the children, such as agreeing to eat an apple every day. From one tutor the researcher learnt how to use "intensive interaction" (Hewett & Nind, 1998). From another tutor, the researcher learnt how to be both "firm" and "kind", in different situations with the children, how and when to love and praise them, and they often suggested physical communication such as cuddling, hugging and kissing. This kind of interaction is reflected in Gibb's (2006) work on teaching and Lang's research (2008) on teaching Maori children and Cooper's work (2004) on empathy, where physical contact is an important part of establishing and modelling an empathic relationship with many students. Concerning the participants' work with computer systems, our fieldwork provides some evidence of the beneficial effects proposed by some of the literature (eg Barry and Pitt, 2006; Moore, 1998).

On the whole our participants enjoyed working with the computer. The argument that the computer can help eliminate distractions (Silver, 2000; NAS, 2005) was evidenced, for example one participant was able to successfully work with the computer, despite the potential distraction of other children nearby singing with their teacher. We found that interacting with the computer in general, and the use of animations in particular, helped prevent the participants from being merely a passive receiver of information and instruction (cf. Silver, 2000). The importance of multi-sensory stimulation in learning with computers has been considered elsewhere (Cooper & Brna, 2002), and is reinforced by the neurological understanding of interaction and learning (Damasio, 1999).

Similarly, we found some evidence to support the argument that the use of a computer keyboard may help create "an awareness of self", for example one participant (Yazan) was surprised when the animated face turned round and the back of the character head appeared instead of its face. The work of four of our participants lends support to Murray's point that through computer use, students with autism may become motivated to read (Murray, 1997). In general, there was some evidence that the work involving the computer did lead to increased attention and rate of learning. Most encouragingly, there was some evidence of lessons being generalised (Elzouki, 2010).

An interesting point not currently discussed in the literature is the possibility of using an interest in the computer as a "reward" during choosing times or break times. Another surprise was that the participants were not happy with an introductory computer tool we built that incorporated photographs of the staff, preferring instead to work with our tool that incorporated human-like computer-based characters. Nimmo (1994) argued that children prefer a computer voice to a human one and interestingly our research tends to show they may prefer a computer face to a human one.

We found no evidence of the "collusion" concern (Parsons and Mitchell, 2002) occurring in practice. This may be because our study of computer-based work was integrated with other aspects of educational provision and also because our collaborative approach meant that in effect the proposal of Higgins and Boone (1996) of the use of "computer buddies" was followed, if only on a de facto basis. Rather than collusion, we tended to find evidence of increased social interaction, between participants and the researcher, between participants and staff and between participants themselves.

Our study highlighted the access problem, however. Even within the relatively affluent UK, with a relatively well funded public education system, access to the technology for the participants was limited, and the expectation is that this will be far worse in many parts of the world. This question of access is raised in many studies on ICT in education (Cooper, 2005).

Some important, further general lessons can be taken from our study. Our results suggest that when working with children with severe autism, it is important to start where the child is, using the child's interests, skills and abilities to attempt to develop suitable computer-based learning activities, rather than attempting to utilise pre-written material. This also marries well with general theories of teaching and learning (Gibbs, 2006; Cooper, 2004; 2008). For example in our field work we incorporated into the computer-based work material from the *Lion King* for one participant, from Old MacDonald's Farm for another, and used specialist hardware (a tablet, pen-based laptop) for another. This poses difficulties for the relatively conventional CBL system that was discussed in Moore's chapter of this book, in which all learning activities are pre-determined and hard-wired into the system, albeit with the possibility of branching facilities. Rather, our evidence suggests that for children with severe autism like our participants, to the extent that one wants to use computer-based learning at all, it needs to be developed and used with the needs of the individual child, at the individual time, in mind. This might lend some support to the Higgins and Boone approach (2006) or to the use of the shell system mentioned in Moore's chapter (cf. Moore, 2009; Evans and Moore, 2007). In this sense students with autism are no different from any others in terms of learning. Just as blanket curricula have been shown to have limited success in terms of meeting learning needs at all levels of education, so the importance of personalisation and valuing the student's own interests have been shown to be central to successful learning. Empathic design of content, processes, software and environments are central to high quality learning and moreover systems need integration into warmly human contexts which enhance the

understanding of each unique person and their specific needs (Cooper & Brna, 2002).

It might be argued that the small number of participants in our study, and the very familiarity of the researcher with those participants, is a threat to the objectivity of the study. However we would argue that only empathic understanding formed through close relationships can guarantee detailed understanding and enable deep reflection on complex subjects such as our participants attempting to operate in educational environments. An empathetic approach with attentiveness to the understandings of the participants is a feature of qualitative research (Miles and Huberman, 1994).

While we would accept that our results need to be treated with caution, we argue that an observer effect is less likely when participants have autism and that our use of different data sources, detailed analysis and subsequent triangulation considerably lessen the threat to objectivity. Further, narrative and descriptive writing about children with autism and adults has been seen as a preferable approach to describe them in a more accurate and realistic way (cf. Klein, 1961; Cohen, 1998; Baron-Cohen, 2008). The understanding of any particular student can illuminate some aspect of learning for others. As Davies (2006, p7) puts it, "We do not claim that these children are representative of all children with autism, but consider them as *individual* cases, from which some generalisations may be made".

Another interesting methodological point concerns ethical issues. To address these, we followed Potter and Whittaker (2001) in seeking to empower participants in the research through serious consideration of their needs and rights at all times. Informed consent was obtained from the parents and the unit's head teacher of the participants involved in the research. Absolute confidentially was guaranteed for participants. The team was committed to the principle that participation in the research should be as enjoyable and meaningful as possible for the participating young people. A child-led model was adopted,

Elzouki, S., Fabri, M., & Moore, D. (2007). Teaching severely autistic children to recognise emotions: Finding a methodology. *Proceedings of the 21st BCS HCI Group Conference. HCI 2007 Volume 2* pp. 137-140. London: BCS.

Evans, R. Moore, D. J. (2007). *A Computer-Based Story Builder Shell*. Internal paper, Leeds Metropolitan University. Available by email from d.moore@leedsmet.ac.uk.

Fabri (2006). *Emotionally Expressive Avatars for Collaborative Virtual Environments*. PhD Thesis. Leeds Metropolitan University.

Fraenkel, J. R., & Wallen, N. E. (2006). *How to Design and Evaluate Research in Education*. New York: Mc Graw – Hill.

Frith, U. (1989). *Autism, Explaining the Enigma*. UK: Basil Blackwell.

Gibbs, C. (2006). *To be a teacher: journeys towards authenticity*. New Zealand: Pearson Education.

Hardy, C., Ogden, J., Newman, J., & Cooper, S. (2002). *Autism and ICT, A guide for teachers and parents*. London: David Fulton.

Hewett, D., & Nind, M. (1998). *Interaction in Action, Reflections on the Use of Intensive Interaction*. London: David Fulton.

Higgins, K., & Boone, R. (1996). Creating Individualised Computer-Assisted Instruction for Students with Autism Using Multimedia Authoring Software. *Focus on Autism and Other Developmental Disabilities, 11*(2), 69–78. doi:10.1177/108835769601100202

Hobbs, D. J., & Moore, D. J. (1998). *Human Computer Interaction*. London: FTK Publishing.

Howlin, P., Baron-Cohen, S., & Hadwin, J. (1999). *Teaching Children with Autism to Mind-Read, A Practical Guide for Teachers and Parents*. London: John Wiley and Sons Irish Autism Society (1995). *A Story of Autism*. Ireland: Irish Autism Society.

Jordan, R. R. (1991). *The National Curriculum: Access for Children with Autism. 1. The Special Educational Needs of Pupils with Autism*. Bristol, UK: The Inge Wakehurst Trust.

Jordan, R. R. (1992). *The National Curriculum: Access for Children with Autism. 3. Mathematics*. Bristol, UK: The Inge Wakehurst Trust.

Jordan, R. R. (2001). *Autism with Severe Learning Difficulties, A Guide for Parents and Professionals*. London: Souvenir Press (Educational & Academic) Ltd.

Klein, M. (1961). *Narrative of a Child Analysis: The Conduct of the Psycho-analysis of children as seen in the treatment of a ten-year-old boy*. London: Virago Press Limited.

Lang, C. (2008). Caring and touch as factors in effective teaching. *Annual Conference of the Scottish Educational Research Association [SERA] Royal George Hotel, Perth, Scotland, 27-29 November 2008*.

Lichtman, M. (2006). *Qualitative Research in Education: A User's Guide*. London: Sage.

Miles, M. B., & Huberman, A. M. (1994). *Qualitative Data Analysis*. London: Sage.

Moore, D. (2005, November). *Collaborative virtual environment technology for people with autism*. Paper presented at the Scottish Autism Research Group Seminar on the Integrated View of Research on Autism: From Theory to Practice, seminar 3: From Socio-cognitive research to information technology for autism spectrum disorders, University of Edinburgh.

Moore, D., Cheng, Y., McGrath, P., & Powell, N. J. (2005). Collaborative virtual environment technology for people with autism'. *Focus on Autism and Other Developmental Disorders, 20*, 231–243. doi:10.1177/10883576050200040501

Moore, D. J. (1998) Computers and People with Autism/Asperger Syndrome. *Communication,* Summer 1998, pp 20-21.

Moore, D. J. (2009) IT and Autism. Keynote speech, The 2009 *International Conference on the Current Trends in Information Technology,* December 15-16 2009, Dubai, United Arab Emirates.

Moore, D. J., & Taylor, J. (2000). Interactive multimedia systems for people with autism. *Journal of Educational Media, 25*(3), 169 177. doi:10.1080/1358165000250302

Moyles, J. (2005). *The Excellence of Play.* Berkshire, UK: Open University Press.

Murray, D. K. C. (1997). Autism and information technology: therapy with computers; in Powell S and Jordan R (eds) (1997) *Autism and Learning: A Guide to Good Practice*; London: David Fulton.

Murray, S. (2007). *An Interactive Classroom Timetable for Children with High-functioning Autism: Development and Qualitative Evaluation of a Computer-Based Timetable.* PhD Thesis. Queen Margaret University, UK.

NAS. (2005). *What is autism?* Retrieved November 10, 2010 from http://www.nas.org.uk/nas/jsp/polopoly.jsp?d=211.

NAS. (2010). *Computers: applications for people with autism.* Retrieved June 30, 2010 from http://www.autism.org.uk/en-gb/working-with/education/educational-professionals-in-schools/resources-for-teachers/computers-applications-for-people-with-autism.aspx.

Nimmo, C. (1994). Autism and Computers. *Communication, 28*(2), 8–9.

Noffke, S. (1997). Professional, personal and political dimensions of action research. *Review of Research in Education, 22*(1), 305–343. doi:10.3102/0091732X022001305

Parsons, S., & Mitchell, P. (2002). The potential of virtual reality in social skills training for people with autistic spectrum disorders. *Journal of Intellectual Disability Research, 46*(5), 430–443. doi:10.1046/j.1365-2788.2002.00425.x

Potter, C., & Whittaker, C. (2001). *Enabling Communication in Children with Autism.* London, Philadelphia: Jessica Kingsley Publishers.

Powell, S., & Jordan, R. (1997). Rationale for the approach. In Powell, S., & Jordan, R. (Eds.), *Autism and Learning - A Guide to Good Practice.* London: David Fulton.

Robson, C. (1993). *Real World Research: A Resource for Social Scientists and Practitioner Researchers.* London: Blackwell.

Robson, C. (2007). *How to Do a Research Project a Guide for Undergraduate Students.* London: Blackwell.

Rock, P. (2001). Symbolic Interactionism and Ethnography. In Atkinson, P. (Eds.), *Handbook of Ethnography* (pp. 26–37). London: Sage.

Silver, M. (2000). *Can people with autistic spectrum disorders be taught emotional understanding? The development and randomised controlled trial of a computer training package.* PhD thesis, University of Hull, UK.

Silver, M., & Oakes, P. (2001). Evaluation of a new computer intervention to teach people with autism or Asperger Syndrome to recognise and predict emotions in others. *Autism, 5*(3), 299–316. doi:10.1177/1362361301005003007

Tantam, D. (1993). *A Mind of One's Own.* London: National Autistic Society.

Williams, J. H. G., Massaro, D. W., Peel, N. J., & Bosseler, A. (2004). Visual-auditory integration during speech imitation in autism. *Research in Developmental Disabilities, 25,* 559–575. doi:10.1016/j.ridd.2004.01.008

Wing, L. (1996). *The Autism Spectrum: A Guide for Parents and Professionals.* London: Constable.

KEY TERMS AND DEFINITIONS

Action Research: When using action research researchers usually conduct several cycles of a research process which includes a) observe events occurring in real life, b) reflect on these and identify that there is a problem, c) plan how the problem could be solved or the situation improved on, and finally d) act and start observing again. A main advantage of using action research is its potential for making changes within real life situations.

Case Study: Case study is a qualitative methodology commonly used in educational contexts to obtain richness and depth of data. When using case study, different methods can be used such as observations, interviews, narrative accounts, documents and records to study the complex issues faced by researchers. A case can be limited to either one individual, one type of situation or a group of people or situations.

Computer-Animated Characters: Animated characters are commonly used in Human Computer Interaction (HCI) where characters perform several types of social behaviours. The potential use of the animated characters to aid social interactions has recently been acknowledged in the HCI literature.

Emotional Literacy: Literacy is defined as the knowledge of a particular subject. Hence, we meant by the emotional literacy in this chapter is the knowledge of the children in recognising emotions.

Empathy: Empathy is a highly complex phenomenon, which develops over time and with frequency of interaction and which is highly dependent on the actors and the context of the interaction. The deepest levels of empathy create strong emotional attachment and a sense of responsibility for others (Cooper, 2002).

Ethnography: In ethnographic research researchers engage with participants in their natural life within their real surroundings to get better understanding. Ethnography requires coming-together of the insider (participant observer) understanding with the outsider (non-participant) observer.

Facial Expressions: Ekman et. al., (1972) found that there are six universal facial expressions which correspond to the following emotions: happiness, sadness, surprise, anger, fear and disgust.

Interviews: Interviews are commonly used in qualitative research. They involve a one-to-one conversation between researchers and participants to get participants' views on any aspects of the research topic.

Observations: Observation is a fundamental method of gathering data to enable researchers collecting real data about participants and their environment in a naturally occurring situation. The researcher can be either participant or non-participant observer based on what he/she wants to know, whereas the observer in non-participant observation is a neutral outsider to avoid the influencing the events taking place.

Severe Autism: Although there is no universally agreed definition for autism, severe autism often refers to people who are at the extreme end of the spectrum (the opposite to Asperger Syndrome), where they usually have the associated learning disabilities linked with autism. Severe autism is usually known as classic autism in the literature.

Theory of Mind: Theory of Mind (ToM) is defined as the ability to mind-read other people's thoughts, where understanding and reasoning about mental states of others is required.

Section 2
Transition

Chapter 7

Let's Get Set for University!
(The Springschool Experience for Disabled Students)

Helen Smith
Leeds Metropolitan University, UK

ABSTRACT

This chapter considers the importance of pro-actively engaging disabled learners in events and activities that seek to encourage their participation in Higher Education. It examines the need to engage these students as early as possible in their educational careers. The impact of government agendas, as well as a discussion of the barriers that such students currently face, will then be addressed. Following this, there will be a detailed analysis of how a West Yorkshire regional partnership has tackled these issues in order to make that transition to university smoother. Particular attention will be made to young people's experience of taking part in two-day workshops known as Springschools.

INTRODUCTION

The purpose of this chapter is to demonstrate that transition to Higher Education (HE) for disabled learners can and should start a long time before a student reaches the point where they are ready to fill in an application form. In many instances, in order that a student even considers university as a possibility, a lot of groundwork needs to be done on the part of schools, colleges, local education authorities, universities and not least the students themselves. Transition to higher education poses many issues for all students, however for students with additional support needs there is no escaping the fact that there are extra barriers that need

DOI: 10.4018/978-1-61350-183-2.ch007

to be dealt with in order that this transition is as smooth as possible.

The chapter will therefore also consider the impact of the government's widening participation agenda on HE participation in recent years, in particular its drive to increase both the numbers of young people participating in higher education and the proportion of people from under-represented groups. An outline description of the current English education system will allow for a fuller understanding of how each part of the system deals with disabled students and how these differences impact on learners. Subsequent barriers to HE will be discussed, including how terminology can potentially cause confusion for education staff as well as students themselves.

Importantly, the bulk of the chapter will be devoted to considering the strategies and activity 'widening participation' have inspired. In particular, it will focus on work undertaken in one particular region, West Yorkshire, UK, to encourage young disabled students into considering higher education as a serious option. The activities and reasoning behind them will be discussed in detail before future developments are outlined in the concluding paragraphs.

BACKGROUND

Brief Summary of the Present Education System in England

Increasing numbers of disabled pupils in England are now educated in a mainstream setting rather than in specialist schools. To better understand the nature of the issues, controversies and problems that surround aspiration and awareness raising work with disabled learners, it is first essential to briefly describe the current school system in England. The same system also operates in Wales.

The school academic year starts on 1ˢᵗ September and runs through to 31ˢᵗ August the following year. Children start school in England in

the academic year in which they will reach the age of 5. Typically a child will attend a primary school between the ages of 4 and 11 followed by attendance at a secondary school or college until the age of 16, when compulsory schooling ends. In some areas middle schools exist which usually see the learner transfer from primary school to middle school at the age of 9 and then from middle school to secondary school at the age of 13.

Some schools and colleges also have post 16 provision which is available to a learner until the age of 19 whilst others require the learner to transfer to a specific post 16 provider, known as a Further Education (FE) college or a Sixth Form college.

The compulsory school years are divided into 4 Key Stages of Learning. The first year of school is called the Foundation Year, typically known as Year Reception. Key Stage 1, (Years 1 and 2) takes place between ages 5 and 7; Key Stage 2, (Years 3, 4, 5 and 6) takes place between ages 7 and 11. Key Stage 3 (traditionally Years, 7, 8 and 9) takes place between ages 11 and 14 with Key Stage 4 (traditionally Years 10 and 11) between ages 14 and 16, culminating in assessment in nationally recognised qualifications such as General Certificates in Secondary Education (GCSEs), BTECs (awarded by the Business and Technology Education Council) and Diplomas.

Until recently in England, National Curriculum Assessment tests, more commonly known as SATs took place in maths, English and science at the end of each of the first three Key Stages followed by GCSE examinations (and/or BTECs or Diplomas) in all subject areas at the end of the final year of compulsory schooling. However, tests at the end of Key Stage 3 were abolished in 2008 following issues with marking. In West Yorkshire at least, this end to Key Stage 3 testing has resulted in a significant number of schools condensing Key Stage 3 learning in to 2 years, thus allowing 3 years, Years 9, 10 and 11 to be devoted to Key Stage 4.

Steps to support change in attitudes can be seen in the government strategy for Special Educational Needs (SEN), 'Removing Barriers to Achievement,' (DfES 2004) It includes four strands, each of which could be said to promote widening participation amongst disabled learners within a school environment. Firstly, early intervention is crucial on the part of schools as with appropriate support from a young age, learners are much more likely to achieve their true potential. Secondly, embedding inclusive practice within the school curriculum will again remove potential barriers and improve academic outcomes. The third and fourth strands focus on the raising of expectations and achievement and working more closely with parents. It is important to consider both of these strands together, as positive partnerships between schools and parents can have a powerful impact on a learner's progress.

- Learners lack confidence in their ability to progress
- Disabled learners achieving academically at a later age

Another reason why disabled learners are regularly missed out of Aimhigher cohorts and opportunities is because their present academic attainment levels do not always reflect their true potential. Diagnosis of a disability does not necessarily happen at birth and it may be that an additional support need is not identified or indeed does not even exist until a child is part way through their school career. Even in such cases where awareness and support has existed since birth, it could be that it takes time to put together effective individual support as a child adapts to the school environment. Also, disabled young people may experience bouts of ill health necessitating prolonged periods of absence from school and regular medical interventions. This naturally impacts on progress academically. The disability may also mean that a young person is unable to work at the same speed as others in the

class. Because of the factors above it may be that some disabled students will not realistically be able to go to university straight from school or college at the age of 18. This does not however mean that they cannot go at a later time in their life. Frequently, such students lack confidence in their ability to progress and it may require extra persuasion on the part of all gatekeepers, in order that they feel comfortable in attending events that may lead them to seriously consider university.

- Few positive role models provided during recruitment

Generally, universities have not traditionally used current disabled undergraduates as 'recruitment tools' at Open Days or campus visit days to encourage others to follow suit or indeed to demonstrate to the wider world that disabled students are part of the university community. This is, of course, a contentious statement as many disabilities are hidden, sometimes deliberately so by the learner themselves. However, the power of empathy between say a deaf school pupil and a deaf university student should not be underestimated.

- Failing to target disabled learners within other groups of under represented learners
- Disabled learners being considered as an homogenous group

The undertaking of the work described in this chapter, frequently highlights one of the inherent dangers that arises from working with disabled learners, that of inadvertently treating them as an homogenous group. The needs of a visually impaired student are vastly different from those with a hearing impairment and hugely different again from those who are wheelchair users. Those with hidden disabilities such as mental health issues, dyslexia, HIV or autism are vastly different again and may not even be considered as disabilities by those who have them. A visually impaired student may have no sight whatsoever or have differing levels of restricted vision, similar may apply to those with hearing impairments. This all demonstrates that above all learners must be treated as individuals with specific learning needs. An event which is simply for disabled learners, may only further alienate students who no more identify with a disabled learner group than they do any other specifically labelled group. The same could equally apply to learners categorised for other reasons such as ethnicity. It is important too to remember that just because a student has been targeted for one reason, eg, their ethnicity, this does not mean they may not have a disability too.

Confusion: Differing Terminology and Practices in the Current Education System

A further barrier to progression also exists simply due to the language used to describe students with additional learning needs in the existing education system.

In schools, such pupils are said to have 'special educational needs' (SEN). This term was originally coined to refer to students with learning difficulties, however this now includes all those impairments that are covered by the Disability Discrimination Act (2001). It is important to note however, that a pupil is not deemed to have a special educational need unless special educational provision is required in order for them to access the school curriculum. Special Educational Needs Co-ordinator (SENCO) is the name given to the teacher who co-ordinates this support in school.

The SEN Code of Practice (2002) recommends schools to implement a 'graduated approach' to support that reflects the individual needs of the learner. Any assistance is recorded in a pupil's Individual Education Plan. This initial support is known as 'School Action' or 'School Action Plus' if additional assistance is sought from external agencies. Even with this support, some pupils may still need further help. In such instances, a pupil will undergo a statutory assessment which may

then result in the preparation of a 'statement of special educational need' on the part of the local education authority and a recommendation for supplementary resources.

Once a student is in post 16 or Further Education, they are then described as 'learners with learning difficulties and/or disabilities' (LLDD) or 'disabled learners'. The resulting support is described as learning support or additional learning support. Support is provided by the college. Funding can also be available for transport provision but this assistance varies depending on the local authority.

In higher education, students are generally referred to as 'disabled students' and are asked to declare their disability on application to university. However non-declaration at this point does not preclude students from disclosure at any other point of the student lifecycle.

HEFCE provides some money to Higher Education Institutions (HEIs) to support disabled students as part of its annual grant to a university. Support is organised differently in each institution but will generally be provided by staff in the disability office, although the names of such offices can vary. The work done by the central Disability Team will be both complemented and supplemented by people in individual academic areas both in an administrative and a course specific capacity. As well as the funding provided by HEFCE, eligible students who have an impairment or condition which will require study support, are entitled to apply for funding under the Disabled Students' Allowance (DSA). This non-means tested funding covers allowances for equipment, travel, general needs and non-medical helpers.

Such differences in terminology create confusion for learners, parents and carers and those working in the different education sectors alike. Learners and their parents have to adapt to the language differences which could result in a student arriving at the application stage to university without ever having been described as or indeed considered themselves to be 'disabled.' They may find themselves both emotionally and literally ill equipped to deal with this change and as a result may at the very least not consider it appropriate for them to tick the relevant disability disclosure box on the Universities and Colleges Admissions Service (UCAS) application form. Rightly or wrongly, the term 'disability' or 'disabled' frequently carries with it quite specific readily identifiable images of impairment and for some to find themselves labelled in the same way is quite difficult to come to terms with. The 'power of the label' is again noted in 'Improving the experiences of disabled students in higher education' (Jacklin, Robinson, O'Meara, Harris, 2007, p.6) which found that although the term 'disabled student' had helped bring about 'legislative changes which had opened doors to HE', its use 'could also be stigmatising.'

Those responsible for young people with additional learning and support needs in each of the respective educational sectors tend to find themselves in the position whereby they have little or no knowledge of the arrangements that exist in the other sectors. They have time only to try their best to provide an accessible education for those young people for whom they are directly responsible. There are few if any opportunities to share knowledge and best practice with others beyond their sector and yet this lack of awareness may have a long lasting impact on the educational outcomes for these same young people. As for the young people themselves, in some instances, a package of educational support may have followed them as they progressed from one Key Stage to the next, yet unless their transition to HE has been properly informed and prepared they may not realise that this move necessitates them to be pro-active in securing the support they need.

Getting There: Transition

Although, encouragingly, the number of students disclosing disabilities appears to be increasing, the National Audit Office (2007-08) reports an increase from 4% to 6% over the past five years for young people under 21, in 'Improving the experiences of disabled students in higher education',(Jacklin, Robinson, O'Meara, Harris, 2007) transition to HE is identified 'as a time of potential vulnerability'. It could be argued that the transition period can be a stressful time for all students as they adapt to living away from home, meeting new people and coming to terms with the different learning styles that are required on higher education courses. However, as stated in 'Improving access to higher education for disabled people' (Adams,Holland, 2006, p.15), often these issues are more complex for disabled students, 'if the individual had previously received personal support from family members, or had developed relationships with personal assistants to meet their needs, they would be additionally adjusting to a new support structure.'

The importance of ongoing information, advice and guidance (IAG) to aid this transition is crucial to successful transition. Clear signposting surrounding who to get in touch with at the university, how to go about obtaining financial support, the possibility of taking part in early induction programmes are vital (Jacklin, Robinson, O'Meara, Harris 2007), (Adams, Holland, 2006).

Working to Redress the Balance: Strategy and Activity Developed in the West Yorkshire Region

In early 2006, West Yorkshire Aimhigher determined to become pro-active in its efforts to redress the balance of HE aspiration raising and awareness activity in favour of disabled students. In particular, it asked HEAR WY (Higher Education Aspiration Raising – West Yorkshire), a collaborative partnership of all the West Yorkshire HEIs, to pilot this work on the grounds that it had an effective track record of producing and delivering innovative widening participation activity. The partnership thus began to look around the country for examples of good practice. In many ways it was not surprising to learn that there were very few specific projects that sought to engage young disabled learners in discovering more about higher education. However, Aimhigher London North, led by Middlesex University, had developed a project which had resulted in them running three-day events called Springschools, aimed at supporting the transition of young people with specific disabilities into higher education.

In an excellent example of sharing good practice, West Yorkshire Aimhigher was invited to observe and take part in the Aimhigher London North Springschool for Visually Impaired students in March 2006. This event sought particularly to engage those who had already taken the first steps towards applying to university, whether that be in the actual submission of an application form or making both general and specific enquiries to particular institutions. The event combined practical information about getting to university, such as preparing for interviews and campus orientation with improving study techniques and an introduction to the latest technology which could best support their particular learning needs. Attendance at the Springschool allowed West Yorkshire staff to become aware of the specific adjustments that would need to be made in order that such an event was fully accessible and also gave them pause to focus on who they particularly wished to target with any activity they might develop. It was decided that as HEAR WY's particular expertise lay in work with pre 16 students, they would develop an event for pupils aged 13 to 15 which would actively encourage the participation of disabled young people in higher education by providing fun, yet informative activities over a two-day period. The workshops would be non-residential. This event would also highlight the benefits of and support within higher education. With permission from Aimhigher London North, the events were entitled Springschools.

The first three West Yorkshire events were delivered in Spring 2007, with a total of 55 pupils taking part. Due to their immediate success four more have subsequently been delivered and other

events have been realised as a result. Springschools were developed for hearing impaired students, visually impaired students and students with specific learning difficulties (SpLD), more particularly students with dyslexia, dyscalculia and dyspraxia. The following paragraphs will focus on the key elements to their successful delivery:

Content of the Days

As the key aims of the days were to encourage disabled learners to make informed choices about higher education in an informal yet educational setting, it was believed to be important that the days contained a mixture of activities that allowed them to consider important generic aspects about HE such as budgeting, accommodation, what courses to choose, social life, whilst at the same time giving learners the chance to take part in academic taster sessions, whether that be in a lecture theatre, IT laboratory or classroom setting which would give them a genuine experience of study in higher education. It was also important for them to realise that there are disabled students already in HE and that study at university is a realistic progression route. This fact was emphasised by asking students with similar disabilities to take part in the events and relate their journey to HE and also by the Disability Services Teams giving short presentations that briefly explained the support that can be available to students. However, it is important to note that these talks were deliberately short as their aim was simply to raise awareness that support existed, rather than to overwhelm young people who would not be coming to university for at least another three years, with figures and facts that may well have altered by the time they apply anyway.

Putting the Programmes
Together – Collaboration

As HEAR WY is a partnership of all seven of the West Yorkshire Higher Education Institutions this meant that it was able to call on the expertise of both disability practitioners and those responsible for working with schools and colleges within each of those institutions. This was particularly helpful as the teams responsible for outreach work were able to provide contacts for local schools and colleges and also provide facilities such as rooms, IT support and current HE students to act as ambassadors and role models during the time the young people were on campus. As they deliver many HE focused days themselves they were also available to give ideas on icebreakers and games to use with the young people.

With regard to the Disability Services Teams, they were able to provide expert knowledge on how to make events fully accessible, from how best we should set up a room so that the lighting would best favour visually impaired students, to the provision of portable induction loops for hearing impaired students moving from room to room.

Both sets of teams were also keen to be involved in the project to develop their own skills and support their own work. Staff within Disability Services Teams, spend most of their time supporting and advising students who are already in higher education. However, all were of the opinion that if more time could be spent preparing students for entry to university then fewer problems would be encountered on arrival as they would have done everything in their power to ensure support was in place from day one of their course. Students would also have realistic expectations as to what university study and life entailed. On the part of the Outreach Teams, the need to amend and adapt some of their activities encouraged them to rethink their planning for events so that their games were more inclusive.

Other staff within universities became involved in the programme. Academic staff were asked to provide workshops and lectures. An example of this was the Carnegie Great Outdoors team at Leeds Metropolitan University (UK). Not only did they provide a lecture on the university's involvement in an attempt to ascend Mount Everest but they also

provided staff to deliver an afternoon of sporting activity including kayaking and a crate stacking activity that involved great teamwork.

Over the two day period students were also given guided tours of the university libraries which gave them the opportunity to familiarise themselves with the resources available. They were also able to try out assistive hardware and software, such as mindmapping, screen magnifiers, audio recording devices and text-to-speech software, which might be useful assistive technologies in an academic setting.

Outside agencies were also crucial to the success of the events. The RNIB (The Royal National Institute of Blind People) provided a member of staff to give specific study skills tips to visually impaired students. Another member of the RNIB team had considerable expertise as a Goalball coach and gave pupils a two hour introductory session to the game. Deaf START, a post 16 support service for Deaf students, provided interpreters and academic support to deaf and hard of hearing students for the entirety of the two-day Springschool experience. Barry Bennett Ltd., a company which supplies specialist equipment for disabled students also attended these early Springschools and provided the students with a very hands-on opportunity to try out the latest technology.

Recruiting the Students

Universities have had Outreach Teams that engage with schools and colleges for many years. The arrival of Aimhigher has allowed such teams to formalise these relationships. At the same time Aimhigher funding has allowed universities, schools and colleges to develop their repertoire of widening participation projects. Many schools and colleges in West Yorkshire now employ an Aimhigher Organiser which makes initial contact easier. However, as detailed earlier in the chapter, frequently disabled students have been seen as the responsibility of SENCOs. This meant that the participation of learners in the Springschool sometimes depended on the Aimhigher Organiser seeking out the SENCO within their school. There are very few schools now in existence that cater purely for the needs of young people with specific disabilities. However, where those schools do exist, invitations were also extended to attend the Springschool. Sensory Impairment teams within each Local Education Authority work with young disabled people on a regular basis and proved to be most helpful in actively recruiting appropriate Springschool participants. We had initially hoped to target pupils in Year 11 as well as Years 9 and 10 but in most instances Year 11 pupils were unable to participate because of the Springschools' proximity to public GCSE Examinations.

Success of the Days

At the start of each Springschool, each pupil was asked to complete a questionnaire. This asked them about their prior knowledge of university, why they wanted to attend the Springschool and what they knew about levels of available support for those with additional needs at university. At the end of the two days, pupils were asked to complete a similar questionnaire thus providing data on whether the event had had any impact on their awareness of what 'going to university' entails, what additional support there was available and indeed whether they now felt more inclined to consider 'going to university' as an option. At the first Springschool for hearing impaired students in March 2007, 100% of participants responded that they had enjoyed the Springschool, with only one person still having any real worries about what life at university might be like. 89% thought that universities provided good support for hearing and impaired students, with 11% not sure.

All those who responded felt they had learned something about university that they did not know before.

Although initially some gatekeepers had expressed concern that such an event be exclusively for young people with a specific disability, in fact

the ability to mix with other people who face the same sort of issues was welcomed by those who took part. As more and more young disabled people are educated in a mainstream school setting, albeit with a tailored support package, it was commented on by staff that sometimes these young people can feel isolated as there are few, if any, other students who can relate to their high school experience. The Springschool allowed people from schools across the region to get to know other people in the same situation as themselves and many swapped email and Facebook contact details to allow them to keep in touch in the future. It also allowed those students who were educated in a specialist school setting, to meet others outside of this environment, giving them the chance to broaden their educational experience.

The use of role models, i.e. HE students who had disabilities similar to those participating in the Springschools, was very effective. Students immediately built a rapport with the pupils and were willing to answer questions about their lives and their journeys to higher education. Other students were also used as 'ambassadors', the same student working with a particular group of 4/5 young people for both days. It was interesting to note that at each Springschool, the atmosphere at the start of the second day was considerably more relaxed and informal than on the first, as both staff and students became familiar with the university environment. Every pupil who has attended the first day of a Springschool, has returned to complete the second day's activities.

A sporting activity formed part of each Springschool programme, so that the university experience was as broad as possible. For some the sporting activity simply provided a very safe and secure environment in which to actually just participate, for others it was a chance to shine, whether that be in football, goalball, running or a teambuilding activity. In some instances, such as goalball, it served as an introduction to a new game which the young people might wish to pursue following the Springschool.

Academics who have delivered taster sessions as part of Springschools have not only enjoyed the experience but feel it has helped them become more aware of how to best deliver more inclusive programmes. Indeed one lecturer asked fellow lecturers in his department if they would attend his Everest talk to deaf and hard of hearing students as an example of staff development.

Above all the Springschools appear to have increased the confidence of those pupils who participated in them. All arrived at Springschool with the potential to progress to higher education, Springschool allowed them to see for themselves that it was a realistic possibility.

Further Activity

The success of the Springschool programme led to the awareness of a need to develop further opportunities for disabled pupils to pro-actively engage with university outreach activity. Work to ease transition to university was also seen as important. The ideal still remained for these young people to take part in activities provided for everybody else in their age and academic interest group, however, it was recognised that such work still needed to be supported by specific interventions.

West Yorkshire Aimhigher Disability Forum

Conscious of its need to engender a collaborative approach to 'widening participation' with regard to disabled learners, West Yorkshire Aimhigher set up a forum consisting of practitioners across the region who wished to make a positive contribution. This consists of representatives from Further Education colleges, HEI Outreach teams and Disability teams, local careers services, Local Education Authorities and Aimhigher District Co-ordinators. This forum provides a means for opinions and knowledge from a variety of different sectors to be voiced and shared, enabling a more coherent approach to be developed regarding disabled learner inclusion in Aimhigher activity. The contribution of this forum and the subsequent activity it has since initiated has further resulted in the establishment of a specific West Yorkshire Aimhigher Disability Strategy which will be discussed below, under the heading 'Future Directions'.

Summer Schools

A natural follow up to a 2-day non-residential Springschool, appeared to be participation in a residential Summer School, alongside 150 other pupils of a similar age. HEFCE saw participation in residential university experiences as an effective way to encourage young people to consider higher education and provided monies to universities in order to facilitate this. Summer Schools give students the chance to stay in university accommodation and to experience all aspects of university life, from academic workshops, to budgeting seminars, from visits to the theatre to a celebratory ball.

The Sensory Impairment Team from Calderdale Local Education Authority (UK) had been enthused by their students' involvement in the Springschools for both visually impaired and hearing impaired pupils. They were therefore keen to take this enthusiasm to the next level by encouraging five of these pupils to attend the residential Summer School that was to be held at Leeds Metropolitan University (UK) in July 2008.

Naturally, the provision of a residential experience for 150 young people takes intense and considerable preparation over many months. The intention of West Yorkshire Aimhigher, HEAR WY and the Calderdale Sensory Impairment Team was to integrate the five young people as much as possible whilst providing the necessary support to allow this to happen. The five pupils participating had visual or hearing impairments and one also had a mobility impairment. The Calderdale Team were able to offer to provide the sign language support themselves, as well as providing a member of staff to act as a guide. The 24 hour care required for one of the pupils was given by the person who normally provided this care at school. The full Summer School residential lasted four nights, the group from Calderdale attended for two nights, arriving half way through the programme.

Participation in the Summer School proved to be an extremely successful experience for all five students. All provided evaluations that indicated that they had been motivated by the residential. Particularly popular was the interaction with other students most notably at the celebratory ball on the final night and the sporting activities. The most important lesson learned was that it would have been better to have included the students from the beginning of the residential rather than introducing them half way through the week. All the other students had had the opportunity to form friendship groups and bond with one another from their arrival on Monday morning. Arriving on Wednesday morning meant that it was somewhat more difficult to break into these groups and establish relationships with other students. In addition to this, the group had necessarily brought adults with them to support their inclusion. Unfortunately this also created barriers. As one visually impaired student commented, it would have been easier to have communicated with fellow students if my guide had been of a similar age, or had been one of the supporting student ambassadors.

The Summer School experience does seem to have provided motivation to entering higher education. Indeed of the five students, one is now at university, one hopes to start in September 2010, with a third hoping to obtain a place in 2011. The other two continue to find language a barrier to further progression currently but are exploring further avenues.

'On the Right Track'

Empowering students to articulate their own support needs is crucial if they are to successfully move from further education into higher education. This was at the heart of a pilot transition project entitled 'On the Right Track', which was run jointly by West Yorkshire Aimhigher and Shipley College, Bradford (UK) from October 2008 to July 2009. The initial aim of the project was to produce a set of learning tools which would gradually and sensitively take students through any barriers which they might face if they were to enter HE. Workshops were planned to cover the following areas: Managing Learning and Anxiety, Living Independently, About my disability, My Learning Needs, Managing my own support. However it soon became evident that individual one to one meetings with learners worked better than the scheduled workshops. This was because the learners were not a homogenous group and did not readily identify themselves as having similar needs, if indeed they recognised that they may need additional support at university at all. These factors altered the course of the 'On the Right Track' project significantly and provoked much debate as to how best to tackle these issues in the future. Further activity in this area is discussed below, under the heading 'Transition Meetings.'

The final activity of the programme was the inclusion of four of the students on a Leeds Metropolitan University residential Summer School in July 2009, very similar to that described earlier in the chapter. Of the four students who attended, three were on the autistic spectrum and one was a wheelchair user. One member of staff from the college attended for the whole of the Summer School, two other members of staff attended at intervals during the period of the residential. Learning from the previous year's experience, the students were asked to attend Summer School for the whole five-day programme. This ensured that the four students became fully integrated into the social groups that were formed and engendered a much more inclusive experience. The fact that a member of Shipley College staff was on hand for the whole time allowed the students to relax into the experience more as he was always available if they felt the need for informal support or just required a little practical advice. Indeed it had originally been planned to provide academic support for 2 of the students on each of the five days. However this proved unnecessary as the students quickly took charge of their own learning experience. A DVD was made of their Summer School experience to encourage others in a similar position to consider attending future residentials. The DVD also provided excellent evidence of the positive learning impact that results from taking part. All four young men subsequently applied to university in the term following their attendance at Summer School.

Taster Days

The success of the Springschools and the advent of the West Yorkshire Aimhigher Disability Forum have allowed more bespoke activity to be developed as relationships between HEIs, Aimhigher, local education authorities and schools have strengthened. An example of such activity is a short HE awareness raising project which took place in 2008-09 with selected pupils from Pinderfields Hospital School, Wakefield (UK). An introductory in-school workshop supported by trained current HE student ambassadors was followed up by a whole day university campus visit that allowed pupils from the school to work with staff and students from the Leeds Metropolitan University Carnegie Great Outdoors team on sporting and teambuilding activities. A final successful follow up in-school workshop further cemented the relationship and a small number of young people are now being supported and mentored by HE students as part of the Aimhigher Associates scheme which will be further discussed in the Future Directions section.

Similar work has been undertaken with young people from St John's School for the Deaf, Boston Spa (UK). The Carnegie Great Outdoors Team has provided an on-campus sporting and teambuilding activity day and a recent hearing impaired graduate

has been in to the school to deliver a talk about his own learning journey and life experiences as part of a Deaf Awareness Event that the school was running.

Collaborative activity has also been undertaken with the Visual Impairment Team in Leeds Local Education Authority. As part of the authority's ongoing 'World of Work' project, two music technology workshops took place, one creating a radio play, one cutting a music CD. Led by undergraduates from Leeds Metropolitan University, these workshops allowed the young people to consider music technology degrees and the subsequent future career opportunities within the music industry.

Drama and Dyslexia Day

A further example of such bespoke work occurred following the approach of a current student who was studying Drama at the University of Huddersfield (UK). Dyslexic herself, she wanted to demonstrate to young people that this did not need to be a barrier to prevent them from going on to higher education. Recruiting the services and skills of fellow drama students, some of whom were also dyslexic, a day of motivational team building and acting workshops were devised for Year 10 students. In May 2010, 42 young people took part in the activities, which also saw input from Aimhigher, as well as the Schools and Colleges Liaison and Disability Services. Feedback was excellent, with 98% of participants responding that they had enjoyed the day, 88% saying that the Taster Day had made them think about going to university and 93% happy to recommend the taster day to other students.

Future Directions

The success of the projects discussed above has resulted in the formalising of the initial groundwork done by the West Yorkshire Aimhigher Disability

Forum. A strategy has been put in place with the following aims:

- To integrate provision for disabled learners into Aimhigher in West Yorkshire.
- To create more possibilities for disabled learners within Aimhigher by sharing good practice across the education sectors.

These aims will be reinforced by the successful achievement of the following objectives:

- To increase the participation in Aimhigher cohorts/Aimhigher activity from amongst disabled students and students with additional support needs.
- To address the key barriers to progression amongst disabled learners.
- To harness the combined talents of the West Yorkshire Aimhigher Disability Forum
- To provide information, guidance and assistance to disabled students and their families/carers before and during inclusion in the Aimhigher cohorts and to give as much support as reasonably possible as they progress with their Aimhigher journey.

A part-time Disability Co-ordinator has been put in place to ensure these aims and objectives are met.

Transition Meetings

An important lesson learned from the On the Right Track project was that transition to HE is a very personal journey for students and encouragement to articulate their needs is much needed. Given this, one to one transition meetings have been taking place between students in Years 12 and 13 in the Calderdale District and the West Yorkshire Aimhigher Disability Co-ordinator. The meetings followed individual letters to students and their parents asking whether they would appreciate a meeting ahead of either submitting a university

application or to help prior to arrival there. At each meeting the importance of declaring a disability at the initial application stage is highlighted. This, together with step by step information and advice on how to get in touch with a university's Disability Advisor, Assessments of Need (a personal interview with an assessor who will make support recommendations to the students' funding body) and the existence of Disabled Students Allowance are then talked through. The first meetings also had in attendance a university Disability Advisor who was able to clearly explain the type of support a student could reasonably expect. This initial input has subsequently allowed the Disability Co-ordinator to conduct meetings alone. The meetings have taken place in either the student's home environment or in school or college. Informal feedback suggests that all meetings have been appreciated by students and parents alike.

However, as successful as these meetings have been, there are insufficient resources available either to sustain them or to roll them out to other areas. An information pack therefore needs to be created which can be given to these students and their parents as well as teachers and other relevant personnel in schools and colleges. They could also form a useful part of the Aimhigher Associates toolkit which will be outlined below.

Aimhigher Associates

A later addition to the Aimhigher initiative has been the creation of the Aimhigher Associates scheme. Aimhigher Associates are university students that have been recruited by Aimhigher to provide school and college pupils between Year 9 and Year 13 with long-term help and support. (Reference www.aimhigher.ac.uk). A small number of disabled university students have so far been recruited to work on this scheme but a greater, more concerted, push to do so is planned for the future. In particular, in future, all Associates could receive training on how best to use the transition toolkit as part of their induction process.

Disabled Voices – Publicity

A positive way to secure successful educational outcomes for young disabled students is to ask them what input they would like and to give them opportunities for their voices to be heard. It is hoped to achieve this in future via the creation of publicity materials designed by the young people themselves which will emphasise the importance of disabled learner inclusion in HE awareness raising activity. This material and its underlying message will then be distributed to all the region's schools and colleges. Voices have also been captured via informal interviews with student ambassadors in a mocked up television studio setting.

Networks

Action on Access, The National Co-ordination Team for Widening Participation has also recognised the importance of recognising best practice and sharing innovative transition ideas with regards to disabled learners and HE. It has encouraged the setting up of cross county networks which will hold regular meetings to promote the aforementioned aims. West Yorkshire and South Yorkshire are now working together to ensure such networking opportunities arise.

CONCLUSION

Regionally, the Springschools have played a significant role in improving the inclusion of disabled learners in programmes of outreach work that encourage transition to higher education. Specifically their success has seen the emergence of a disability strand with clear objectives as well as a budget, forum and part-time outreach co-ordinator to allow strategy and activity to dovetail with one another. This system of organisation means that those interested in knowing more about disabled learner transition to university know who, and

where, to go to find out more. Crucially it has allowed stakeholders to broker new ideas to develop ever more effective workshops and activities.

As the impact of this, and the work of many other regions, is felt nationally, so is the need to capture this best practice and share it with others, hence the development of broader regional and national disability networks. There is growing awareness that for greater inclusion of disabled learners in higher education to be achieved, such students cannot remain the exclusive responsibility of one gatekeeper. For truly successful long term outcomes to be achieved, families and services need to work together to provide the individual learner with support they both want and need.

Finally, and most importantly, a pool of previously untapped talent is now increasingly able to access relevant activity and information that will empower them to make informed decisions about their own future, broadening their horizons. It is to be hoped that in future months and years, this momentum can be maintained.

REFERENCES

Adams, M., & Brown, S. (Eds.). (2006). *Towards Inclusive Learning in Higher Education: developing curricula for disabled students. Abingdon.* Routledge.

Adams, M., & Holland, S. (2006). Improving access to higher education. In Adams, M., & Brown, S. (Eds.), *Towards Inclusive Learning in Higher Education: developing curricula for disabled students. Abingdon* (p. 15). Routledge.

DDA. (1995). *Disability Discrimination Act.* Retrieved July 03, 2010, from http://www.opsi.gov.uk/acts/acts1995/ukpga_19950050_en_1

Department for Education and Skills (DfES) (2002). *Special Educational Needs Code of Practice.*

Department for Education and Skills (DfES) (2004). *Removing Barriers to Achievement: The Government's Strategy for SEN.*

Elliott, T., & Wilson, C. (2007). *Targeting and recruitment of disabled learners.* Aimhigher.

Higher Education Funding Council for England (HEFCE) (2007). *Higher education outreach: targeting disadvantaged learners, Guidance for Aimhigher partnerships and higher education providers*

Higher Education Funding Council for England (HEFCE). (2009). *Strategic Plan 2006-11, Widening Participation and Fair Access.* Updated June 2009. Retrieved November 26, 2010, from http://195.194.167.100/Pubs/hefce/2009/09_21/09_21.pdf

Jacklin, A., Robinson, C., O'Meara, L., & Harris, A. (2007). *Improving the experiences of disabled students in higher education* (p. 6). Higher Education Academy.

NAO National Audit Office (2002). *Widening Participation in Higher Education in England.*

NAO National Audit Office. (2007). *Staying the course: the retention of students in higher education. Senda Special Educational Needs and Disability Act 2001 (2001).* Retrieved November 26, 2010, from http://www.legislation.gov.uk/ukpga/2001/10/contents

NAO National Audit Office (2008). *Widening Participation in Higher Education.*

National Disability Team (NDT) and Skill: National Bureau for Students with Disabilities (2004). *Aspiration raising and transition of disabled students from Further Education to Higher Education.*

ADDITIONAL READING

Action on Access., (2009). *Induction and Disabled Learners.* Ormskirk: Action on Access. Marriott, J., (2007). *Post 16 Education and Disabled Learners: A guide for schools, colleges and information, advice and guidance workers.* Ormskirk: Action on Access.

Tomlinson, J. (1996). *Inclusive Learning: principles and recommendations.* Coventry: The Further Education Funding Council.

KEY TERMS AND DEFINITIONS

Aimhigher: The main driver in the government's effort to widen participation in HE. It has as its goal to raise the awareness, aspirations and attainment of young people who are currently under represented in HE.

Aspiration and Awareness Raising Activity: Events, projects, campus visits that seek to encourage young people to make informed decisions about higher education.

Springschools: Two day workshops at a university campus for disabled students (pre 16) that seek to provide a fun yet informative introduction to higher education.

Transition to HE for Disabled Students: The whole process of moving to higher education, including, HE campus visits, application, induction, provision of support and ongoing student life.

Widening Participation: Is concerned with addressing the imbalance between the uptake of HE opportunities from different social groups. It seeks to engage with groups of people who are currently under-represented in HE in the UK.

Chapter 8
Students with Autism in Higher Education

Salima Y. Awad Elzouki
Leeds Metropolitan University, UK

Elizabeth Guest
Leeds Metropolitan University, UK

Chris Adams
Leeds Metropolitan University, UK

ABSTRACT

Recently there has been an increasing awareness of disability issues in the UK. In line with this, there is an increasing concern to enhance the learning of students with disability in higher education (HE) and an acknowledgement that more research is needed to investigate the practical issues faced by students with disabilities. This recent increase in research has, however, tended to ignore issues faced by students with autism in HE. It was this that motivated the research discussed in this chapter. The chapter starts by arguing for the importance of catering for students with autism in HE. Next the authors consider the practical issues that students with autism might face in HE. The authors do this through three means: a narrative account of two students, a case study of another student written by his close social worker and a case study concerning a specific UK University.

INTRODUCTION

This chapter discusses the impact that autism might have on students, both academically and socially, while they are at University. This is done via three accounts; a narrative account of student experience and two case studies. The narrative

DOI: 10.4018/978-1-61350-183-2.ch008

involves a set of scenarios that have been put together from a set of real experiences to illustrate the kinds of issues that students with autism experience. Because individuals on the autistic spectrum vary widely in how they perceive the world, these experiences have been crystallized into two characters, Bob and Sam, who think quite differently from each other but who experience similar difficulties. These scenarios set the scene for the first case study concerning a student with Asperger Syndrome. This case is written by the support worker who supported the student for 40 hours a week for the duration of the student's course. Finally, we provide another case study of a major UK University, including an interview with the University's Disability Services Manager (DSM) and a collection of documents and information in relation to students with disability in this University. Finally, based on the above three accounts we conclude with a set of recommendations that we hope will enhance the support of students with autism in HE. All names used in the chapter, including the University name, are anonymous, for ethical reasons.

BACKGROUND

The Importance of Catering for People with Autism in HE

Recruiting more students into HE has become one of the most important items on the political agenda in the UK (Riddell et. al., 2005). In particular, there is an increasing interest in research concerning the participation of students with disabilities in HE (cf. Riddell et. al., 2005), and there is an increasing interest in recruiting more students with disabilities into HE (Brown, 2005).

As well as an obvious ethical obligation to cater appropriately for students with disabilities, these students are protected by law against any discrimination in UK Higher Education Institutions (HEIs) (Disability Rights Commission, 2007). Consequently, a Widening Participation agenda becomes essential in HE to guarantee fair opportunity for all students with disabilities and to ensure that they achieve their full potential (HEFCE, 2008). For example, after publishing the tenth set of UK HE performance indicators in 2008, Professor David Eastwood, HEFCE (Higher Education Funding Council for England) Chief Executive said: 'Widening participation in higher

education is vital to ensuring a fair and equitable society. HEFCE and the Higher Education sector are determined to increase the number of students entering higher education from under-represented groups' (HEFCE, 2008). In the light of this, there is an increasing awareness by UK universities of their responsibility to offer appropriate provision for students with disabilities, and students with disabilities are encouraged to seek and choose universities that can offer suitable support (Directgov, 2010).

Despite such measures, however, people with autism still face a considerable amount of discrimination. For example, a survey by the UK National Autistic Society (NAS) 2001 *Ignored or Ineligible? The Reality for Adults with Autism Spectrum Disorders* suggests that adults with autism are "vulnerable" and "excluded", many are dependent on their parents or carers and often "fall through the gap between mental health and learning disability" (NAS, 2001, p. 6). An NAS report (NAS, 2008), *I Exist: The Message from Adults with Autism in England,* showed that adults with autism were "scared" about their future and feel they do not get the appropriate support as a result of people "misunderstanding" autism. Similarly, Beardon & Edmonds (2007) argue that there is little information concerning the needs of adults with autism.

The passing of the Autism Act in November 2009 by the UK government was an acknowledgement that adults with autism have received inadequate care in the past and a commitment to improve on this in the future. Similarly, after the publication of the first Bill of Scotland for Autism (We Exist) in 2010, Carol Evans, the NAS National Director for Scotland, said that people with autism's "needs are great and have been very much ignored" (NAS Scotland, 2010).

The research outlined in this chapter aims to contribute to attempts to address this imbalance concerning the needs of adults with autism. Specifically, we will address a particular population of adults with autism i.e. students with autism in higher education (HE). Such students have been thus far under-represented in HE. Indeed, it is worth noting that the category for such students did not even exist as a valid entry for disability in statistics collected by the UK Higher Education Statistics Agency (HESA) until 2003/04. Concerning the few students with autism who do get to University, Baron-Cohen (2008) suggests that they may be more prone to drop out than their peers who do not have autism, as a result of the inflexible learning environments available. In this chapter, therefore, we focus on the needs and difficulties that might be faced by students with autism.

Autism in HE: Under-Representation

We start by arguing that people with autism are disproportionately under-represented in HE. A pre-requisite is an understanding of the concept of autism.

Autism Spectrum Conditions

A commonly held view of the nature of autism is that it involves a "triad of impairments" (Wing, 1996). The triad of impairments involves social, communication and imagination difficulties, as discussed in more detail in Moore's chapter in this book. 'Asperger Syndrome' (eg Attwood, 2007) generally refers to a mild form of autism in that people with Asperger Syndrome may have "fewer problems" with language than people with autism (NAS, 2010a). Asperger Syndrome is also described as a 'hidden disability' (eg NAS, 2010a), because of the lack of obvious physical manifestations. Although people with Asperger Syndrome generally do not have the associated "learning disabilities" sometimes linked with autism, they might have some specific difficulties such as "dyslexia and dyspraxia or other conditions such as attention deficit hyperactivity disorder (ADHD) and epilepsy" (NAS, 2010a).

Wing (2002) suggests that it is useful to see autism as a spectrum, often known as "autism spectrum disorder" (ASD). Attwood, (2007) suggests that the mild end of the spectrum is known as 'Asperger Syndrome' and Baron-Cohen, (2008) suggests that the severe end of the spectrum is known as 'classic autism'. Recently, the term "autism spectrum condition" (ASC) has started to come into vogue, (e.g. Baron-Cohen, 2008).

The Number of People with ASC

The incidence of ASC appears to be increasing all over the world. For example, in the US autism is estimated to have risen recently from 1 in 500 to 1 in 150 (cf. NIMH, 2010) and to 1 per 100 in the UK (NAS, 2010b). Further, a recent study conducted by Baron-Cohen, et al. (2009) concerning the prevalence of autism in children aged 5–9 in the UK suggests that the proportion is slightly above 1%. The UK NAS (2010b) reports that "there is no prevalence rate for ASD in adults". Baron-Cohen, (2008) has related the apparent increase in the incidence of ASC to the improved detection rates of autism and to the recent addition of many "milder cases" of ASC in the diagnostic criteria.

Many developing countries seemed until recently not to recognise ASC (cf. Lotter, 1978). For example, Libya, which previously appeared not to recognise ASC now sees it as a separate diagnosis. Recently, the government, professionals and parents in Libya have tried to gather as much information about ASC as possible and have created charities and special units for children with ASC. However, figures for incidence are not yet available (cf. Elzouki et. al., 2007).

The Number of Students with ASC in HE

Table 1 shows figures for ASC students in HE in the UK, starting from 2003/04 (the year that autism was recorded as a valid entry for disability in HEIs in the UK). Table 1 also shows figures of students with dyslexia and mental health difficulties. These categories are of interest partly because the diagnosis of autism in adults is often seen as falling in the gap between learning disability and mental health difficulties and partly because adults with AS may also have some learning difficulties such as dyslexia as well as their ASC diagnosis.

As Table 1 shows, the percentage of ASC in HE ranges from 0.01% to 0.08%. Given that, as seen earlier, the percentage of the total population that has ASC is estimated at up to 1% or more, it seems clear that ASC students are under-represented in HE, in the UK at least. The ASC percentage figure in Table 1 does grow, year or year, but remains far below what it should be were ASC people to be proportionately represented in HE.

One possible reason behind this is that people with ASC and their carers may not believe that HE is a realistic possibility for them. For this reason awareness raising initiatives such as those discussed by Smith elsewhere in this book are likely to be very important. A second possible reason for the under-representation of ASC people in HE is that the literature suggests a major problem for

most adults with AS to get a formal diagnosis. For example, the results of a survey conducted by Beardon and Edmonds (2007) showed that many people have difficulty in obtaining a diagnosis at all, and many get theirs relatively late in life (with an average age of 29 years). A third possible reason is that some students with a disability do not join disability services, since they are not obliged to report their disability. Such students will not be counted under HESA returns. For this reason, Beardon & Edmonds (2007) recommend encouraging such students to declare their autism, with a view to getting the support they may need. As seen earlier, Baron-Cohen (2008) discusses ASC students who leave universities as a result of the inflexible learning environments available, and this may be another reason for the underrepresentation of students with ASC in HE.

If universities are to provide the sort of educational opportunity to people with ASC that we would argue they should, legally and ethically, provide, it is important to understand how his or her ASC might affect a student's daily life at University. Given this, we now provide a narrative account of two students with ASC.

Table 1. Number of UK students with ASD, Mental Health Difficulties & Dyslexia according to the 2003/04-2008/09 HESA Student Returns

Year	Total number of students	Students with ASC		Students with Mental Health Difficulties		Students with Dyslexia	
		Number	% of total	Number	% of total	Number	% of total
2003/04	2247440	145	0.01	5,270	0.23	49945	2.22
2004/05	2287540	535	0.02	6,240	0.27	57900	2.53
2005/06	2336110	1120	0.05	7,035	0.30	64880	2.78
2006/07	2362815	1035	0.04	8,210	0.35	72050	3.05
2007/08	2306105	1455	0.06	9675	0.42	*76385	3.31
2008/09	2396050	1925	0.08	11200	0.47	82860	3.46

* The 'Dyslexia' category was expanded for 2007/08 onwards to allow for the inclusion of students with similar categories such as a learning difficulty not identified as dyslexia.

A NARRATIVE AND TWO CASE STUDIES

A Narrative of Bob & Sam: What it is Like to be a Student with ASC

From a set of personal experiences of students on the autistic spectrum, we have crystallized two characters, Bob and Sam We will use these characters in a set of scenarios in order to illustrate what it is like to be a student on the autistic spectrum, from their point of view. These scenarios are based on real events. Bob studied Computing and Sam studied English. Each scenario is followed by a reflection that provides a commentary based on relevant ASC literature. The narrative approach adopted in this section is similar to that used by Fitzgerald et al., elsewhere in this book.

The Social Scene

Bob and Sam know that they are not good at making friends, so they sign up for a number of clubs. Bob likes being outdoors, he signs up for canoeing and running. Sam also signs up for canoeing, but is also interested in scuba diving. Both students attend club events regularly, but find that although other members of the club are friendly and will talk to them during activities, no real friends result. Both find relaxing in the pub after activities hard going. They both find it hard to understand and join in with the banter. In addition, Bob finds pubs too dark and noisy, and while Sam likes the dim light, he finds trying to follow one conversation while others are going on nearby almost impossible. Unless he concentrates very hard, sentences become an incomprehensible mixture of all the sentences being uttered around him.

Reflection

The social scene highlighted above reflects the common view of autism in the literature. Difficulties with social proficiencies is considered to be the cornerstone of autism (see the background section above). Bob and Sam's social scene is typical of the view of many people with ASC about social difficulties they encounter. For example, Donna Williams a professional writer with Asperger Syndrome (AS) states in one of her books *Autism: An Inside – Out Approach* that the world to people with AS "is a mass of people, places and events which they struggle to make sense of, and which can cause them considerable anxiety" (Williams, 1996). Also, she notes that anxiety is one of the difficulties that affect her 'tolerance'. Similarly, Attwood (1998, p26) argues that "many young adults with Asperger's Syndrome report intense feelings of anxiety", after several attempts of trying to engage in different social interactions. Further, the survey mentioned above conducted by Beardon & Edmonds (2007) suggests that participants found social situations such as public transport experiences either extremely or very stressful. The survey also shows that 68% of the 237 participants with ASC have had contact with Mental Health services, and 38% did so as a result of depression and 12% as a result of anxiety.

The high level of anxiety around social interaction can lead to isolation of the student. This can be particularly acute when the student has left home to go to University. Moving away from home to live independently for the first time could be an issue for anyone, but for disabled students it is often more complicated (Adams & Brown, 2006). We argue that this transition is even more complex for students with autism as they are likely to feel isolated because of their social difficulties. Hence, they may need support in social arrangements when they move residence to live in or close to University.

Thinking and Adaptations

Both Bob and Sam are conscientious students. They have chosen to study subjects that interest them and are keen to learn. Bob and Sam think and learn in different ways. Bob loves pictures and learns best when things are explained via diagrams and pictures rather than just words. Sam really loves words and is fascinated by them. He likes the sound of them and loves finding just the right word to produce the right "feel" to a sentence. To him, words make much more sense than pictures and he likes communicating via forums and second life. Sam likes these forms of communication because it takes away gestures and tone of voice, which as far as Sam is concerned, just confuse verbal communication. Bob, however, does not like internet forums and Second Life, an online virtual world, and engages with them as little as possible. When he does engage it is more as an observer than a participant. Bob is also dyslexic and finds that typing in responses is a slow and laborious process. He has tried out 'Dragon Naturally Speaking', speech-to-text dictation software, in the resources room for disabled students in the library, but does not get on well with it because he hates hearing the sound of his own voice when it is not part of a two way conversation. Assignments cause Bob and Sam a certain amount of puzzlement. They wonder why many students do their assignments at the last minute. Both have learnt that if they do not really want to do something it is better to get it out of the way so that you can stop worrying about it. They are both inclined to become anxious about tasks that they are required to do, but which do not interest them. However, this does not mean that they simply sail through their assignments: they each have their own particular difficulties.

Sam generally likes his assignments and finds them interesting, but there is always more to read, and more to find out about the topic. Sam finds it hard to know when to stop gathering information and opinion about the topic and to start writing. Then he has a tendency to spend too long on trying to find just the right way to say something. The result is that although he has worked steadily on the assignment from the beginning, he too finds himself working extra hard before the deadline. He then gets very anxious after he has handed his work in as he thinks of something else he could have put in it, or a better way of phrasing something. In addition, he does not understand why he often gets very high marks (above 70%) but sometimes gets low marks (40-47%). As far as he could tell he had the same understanding of the material and put in the same amount of effort. What is happening is that when the topic is about romance, or complex relationships between people, he tends to misunderstand the issues involved and thus does not do as well. In these cases, he also tends to misunderstand the question. Luckily, as he progresses in his studies he is able to choose modules that relate to his strengths. He finds that he is particularly good when it comes to studying material written for children.

Bob too is able to choose modules that play to his strengths as he progresses through his studies, but he has different issues with his assignments. He has difficulty in getting to grips with the various software programs he is required to use, but finds that once you know a few, learning more becomes less of an issue. In addition, despite his dyslexia causing problems with syntax and variable names, he finds that he takes to programming very well. He likes the challenge of working out how to get a computer to do something, especially when it is not immediately obvious how to do it. He discovers that he is better at design than he would ever have expected. Because he enjoys playing with the software to see what he can get it do and, and because he is always tweaking his design or his code, Bob finds that he is often pushed for time with his report at the end – especially as he does not like writing. He finds that the oral type of examination for his programming courses works better than just relying on a report. Luckily he gets help from student disability support who put him in touch with someone who monitors his progress with his assignments and who can tell him when to stop tweaking and start writing. By the end of his studies, he has learnt to manage the balance by himself.

Reflection

The above narrative about the thinking and adaptations of Bob and Sam reflects some of the views in the literature concerning the ability and learning skills of people with ASC. For example, Jordan & Jones, (1999) and the UK NAS (2010a) suggest that students with AS can be very talented in their chosen areas of study. Baron-Cohen (2008) relates this to the fact that many people with ASC have a high IQ, and this has led others to suggest that people with AS might not be affected by general learning difficulties (Jordan & Jones, 1999; NAS, 2010a). However people with a high IQ are more likely to find methods of coping with learning disabilities such as dyslexia by themselves as they progress through school. This can make it appear that AS adults do not actually suffer from these learning difficulties and this in turn might affect their getting the appropriate diagnosis.

Some people on the autistic spectrum may have preferred learning styles to the extent that they find it extremely hard to handle other styles of learning. We see this with Bob, who is very visual and Sam, who relates to words rather than pictures. In the same vein, Temple Grandin, a professional scientist who has ASC, states in her article *Thinking in Pictures* that "I THINK IN PICTURES. Words are like a second language to me" (Grandin, 2006). Jordan in her article *A rose by any other name?* suggests that the 'different' way people with ASC understand and interact with the world is 'part of human functioning', and links this to learning styles (Jordan, 2007, p11). She argues that whatever learning style people with ASC might have it needs to be accommodated in any educational system, and Baron-Cohen, (2008) argues for the importance of making the learning styles flexible in University, to support students with ASC.

In this context, it is interesting to note that as long ago as 1994 Hans Asperger discussed the academic levels that students with AS might reach if their needs are supported correctly:

able autistic individuals can rise to eminent positions with such outstanding success that one may conclude that only such people are capable of certain achievements. Their unswerving determination and penetrating intellectual powers, part of their spontaneous and original mental activity, their narrowness and single-mindedness, as manifested in their special interests, can be immensely valuable and can lead to outstanding achievements in their chosen areas. (Asperger, 1991, p. 88)

Experience of Classes

Both Bob and Sam attend classes regularly. Neither understands why many other students do not attend regularly and do not appear to be interested in what they have chosen to study. They are especially puzzled as to why those who do attend want to be connected to their mates all the time, including during classes. They cannot understand why their classmates think it is perfectly acceptable to send text messages during classes. Sam likes texting, but much prefers to keep his phone switched off much of the time so that he can answer texts when he is ready to do so. He finds receiving and sending texts all the time very distracting and it makes him anxious because he is not managing to get the things he wanted to do done. So he answers his texts when he is ready and this enables him to settle down and get his work done. He wonders if this is why other students struggle to get their work done on time, although when he asks his fellow students they assure him that texting has nothing to do with it.

By contrast, Bob finds texting hard and does not engage with this for social purposes. As far as he is concerned, a mobile phone is for emergencies or when you need to get a message to someone urgently. He is totally baffled by the concept of using them for everyday social interaction. Isn't it much easier just to talk to people when you see them? And why do they want to know about the minutiae of the lives of all their mates? Isn't this just boring?

Bob spends a lot of time in labs. When in a lab, he tries to get a computer in a quiet corner so that he can work with few interruptions. It is common practice for tutors to let other students use any free machines in the lab. This is institutional policy as it reduces the pressure on public machines and allows more access to specialist software. Bob finds this hard because then the lab is full, and often becomes noisy. In addition, the extra students tend to wander in and out of the lab quite a lot. The extra visual information combined with the extra noise, often makes labs a difficult, stressful and tiring environment for Bob. He has no idea how everyone else manages to cope, and why they think that this kind of behaviour is acceptable.

Bob's course incorporates elements of group work. While he quite likes working in small groups in classes, he experiences quite severe difficulties when it comes to group assignments. He finds it very hard to handle the logistics of trying to arrange a time when everyone is prepared to meet. When it comes to deciding on a location to meet, he tends to give up and wait for the rest of the group to tell him. When these meetings suddenly change or get postponed he gets very upset. He also finds it frustrating when people do not turn up, or have not the work that they agreed to do. The result of all the uncertainty around others' behaviour makes group work extremely stressful for Bob. However, he tries very hard to complete the work he agreed to do. In the end he usually gets a good mark for the work, but it is by no means a positive experience for him. As the course progresses, Bob discovers that there are a couple of other students with whom he can discuss the content of learning materials to the mutual benefit of both. In fact, due to his good memory some students get into the habit of asking him when they get stuck. Bob can normally remember the answer, or knows where to find the answer. Eventually Bob finds that he can work in

partnership and on an equal basis with one other student on assignments. He learns to enjoy the interaction of ideas that can come from working with someone of similar ability.

Reflection

Hypersensitivities to noise, smells, touch and movement can make an ordinary classroom quite an ordeal and hard to deal with for a student with autism. But it could seem quite normal from the point of view of students without disabilities. As a result, UK legislation, in particular the Special Educational Needs and Disability Act (SENDA) 2001 places the responsibility of making reasonable adjustments for all disabled students on HEIs (Herrington, 2002; Adams & Brown, 2006). Prior to that, reasonable adjustments were mentioned by the Quality Assurance Agency (QAA) Code of Practice in 2000, and the extension of the Disability Discrimination Act (DDA) in 1995 to education by the SENDA in 2001, then included into Part IV of the DDA in 2005 (cf. Adams & Brown, 2006; Brown, 2005).

In contrast to the 'reasonable adjustments' approach, others in the literature argue that learning processes should be inclusive and that therefore, no special adjustments should be needed as all students should get equal and similar opportunities. For example, Brown (2005) argues that if an institution needs to offer special assessments for students with disabilities, this suggests that the institution does not have a good plan for their assessment, learning and teaching strategies. She also suggests that reasonable assessments should be given to all disabled students and argues that 'good practice in inclusive assessment is good for everyone'. In line with this Adams & Brown (2006) support the idea of involving many staff across one institution, e.g. academic and disability service staff, to develop inclusive learning.

Whilst we agree that this idea is worth striving for, we are not convinced that it is possible to cater for everyone all of the time, especially when there are conflicting needs as a result of various disabilities. For example, if students are asked to do a presentation, assessing the work partly on the design of the slides and the variation in the tone of voice may well be appropriate, but perhaps not fair for students with ASC. One might argue that presentations for students with ASC be avoided, but that would deprive students of the chance to develop these skills before they get to the workplace.

Communications

Because of different ways of thinking, it is not unusual for complete misunderstandings to occur between staff and students with ASC in the classroom environment. It has happened that an experienced lecturer has not been able to work out what has broken down in his communication with Bob. Since Bob is a visual learner he registered for a one day training session to improve his writing skills. In the morning he seemed enthusiastic to learn new skills. When the tutor gave the first task Bob did the task, similarly to the other students. However, at the second task Bob seemed to misunderstand what the lecturer said was required. Bob stopped working and asked the lecturer to explain the second task again. The lecturer tried to explain the task for Bob twice but Bob was still confused. His confusion appeared clearly on his face though he tried to ask for help for the third time. The lecturer could not explain the task any more. Then the student (Alice) who sometimes used to work collaboratively with Bob tried to help. However, neither Alice's nor the lecturer's explanation helped, since Bob misunderstood the task from the beginning and could not change to what the lecturer wanted him to do. Although Bob appeared upset and anxious other students continued working with the tasks given to them, apart from Alice. She empathised with Bob and tried to make him calm down. Simultaneously, Alice tried to explain to the lecturer that Bob has Asperger Syndrome and was surprised when the

lecturer said that he was aware of Bob's disability but he could not offer any more help. Finally, Bob used his way (visual learning) to work out the tasks and later he left the class very upset and apathetic, feeling that he would not learn any more from the lecturer.

Reflection

Such an experience can be very distressing not only for Bob but for any student with disabilities when it seems that their needs are not understood or provided for. In the light of this, Beardon & Edmonds (2007) recommend offering support that is particular to the individual requirements, rather than general support for people with autism, and Baron-Cohen (2008) suggests that learning environments should be flexible to meet the different needs of students with autism.

Happy Endings

At the end of their studies both students graduate with first class honours. During the later years they have been able to tailor their modules to their strengths and both students have done well. Both have been able to secure jobs. Bob gets a job at the UK Government Communications Headquarters (GCHQ), where Asperger Syndrome is well understood. Sam gets a job writing text books for primary school children with a major publisher. He plans to write stories for children in the future.

Reflection

Bob and Sam were both extremely good at their chosen subjects. Although they had to deal with many issues while studying, they managed to pick up enough social skills (perhaps through their extra-curricular activities) in order to get through interviews. They were both able to get jobs to which they are well suited and which give them the freedom to complete tasks in the way that works best for them. This is the ideal scenario, but unfortunately is not experienced by many graduates with ASC. Many graduates on the autistic spectrum do not get jobs because of their lack of social skills or simply because they come across as odd. Only 15% of adults (NAS 2010c) on the autistic spectrum are in employment.

Unfortunately, there is no guarantee that Bob and Sam will manage to stay in employment. There is a very high chance that the cumulative stress of coping with life and work without any form of support will result in ill health or some kind of mental breakdown. Although it is outside the scope of this chapter, it is essential that people on the autistic spectrum are able to access appropriate support once they have left full time education.

As is perhaps clear from the Bob and Sam narratives, and the preceding discussion in this chapter, students with ASC in the UK are entitled to support because of their disability while at University. The nature of support received may well be a crucial factor in the success or otherwise of a University education. Given this, we turn now to examine the experience of a support worker who supported a student with ASC for 40 hours a week for the duration of his three year degree course. This experience is written by the support worker to illustrate the difficulties that may be faced by students with ASC, from the point of view of someone who worked closely with them. We argue that this case study approach enables us to achieve the richness and depth of data available needed to explore lived educational experience of a student with ASC.

Case Study: A Personal Reflection on Supporting a Student with ASC, by His Learning Support Worker

About the Support Worker

From September 2007 until June 2010 I worked as a learning facilitator for a student with ASC, at a large higher education institution in the UK. Throughout this time I have been given a unique insight into the nature of autism and its complexities. I have been able to observe how a student with ASC develops coping strategies both in an academic learning context and, additionally, when faced with the challenges of independent living for the first time. Throughout this time I have also been able to develop my own strategies in order to facilitate the learning experience for a student with ASC.

Firstly I present a brief overview of how I found myself working in such close proximity to this young man. I have worked in Disability Support in Higher Education for over 10 years, initially as a 'stop gap' after graduating from University. I graduated with a Microbiology degree and intended to pursue either research or teaching. However, I soon found that working as a learning facilitator was a rewarding and challenging experience. Over the years I have assisted students with a wide range of disabilities including visually and hearing impaired students, students with physical support needs, students with dyslexia, and those with Obsessive Compulsive Disorder and Autistic Spectrum Conditions. Each student is usually granted a certain amount of hours from their Disabled Students' Allowance (DSA) where I will be available to facilitate their learning. The nature of this facilitation can differ greatly between students, mainly according to the differing nature of their disabilities. Generally, though, I assist with time keeping and planning, I liaise with academic staff on the student's behalf, liaise with their peers and do whatever I can in order for them to deliver academic work to the best of their ability. I usually have a small cohort of students but at the start of the 2007 academic term this was all about to change.

Initial Steps and Preparations

In June 2007 as I was asked if I would like to support only one student rather than my usual cohort and, in addition, whether I would be able to commit to this for the full three academic

you have to be extraordinarily patient. The changes were so gradual they were sometimes hardly noticeable but it was very satisfying to start to spot when he initiated conversations and particularly when he began asking me about my activities outside work or my social life. It really felt that there was a trust developing and this was further helped by us also sharing the same interests. We could fill the long waits between lectures discussing a host of TV programmes we both enjoyed and he could explain to me some of the intricacies of the sports he so enjoyed playing. I must stress that in my opinion this 'downtime' was equally as important as, for example, working on an essay together—we had to develop an overall trust and the rest very gradually started to click into place.

I have mentioned routine and consistency already and I felt this was a key element. We planned out days and tried to avoid any surprise deadlines or situations where the normal status quo would be disrupted. An example of how this could be problematic was when a lecturer wasn't clear on the word limit of an essay. The limit had been set at 4000 words but, after discussion with the students (who felt they needed more to work with), the limit was changed to 'either 4000 or 5000 words'. This caused much confusion to the student, as did the inconsistencies regarding the 'plus or minus 10%' word limit—some lecturers endorsed it, some did not allow it—and this lack of clarity and boundaries is one example of how a student with ASC can become destabilised and confused.

Strategies

Here I discuss key things that I believe helped the student develop throughout the three years; split into those provided by the University followed by coping strategies devised by the student and my own observations. Firstly, with regard to the former, the University did a tremendous amount. His DSA equipment and facilitator (myself) were in place for his arrival meaning that he had his IT equipment ready and I was given plenty of time to prepare for his arrival. Furthermore he was allowed to stay in the same room in his Halls of Residence for three years rather than have the additional upheaval of finding private shared accommodation in his second and third year. This meant he felt settled and had the additional bonus of widening his friendship group (with each new student intake) whilst also maintaining his course and sports related peers.

The consistency I could provide him was greatly assisted by the University granting me the freedom to use our weekly hourly allowance as the student and I agreed. I never felt I had to say 'no' to any activities as we were given a generous allowance of time to work with; I could essentially be there if and when he needed me. With regards to his anxieties concerning transportation we were given a budget to spend on taxis. This was intended for an initial period but it became a hard habit to break (I will expand on this later) as he was more anxious about transportation than I had realised (describing it to his psychologist as his number one concern in a 'triangle of anxieties'). The University had excellent gym facilities on campus and an ample one at his Halls of Residence. This allowed the student to regularly exercise and this not only kept him match ready for his various sports but additionally, I generally observed a more relaxed yet alert student emerging after a long gym session. This observation is congruent with the advice from his parents that some of his medication can be reduced during heavy periods of exercise due to the positive effect exercise promotes on his mental health. Additionally University staff were patient, approachable and flexible, with deadlines being extended as per his Disability Support contract with the minimum of fuss.

With regards to the student's coping strategies he increasingly began planning his own days. He'd say to me in the taxi to University what he planned to do that day. This extended beyond his academic study; he'd plan in sports training and look ahead to social events (for example, planning in the collection and return of fancy dress costumes). It felt that as he became more settled in his new life his confidence began to grow.

As a final point concerning my strategies, I present a scenario which demonstrates both autistic traits in the student and additionally why having a learning facilitator on hand was useful. There was an occasion in a lesson where the lecturer asked the class not to write whilst he was talking. He then paused to turn the pages in front of him and the student wrote something at that time. He was, predictably, told off for it. I felt he was a little troubled by it and when pressed said, *"The lecturer said not to write whilst he was talking but he wasn't actually talking at the time"*. This very literal interpretation of the lecturer's instructions landed him in trouble. I think that if I hadn't been there to reflect on the incident with him and discuss it with the lecturer it could have become disproportionately problematic. The student may have taken a dislike to the lecturer as he felt he was *"wronged"* and this may have had further implications. The incident served as a reminder to me to be very clear and direct with my language with the student, something that I had been advised to do prior to working with him. This coupled with routine were the main strategies I employed with him.

Extra Curricular Activities, Social Interaction and Independence

The student being discussed was a very keen sportsman and I felt that his love of sport was key in his personal development. Not only was it noticeably good for his mood and overall health, it allowed him to interact with his peers. I think this is an overwhelmingly positive thing for someone with ASC. He gained respect from his peers and confidence and a social scene was also opened up to him. He very quickly became a sought after American football player. American football relies on discipline and clearly defined set plays. I feel

that this suited his personality and he loved playing the game. It also helped him confront some of his issues around transportation as he had to travel with the team to away matches. For many months I accompanied him to his training sessions three times a week but gradually he began organising his own lifts and even suggesting I go home once he was at the pitch as he was confident someone would accompany him back.

One of my goals was to reduce his reliance on taxis. I discussed this with his psychologist and she suggested progressively building up the student's confidence with smaller walks to the shops before tackling the walk to University. She referred to this as a "progressive desensitisation" approach. Regrettably, we never ended up regularly walking the full journey to University and back but the student did walk to the local shops with me. By the end of the third year he was even suggesting walks to the sandwich or video shop. Fortunately this particular journey passed what is now to be his new flat so I'm confident he will become much more comfortable traveling to University and home on his own.

Academic Achievements

The student's BA (Hons) was a course which was both academically challenging and involved significant vocational elements (for example work experience and community interaction). I feel it was an excellent choice of course for the student. The academic work was regular and varied (essays, presentations, poster projects etc) leading to a Major Independent Study in Year 3. The student was able to do work experience in schools and this lead him to deciding on his career path—to become a teacher.

It was his completion of the Major Independent Study (MIS) which was most fascinating to observe. It was a substantial piece of work (10,000 words) in which he had to set his own subject of investigation, collect data and present his findings, reporting his progress to his MIS supervisor. He decided to study whether there is any common teaching pedagogy developed by teachers when educating students with ASC. To complete this he had to present a literature review in relation to what is currently known about the condition. Furthermore, he visited a specialist school (which, incidentally, he used to attend) to interview teachers about their experiences and pedagogical strategies regarding teaching children with ASC. What emerged was a young man thriving in higher education, with higher education giving him a chance to understand more about himself, whilst also equipping himself with the tools to reach towards his career goal. His work on his MIS was outstanding and by this point we had developed an exceptional working relationship. My role was merely to oversee his project, his enthusiasm and obvious engagement with his chosen subject allowed him to gain a first class mark for this piece of work.

Future Goals and Reflections

The student gained his degree and has been given an unconditional offer to do a Masters degree. He is continuing playing his favourite sport and has moved into his own private flat. After this he intends to do a Postgraduate Certificate in Education (PGCE – a teaching qualification in the UK) before realising his dream of becoming a teacher, ideally working with students with ASC. I intend to work with him for the next two years. I am certain that he will gradually rely on me less and less, becoming the independent young man he is capable of being. He has overcome a tremendous number of obstacles in his life with good humour and optimism. I think that engaging in HE has given him the life skills and knowledge he needs to become more self aware, more socially confident and able to live an independent life with a career he will undoubtedly excel in. The student gave permission for me to write this case study, and hopes it will encourage other students with ASC to enter University to succeed once there.

Reflection on the Support Worker Case Study

In this case study given by the support worker, we saw many similar issues cropping up that were highlighted in the Bob and Sam scenarios. For instance, social issues and issues to do with different ways of thinking were especially prominent and led to a significant level of anxiety, which the support worker was able to lower over time. However, we argue that the support worker did not acquire this ability straightforwardly, as he needed to get to know the student very well over a long period of time to understand his needs and to be able to support him effectively. He took the challenge to move this student from a completely dependent student when he arrived at University to a more confident independent student at the end of his study. The potentially positive effect of forming good relationships with students with ASC is also mentioned elsewhere in this book (see the chapter by Elzouki & Cooper). The high standard of the student's achievements in HE relates well the description given by Asperger to such students, cited earlier.

The extent to which all students with ASC can have a similar positive experience and support in HE is investigated next. To understand the institutional level challenges of meeting the needs of students with ASC, we look at the issues from the perspective of one of the UK's largest higher education institutions.

Case Study: A Specific UK University

In this section we will review the provision for students with ASC in a large UK University. The case study was conducted via a general document review, an investigation of the numbers of students with ASC, and an interview with the manager of the University disability service. Each of these three aspects will be considered in turn.

Information from Documents

This University's widening participation strategy includes a commitment to:

- Recruiting more disabled students
- Providing all students with a positive and effective learning experience
- Helping all students to participate in learning in exciting, flexible and stimulating environments
- Inclusive learning.

The University Disability Service (DS) is the initial point of contact for disabled students to discuss their needs either for "reasonable adjustments" or to communicate with academic staff regarding any alternative arrangements. All disabled students are advised to contact the DS before they start their course to identify the appropriate reasonable adjustments they might need. After that, they are advised to communicate directly with academic staff members to ensure that their learning needs are met. If they experience any difficulties they are recommended to contact the DS staff for assistance.

The support made available includes, for example, extra time and/or separate rooms during examinations, use of recording equipment to record lecturers, and access to a note taker and British Sign Language Interpreter. Further, the University web site has information for all students with disabilities. Most attention is paid towards increasing awareness about support and assessment of students with dyslexia, because of the high number of students with dyslexia in HEIs in general and in this University in particular.

In addition, the DS also provides specific information to academic staff concerning students with ASC, partly in order to increase awareness of this disability and partly to decrease the level of anxiety that students with ASC might face and help to establish a good relationship between them and the academic staff. The information outlines some characteristics of people with ASC, as follows:

- Staff are advised to understand that students with ASC might be limited in their use of eye contact, and that therefore contact with such students via email might provide a better vehicle for feedback and discussion.
- As students with ASC tend to analyse conversation literally, academic staff are advised to communicate clearly and directly with such students. In particular they are advised to avoid sarcasm and figures of speech.
- Students with ASC may have difficulty in interacting socially with others and therefore, they may not be able to make friends, and even if they do they might find it hard to keep that relationship.
- Identifying particular staff name(s) is recommended, to facilitate students in contacting the staff when they need help. The contact staff could be one academic and one from the Disability Service. If the enquiry is dealt with by the staff quickly this will relieve a lot of any stress the student might encounter in the University.
- As people with ASC may have some difficulties in reading other people's perspectives, they might find it difficult to sustain academic argument. Similarly, since people with ASC do not pick up verbal signs, getting their collaboration does not come effortlessly.
- Many students on the autistic spectrum have a particular interest and may expect others to share the same interest with them. If others are not interested in this particular topic, the student may feel misunderstood and think that others (staff or peers) do not like them.

Reflection

The staff information suggests some similarities with the narrative scenarios and case study we outlined above such as social issues concerning limitations in eye contact and communication with people with ASC. The benefit of using the technology such as emails to communicate with students with ASC is also highlighted. The pros and cons of sharing their interests with people with ASC are also highlighted, and are also discussed elsewhere in this book (see the chapter by Elzouki & Cooper). The amount of information concerning ASC contained in the University's documentations and leaflets that are available to students, is relatively small compared to mental health difficulties and dyslexia. This is in keeping with the currently relatively low number of students in the University with ASC, an issue to which we now turn.

The Number of Students in the University with ASC, Mental Health Difficulties and Dyslexia

The University student population between 2002/03 and 2008/09 was given by the University Planning and Registry Services. The population of students with disabilities was given by the University's Disability Service, based on the students who disclosed their disability and provided evidence of their diagnosis.

Reflection

Table 2 suggests that, as with UK HEI in general, dyslexia is the largest category of students with disability. More significantly in the current context, the table also shows that the general under-representation of students with ASC in UK HEI (as shown in Table 1 earlier) is also in evidence in our case study University. Below we discuss some factors that might contribute to this under-representation:

- The Disability Service in any HEI needs a disclosure from students about their disabilities. Since an existing formal diagnosis of ASC is unattainable for many young adults with ASC, we argue that this contributes negatively towards the exact records of students with ASC.
- The University Disability Service is not authorised to offer an autism diagnostic service to students, although they may advise students who might benefit from a

Table 2. Percentage of students with ASC, mental health difficulties and dyslexia compared to the number of the University students and students with disabilities in the University

Academic Year	Students with ASC as a % of total students and of students registered with the Disability Service (DS)		Students with Mental Health Difficulties as a % of total students and of students registered with DS		Students with Dyslexia as a % of total students and of students registered with DS	
	% University	% DS	% University	% DS	% University	% DS
2003/04	0.01	0.2	0.2	3.6	2.4	55.9
2004/05	0.004	0.1	0.2	4.6	2.3	55.8
2005/06	0	0	0.2	3.8	2.7	62.2
2006/07	0.03	0.7	0.2	4	2.9	60.5
2007/08	0.05	1	0.3	5	3.1	60
2008/09	0.06	1.1	0.3	4.9	3.3	63.4

diagnosis to pursue this with their doctor. If they get a diagnosis of ASC this will enable them to get the appropriate support they need.

- Students make their own decisions to choose the appropriate category which best describes their disability or impairment. For example, sometimes they describe themselves as having an "Unseen Disability". As a result there might be cases of misreporting. This system is widely used across other UK Universities.

Although there are relatively few students with ASC in the University, it is of course important that the students who are there are helped to achieve to their full potential. To explore how the Disability Service seeks to help achieve this, the lead author of this chapter conducted an interview with the Disability Services Manager (DSM).

An Interview with the University's Disability Services Manager

The interview with the DSM took place during the academic year 2007–2008, the year this research was started. The interviewer started by explaining the research idea to the interviewee. Below we summarise some of the key lessons from the interview.

- As mentioned above, the Disability Service is the first contact for disabled students once they register with the University. There are different disability advisers for the different University faculties. The students are advised to meet the appropriate Disability Service adviser, in order to register with the service and to discuss their needs. The disability advisers then verify the student's needs and set in place suitable provision. They also monitor how these needs are met by getting feedback from

students by phone or email and by contacting their support workers.

- Since the Disability Service does not want students with disabilities to feel that the service is "*intrusive*", they follow a strategy with all students with disability that deals with them as '*adults*'. As a result, it is the "*student's responsibility*" to accept/ refuse the support that is offered to them and to inform the Disability Service of any other support they might need.

- Concerning whether this strategy would work well with students with ASC the DSM suggested "*It might not work with them but that's where the role of the disability support workers comes in*". The disability support workers, however, are not specialists in autism but they are able to work on all areas of disability, as they have to attend some specific workshops and courses prior to their employment. Below are some examples of specific cases of support, which may illustrate the way the support role works in practice:

  ○ A student with ASC came to register with the Disability Service. He liked to live in the University accommodation and needed help in keeping himself and his room clean. The student also needed help to familiarise himself with the new accommodation as well as how and where to do his shopping. After discussing these needs with the student, the student's social worker and his parents, the Disability Service arranged a full time support for him with one of the University support workers. The social services and the education authority were to pay the cost of this support. However, since full time support is expensive it was hoped to reduce the support time as and when the student becomes familiar with the new University environment.

○ Another student came to the initial meeting with the Disability Service along with one of his parents. The DSM did not know how to communicate with the student as he refused to respond to any questions. The DSM *'tried his best to make the student respond to clarify his needs but he didn't'*. Then the student's parent asked to be kept informed daily regarding what happens with the student. Since this was not one of the Disability Service strategies, an arrangement was made to enable the parent to contact the Disability Service to get informed about what is happening with the student.

Reflection

The interview illustrates the good service and valuable support this University Disability Service tries to provide to all students including those with ASC. However, the interview also highlights difficulties in communication with students with ASC, including finding out what they really need. This is where the importance of involving a student's parents and social workers as well as the University support workers in the initial meeting may be beneficial. In addition, there are issues concerning the cost and level of support to fund the needs of students on the autistic spectrum since they may need support that addresses far more than the academic side of HE degree study. These issues are also highlighted within our narrative and the case study written by the support worker.

RECOMMENDATIONS

Based on the empirical work discussed above, namely the narrative accounts of Bob and Sam,

the case study of a student written by his support worker, and the institutional case study, we offer some tentative recommendations that might help Universities that expect to include more students with ASC. Since people on the spectrum are varied we suggest, however, that these recommendations need to be considered against the background of the specific needs of any given student. Each student is an individual and it is not possible to come up with a 'one size fits all' strategy for students with ASC. Bearing this caveat in mind, our recommendations are as follows:

We saw examples of understanding and misunderstanding students with autism by their tutors and peers within our narrative and the case study written by the support worker. Because of the complexity of the condition, therefore, we recommend that all academic and support staff at a University should attend training session(s) about the characteristics and needs of people with autism. The peers of students with ASC might need to know about autism as well. We advise that such training sessions should ideally include a trainer who is on the autistic spectrum, in line with Breakey's (2001, p 13) claim: "we neuro-typical people, if we really want to learn more about autism, must listen to what autistic people tell us".

The literature concerning teaching and assessment arrangements made for students with disabilities suggests that teaching and learning is the main area of concern to improve the quality of participation in HE by students with disabilities. It could be argued that HEIs should support students by providing an inclusive environment for all of them. This might be facilitated by looking at individual support/arrangements first, then including these personal arrangements into a new welcoming inclusive learning environment for all students, including students with ASC. However, we must consider that students with ASC are likely to need holistic support, rather than just support aimed at their academic studies. Ironically, the academic aspect of being a student may well cause the fewest issues for students with ASC. Issues to do with socialising and everyday life could well cause these students the most problems. This is a real challenge for student support systems.

It was shown above that depression, stress and anxiety are likely to appear frequently in people with ASC. It is important, therefore, to notify depressed students of the appropriate services available to contact within their University. In our case study University, for example, depressed students are advised to contact counselling or disability service to provide them with the appropriate support to manage their stress while studying.

All students with disabilities, including students with ASC need to be encouraged to state their diagnoses to disability services to get access to the support they need. Some students with ASC may need access to quiet places to study and relax, which means that suitable places should be provided. In fact, at our case study University, there is a special room that is prepared for students with disabilities to study in the library. However, there is some indication to suggest that the canteen area is a very challenging one for many students with ASC because of the noise, movement, and smells.

Care should be taken to ease the transition between school and University as much a possible. This may well involve liaising with the student, their parents, and any professionals that have been involved with their support at school.

Directions around University campuses should be clear and maps should be readily available. Exceptional care should be taken within buildings directions to ensure that it is easy to find the correct floor and room. For example, colour coding floors and wings is likely to be very helpful since some students with ASC are visual learners.

It might be wise to allow students with ASC to choose where they want to sit in a class and ensure that this space is always available if they want it. This is especially important if other students are allowed access to facilities such as computers while a class is in progress.

Mental health and dyslexia disability support advisors should be aware of autism and able

therefore to consider the possibility that some students may have ASC as well as dyslexia or mental health difficulty. The support advisors should have specific training in ASC. Ideally, there should be at least one specialist in the condition.

Considering the difficulties that students with ASC may have with some audio/visual materials and presentation could help students with learning difficulties and/or dyslexia. Conversely, it could be recommended that student with ASC should be advised to use the software "Quick Scan" (which is aimed primarily at students who are dyslexic) as it might give them some indications about their learning styles.

Similarly, good teaching and learning practices e.g. the provision of good handouts in different formats, written, oral and online would potentially benefit all students, not only students with ASC. For example, in our case study University there are learning workshops that might help students with autism as well as other students. However, if students with ASC prefer to have these workshops individually or if the group workshops are unsuitable, one-one tutorials should ideally be available for them.

Similarly, the library tours that take place in some universities at the beginning of the academic year could be useful for students with ASC as well. However, it might be more appropriate for students with ASC to be offered individual or small number tours. It might be wise to do the tours at times other than lunch or break times when the library and corridors may be full and busy with many students.

Disability leaflets available in University common rooms and communal areas might benefit students with ASC. However, copies should also be available online or sent to students with ASC as the communal areas may be busy and crowded. Indeed, providing online information might benefit all students particularly new students prior to their arrival at University, to familiarise them with the new environment they will shortly be joining. As Williams (1996) suggests, 'chronic stress' may be caused by different sources of life problems not necessarily by ASC. Thus social and academic arrangements that aim to reduce students' stress and anxiety would not help students with ASC only.

Students with ASC will need support finding suitable accommodation. Any rules about the length of time a student may spend in University accommodation should be relaxed for these students if it turns out that this kind of accommodation provides the least stress.

Sudden changes in routine should be avoided. If a class has to be cancelled then the student should be informed immediately so that they can change their plans for the day. Arriving to discover a cancelled class may cause a student with ASC considerable stress. Similarly, a change of location and/or staff member should also be communicated to them as soon as possible.

Students with ASC should be encouraged to join some of the clubs and societies available at University. This should provide them with more structured social contact, improve their social skill, and make loneliness and isolation less likely.

Relevant academic staff such as course leader or year tutor would ideally be involved in the meetings that the student has with the disability support services.

More generally, it is likely to be useful to provide academic staff with information about students with ASC, in a similar manner to the sheet provided by our case study University above.

Staff should be advised to check the student's understanding of assignment tasks and course material as the student may experience frustration if they do not understand or record what actually they have been asked for. This could be done by emails which might also be an appropriate means of giving feedback to students with ASC.

Structured context is very important for people with ASC and therefore, instructions must be clear and unambiguous. Further, assistance with prioritising and organising work is essential to support students with ASC as they may choose other priorities rather than the most imminent deadline.

Students with ASC need careful supervision in areas that have options so that their anxiety can be managed when choosing suitable topics. Finally, students with ASC might need some short breaks during assessment time as they might benefit from refreshing their concentration. They may also benefit from extra time to accommodate delayed processing of information.

FUTURE RESEARCH DIRECTIONS

As well as these recommendations for practice, we also suggest areas that we believe warrant further research:

Riddell, et. al. (2005) argue that 'Until institutions listen to their disabled students themselves to collect data and feedback they will remain ignorant of the difficulties and barriers faced by disabled students as they go about their daily business'. Similarly, a report published by Plymouth University (2010)- in the UK, entitled *Twenty-one things you need to know about current assessment practice for disabled students when considering inclusiveness* suggests that qualitative student feedback is the 'gold dust' of projects in this area. In line with this, we recommend that future research include the voices of students with ASC (cf. Madriaga, 2007, and the chapter by Adams at the end of this book).

In addition, an action research approach could usefully be applied in similar research conducted with students with ASC, to investigate whether any 'reasonable adjustments' made actually fit the particular students' needs. More generally, action research could be used to identify different forms of inclusive assessments and their efficacy for each student.

CONCLUSION

In summary, this chapter has discussed the effects that ASC may have on students, both academically and socially while they are at University. To explore this, we looked at the issues from the perspectives of two students with ASC, a support worker who worked with a student with ASC and at the inclusivity practices at one of the UK's largest universities. In terms of the themes of this book, namely technology, transition and inclusivity, this chapter is concerned chiefly with the inclusivity issue. Achieving inclusivity for students with ASC is a challenge for the institution and the students, but we hope that this chapter has given insights into ways of achieving the very important goal of achieving such inclusivity. There is still much to be done but we hope that this chapter may make a contribution to the helping people with autism enter and succeed in HE.

REFERENCES

Adams, M., & Brown, S. (2006). *Towards Inclusive Learning in Higher Education: Developing curricula for disabled students*. London, New York: Routledge.

Asperger, H. (1991). 'Autistic psychopathy' in childhood. In *Frith, U. (1991). Autism and Asperger Syndrome*. Cambridge, UK: Cambridge University Press. doi:10.1017/CBO9780511526770.002

Attwood, T. (1998). *Asperger Syndrome, A Guide for Parents and Professionals* (2nd ed.). London, UK: Jessica Kingsley.

Attwood, T. (2007). *The Complete Guide to Asperger's Syndrome*. London, UK: Jessica Kingsley.

Baron-Cohen, S. (2008). *Autism and Asperger syndrome: the facts; all the information you need, straight from the experts*. UK: Oxford University.

Baron-Cohen, S., Scott, F. J., Allison, C., Williams, J., Bolton, P., Matthews, F. E., & Brayne, C. (2009). Prevalence of autism-spectrum conditions: UK school-based population study. *The British Journal of Psychiatry, 194*, 500–509. doi:10.1192/bjp.bp.108.059345

Beardon, L., & Edmonds, G. (2007). *The Needs of Adults with Asperger Syndrome*. Uk: National ASPECT Consultancy. Retrieved October 30, 2010, from http://www.aspectaction.org.uk/ASPECT%20Consultancy%20report.pdf.

Breakey, C. (2006). *The Autism Spectrum and Further Education: a Guide to Good Practice*. London, UK: Jessica Kingsley.

Brown, S. (2005). How can we make the Higher Education Learning Experience Inclusive? The role of Staff and Educational Development. *Proceeding of TechDis Higher Education Conference (2005)*.

Directgov, (2010). *Disability support in higher education*. Retrieved October 25, 2010, from http://www.direct.gov.uk/en/DisabledPeople/EducationAndTraining/HigherEducation/DG_4000917

Disability Rights Commission. (2007). *Understanding the Disability Discrimination Act: A Guide for colleges, universities and adult community learning providers in Great Britain*. UK: Skill.

Grandin, T. (2006) *THINKING IN PICTURES with 2006 Updates from the Expanded Edition*. Retrieved October 21, 2010, from http://www.grandin.com/inc/visual.thinking.html

HEFCE. (2008). *Widening participation indicators for higher education are improving*. Retrieved January 13, 2009, from http://www.hefce.ac.uk/news/hefce/2008/wp.htm#note1

Jordan, R. (2007). A rose by any other name? In *Communication*, winter 2007 pp 10-12.

Jordan, R., & Jones, G. (1999). Review of research into educational interventions for children with autism in the UK. *Autism, 3*(1), 101–110. doi:10.1177/1362361399003001009

Lotter, V. (1978). Childhood Autism in Africa. *Journal of psychology and psychiatry, 19*(3), pp 231-244.

Madriaga, M., Goodley, D., Hodge, N., & Martin, N. (2007). *Enabling transition into higher education for students with Asperger Syndrome.* Retrieved January 12, 2009, from http://www.heacademy.ac.uk/assets/York/documents/manuel_madriaga_report.pdf

NAS. (2001). *Ignored or ineligible? The reality for adults with autism spectrum disorders.* Retrieved October 15, 2010 from http://www.nas.org.uk/content/1/c4/28/61/ignored.pdf

NAS. (2008). *I Exist: The Message from Adults with Autism in England.* Retrieved November 12, 2010, from http://www.autism.org.uk/global/content/search%20results.aspx?q=I%20exist

NAS. Scotland (2010). *We Exist A Bill for Autism, A Bill for Scotland: Accept difference. Not indifference.* Retrieved October 14, 2010, from www.autism.org.uk/scotland

NAS. (2010a). *What is Asperger syndrome?* Retrieved September 15, 2010, from http://www.autism.org.uk/en-gb/about-autism/autism-and-asperger-syndrome-an-introduction/what-is-asperger-syndrome.aspx

NAS. (2010b). *Statistics: how many people have autistic spectrum disorders?* Retrieved October 30, 2010, fromhttp://www.autism.org.uk/About-autism/Some-facts-and-statistics/Statistics-how-many-people-have-autism-spectrum-disorders.aspx

NAS. (2010c). *Employment.* Retrieved November 1st, 2010, from http://www.autism.org.uk/living-with-autism/employment.aspx

NIMH. (2010). *Autism Spectrum Disorders (Prevalence Developmental Disorders).* Retrieved November 20, 2010, from http://www.nimh.nih.gov/health/publications/autism/complete-index.shtml

Plymouth University. (2010). *Twenty-one things you need to know about current assessment practice for disabled students when considering inclusiveness.* Retrieved November 15, 2010, from http://www.plymouth.ac.uk/files/extranet/docs/SWA/3.%20Twenty-one%20things%20you%20need%20to%20know%20about%20current%20assessment%20practice%20for%20disabled%20students%20when%20considering%20inclusiveness.pdf

Riddell, S., Tinklin, T., & Wilson, A. (2005). *Disabled Students in Higher Education; Perspective on widening access and changing policy.* London, New York: Routledge.

Williams, D. (1996). *Autism An Inside – Out Approach: An innovative look at the mechanics of autism and its developmental cousins.* London and Bristol, UK: Jessica Kingsley.

Wing, L. (1996). *The Autism Spectrum: A Guide for Parents and Professionals.* London: Constable.

Wing, L. (2002). *The autistic spectrum: a guide for parents and professionals.* London: Robinson.

ADDITIONAL READING

Frith, U. (1991). *Autism and Asperger Syndrome.* UK: Cambridge University Press. doi:10.1017/CBO9780511526770

Healey, M., Bradley, A., Fuller, M., & Hall, T. (2006). *Listening to students The experinces of disabled students of learning at University in Adams; Mike & Brown; Sally (2006). Towards Inclusive Learning in Higher Education: Developing curricula for disabled students.* London, New York: Routhledge.

HEFCE. (2001). *Strategies for widening participation in higher education, a guide to good practice (2001).* Retrieved January 13, 2009, from http://www.hefce.ac.uk/Pubs/hefce/2001/01_36.htm

Herrington, M., & Simpson, D. (2002). *Making Reasonable Adjustments with Disabled Students in Higher Education. Staff Development Materials: Case Studies and Exercises*. UK: University of Nottingham.

Hills, M., & Healey, M. (2006). *Developing an inclusive curriculum for a) students with mental health issues b) students with Asperger Syndrome*. Geography Discipline Network, University of Gloucestershire. Retrieved September 15 2009 from www2.glos.ac.uk/gdn/icp/

Howlin, P. (1997). *Autism: preparing for adulthood (winner of the 1997 NASEN Special educational Needs Book Award)*. London, new York: Routledge.

NAS. (2008). *University: how to support students with Asperger syndrome*. Retrieved October 20, 2008, from http://www.autism.org.uk/nas/jsp/polopoly.jsp?d=1011&a=12205&view=print

NAS. (2008). *What can I do to help improve my study skills?* Retrieved October 20, 2008, from http://www.autism.org.uk/nas/jsp/polopolyjsp?d=1274&a=12599&view=print

NAS. (2008). *Education: the needs of students with autism and Asperger syndrome*. Retrieved October 20, 2008, from http://www.autism.org.uk/nas/jsp/polopolyjsp?d=1011&a=4525&view=print

NAS. (2008). *What can I expect in the first week?* Retrieved October 20, 2008, from http://www.autism.org.uk/nas^sp/polopoly.jsp?d=1274&a=12598&view=print

NAS. (2008). *Prospects student support service*. Retrieved October 20, 2008, from http://www.autism.org.uk/nas/jsp/polopolyjsp?d=1273&a=12594&view=print

NAS. (2009). *Think differently act positively*. Retrieved January 7, 2009, from http://www.autism.org.uk/nas/jsp/polopoly.jsp?d=160&a=14720

NAS. (2010). *Supporting adults with autism: a good practice guide* Retrieved November 20, 2010, from http://www.autism.org.uk/about-autism/autism-library/magazines-articles-and-reports/reports/our-reports/supporting-adults-with-autism-a-guide.aspx

Powell, A. (2002). *Good Practice Guidelines for Universities. an extract from "Taking Responsibility: Good practice guidelines for services -adults with Asperger syndrome"*. London, UK: National Autistic Society,2002, funded by the Department of Health. Retrieved October 20, 2008, from http://www.users.dircon.co.uk/~cns/guidelines.html last accessed

KEY TERMS AND DEFINITIONS

Action Research: When using action research researchers usually conduct several cycles of a research process which includes a) observe events occurring in real life, b) reflect on these and identify that there is a problem, c) plan how the problem could be solved or the situation improved on, and finally d) act and start observing again. A main advantage of using action research is its potential for making changes within real life situations.

Asperger Syndrome: Again, there is no universally agreed definition, but Asperger Syndrome is often regarded as a mild form of autism.

Autism: This involves a "triad of impairments" or a triad of "differences": (i) there is a social difference: someone with autism may find it hard to relate to other people (ii) there is a communication difference: someone with autism may find it hard to understand and use verbal and non-verbal communication (iii) there is a possible difficulty with social imagination. Much current thinking is that this triad of differences is at least partly underpinned by a "theory of mind" difference - people with autism may have a difficulty in understanding mental states and in ascribing them to themselves or to others.

Autism Spectrum Disorder: Autism is usually seen as a 'spectrum condition': it varies in degree of severity, from severe autism, displaying the above triad to a large extent, to mild autism. Because of this the expression 'autism spectrum condition' or 'autism spectrum disorder' is often used rather than just 'autism'.

Case Study: Case study is a qualitative methodology commonly used in educational contexts to obtain richness and depth of data. When using case study, different methods can be used such as observations, interviews, narrative accounts, documents and records to study the complex issues faced by researchers. A case can be limited to either one individual, one type of situation or a group of people or situations.

Higher Education: In the UK this refers to degree level education, typically in a higher education institute such as a university and typically post 18 years of age. In the UK such education is non-compulsory.

Interviews: Interviews are commonly used in qualitative research. They involve a one-to-one conversation between researchers and participants to get participants' views on any aspects of the research topic.

Chapter 9

Reappraising the Social Model of Disability:
A Foucauldian Reprise

William J. Penson
Leeds Metropolitan University, UK

ABSTRACT

The social model of disability is widely accepted as a contemporary and progressive way to understand the experience of disabled people and is also seen as a means by which there can be a response to the discrimination that arises out of impairment. However, this chapter argues that there has been/is a process of assimilation, which has claimed the social model of disability within a dominant medico-legal discourse. Using Foucault's work on biopower and docility this chapter exposes the human body as the means by which institutions and disciplines continue to define the experience of disabled people. The process of assimilation requires the propagation by medico-legal disciplines of a certain privileged knowledge of the body, which is presented in ways that suggest objective neutrality. Taking a focus on psychiatry we can see that disciplinary constructions of the body, impairment and disability are problematic.

INTRODUCTION

This chapter will problematise current disability theory with reference to a number of Foucault's texts but in particular 'Docile bodies' (Foucault, 1975; 1991). The purpose of terming this chapter

DOI: 10.4018/978-1-61350-183-2.ch009

a *reprise* is in recognition of the previous critiques that have been raised through applying Foucauldian theory in disability discourse and in understanding the lived experience of disabled people (see Tremain (2009) for a particularly relevant coverage). This is most significantly applied in relation to constructions of impairment, the body and the mind, the primacy given to such constructions, ontological conflicts and indeed the social model of disability as a practice that follows. There remains some merit in further developing the synthesis of Foucault's work and disability theory, and at points I speculate on the use of postcolonial perspectives in disability as an allied area of post-structuralism, given that Foucault is often associated with the post-structuralist school.

Before expanding on this argument it is necessary to explain why this might be of interest in a discussion of education for adult learners, given that adult learning in higher education is of most concern for this book. I would suggest that the relevance of this chapter could be seen in four ways. Firstly, that education is organised within disciplines and institutions and so an exploration and critique of such an organising system is crucial to understanding educational operations. Secondly, that generally the social model of disability is viewed as a progressive, contemporary approach to understanding disability and responding to the needs of disabled learners. Given the status of the social model of disability, it is important that it is discussed in terms of its limitations and benefits. Thirdly, that the activities of taxonomy, that is the activities of 'empowered description', are applied to adult learners and that this application has a power effect in designating learners as 'bright', 'dyslexic', 'introverted', 'failing', for instance. These ways of separating different kinds of learner have an impact on the learner and the operations of education. I coin the term 'empowered description' as a way of denoting systems of arbitrary taxonomy that have an organising effect and are privileged with, and through, authority. I would consider the term 'empowered description' to be one that most accurately reflects practices that can otherwise be camouflaged in the use of the word 'taxonomy' behind an implied legitimacy, obscuring the partiality of the word. Finally, I suggest that Higher Education is a key location for the disability discourse to develop as a critical perspective, in the interests of disabled people. However, both inside the higher learning institu-

tion, and outside, disability activism and discourse is offered a limited regard, and as such, disability discourse is a 'subjugated knowledge', that is, as a certain category of knowledge claim that is/are seen as less viable than other knowledge claims such as medicine. Higher education is crucial as a place from which resistance can be mobilised in response to disciplinary power. It is beyond the scope of this chapter to offer a Foucauldian analysis of Higher Education as a whole, indeed this may be contraindicated given it would be an attempt at a unifying, generalised perspective, but rather the critique I do proffer is problematising the social model of disability, and that is through a lens that I apply to the practices of psychiatry.

My choice of psychiatry is because of how mental illness has come to be understood as a disability, and some of the questions this raises. The reader may therefore see a similarity in how disciplinary power operates across a number of institutions and disciplines, and should see that there are currently limitations in the application of the social model of disability. The reader may also question the psychiatric model, and also the arrangement of people that are in distress and are inducted into the field of mental health. By 'arrangement' I refer to the deployment of people within systems of knowledge and power, which will be expanded in later parts of this chapter when I discuss subjugation and docility. It is important to note that in my discussion of the disciplinary power of psychiatry and psychology, that we recognise that there is dissent and resistance in these disciplines also, such as the critical psychiatry movement and radical psychologists. Such movements do not necessarily coalesce in one place, or time, but refer to activities of resistance and disavowal, that mobilise, disperse, and regroup in response to the exercise of disciplinary power. However, while such acts of resistance are noted, it should also be considered that these groups, and their areas of discourse, do remain interested in the research and *knowing* of the person. Even though I am being mindful of the ethical practice of critical psychiatrists and radical psychologists, there is still an exertion of disciplinary knowledge, and therefore of disciplinary power.

Foucault's work is often associated with power, its relationship to the provisional nature of knowledge, modes and acts of resistance and subversion. This complicates my discussion somewhat in that an introduction should, to some extent, set out key terms and principles for the work that follows, but in relation to the term 'disability', I will, in the spirit of refusing a totalising, summative position, avoid doing this. Any definition would fall short of both the lived subjectivity and complexity of disability, and current definitions tend to be of a medico-legal orientation. The reader may need to tolerate the uncertainty of the word disability throughout this chapter, but in doing so; they will have entered into the spirit of avoiding a totalising position on disability. In many ways this is at the heart of why this chapter discusses disability. My consideration of disability tends towards a wide, inclusive practice wherein disability includes people designated as having learning disabilities and people with mental health problems (Hughes, 2004). I would also suggest, given the points so far raised, that disability is not an act of self-definition, but rather a complex process, and a fluid interaction between the individual judged to have impairment and their transactions with disciplinary power. What follows is some context on Foucault's work on docility and biopower, a tentative theorising of the mechanisms that underpin disability and an application of these ideas in a discussion about psychiatry as a discipline involved in disability. Foucault did not explicitly refer to disability in his explanation of docility. In my coverage of 'docile bodies' it may seem that disability is absent, but it is important to hold a premise in mind; disability as a category of person and experience evolves from the exercise of power in/through efforts to construct the knowing and being of the body. Reference to docility refers to any subjugation that orders and regulates the body, and there is a caution to be taken, that is, by applying this

Foucault's work too tightly to disability in the first instance, accepts the premise of disability before the power effects involved in constituting the body and mind have been revealed. Without the preamble, 'disability' appears, without question, as a natural category.

BACKGROUND

At the heart of the problem with the current application of the social model of disability is a paradox that seems inherent in disability activism. The movement towards valued inclusion and participation in society, through having access to and adopting the structures and means of that society, for example access to employment, rights of parenthood and education, are the means by which disabled people, are in fact segregated, measured and deployed. The anticipated social and material change desired by early disability activism, and the subsequent formulation of the social model of disability has been appropriated into politico-legal and medical discourse, rendering it an assimilated domain or interest. As a result, such assimilation renders activism as reduced, less potent, in proximity to the very thing is resists, and this is through, and by the induction of the interests and concerns of disability activism into the socio-medico symbolic order. This assimilation, at least in part, operates through the concessionary responses offered in negotiation with mainstream discourse/interests resulting in negligible gains for most disabled people. As disability activists, in whatever way we presume, we might borrow an insightful phrasing of our dilemma from the postcolonial canon, which locates the tension in responding to a colonising presence:

However, to achieve autonomy people had to first find the means to articulate it. To win self-determination they had to develop ways of dealing with the negation, self-alienation, and internal hatred produced by colonialist rule. It was at

this point, where they were confronted by their own self-contradiction, that many had creative recourse to the very predicament that entrapped them — self repetition or mimicry. (Boehmer, 2005, p.162)

Models of disability remain predicated on what Campbell (2009) recalls as the tragedy model of disability in interaction with what she calls 'negative ontologies' (Campbell, 2009, p.108). I argue that negative ontology is in the company of a dominant discursive mode constituted through socially empowered, and valued, notions of normalcy and autonomy. In addition to Campbell's (2009) proposition, her view of negative ontologies, there is in operation a 'teleological fantasy' that supposes a steadily progressive design and trajectory towards a better state of being or anticipated endpoint. This teleological fantasy underpins activities aimed to recover function, to rehabilitate impairment, and reduce disruption; these activities and practices include screening, surgery, adaptation, rehabilitation, therapy (physio-, occupational and psycho-), and building prosthetics and aids. These activities and practices are contingent on ideas of normalcy and on the ideal of achieving autonomy, and they are teleological in that that they are applied within the assumption that remediation and reparation lead to a better way of living, in fact, that there is a better way of living that the able bodied do model. Such dominant discursive motifs underpin a range of diagnostic and reparative practices to ameliorate the impaired and disabled closer to the accepted norm for physical and psychological wholeness and function. And it is this that underpins ableism and which makes Foucault's work theoretically best placed to mount a critique or counter position.

I suggest the term 'disabling triangle' is descriptive of the interaction between three areas of dominant discourse that maintain disability as a subjugated experience and population, and the disabling triangle underpins the disabled identity arising out of a mode of empowered description.

The first angle in the triangle is that beliefs are in circulation and operation about the worth, wholeness and humanness of the disabled person that is predicated on a tragic or negative orientation — a 'negative ontology' (Campbell, 2009). Secondly, this interacts with 'myths of normalcy' that construe the statistical phenomena of the normal distribution curve as being preferred and therefore privileged. The 'myth of normalcy' is enacted through acts of measurement which are themselves socially constituted. So the act of measurement that underpins the organisation of data under the normative rubric is also culturally bound, and as such tends to be disproportionably applied to populations under surveillance by disciplinary power, of which the disabled are one. Here then, a data set is actually a value statement, which is numerically articulated. A departure from normalcy is the quality, concealed as a quantity that enunciates the disabled difference. Finally, these two angles of the triangle are bound-up with notions of 'autonomy' that assume autonomy is a natural human state, denied at least in part to the disabled, as a function of their (our) impairment. In fact, autonomy is predicated on a range of medico-legal and socio-economic definitions and factors that become unevenly attributed to the disabled population. Autonomy relies primarily on socially mediated factors such as financial income, cultural expectations of beauty, participation in employment, and property ownership. So autonomy is not a property of the individual that is optimised without recourse to social and cultural dimensions. In summary, I suggest that the activity and practice of disabling is contingent on the circulation, and interaction, of three qualities, as beliefs, that are operationalised socially and culturally. These three beliefs, the disabling triangle, are a negative ontology ('the disabled are fundamentally tragic'), a 'myth of normalcy' ('normal people are constant in their ability, role and function; disabled people are constant in their dysfunction') and notions of autonomy ('the disabled cannot self determine and manage for themselves like normal people can').

Later in this chapter I will make use of the field of mental health as an exemplar of the mechanics of power, which offers insights into the modelling of disability based on two qualities of the mental health field: firstly, its relatively recent admission to the legitimised (as opposed to a subjective, subversive) domain of disability; and secondly, on epistemological grounds in that critics employing a method of immanent criticism have convincingly demonstrated the poor construct validity of key psychiatric constructs (Boyle, 1990). The poor construct validity is concurrent with the lack of a viable, definitive physical location or impairment, but this exists without any discernible changes in the disciplinary power of psychiatry. This is worth labouring: psychiatry has yet to deliver sound evidence, and an indisputable position, for any of its knowledge claims about mental illness; however, despite this, its disciplinary power has in fact grown and has extended into a range of social milieu, including legislated powers of detention and compulsory treatment.

As a research activity this chapter also demonstrates the importance of interdisciplinary argument, in that critical perspectives in an area of concern like disability are often subjugated then appropriated by social care and medical disciplines. So by turning to theoretical positions and methodologies found in philosophy, cultural studies, arts and humanities, which in relation to medicine and law can be argued in terms of a subjugated knowledge, we can expand critical analysis and from the point of view of activism, and articulate resistance to the dominating views of disability that subjugate the experience and lives of the disabled. In this spirit Allen suggests:

When one inhabits a system of thought, belief, or concepts, it [knowledge] appears self evident; effective contrast to another system, equally self-evident to its contemporaries, allows one to see

the unity of present knowledge as an arbitrarily enforced exclusion (Allen, 2009, p.102)

As Allen (2009) suggests, when one is inducted into a disciplinary area, one comes to accept the parameters and discourse of that area, and the foundations of that discipline come to seem self-evident. Aside from Allen's invitation to view disciplines from without, there is an echo of Foucault's concern about the dangers of unifying, totalising theory, and what is excluded in the process of uni-disciplinarity.

Foucault's Work

While Foucault's treatment of the body, across a number of his texts, provides a critical theory of how and what forces and powers act upon the body, and appears to have informed to some extent the social model of disability as an early activist model of disability. Application of Foucault's theory to this area remains troublesome, for instance as a 'weak' formulation of social constructionism (Siebers, 2006). In exploring the application of Foucault's texts to the field of disability I will work through two areas. Firstly, I provide a review of Foucault's notion of 'docile bodies' and secondly, I will make use of some key essays in the disability studies canon, which draw on Foucault's work.

In a number of his texts Foucault makes use of notions of physicality and space, and this is seen as a key motif in his work (Driver, 1994). This is significant insofar as the body is the only true point for forces, and expressed power, to act upon and in. The physical matter of the human body therefore becomes the locus of governmentality; that is the 'conduct of conduct', through which there is a location of the soul and psyche, sexuality, madness, character, motivation, industry and normalcy. Foucault takes to task the practices in a given discourse, and scrutinises these, less in a linear, traditionally historiographical way, and more in the sense of examining multiple points of interest and application in a given temporality. He poses the question:

Is it not possible to make a structural analysis of discourses that would evade the commentary by supposing no remainder, nothing in excess of what has been said, but only the fact of its historical appearance? [...]The meaning of a statement would be defined not by the treasure of intentions that it might contain, revealing and concealing it at the same time, but by the difference that articulates it upon the other real or possible statements' (Foucault, 1963: 2010, p. xix).

In this quote Foucault is setting out, it seems, his purpose and he is also indicating his methodology, certainly in *The Birth of the Clinic* (Foucault, 1963:2010). In the first sentence he is indicating that analysis of a given area might be undertaken without recourse to the identification of sub-structures, for instance psychological drives in psychological theory, but instead, enquiry can focus on the relationships, transactions and events of that moment. He goes on to expand this in the sense that he disavows the use of speculation beyond what was/is evident and is rather more interested in the connection and relationships between combinations of individuals and groups, in a given time and a given space. We get a sense here that Foucault's work is less interested in describing structures, and more interested in what practices are *between* them. It follows that his action involves enquiring into 'the meaning of a statement that articulates it upon the other' (Foucault, 1963: 2010, p.xix). Any further attempt to reduce Foucault's work thematically is likely to do it a disservice and in fact he was cautious himself of 'the limitations of general theories' (Driver, 1994, p.117). So, Foucault's methodology, although he tended to avoid this word as a way to describe his activity, suggests we can illuminate power effects by looking at what is evident rather than seeking below the surface for intentions, motivations etc. Unifying theory fails

to describe adequately the reality of the inconsistency, plurality, multiplicity and dynamism of experience and being, especially so in the human sciences. Rather, such theory, and any activity that follows, indicates an interest, which is empowered to describe, along the lines of its interest, and so is limited and limiting. However, this does offer a point of access to his chapter 'Docile Bodies' (Foucault 1975; 1991).

ISSUES, CONTROVERSIES AND DEBATES

The Foucauldian Docile Body and Disability

Using the idealised image of a soldier, constructed piece-by-piece (Foucault 1975; 1991, p.135), Foucault notes that from the late 1700s 'the classical age discovered the body as object and target of power' (Foucault 1975; 1991, p.136). The emerging knowledge of the body as a machine was typified in two ways, what Foucault calls 'registers', which are construed as the 'anatomico-metaphysical' (body, thought and spirit) and the 'technico-political' (the social structuring of the regulation and correcting of the body). Arguably these registers act along their own axes, and although Foucault notes these registers as distinct, he suggests also that they have some points of overlap. These points of overlap become the spaces for the origination of regulation, certainly the concentration of such (Osbourne, 1994). The school, hospital, monastery, barrack and prison, are the physical points, the location, of the overlap of these registers that are intended to extend into the similarly socio-culturally formulated domain of the psychological. So the matter and space of the body, within the context of an institution locating disciplinary power, becomes the route to the soul, to motivation, learning, loyalty and the psyche.

Murray (2008) suggests there is a primacy given to physical difference in disability discourse over psychological difference. However, 'docile bodies' are constituted to enhance their productivity and subjugation, a theme that will be returned to later in the chapter. Foucault suggests that this corporeal subjugation is with the intention of gaining influence over the soul, psyche, motivation and personality (Foucault, 1991, pp.130-131), which in part may explain the importance of the primacy of physicality. The power exerted at the point where the registers overlap, the location and the concentration, are *intended* to generate an effect in the sense that the body is a purposeful site of a given institution's training, discipline and deployment. Physical matter and spaces are key to both Foucault's thesis in itself, and the application of his thesis to understanding disability, in that what Foucault refers to as 'disciplinary power', with these registers in mind, is power that is constructive, in that it is constitutive - it forms, surveys and maintains. Without institutional spaces within which disciplinary power can be expressed, having worked around, on and in the body, such disciplinary power would not be (Armstrong, 1994). Being mindful of this, Foucault also suggests: 'we believe, in any event, that the body obeys the exclusive laws of physiology and that it escapes the influence of history, but this too is false' (Foucault, 1971:1984, p.87). Here Foucault is noting a problem in treating the body as *ahistorical*, *acultural* and also *atheoretical* in that scientific efforts to measure, map and explain the body are actually located within culture, and time, and do not exist neutrally beyond time, place and culture.

Subsequently the body, and the science of the body, anatomy and physiology, are in communication with human construction and this knowledge does not ever sit outside its constitution by humans. For instance, the understanding of the anatomy, functions and workings of the human heart reflect the time and place of enquiry. A heart is present, for most people, irrespective of time and place, but our knowledge of it is not. But the heart changes, and defies our knowledge of

it; in the thirteenth as compared to the twentieth century, across the lifespan, it responds differently to stressors, it changes within the context of the whole human organism, speeds with excitement, varies with lifestyle and socio-economic factors, can be removed and kept alive, can be replaced, weighs heavy in sadness and is an emblem for courage and love.

We note that this constituent or constructing effect and property of disciplinary power is at once affiliated to the adage *knowledge is power*, but significantly, perhaps more so, also that *power is knowledge*. Bhabha (1994) draws our attention to what follows, in that if power is knowledge it is also partial and provisional, and subject to negotiation, in what he refers to as the 'third space of enunciation'; the space between *I* and *you* where negotiation is made, resistance is played, renewal and hybridity is generated. By 'hybridity' I refer to the state of flux and mobility with which Bhabha views identity and culture, that defies fixity and the totalising positions of authority. In thinking about *power/knowledge* Allen offers a succinct explanation:

The virgule, or slash, in Foucault's neologism power/knowledge does not equate these two terms; rather it divides, and distinguishes power from knowledge, and then relates them to each other in a reciprocal economy. Each of these terms grows with and through the other one; they confirm each other, reproduce each other, and sustain each other's authority. (Allen, 2009, p. 95)

Disciplinary power as exerted through surveillance and monitoring, interacts with, and informs notions of the body as both knowable and known, and this perpetuates the fallacy of the body as a *constant* existing beyond culture, and this *power/knowledge* provides the rationale for a range of activities, such as assessment, both in and beyond the institution. This may also begin to constitute what Foucault refers to as 'diffusion' (Driver, 1994), disciplinary power working outwards from the institution, that the act of observation, the clinical contact itself constitutes the exercise of power. Perhaps this is seen in the advent of community and medical social work, district nursing, community psychiatric services, intermediate care services and midwifery, which operate and enable surveillance (Osbourne, 1994). Furthermore, diffusion provides the scaffold that supports the social product that is the practice of *acultural* knowing. As Foucault writes that 'the exercise of discipline presupposes a mechanism that coerces by means of observation; an apparatus in which the techniques that make it possible to see induce effects of power, and in which, conversely the means of coercion make those on whom they are applied clearly visible' (Foucault, 1975:1991, pp.170-171). Such disciplinary practices demonstrate diffusion in health and social care as a transactional and negotiable practice of power relations, in that at some point, and in response to some resistance, the institution as a physical locale of disciplinary power had shifted, with the arrival of new practices of entering the community and becoming mobile. The effect overall, is a maintenance in disciplinary power despite the shift from institution to home and community.

While Foucault's work in *Discipline and Punish* (1975; 1991) concerns the mid seventeenth century late the eighteenth century, his historical analysis is understood as being revealing of contemporary concerns. Foucault suggests that the overlap in the aforementioned registers has a tension in that the first register is concerned with 'submission and use' (the anatomico-metaphysical register) and the second register with 'functioning and understanding' (the technico-political register), and so, 'there was a useful body and an intelligible body' (Foucault, 1975; 1991, p.136). It is significant that these registers may operate at points in concert, though not necessarily intentionally so. I would argue that the point at which these two registers act in concert, may be where we see the modern construction of the body; the body is efficient, to optimize the performance of

prescribed activities, and also the body is known and knowable. So in effect the greatest societal gain, for current social organisation, is to have a knowledge of the body that firstly maintains the privilege of certain institutions (institutions refer also to disciplines)—medicine, biology, physiology, sports science, physiotherapy, the human sciences—and secondly to have these institutions and disciplines interact with, inform and complement the discourse of efficiency (such as employment practices, occupational science and welfare provision).

Herein we see that *power/knowledge* acts to constrain and direct the body—so physical potency becomes harnessed and purposeful; it is subjugated as it is employed and made industrious, and so it is not emancipatory. Hughes (2009) notes this, and adds a proposition that '[T]he central contradiction of the human body is this: it is, simultaneously, a potential source of our enslavement and of our freedom' (Hughes, 2009, p.89) and he goes on to suggest that Foucault would not consider the body to be a source of freedom. I would argue otherwise in that Foucault's position seems to be that freedoms do not arise from the body, rather, freedoms and enslavement arise from the exercising of *power/knowledge* of the body. However, what initially appears to be the emergence of freedoms is over time compensated for, and regulated through new technologies of power, which emerge also. Such freedoms, possibly arising out of formerly subjugated interests, and I am thinking particularly of disability activism here, are assimilated following their recent, now historical, resistance, which is perhaps resonant with Campbell's (2009) notion of a *regulated liberty*.

Given that Foucault maintained a view of disciplinary power that was positive, in that it was constitutive, by extension it also has to be mobile and dynamic, as argued earlier in the notion of diffusion. Foucault suggests that the expression of power as a technology is assimilative, which can be construed, perhaps mistakenly, in teleological terms as progress. Foucault gives the example of changing views of practices of sexuality over time, which may come to be owned by institutions as a means to retaining a position in power relations (Foucault, 1980). However, this merely reiterates his earlier arguments in not moralising nor favouring a given expression of power, but rather in examining the way in which technology shifts in relation to diverse applications and resistances: 'to disentangle the conditions of history from the density of discourse' (Foucault, 1963: 2010, p. xxii)

With regard to disability, through 'Docile Bodies' we can begin to understand the significance of bodies without efficiency – those with disease and dysfunction, that fall outside of prescribed production and are thus seen as having dubious worth, other than to offer a route to understanding normalcy and functionality; a hierarchy of binary oppositions, one privileged over the other (Powell, 1997); healthy>diseased; function> dysfunction; efficiency> inefficiency; desirable> undesirable; symmetrical> asymmetrical.

In this binary opposition, the disabled body is in one sense constituted within the institution, and paradoxically becomes the site of resistance to disciplinary power and the clinical gaze, and to docility. Disabled bodies cannot totally comply with the demands of the technico-political register as a machine moving in the direction of efficiency, or the regulatory demands of self sufficiency, leaving the institution with the options of greater surveillance and regulation, or assimilation into an alternative view: what else can the institution do when the contracted limb refuses to straighten or the amputee, with an ill-fitting prosthetic, fails in rehabilitation? Indeed, the disabled body also fails in the anatomico-metaphysical register, in that it neither situates reason nor reflects normalcy, all of which operate within a false premise of physical constancy.

In later work Foucault locates some of his theorising on disciplinary power acting in a physical space, and on/in bodies, in the term 'bio-power', which is characterised as beginning with 'the endeavour to rationalize the problems that the phenomena characteristic of a group of living human beings, when constituted as a population, pose to governmental practice (Tremain, 2006, p. 185). Biopower, as applied to disability, goes on to involve a 'strategic movement' (Tremain, 2006, p. 185) within forms of *power/knowledge* in the monitoring, surveillance and management of the problems of this given population, and the individuals that constitute it: in this case, the disabled. This might be seen in a raft of policy and legislative changes that come to typify definitions of the disabled, their induction into receiving help and the audit made of said help.

So it is the space as rendered, either in a concentrating location, or in a diffused place of practice, where disciplinary power is expressed, in transaction with methods and models for understanding (knowledge) which in the first instance construct normalcy as a neutral given, when in fact, Foucault's proposition is that bodies are 'written upon' (Foucault, 1971:1984, p.83), culturally and socially inscribed, and are not static. In the second instance, disciplinary power fabricates normalcy as 'a location of bio-power' (Davis, 1995, p.128). With this power come the contingent privileges that are afforded normalcy, not least the perpetuation of its own illusion. The illusion being that there is a norm that is both a natural phenomenon, and that it is contingent on forms of measurement that are not culturally and socially constituted. This is a good point to speculate, given the limits of finding a definitive historical point of origin, on the birth of modern ideas of disability.

Davis (1995) describes the Venus de Milo statue, considered an object of great beauty, and juxtaposes this with a description of Pam Herbert, a quadriplegic with muscular dystrophy, on her wedding night, and asks the question: 'Why does the impairment of the Venus de Milo in no way prevent 'normal' people from considering her beauty, while Pam Herbert's disability become the focal point for horror and pity?' (Davis, 1995, p.128). A response to Lennard Davis' question may be constructed, in part, from the chapter 'Open up a few corpses' (Foucault, 1963: 2010) wherein Foucault is noting the shift in the pursuit of pathological anatomy, from viewing diseases that act in and on the body as invading species, to a view wherein they are transposed into the body, as a dysfunctional property of organs, tissue or the whole. This leads, and is lead by, the practice through which:

[T]he only pathological fact is a comparative fact [and] one must compare subjects who have died of the same disease [...] accepting the old principle [...] that alterations observed on all bodies define, if not the cause, at least the seat of the disease and perhaps its nature (Foucault, 1963: 2010, p.165).

This has a double significance in understanding what may be the birth point of modern constructions of disability in that firstly, the body becomes a constituted part of, as well as the site of, illness and dysfunction. Secondly, this is described and recorded through comparison with other bodies, which in turn requires a notion of, and the construction of, normalcy from which to differentiate. The process of empowered description, as employed through disciplinary power, then requires a language to make its discoveries known, to confirm its mystique, and to accent the difference that it notes. This process perhaps leads to descriptions of a given physical state becoming referential of, and attached to, the whole human—a 'cripple', a 'spastic', a 'mongoloid', an 'idiot', a 'schizophrenic'. Such terms are summative constructions in the way Foucault describes what happens in the *invention* of the homosexual (Foucault, 1976, p.43), and they are terms and inventions through which the whole of that human is viewed, all the time. Certainly Snyder & Mitchell (2006, p.117) and Davis (1995, p.30) note the significance of differentiation as the root of the statistical norm, or average, as conceptualised by early statisticians, many of who were also eugenicists. The

concept of norm, as applied to populations, becomes a means to identify those that fall too far beyond it—outside of the standard deviation. We might demarcate common terms, some of which feature in the list above, used by the layperson; a 'commonsense' use of language in the circulation of common knowledge (Berger & Luckman, 1966:1991), and differentiate it from the specialist language of the clinician, administrator and researcher. What is being objected to here is not a given word or phrase in itself, but the totalising effect of the *use* of a word or phrase. Some words like 'spastic' are still in circulation but may be frowned upon as denigrating, however, clinical language may also have an effect that erodes the dignity of the person, but because of its location in a professional lexicon, it is found to be acceptable, when in fact it is merely sanitised. To paraphrase Wittgenstein, its is the use of a word that demonstrates its meaning.

The low economic worth of the impaired necessitates their seclusion away from the normal population, especially given the fears of the period (the eighteenth and nineteenth centuries) for how sub- and abnormality might be communicated; a process we now refer to as exclusion, and which can be enacted without recourse to remove the individual to an institution. Such segregation requires surveillance, and involves rehabilitation, and so there is a cyclical relation that seems to legitimise the presence of the professional discipline:

Disciplines will define not a code of law, but a code of normalization, and they will necessarily refer to a theoretical horizon that is not the edifice of law, but the field of human sciences. And the jurisprudence of these disciplines will be that of a clinical knowledge. (Foucault, 2004, p.38)

In effect, the professions of segregation, those responsible for the institution, do police those people outside of the prescribed norm who are intolerable for whatever reason. Clinical knowledge acts as the law that legitimises the professional presence, which ensures that the clinical space and clinical practices are maintained. While Foucault is describing historically the differentiation of power, he does this to illuminate contemporary power effects; 'my objective […] has been to create a history of the different modes by which, in our culture, *human beings are made subjects*' (Foucault, 2002, p.326, my emphasis).

The practices that evoke a range of taxonomic ventures through the eighteenth and nineteenth centuries use *difference* as the key to the construction of hierarchies, which tended to normalise the interests of white, European imperialists. Concurrent with taxonomy was an investment in new sciences of population, demography, and alongside these, the development of statistics and its discovery of the normal distribution curve and of the idea of the average (Davis, 2006). The mean and average become the tools to support a notion of the authentic. With this authentic, traditional, 'as it should be' body, what might be termed the 'benchmark man' (Campbell, 2009), the means to settle an otherwise intolerably unstable and provisional knowledge (Boehmer, 2005) becomes available.

While natural scientists laboured under the impression of empirical objectivity, they were in fact operating entirely within social and cultural constructed norms. Foucault explains that while 'we believe, in any event, that the body obeys the exclusive laws of physiology and that it escapes the influence of history […] this too is false' (Foucault, 1984, p.87). Questioning the rationality of science, especially the human sciences, begins with the subject/object designation. That is that the assumption of a dynamic, not fully known, but knowable, object that is to be studied by the constant subject/researcher with an assumption of neutrality on the part of the subject (Foucault, 2000, p.257). Steadily there is an organising tendency for the disciplines in that they began to identify domains of expertise and knowledge claims, within which they operate(d), as well as systems by which they may organise the bodies

they come to subjugate. While on the surface, this may look to be an argument in support of the social model of disability, and to some extent that is true certainly for the early iterations of the model; it is in fact demonstrating that the body is an inconstant place. So basing disability in the assumption that the body, and thus impairment is constant, and denoting the variable social responses neglects the disciplinary power exerted in constructing the body. Both the body and its social presence are culturally located.

The Institution and the Disciplines

In relation to the purpose of the institution, Foucault suggests 'the bourgeoisie is not interested in the mad, but it is interested in power over the mad' and links this interest as being with regard to 'a certain economic profit' (Foucault, 1976:2004, p.33) that such a surveillance and segregation might impart. This is true for the disabled generally. The value, economic or otherwise, of institutional segregation appears here to be threefold. Firstly, in providing employment for the surveyors; secondly, in its complementarity with other acts of domination; thirdly, there is value in reducing the presence of the unproductive mad in an otherwise productive population. This sits concurrently with the natural scientist's exploration of the body, as they began to work with the notion of norms (Davis, 1995).

Dwelling on institutional practices, during this period of the growth of human sciences, Foucault (1975:1991) notes the systems and structures by which disciplinary power is administered in and through physical distribution. He explores how subjugation is enacted in the organisation of subjects through enclosure, partitioning and functionality of space. Then in the control of activity there is the application of timetabling, ordinal organisation, the finessing of motor performance, and the full occupation of time.

While Foucault draws on military training to exemplify this administration, it becomes evocative of any institutional delivery. Arguably this is also a 'juridico-discursive' exertion of power, which Tremain (2006) refers to as 'fundamentally repressive' (Tremain, 2006, p.186). Foucault's use of the phrase 'juridico-discursive' is usually in reference to a legal and state mechanism of repression. In noting the interconnectedness of networks of exertions of power and influence, it is significant that the status of disabled people is in reference to juridico-discursive exertion through either a direct construction of them (us) as non-people, who by extension may not have been permitted to participate in activities like voting. There is also a complicity in the privileging of medico-political acts such as detention and treatment against one's consent. It is most significant that legislation such as the Disability Discrimination Act (DDA)(Office of Public Sector Information, 2005) and the Mental Health Act (Amended) (MHA) (Office of Public Sector Information, 2007) are generated in government, through dialogue with experts, and enacted in social and healthcare contexts. These laws define the terms of reference for the experience that follows in other modes. So while it may be argued that the expression of power is in one sense constitutive, it is also arguably still fundamentally repressive. On first appearance the DDA does not look to be repressive, however, beyond its statements of intent, it relies on expert opinion to endorse the presence of an impairment thus undermining of the process of self-definition and it introduces the idea of reasonable adjustment, which requires services/employers to act to only an extent. The repression is obscured, but we might ask, to what extent has the lives of disabled people really changed in the UK since the DDA became law? As Boehmer (2005) suggests, subjugated populations are left with the dilemma of how to resist their subjugation when the language and structures by which resistance might performed are already known and designated, for instance in the DDA and MHA. For the disabled, juridico-legal and socio-medical powers are brought to bear operating at overlapping

junctures to ensconce the definition of disability in law that both constitutes the disabled state, and for some people, enables the application of clinical powers. Certainly, mental health appears unique in healthcare as an area of practice that has the powers to remove liberty, forcibly treat and recall to the clinical space for treatment. In doing so, health and social care professionals may call upon police powers to invoke and enact an arrest.

In theorising institutional practices, we note the mode of action as having been primarily in performing 'dividing practices' (Tremain, 2006, p.186), that is, through segregation within institutions, in the ways Foucault outlines above. This has formerly been segregation in asylums, and more recently in hospitals and homes, often in dormitory accommodation or single rooms, and most often with a regimented daily structure (meal times, weekly baths, times for hot drinks), including industrial or occupational therapies, and communal living (dining rooms combining function and space). It is important to note that institutional practices have tended, certainly in the past, to be overinclusive in their admissions including a range of people; the poor and destitute, 'morally corrupt', the mad. And while at this point we are considering psychiatric asylums, Foucault refers to any site of institutional power, including the hospital, barracks, prison, monastery, and school. At their worst institutional spaces, and dividing practices, have combined with a eugenic ethos, or rather extended what was already a separation into elimination. For instance between 1939 and 1941, 70,000 people were thought to have been killed in German mental institutions, which by the end of the Second World War was thought to be 250,000 killed through gassing with carbon monoxide, and a further 40,000 starved to death in French hospitals (Read & Masson, 2004). The technology for extermination, developed in German institutions, by psychiatrists and their colleagues, was transported to the death camps (Read & Masson, 2004). And it is the effectiveness of the institution in producing and maintaining docility, and in exerting bio-power, that in turn allows it to undertake its activities locally.

A process of deinstitutionalization, form the 1950s onwards in Western societies, has seen a shift from institution to community. This is in many senses progressive but it is also the mode of diffusion of institutional practices. Debate about the success of deinstitutionalization is of interest in itself, in that it has allowed for speculation by the public and disciplines on whether the intrinsic 'abnormality' of the ill and impaired can be accommodated outside of a specialist setting. Such discussion seems to maintain a view commensurate with the disabling triangle, assumes the good quality of life of those people who would never have lived in an institution, camouflages diffusion and re-locates problems in living, not as a social factor, but as an inherent property of the disabled individual.

Psychiatry and Psychosis—
Subjugation in Action

Focusing on psychosis, or rather the body of the psychotic is central to my argument in that it offers us a locale of both domination and resistance within the discourse of psychiatry. In the same way that Foucault expanded the processes of knowledge/power in areas of disciplinary activity, an examination of contemporary psychiatry might on the first hand offer a necessary critique of psychiatry as a disciplinary power with a potent presence in Western thinking, policy and practice. But an examination of psychiatry will also offer a point from which we might track along the argument and see the fault lines in other areas of disciplinary exertion over disabled people, for instance the networks of power that flow through psychiatry, into the legislature, through policy making, in pharmaceutical industries, and expert commentary on 'real life'. While the starting point of this focus is psychiatry the exercise of power is linked though an extensive network. In brief my argument is that in the absence of impairment, on

the basis of psychiatry's exertion of disciplinary power, madness has been inducted into the field of disability. This illuminates the contemporary application of the social model of disability as having been assimilated into medical discourse, and not necessarily to the gain of the disabled. Disciplinary power within psychiatry is perhaps one of the most convincing exemplars of both the mechanics of subjugation and of diffusion, and *making* psychiatry interact with the critical elements disability discourse, may yield tremendous insights (Lewis, 2006).

Recent writers such as Mary Boyle (1990) and Richard Bentall (2009) have posited robust criticisms of the psychiatric taxonomic system and all that follows from the privileging of such a system. Such privilege is surprising given the paucity of scientific rigour through which illness constructs like schizophrenia are invented. The collective view of these critics might best be articulated as being that psychotic illnesses such as schizophrenia fail to meet medicine's own requirements of construct validity, which demand that diseases should offer a discernible pattern and then a series of predictions that can be tested, with greater and more reliable knowledge accrued through a scientific enquiry (Boyle, 1990). Indeed, Bentall suggests that mental illness constructs have the same level of rigour as astrology (Bentall, 2009, p.110). For instance, there is not an agreed causal explanation of schizophrenia or psychosis. However, the explanatory models that are currently promulgated tend towards a supposition of personal vulnerability or defect that interacts with environmental stresses (a negative ontology), which in reality offers a perspective only a little beyond basic evolutionary theory and so lacks specificity for the range of phenomena grouped under the schizophrenia diagnosis.

Without a sound scientific basis from which to justify the intrusion into, and the policing of, people's psychological states, the activities of psychiatry and psychology are continuations of the colonial venture: an impassioned drive towards civilising (through cure, rehabilitation and containment) the mad in the service of industry. This resonates through the role that psychology plays in racist discourses for instance intelligence testing that was supposed to find inferiority in black participants as compared to white participants; a line of thought which continues to resurface (Reicher, 2001). The industries I refer to are petrochemical, pharmaceutical, psychotherapeutic, health and social care, psychological screening and therapy, and industry is in the service of maintaining professional expertise. The colonisation of the mind is perhaps most perfidiously present in the maintenance of the illusion that there has been a scientific fixing of psychological normalcy (the myth of normalcy), but in fact this is merely the production of a modern consumable. By this I mean that the assumption of psychological normalcy and the constructs of psychological abnormality provide a socially articulated position to demarcate abnormality. Contingent on this is an opportunity for industry, which aims to both sell products that maintain normalcy, (through screening, assessment, low-intensity psychological therapy and prophylactic medication), and to correct abnormality (diagnosis and treatment in a range of modalities such as intensive psychotherapy and tranquillising medication).

Psychiatry has staked a claim, that it has access to the impairment that sits beneath schizophrenia. Relating this to disability discourse, we can see that psychiatry has claimed the impairment that is the medical pre-requisite that institutes the state of disability. The suggested impairment endorses the subsequent disability, which in turn makes certain human experiences, such as hearing voices, amenable to various disciplinary powers such as welfare state benefits, public protection, vulnerable adult procedures, risk assessment and care planning (the myth of autonomy). However, there is not an identified site for schizophrenia in the body or brain, and if there were, presumably this would be a site in the central nervous system, making psychiatry redundant in favour of neurol-

ogy. Despite a lack of identifiable and predictable impairment, schizophrenia and its allied conditions are counted as disabilities in policies such as the DDA. Absence of a clear causality and a poor predictability from the schizophrenia construct do not prevent attempts, often wrong, and wrongful, at diagnosis, especially in the absence of a verifiable set of signs. That is, there is no objective test for the presence of pathology such as you might see in testing for a neurological disorder. Diagnosis is made on the basis of observation and self-report—the schizophrenic is co-opted into providing the evidence of their illness, while a positive diagnosis will immediately question the schizophrenic's capacity to be rational; not unlike the effect of the panopticon in enabling a discrete but totalising view of the human subject, before soliciting their own internal self-monitoring and self-censorship to aid rehabilitation. To supplement the patient's self report, the practitioner may turn on the clinical gaze, presumed to be unenculturated, unimpassioned and reliable, for an objective view of the patient's state. What follows are treatments that include potent and damaging psychotropic substances with dubious effectiveness (Bentall, 2009).

In conjunction with the coverage of disciplines and institutions, there is an apparent intellectual domination over the human experience of psychotic phenomena that is operationalized through medicine. In effect, we have a self-serving and self-perpetuating cycle, a nominalist nightmare, and paradoxically an essentialist nightmare; psychiatry exists to treat schizophrenia and schizophrenia exists because psychiatry says it does. The legitimacy of this circularity in *power/knowledge* terms allows for the constitution then segregation of a population—the insane—and their treatment and surveillance. *Power/knowledge* being a Foucauldian equation for the almost inseparable relationship between power and knowledge in that each closely constitutes the other. The tools of the trade are a range of clinical/diagnostic and administrative/legal operations most likely to include risk assessment and management. Risk management will relate most urgently to assessments of the potential for harm to others, harm to oneself and self-neglect and rarely iatrogenic risks arising from treatment and exposure to psychiatric settings; risk of stigma and social risks such as cycles of poverty. Families, where they are involved, will be acculturated into an expanded mental health practice community wherein their lived subjectivity is neutralised in favour of a surveillance role directed at the patient. This is operating within the supposition that there is a disease state that manifests in relation to environmental stressors and that early detection will reduce the toxicity of the experience. The strongest claim that can be made of such phenomena is correlative. Causality, underlying mechanisms and processes can only be theorised, at best tentatively, in a correlative relationship.

So far this account speaks clearly to Foucault's notion of *docile bodies*, that is the practices of psychiatry are about having power over the mad, subjugation, and in accruing what comes with such power, rather than necessarily being in a position to help or repair. When we come to think of diffusion I have previously cited the partial shift from asylum to community practices centred in the patient's home. I might take a moment to reflect on assimilation, bearing in mind the objections to the schizophrenia and psychosis label above. Take the most recent guidance commissioned by the UK National Institute for Clinical Excellence (NICE):

Schizophrenia is one of the terms used to describe a major psychiatric disorder (or cluster of disorders) that alters an individual's perception, thoughts, affect and behaviour. Individuals who develop schizophrenia will each have their own unique combination of symptoms and experiences, the precise pattern of which will be influenced by their particular circumstances (National Collaborating Centre for Mental Health, 2009, p.17, my emphasis).

It is here that we see the assimilation of the aforementioned objections to schizophrenia and the critical perspectives. Little in the NICE guidance may be noted as a direct response to the critical authors, Bentall and Boyle, but one may see the evidence of their perspectives; the resistance has been met, understood in terms of its convincing arguments, and an attempt is made to neutralise this through psychiatry taking it as its own. Here I am conflating the discipline of psychiatry with the interests of NICE. In effect disciplinary power in psychiatry is applied through a method of empowered description, to a disparate set of phenomena, arising out of a disparate field of contributory factors, which somehow allows for diagnosis and treatment. It should be noted that perhaps unlike any other disease or illness state NICE emphasises the unique pattern in response to idiosyncratic circumstances which covers many possibilities without entering into a shift in the *power/knowledge* of the psychiatric disciplines. In short, having constituted the body as the site of madness/psychosis in the first instance, psychiatry acts upon the body to influence the wellness of the mind, and in the second instance psychiatry notes the social and psychological substrates of mental illness, which offers the rationale and a basis for psychiatric power to diffuse

SOLUTIONS AND RECOMMENDATIONS

Reappraising the Social Model of Disability

The 'social model of disability' is the formulation largely preferred by disability activists and to large degree policy makers in Europe and the U.S. for conceptualising disability. Shakespeare (2004) explains that following earlier civil rights movements, the social model makes a separation between what otherwise has been a conflation of identity and problems. In this case it is the separation of the impairment (the dysfunction, missing element) and the social experience of disadvantage and stigma. Disability arises when the environment, including prejudicial attitudes, prevents full participation. While this conceptualisation is thought to have resulted in material gains for some disabled people its premise is problematic.

Tremain (2004) suggests that the current articulation of the social model of disability assumes a somewhat static and neutral notion of impairment. As argued earlier, if we accept that impairment is socially and culturally constituted through the application of disciplinary influence through bio-power, we may note that impairment is an effect of *power/knowledge*, and is not in fact a constant that sits outside of its social constitution. The implication of this is we have come to accept impairment as a neutral measurable and that disability follows the definition of impairment as the socially reliant experience; in fact both impairment and disability are socially constituted. For example some physical differences have been treated as an indicator of inferiority but not on the basis of disability such as skin colour. As already suggested, the disabled body is *written upon* (Foucault, 1971:1984, p.83) and so too is impairment, and thus it exists in time and in culture, and in service to the institution and discipline. Impairment is in service to the institution and discipline in the sense that without impairment, there is no need for rehabilitative and support services, so the discipline will continue to define what it needs to exist. Furthermore, while separation is given to impairment and disability, this renders the former as still under the jurisdiction of biomedical practice and interpretation. The static status of impairment does not withstand scrutiny, one needs to look only at the institutions expedient use of 'trades, workshops and factories' (Foucault, 1961:1987, p.44) and workhouses for all but the contagious, and later the use of the 'insane' as a ready workforce in wartime (Warner, 1985: 2004). In both these examples, impairment,

though a reason for segregation, did not preclude productivity when prescribed by the institution. Furthermore, despite the assimilation of the mental health field, through policy, into the construct of disability, psychiatric impairment resists fixing through anatomy or physiology — for functional mental health problems there is no discernible, originary impairment.

FUTURE RESEARCH DIRECTIONS

At a recent conference I presented a much shortened variation of this chapter and I would care to note that a question from the floor should be given a provisional response. The question was 'if we don't have the social model of disability what do we have?' I have three options available for discussion and perhaps the latter two points must always follow the first.

Firstly, we need to continue to create a space where disabled people, activists and theorists might meet to take to task the theoretical assumptions, perhaps both in the social model of disability itself, and how it has been assimilated and operationalised. The commensurate changes anticipated through the rhetoric of various governments and governing bodies have not been materialised in the quality of life and the prospects of disabled people to a great degree. However, this does not mean that there are not pockets of practice in education, given the subject of this text, that show a high degree of sophistication and responsivity to disabled learners.

Secondly, that having created a space for discussion and activism, at least part of this discussion ought to include noting the points where there is mainstream assimilation of disability discourse that undermines equality for the disabled, not unlike what I have argued happens in psychiatry and the field of mental health. Then a resistive action can be mobilised in response: we need not let our lived subjectivities be appropriated. This may be made at the level of local political representation, by demanding a presence in policy development, and through producing challenging research on the terms of disabled people.

Finally, if as I have argued, the body, impairment and disability are provisional states of knowledge as well as lived subjectivities, perhaps the time has come to re-orientate away from the politics of personality and oppression and note that at some point in most people's lives they will need assistance and support. The term 'disability' can be made descriptive less of trait and more of a state; if people are trusted to express their needs for assistance and adaptation at the point they have them, and for some this may mean much of their life, then the onus shifts from the insufficiency of the person, the medical model of disability, as originally envisaged through the social model, to the capability of society to respond. A medical authentication of impairment only serves to sow suspicion and mistrust about the deserving and the not deserving, it undermines self-definition as useful starting point in the process of gaining access, and conceals the lack of resources made available to a range of people who otherwise might have their needs met, and their lives transformed.

Given this, it would be inappropriate for me to suggest an alternative to the current use of the social model of disability. It is sufficient to mount a critique, and those people who suggest one should not critique without offering an alternative or a solution, unerringly serve the status quo, they favour the individual as being entirely responsible, and undermine the possibilities of collective response through not allowing time for discussion, and an evolution of ideas and practices.

CONCLUSION

Foucault's formulation of *docile bodies* allows for a systematic dissembling of constructions of psychological and physical normalcy. Such constructions are enacted through institutional engagement in taxonomy and culturally generated notations of difference, which camouflage themselves in a field of neutrality. Disciplinary power in the pursuit of subjugation (docility) is applied to a pathological population, which have become known as *the disabled*. In doing so perhaps physical and psychological normalcy becomes a site of blindness to disciplinary power, whereas impairment and disability, through both their construction and their lived reality, are prime sites of resistance, renegotiation and reprise. Social and economic integration and participation become the promise by which the biomedical construct of impairment is socially operated, and it has recently succeeded in extending itself into a discourse on disability activism by responding to calls for a restructuring of the means to social access. But in doing so medicine has also retained jurisdiction over what it means to be healthy and whole. To some degree the social model is flawed in two directions which activists and thinkers can act along; firstly there is a need to refocus backwards towards the assumption of impairment as a given, this would question medical jurisdiction. Secondly, thinking forwards, the social model of disability needs to be disentangled from the multitude of practices that have come to fall under its rubric; the model may be mostly sound with the problem being assimilation and practice

Given the period that Foucault works with across a number of his texts, the Europe of the seventeenth and eighteenth centuries, there is some further work that might be undertaken theorising disability as a colonised state. Definitions of disability arise from a context and history of geographical segregation, eugenics, philanthropy, treatment and rehabilitation. Race, disability and criminality have actual and thematic relations in the eighteenth century colonial Europe. For instance, constructions of the 'throwback' were seen as influential in theories of criminality, such as Lombroso's work in the late eighteenth century, which linked 'criminals, savages and apes' (Pick, 1989, p.122). Such a 'theory of atavism' equates, and then taxonomizes, delinquency, racial difference and 'anatomical difference' (Pick, 1989, p.122). In the case of disability, this colonising presence relies on a discourse of the disability triangle: negative ontology, myths of normalcy and autonomy.

We are yet to integrate the idea of the fluidity of the lived experience of impairment and disability across the lifespan (Davis, 1995) and as such, 'disabled' has become an identity with questionable merit. On the one hand disability is a rallying call for political activism and for some people there are material benefits, and on the other hand, disability is a category of insufficiency that for many people bars them from full social participation. As Davis (1995) suggests only about 15% of people are born with an impairment that makes disability a somewhat mobile and fluid experience for many people. What we do know, and what Foucault's work suggests, is that there is unlikely to be a paradigmatic shift that fundamentally changes the lived experience of disabled people. Rather, there will continue to be subjugation and domination that is resisted and negotiated with. Power will and does circulate and should disabled people come to exercise it, this may need to be in ways that are strategic and that aim to impact upon the disability triangle.

REFERENCES

Allen, B. (2009). Foucault's Nominalism. In Tremain, S. (Ed.), *Foucault and the Government of Disability*. Michigan: The University of Michigan Press.

Armstrong, D. (1994). Bodies of Knowledge/ knowledge of bodies. In Jones, C., & Porter, R. (Eds.), *Reassessing Foucault: Power, Medicine and the Body*. London: Routledge.

Bentall, R. P. (2009). *Doctoring the Mind: Why psychiatric treatments fail*. London: Penguin.

Berger, P., & Luckman, T. (1966;1991). *The Social Construction of Reality: A Treatise in the Sociology of Knowledge*. London: Penguin.

Bhabha, H. (1994). *The Location of Culture*. London: Routledge.

Boehmer, E. (2005). *Colonial and Postcolonial Literature: Migrant Metaphors*. Oxford, UK: Oxford University Press.

Boyle, M. (1990). *Schizophrenia: A Scientific Delusion*. London: Routledge.

Campbell, F. K. (2009). 'Legislating Disability: Negative Ontologies and the Government of Legal Identities'. In S. Tremain, S. (Ed.) *Foucault and the Government of Disability*. Michigan: The University of Michigan Press.

Davis, L. (1995). *Enforcing Normalcy: Disability, Deafness and the Body*. London: Verso.

Davis, L. (2006). Constructing Normalcy: The Bell Curve, the Novel, and the Invention of the Disabled Body in the Nineteenth Century. In Davis, L. (Ed.), *The Disability Studies Reader* (2nd ed.). London: Routledge.

Driver, F. (1994). Bodies in Space: Foucault's account of disciplinary power. C. Jones, & R. Porter, (Eds.). *Reassessing Foucault: Power, Medicine and the Body*. London: Routledge.

Foucault, M. (1979). *The History of Sexuality 1: the will to knowledge*. London: Penguin.

Foucault, M. (1980). Body/power. In Gordon, C. (Ed.), *Michel Foucault: Power/Knowledge- Selected Interviews and Other Writings 1972-1977*. London: Harvester Wheatsheaf.

Foucault, M. (1961, 1987). *Madness and Civilization: A History of Insanity in the Age of Reason*. London: Tavistock/Routledge.

Foucault, M. (1975:1991). *Discipline and Punish: The Birth of the Prison*. London: Penguin.

Foucault, M. (2000). Interview with Michel Foucault. In Faubion, J. D. (Ed.), *Power: essential works of Foucault 1954-1984 (Vol. 3)*. London: Penguin.

Foucault, M. (1976: 2004). *Society Must Be Defended*. London: Penguin.

Foucault, M. (1963: 2010). *The Birth of the Clinic*. London: Routledge.

Foucault, (1971;1984). 'Neitzsche, Genealogy, History' In P Rabinow,(Ed). *The Foucault Reader*. London: Penguin.

Hughes, B. (2004). Disability and the body. In Swain, J., French, S., Barnes, C., & Thomas, C. (Eds.), *Disabling barriers- Enabling Environments*. London: SAGE.

Hughs, B. (2009). What Can a Foucauldian Analysis Contribute to Disability Theory? In Tremain, S. (Ed.), *Foucault and the Government of Disability*. Michigan: The University of Michigan Press.

Lewis, B. (2006). *Moving Beyond Prozac, DSM, and the New Psychiatry: The Birth of Postpsychiatry*. Michigan: The University of Michigan Press.

National Collaborating Centre for Mental Health. (2009). *Schizophrenia Core interventions in the treatment and management of schizophrenia in primary and secondary care*. London: The British Psychological Society /The Royal College of Psychiatrists.

Office of Public Sector Information. (2005). *Disability Discrimination Act (2005)*. Accessed at http://www.opsi.gov.uk/acts/acts1995., 1431, 19th March, 2010.

Office of Public Sector Information. (2007). *Mental Health Act (Amended) (2007)* Accessed http://www.opsi.gov.uk/acts/acts2007/ukpga 1435, 19th March, 2010.

Osbourne, T. (1994). On Anti-medicine and clinical reason. In Jones, C., & Porter, R. (Eds.), *Reassessing Foucault: Power, Medicine and the Body*. London: Routledge.

Pick, D. (1989). *Faces of Degeneration: A European Disorder, c.1848-c1918*. Cambridge: Cambridge University Press. doi:10.1017/CBO9780511558573

Powell, J. (1997). *Derrida for Beginners*. Danbury: For Beginners LLC.

Read, J., & Masson, J. (2004). Genetics, eugenics and mass murder. In Read, J., Mosher, L., & Bentall, R. P. (Eds.), *Models of Madness: Psychological, Social and Biological Approaches to Schizophrenia*. Hove: Brunner Routledge. doi:10.4324/9780203420393_chapter_4

Reicher, S. (2001). Studying Psychology Studying Racism. In Augoustinos, M., & Reynolds, K. J. (Eds.), *Understanding Prejudice, Racism, and Social Conflict*. London: SAGE.

Shakespeare, T. (2004). The social model of disability. In Davis, L. (Ed.), *The Disability Studies Reader* (2nd ed.). London: Routledge.

Siebers, T. (2006). Disability in Theory: From Social Constructionism to the New Realism of the Body. In Davis, L. (Ed.), *The Disability Studies Reader* (2nd ed.). London: Routledge.

Snyder, S. L., & Mitchell, D. T. (2006). *Cultural Locations of Disability*. Chicago: The University of Chicago Press.

Tremain, S. (2006). On the Government of Disability: Foucault, Power, and the Subject of Impairment. In Davis, L. (Ed.), *The Disability Studies Reader* (2nd ed.). London: Routledge.

Tremain, S. (Ed.). (2009). *Foucault and the Government of Disability*. Michigan: The University of Michigan Press.

Warner, R. (1985: 2004). Recovery of Schizophrenia: Psychiatry and Political Economy. Hove: Brunner Routledge.

KEY TERMS AND DEFINITIONS

Activist Models of Disability: those models that arise out of political and social action taken by disabled people and their allies. These might be differentiated from models that explain, and describe disabled people from other interested views such as social science and medicine.

Autonomy: A self sufficiency in thought and action.

Biopower: A term coined by Foucault in his later works referring to the exercise of disciplinary power in, on and around the corporeal body.

Diffusion: The process by which disciplinary power extends beyond a concentrated institutional location along networks of power.

Disability: Commonly refers to the disadvantages that arises from a physical or mental impairment.

Disciplinary Power: The power this is exerted through the power/knowledge constituted within certain disciplines that are organised around privileged discourse.

Docility: The intended state of *being* following and during subjugation by disciplinary power.

Docile Bodies: This is Foucault term to describe the effect of subjugation towards docility and notes that to subjugate the person one must act upon the body for example to make someone very busy or to segregate them.

Foucauldian: A catchall term for thinking that falls into the broad area of Foucault's work and methods. Probably this will refer in some way to power and the exercise of power.

Impairment: An absence or disruption of anatomy or process in the physical or psychological functioning of the person.

Normalcy: A value that is conferred on the basis of a privileging of the statistical phenomena of the mean or average.

Medical Model of Disability: The belief arising from medicine that disability and impairment are\the same thing and are located in the individual, not in society and structures.

Social Model of Disability: The belief that impairment leads to disability because societal processes and structures are arranged in such a way that some impaired people cannot participate. This includes attitudes not just physical barriers.

Section 3
Inclusivity

Chapter 10
Support for Disabled Students in Higher Education:
A Move Towards Inclusion

John Reaney
Leeds Metropolitan University, UK

Andrea Gorra
Leeds Metropolitan University, UK

Hanim Hassan
Leeds Metropolitan University, UK

ABSTRACT

Disabled students can expect adjustments and practical support when commencing their studies at a university in the United Kingdom. Many institutions, however, strive to provide disabled students with an 'inclusive' experience, beyond that which is required legally.

In this chapter, the authors will offer an insight into how disabled students are supported at Leeds Metropolitan University in the North of England. After introducing the relevant legislative framework, they outline how this has been interpreted at Leeds Metropolitan University. The authors then discuss the challenges that a higher education institution faces when striving to be an inclusive university and argue that there is a dichotomy between the current individual funding model and inclusive university provision. Finally, they look to the future of support for disabled students and make suggestions for further research.

INTRODUCTION

In this chapter we provide an insight into how disabled students are supported at a large higher education institution in the United Kingdom (UK), using Leeds Metropolitan University as a case study. We discuss how a higher education institution the size of Leeds Metropolitan University can make adjustments for disabled students and we outline some of the adjustments currently in place as the university strives to be inclusive to all students, including those with disabilities.

The chapter begins by introducing two models of disability—the medical and social model—which

DOI: 10.4018/978-1-61350-183-2.ch010

are commonly used to theorise about disability. We then introduce a third term, inclusion, by which we mean the equitable participation of diverse students in higher education (see also HEA, 2010). Following this, we offer some background to the legislative framework relevant to the area of higher education in the context of Great Britain and Northern Ireland. The legislative landscape regarding the provision of education to disabled students has changed significantly over the past twenty years and in this chapter we draw attention to the most relevant points. This includes a critical review of the United Kingdom's current funding model.

We consider how the complex legislative framework has been interpreted by the higher education sector as well as the practical steps that have been implemented at Leeds Metropolitan University to conform to legislative requirements. We then provide some background information to the university as well as a detailed outline of the structure of the disability services provided by Leeds Metropolitan University to allow the reader to make a comparison to their own experience.

Following this we highlight a number of issues and controversies around the concept of inclusion, disabled learners' identity and the current funding model for disabled students. We discuss whether higher education institutions can be fully inclusive in terms of their provision and we consider the dichotomy between the concept of inclusion and the current individual funding model operated by the current funding bodies.

Finally, we argue that inclusivity should be built into a university's service provision which would mean that adjustments would not need to be made specifically for every disabled student's needs. But instead the university is adjusted to meet the needs of all students, including those with disabilities.

We conclude by looking to the future and offering a view to a possible solution to achieve the aim of providing an inclusive university to disabled students.

BACKGROUND

Disabled or Impaired? A Clarification of Terminology

Traditionally disabled people were described in what we now consider to be negative terms. Terms such as cripple, handicapped, deaf and dumb are just a few examples of words used to describe, and define, people with a specific disability. One of the problems with these and similar terms is that they are frequently used to define the whole person. By that we mean that a cripple was just that, the person was lost within the term and whatever else they may have become becomes irrelevant. This leads to a debate as to what do we describe people as today. In the UK the term 'impairment' has gathered favour, for example it is used by the Quality Assurance Agency (2010) and the Disability Discrimination Act (1995). Hence people may be described as having physical impairments, or perhaps sensory impairments, and this is the term we will use in this chapter. A further debate in the UK centres on the two descriptions 'person with a disability' and the alternative 'disabled person'. We use the second of these descriptions throughout this chapter, following the social model convention that a person is disabled by society therefore it is through their interactions with society that they become a disabled person. We describe this model in more detail in the next section of our chapter.

Models of Disability

There are different ways of thinking and theorising about disability and the experiences of disabled people. An acknowledgement and brief explanation of two of the main models of disability, the medical or individual model and the social model, provides a starting point for our discussion on disability. The origin of these two models lies with disabled people in the United Kingdom who began articulating their experiences from a social interpretation perspective, notably by Oliver (1983) amongst others. Conventional thinking at this time was that disabled people, as a result of their impairment, would find it difficult and challenging to perform many of what were considered to be 'normal' activities. This perspective locates disability within the individual with society's response aimed at correcting the impairment in some way or at least mediating the effects to enable the individual to function at some level (Priestley, 2003). Society therefore needs to do very little to address inequalities, it was the medical profession's responsibility to 'cure' those it could, whilst those who could not be cured but could 'fit in' to mainstream life did so. We suggest that this individual approach promotes a policy of integration, with the disabled person adjusting to and accepting that the problems that they encounter regarding inaccessible transport, services, employment and education are their problem. In terms of education this was discussed recently by Adams and Brown (2006) who pointed out that commonly education provider's responses to disabled students were that they had to 'fit in' to the traditional education model offered.

The social model offers an alternative viewpoint (Priestley, 2003). Exponents accept that an individual may have a physical, sensory or cognitive impairment but argue that it is society's response to this which creates the disability. It is the inaccessible transport, services, employment and education which is the problem, not the individual. Disability arises when society fails to accommodate difference, so it is the flight of steps which disables a wheelchair user, not the fact that they have a physical impairment and are in a wheelchair. This is the main distinction between the medical and social models; it takes away the problem from the individual and puts it firmly within the remit of society. The social model suggests that society is responsible for disabling people; and it is therefore society's responsibility to remove as far as possible the artificial barriers which it has created.

What an understanding of these two different models can do is to enable us to move beyond the binary opposites of medical and social, give us a theoretical underpinning for examining where current practice is located, and introduce a third term in to the frame. That third term is inclusion and we explain what we understand by 'inclusion' in the next section.

Inclusion and Equity

We follow the Higher Education Academy's (HEA) definition of the term 'inclusion', which means the full and equitable participation of diverse students in higher education (HEA, 2010). The key term here is equitable, for the purposes of this chapter we consider equity to mean the access, participation and experience of diverse students in higher education. The concept of equity is essentially about fairness and social justice and has both a moral and an ethical dimension (Whitehead, 1990), which includes but also goes beyond the issue of equality. The pursuit of equality is laudable, but for disabled students often what is needed is something else, a little bit extra, and that extra is equity. Taking this argument a little further we would suggest that it is through the requirement to make reasonable adjustments that equity is achieved. A student with a visual impairment, for example, is treated with equality and given equal access to the library facilities. Nevertheless they still cannot access the printed material, what is required is a reasonable adjustment to have access to the material in an alternative format. That is what we understand by the term equity.

Policy Developments in the Higher Education Sector: A UK Perspective

In this section we outline the development of the practice of supporting disabled students in higher education, with reference to early sector wide guidance. We describe ways in which professionals working to support disabled students have themselves been supported by a range of sector wide initiatives.

The practice of making adjustments and offering practical support to disabled students in the United Kingdom's higher education system began many years before the legal requirement to do so was introduced in 2001. Pockets of good practice were developing across the sector as higher education institutions were becoming more aware of the needs of their disabled students and were discovering ways to meet those needs. In Leeds Metropolitan University for example the post of Disability Co-ordinator was set up in the early 1990s and some provision was already established by that time in other higher education institutions.

An influential driver for the sector in the early days was Skill, The National Bureau for Students with Disabilities. Their Coordinator's Handbook (Skill, 1997) combined a section devoted to guidance on setting up a disability service within an education institution, with a separate section offering background information about different disabilities and the types of support which may be suitable. In pre-legislation days this handbook offered answers to many questions for early disability support practitioners. Issues around funding disabled students, funding a disability service, and guidance on arguing the case for equal access for disabled students were some of the topics covered.

Another example of the way in which the development of practice within higher education institutions was shared and good practice discussed was through a tool called Dis-Forum, an on-line discussion board hosted by the National Academic Mailing List Service, known as JISCMail (2010). This service was widely used by practitioners. The earliest archives date back to 1996 and it is still a thriving and lively source of help and inspiration for many working in the disability sector in higher education.

Although the DDA (Disability Discrimination Act 1995) largely excluded education from its remit it did place a duty on the Higher Education Funding Councils in England and Wales, and

Scotland to take account of the needs of disabled students and to require institutions funded by them to provide disability statements (Minister for Disabled People, 1996). The purpose of a disability statement was to give information about an institution's facilities for disabled students, including information about their admission arrangements. Institutions were also required to give a named contact so that disabled people could find out further details relevant to their impairment. Institutions were required to structure information under three headings: policy, current provision and planned developments (HEFCE, 1996). The first statements were required by the funding councils in January 1997, with a revision due three years later in 2000. However, the HEFCE requirement for institutions to produce Disability Statements was overtaken by the introduction of the amendments to the DDA in 2001 and the practice ceased. This amendment to the DDA was through the Special Educational Needs and Disability Act 2001 which formed Part 4 of the DDA.

Higher Education Funding Council for England

Just before the DDA 2001 (Senda, 2001) was introduced two highly influential documents were published which have had a significant impact upon disability and higher education.

In January 1999 the Higher Education Funding Council for England (HEFCE) and the Higher Education Funding Council for Wales (HEFCW) issued a joint report which set out the funding council's position on what they expected higher education institutions to offer as the base level provision for disabled students. What they meant by base level provision was that this would be the minimum level of support available at a higher education institution. This report can be seen as one of the key influential policy drivers for disabled students in higher education and its influence is still significant today.

The report was based upon research evidence gathered from the higher education sector, and whilst they found that many institutions gave effective support to individual students the findings also showed that for some students disability had been a barrier to higher education (HEFCE, 1999). They recommended that the higher education sector should be continuously striving for student-centred inclusive learning (HEFCE, 1999).

One recommendation to facilitate inclusion was for additional funding, a weighted premium which would be allocated annually to institutions based upon their numbers of disabled students. This recommendation was accepted and implemented and continues through to today. In 2009/10 HEFCE allocated a total of £13.3 million for the sector through this weighted premium funding.

Bearing in mind this 1999 report predates the 2001 DDA and legal obligations for institutions; it interestingly raises questions around institutional obligations and individual responsibilities. It does clearly value the Disabled Student Allowance (DSA) which is a grant given by the government to students who have extra costs in attending their course because of a disability. Part of the value of the DSA is seen as coming from the student having resources with which they can buy technology and services. They acknowledge that some of the, arrangements at that time needed to be improved but state that DSA is positive and enhances the role of the student as a consumer (HEFCE, 1999). More than ten years later we must acknowledge that services have improved. But if we accept that students are consumers the important bit HEFCE leave out is the possibility that a student would rather consume a holistic inclusive experience rather than be driven to buy additional services to enable them to access the product.

In 2009 HEFCE reviewed their 1999 guidance in light of legislative changes, notably the DDA, which had been introduced in 2001. Their research found that there had been significant progress in support for disabled students but there was still more work to do to move towards disability equal-ity (HEFCE, 2009). Controversially, they also found that their funding methodology remained fit for purpose and therefore they had no plans to undertake any immediate revision (HEFCE, 2009).

Quality Assurance Agency

In the UK the Quality Assurance Agency (QAA) produces codes of practice for the assurance of academic quality standards in higher education. Section 3 of the code relates to disabled students and was first published in 1999, thereby predating part 4 of the DDA. Alongside other codes section 3 was revised and the second edition published in 2010. Whilst this Code of Practice has no legal status it is a statement of good practice and hence a useful tool which higher education institutions can use to measure their performance against agreed sector wide precepts.

The QAA (2010) rightly points out that the DDA requires institutions to consider provision for disabled students as an entitlement rather than on a needs basis. They note, however, that barriers to equal opportunities still remain. The QAA section 3 is an important and valuable document in terms of guidance for institutions. If followed, the 21 precepts (QAA, 2010) will ensure an institution's approach to disability is consistently inclusive.

We noted above the influence and value of the HEFCE report, we likewise consider the QAA Code of Practice to have equal significance, especially for inclusion. Throughout the code the focus is upon helping education institutions to identify potential barriers to the participation of disabled students and hence advice on how to remove these. Strong recommendation is given to the involvement of disabled students in this process. This can be seen both in the original 1999 edition and in the later 2010 revision which follows the requirements institutions have under the Disability Equality Duty (DED) which came in to force in December 2006.

National Association of Disability Practitioners

The National Association of Disability Practitioners (NADP), formerly the National Association of Disability Officers, began life in 2000. It is a professional association for those working in the tertiary education sector involved in the management or delivery of services for disabled students. The value of a professional organization for those working in the sector is potentially large. NADP works to organize events and conferences to enable practitioners to gain valuable continuing professional development. It enables members to share issues of concern, and it acts as a voice for those with responsibility for disabled students. Recently it has been working with others to address issues raised by the funding difficulties UK students have encountered as the responsibility moves from Local Authority control to that of the Student Loans Company.

Disability Policy in Higher Education Post 2001

When the Disability Discrimination Act was formulated in 1995, post-16 education was largely excluded (Adams and Brown, 2006) until the implementation of the Special Education Needs and Disability Act (SENDA) in 2001. SENDA now forms Part IV of the DDA and from September 2002, provisions of the act affected the teaching, learning and assessment of disabled students in higher education. Fuller et. al., (2009) suggests that the introduction of Part IV of the DDA has shifted the focus of higher education institutions from concentrating their efforts on physical access barriers for disabled students towards the removal of barriers related to teaching, learning and assessment. Adams and Brown (2000) argue that this move to focus on teaching, learning and assessment is crucial as it will enable disability issues to become part of mainstream learning and

teaching, and not just lie within specialist student services units.

Through DDA, it is unlawful for UK higher education institutions to discriminate against disabled students. It is now the institution's responsibilities to make reasonable adjustment for disabled students as well as ensuring that disabled students are not being discriminated against in any way.

As a result, higher education institutions are required to plan more strategic approaches to support disabled students in their institutions. This includes identifying reasonable adjustments in their teaching, learning and assessment (DRC, 2005). Research carried out by DRC (2005) reveals that although the DDA was introduced in 1995, there remains a big gap between the life experiences of disabled people compared to non-disabled people. The DDA was amended in 2005 by the Disability Equality Duty (DED). The definition of disability was broadened and a wider range of people were covered by the duty including people with MS, HIV, non clinical mental illness or cancer. The DED gave more responsibility to the higher education institutions to make reasonable adjustments for students with disabilities and to involve disabled students in policy formulation (Madriaga, 2007), therefore widening their participation in higher education (Goode, 2007). The focus is no longer on an individual student's case but more on improving services and policies as a whole for disabled students (DRC, 2009).

Since 2001, disability policy for disabled students in higher education has gone through various phases of development, from focussing on the support for individual students in DDA 2001 to a more institutional holistic approach with the introduction of the DED in 2005. In October 2010 the Equality Act was introduced, bringing together all aspects of anti-discrimination legislation in the United Kingdom including disability. The effects of this single piece of anti-discrimination legislation have yet to be fully understood in terms of UK higher education institutions, it could be the case that disability issues are somewhat sidelined as other equality strands are put in the foreground. Disabled people and those working with them will need to ensure their voice is heard to embed those improvements in access to higher education which have already been achieved, and to drive forward the move to inclusion.

Having outlined the wider picture within the UK in terms of supporting disabled students in higher education and the policies which can seen as drivers towards full inclusion, we will now move to considering the situation in one particular institution.

SUPPORTING DISABLED STUDENTS IN HIGHER EDUCATION–DEVELOPMENT OF PRACTICE AT LEEDS METROPOLITAN UNIVERSITY

Leeds Metropolitan University is based in Yorkshire in the north of the United Kingdom. The university offers a range of undergraduate and postgraduate courses across six faculties, covering the subject areas of arts, business, computing, education, health and sport (Leeds Met, 2010). Predecessor institutions of Leeds Metropolitan University data back as far as 1824 when the Leeds Mechanics Institute was founded. The institution has provided over a century of teacher training education. In 1992 the institution became Leeds Metropolitan University and was given degree awarding power. Today the university has almost 30,000 students, 3,000 staff and 300,000 associate students through its Regional University Network of 24 partner colleges.

The university states in its assessment, learning and teaching strategy 2008-2012 (ALT, 2010) that it promotes inclusive approaches, recognizes the diversity of students and works to ensure that teaching practice is inclusive. Recruitment of disabled students is encouraged and there is a range of specialist IT equipment and software available to support disabled and dyslexic students as well as staff.

The Disability Service at Leeds Metropolitan University came in to being during the early 1990s. The post of Disability Co-ordinator was set up as the result of the funding provision offered by HEFCE. The aim of Leeds Metropolitan University Disability Services team is to deliver a responsive, flexible, fast and professional service, working within University regulations and policies to ensure that the support needs of disabled students are identified, resourced and delivered in a timely manner consistent with our obligation to make reasonable adjustments for disabled people.

To meet this aim the Disability Services Team is divided into six related but different functions. Includes the Disability Advisers, the Assessment Centre, Dyslexia Tutors, and the Senior Student Adviser. The work of these four areas is supported by an Administration team. The West Yorkshire Aim Higher Disability Co-ordinator is additionally part of the team. The team is managed by one Disability Services Manager who has responsibility for all functions of the team.

The work of the Disability Services Team encompasses the following functions:

Disability Advisers

Disability Advisers are responsible for evaluating and implementing a range of strategies which will enable individual disabled students to participate fully in their course. Funding options will be considered and the student advised to apply for DSA, where appropriate, so that a needs assessment can be undertaken. One outcome of this process is an Advice on Reasonable Adjustments document which summarises the advice, recommendations and support needs of the student, this is circulated, with the student's approval, to relevant colleagues within the University.

Assessment Centre

As well as working within university regulations the Assessment Centre and its Assessors also have to work to United Kingdom government initiated and Student Loans Company driven Quality Assurance Group frameworks. The role of the Assessors is to assess the study support needs of disabled clients, including internal and external students, and to produce reports which meet the needs of clients, funding bodies and the University. The resulting document which is a Needs Assessment Report is a key document for all stakeholders.

Disability Support Worker Scheme

The Support Worker Scheme employs and coordinates the activities of a range of non-medical helpers providing services to disabled students at the university.

Dyslexia Tutors

Dyslexia Tutors have responsibility for providing specialist tuition and guidance for dyslexic students. To do this they provide a tutorial drop-in facility where dyslexic students can ask questions and raise issues relating to their study.

Senior Student Adviser

The role of the Senior Student Adviser is to act as a point of referral for students presenting with serious personal problems, especially those arising from mental health issues. Referrals can come from either colleagues within Student Services or others from across the University. The service is delivered on a one-to-one basis and can involve the participation of external agencies as necessary. The role is also important in terms of offering guidance and support to staff throughout the University in their work with students.

Administration

The role of the Administration team is to provide administrative support to the entire Disability Services Team. Each section of the Disability Services Team collaborates and interfaces to provide a range of services to disabled students, it is the Administration team which provides the administrative services to support this work.

West Yorkshire Aim Higher Disability Co-Ordinator

The post of the Disability Coordinator is externally funded although the post holder works as part of the disability team. The role is a strategic one for Aim Higher and provides opportunities to consider raising aspirations amongst disabled school children whilst also giving attention to the key issue of transition.

The Disability Services team has an ever increasing case load of around 1700 disabled students each year. On average 60% of these students will disclose dyslexia, with the remainder spread across the other impairments. Over the past four academic years from 2005/6 to 2008/09 the average percentage of students who declared a disability to the university was 6.88% (Quality Enhancement Committee, 2010). The following table shows the number of students who disclosed to Leeds Metropolitan University as at 31 July 2010 for the academic year 2009/10.

UCAS are the organization responsible for managing applications to higher education courses in the UK. Leeds Metropolitan University uses the UCAS classification of impairments.

Several research projects and audits have taken place at the university to date to investigate the motivations, preferences and experiences of disabled students.

A recent audit (Quality Enhancement Committee, 2010) was commissioned by Leeds Metropolitan University's Disability Strategy Group with the aim of investigating the experiences of

Table 1. Number of students disclosing an impairment (academic year 2009/10)

Code	Nature of Impairment	Number (%) students with a disability
		31-07-10
02	Visual Impairment	46 (2.6)
03	Hearing Impairment	63 (3.6)
04	Wheelchair/Mobility Impairment	59 (3.3)
05	Personal Care Support	0 (0)
06	Mental Health Difficulties	88 (5.0)
07	Unseen Disability	192 (10.9)
08	Multiple Disabilities	57 (3.2)
10	Autistic Spectrum Disorder	19 (1.1)
11	Specific Learning Difficulty	1191 (67.6)
96	Disability not listed above	47 (2.7)
Total		**1762 (100)**

disabled students at the university. A range of perspectives were considered in order to establish how the day-to-day practice provision for disabled students compares to the university's aims for inclusion. Reflecting on both strategic and operational issues, good practice has been identified and recommendations have been established. An aim of the report has been to promote good practice and to work towards compliance with the DDA.

The audit used a sampling approach and investigated the views of staff and students in two faculties of the university (Sport and Health faculty). Although only a small number of students responded (12) a more substantial number of staff (40) took part. Important observations were made from the 52 responses received, for example, the Good practice demonstrated by the Disability Services Team and the flexible support available in the library areas was noted by students. However, student responses also indicated a clear need for the further enhancement of inclusive practice. For example, one conclusion was that staff need to have a greater level of awareness regarding the impact impairments have on assessment, teaching and learning. Alan Hurst's chapter in this book makes some practical suggestions on how to

support academic staff development in this area. Another conclusion of the report was that good practice in classrooms needed to be made more consistent in order for Leeds Metropolitan University to become a 'fully inclusive' university.

A survey conducted by the 'Centre for Excellence in Teaching and Learning – Active Learning in Computing' and Disability Services from 2007 identified the reasons why disabled students chose to study at Leeds Metropolitan University. The survey had a total of 53 respondents and was distributed via disability advisors and dyslexia support tutors to students studying different courses at a range of levels. Students could choose more than one answer to each question. Seventy percent of respondents stated that they choose the university for 'Choice of course.' This was followed by 'Support for disability' (43%), 'Leeds as a city' (38%) and 'close to home' (36%). 42% of respondents stated that the support for disabled students had influenced their choice of university, compared to 58% who said it had not.

This very positive response from students indicates that the university has an established reputation for taking disability support and inclusion seriously with almost half of the respondents choosing the university for the support offered to disabled students. As well as this we must consider the possibility that some of the students who did not choose this response may have chosen the university because they viewed it as sufficiently inclusive to allow them to successfully complete their studies without the additional services offered by the disability team.

However, as we will discuss in the next section the move towards inclusion is not always helped by UK government policy.

ISSUES, CONTROVERSIES, PROBLEMS

The Dichotomy Between Inclusive University Education and the Current Individual Funding Model for Disabled Students

In this section we will consider how far the higher education sector has moved towards inclusive learning for disabled students. We begin by considering one of the key aspects of the DDA, the concept of reasonable adjustment. We will argue that the DDA can be used as a valuable tool in driving forward an inclusive agenda and practice within higher education institutions. We explain the main funding method for disabled students in higher education, the DSA, and go on to raise the issue of 'disability identity'. Finally we will explain how the funding of disabled students in the UK through the DSA presents a dichotomy for institutions striving for inclusion, through its individual funding model.

The Disability Discrimination Act and Reasonable Adjustment

Central to the Disability Discrimination Act is the concept of 'reasonable adjustment' (DDA 1995, 2001, 2006). For education providers this means that they have to ensure that they take reasonable

steps to enable disabled people to access education. This relates to both physical access and access to services. The DDA does not define 'reasonable' nor specify the factors which institutions should consider when determining what is reasonable. A definition of reasonable would be decided in the law courts as they debate individual cases and make judgements on case law. What is reasonable is variable and depends upon a range of circumstances which are listed in Section 5.37 of the code:

- whether taking any particular steps would be effective in overcoming the difficulty that disabled people face in accessing the student services in question
- the type of service being provided
- the nature of the institution or service and its size and resources
- the effect of the disability on the individual disabled person or student
- the extent to which it is practicable for the education provider to take the steps
- the financial and other costs of making the adjustment
- the financial resources available to the education provider
- the availability of grants, loans and other assistance to disabled students (and only disabled students) for the purpose of enabling them to receive student services (such as Disabled Students' Allowances)
- the extent to which aids and services will otherwise be provided to disabled people or students
- health and safety requirements; and
- the relevant interests of other people including other students.

(Disability Rights Commission, 2007, p.79)

Basically, issues such as the cost of the adjustment, the interests of other students, health and safety factors and whether academic standards are maintained will all be taken into account in deciding whether an adjustment is reasonable. So far there has been very little in the way of case law to guide institutions as to what reasonable adjustments are. The Code of Practice to Part 4 (Disability Rights Commission, 2007) outlines some examples which are an excellent guide to this issue and if followed and adapted to the particular circumstances will go a long way to ensuring providers stay within the law.

Perhaps what is more important than case law is that higher education institutions have policies and procedures in place to consider individual requests from disabled students. In practice, for example at Leeds Metropolitan University, guidance on what might be reasonable adjustments for individual students will often come from the Disability Services Team. The experience of the Disability Services Team would suggest that often students who disclose a disability are not aware of what they are entitled to or what they need. The quality of the guidance and support given to students at this stage is often dependant on the skills and experience of the professionals, built up over many years of working in the sector and their work in sharing best practice, as well as keeping up to date with legal requirements and developments in inclusive education.

A key element of the experience which Disability Services Teams across the UK higher education sector have developed relates to sources of funding for disabled students. Disabled students allowances have been around for twenty years and their importance and influences is discussed in the following section.

Individual Student Funding and Disability Identity

Disabled Students' Allowances is a United Kingdom wide allowance given to individual disabled students who have proved to the satisfaction of their funding body that they have extra costs because of their disability. The extra costs which a student may encounter will arise from inacces-

sible elements of their course. DSAs have been available for disabled students in the UK since 1990. Prior to this, disabled undergraduates were eligible to receive a single payment of £765 from their Local Authority to help support their studies (Laycock, 1996). The introduction of DSA by the UK government was followed by a steady year on year expansion in the numbers of disabled students disclosing a disability. For example, in 1994/95 which is the first year data became available, the percentage of disabled undergraduates in UK institutions was 3.1%, by 2000/01 this had risen to 4.3% and by 2008/09 it was 7.4% (HESA). Whilst it would be naive to credit DSA as the sole cause of the increase it may nevertheless have been a contributing factor.

Twenty years later DSA remains the major source of funding for disabled students in UK higher education institutions. The allowances are intended to cover any extra costs a disabled student may have as a result of their disability and attendance on a course of higher education. Whilst there have been some changes over time, part time and post graduate students are now eligible for example, although international students are still excluded, the process of application remains largely unchanged.

To access DSA students have to establish their eligibility by providing evidence of their disability to their funding body who will then require them to have what is called a Needs Assessment to determine the level of support needed (Bridging the Gap, 2010). The funding they are allocated can then be used to purchase items of technology, both hardware and software, it can be used to pay for what is termed a non-medical helper (Bridging the Gap, 2010), and it can be used to cover extra costs associated with travel.

To obtain reasonable adjustments or DSA a student is required to take an important step, that of taking on an identity as a disabled student. All students entering higher education have to construct and negotiate an identity as a student, for those with an impairment this is a complex decision, (Jacklin et al., 2007). A majority of students in higher education have hidden impairments (HESA 2009) such as medical conditions, mental ill health, and by far the largest number who have dyslexia. These people may have been unaware that their impairment was considered to be a disability, they may also have been unaware that to have equal access to higher education they would have to disclose their condition and assume the identity of a disabled person.

One issue with a disability identity is the baggage of negative connotations with which the term disability is associated. A disabled person has a lack of something, they are less than normal; they are objects of pity requiring help. These and other statements and representations of disability are what Foucault would call a 'discursive formation', a collection of discourses which constitute our knowledge of the term disability (Foucault, 1979). Foucault explains that the discourses are not neutral nor value free, they are located within a series of power relations. Whilst this knowledge of disability is contested it does nevertheless present a student with a difficult choice, to be disabled and receive adjustments and funding, or to remain outside the system and possibly struggle. To be part of a minority group, or to stay safe, relatively, with the majority, that is the question that disabled students need to address.

Debates about disability identity bring into focus the contested meanings of disability which can be seen through the perspectives of the medical model of disability on the one hand and the social model on the other and are why we argue for a move to the term inclusion. This issue involves much more than a difference between a medical or social model, what is really important here is that an issue of identity becomes a major transitional issue. As all students move from college, work or home into higher education they enter a period of vulnerability, (Jacklin et al., 2007). For disabled students this is magnified by barriers they encounter, funding applications they have to negotiate, new processes to learn in order to find

the support they need. Becoming a disabled person (student) is a huge decision which some students are not comfortable with, and yet we insist upon it in order to put interventions in place which aim to minimise the effect of the impairment. This is surely an issue which demands further debate at the highest level with input from students who have had to make this decision.

SOLUTIONS AND RECOMMENDATIONS

Inclusion–Creating a Better University Experience for All

Many writers have stressed the importance of and argued the reasons why higher education providers should be following an agenda of inclusive practice for all students. Tomlinson (1996) argued for an approach which moved away from the location of the difficulty or deficit within an individual, and instead put the responsibility on the educational provider to understand and respond to the individual learner's needs and requirements. Shakespeare (1997) expanded on this and argued for an understanding of the difference between integration and inclusion. Integration implies that the individual will fit into the system whilst inclusion is the opposite with the system itself acknowledging the ways in which it excludes and creates barriers for disabled people.

Consider this, a higher education institution makes adjustments to its physical estate to ensure it is accessible to a range of people. That might for example involve the installation of a ramp or lift to ensure that people are not disabled by a flight of steps at the entrance to a building. No one asks whether someone has a disability before they are allowed to use the ramp or lift, the feature is there for anyone to use irrespective of their need, this is an example of inclusive practice. However, contrast that with a student's experience once inside a building. Students are required to disclose a disability, accept a disability identity, request adjustments and apply for additional funding to pay for some of those adjustments. Although staff may be attempting to support the students and to ensure that they get all the support they need, they must work within the current funding requirements and it is at this point that the institution can no longer be considered to be inclusive for students with a disability.

Institutions must begin to focus on the barriers which disabled students face. Research by Fuller et al., (2004) suggests that barriers exist in most areas of a student's experience of higher education. Barriers to learning, barriers to assessment and attitudinal barriers from staff were all issues raised by disabled student as part of this research. It has been suggested that the current model of provision for disabled students in higher education focuses more on assisting students to overcome the barriers they face rather than working to remove them, (Tinklin and Hall, 1999). Whilst we acknowledge the work carried out by higher education institutions to address some of the barriers identified, we must also emphasise that further work is urgently required to address the issues which are identified consistently across the sector by both staff and students alike.

We argue that the Disability Discrimination Act can be a valuable tool in driving forwards the inclusive agenda. However, a key element of the duty to make reasonable adjustments is that education providers have an anticipatory duty owed to disabled people and students at large (Code of Practice, 2007). The way in which it is intended this duty will work can be seen quite clearly in issues of physical access. It will be too late for an education provider to consider physical access when a wheelchair user presents themselves at the foot of a flight of steps. The provider should have anticipated that mobility impaired people were going to engage and interact with them and should therefore have anticipated their access needs by providing an alternative such as a ramp or lift. Equally students having requirements to

access material in a range of alternative formats should have their needs anticipated and provision for such material arranged in advance. This firmly adheres to the social model of disability, which locates disability with society's approach to a person's impairment; where the flight of steps is considered to be the disability and not the individual.

FUTURE RESEARCH DIRECTIONS

If we were to choose one single initiative which has had the most significant impact upon disability and higher education it would be DSA. The importance and value which DSA has brought to disabled students in the United Kingdom is enormous and we must acknowledge this. What we would suggest is that the time has come for a fresh look at funding for higher education institutions and their disabled students.

This is where a blurring of responsibility occurs, at the boundary between an institution's duties under the DDA which requires institutions to make reasonable adjustments and the extent to which DSA can be used by individual students to fund these adjustments. Therein lays the problem, for if a student purchases support through DSA to make the course accessible for them is a very positive step for the student but this has no impact at an institution level. For example, there is no obligation for an institution to look at its policies and practices to ensure accessibility and inclusion is in place for the next student. The question as for example put by the Scottish government in their review of DSA is whether a student has entitlement to DSA or whether their entitlement is to access higher education (The Scottish Government, 2007).

In England the Department for Education and Skills as it was then called made reference to the likelihood of confusion at the boundary of responsibility between institutions and DSA and they called for a review of the funding policy

(DfES 2006, point 84). Some tension is clearly evident within policy makers as they grapple with the issue of funding higher education institutions and their disabled students.

Conversely, the National Audit Office, whilst reporting on their investigation into the retention of students in higher education, found that students in receipt of DSA were more likely to continue on their course than those not receiving DSA (NAO, 2007). This finding may indicate a number of issues. Students with DSA may be putting more commitment in to their studies, or possibly the award of DSA enables students to purchase adjustments which really do make a difference to their participation on their course. Further work needs to be undertaken in this area to uncover the reasons behind this statistic. Nevertheless the NAO findings do point to an important benefit to those students for whom DSA is available.

The anticipatory duty by education providers to make reasonable adjustments for disabled students is part of a drive towards inclusion and can make a substantial difference to the educational experiences of disabled students. If providers take a strategic approach and continually plan for adjustments which may need to be made there is less of the need to be reactive to the needs of students. To a greater degree inclusivity becomes built into the provider's culture. It is not the case, however, that providers can anticipate the needs of all students. Disabled people are not a homogenous group; they are as diverse and different as the whole population. The DDA recognises this and acknowledges that in some cases it is appropriate to ask students to identify if they have any particular requirements and consequently what adjustments they require. This does not detract from inclusion nor signal a return to a deficit model; instead it recognises diversity and locates the solution, not the problem, within an individual. This demonstrates inclusion and equity as a result of a reasonable adjustment. Yes the DDA has its problems and its detractors, but we feel that it can be a real motivator for change within higher education. If the higher education

sector can utilise the DDA, the recent Equality Act of 2010, and the QAA Code of Practice, we are confident a real change can be brought about within UK higher education institutions.

It might also be argued that the current funding methodology, in particular the DSA, actually mediates against institutional change through its continued pursuit of an individual model. A student funded individually through DSA does nothing to enhance access and inclusion for any following students. In this chapter we have questioned whether it is right to require students to adopt a disability identity in order to be able to access their course. We acknowledge that some research, the NAO report for example, points to increased retention amongst students in receipt of DSA, but we now recommend a full review of current funding policies, and the implications of the current nature of DSA funding because as we have argued too much reliance on DSA being to the detriment of inclusion.

Therefore, we can identify as a possible future research direction the assessment of the value of DSA by comparing the experiences of disabled students in receipt of DSA and those without funding. Current research (NAO, 2007) indicates that students in receipt of DSA stay longer on their chosen university course. However, a correlation is not causation and it would be of value to further investigate this area and disabled students experiences and motivations to identify whether it is really the individual funding, DSA, which students receive or whether other factors are more prevalent.

CONCLUSION

In this chapter we have offered an insight into how disabled students are supported at Leeds Metropolitan University in the United Kingdom. We have explained the concept of an 'inclusive' university and the benefits of this concept for all stakeholders involved. After introducing the relevant legislative framework that surrounds higher education we have compared and contrasted the impact of this prevailing individual funding model with the aim of Leeds Metropolitan University to become a truly inclusive university. We have elaborated on the dichotomy that we perceived between individual funding for disabled students and the concept of the inclusive university education.

One solution for the dichotomy argued above would be to change the funding model for disabled students away from an individual funding model towards a model in which the university receives funding for its disabled students. Universities would then be required to use the funding towards measures that make the university environment, including its assessment, learning and teaching provisions more inclusive. This could for example encompass the use of a range of assessment methods, as well as the provision of inclusive teaching material for all students.

An inclusive university is one in which all students are treated with equity, where students will not be required to adopt and negotiate a disability identity. Currently students have to disclose a disability, provide evidence of the condition or impairment. There would be no requirement for disabled students to apply for external funding in order to purchase their own reasonable adjustments as it is currently required under DSA.

We must acknowledge the fact that the whole student body can benefit from the adjustments made for disabled students. For example, Leeds Metropolitan University's use of a virtual learning environment offers enormous benefits to disabled students as it delivers materials electronically at a time to suit their learning. This benefit is also widely used and appreciated by all students.

The legal requirements have and will continue to drive forward the march towards inclusive education. Much progress has already been made in the UK higher education sector but as we have argued above further work still needs to be carried out to offer all students an equitable inclusive university experience.

REFERENCES

Adams, M., & Brown, S. (2006). *Towards Inclusive Learning in Higher Education: developing curricula for disabled students. Abingdon.* Routledge.

ALT. (2010). *Assessment, Learning and Teaching Strategy 2008-12 Leeds Metropolitan University.* Retrieved July 03, 2010, from http://www.leedsmet.ac.uk/ALT_Strategy_2008-12.pdf

Bridging the gap (2010). *A guide to Disabled Students' Allowances (DSAs) in higher education.* Retrieved August 03, 2010, from http://www.direct.gov.uk/prod_consum_dg/groups/dg_digitalassets/@dg/@en/@educ/documents/digitalasset/dg_183900.pdf

CoP. (2007). *Code of Practice: Post-16 Education.* DRC, 2007. London: The Stationery Office. Retrieved August 03, 2010, from http://www.opsi.gov.uk/si/si2007/uksi_20071496_en_1.

DDA. (1995). *Disability Discrimination Act.* Retrived July 03, 2010, from http://www.opsi.gov.uk/acts/acts1995/ukpga_19950050_en_1.

DfES - Department for Education and Skills Great Britain. (2006). *Report of the Review of Higher Education Student Finance Delivery in England.* London: DfES.

DRC - Disability Rights Commission. (2005). *The Duty to Promote Disability Equality: Statutory Code of Practice.* London: DRC.

DRC - Disability Rights Commission. (2009). *Involving Disabled People.* Retrieved February 26, 2009, from http://www.dotheduty.org/. London: DRC.

Education and Skills Committee. (2006). *Clarification of inclusion policy.* London, HMSO. Retrieved August 03, 2010, from http://www.publications.parliament.uk/pa/cm200506/cmselect/cmeduski/478/47807.htm

Equality Challenge Unit. (2010). Retrieved August 03, 2010, from http://www.ecu.ac.uk/

Foucault, M. (1979). *The History of Sexuality 1: the will to knowledge*. London: Penguin.

Fuller, M., Healey, M., Bradley, A., & Hall, T. (2004). Barriers to learning: a systematic study of the experience of disabled students in one university. *Studies in Higher Education, 29*(3), 303–318. doi:10.1080/03075070410001682592

Goode, J. (2007). Managing disability: early experiences of university students with disabilitie*s. Disability & Society, 22*(1), 35–48. doi:10.1080/09687590601056204

HESA - Higher Education Statistics Agency. (2009). *Students and Qualifiers Data Tables*. Retrieved July 01, 2010, from http://www.hesa.ac.uk/index.php?option=com_datatables&Itemid=121&task=show_category&catdex=3#disab

Higher Education Academy. (2010). Retrieved July 01, 2010, from http://www.heacademy.ac.uk/

Higher Education Funding Council for England (HEFCE). (1996). Specification for Disability Statements required from Institutions. *HEFCE Ref 1996/8*. Retrieved July 01, 2010, from http://www.hefce.ac.uk/pubs/hefce/1996/c8_96.htm

Higher Education Funding Council for England (HEFCE). (2009). Outcomes of HEFCE review of its policy as it relates to disabled students. *HEFCE Ref 2009/49*. Retrieved July 01, 2010, from http://www.hefce.ac.uk/widen/sldd/allocat.asp.

Higher Education Funding Council for England (HEFCE) and the Higher Education Funding Council for Wales. (HEFCW) (1999). Guidance on base-level provision for disabled students in higher education institutions. *HEFCE Ref 99/04*. Retrieved November 18, 2010, from http://www.hefce.ac.uk/pubs/hefce/1999/99_04.htm.

Jacklin, A., Robinson, C., O'Meara, L., & Harris, A. (2007). *Improving the experiences of disabled students in higher education*. Higher Education Academy.

JISCMail. (2010). *Discussion list for disabled students and their support staff*. Retrieved July 03, 2010, from www.jiscmail.ac.uk/lists/disforum.html.

Laycock, D. (1996). *Surveys into the Operation of the Disabled Students' Allowances*. London: University of Westminster Press.

Leeds Metropolitan University. (2010). *About Leeds Metropolitan University*. Retrieved July 03, 2010, from http://www.leedsmet.ac.uk/vco/index_about.htm

Madriaga, M. (2007). Enduring disabilism: students with dyslexia and their pathways into UK higher education and beyond. *Disability & Society, 22*(4), 399–412. doi:10.1080/09687590701337942

NAO - National Audit Office. (2007). *Staying the course: the retention of students in higher education*. Retrieved July 03, 2010, from http://www.nao.org.uk/publications/0607/student_retention_in_higher_ed.aspx

Oliver, M. (1983). *Social Work and Disabled People*. Basingstoke: Macmillan.

Priestly, M. (2003). *Disability*. Cambridge, UK: Polity Press.

Quality Assurance Agency for Higher Education. second edition (2010*). Code of Practice for the Assurance of Academic Quality and Standards in Higher Education. Section 3: students with disabilities*. Gloucester: QAA.

Quality Enhancement Committee. (2010). *A report on the quality enhancement audit on the experiences of disabled students*. Academic Board Leeds Metropolitan University.

Senda Special Educational Needs and Disability Act 2001 (2001). Retrieved November 01, 2010, from http://www.legislation.gov.uk/ukpga/2001/10/contents

Shakespeare, T. (1997). Reviewing the Past, Developing the Future. *Skill Journal, 58*, 8–10.

Skill (1997). *The Coordinator's Handbook*. London, Skill: National Bureau for Students with Disabilities.

The Scottish Government. (2007). *Review of disabled students allowance project*. Retrieved August 03, 2010, from http://www.scotland.gov.uk/Resource/Doc/82254/0054157.pdf

Tinklin, T., & Hall, J. (1999). Getting round obstacles: Disabled students' experiences in higher education in Scotland. *Studies in Higher Education, 2*(24), 183–194. doi:10.1080/03075079912331379878

Tomlinson, J. (1996). *Inclusive Learning: principles and recommendations*. Coventry: The Further Education Funding Council.

Whitehead, M. (1990). *The concepts and principles Equity and Health*. Copenhagen: World Health Organisation. Retrieved August 03, 2010, from http://www.dhsspsni.gov.uk/ehr-introduction.pdf

ADDITIONAL READING

Benson, S. (1997). The Body, Health and Eating Disorders. In Woodward, K. (Ed.), *Identity and Difference*. London: Sage.

Bhabha, H. (1990). The Third Space. In Rutherford, J. (Ed.), *Identity, Community, Culture, Difference*. London: Lawrence & Wishart.

Fairclough, N. (1989). *Language and Power*. London: Longman.

Hall, S. (Ed.), *Representation*. London: Sage.

Said, E. W. (1995). *Orientalism*. London: Penguin.

Woodward, K. (1997). *Identity and Difference*. London: Sage.

KEY TERMS AND DEFINITIONS

Disabled Student: Any student coming with the definitions of disability in the Equality Act 2010 (UK).

Disabled Students' Allowance: A grant given by the UK government to higher education students who have extra costs because of their disability.

Funding Methodology: The UK government's policy on funding disabled students in higher education.

Inclusion: The full and equitable participation of all.

Medical Model: Placing the location of the disability within the disabled person.

Social Model: Places the location of disability within society's practices.

Chapter 11

Disabled Students in Higher Education:
Lessons from Establishing a Staff Disability Forum

Ian Clarke
Leeds Metropolitan University, UK

ABSTRACT

This chapter contains a case study, set in a major UK University, concerning the evolution, progress and actions resulting from establishing a staff disability forum. The discussion of the case study enables us to offer a series of recommendations for other organisations wishing to establish such a forum. The forum was initially established as a means of consulting with disabled staff but it rapidly evolved into an action group with a remit of initiating and monitoring key actions such as reviewing disability education, running major consultation events and organising a Quality Enhancement Audit, which includes the important issue of seeking to avoid unwitting discrimination in policies or procedures.

INTRODUCTION

Leeds Metropolitan University has a stated commitment to eliminate unlawful discrimination and harassment and to promote equality of opportunity and positive attitudes towards disabled people. The

DOI: 10.4018/978-1-61350-183-2.ch011

University is also committed to consult with both disabled students and staff. One practical means of doing this was to establish a 'Disability Action Group' (DAG). This was first convened in 2007 with the following agreed terms of reference: (i) To provide a safe and supportive environment in which to discuss issues relating to disability. (ii) To provide support and networking. (iii) To share best practice. (iv) To contribute to policy development across the University. (v) To contribute to staff development and awareness raising in relation to equality and diversity. (vi) To ensure the group has a credible presence for the disabled community through the membership and participation of disabled people.

The mode of operation was to meet four to six times a year and to report to the University's 'Disability Strategy Group'. This latter group provided a strategic steer for the University, with DAG undertaking projects or acting as a 'sounding board' on behalf of the Strategy Group. DAG is made open to all staff and students of the University who are willing to make a commitment to the group and the role and responsibilities of membership and encourages both disabled participants and others with a personal or research interest in disability to participate.

DAG has evolved since its inception in 2007, responding to changes in the University structure, to governance changes and to changes in equality and diversity legalisation, for example in the UK the 2010 Equality Act (ECU, 2010). This chapter will chart the progress of DAG, serving as a case study which it is believed will be of interest to other higher education institutions (HEI), and will offer a series of recommendations, based upon our experience, as to how to establish and maintain such a group. The following sections outline the key actions of the group.

The Work of the Disability Action Group: Consultation

In 2007, DAG supervised and supported a 'Garden Party', primarily to facilitate consultation with a range of disabled people in the local community, enabling feedback concerning what the University was doing well and what could be improved upon. Here we present the publicity used for the event, in the expectation that this might serve as a useful starting point for other HEIs who may be considering a similar approach:

On Friday the 31st of August 2007 the beautiful grounds of our Headingley Campus will play host to the Leeds Metropolitan University Community Garden Party. The event is being organised by our Equality & Diversity Unit and its purpose is to forge partnerships with people from the university and the wider community that are affected by disability issues. We hope that the spirit of the event will encourage informal discussions about the obstacles faced by potential students and employees due to a disability. As a dedicated equal opportunities employer and firm promoter of widening participation in education, we hope to use what we learn to feed into a review of how we recruit and support disabled staff and students.

A number of useful recommendations arose from the consultation exercise. These recommendations may provide a useful 'checklist' for other HEIs, so it is worth articulating them in full here:

1. All University departments should complete 'Equality Impact Assessments', in order to ensure that accessibility to all buildings and services is not discriminatory against people with mobility impairments.

2. Halls of residence that have suitable scope for development into accommodation that includes adequate facilities for 24 hour carers should be identified.

3. A sustainable model of accessibility for disabled university students is required. The model should use technology and innovative adaptation programmes to create an economically sound business model for inclusion of disabled students.

4. Navigation issues for disabled student access to buildings and services should be addressed.

5. Equality groups should evaluate proposals to make new buildings accessible 'beyond compliance' in terms of suitable signage in various alternative formats, induction loops and accessibility systems.

6. The University should adopt an institution-wide graphics style that uses designated symbols to guide staff and students with visual impairments and/or learning difficulties around university sites and services. These symbols should be also be used in all university signage, printed literature and digital media.

7. It is important to develop unique and innovative training programmes to increase organisational awareness of disability issues In order to create an inclusive culture within the organisation.

8. Existing community partnerships that enhance disability visibility within the institution should be built upon. New involvement projects that engage further with the disabled community will help to develop trust and assurances that the institution is fair and respectful of diversity in its workforce and student body.

9. Innovative ways to overcome the perceived barriers to higher education and employment for disabled people and their families should be researched. This could include tailored marketing plans that use accessible information resources or specific publications for the disabled community or outreach programmes into schools and community groups that raise awareness of the University's inclusive culture.

The consultation work of DAG was continued via a further major event, held in 2008, entitled 'Celebrating Diversity at Leeds Metropolitan University—Community Carnival Garden Party'. As the name suggests, the event was designed to encompass all strands of equality and diversity, which were seen as comprising disability, race, gender, sexual orientation, age and faith. This subsuming of disability concerns within a broader equality narrative is a specific example of a general trend discussed by Adams and Brown in the final chapter of this book. The event gave staff and students the opportunity to look at how strands of diversity overlap and to examine the issues associated with dual discrimination. A further aim of the event was to interact with the local community and to enable them to share their experiences and expectations concerning working or studying in a HEI.

An important outcome was a strong recommendation from local groups, especially MIND, a UK mental health charity, that greater awareness of mental health issues be promoted. In particular, the event provided impetus to deliver a stress management strategy at Leeds Metropolitan University, including a requirement for all managers and teams to complete and act upon stress risk assessment. Additionally, it resulted in a first pilot cohort of staff completing a 'Mental Health First Aid' programme and the University subscribing to the 'scheme (Mindful Employer, 2010). This scheme acknowledges that people who have mental health issues may have experienced discrimination in recruitment and selection procedures. The scheme also recognises, and seeks to counter, the phenomenon that whilst some people will acknowledge their experience of mental health issues in a frank and open way, others fear that stigma will jeopardise their chances of gaining employment. Equally important, the scheme makes it clear that, given appropriate support, the vast majority of people who have experienced mental ill health continue to work successfully, as do many with ongoing issues.

The Work of the Disability Action Group: Disability Education

As is argued in the Preface to this book, a vitally important aspect of the success or otherwise of disabled students is the ability of their teaching staff to cater for their specific needs; as with all students, their day to day educational experience in the tutorial room or lecturer theatre is of paramount importance. A similar point applies, of course, to the administrative and support staff with whom students may be working whilst at University. In the light of such considerations, an important aspect of the work of DAG is to contribute to the development of staff in terms of their disability-related practice (cf. also the chapters in this book by Hurst and by Gray et al.).

In the case of DAG, this work involves two strands. One is the publication on the University web site of 'reflections' raising disability-related issues and dilemmas. The second is designing and running formal disability education sessions for staff. Each of these strands will be considered in turn.

Reflections

Short (200 word) reflections on disability issues are published by DAG members on a weekly basis. The aim of the reflections is to raise complex and challenging issues and engage the community in debate on these issues. Here we give three exemplar reflections. We quote them here in full here partly as exemplars and partly because the issues they raise are likely to be crucial in the working and every day lives of readers of this book.

The first reflection is entitled 'Challenging prejudice and respecting needs':

At a recent Disability Action Group meeting, a student who has diabetes talked about feeling stigmatised after being verbally abused when administering insulin in public spaces. My immediate response was to feel protective towards her, to think that the university should provide safe, convenient and private places in which those who need to can 'see to' their medical needs. However, the student's view was that rather than helping, to do so would actually further stigmatise people with diabetes, by hiding the realities of their condition. The alternative to simply protecting those with particular needs is to challenge prejudice and to educate the community, so that they understand the nature of some common conditions. In the case of diabetes, doing so would involve persuading

students and staff alike that injecting insulin is neither rude nor scary, but routine and essential.

My assumption when faced with the situation described was plainly mistaken. I had thought that what were necessary was private and safe places where this student could inject insulin. In reality the issue was about equality and diversity - about the importance of respecting the needs of individuals, even when they act in ways that we don't understand.

The second reflection is entitled 'Caring for others: equality, diversity and respect for all':

If a colleague demonstrates behaviour that disturbs us, how should we respond? Care is needed in reflecting on such behaviours and our responses to them, especially when they may be underpinned by issues and experiences that we do not know about. In the above reflection I drew attention to the importance of respecting the needs of individuals, even when they act in ways that we simply don't understand. I was referring to behaviours arising from physical needs, but things can be more difficult if a person's behaviour may be underpinned by mental health issues.

If a person with a visible disability is experiencing difficulties, our immediate response may be to act so as to protect them. In the case of personal issues that manifest themselves in behaviour that disturbs us, the response will often be to distance ourselves from them, leaving them to fend for themselves rather than offering support and understanding. Universities need to be beacons in recognising and accommodating differences that result from a range of issues, however challenging. Finding ways of valuing everyone and building a culture of courtesy and respect is a real test of an organisation's commitment to equality, diversity and care for all.

The third reflection we have chosen is written by Gavin Fairburn, a Professor of Ethics and language. The reflection concerns the important issue of use of language, in particular the use of 'person first' vocabulary:

Recently I taught a class about issues in language, disability and ethics to students of rehabilitative psychology at the Catholic University of Dublin. My preference for conversational teaching is difficult to achieve with a hundred or so students whose native language is one in which I am a mere fledgling, especially in an educational culture in which, generally speaking, teachers are still expected to talk while students listen. Nonetheless, there was animated conversation - prompted, for example, by my asking which of two terms: 'disabled person' and 'person with a disability', they thought we should use. 'Is one a better, that is, a more accurate description of the physical or social facts?' I asked, 'Is one more respectful and hence ethically preferable to the other?'

The answers I received were unanimous on all counts. 'Person with a disability' they thought was preferable, because it puts the person first and recognises that their disability is just something that they have. This answer, which fits very well with my own view, contrasts markedly with the UK, where the influence of the Social Model of Disability is still so strong that 'disabled person' is for many, not only the preferred, but the expected term.

Such emails prompted response and debate, chiefly via on-line means. The third reflection above, for example, prompted debate about the social model of disability in a university context. Further, the reflection is used regularly as a starting point for our disability education sessions, for instance, to illustrate the differences between the social and the medical model of disability, which are of course widely discussed in the literature (e.g.

ODI, 2010; Bishop, 2003). We turn now to discuss these disability education sessions in more detail.

Formal Disability Education Sessions

A range of formal sessions on disability education is offered to staff, from an introductory 'Becoming Disability Confident' programme to more advanced 'Disability education' sessions. The entry level 'Becoming Disability Confident' programme posits four main aims for participants in the programme: (i)To understand and use acceptable language in relation to disability. (ii) To understand the definition of 'disability'. (iii) To understand the various models of disability. (iv) To identify areas for further development.

The next level of Disability Education examines legal and other definitions of disability, including the social and the medical models. Participants also discuss disability at work, making reasonable adjustment and sources of support. The sessions are interactive and often incorporate a short DVD produced by a student with a mental health issue who had experienced significant challenges during her University career. Her needs in terms of assessment, teaching and learning had been fully met by collaborative work with academic staff and Disability Services. This meant flexible attendance at taught sessions and the recognition that she might need 'time out' of taught sessions on occasions. However, her openness and honesty caused problems in the halls of residence that the University had provided. She disclosed her disability and was consequently ostracised by students with parents of fellow residents contacting the university to complain about her. The student's response was to produce a short DVD highlighting what it is like to see things from her perspective. This has resonance with the 'lived experience' theme discussed in the chapters in the book by Fitzgerald et al, Elzouki and Cooper and Elzouki et al.

The student wanted the DVD she had made to be used as widely as possible. It was used regularly in staff development sessions and promoted awareness that needs can be met in academic spheres but illustrated how there are often negative consequences when someone is open about their particular issues.

At the end of each session participants are asked to suggest areas for further development. For instance, Speech and Language Therapy staff were very keen to look at their responsibility regarding the work placement of students, potentially a key area for disabled students (Fell & Wray, 2006). This also led to discussion and action regarding the core competencies of these programmes. As a result, many staff also requested further updates on the work of the University's Disability Services. This in turn led to further bespoke disability education sessions incorporating the operation of Disability Services and how staff and students access this. It also helped to clarify what Disability Services do and what is expected of teaching staff.

The Work of the Disability Action Group: Student Induction Events

In tandem with Disability Services, the Student Union and the Equality and Diversity Team, DAG organises a student induction event at the start of the academic year. The event has five main aims: (i) To provide new disabled students with the opportunity to meet with the Disability Services team and other relevant university personnel, such as dyslexia tutors and library staff. (ii) To allow relevant university personnel to become acquainted earlier with new students, with a view to addressing potential issues before they become barriers. (iii) To raise students' awareness of the support that can be made available to them and provide them with literature, informal drop-in sessions and a paperwork clinic. (iv) To provide bespoke campus orientation tours that better fit particular students' needs than does the general tour. (v) To provide bespoke library tours that also concentrate on the Disability Resource Area and its assistive technologies. In parallel with

this induction event the Students' Union and the Equality and Diversity Team run a campaign to raise awareness of the rights of students under the UK Disability Discrimination Act.

The Work of the Disability Action Group: Quality Enhancement Audit

A further important role of DAG is to assist with the conduct of quality enhancement audits, which aim to examine, from a range of perspectives, the extent to which University policy is successfully operationalised in practice. It also examines the extent to which policies, eg the 'Equality Scheme' (Leeds Met, 2009) are in keeping with national level policy as laid down by the legislation, by the disability equality duty (Disability Rights Commission, 2010) and Quality Assurance Agency (QAA) precepts (QAA, 2010).

This audit process is important in that it leads to the identification and dissemination of good practice and where appropriate to recommendations to improve provision. The audits are conducted in part via focus groups with staff and students and open-ended questionnaires. The case study University is generally regarded, and rightly so, as a highly inclusive organisation, a view that was supported by respondents to the audit process. Even so, concerns were raised from the audits. Key lessons from these audits are detailed here, since they may be relevant to other HEIs. An enhancement of the role of the 'faculty disability coordinator' was required. This was followed by both formal and informal staff development in the individual faculties on the role of the faculty disability co-coordinator. The staff development programme could potentially be used for 'case conference' meetings for staff to discuss differentiation and inclusion. A range of staff development activities to promote greater staff awareness of how disabilities affect teaching, learning and assessment should be delivered (cf. the chapter by Hurst in this book). It is believed that this should be a mandatory programme for staff. A further outcome from the audit was that services and teams across the university would benefit from awareness-raising in relation to the work of Disability Services and such sessions might routinely form a part of the staff induction and be delivered as part of the disability confident sessions. In general, mechanisms for disseminating best practice are needed.

A campaign in conjunction with the Students Union to raise awareness of the needs of disabled students amongst the general student body has taken place in previous years as part of Freshers' events. These are events that are tailored towards first year students new to studying at the University. Evidence from the audit as well as recorded stories from students indicates the value of this work.

Ongoing impact assessments of teaching accommodation should be undertaken to review its fitness for purpose for disabled students.

The Work of the Disability Action Group: Impact Assessment

The Disability Action Group has a key role in delivering 'equality impact assessments'. This involves a critical review of policies and procedures to see if they unwittingly discriminate against disabled people. There is a danger that this could be seen as a bureaucratic or 'tick box' exercise. To help avoid this, DAG developed a practical, very easy to use and accessible on-line tool, and the Equality and Diversity team produced a procedure and a document to support this.

RECOMMENDATIONS

Higher education institutions in the UK have seen a marked increase in the proportion of students disclosing a disability—students known to have a disability, as a proportion of the entire student population increased from 6.5% in 2004/05 to 8% in 2008/09 (Higher Education Statistics Agency,

2009). While this is a very welcome trend, it carries implications for the disability Support workloads of academic departments, student services and Disability Services. Our experience has been that the formation and operation of a group specifically to investigate such issues on the ground, with a view to maximising the educational experience for all students, is a very beneficial approach. Given this, we conclude with some practical lessons and recommendations that we believe will be useful for other organisations, specifically higher education institutions.

1. It is imperative to begin with a clear remit to embed the group into a university wide structure that actually does something practical. It is good to start this group off as a safe and supportive environment in which to discuss issues relating to disability but it should quickly evolve into an action group with measurable outcomes.

2. Align the group's work to the strategic aims of the organisation.

3. Give the group a legal compliance role. For instance, it could have the task of overseeing, or providing a 'sounding board' for compliance with new legislation. It could also serve to highlight risks or potential for unwitting discrimination.

4. 'Equality Impact Assessments' can provide a clear focus for such a group. This is especially good if this is embedded into a governance or formal structure where the work is incorporated into amending policies or escalating issues in order to achieve compliance or great accessibility. Looking for potential unwitting discrimination in policies and procedures is a good starting point.

5. The group should contribute to staff development and awareness raising in relation to disability issues specifically and equality and diversity generally.

6. It is important to try to ensure that the group has a credible presence across and beyond the University, by high profile campaigning or consultation as appropriate.
7. Contribute to University and external publications as appropriate.
8. Use social media to attract new members and to publicise work.
9. Look for common themes across forums or action groups and be mindful that the work of forums may well overlap.
10. Campaign for and celebrate disability issues.

CONCLUSION

The Disability Action Group has evolved into a dynamic forum to represent, campaign for and raise awareness of the needs of disabled people in the university. It has become the lynchpin in the process of equality impact assessment and therefore underpins the organisational governance structure of equality and diversity. The DAG is a key player in establishing and maintaining a disability mindset in all staff when considering all aspects of policy and procedure, whether these are formal or informal. The DAG has initiated several events detailed in this chapter, such as consultations with disabled people in the local community, disability education for staff and audits that examined whether the university's 'Equality Scheme' was kept in line with national level policy. The ultimate aim is for all staff to be disability confident and for disability to be part of the unconscious competence of all staff. We believe this to be an essential aspect of working life in general and of educational communities in particular, and hope that this chapter, by sharing our experiences and recommendations, will play a part in helping other organisations achieve these goals.

REFERENCES

Bishop, J. (2003). The Internet for educating individuals with social impairments. *Journal of Computer Assisted Learning*, *19*, 546–556. doi:10.1046/j.0266-4909.2003.00057.x

Disability Rights Commission. (2010). *Disability equality duty*. Retrieved December 9, 2010 from http://www.dotheduty.org/.

ECU. (2010). *Equality Challenge Unit Briefing, May 2010: Equality Act 2010, Implications for higher education institutions*. Retrieved December 9, 2010 from http://www.leedsmet.ac.uk/rso/downloads/ECU_EqualityAct2010-Briefing.pdf.

Fell, B., & Wray, J. (2006). Supporting disabled students on placement. In Adams, M., & Brown, S. (Eds.), *Towards Inclusive Higher Learning in Higher Education – Developing Curricula for disabled students*. Abingdon. Routledge.

Higher Education Statistics Agency. (2009). *Performance Indicators 2008/09: Summary tables and charts*. Retrieved December 10, 2010, from: http://www.hesa.ac.uk/index.php?option=com_content&task=view&id=1706&Itemid=141

Leeds Met. (2009). *Leeds Metropolitan University Equality Scheme*. Retrieved December 9, 2010 from http://www.leedsmet.ac.uk/rso/downloads/LM_EqDiv_SES_Disability.pdf.

Mindful Employer. (2010). *Charter for Employers*. Retrieved December 17, 2010, from: http://www.mindfulemployer.net/charter.html

ODI. (2010). *The social model of disability*. Retrieved December 10, 2010 from: http://www.officefordisability.gov.uk/about-the-odi/the-social-model.php.

QAA. (2010). *Code of practice for the assurance of academic quality and standards in higher education*. Retrieved December 9, 2010 from http://www.admin.cam.ac.uk/univ/disability/practice/pdf/qaa.pdf.

Chapter 12
Supporting Learning in Further & Higher Education in Northern Ireland

Pauline Dowd
Belfast Metropolitan College, Northern Ireland

ABSTRACT

The research, on which this chapter is based, was undertaken to provide baseline details which would help determine the nature and level of support required by the Further and Higher Education sectors in Northern Ireland in advance of the Special Educational Needs Disability Order Northern Ireland (SENDO NI) which became law in September 2005.

The fieldwork for this research took place at the end of 2004 and the beginning of 2005 and the research addressed the following questions: How much progress has been made by the main adult education providers in Northern Ireland towards providing a whole institute strategic approach which will ensure equity of access to all services for adults with a disability? What represents best practice in both the Further and Higher Education sectors? What further action is required in the Further and Higher Education sectors to further improve the nature and level of support for people with a disability?

The findings would suggest that while much progress has been made across both sectors in terms of physical accessibility much work is still required particularly across the further education sector to establish a strategic approach to the provision of a high quality service which meets the requirements of the SEND legislation. Aspects of a high quality service were found in both sectors, however, with regard to funding, policy and planning, management of service and resourcing the Higher Education sector demonstrated best practice most often. In the research it is recognised that the sharing of best practice and the establishment and extension of structures to improve regular communication within and between sectors is crucial. Input from external specialists is also identified as vital in the drive to provide a high quality service accessible by all students with a disability who require support.

DOI: 10.4018/978-1-61350-183-2.ch012

INTRODUCTION

This chapter will outline the circumstances in which a need for research was identified, research that would outline the changing context of disability support in Northern Ireland, describe approaches to disability support in both the Further and Higher Education sectors and identify associated best practice, good practice or needs. It will set the context examining the scale of engagement and relevant funding mechanisms. It will then outline the findings of the research in the following areas:

- Policy & Planning
- Management of Service
- Physical Accessibility
- Resourcing
- Staff Development
- Referral
- Initial Needs Assessment
- Teaching and Learning
- Assessment
- Quality Assurance
- Communication and Networking

The chapter will outline the perceptions of disability support amongst staff and students and examine the evidence-based recommendations which evolved from the findings of the research. It will detail a range of significant differences between the Further and Higher Education sectors. It will analyse the findings of the research in terms of the distance to travel before either sector can confidently claim to be fully prepared for the implications of the SEND legislation. Finally the chapter will briefly outline the main sector-wide changes made in the FE sector since the research in 2005 as well as changes made at institute level at the Belfast Metropolitan College (previously Belfast Institute and Castlereagh) which was at the time of the research and remains the largest college in Northern Ireland.

BACKGROUND

As adults with disabilities are increasingly included in all aspects of mainstream society so colleges and universities in Northern Ireland have made significant progress in ensuring that students with a disability have access to the full curriculum offer of each institute as well as all related student support services. This is immediately obvious in terms of physical adjustments, the existence of a disability support unit in each establishment and statements on marketing materials. It can now reasonably be argued that this process of 'inclusion' has greatly enriched the adult education environment in our colleges, university colleges and universities for all students and staff.

The debate around the medical model of disability versus the social model is an important element of the drive for inclusion. Barbara Waters, in an address to the 'Universities UK Policy Conference' (Waters, 2002) suggests that there is now wide acceptance of the social model of disability which suggests that disabled people's restricted participation in society is no longer as a result of physical limitations or impairments but a socially created barrier, where people are disadvantaged by their environment and the policies, practices and procedures associated with the delivery of services. This model is preferred by a range of organisations across the UK including the Red Cross who explain that "instead of emphasising the disability, the social model puts the person at the forefront and emphasises dignity, independence, choice and privacy." (Red Cross, 2010) The Office of Disability Issues HM Government (ODI) which leads the UK government's vision of achieving equality for disabled people also uses and encourages others to use the social model of disability. (ODI, 2010)

Many of the improvements and adjustments made in the FE and HE sectors to date fit into the social model of disability and it is of course important that the removal of physical barriers continues and that access remains a key element of planning for all building and refurbishment projects. However, it seems reasonable to suggest that improvements in physical access must be accompanied by a strategic plan which requires each individual to take responsibility for removing barriers to inclusion at all stages of the student pathway.

A visit to any of the FE or HE institutes will demonstrate that colleges, university colleges and universities in Northern Ireland, as suggested earlier, have invested significant resources in improving access to their buildings as evidenced in new build and refurbishment programmes. Marketing materials and in-house signage also demonstrate the existence of a disability support service in each institute with systems for identifying and supporting individual students. However, the introduction of the SEND legislation in 2005 which required 'reasonable adjustment' in the classroom and beyond, presented further challenges for both the Further and Higher Education sectors.

A 'reasonable adjustment' is defined in the Disability Discrimination Act of 1995 (www.opsi. gov.uk) as 'a reasonable step taken to prevent a disabled person suffering a substantial disadvantage compared with people who are not disabled.' However, the development of a culture of inclusion where 'reasonable adjustment' is automatic or at least an option, requires the full support, commitment and enthusiasm of governing bodies, senior managers and curriculum managers as well as lecturers and support staff. This commitment must then be supported by a range of resources both at government department level and at individual institute level.

It seems useful at this point to briefly review the historical background to current policy regarding inclusion in Northern Ireland. The 1947 Education Act (NI) brought legislation to Northern Ireland similar to that in place in the UK from 1944. With this legislation local education authorities were responsible for determining the special educational needs of children with learning difficulties and children who were 'uneducable' became the re-

sponsibility of the Department of Health & Social Services. In an article entitled 'The Development of Education for Children with Special Educational Needs (NI)' (SCOTENS, 2010) it is estimated that by the 1970s more than 2,500 pupils were attending 'Special Schools' of which there were 30 and 200 pupils with less severe learning difficulties were attending units in mainstream schools. Interestingly it is also noted in this article that at this time there was no qualification required to teach in a 'Special School.'

In the Warnock Report (Warnock 1978) a new way of thinking about the area of 'special educational needs' was recommended, with the removal of offensive labels and clear recommendations that as many children as possible should be educated in mainstream schools and that provision should be put in place to facilitate this. Following legislative change in the rest of the United Kingdom, the concept of 'special education needs' was introduced into education legislation in Northern Ireland by the Education and Libraries (NI) Order 1986. All children and young people up to 19 years of age were to be identified, assessed and provided with suitable education, regardless of ability or disability.

In 1991 the UK (including Northern Ireland) adopted the United Nations Convention on the Rights of the Child. Article 23 states that the disabled child should have effective access to and receive education which encourages the fullest possible social integration and individual development. The Children (Northern Ireland) Order of 1995 increased the rights of parents to have more choice in the education and welfare of their children including in their educational provision. Throughout the 1990s and beyond, the debate about the segregation of disabled children in special schools or their inclusion in mainstream schools continued. A child may be described as 'statemented' if a statutory assessment has been carried out and a formal statement of special educational need issued, this is a legal document and determines how a child will be schooled. The

Department of Education issued figures in 2001 which indicated that the percentage of statemented children attending special schools in Northern Ireland dropped from 54% to 49% between the academic years of 1997/98 and 2000/01 and the number of statemented children attending mainstream schools increased from 27% to 33%.

The participation of students with a disability within both the FE and the HE sectors was greatly enhanced in the 1990s by the advent of the Disabled Students' Allowance (DSA) in 1990 for students on higher education designated courses and the Additional Support Fund (ASF) in 1998 for students on further education designated courses.

In 1995 the Disability Discrimination Act provided comprehensible and enforceable civil rights for disabled people. The main focus of the act was employment and access to goods and services, this covered non-teaching provision in FE and HE institutes including student services and there was a requirement for institutes to publish Disability Statements, however, adjustments in the classroom were not required.

In 1996 Professor John Tomlinson published his report on further education for learners with disabilities and/or learning difficulties (Tomlinson 1996). He identified the change needed to put the learner at the centre of provision and for programmes to be designed around the learner's needs and he defined 'inclusive learning' as 'the greatest degree of match or fit between the individual learner's requirements and the provision that is made for them.'

In 1996 The Education (NI) Order provided a legal framework for the assessment and development of special education provision. Although designed to improve the quality of provision for children with special educational needs by making it a legal responsibility to provide appropriate education, this legislation was weakened by the proviso that the provision was dependent on it not impacting adversely on other pupils in the class and also on the efficient use of resources. Schools were also required to draw up policies and arrange-

ments for pupils with special educational needs. Education and Library Boards were required to advise parents and to consult them about proposed provision, and parents were given the opportunity to appeal decisions.

Section 75 of the Northern Ireland Act (1998) required public authorities to have regard to equality of opportunity for those with disabilities and those without. The Equality Act in Northern Ireland in 2000 (Equality Act (NI) Order 2000) ensured that people with disabilities had the same rights as others in the United Kingdom and Northern Ireland.

With the introduction of the Special Educational Needs and Disability (SEND) legislation in 2005, the Disability Discrimination Act 1995 was in effect extended to cover FE and HE. 'Reasonable adjustment' was required to ensure the inclusion of all individuals across the curriculum offer and for all services provided within FE and HE throughout Northern Ireland.

This, then, is the context in which the empirical work discussed in this chapter was carried out. Up to this point there was no sector-wide research concerning educational provision for disabled people in FE and HE institutes in Northern Ireland although some important work was carried out by the Education and Training Inspectorate (Education and Training Inspectorate, 2004). A report by the ETI in the academic year 2003/04 (Education and Training Inspectorate, 2004) which examined the provision for students with a disability in FE Colleges in Northern Ireland began by reiterating the strengths identified in a previous survey carried out in the 2001/02 academic year. These strengths included:

- The good quality of much of the teaching.
- The excellent relationships between students and tutors.
- The many opportunities for social interaction.
- The well-documented outcomes for the majority of students.

However, the variation in interpreting the funding mechanism, for students with a disability, was noted as a weakness.

The 2003/04 inspection focussed on 5 of the 16 colleges and included classroom observation as well as discussions with students, college support staff, course tutors and management. In the report on this work, improvements since the previous survey two years earlier were identified and included the following:

- Use of enrolment forms to identify students' learning needs.
- The high quality of teaching.
- Better use of Individual Student Learner Agreements in relation to decisions about accreditation and career opportunities.
- Effective use of the Learning Support Fund to support participation in mainstream courses.
- The increased interest and support of college Senior Management Teams.
- The developing culture of inclusion and increased access.
- The increased enrolments of students with a disability and their success in an increasing range of accredited courses.
- In 2 colleges, the enhanced role of the Learning Support Coordinator and a whole college approach were also noted.

This report concluded that 4 significant areas remained in need of improvement these were:

- The need to develop learning support services which include all departments and facilities and which facilitate a culture of participation and inclusion for the most vulnerable students.
- The need for staff development on special education issues across the vocational areas within colleges, with part-time staff included.

- The need for the provision of courses with appropriate and nationally recognised qualifications for students with more severe learning difficulties.
- The standard of the careers advice given to students with a disability.

This report concluded:

"It is clear that there have been positive developments in the provision made for students with learning difficulties and disabilities over the past few years... There is a greater sense of inclusion and an increasing willingness on the part of colleges to meet the diverse needs of those who require support to access the available courses. As a result there is also an increasing range of accreditation and progression routes available to these students."

In 2005 there was no comparable study which examined disability support and inclusive learning in the FE and HE sectors in Northern Ireland. While it was useful to read the brief findings of the ETI from 2002 and 2004 it was immediately obvious that the scope of the research on which this chapter is based needed to be more comprehensive in terms of the institutes included and more complex in terms of methodology. The research of 2005 therefore included all of the FE and HE institutes in Northern Ireland and examined the issues discussed previously by the ETI, including teaching and learning, funding mechanisms, management of the service, staff development as well as others which needed to be in place if institutes were to meet the requirements of the forthcoming SEND legislation. It also attempted to establish how effective the providers of FE and/or HE were in ensuring that the services offered were open to, and accessible to students with a disability.

ISSUES CONTROVERSIES PROBLEMS

Methodology

The 2005 research project on which this chapter is based was led by the Research Centre of the Belfast Institute of Further & Higher Education (now Belfast Metropolitan College - BMC) and was managed by a project team on which the individual universities, the Further Education sector, the National Bureau for Students with Disabilities - SKILLNI and the Department for Employment and Learning were represented.

All 16 FE colleges and all 5 Higher Education institutes, including the University of Ulster, Queen's University Belfast, the Open University, Stranmillis University College and St Mary's University College, took part in at least one aspect of the research. Of the 21 institutes making up the FE and HE sectors in Northern Ireland 16 completed an institute questionnaire and a stratified sample of 490 staff from 20 institutes completed the staff questionnaire. Representatives from 8 governing bodies completed the governing body questionnaire. A total of 194 disabled students took part in the 31 focus groups and a further 56 disabled students completed a student survey.

The aim of the *institute questionnaire* was to collect both quantitative and qualitative data regarding the scale and nature of engagement of the FE and HE sectors with people with a disability. The institute questionnaire included the following sections:

- Background information
- Enrolments details
- Inclusive learning practice
  ○ resourcing
  ○ quality assurance
  ○ management, strategic planning and legislative requirements
  ○ staff development and training
  ○ referral and initial needs assessment
  ○ accessibility
  ○ assessment

In each institute the Learning Support Co-ordinator/Disability Support Manager took responsibility for the completion of this 16 page questionnaire. As well as qualitative information, this detailed survey required basic statistics relating to the whole student body and those students who had declared a disability.

These statistics included the following:

- part-time and full-time enrolment numbers
- age profile
- gender profile
- mode of attendance
- academic department breakdown
- staff time allocation
- nature of disability and numbers
- nature of financial support

It should be noted that some institutes were unable to source data to enable them to provide these statistics. This suggests that at this time, some institutes may have lacked the necessary information base to engage in fully effective review and forward planning.

The *staff survey* aimed to capture perceptions of both academic and support staff regarding their institute's response to students with a disability. All heads of department in each institute were invited to take part in the research and they were asked to randomly select one full-time and one part-time member of staff from their department to take part.

Each member of staff was presented with a set of statements and asked to rate them for agreement using a 0-10 scale. A précised version of the statements is as follows:

1. Fully aware of policies and procedures
2. Always briefed in advance of work with a student
3. Fully aware of initial assessment procedures

4. Appropriate facilities and equipment
5. Appropriate professional support from experts
6. Left to me to decide how best to work with student
7. Not appropriate to change our way of working
8. More should be done to support students
9. I've been involved in a particularly successful support approach

In an attempt to analyse the organisation and culture, staff were then invited to consider a series of 6 descriptors around the following 10 areas:

- organisational support
- management support
- access and support
- wider organisational support
- examination and assessment support
- teaching and learning practice
- staff development
- initial needs assessment
- funding arrangements
- system for record keeping

The descriptors ranged from weak practice to best practice and staff were asked to identify for each area, which descriptor best reflected current practice in their institute with regard to this area. Support staff were not expected to respond to any area which they felt was outside of their job role. All staff were then asked to select, from a list of 10, the 3 most significant barriers to students choosing to study at their institute. All staff were asked to indicate the most significant improvements in their institute which had facilitated the participation of disabled students, the opportunity to make additional comments was also given. As well as issuing hard copy questionnaires the research team also visited each institute at a pre-arranged time, date and venue to offer one-to-one support and assistance with the completion of the questionnaire and to clarify and provide informa-

tion where necessary. None of the HE institutes required this support.

The *Boards of Governors questionnaire* requested background information and comments on the level of priority given, at their meetings, to the issue of inclusive learning and disability support. They were also asked if the implications, for their institute, of the forthcoming SEND legislation had been considered at Board of Governors or Education Committee level.

Fifteen external experts working in this area took part in *confidential interviews*, the groups represented included:

- SKILLNI (National Bureau for Students with Disabilities)
- RNIB (Royal National Institute of Blind People)
- RNID (Royal National Institute for Deaf People)
- PHAB (A charity which encourages people of all abilities to come together on equal terms to achieve inclusion in the wider community)
- MENCAP (The Voice of Learning Disability)
- British Dyslexia Association
- Special Schools
- Belfast Education and Library Board

Findings

The findings of the research then indicate the scale of engagement and the nature of the funding mechanisms before considering the policy, planning and management of the service, resourcing, teaching, learning and assessment, quality assurance and the sharing of best practice.

In 2003 the Department of Enterprise, Trade and Investment (DETI, 2003) estimated that approximately 20.5% of people of working age and 10.5% of 18-30 year olds across Northern Ireland had a disability. The research fieldwork in 2005 indicated that between 1% and 4% of students recruited by FE colleges had a disability and approximately 2% of students recruited by HE institutes had a disability with approximately 7% of students recruited by the Open University in Northern Ireland having a disability.

While numbers of students with a disability, being supported across both sectors, are below the national rate of disability it is important to note that some students declare their disability but do not require support. Although still below this national rate of disability, the Open University in Northern Ireland had more than 3 times the rate of enrolments of students with a disability than any other HE institute. The structure and support systems offered by the Open University facilitate the involvement of people with certain disabilities as the courses are normally completed via distance learning and there is no need to regularly attend a university campus. Students can also study when they choose and make use of the range of teaching materials and avail themselves of the study support systems as required.

In the FE sector at this time, 55% of students with a disability were funded by the Additional Support Fund (ASF) or the Disabled Students' Allowance (DSA), 42% were funded by enhanced Full Time Equivalent funding – (the funding unit used by the Department for Employment and Learning) and 3% were funded from other sources. In the Higher Education sector 96% of students with a disability were funded through DSA and 4% were funded from other sources.

The introduction of the Additional Support Fund (ASF) and the Disabled Students' Allowance (DSA) gave staff in the FE sector the opportunity to work with smaller groups or on a one-to-one basis, it also enhanced the development of the provision and allowed for the involvement of more appropriately qualified staff. With regard to these financial arrangements, there was the suggestion from within this sector that funding should be extended to support 14-19 year olds on school links provision. It was also suggested that the ASF should be for additional support, not

instead of other support and that the structure of this particular funding system presented difficulties for forward planning. Other suggestions from the FE sector for improving the service were that there should be one funding formula for all, that there should be specific funding for care needs and that there should be a reduction in waiting time between enrolment and the arrival of funding. Concern was also expressed that the strict interpretation of rules by management in some colleges caused some students with undeclared mental health issues to miss out on support.

Within the HE sector it was felt that although the funding system supported a lot of work, it should be paid per capita, it was also suggested that as funding follows the student, institutes had difficulty developing a centralised bank of resources. In the HE sector there were concerns that DSA was rarely sufficient to cover support costs for profoundly deaf students. In an interview during the research fieldwork, a representative from the Royal National Institute for Deaf People (RNID) supported this view; they saw lack of funding as one of the main barriers to students with a hearing impairment beginning or completing a course. In general, external organisations expressed the view, in interviews, that the HE sector was better funded in the area of disability support than the FE sector and the former was therefore more able to provide a more comprehensive service.

To enable FE or HE institutes to comply with the underlying principle of the 2005 SEND legislation, that: 'Disabled people should have the same opportunities as non-disabled people to benefit wherever possible from whatever education or other related provision is available,' and to develop a culture of inclusive learning, institutes require the engagement of a range of senior staff across the institute. These staff must include senior management and estate management with oversight provided by the Board of Governors. One indication of the involvement of such senior staff, is the extent to which reference is made to inclusive learning/disability support in key strategic and operational documentation as well as the existence of a clear disability statement. Another indicator of the desire to create a culture of inclusion is the extent to which staff are kept informed and up-skilled to enable them to fully support inclusive practice.

Seven FE colleges stated that they made reference to provision for students with a disability in all strategic planning and operational documentation. The remaining 5 FE colleges made reference to provision in a selection of these documents. All of the HE institutes stated that they made reference to provision for disability support in strategic documents. All of the responding HE institutes and 10 of the 12 FE colleges, stated that they had a disability statement.

The disability section of the strategic plan of 7 FE and 2 HE institutes was formulated after seeking advice from disability specialists within their institute. In 2 FE colleges the strategic plan was written after taking account of formal reviews or audits of provision. One FE college and 2 HE institutes agreed that their strategic plan was formulated following specialist advice and formal reviews and audits of provision. The strategic plan of one FE college was not informed by either specialist opinion or formal reviews. Only 27% of FE staff and 35% of HE staff stated that in their view, either management ensures that good practice is adopted throughout the organisation or that their organisation gives a high priority in its future planning to the needs of students with a disability.

Of the 8 questionnaires completed by the Governing Bodies of institutes across both sectors, 7 stated that they gave disability support high priority in their Institute Development Plan, the other institute gave this moderate priority. Six Governing Bodies/Education Committees stated that 'the implications of the SEND legislation' was an item on their agenda.

Evidence from the research would indicate that prior to the introduction of the SEND legislation the senior staff and the Boards of Governors in

most FE and HE institutes had engaged with the process of disability support. However, the use of external disability experts to help inform the development of policy and planning documents is low, 16% in FE and 13.5% in HE. In terms of contributions to departmental future planning only 11% of FE staff and 18% of HE staff stated that their organisation included the disability support department in the forward planning of disability policies.

At the time of this research, representatives from external organisations expressed their views on policy and planning, the Royal National Institute of Blind People (RNIB) felt that the FE sector was not planning strategically for students with a visual impairment in mind. There was also concern expressed by MENCAP (a UK charity for people with a learning disability) regarding the Department for Employment and Learning's change in strategic direction for the FE sector with the introduction of 'FE Means Business' (DEL, 2006). They felt that this would have a negative effect on provision for students with a disability who would not always fit neatly into the implementation of a strategy which was to focus on raising skills and qualifications levels to meet local economic needs while ensuring that curriculum provision focussed on economic and workforce needs.

The nature of the line management and the level of support from management has implications for the quality and success of any service. It was the view of the Learning Support Coordinators, who expressed an opinion, that the investment in staff to manage the disability support service was some indication of the level of importance placed on the area of disability support by their Senior Management Teams.

The number of students attending the FE colleges at the time of the research including full-time, part-time and short course enrolments was higher than in the HE sector, as high as 40,000 in the biggest college—Belfast Institute of Further and Higher Education (now Belfast Metropolitan

College). Also most of the FE colleges had more than one campus and a range of out-centres, at this time the Belfast Institute had more than 100 out-centres used for evening classes. This range of learners and spread of locations presented a huge challenge to the disability support teams in terms of communicating information to all students. This was further complicated by the fact that declaration of disability in the FE sector tended to be late August or early September in the vast majority of cases as students enrol or apply for courses. Since UK courses start in September, this gave very little time to put provision in place. In addition to this, in the FE sector there is a much greater range of levels of courses and of duration than is the case in the HE sector. This again added to the complexity of ensuring that all students with specific support needs were identified and properly supported.

The circumstances in the HE sector, excluding the Open University, are different, provision is predominantly on a full-time basis although there is substantial part-time provision in two institutes. Two of the HE institutes also make use of numerous sites and out-centres and faced a similar challenge to the FE sector in terms of communication with all students. UCAS is the organisation responsible for managing applications to UK HE courses, the HE sector in Northern Ireland, has the advantage of full-time students declaring their disability on UCAS forms which facilitates the initial steps in the organisation of support as early as the February before a September start.

The status of the Learning Support Co-ordinator or day-to-day manager of disability services in HE and the time allocation afforded to this role are clear indicators of the extent of the investment in the inclusion process by these institutes. Another indicator of this commitment is the actual involvement of senior managers on an on-going basis monitoring and reviewing the service with the team and supporting changes and developments as the need arises.

All 12 FE colleges and 3 HE institutes had a designated member of staff responsible for the day-to-day management of support services for students with a disability. In 5 of the FE colleges and 3 of the HE institutes the member of staff was full-time, but in the remaining FE colleges the member of staff was employed on a part-time basis with dedicated student contact hours ranging from 0 to 20 per week. In some FE colleges, services were managed by untrained administrative staff and some academic and support staff believed that they themselves were often left to decide how best to provide assistance to students with a disability. During fieldwork interviews, senior staff at SkillNI—the Northern Ireland branch of the national bureau for students with disabilities, explained that they had previously expressed concern regarding the role and status of the Learning Support Co-ordinator in the FE sector and that these concerns had not been addressed.

In 9 of the FE colleges members of the Senior Management Team were involved in the area of disability support on a regular basis. In the other colleges the involvement of the SMT was described by staff as 'ad hoc' or in response to serious difficulties. In all 4 HE institutes at least 1 member of the Senior Management Team took an active role in the disability support service. In the HE sector the management of disability support seemed to be well organised, with adequate staff hours and with regular support and involvement from the Senior Management Team.

Physical Accessibility

Physical access to a building and to the services within that building is crucial if students with a disability are to participate on an equal footing with non-disabled students. Access issues such as lack of ramps, lifts, car parking, adapted toilets and brailled signage or documents available in a variety of formats were amongst the most significant barriers to student participation according to 21% of FE staff and 15% of HE staff. In both sectors a significant number of staff (FE 31% and HE 24%) stated that some parts of their buildings were not accessible to those with physical disabilities.

However, it became clear during institute visits undertaken as part of the research, and from input from students with a disability that major steps had been taken to improve physical accessibility. All participating institutes stated that their libraries and resource centres were suitable for access by students with a physical disability, students agreed. Eleven of the 12 FE colleges and all 4 HE institutes stated that student services facilities such as canteens and students' unions were suitable for access by students with a physical disability, again students agreed.

Nine FE colleges and 2 HE institutes stated that they had appropriate signage in buildings to facilitate students with a visual impairment. However, a representative from the RNIB believed that there had been a lack of physical change to aid the access into and around buildings for the visually impaired in both the FE and HE sectors and that an institute audit would clearly identify this problem.

Improvements in physical access over the past 2 years were noted by 75% of FE staff and 71% of HE staff. These improvements are obvious and measurable and people quite rightly expect them to be in place. In discussions with students about their most pressing needs, access issues were rarely mentioned. Their most pressing needs usually concerned teaching, learning and assessment. When students did raise access issues it was usually in relation to bad practice such as electronic doors being switched off, lifts being out of order for lengthy periods or disabled toilets being used as store rooms, all of which were very frustrating to students and rendered the numerous and often expensive adaptations pointless.

The research findings suggested that, to support the adjustments made to improve physical access, an efficient system of reviewing facilities and reporting problems also needed to be in place for optimum results. In the HE sector the system of

review seemed to be effective and completed on a regular basis involving the Director of Student Services, a senior student affairs tutor or disability services staff, estates and student affairs and a member of the disability support team. However, there was a lack of consistency within the FE sector regarding the regular review of access needs and providing effective feedback channels for the reporting of needs.

As well as being able to access a building and its facilities, students with a disability also need to be able to safely evacuate the building in an emergency. All 12 FE colleges and 2 HE institutes outlined their specific evacuation procedures for students with a disability. However, discussions during student focus groups revealed that frequently students with a disability were not aware of these procedures and some had concerns about aspects of the procedures such as being left in a designated room, alone during an emergency.

Resourcing

During interviews, experts in the field of disability agreed that to be effective and sustainable, resourcing needs to be on-going rather than intermittent and it must be systematically organised. It was also agreed that it must be reviewed regularly and that external specialists should be involved in the process. It was also suggested that suitable accommodation is a basic requirement for a quality disability support service.

In relation to accommodation, 6 of the FE colleges and 1 HE institute did not have a designated space exclusively for use by the disability support team. However most of the FE colleges and all of the HE institutes had some access to a space suitable for confidential assessment, half of the FE colleges and all of the HE institutes had some access to a space suitable for meetings and 3 FE colleges and all of the HE institutes also have some access to a space suitable for staff training. Once more, there was much more consistency of provision within the HE sector than within the FE sector.

In some FE colleges disability support staff expressed concern regarding the exclusive use of accommodation so that appointments and initial needs assessment of students sometimes had to be delayed because rooms had to be pre-booked. This delay in assessment was often substantial and also had repercussions for the process of organising the necessary support mechanisms and equipment and claiming funding; all of which affected the quality of the service to students. There were also concerns about confidentiality and the appropriateness of some rooms.

The process of identifying resource requirements is important and needs to be clear, structured and comprehensive. Some colleges stated that they identified resource requirements as part of the on-going student needs assessment process, whereas other colleges identified these requirements in relation to individual need and made general requisition requests annually. In one FE college this process was viewed by staff to be 'ad hoc' and without a budget. Once again, there was widely varying practice within the FE sector. In the HE sector 2 institutes identified resourcing requirements at regular meetings which involved a variety of staff including senior managers. The other 2 HE institutes carried out this function at annual reviews where there was an opportunity to make recommendations about expenditure.

In examining the issue of resourcing, all FE and HE institutes identified their most urgent resourcing requirements. In the FE sector these needs included more specialist staff, an adequate room allocation, assistive technology, more technical support and training for disability support staff and the availability of funding for assessment of all students requesting it. The issue of resourcing and facilities available at out-centres was also raised as was the issue of the time allocated to the Learning Support Co-ordinators within the FE sector.

In the HE sector the staff development needs of academic staff was an urgent issue as was the need for more physical resources and the need for financial support to allow institutes to meet the needs of part-time and international students who were not entitled to DSA.

Although all institutes recognised the value of multi-format materials, they also recognised that the cost of hard copy production was very high and the demand very low or non-existent. Some institutes preferred to use their limited resources for other types of support and offered one-to-one support to those who required help with written materials.

Access to the institute website and intranet is important to students throughout the student pathway in terms of accessing general information and the institute virtual learning environment (VLE) which is important for accessing materials which support the curriculum. A description of the various standards which measure accessibility can be found at www.W3.org, http://www-03.ibm.com and http://webaccessibility.jhu.edu. Seven FE and 3 HE institutes indicated that their web site conformed to standards which measured accessibility, the standards identified by the institutes included BOBBY, W3C, conformance level A, AA and AAA and BETSIE (BBC Education Text to Speech Internet Enhancer) a piece of software which creates a text version of a webpage.

Staff Development

If the disability support service is to be effective the manager and staff working in the centre will ideally need to be aware of current legislation, the results of reviews and internal procedures and the latest developments in equipment, software and enabling technology. Further, if an institute is to take inclusion and disability support seriously all academic and support staff also need to be aware of relevant legislation and institute priorities with regard to disability support and they need to be clear about their role and responsibilities. Within the FE sector 43% of academic staff and 26% of support staff claimed to have received training in the previous 2 years in relation to supporting students with disabilities, in the HE sector this figure was 34% for academic staff and 41% for support staff. A substantial 44% of staff in the FE sector claimed to be unaware of staff development opportunities or to believe that staff development relating to disability support is not a high priority in their institute, this was also the case for 29% of HE staff.

In terms of teaching and learning, students provided examples of good practice in the classroom across both sectors, students were also able to provide examples of poor practice across both sectors. During one-to-one support sessions with the research team, some lecturers in both sectors stated that they did not see disability support as their responsibility. Both of these issues – classroom practice and lecturers acknowledging their role in disability support and creating an inclusive environment - have implications for awareness raising and staff development.

Representatives from external organisations working with people with a disability expressed the view that there was a serious lack of staff development across the FE sector, particularly in relation to students with specific disabilities such as visual impairment, hearing impairment and mental health issues.

Referral

Across both sectors the majority of responding students were not aware of the support available before enrolling or applying to a course nor were they aware of pre-course information which was available.

The manner and timing of student referral has implications for the quality of service students receive at the beginning of a course. As mentioned earlier, declaration on UCAS forms the February before a September start in the HE sector allows more time to do initial assessment, make a funding

application and to organise assistive technology and enabling software, and more general support. Referral in the FE sector, however, was and remains predominantly in late August or early September. This greatly reduced the time available to put the various support mechanisms in place before the start of classes. There was also a significant number of students in the FE sector who did not declare their disability until after the course had started.

Self-referral was the most common system of referral across both sectors but it is a matter of some concern that most institutes believed that it was likely that the current referral systems failed to identify some students in need of support. In terms of support for lecturers, HE academic staff were significantly more positive than FE staff in relation to believing that they were always appropriately briefed in advance of working with students with a disability.

Initial Needs Assessment

Across both sectors 99% of staff were aware that there were initial needs assessment services available in their institute to identify students with a disability. However, there were no common standards required of staff, at the time of this research, in relation to initial needs assessment. While some institutes gave a lengthy account of their processes and the steps involved from declaration to support arrangements, other institutes struggled to do initial needs assessments mainly due to the restricted time allocation of the Learning Support Coordinator. In 1 HE institute and 1 FE college, initial assessment was carried out by people who had no experience or qualifications in the area of disability support. Evidence showed a wide variety of practice, although clearer and more robust initial assessment procedures existed in the HE sector compared to the FE sector. The initial assessment procedures experienced by some students in the FE sector were described by the students themselves, as 'ad hoc,' casual or non-existent while students in the HE sector stated that the initial assessment process started early and support was normally in place when the course began.

Teaching & Learning

Student views suggested considerable variance in the quality of on-going support available in the classroom. In both the FE and HE sectors, students gave examples of teaching which demonstrated that the staff were aware of the needs of students with a disability and endeavoured to meet their academic and personal needs at every opportunity. This included flexibility in assessment methods as well as style of teaching and addressing specific issues as they arose. The examples of good practice given by students included the distribution of notes a week in advance, the availability of lecture notes in a variety of formats and the use of individual tutorials to ensure that needs were being met. There was also evidence that in some cases course teams had been informed by the disability support team of the needs of particular students and had made appropriate adjustments consistently across the course modules.

However, students also cited examples of classroom situations which would suggest that the lecturer was either unwilling or did not have the skills or knowledge to provide equality of opportunity by meeting additional needs. Some examples were given by students of practices in the classroom that need urgent attention, for example, it was often the case in the FE sector that information regarding additional needs had not been shared with course teams, so students had to inform individual staff of their disability. In the HE sector however, 80% of students responding to the survey stated that lecturers were made aware of their disability by the institute, this was also the experience shared by HE students in focus groups. One student from the FE sector and 1 student from the HE sector declared their disability directly to teaching staff and the response

suggested that the lecturer did not consider their condition to be debilitating and therefore refused to make adjustments to meet the additional needs of the student.

These difficulties experienced by students are perhaps explained by the views of some academic staff in response to the survey, where 36.4% of FE academic staff and 26.4% of HE academic staff stated that when students with a disability were present, either teaching and learning practice was not affected or it was left entirely to the response of individual teachers.

Issues raised by dissatisfied students also included lecturers not having time to discuss the student's needs even at the outset of the course. Some students complained about the attitude of teaching staff towards them and others simply got frustrated because teaching staff refused to make reasonable adjustments. Student views would suggest that opportunities for reasonable adjustment in the classroom which require planning or a small amount of effort were missed across both sectors. It would also seem that this classroom based support lacks co-ordination in both sectors. For example, students with dyslexia in some HE institutes are given allowances for spelling and grammar in assignments while in other HE institutes students are not given this support. No FE students indicated that they were given allowances for spelling and grammar. This indicates a need for clarification of policies and practices.

In terms of adapting teaching styles to meet student needs in the HE sector, 21% of respondents indicated that they were not experiencing any adaptations to teaching styles by lecturers. Where it did occur, the most common adaptation was the availability of class notes in advance which was stated by 32% of students, while 16% of students identified the availability of class notes in multiple formats as the most important adaptation. Use of enabling technology was an important adaptation for 12% of respondents and 19% of HE students experienced some other adaptation of teaching style including the use of Power Point and video, on-line conferencing and a change to the speed of lectures. Students also appreciated the opportunity to move around the room, the availability of extra support after class, or the opportunity to receive notes missed due to absence.

Some HE students attending focus groups expressed frustration that some lecturers refused to adapt their teaching style to meet their needs. Class notes in advance was the most common request while other students who frequently made use of enabling technology in other classes would have appreciated its consistent use across their institute. Some FE students taking part in focus groups indicated that they received lecture notes in advance or in a different format and several lecturers also made themselves available after class for one-to-one support.

While some adaptation of teaching style is common in HE, there is an opportunity for development in terms of use of enabling technology, power point, video and on-line conferencing. Each of these facilities is currently available in less than one fifth of lectures based on feedback from students. The British Dyslexia Association suggested that computer based learning techniques should be more widely used to support students with dyslexia. This is further evidence that HE and FE academic staff could benefit from awareness raising which should include the importance to students of reasonable adjustments such as notes in advance and notes in a variety of formats as well as the availability of enabling technology and computer based learning techniques.

Assessment

Ideally students should have the opportunity to avail themselves of a range of adjustments in exam structure, additional time allowance for exams and flexibility in assessment methods, depending on their disability. All FE and HE institutes had special examination and assessment policies for students with a disability. However, a substantial number of students across both sectors were not offered an alternative form of assessment when they experienced difficulties and students in both sectors felt that staff tended to make adjustments to existing forms of assessment rather than making available alternative and more suitable forms of assessment. Students also experienced difficulties with adjustments for exams, there was no agreement that this was set up in an organised manner and that it was easily available in all institutes.

Quality Assurance

A clear and effective quality assurance process is another important aspect of an effective service which should develop in line with legislative change, student demand and expanding numbers. In 10 of the FE colleges a deputy director had sole or shared responsibility for quality assurance in relation to disability support, in 1 FE college there was no quality assurance process. Across the HE sector members of the Senior Management Team were involved in implementing and overseeing the quality assurance process. There were a variety of standards in use for quality assurance purposes with most institutes adopting at least one. For example, most HE institutes and most FE colleges had some process of capturing student feedback in relation to disability support services. The results of this student feedback were put to a variety of uses but there did not seem to be a consistent use of this feedback across the FE sector in particular.

Communications & Networking

There is considerable variation in relation to the extent to which individual institutes engage in external networking, including building relationships with specialist organisations and attending conferences. Although all participating institutes stated that they had contact with a range of external organisations, some external organisations indicated a desire to provide further assistance and expertise to the FE sector to help strengthen provision and they expressed concern that some FE colleges did not engage with them already. They suggested that this involvement might include advice on the purchase of software and enabling technology or involvement with training tutors as well as on-going advice and guidance.

Attendance at conferences and events dealing with issues in the area of disability support was not common or frequent although some institutes did support this activity. Some managers of disability services regularly attended the Learning Support Coordinators' Forum, a group which meets every month to discuss common issues, and they found it invaluable in terms of sharing best practice and agreeing responses to priority issues in the area of disability support which were cross-sectoral. Other disability support managers who were not working full-time, were not released to attend this forum on a regular basis, this caused a level of frustration and was identified as a missed opportunity for their institute.

SOLUTIONS & RECOMMENDATIONS

The evidence collected during this research confirmed that, in Northern Ireland, both HE and FE sectors had some distance to travel before they could confidently claim to be fully prepared for the implications of the SEND legislation. In terms of the scale of engagement a comparison of statistics provided by the Department of Enterprise, Trade and Investment (DETI) with participation rates submitted as part of the research would suggest that at the time of the research the rates of involvement, of people with a disability, in both the HE and the FE sectors, was far short of the national average. As part of the final reporting mechanism of the research project, detailed observations were fed back to individual colleges and universities and general recommendations were made. This was an attempt to help guide institutes towards the higher standards and 'reasonable adjustment' in the classroom required by the SEND legisla-

tion of 2005 to meet the needs of students with a disability.

Funding

The findings of the research strongly suggested that the funding of students with a disability should be reviewed, the main HE funding system (DSA) represents best practice and there is a need to ensure equity for all students within each sector and across sectors regardless of whether the course of study is a HE course or an FE course.

Policy & Planning

Although the majority of institutes stated that they included disability statements within high level policy and planning documents, there is still some distance to be travelled to ensure that staff are both aware of the requirements and aware of how this must be turned into practice on the ground.

The consistent level of involvement of senior management teams and governing bodies is some indication of the degree of importance given to disability support at a strategic level and is crucial as decisions regarding resourcing and staffing are also made at this level. There was evidence that some institutes used external disability experts to help inform the development of policy and planning documents and the disability support department was also included in forward planning of disability policies. The figures indicated best practice in two significant areas of consultation, in the future planning within departments and in the forward planning of disability policies. However, it was a matter of some concern that 2 FE colleges did not have a disability statement and the strategic plan of one institute was not informed by specialist opinion or formal reviews or audits of provision.

It was obvious at this time that support needed to be provided to some institutes in order to ensure that their policies and strategies fully complied with the SEND legislation. Given that this reflected the position of some of those institutes that responded to the institutional review, this also indicated a need to review all policy and strategy documents of non-respondents.

Management of Service

The research made it very clear that the demands placed on the Learning Support Co-ordinators in the FE sector were numerous, time-consuming and crucial to the success of development in this area. In the HE sector it seemed that there was often a clearly defined team with processes and procedure in place to support students with a disability. However, this was not the case in the FE sector.

Late declaration by students of disability, had and still has implications for the level and quality of support in the FE sector during the early period of each academic year. Given the complexity of FE sector provision, it might have been expected that the sector would have put clearer and more robust procedures in place than the HE sector. This did not appear to be the case.

It is a matter of particular concern that several Learning Support Co-ordinators in the FE sector carried out a lengthy list of duties supporting disabled students with only a small number of student contact hours or in their non-contact time only. It was also a concern that in 2 FE colleges the day-to-day manager was not professionally trained in the area of disability support and in some colleges senior managers did not yet see disability support as a priority and reacted to issues rather than planning strategically.

The HE sector was more consistent in providing full-time management of learning/disability support services and they were more likely to locate the management of the service within the academic community. The HE sector also had a more consistent and strategic response than the FE sector to the management of services for students with a disability.

Physical Accessibility

There was considerable evidence of significant efforts having been made to improve physical access in both the FE and HE sectors. This was reinforced by the fact that students rarely mentioned physical accessibility as their most pressing concern. However, there were areas of some institutes which remained inaccessible thus indicating a need to ensure that access remains a priority for new build and refurbishment projects. Although all institutes felt that they had made reasonable adjustment in terms of signage the RNIB expressed some reservations regarding the extent of adjustments to meet the needs of a person with sight impairment. It was suggested in the recommendations that the institutes in question would benefit from a review of these facilities with input and support from the RNIB. With regard to general physical accessibility there was again, more consistent practice in most areas within the HE sector and again an opportunity for the sharing of best practice.

As well as the improvements to access, a system of review of physical access is crucial if standards are to be maintained and improved, the review procedures must be regular and flexible and should feed into the decision making process at a high level. There is a need for FE colleges to consider how they can best incorporate this aspect of review into their overall review process. In terms of evacuation procedures, some institutes needed to address the concerns raised by students, students themselves need to be involved in agreeing a procedure which meets requirements as well as their needs.

Resourcing

In the FE sector, very basic needs, such as having designated staff and access to appropriate rooms, were identified as urgent requirements. HE sector needs were more likely to focus on qualitative improvements to existing resources or procedures.

This feedback gave a clear indication of the general position of each of the sectors in terms of preparation for and readiness for the SEND legislation and the work still required across the FE sector.

The importance of the provision of multi-format materials and access to the institute website should not be underestimated as failure at this point to provide adequate information in a format which is accessible might be the sole reason for a person not enrolling on a course. Alternative formats which do not require resources to produce hard copy or one to one contact should be investigated as should the possibility of colleges sharing software and specialised hardware across the sector to meet this need. For example, the DAISY (Digital Accessible Information System) software and reader allows people who are blind to navigate recorded and electronic documents including an institute prospectus.

In terms of website accessibility the figures indicated that 5 FE and 1 HE institute did not conform to any standard for accessibility, they also indicated that there was no common standard to which each sector was working towards, an appropriate agreed standard is crucially important.

With regard to the resourcing of the disability support service across both sectors, there is an important place in this process for annual review, where the growth and development of the service can be considered in depth as part of the annual requisition and budget allocation processes. However, this alone would limit the effectiveness of the service as the system must also be flexible enough to respond to urgent need as it is identified, whatever the time of year. This flexibility and support was evident in some institutes, but not in others particularly within the FE sector and therefore required urgent review. In summary, the research indicated a varying picture regarding resourcing across the sectors. The greatest variation in standards of resources was within the FE sector.

Staff Development

It was worrying that so many staff across both sectors were unaware of staff development opportunities or they believed that staff development relating to disability support was not given a high priority by their institute. As good practice is at least partially dependent on appropriate training it was clear that an awareness raising programme around the area of disability support was urgently required for all staff followed by specific training appropriate to job role. It was recommended that all staff should be made aware of the implications of the SEND legislation with training which clearly indicated their individual responsibilities as part of the drive to create an inclusive environment for all students. It was suggested that external disability specialists should be consulted in terms of the focus of this training and be invited to be involved in the delivery of the training.

Referral

There was a very obvious need to establish effective internal referral systems, to facilitate the referral of disabled students for support, which were understood by all staff and ensured that all staff were aware of the importance of students with a disability disclosing their disability. It was also recommended that the benefits of disclosure should be explained in student induction materials and that the availability of pre-entry guidance should be more widely publicised particularly on each institute website. There was an urgent need to ensure that an adequate staff allocation was in place during the August/September period when the majority of referrals to the disability support service in the FE sector take place. Finally, exclusive use of appropriate space for confidential disclosure was required by the disability support team, at least at these peak times. In terms of the follow up action it was also recommended that lecturers should be given as much information as is available at the earliest opportunity to enable them to fully prepare to support a student with a disability.

Initial Needs Assessment

There was evidence that all institutes had made serious efforts to create a more inclusive environment by improving initial assessment arrangements, although the progress made towards this target varied considerably amongst institutes. Staff in all institutes were aware that there was an initial needs assessment process in place for students with a disability. However, basic common standards in terms of the nature of the assessment and the minimum experience and qualifications required of those carrying out the assessment were not in place, the establishment of such standards was a priority. As suggested above, the problems caused by the late declaration of a disability by students in FE must be urgently addressed by making use of additional staff to carry out initial assessments at this very busy time, to ensure that support is in place as close to the beginning of term as is possible.

Assessment

All FE and HE institutes had arrangements in place to support students with a disability in terms of examinations and assessments, however the views of staff and students suggested a wide range of practice, albeit with examples of good practice in some institutes.

It was recommended that assessment arrangements should be coordinated and standardised within each institute and best practice shared across both sectors, this is particularly important in terms of the use of alternative forms of assessment which requires some development.

Quality Assurance

Within the FE sector there were a variety of standards being used by disability support staff to benchmark the quality of their work with disabled students, in some FE colleges there were no such standards. The capture of student feedback should have been an important aspect of the quality assurance process but this was not part of the process in all institutes. It was agreed that a common and robust set of standards for disability support work, that met the requirements of the SEND legislation, must be agreed across the sector urgently with senior managers taking responsibility for implementing and reviewing the process.

Communication and Networking

If disability support managers and staff are to keep up to date with legislative changes and developments in the area of disability support, they need to attend external conferences and events. Also, the input from external specialist agencies is invaluable and disability support managers and staff should be given the time to build relationships with these organisations; with a view to developing an effective network of external expertise that can contribute to the development of institutional expertise and improve the quality of the service they offer to students.

It was recommended that the role of the learning support forum should be secured and developed, the HE sector should also be represented on the forum and it should have an advisory role in the area of policy and best practice. This forum should also regularly consider the sharing of best practice and the review of emerging issues across both sectors, as part of its routine business. There should also be an agreed role in the forum for external agencies, to help meet the needs of the institutes, the staff and most importantly the student.

Finally it was recommended that each institute should consider establishing an advisory review group to which students and external experts are willing to contribute and this group should report annually to the Institute's Senior Management Team prior to the preparation of the each institute's annual Development Plan (IDP), if this is not done already.

In summary then, the findings of the research would suggest that at this time students with a disability were underrepresented in both the FE and HE sectors in Northern Ireland and that the funding mechanisms needed to be reviewed to ensure equality across both sectors.

The research identified clear opportunities for the sharing of best practice within each sector and across the sectors and the need for the support of government, governing bodies and senior management teams. This is particularly relevant to the issues of funding and the strategic management of the service. This support would enable disability support managers to advise on areas which require attention from policy and planning to resourcing and delivery to staff development and awareness raising. Support from the top level would also facilitate the raising of standards of practice at an operational level from referral and initial assessment to delivery and quality assurance. It would further allow staff specialising in the area of disability support to support and empower all staff both support and academic to become fully involved in the area of disability support. It would also facilitate the involvement of external disability support organisations and enable institutes to make best use of the specialist skills and knowledge available within these organisations which are often so generously offered on a voluntary basis. Only with this level of support and cooperation will it be possible to develop a culture of inclusivity with all staff and students working together with sufficient awareness, relevant knowledge, energy and confidence to ensure the full participation of all students.

FUTURE RESEARCH DIRECTIONS

Before looking to the future it seems appropriate to summarise some of the significant recent changes which have taken place within the Northern Ireland FE sector since the cross-sectoral research project. Across the Northern Ireland FE sector:

- there has been a restructure with the 16 colleges amalgamating to form 6 colleges.
- the Department for Employment and Learning (DEL) now provides the 'Additional Support Fund' a ring fenced budget for all colleges to support students not eligible for DSA.
- a Disabled Students' Allowance (DSA) user group has been set up with representation from the FE colleges, universities and the Education and Library Boards, to deal with both operational and strategic issues.
- the BRITE organisation (Beattie Resources for Inclusiveness in Technology and Education), have provided assessor training for 16 staff across all 6 colleges and the 2 universities.
- each college has a learning/disability support coordinator.
- the learning support coordinators' forum has been restructured to include representatives from DEL, all 6 colleges, the 2 universities and the agricultural colleges.

In an attempt to outline progress and development at an institute level, the Disability Support Coordinator of Belfast Metropolitan College which is the biggest FE/HE institute in Northern Ireland, was invited to summarise the main changes which she had been observed over the past 5 years. At Belfast Metropolitan College:

- details of the disability support services are now available on the college website and are regularly updated.
- details of disability support services are given on all college marketing materials.
- details of disability support services are given at all college information events.
- extensive support materials are now available to all staff on the college intranet.

- each curriculum area now has an agreed procedure for handling disclosure and sharing information.
- the Disability Support Team is now involved in the annual business planning cycle and service review.
- all staff - management, academic and support, have been required to attend SEND awareness raising sessions.
- all newly appointed staff are required to attend SEND awareness raising sessions.
- SEND updates training sessions are made available to all staff.
- the Disability Support Team provide an ongoing staff training programme in specific areas of disability which is open to all staff.
- the Disability Support Team, supported by external specialists, offer bespoke training to individual course teams on request.
- links with both statutory and voluntary external disability organisations have been strengthened.
- improvements in the Disability Support Service have been recognised by the Education & Training Inspectorate in their 2007-08 report.

In terms of future research, disability support staff in the FE sector have expressed an interest in follow up research which would build on the evidence collected in 2005. This would enable managers and staff to observe progress and action required and would be useful to the Learning Support Coordinators' Forum in terms of planning, addressing issues and sharing best practice. It would also be interesting to compare the current rates of participation and feedback from both staff and students, with those of 2005 considering the work that has been done and the perceived progress made over this period.

During the research on which this chapter is based, the RNIB expressed concern about the support of visually impaired students and suggested

an audit. Such an audit could be integrated into the research project with guidance from RNIB.

REFLECTIONS

There is considerable variation of practice amongst institutions and particularly within the FE sector and ensuring inclusion depends on the effective management and coordination of a wide range of inputs and processes. Good practice and legislative requirements call for the creation of institutional cultures where there is an over-riding duty to act in the best interests of all learners. This a need for action at all professional levels including government, institute senior management, disability support staff, lecturing and support staff.

In light of the Disability Discrimination Act, the Tomlinson Report and the SEND legislation, a wide range of measures have been put in place across both the FE and HE sectors. These measures include physical access improvements, staff awareness raising, and staff development and targeted training in a range of institutes. In other institutes links have been developed with external organisations, policies and procedures have been updated and equality committees have been established. The data gathered as part of the research suggests that there is real scope for further reflection in all institutes including those which did not take part in all aspects of the research. It would also be interesting to track progress since the findings and recommendations were fed back to individual institutes and the SEND legislation was implemented.

This chapter has reported on a large scale empirical research study of the educational support for disabled students in further and higher education, as practised in Northern Ireland. In terms of the overall themes of the book, the chapter has important things to say concerning technology, since concerns were raised about the extent of knowledge of, and compliance with, accessibility standards in, for example, the institutes' web sites. More importantly, though, the chapter gives interesting practical insights into the demanding challenge of inclusivity in a complex further and higher education system.

REFERENCES

DEL. (2006). *FE Means Business - A programme for Implementation 2006*, Retrieved October 10 2010, from www.del.gov.uk.

DETI. (2003). *Department of Enterprise, Trade & Investment; Northern Ireland Labour Force Survey (LFS) Autumn 2003*. Retrieved June 10, 2010 from www.deti.gov.uk.

Education and Training Inspectorate. (2004). *Survey of Provision for Students with Learning Difficulties and/or Disabilities (SLDD) in Colleges of Further Education in Northern Ireland*. Retrieved November 28, 2010, from http://www.etini.gov.uk/report-of-a-survey-of-provision-for-students-with-learning-difficulties-and-or-disabilities-in-colleges-of-further-education-in-northern-ireland.pdf

ODI. (2010). *The social model of disability*. Retrieved November 28 2010 from http://www.officefordisability.gov.uk/about-the-odi/the-social-model.php.

Red Cross. (2010). *The social model of disability*. Retrieved November 28, 2010 from http://www.redcross.org.uk/What-we-do/Teaching-resources/Teacher-briefings/Disability.

SCOTENS. (2010). *The Development of Education for Children with Special Educational Needs (NI)*. Retrieved November 28, 2010 from http://scotens.org/sen/articles/develofspecialedni.pdf

Tomlinson, J. (1996). *Inclusive FE, Report of the Learning Difficulties and/or Disabilities Committee, FEFC*. Retrieved November 28, 2010 from http://www.csie.org.uk/publications/tomlinson-96.pdf

Warnock, M. (1978). *The Warnock Report: Special Educational Needs: Report of the Committee of Enquiry into the Education of Handicapped Children and Young People*. London: HMSO.

Waters, B. (2002). *Inclusion, Independence and Choice*, Address to the Universities UK Policy Conference, London 2002.

Chapter 13
Modeling and Developing a Dyslexia Support System

Tim Deignan
Independent Consultant, UK

ABSTRACT

This chapter reports on an exploratory study investigating the views of dyslexic university students and their learning support staff (N=33) in relation to dyslexia support provision. The research design used an innovative blend of Q methodology, a technique to examine human subjectivity, and socio-cultural theory to model subjectivity and activity in relation to the support provided. Four different viewpoints on the issues were interpreted. The study considers the findings in relation to the potential implications for policy and practice, and suggests how the views of students, educators and other stakeholders could be used to inform and improve the future development of learning support provision at a range of levels. The methodology, findings and recommendations will be of interest and relevance to front-line educators, researchers, strategists and policy-makers.

INTRODUCTION

There is ongoing debate and discussion on how best to support university students who have been diagnosed as dyslexic. The activity of learning support practitioners in universities takes place against a changing higher education policy landscape involving various actors and forces.

DOI: 10.4018/978-1-61350-183-2.ch013

The ways in which learning support issues are perceived by stakeholders, including students, practitioners, academics and policy-makers are all factors affecting the nature and efficacy of the support provided. The study reported on here was carried out in a new university, previously a polytechnic, in the north of England. The study considered learning support from a sociocultural perspective, where the activity of dyslexic students and their university support staff is seen as taking place in a particular social and cultural context. The study sought to model this dyslexia support by using a holistic, system-based approach where the values and viewpoints of the stakeholders were given a central place in the modelling process. By modelling the activity and the subjectivity within the system, the study sought to identify tensions and related opportunities to develop learning support provision at a range of levels.

BACKGROUND

A report commissioned by the UK government, the Rose (2009) review of dyslexia and literacy difficulties, defines dyslexia as "a learning difficulty that primarily affects the skills involved in accurate and fluent word reading and spelling" (p.30). The Rose Report notes that there is generally wide acceptance of both dyslexia as an identifiable developmental difficulty and of the need to provide learning support for dyslexic students. However, there are some who question the rationale of this argument, holding the view that 'dyslexia' as a concept lacks validity. For example, Professor Julian Elliot of Durham University, speaking about dyslexia on a Channel 4 (2005) TV program entitled 'The Dyslexia Myth', commented, 'I can't define it'. Other academics interviewed on the program have argued that it is not helpful to isolate a special group of poor readers and to identify them as dyslexic. They do not deny the difficulties experienced by individuals classified as dyslexic, but challenge the validity of dyslexia as a construct to explain and remediate these difficulties. In oral evidence to the UK House of Commons, Elliot has argued that

there is no test in neuroscience to identify an individual child who you might want to describe as dyslexic or whatever. These are pipedreams... Then there is a whole range of symptoms and like a horoscope, if you look at a horoscope whichever one you look at you will find you fit... The

idea that you can sub-divide the population of people struggling to learn to read into dyslexics and non-dyslexics is untenable... the term itself is conceptually flawed. (Elliot, 2009)

The argument against identifying and supporting dyslexic learners relates to issues of equality and also of cost-effectiveness, that funding should be diverted away from so-called 'dyslexics' to instead provide interventions for all learners with poor reading skills. However, dyslexia organizations, such as the Dyslexia Institute and the British Dyslexia Association, have criticized the 'dyslexia myth' argument for being too narrowly focused and for not recognising that dyslexia is not associated solely with reading difficulties. These criticisms notwithstanding, similar arguments in relation to validity and cost-effectiveness are played out in the higher education sector. David Lammy (2009), then UK Minister for Higher Education and Intellectual Property, put the annual cost of student support in higher education at £5 billion. Disabled Student Allowances (DSAs) make up a significant part of this support cost. Skill (2009), the National Bureau for Students with Disabilities, describe how the DSA was "first introduced by the Department of Education and Employment (DfEE) in 1987, and formalized as DSA in 1991" (p.30). The then UK Department for Innovation, Universities and Skills (DIUS) (2009) [now Business, Innovation and Skills (BIS)] stated that, "overall, 49% of students who report a disability are also in receipt of DSA". According to the National Association of Disability Practitioners (NADP, 2009a), "the vast majority of DSAs applicants are dyslexic" (p.12).

NADP (2009a) note that the regulations governing DSAs "do not explicitly define disability" (p.11), although "overall each year, students with Specific Learning Differences (SpLDs such as dyslexia and dyspraxia) typically form the largest sub-group of disabled students and people with the 'unseen' chronic medical conditions" (p.2). Critics of the DSA support system have included at least one member of the 2009 Parliamentary Labour Party; Graham Stringer (2009), Labour Member of Parliament for Manchester Blackley, commented that, "35,500 students are receiving disability allowances for dyslexia. Last year this cost £78.4 million…it is time that the dyslexia industry was killed off". Stringer cited sceptical comments by Elliot to support his own criticisms of dyslexia support funding. Clearly, while there is broad professional consensus on both the concept of dyslexia and the funding of learning support for students diagnosed as dyslexic (e.g. Rose, 2009), these remain contested issues.

In relation to dyslexia as a concept, there are indeed scores of definitions of the term 'dyslexia' (e.g. Rice & Brooks, 2004, pp.133-146). However, this proliferation can in part be understood by considering the different perspectives of those behind the definitions. For example, Nicolson (2002) describes the dyslexia community as an "ecosystem", with different conceptions of dyslexia, and different definitions, related to the sometimes conflicting roles and interests of its members. In relation to learning support for university students, the Report of the National Working Party on Dyslexia in Higher Education (1999), cited in a DIUS (2007) guidance document, identifies two forms of dyslexia:

1. **Developmental Dyslexia:** a problem with particular aspects of learning despite adequate intelligence and general learning skills. Developmental dyslexia is the more common form of dyslexia. This type is usually inherited and neurologically based; and
2. **Acquired Dyslexia**: is characterized by a loss of literacy skills as a result of a neurological trauma, illness or brain disease. (DIUS, 2007)

The DIUS (ibid.) guidance notes that, "dyslexia is a variable condition and not all students with dyslexia will display the same difficulties or characteristics". The document describes and

explains the purpose of study skills support for dyslexic university students as follows:

Study skills tuition to help with basic study skills to manage dyslexic thinking styles and difficulties within higher education, language and numeracy. Individual study support sessions may be required because generalized advice offered by a department may not take into account different learning skills…the aim of such support should be to impart generic skills which, together with any specialist equipment that has been provided, will allow the student to become an independent learner. Therefore, any study skills support recommended should be tailored to the student's individual needs, setting out clear goals and timescales for achieving those goals. (DIUS, 2007)

Commentators (e.g. Calder, 2001; ADSHE, 2009) have stressed the importance of developing the study skills of dyslexic learners to help them access the curriculum. Students with dyslexia often have weak organisational skills and have difficulty checking their work (e.g. Fawcett, 2002). Ott (1997) lists reading, writing, proof-reading, note-taking, time management, and examination tactics among the study skills required in higher education. Pumfrey & Reason (1997) note the importance of emotional and social factors in supporting dyslexic learners and argue that practitioners should "take account of the views of the learner not only with regard to initial feelings but also in relation to ongoing methods of intervention" (p.65). Rice & Brooks (2004) argue that "no generalization is valid for each and every member of the population of adults who have been identified [or who have identified themselves] as 'dyslexic'" (p.40). Tailoring provision to the needs of the individual student is therefore considered by practitioners to be an important part of learning support for dyslexic students (e.g. ADSHE, 2009).

Study skills tuition for dyslexic students is funded through the DSA (DfES, 2005). From their introduction in the early 1990s until the end of

2008, most DSA applications were processed by the individual student's Local Education Authority (LEA), since renamed as Local Authorities (LAs). A transfer of responsibility occurred with effect from the 2009-2010 funding cycle, when the Student Loan Company (SLC), also known as Student Finance England (SFE), took over the administration of the DSA application process for all Year 1 undergraduate and postgraduate students (NADP, 2009a:p3). In a letter of guidance to the sector, the SLC (2008) stated, that "for the majority of customers [i.e. students] 10 hours study skills should be sufficient to meet their needs". No evidence was provided in the guidance letter to justify this notional ten hour figure. The SLC advised that while there was no official ceiling on support in individual cases, only ten hours was deemed sufficient for the majority of students to become independent. Support tutors were expected to develop dyslexic students' study skills against specified learning outcomes (e.g. research, composition, proof-reading, note-taking, time management, and examinations). Requests for additional hours, the guidance explained, would only be considered by the SLC if supported by evidence such as individual learning plans and reviews of student learning outcomes. It was noted in the letter of guidance that any request for further hours had to meet internal criteria set by the SLC. These proposed changes, along with other aspects of the SLC's service to disabled students, drew considerable criticism from dyslexia organizations.

The study reported on here, looking at the views of dyslexic university students and their support staff in relation to learning support, was conducted at the time of transition described above, shortly before responsibility for the administration of DSAs was passed from LAs to SFE. The study was carried out at a new university in the north of England. There was no specific institutional policy at the time relating to dyslexia support other than the university's Equal Opportunities Statement, which was general in nature. However dyslexia support tutors were expected to follow the university's guidelines on their role, which included, for example, the need to take into account the student support recommendations made in educational psychologists' reports. There was no subject syllabus, as such, that dyslexia support tutors were expected to teach as it was recognized that dyslexic students have individual profiles of strengths and weaknesses, and the level and content of their main programs of study also varied widely. In relation to individuals and context, Oliver (1992), a figure associated with the development of the 'social model' theory of disability, has argued that "disability cannot be abstracted from the social world which produces it" (p.101). In this regard, the curriculum in relation to learning support can be conceived of as broad and encompassing the various activities undertaken, and the relationships between staff and students in their learning communities (Cornbleth, 1990).

METHODS, FINDINGS AND DISCUSSION

Conceptual Framework and Methodology

Consistent with a social model approach to dyslexia and learning support, the conceptual framework for the study reported on here treated teaching and learning as activity that is socially situated (Engeström, 1999) and explored the perspectives of the study participants in relation to their communities of practice (Lave & Wenger, 1991; Wenger, 1998). Guile & Young (1998, p.185) comment that both Engeström and Wenger regard learning as a fundamentally social and reflexive process. Roth & Lee (2006) note that the concept of "communities of practice" originates from "a cultural-historical theory of activity, or, as Lev Vygotsky called it, in a 'concrete human [social] psychology'" (p.27). "Socioculturalists argue that the individual learner cannot be meaningfully separated from the social and cultural context of learning" (Sawyer, 2002, p.283). Taking a socio-cultural approach, the present study used an activity theory framework (Engeström, 1993), which is grounded in the notion that human beings use tools to work on an object, or problem space, in order to achieve a desired outcome.

Stetsenko (2005), in relation to activity theory, comments that "Cultural-Historical Activity Theory (CHAT) is one among a number of approaches that move away from the individualist and mentalist notions of human development, toward viewing it as embedded within sociocultural contexts and intrinsically interwoven with them" (p.70). In this approach, development, activity, and context are inseparable. "Contexts", as defined by Engeström (1993), "are activity systems. An activity system integrates the subject, the object, and the instruments (material tools as well as signs and symbols) into a unified whole" (p.67). With regard to such instruments, Engeström (1999) notes the central role of mediation in activity theory and cites Wartofsky's (1979, p.205) view that, "the *artifact* is to cultural evolution what the *gene* is to biological evolution" (p.29).

The concept of activity highlights the complex interactions and relationships between individual and community. Engeström (2000) comments that, "a collective activity system is driven by deeply communal motives. The motive is embedded in the object of the activity" (p.964). Foot (2002) suggests that an activity system's object can be identified through the varying perspectives of multiple participants and that this can be achieved "by 'catching' facets of the object as it is conceived of and engaged by the participants in an activity system through empirical research" (p.132). Engeström (1993) suggests that the object in activity theory functions as the "problem space". For example, the problem space in the present study may be viewed from the perspective of the university, where dyslexia support may be seen as a tool to address students' needs as learners and to provide equality of opportunity. Students

with dyslexia can thus be seen as the 'object' of dyslexia support activity. A student with dyslexia carries the cultural motive of tackling the issue of equal opportunities, as the university aims to develop the students' ability to survive and achieve in the university and beyond. This dynamic is represented in Figure 1.

The model in Figure 1 is also consistent with Stake's (1995) emphasis on the system as a unit of analysis, and speaks to the point made by Riddell et al (2005) that "policy formation and implementation are clearly dynamic processes" (p.83). The lightning bolt icons in Figure 1 are significant in that they indicate potential "contradictions" between the different elements. Such contradictions can occur anywhere in the system. Engeström (1999) emphasizes the importance of analyzing internal contradictions within an activity system. Kangasoja (2002) describes contradictions as, "the driving force of development. They are manifest in the daily practices as breakdowns, tensions, ruptures and innovations. They call for reworking, both conceptually and very concretely, the objects and motives that sustain the activity, and for re-mediating the activity system by way of improving and inventing new tools" (p.200). Engeström (1999) notes that actions involve "failures, disruptions and unexpected innovations", and recommends analyzing the entire activity system in order to "illuminate the underlying contradictions that give rise to those failures and innovations as if 'behind the backs' of the conscious actors" (p.32).

In relation to modeling different perspectives, Engeström (1999:20) argues for a multi-voiced theory of activity in which internal contradictions and debates are an essential focus of analysis. This is consistent with the view of Riddell et al (2005) on the "importance of examining fine grained experience at local level" (p.84). Similarly, Ozga (2000) suggests that we can contribute to our understanding of education policy through "documentation and analysis of the 'voices' of the major 'actors' in the system" (p.128); Ozga

Figure 1. Object-oriented activity: dyslexia support in the university (after Engeström, 1993)

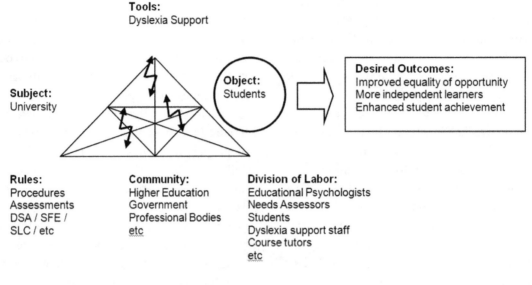

DSA Disabled Students Allowance
SFE Student Finance England
SLC Student Loans Company

argues that "complex realities can be modeled and applied in ways that may be widely understood" (p.81). In line with the above, the study reported here sought to explore and model participants' views on the issues involved in learning support for dyslexic students in a university context.

In relation to the research process, Vincent & Warren (2005) argue that it is "as crucial to theorize the process of data collection as to theorize about the data itself" (p.113). With regard to data collection, and consistent with the need to adopt a multi-voiced approach, Q methodology was used to model the subjectivities, or viewpoints, of the research study participants. Q methodology (Stephenson, 1935, 1953; Brown, 1980) was chosen for the study as it offered a theoretical basis for understanding the diversity of views on dyslexia learning support within the participants' communities of practice. Community in this sense is defined by engagement in a practice, where "human engagement in the world is first and foremost a process of negotiating meaning", which includes

"the engagement of a multiplicity of factors and perspectives" (Wenger, 1998, p.53). Wenger (1998) also refers to a community of practice as "a living context" (p.214) and describes the benefits of bringing "various perspectives together in the process of creating some coordination between them" (p.218).

The context of the study reported here involved dyslexic students on a range of degree programs at the university, accessing dyslexia support to help ensure equality of opportunity and to develop their effectiveness and independence as learners. In a previous dyslexia study using Q methodology, Paradice (2001) investigated understandings of dyslexia among parents of school children with dyslexia, educational psychologists and special educational needs co-ordinators. Paradice's research evidence suggests that there are differences in the way people view dyslexia, and that these differences could result in communication difficulties. Paradice (p.224) concludes that, "it is therefore important to establish areas of common understanding between parents and profession-als". The study reported in this chapter also used Q methodology to investigate perspectives on dyslexia, but with the focus instead on the views of dyslexic university students and their disability support staff in relation to learning support in higher education.

A Q methodology study typically involves par-ticipants sorting items, usually a set of statements, to express their views on any given issue. Their ranking of the items is then subjected to correla-tional and factor analysis. As described by Brown (1980), "Q technique and its methodology…was designed to assist in the orderly examination of human subjectivity" (p.5). Brown (1997) describes the purpose of Q as being, "to enable the person to represent his or her vantage point…for inspection and comparison" (p.14). Q methodology refers to the use of Q-sorting as a data collection technique and also to Q-factor analysis, a procedure for statistical analysis. Q-sorting and Q-factor analy-sis can be combined with post-sort interviews, allowing researchers to benefit from a blend of qualitative and quantitative research approaches; in relation to this blend, Q methodology has been described as "quali-quantological" by Watts & Stenner (2005). Q methodology has been used increasingly in a wide range of subject areas, with studies reported in numerous academic journals (e.g. Barker, 2008; Deignan, 2009; La Paro et al, 2009). As described by Barry & Proops (1999), "the basic distinctiveness of Q methodology is that, unlike standard survey analysis, it is interested in establishing patterns within and across individuals rather than patterns across individual traits, such as gender, age, class, etc." (p.339).

Procedurally, Q-sorting involves the partici-pants representing their subjective viewpoints by rank ordering the set of items, usually statements, known as a 'Q-sample'. To generate the Q-sample for the study reported here, which comprised forty-eight statements, diverse views on dyslexia sup-port were collected from a wide range of sources including the academic literature, and communica-tions with dyslexic students and other individuals from a range of backgrounds who had personal experience of inclusion policy and dyslexia sup-port in university settings. In selecting the final set of statements, care was taken to ensure that the forty-eight items provided thematic coverage of the different elements of the activity system as depicted in Figure 1. Accordingly, statements were selected which related to the subject, tools, object, outcomes, rules, community and division of labor. These relations were not exclusive; the individual statements can be related to more than one aspect, reflecting the dynamic and inter-connected nature of the elements in the activity system. Below are some examples of the final set of forty-eight statements which were sorted by the thirty-three participants in the study:

- Students with dyslexia should be seen as having learning differences, not 'learn-ing difficulties'. (statement 1, relating to the *object*)
- Dyslexia support provision should be standardized to meet the needs of all dys-lexic students. (statement 10, relating to the *tools*)
- There is a danger of dyslexia support tutors doing their students' work for them. (state-ment 36, relating to the division of *labor*)

In seeking to include diverse viewpoints, the research design followed the principles of inclu-sive research espoused by commentators (e.g. Williams, 2003; Stalker, 1998). However there are conflicting motives and principles within both inclusive research and education (e.g. Howe & Welner, 2005). Acknowledging these differ-ences, a central element of the approach used in the present study was a systematic exploration of the participants' subjectivity in relation to the learning support activity system. With regard to its utility in this respect, Van Eeten (2001) argues that Q methodology can identify stakeholders' arguments without forcing a specific problem definition upon them: "Q-methodology is especially suited to the task of uncovering positions really held by participants in a debate rather than accepting decision-makers', analysts', or even the participants' predefined categories" (pp.395-396). Van Eeten (2001) suggests further that "an in-depth analysis of the stakeholders' arguments and their relations, applying Q-methodology, can be used to come to an action-forcing reconception of a controversy" (p.392).

With regard to the focus of the study on activity and subjectivity, in Figure 2, the triangle and the black oval represent an activity system and its object. The grey elliptical shapes around the triangle represent the subjectivity, or viewpoints, to be modeled within the activity system (Deignan, 2005 & 2006). These elliptical shapes have been blended with the basic Engeström triangle to emphasize the relevance of, and focus of the study on, diverse values and viewpoints in an activity system. The understanding of subjectivity is particularly relevant to both activity theory and to the communities of practice literature. Lave and Wenger (1991) regard multiple viewpoints as a characteristic feature of participation in a community of practice (p.113). They describe how "objective forms and systems of activity, on the one hand, and agents' subjective and intersubjective understandings of them, on the other, mutually constitute both the world and its experienced forms" (p.51).

With regard to activity and subjectivity, the use of Q methodology in the research design for the present study addresses a significant scholarship gap in that subjectivity has been under-theorized in the activity theory and communities of practice literature. For example, Engeström (2000) emphasizes the importance of making manifest the multi-voicedness inherent in a collectively constructed activity system, but acknowledges that a methodological approach for analyzing the perspectives involved has been lacking. Similarly, Roth et al (2004) suggest that subjectivity is an important but overlooked feature of activity-

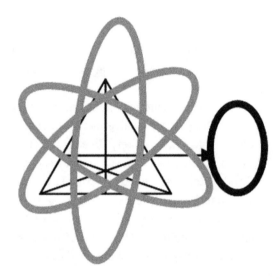

Figure 2. Activity and Subjectivity

theoretic studies, and emphasize the importance of a better understanding of subjective realities in activity systems. Likewise, Billett (2006) has criticized "theories of thinking and acting (i.e. learning) that emphasize the social contributions to human cognition, yet in which the position of the subject is denied, minimized or otherwise under-played, such as communities of practice (Wenger 1998), activity systems (Engeström 1993) and distributed cognition (Salomon 1997)" (p.11).

Incorporating Q methodology into a socio-cultural analysis addresses this gap by specifically exploring subjectivity within the activity system. Subjectivity and activity are the inter-related foci of the study. The research design also respects the view of a pioneer in activity theory, Leontyev (2009), who, considering the "psychology of experience", suggests that "although a scientific psychology must never lose sight of man's [sic] inner world, the study of this inner world cannot be divorced from a study of his activity" (p.419). The methods used in the study reported here gave each participant the experience of expressing their views by doing a Q-sort in a way consistent with that described by Leontyev, "to compel him to stop

Table 1. Distribution of the forty-eight statements

- 3	- 2	- 1	0	+ 1	+ 2	+ 3
Strongly Disagree	Moderately Disagree	Mildly Disagree	Neutral	Mildly Agree	Moderately Agree	Strongly Agree
4 statements	6 statements	9 statements	10 statements	9 statements	6 statements	4 statements

for a moment, as it were, the flow of his activity and examine the essential values that have formed in his mind, in order to find himself in them or, perhaps, to revise them".

There were thirty-three participants in the study, comprising fourteen disability support staff and nineteen students with dyslexia. The study participants were asked to sort the forty-eight Q-sample statements under seven headings, ranging from 'disagree strongly' to 'agree strongly', following the quasi-normal distribution shown in Table 1. Using a quasi-normal, forced distribution is a common practice in Q studies and has little if any impact on the statistical outcomes when compared with results using a 'free' distribution of the items by the participants in a study (e.g. Block, 1956; Brown, 1971; McKeown & Thomas, 1988). The forty-eight statements were printed on individual pieces of paper resembling a deck of playing cards and the column headings, i.e. -3 to +3, were laid out across a table in front of the participants. An amanuensis was made available to the participants to help them complete the Q-sort, if required. McKeown & Thomas (1988) emphasize the fact that, in Q methodology, "variables are the people performing the Q-sorts, not Q-sample statements" (p.17). This is in contrast to the more usual approach, referred to as R-methodology (McKeown & Thomas, 1988; Stephenson, 1953). R-factor analysis, rather than identifying groups of individuals with similar perceptions, deals with groups of related items within a questionnaire. Brown (1980) notes that, in Q methodology, "the resultant factors point to…persons bearing family resemblances in terms of subjectively shared viewpoints" (p.6). In the

present study, to aid transparency in relation to the question of researcher bias, the researcher / author, Tim Deignan, also completed a Q-sort and this was included in the data analysis (see participant Q-sort 14 in Table 2).

After sorting the statements, participants were asked to comment on their Q-sort, particularly in relation to the items with which they agreed strongly or disagreed strongly. The interviews were audio-recorded. The unique distributions, or ranking, of the statements by each participant were recorded and these individual Q-sorts provided the units of data for subsequent statistical analysis. PQMethod, a software package designed specifically for application with Q methodology, was used for correlational and factor analyses of the data. A basic assumption of factor analysis is that underlying dimensions, or factors, can be used to explain complex phenomena. The statistical operations applied to the thirty-three participants' Q-sort data resulted in the interpretation of four underlying factors. The viewpoints associated with each of these factors were then modeled by generating four synthetic Q-sorts, each of these being a composite of those individual Q-sorts which were associated strongly with each of the respective factors.

Results

Four distinct factors, or viewpoints on the issues, were interpreted, based on their respective values as reflected in the differences in their rankings of the forty-eight Q-sample statements relating to dyslexia support. The four interpreted viewpoints were derived from correlational and factor analysis

Table 2. Factor Matrix, with an 'X' Indicating a Defining Sort

Factor Loadings				
Q-sorts	Factor 1	Factor 2	Factor 3	Factor 4
1 mos01	0.0945	0.2609	0.8109x	0.1132
2 mos02	0.1611	0.5710	0.5710	0.3800
3 mos03	0.2857	0.1918	0.1505	0.6879x
4 mos04	-0.1349	0.2479	0.5406	0.2440
5 mos05	0.3561	0.0876	0.5421	0.4754
6 mos06	0.3625	0.0422	0.6304	0.4042
7 mos07	0.0439	0.2914	0.2775	0.7791x
8 mos08	0.7387x	0.2397	0.2839	0.1462
9 mos09	0.5256	0.3772	0.2434	0.3772
10 mos10	0.2351	0.3322	0.1582	0.4658
11 mos11	0.2635	0.0036	0.4929	0.5663
12 mos12	0.1378	0.3880	0.2282	0.5985
13 mos13	0.3587	0.3602	0.1027	0.6456
14 mos14	0.1488	0.3018	0.4086	0.5757
15 stu01	0.6619x	0.2675	0.2404	0.3674
16 stu02	0.0498	0.7063x	0.1042	0.3315
17 stu03	0.3676	0.5472	0.1767	0.3758
18 stu04	0.2415	0.2376	0.6806x	0.1707
19 stu05	0.0951	0.1028	0.5037	0.1867
20 stu06	0.2175	0.0127	0.2726	0.0993
21 stu07	0.3887	0.2887	0.3289	0.4351
22 stu08	0.3178	0.3477	0.1266	0.4146
23 stu09	0.1183	0.1045	0.1995	0.4382
24 stu10	0.2233	0.7026x	0.1523	0.2844
25 stu11	0.3097	0.3334	0.2870	0.2370
26 stu12	0.0682	0.2726	0.0684	0.1305
27 stu13	0.4278	0.3588	0.4708	0.2607
28 stu14	0.1845	0.1786	0.0939	0.3047
29 stu15	0.4158	0.1549	0.3225	0.0944
30 stu16	0.3738	0.2798	0.6080	0.1930
31 stu17	-0.0436	0.2146	-0.0774	0.1579
32 stu18	0.1275	0.6950x	0.2374	0.3309
33 stu19	0.2262	0.7472x	0.2767	-0.0881

Note: The columns show the loadings of the participants' Q-sorts across the four factors, which were interpreted using Principal Components Analysis and Varimax Rotation. With regard to the participants' Q-sort identifiers, "mos" = member of staff, and "stu" = student. The researcher / author was participant 14 in the study; mos14 refers to his Q-sort.

of the thirty-three participants' Q-sorts. Principal Components Analysis revealed factors with an eigenvalue greater than 1.00 and this figure was used as a criterion to guide the selection of factors for rotation (Thomas & Watson, 2002; Donner, 2001; Wigger & Mrtek, 1994). The second criterion was that a minimum of two Q-sorts should load significantly on each factor. When selecting individual Q-sorts for merging into a representative factor, commentators (e.g. Comrey & Lee, 1992; Tabachnick & Fidell, 2001) consider 0.6 to be a very good correlation, while 0.3 is considered to be a poor correlation. The four selected factors were rotated using Varimax, which Brown (1980) notes may be used when researchers wish to avoid imposing a priori categories on the data. The resulting factors are a synthetic composite of those defining Q-sorts, marked with an X in Table 2, which loaded strongly and relatively cleanly on each factor. The four Factor arrays are shown in Table 3. Key differences in emphasis between these four perspectives are headlined below.

- **Factor 1:** Dyslexic students are frustrated and isolated - they need unorthodox teaching methods to help them cope
- **Factor 2:** Dyslexic university students have learning difficulties - their study skills need to be good enough to cope on entry to university
- **Factor 3:** Dyslexic students are unprepared for university – course tutors are aware of their needs but don't address them
- **Factor 4:** University does too little for dyslexic students - dyslexia support tutors can do too much

The loadings of each Q-sort across each of the factors is shown in Table 2. Each participant with a defining Q-sort, marked with an X, can be considered as a spokesperson for the viewpoint which their factor represents. For example, the rankings of the forty-eight statements in the Q-sample by participant 1, a member of staff, and

by participant 18, a student, emerged statistically as representing a distinct perspective in relation to dyslexia support. The extent to which all of the thirty-three participants' Q-sorts relate to, or load on, Factor 3 can be seen in the Factor Matrix in Table 2. The matrix shows that the Q-sorts of participants 1 and 18 load strongly on Factor 3, with a correlation in both cases above the 0.6 level. By contrast, their respective loadings on Factors 1, 2 and 4 are relatively weak, with correlations below 0.3 in each case. Q-sorts 1 and 18 therefore load relatively cleanly on Factor 3. This is not the case with the other Q-sorts in relation to Factor 3. For example, Q-sort 6 loads strongly on Factor 3 but also shows a 0.4 correlation with Factor 4. Because of this cross-loading, Q-sort 6 has not been selected as a defining sort for Factor 3; only Q-sorts 1 and 18 were selected for this purpose. Their respective Q-sorts were therefore selected and merged into a single synthetic Q-sort, which is displayed among the factor array columns in Table 3.

Table 3 shows the synthetic Q-sort values for each of the four factors interpreted. The four factor arrays are a product of the merging of those particular Q-sorts, marked with an X in Table 2, which were associated with each factor. In Table 3, 'N' indicates the number of Q-sorts in the study that were used to exemplify the viewpoint of each factor (two, four, two, and two, respectively). The number of individual Q-sorts exemplifying each factor does not necessarily reflect the prevalence of each factor viewpoint in the wider population, and no claims regarding generalisability are made in that regard. As Robbins (2005) notes, Q methodology reveals "characteristics of subjectivity rather than characteristics of populations" (p.215).

In modelling the subjectivity of the study participants, the particular four factor solution described here was arrived at using Principal Components Analysis and Varimax rotation. While this offers a mathematically informative solution, it should be noted that an alternative Centroid technique of factor analysis is also

Table 3. Q-sort values for Factors 1 - 4

0=neutral -/+1=mildly dis/agree -/+2=moderately dis/agree -/+3= strongly dis/agree				
Note: Statements in bold italics indicate a consensus in the responses to that item (i.e. the values are all positive, all negative, or all neutral). Shaded cell values in the factor array columns indicate an item ranking difference of two or more points relative to the other three factors.	Factor Arrays			
	F1	F2	F3	F4
	N=2	N=4	N=2	N=2
Students with dyslexia should be seen as having learning differences, not 'learning difficulties'. (1)	2	-2	0	3
Dyslexia support should concentrate on improving students' spelling. (2)	-1	-3	0	-2
Getting clear assignment feedback from course tutors is important to dyslexic students. (3)	3	3	0	2
Course tutors understand how to support students with dyslexia. (4)	-1	-2	-2	-2
With learning support provision, dyslexic students have a better chance of coping at university than non-dyslexic students. (5)	-3	-1	0	0
The main priority for dyslexic students is getting through their course. (6)	0	0	3	-1
Providing alternative forms of assessment for dyslexic students can undermine academic standards. (7)	0	0	-2	-3
Dyslexic students need help with developing their study skills. (8)	3	3	2	1
The university values the contribution that students with dyslexia can make. (9)	0	0	-1	0
Dyslexia support provision should be standardized to meet the needs of all dyslexic students. (10)	-2	-2	-1	-1
Dyslexia support should be mapped against critical moments in the student's learning program. (11)	-1	1	1	0
Dyslexic students get the coursework grades that they deserve. (12)	-3	1	-2	0
Students with dyslexia can learn from hearing other students talk about their experiences of coping at university. (13)	1	0	0	1
The quality of dyslexia support provision in the university is satisfactory. (14)	0	1	1	0
Course tutors are explicit about what they expect from students. (15)	-1	0	-1	-2
Having effective learning support is important to dyslexic students. (16)	3	3	2	2
Course tutors incorporate the needs of dyslexic students into the design and delivery of programs. (17)	-1	-1	-3	-1
Dyslexia support should involve human contact, including counseling, so that the emotional effects on students' learning can be addressed. (18)	2	0	0	2
Course tutors have the training needed to support students with dyslexia. (19)	-2	-2	-2	-2
Students need specific help with understanding how dyslexia affects their learning. (20)	2	2	2	2
Dyslexia support provision should aim to reduce academic culture shock. (21)	0	0	0	0
The academic culture of the university makes it easy for dyslexic students to talk to other students and staff about their concerns. (22)	0	0	1	-1
The university's dyslexia support provision helps students to progress through their program of learning. (23)	0	1	2	1
The importance of course tutors needing to take account of students' different learning styles is exaggerated. (24)	-1	-1	0	-2
Students with dyslexia waste time and energy because they don't know the best way to do things. (25)	2	3	2	1
Dyslexia support is really just about spoon-feeding weak students. (26)	-3	-3	-3	-3
Dyslexic students worry about not meeting their course tutors' expectations. (27)	2	1	2	0
The university meets all the needs of its dyslexic students. (28)	0	-1	-1	-3
Course tutors should help dyslexic students to improve their study skills. (29)	0	1	1	-1
Dyslexic students can be empowered by learning how to use appropriate information and communication technology. (30)	1	1	1	1

continued on following page

Table 3. continued

0=neutral -/+1=mildly dis/agree -/+2=moderately dis/agree -/+3= strongly dis/agree				
The informal peer support that dyslexic students get is more effective than the support provided by the university. (31)	0	-1	0	0
Dyslexia support should help students to cope holistically with the combinations of complex challenges that face them. (32)	0	2	2	3
Course tutors are aware of their dyslexic students' support needs. (33)	-2	-2	1	-1
On entry to a programme, a student's study skills should be good enough to cope with the academic demands of their course. (34)	-1	1	-1	-1
Students with dyslexia are sometimes unprepared for the academic demands of their university programme. (35)	1	0	3	1
There is a danger of dyslexia support tutors doing their students' work for them. (36)	-3	-3	-2	1
Dyslexia is a vague concept. (37)	-3	2	-3	2
The support that dyslexia tutors can provide over an academic year is not enough to substantially improve a student's academic performance. (38)	1	-2	-1	0
To combat the effects of dyslexia, non-standard or unorthodox methods of teaching are needed. (39)	1	-1	-1	-2
The transition from school or college to university is equally challenging for dyslexic and for non-dyslexic students. (40)	1	1	1	2
By being 'dyslexic-friendly', course tutors can actually discriminate against non-dyslexic students. (41)	-2	-3	-1	-1
The co-ordination between dyslexic students' Local Education Authorities and the university is satisfactory. (42)	-1	-1	-1	-1
The learning support offered to dyslexic students should help them to become independent learners. (43)	-1	2	1	3
Dyslexic students play a central role in determining the nature of the learning support they receive. (44)	1	2	0	0
When marking assignments, course tutors make sufficient allowance for the effects of dyslexia on their students' written work. (45)	1	-2	-3	0
University can be a frustrating and isolating experience for dyslexic students. (46)	3	0	1	1
Meeting the needs of dyslexic students requires huge amounts of additional work by course tutors. (47)	-2	-1	-2	-3
To be effective, university learning support needs a holistic and coherent approach to policy design which engages all those involved, including dyslexic students, non-dyslexic students, course tutors and support staff. (48)	1	2	2	3

used in Q studies (Stephenson, 1953). Using that technique, judgmental or 'manual' rotation of the factors allows the researcher to take account of theoretical considerations relating to the topic under investigation when arriving at the final factor structure. The number of solutions using the Centroid method is potentially infinite. The four factor structure arrived at in the present study is therefore offered as 'a' solution rather than 'the' solution; the procedure used provides a theoretical basis for delineating the viewpoints interpreted below.

Following Brown (1980), the factor arrays shown in Table 3 were "placed side by side and compared, the differences and similarities in scores providing the bases for description and theorizing" (p.262). Accordingly, areas of consensus, together with participants' post-sort interview comments and also differences between the four interpreted viewpoints are described below. Note: The relevant Q-sample statement numbers (1-48) are referenced in brackets, e.g. (16).

Areas of Consensus Among the Four Viewpoints

All four of the interpreted viewpoints (i.e. those synthetic viewpoints associated with factors 1-4 in the Factor Matrix) believed that having effective learning support is important to dyslexic students (16). Mos13, for example, commented, "It's key. It's central to it really. If the learning support isn't there, then they are going to face all sorts of difficulties". Mos10 agreed, saying "if the support is effective, then they'll learn the skills of managing their study". Stu03 remarked, "it helps you to fit in, to do the assignments, and to have strategies to help you remember". Stu02 felt that learning support could help not just dyslexic students but all students. Mos09 commented, "when I've been studying dyslexia, the methods…and the strategies that I've taught my students and I've learned along the way, I wish I'd known them as a non-dyslexic going to school. I think my grades would have been greatly enhanced". The four viewpoints all believed that students with dyslexia waste time and energy because they don't know the best way to do things (25). Stu19 commented, "I do think students with dyslexia waste their time trying to get to the solution without any help. But it's much easier with the help"; he added that planning an assignment "is damn near impossible as a dyslexic", but with a dyslexia support tutor, "I thought I was in a much better, more confident, and in a fair mind to answer the question required".

All four viewpoints felt that the transition from school or college to university is equally challenging for dyslexic and for non-dyslexic students (40). In relation to the purpose of support, they were neutral on the question of whether dyslexia support provision should aim to reduce academic culture shock (21). They did however believe that students need specific help with understanding how dyslexia affects their learning (20). They also felt that dyslexic students need help with developing their study skills (8). Mos09 argued that, "all dyslexic students need help with

developing effective study skills. I've not met a dyslexic student yet that's come with ideal study skills". All four viewpoints disagreed with the notion that dyslexia support provision should be standardized to meet the needs of all dyslexic students (10).

All four viewpoints rejected the suggestion that dyslexia support is really just about spoon-feeding weak students (26). Stu02 commented that "you can't be spoon-fed anything". Stu03 rejected the view of teaching and learning which she felt was implicit in the statement, commenting that "it's like saying you'll just sit there and we'll give you all the answers"; she insisted that dyslexia support was "about giving students strategies". Stu19 argued that "if it was spoon-fed then your dyslexia tutor would write all your essays or your dissertation for you". Some of the support staff echoed the students' comments. Mos10 said, "I think there's a lot of misunderstanding about what dyslexia means and people just think it means bad spelling or you're lazy or something". Mos12 commented "they can actually be highly capable students if they are given the right type of support. So that's a complete myth" (26).

Mos03 agreed, saying "It's about them learning differently…They just have different needs". Mos01 remarked that he had "never met a weak dyslexic student". Mos05 argued that dyslexia support is really about "giving them strategies, empowering them to do it themselves". Mos09 insisted that "even if you wanted to, you couldn't do [the student's work for them] because we're not specialists in all subject areas. We're there to help them become more independent learners". The four viewpoints believed that dyslexic students can be empowered by learning how to use appropriate information and communication technology (30). Mos10 remarked, "I think there's really good software out there that can help with all sorts of things…I would qualify that by saying, 'where it suits them'. Those that are interested and motivated to use the technology, I think can benefit tremendously, but it doesn't suit all of them…some are a bit phobic".

In relation to course tutors (i.e. not dyslexia support tutors, but subject tutors on a student's main programme of study), the four viewpoints do not believe that course tutors incorporate the needs of dyslexic students into the design and delivery of programmes (17). Mos01 commented, "I do believe that eventually there will be legal challenges…I don't believe they [universities generally] are making reasonable adjustments". The four viewpoints rejected the suggestion that meeting the needs of dyslexic students requires huge amounts of additional work by course tutors (47). They also rejected the view that, by being "dyslexic-friendly", course tutors can actually discriminate against non-dyslexic students (41). Mos12 commented, "by using dyslexic-friendly approaches to teaching and teaching materials, it doesn't undermine non-dyslexic students or cause any form of discrimination against them". The four viewpoints all felt that course tutors do not have the training needed to support students with dyslexia (19) and do not understand how to support them (4). Mos03 commented, "I think some course tutors do not have a clue. They don't understand what dyslexia is". Mos09 felt that "most course tutors seem to have little or no experience regarding dyslexia…they feel quite disabled by that in my experience and that's the impression I get from students as well…when I've done dyslexia awareness [staff training] in the past…that's the message that's come across".

In relation to administrative systems, the four viewpoints believe that the co-ordination between dyslexic students' Local Education Authorities and the university could be improved (42), and that, to be effective, university learning support needs a holistic and coherent approach to policy design which engages all those involved, including dyslexic students, non-dyslexic students, course tutors and support staff (48).

Areas of Difference Between the Four Viewpoints

While there were clear areas of consensus among the four viewpoints, as outlined above, there were also points of difference between them. The four viewpoints are contrasted below. To help distinguish them one from another, a profile for each is provided. The profiles for the four factors, or synthetic viewpoints, are titled in a way that reflects differences in their orientation, based on the differences between their respective statement rankings as shown in the factor arrays in Table 3. NB: The relevant Q-sample statement numbers (1-48) are referenced below in brackets, e.g. (46).

Factor 1: *Dyslexic students are frustrated and isolated - they need unorthodox teaching methods to help them cope*

The Q-sorts of participants mos08 and stu01 exemplified this viewpoint. Factor 1 feels more strongly than any other that university can be a frustrating and isolating experience for dyslexic students (46). This viewpoint disagreed more strongly than any other with the suggestion that, with learning support provision, dyslexic students have a better chance of coping at university than non-dyslexic students (5). It was the only viewpoint with a neutral response to the suggestion that dyslexia support should help students to cope holistically with the combinations of complex challenges that face them (32). Factor 1 was the only viewpoint to agree with the suggestion that, to combat the effects of dyslexia, non-standard or unorthodox methods of teaching are needed (39). It is the only viewpoint to disagree with the suggestion that the learning support offered to dyslexic students should help them to become independent learners (43).

Factor 2: *Dyslexic university students have learning difficulties - their study skills need to be good enough to cope on entry to university*

The Q-sorts of participants stu02, stu10, stu18 and stu19 exemplified this viewpoint. Factor 2 was the only viewpoint to disagree with the suggestion that students with dyslexia should be seen as having learning differences, not learning difficulties (1). It was also the only viewpoint to agree with the suggestion that, on entry to a programme, a student's study skills should be good enough to cope with the academic demands of their course (34).

Factor 3: *Dyslexic students are unprepared for university – course tutors are aware of their needs but don't address them*

The Q-sorts of participants mos01 and stu04 exemplified this viewpoint. Factor 3 felt more strongly than any other viewpoint that students with dyslexia are sometimes unprepared for the academic demands of their university programme (35). Factor 3 was the only viewpoint which agreed that course tutors are aware of their dyslexic students' support needs (33). However, Factor 3 disagreed more strongly than any other with the suggestion that course tutors incorporate the needs of dyslexic students into the design and delivery of programmes (17). Factor 3 was the only viewpoint to respond neutrally to the suggestion that students with dyslexia should be seen as having learning differences, not learning difficulties (1). Similarly, it was the only viewpoint to respond neutrally to the suggestion that getting clear assignment feedback from course tutors is important to dyslexic students (3).

Factor 4: *University does too little for dyslexic students - dyslexia support tutors can do too much*

The Q-sorts of participants mos03 and mos07 exemplified this viewpoint. Factor 4 disagreed more strongly than any other with the suggestion that the university met all the needs of its dyslexic students (28). It was the only viewpoint to agree with the suggestion that there is a danger

of dyslexia support tutors doing their students' work for them (36).

Finally, as participant 14 (mos14) in the study, the author also completed a Q-sort to model his views on the issues. As can be seen in Table 2, the author's Q-sort correlates poorly with factors 1 and 2, slightly more positively with factor 3, and most strongly with factor 4. For example, the author's Q-sort, as did factor 4, ranked item 28 under disagree, and item 36 under agree. Similarly, and consistent with the viewpoint associated with factor 4, the author feels that the university where the study took place could do more to support dyslexic students, and indeed feels that this is probably true of most universities. Again consistent with the factor 4 viewpoint, the author feels that some dyslexia support tutors can sometimes do too much for students, either inadvertently or deliberately, and in doing so provide inappropriate levels of support.

The author's Q-sort also showed similarities to the interpreted viewpoints in relation to those statements that were consensus items for the four factors. In Table 3, the four factor arrays are shown with the consensus items marked in bold italics. There are sixteen such consensus items, where the rankings of a statement are consensual in that they are all positive, all negative, or all neutral. The author's own Q-sort ranked twelve of these sixteen items in the same way as the rankings of the four factors. In summary, as with the majority of the participants in the study, the author's viewpoint as reflected in his Q-sort can be seen as having varying degrees of correlation with the four synthetic viewpoints associated with the four factors. However, as with most of the participants' Q-sorts, the author's was not correlated strongly and cleanly enough to be selected as a defining sort for any one of the four factors.

Issues Arising from the Data

The factor arrays, which show the rankings of the statements by the four interpreted viewpoints, when considered together with the participants' post-sort interview comments, suggest that a number of issues are seen as significant in terms of the theory and practice of dyslexia support. These issues, which are outlined below, include: understandings of terminology relating to dyslexia and learning differences, the importance of spelling and curriculum content in dyslexia support tutorials, and the awareness and response of course tutors in relation to students' needs.

In relation to terminology, there was near polarization of the four viewpoints in the ranking of item 37, which stated that "dyslexia is a vague concept" (see Table 4). Factors 1 and 3 disagreed strongly with this statement, while Factors 2 and 4 agreed moderately with it. Mos01 disagreed strongly with statement 37, and attributed such a view to "people with their own internal political agendas". He commented that dyslexia "is not a middle class construct" and added that statement 37 was "one of the most insulting comments I've heard in a long time". Other participants saw it differently. Stu02 remarked that, "it just seems to be a label. It doesn't tell you specifically how everyone's affected. Everyone's affected differently and cope with that effect differently to varying degrees".

Another item relating to labeling and definitional issues was statement 1 (see Table 5), which suggested that "students with dyslexia should be seen as having learning differences and not learning difficulties". One student (stu06) felt that "differences" was a more appropriate description than "difficulties", commenting that, "in some classes, if things are done differently, like the way a teacher does a lesson, I work better and if they're done a different way then sometimes I don't" The connotations of different terms were also mentioned. Stu05 commented that, "some people's ideas of what dyslexia is can really hold you back...I've come across students and tutors who just think because you are bad at spelling you are not intelligent".

Participants' views also differed in relation to the question of curriculum content in dyslexia tuition. Most participants were dismissive of statement 2 (see Table 6), which suggested that dyslexia support should concentrate on improving students' spelling. Mos03 commented, "it's not just about spelling...It's a whole host of other things they might have problems with or, you know, do differently". Mos13 felt that, "spelling is, you know, the least of it as far as I'm concerned. It's much more to do with, you know, how you

Table 4. The rankings of statement 37 by the four factors

Dyslexia is a vague concept. (37)						
Strongly Disagree	Moderately Disagree	Mildly Disagree	Neutral	Mildly Agree	Moderately Agree	Strongly Agree
Factor 1 Factor 3			*Author*		Factor 2 Factor 4	

Note: For the sake of transparency, the ranking of this statement by the author / researcher in his Q-sort is also shown.

Table 5. The rankings of statement 1 by the four factors

Students with dyslexia should be seen as having learning differences, not 'learning difficulties'. (1)						
Strongly Disagree	Moderately Disagree	Mildly Disagree	Neutral	Mildly Agree	Moderately Agree	Strongly Agree
	Factor 2		Factor 3	*Author*	Factor 1	Factor 4

Table 6. The rankings of statement 2 by the four factors

Dyslexia support should concentrate on improving students' spelling. (2)						
Strongly Disagree	Moderately Disagree	Mildly Disagree	Neutral	Mildly Agree	Moderately Agree	Strongly Agree
Factor 2 *Author*	Factor 4	Factor 1	Factor 3			

organize your thoughts, how you organize your work and prepare yourself for your work and that sort of thing". Stu01 felt

that, "it's a lot of different issues. Too many people concentrate on the spelling aspect". Similarly, stu02 strongly disagreed with statement (2), saying "it's that stereotypical comment". Stu19 remarked, "I think there's more issues at higher education level than spelling…planning your time management, planning essays, planning dissertations". One student (stu13) explained how he very nearly did not come for dyslexia support at all in the final year of his degree programme as he was concerned that the support tutor might focus on improving his spelling.

I can go into ways that dyslexia support has not helped me…previous dyslexia tutors have worked on things like spelling and reading certain words. I don't really think that is what my problem is at all. You know, my problem is organizing stuff – organizing written work, structuring it – I think that's where my problems lie…Certainly in the first year of uni it were just a bit of a waste looking at certain spellings of words and stuff. It's just not what I needed at all really…I very nearly didn't come for any support this year based on all the things that have happened previous. (stu13)

While none of the four interpreted factors, or viewpoints, felt that improving students' spelling should be a priority (2), one individual student and one member of staff did agree with this item; mos04 commented that spelling was "important in an academic setting", and that poor spelling could "create an impression on the tutor" when marking

assignments. Course tutors' awareness of dyslexia and their attitudes to dyslexic students were seen as problematic by many of the participants. There was a perception that course tutors do not make sufficient allowance for the effects of dyslexia on their students' written work (45) (see Table 7). Stu19 commented in respect of course tutors that, "they don't know you are dyslexic", and suggested that this might be because of communication problems between disability services and academic staff. Criticising written feedback from course tutors on his assignments, stu04 described how, "a fair few of my tutors, their writing is so bad I couldn't understand it". Stu10 gave an example of negative feedback from a tutor, commenting that, "she didn't actually take into account that I was dyslexic so the feedback that she'd given.. it was a bit of a kick in the balls really…with hindsight I think she should have been notified that I was [dyslexic] because I think they would have had it written down, or I assume they would have had it written down somewhere".

Criticisms were also made of course materials. Mos01 suggested that because of "academic snobbery" among some course tutors, course materials were too often inaccessible to dyslexic students. Mos02 felt that course tutors needed to use more multi-sensory approaches in their teaching. Stu03 described how course tutors had given her handouts in size 6 font on white paper which she found impossible to read; she commented, "if they just discussed how you are coping, how they could help you in their lectures". Stu04 described how, "some of them didn't do anything really…it was a case of 'just get on with it', which wasn't very helpful". Examinations could also be problem-

Table 7. The rankings of statement 45 by the four factors

When marking assignments, course tutors make sufficient allowance for the effects of dyslexia on their students' written work. (45)						
Strongly Disagree	Moderately Disagree	Mildly Disagree	Neutral	Mildly Agree	Moderately Agree	Strongly Agree
Factor 3	Factor 2 *Author*		Factor 4	Factor 1		

atic. Stu01 described a situation where he felt his request for an amanuensis had been handled insensitively by his tutor. In relation to these perceived shortcomings, three of the four viewpoints interpreted felt that course tutors were not aware of their dyslexic students' needs (33) (see Table 8).

Stu04 remarked that, "in my opinion I'm treated as if I'm thick by the majority of tutors I come across, and there's only one who is very understanding because he is dyslexic himself". Asked how he thought this situation could be improved, he replied that, "if there was a way of giving them dyslexia for a couple of weeks it would be very useful".

Discussion

From an activity theory perspective, Stetsenko (2005) points out that "one of the central pillars of CHAT [Cultural Historical Activity Theory] is the idea that human development is based on active transformations of existing environments and creation of new ones achieved through collaborative processes of producing and deploying tools" (p.72). In relation to transforming dyslexia support in higher education, the findings of the study reported on in this chapter have implications for those responsible for decision-making at a range of levels, from individual dyslexia support tutors to government ministers. This section will suggest how such transformations might be made, and argues that to be effective, the development process must incorporate three features; complexity, polyphony (or multi-voicedness) and reflexivity, in order to achieve the desired outcomes.

Each of these three features is important. Firstly, complex issues and environments need to be acknowledged as such, and modeled clearly, in order to reduce the likelihood of simplistic pseudo-solutions being imposed on a poorly understood problem. Secondly, the process of framing the problem space will benefit greatly from the inclusion of different voices and values relating to the issues under consideration. Thirdly, while acknowledging complexity and incorporating multiple perspectives is necessary, they alone will not be sufficient to tackle the issues identified. To do this, awareness of the often diverse understandings of different stakeholders must also be used reflexively to transform the system by developing existing, enhanced, or new tools.

To consider further the development issues involved, the data from the Q-methodology study

Table 8. The rankings of statement 33 by the four factors

Course tutors are aware of their dyslexic students' support needs. (33)						
Strongly Disagree	Moderately Disagree	Mildly Disagree	Neutral	Mildly Agree	Moderately Agree	Strongly Agree
	Factor 1 Factor 2	Factor 4 *Author*		Factor 3		

were analyzed using an activity theory framework (see Figure 1). The sorting of the Q-sample statements by the study participants together with the participants' post-sort interview comments as to why they ranked the statements in the way that they did suggest that a number of tensions are likely to impact on the levels of success achieved by dyslexia support initiatives in any given higher education context. The study findings suggest that there are potentially many 'contradictions' or tensions between dyslexia support as a *tool* and other elements of the activity system in a higher education context. Some of these tensions are highlighted in Figure 3.

Listed inside each of the boxes in Figure 3 (i.e. tools, rules, etc.) are some of the potential tensions relating to the different interacting elements of the activity system. These are variables which will impact on the success of learning support provision for dyslexic students in a university context. They are suggestive only, as local practices will apply within specific activity systems, and in any given institutional context the elements will interact with each other in a way that reflects

the unique nature of that individual system. Figure 3 highlights only potential tensions between the *tool* and the other elements in the activity system. There may also be tensions within and between other elements of the activity system. For example, tensions may be found in the dynamic relationship between the *community*, the *rules*, and the *division of labour*. The study findings and issues outlined in the results section above and the tensions summarized graphically in Figure 3 are now considered with regard to possible interventions and system development.

In relation to complexity, terms such as 'disability', 'dyslexia' and 'learning difficulties' will have different meanings for different people. For example, individual students, individual dyslexia support tutors, individual course tutors, and individual policymakers may have different understandings of these terms and different perspectives on the issues. The complexity of the terms and concepts involved, and how this complexity relates to individual value systems needs to be recognized. Valsiner (2008) comments that, "values are internal subjective meaning fields

Figure 3. Some potential tool-related tensions, illustrated by lightning bolts, in a dyslexia support activity system

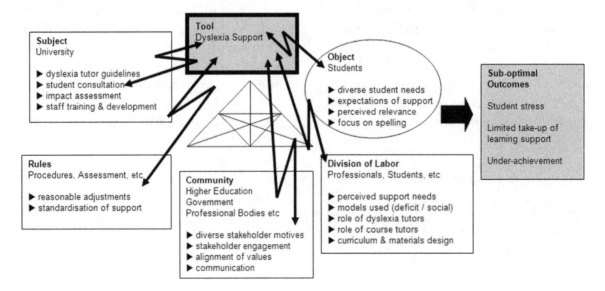

that totally capture and guide the person who has constructed them" (p.73). This is an important point, as decisions regarding dyslexia support interventions will inevitably be influenced by how decision makers, from micro to macro-level, define the problem space and how they perceive that which they seek to transform.

The above point can be illustrated, for example, with reference to the present study and the evident differences in the perceived importance of spelling in dyslexia support. Many dyslexic students do not spell accurately and consistently, and this is often noted in Educational Psychologist's reports as an issue requiring intervention. At the university where the study reported here was conducted, the guidelines for dyslexia support tutors put a particular emphasis on following the recommendations made in Educational Psychologists' reports:

Ensure any support you offer is in line with the student's educational psychologist's report...For example, if the report suggests that the student's spelling is poor, the aim is to help them find ways to overcome this and not to continually correct their spelling...Your role is one of support to help minimize as far as possible the effects of their dyslexia.

With regard to such guidelines, there is a danger as noted by Dyson (2005) that, "'special needs' are held somehow to emerge from the individual assessment process and the means of 'meeting' those needs become self-evident once the needs themselves are specified" (p.123). Accordingly, defining the problem space as one of poor spelling requiring spelling intervention carries a risk; the case of stu13 above exemplifies how an emphasis on spelling may in fact discourage students from attending learning support. Clearly, dyslexia support tutors' views on teaching spelling have implications; teachers' beliefs, as noted by Carrington & Elkins (2005), "influence the ways students are taught and correspondingly the model of supporting students with diverse learning needs" (p.86).

Policy makers' beliefs are equally salient in relation to how the defining of the problem space can influence the way in which interventions are conceived. For example, Student Finance England (SFE) have recommended introducing a standardized support package for dyslexic students in higher education. Such an intervention, narrowly defining the problem space as one involving inconsistency of provision requiring standardized support for all dyslexic students, also carries a risk. There is a danger that a 'one size fits all' approach may result in support not being sufficiently customized to meet individual students' needs. Indeed, the findings from the present study (see Table 3, statement 10) suggest that dyslexic students and their support staff may not want such standardized packages. Similarly, dyslexia organisations have spoken out strongly against the SFE standardization proposal (DSA-QAG, 2010, p.4).

The above examples point to the need for a holistic, systemic analysis of dyslexia support policy and practice which respects the complexity of the issues involved. Riddell et al (2005) explain that "policy is not simply made by elected representatives nor in public fora, but also in the daily interactions and negotiations of service users and professionals" (p.72). Policy in itself does not empower or liberate learners, and as Benjamin (2005) notes, "'valuing diversity' is inadequate for the task of illuminating present injustices or producing radical alternatives" (p.187). Clegg & McNulty (2005) note that, "inclusion, and barriers to inclusion, operates at the micro level as well as in the broader sphere" (p.219). The issues are complex, and effective intervention requires more than mere rhetoric or policy statements. In fact, the findings of the present study suggest that the situation described by the Quality Assurance Agency (QAA) more than twenty years ago may still persist in that,

disabled people...have been excluded by teaching methods that do not take full account of their needs (precept 9)...Their participation at every stage of provision, from design to evaluation, is likely to ensure that developments are both effective and efficient in increasing access and improving the quality of disabled students' experience of higher education (precept 12). (QAA, 1999)

The inclusion of stakeholder perspectives in the development of provision necessitates respect for and incorporation of polyphony, or multi-voicedness, in any analysis of the issues. In relation to activity theoretical studies, Lantolf and Thorne (2006) comment that, "though an analyst produces systemic representations 'from above' as it were, s/he must also attempt to render the participant relative perspective of the situation" (p.212). The study reported on here does this by modeling the participants' perspectives using Q methodology. The participants' individual Q-sorts can be seen as an example of what Thomas (2010) refers to as "a particular representation given in context and understood in that context" (p.578), while the author's interpretation of the data "offers understanding presented from another's horizon of meaning but understood from one's own" (p.579). A respect for multi-voicedness is central to Q methodology, and can illuminate perspectives on a problem space in ways that raise awareness and inform the design of effective interventions. This respect for polyphony is also in keeping with the government's requirement that professionals "consult with students who need learning support to ensure that that support enables them to participate in learning" (DfEE, 2001, p.14). Such consultation necessarily requires a respect for the voice and values of the student and should include consideration of how students' values relate to those of their tutors.

Problematically, the findings of the present study provide evidence of dyslexia support tutors offering help which may be perceived by their students as inappropriate (e.g. in relation to the teaching of spelling). It is understandable that practitioners in different contexts may have quite different perceptions of the problem space and of the various tools which mediate their practice. Their views will be shaped by the different contexts in which they operate. They will have different insights, understandings, and values in relation to their particular contexts and in relation to what is required for dyslexic students to access and succeed in their particular learning contexts. These different views may in part be a result of differences in the background and training of tutors. For example, a dyslexia tutor trained to support primary school children may have a different approach to working with university students than a colleague who has been trained specifically to support dyslexic adults. In any case, regardless of the rationale for, and potential efficacy of the support provided, if it is perceived as inappropriate by the student then there is a real risk of disengagement by the student no matter how well-intentioned or potentially effective the support offered.

To be inclusive, a learning support system must respect and include the experiences and views of students. This process is important in getting what Kellet and Nind (2003) refer to as an "interactive fit" between the learner and the curriculum. The fit should also include a balance between cognition and emotion (Collins et al, 2002), and should empower students in their learning. One practical way to help minimize student disengagement with tutorial support would be for dyslexia support tutors to use the Q-sample of statements designed for the present study, or a variation of it tailored to suit their particular context. The dyslexia support tutor and the student could each complete a Q-sort, followed by a comparing and contrasting of their respective rankings of the statements. This process could generate useful discussion and insight into how they each perceive the challenges facing the student and the role of the support tutor in meeting those challenges. Furthermore, it could provide a basis for collaborative negotiation and individualized planning to meet the students' needs in a way that both the student and the support tutor feel is appropriate.

FUTURE RESEARCH DIRECTIONS

Inclusion requires giving more power to the voices of the excluded. Developing a maximally inclusive learning support system requires dialogue and understanding between stakeholders at a range of levels. Rix & Simmons (2005) argue that "inclusion and exclusion are, of course, fundamentally tied up with power" (p.8). Similarly, Lantolf and Thorne (2006) ask, "who decides what the object of activity is? How will the outcome be evaluated, and by whom, and with what effects?" (p.223). Power is not distributed evenly among all stakeholders. However, asymmetries of power may be ameliorated through the better identification and pursuit of shared interests. The approach used in the study reported here, if applied to other aspects of the system, could illuminate multiple perspectives on dyslexia support, and help to build consensus, co-producing a shared object for all partners to work on.

It is important to understand the variety of viewpoints on learning support issues, and to use this understanding to inform policy and practice. The previous section suggested a practical way for students and support tutors to use the Q-sort process to improve their teaching and learning. Other professionals could also use Q-sorts to engage more effectively with dyslexic students. For example, the study findings suggest that course tutors can be perceived by students and support staff as not understanding or catering for their dyslexic students' needs. To investigate this further in any given university context, a Q-study of course tutors' views on the issues could be undertaken and used to inform better staff training and development, where needed, in relation to inclusive education for dyslexic students. A further related Q-study could be carried out to investigate in more detail how dyslexia and its

specific effects are perceived by university students with dyslexia. Also, survey research could be undertaken to investigate the prevalence of the four perspectives interpreted in the present study among the wider population of students with dyslexia and their support staff in universities. These are just some of the possible directions for future research.

There is also a need at a national level to explore multiple perspectives in relation to the various organizational stakeholders, including the Student Loan Company (SLC) and Student Finance England (SFE}, and groups representing dyslexic students and dyslexia support professionals. While all of these different stakeholders are part of the dyslexia support landscape, their motives will not be entirely congruent. Leontyev (2009) comments that, "the scientific investigation of activity necessarily demands the discovery of its object" (p.397). In a complex policy landscape, the object or problem space will be perceived differently by different stakeholders. There will almost certainly be tensions between the respective objects of their activity. In this regard, Leontyev (2009) comments that "the main thing that distinguishes one activity from another lies in the difference between their objects. It is the object of activity that endows it with a certain orientation...the object of activity is its motive" (p.400).

For example, in relation to system performance, the SLC may or may not put a higher value on the cost-effectiveness of learning support provision than do dyslexia support organizations. The BIS may or may not put a higher value on national university performance results than on the experiences of individual students. Subtle and not so subtle differences between values can generate tensions within the system and affect communication between stakeholders. As a graphic illustration of this point, an interacting network of activity systems, with tensions between their objects, is shown in Figure 4. While the different activity systems illustrated may have some declared shared interests, the differences in their respective objects and the associated tensions need to be identified and addressed. Such tensions are natural features of activity systems. Roth et al (2004) describe contradictions as "potential growth points that allow the system to improve" (pp.50-51). Identifying tensions through values-focused research and working in partnership to develop a shared object would help to improve the likelihood of the different national stakeholder organizations collectively achieving mutually beneficial outcomes.

Failure to acknowledge, value and address system tensions carries a risk. The potentially serious consequences of limited stakeholder collaboration and poor communication can be seen in the case of the recent management of DSAs. Following the transfer of DSA administration to the SLC, disability organisations and others were critical of the SLC's DSA service provision. NADP (The National Association of Disability Practitioners) (2009b) felt that SLC staff appeared to "lack

understanding of the general HE student environment" (p.4); they also suggested (2009b) that the SLC had "failed to engage appropriately and in a coordinated fashion with key stakeholder organizations" (p.8). Similarly, Skill (2009) referred to "a breakdown of trust between the stakeholders" (p.1). Following the widespread concerns about its service, the Hopkin Review (2009) was commissioned by the government to investigate SLC provision. Hopkin (2009) stated that "rebuilding trust and confidence in the Student Loans Company amongst external stakeholders will be a challenging but essential task", and recommended that the SLC "should work closely with key stakeholders in the higher education sector to ensure they are well sighted on possible risks and emerging issues and are able to work together to overcome them" (p.39). Lack of trust was also mentioned in a report by the National Audit Office (NAO) into the service provided by the SLC. The NAO (2009) recommended that

Figure 4. Interacting activity systems with different objects causing system tensions

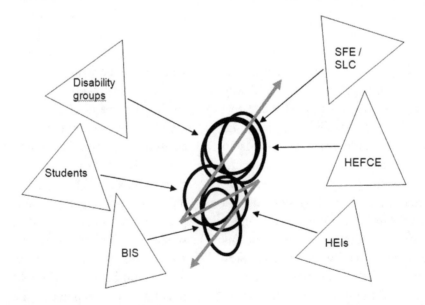

SFE Student Finance England
SLC Student Loans Company
HEFCE Higher Education Funding Council for England
HEIs Higher Education Institutions
BIS Department for Business, Innovation and Skills

BIS and the SLC "urgently need to strengthen their relationship so that there is mutual trust, open communication and shared understanding of how to deliver the service" (p.10). Following these criticisms, the Chief Executive and the Chairman of the SLC both resigned (BBC News, 2010). In summary, while trust and confidence are to be welcomed, actually developing a complex system in a way that effectively promotes stakeholder trust and confidence is a real challenge. To achieve the desired outcomes, complexity, polyphony and reflexivity should be acknowledged as required design features of, and actively incorporated in, the development process.

CONCLUSION

We should listen carefully to dyslexic students (e.g. Hancock & Mansfield, 2002) to hear what is significant to them, and to critically reflect on how we incorporate their perspectives into the ways we support them. Swain & Cook (2005) argue that "the starting point for democratization is the recognition that those directly involved have legitimate perspectives that can inform and shape moves towards inclusion" (p.70). However, not only do individual dyslexic students face complex challenges; universities and other organizations face complex challenges in meeting the needs of the students they serve. To tackle these challenges, in relation to activity theory and the design

of educational systems, Jenlink (2001), argues that "the embodiment of participants' subjectivity is a critical element of the social change or transformation process" (p.350), and comments that, "stakeholder subjectivity is recognized as a primary tool in the generative process of creating an "ideal" system" (p.358).

Sociocultural analysis of stakeholder subjectivities employing Q methodology and activity theory could lead to new models and understandings of the issues, and inform the further development of policy and practice in dyslexia support including new tools to support student transition and progression. Such studies might contribute to the field in a way which "illuminates policy and enhances practice" (Bassey, 1999:7). This chapter makes recommendations to address and go beyond the tensions and challenges identified within dyslexia support. To that extent, it may go some way towards meeting the criteria set by Rix & Simmons (2005), who comment that, "at best we can attempt to examine tensions that are prevalent in the initiation and implementation of inclusive policies and systems, and to highlight areas in which there is still much to be done" (p.8).

By expanding our knowledge and appreciation of different stakeholders' perspectives, we can build shared values into the tools that we use. Tools designed to meet a collective need are more likely to be used, and are more likely to be effective in achieving the changes desired, if they reflect and carry the values of their user-communities.

Figure 5. Satisfying different stakeholder needs by designing shared values into the system

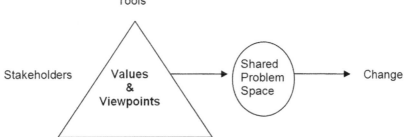

Achieving this requires modeling and incorporating a range of individual perspectives on the issues. As Wenger (1998) comments, "connecting the formation of collectivity and the experience of subjectivity…highlights the inseparable duality of the social and the individual" (p.14). Making connections between individual subjectivities and using these to develop the social good requires planning. An inclusive process of building diverse user values into tools, by combining Q methodology and activity theory, is represented schematically in Figure 5. This is a simplified version of Figure 1, but amended to signify a central place for the values and viewpoints of multiple stakeholders, which should be investigated and modeled to inform planning and development.

More values-focused research will point to key areas of consensus between stakeholders and also to areas where differences of opinion exist. This information can then be used to help shape consensus and partnership by recognizing and building on common values. The approach is consistent with Bottery's (2006) emphasis on "valuing and respecting others' (similarly provisional) views and opinions, and, crucially, of recognizing that such views are sufficiently important as needing to be captured" (p.110). Finally, while this chapter has focused on dyslexia and learning support, the same approach to modeling activity and subjectivity could be applied usefully in a wide range of policy and development contexts.

REFERENCES

ADSHE. (2009). *Guidelines for Quality Assurance in Specialist Support for Students with SpLDs in Higher Education*. Retrieved September 29, 2010, from http://adshe.org.uk/wp-content/uploads/ADSHE-Guidelines-June-20091.pdf

Barker, J. H. (2008). Q-methodology: An alternative approach to research in nurse education. *Nurse Education Today*, *28*(8), 917–925. doi:10.1016/j.nedt.2008.05.010

Barry, J.[a] & Proops, J. (1999). Seeking sustainability discourses with Q methodology. [b,*]. *Ecological Economics*, *28*(3), 337–345. doi:10.1016/S0921-8009(98)00053-6

Bassey, M. (1999). *Case Study Research in Educational Settings*. Buckingham: The Open University Press.

Benjamin, S. (2005). Valuing diversity' – a cliché for the twenty-first century? In Rix, J. (Eds.), *Policy and power in inclusive education: Values into practice* (pp. 175–190). London: Open University.

Billett, S. (2006). Work, Subjectivity and Learning. In Billett, S., Fenwick, T., & Somerville, M. (Eds.), *Work, Subjectivity and Learning* (pp. 1–20). Dordrecht: Springer. doi:10.1007/1-4020-5360-6_1

Block, J. (1956). A comparison of the forced and unforced Q sorting procedures. *Educational and Psychological Measurement*, *16*(4), 481–493. doi:10.1177/001316445601600406

Bottery, M. (2006). Education and globalization: redefining the role of the educational professional. *Educational Review*, *58*(1), 95–113. doi:10.1080/00131910500352804

Brown, S. R. (1971). The forced-free distinction in Q-technique. *Journal of Educational Measurement*, *8*(4), 283–287. doi:10.1111/j.1745-3984.1971.tb00939.x

Brown, S. R. (1980). *Political Subjectivity – Applications of Q Methodology in Political Science*. New Haven, London: Yale University Press.

Brown, S. R. (1997). *The History and Principles of Q Methodology in Psychology and the Social Sciences*. Retrieved April 12, 2004, from http://facstaff.uww.edu/cottlec/QArchive/Bps.htm

Calder, I. (2001). Dyslexia across the curriculum. In Peer, L., & Reid, G. (Eds.), *Dyslexia – Successful Inclusion in the Secondary School* (pp. 174–181). London: David Fulton Publishers / BDA.

Carrington, S., & Elkins, J. (2005). Comparison of a traditional and an inclusive secondary school culture. In Rix, J., Simmons, K., Nind, M., & Sheehy, K. (Eds.), *Policy and power in inclusive education: Values into practice* (pp. 85–95). London: Open University.

Channel 4 (2005). *The Dyslexia Myth*. Broadcast September 8, 2005, Dispatches series. London: Channel 4.

Clegg, S., & McNulty, K. (2005). The creation of learner identities as part of social inclusion. In Rix, J. (Eds.), *Policy and power in inclusive education: Values into practice* (pp. 213–222). London: Open University.

Collins, J., Harkin, J., & Nind, M. (2002). *Manifesto for Learning*. London: Continuum.

Comrey, A. L., & Lee, H. B. (1992). *A first course in factor analysis*. Hillsdale, NJ: Lawrence Erlbaum.

Cornbleth, C. (1990). *Curriculum in Context*. Basingstoke, UK: Falmer Press.

Deignan, T. (2005). (2005, September). *Transferable People: reframing the object in UK post-compulsory education and training*. Paper presented at the University of Manchester conference on Sociocultural Theory in Educational Research and Practice, Manchester, UK.

Deignan, T. (2006). *Transferable People: reframing the object in post-compulsory education and training*. PhD thesis, University of Manchester: UK.

Deignan, T. (2009). Enquiry-based learning: Perspectives on practice. *Teaching in Higher Education*, *14*(1), 13–28. doi:10.1080/13562510802602467

DfEE. (2001). *Code of Practice on the Identification and Assessment of Special Educational Needs. Department for Education*. London: Central Office of Information.

DIUS. (2007, March). *Disabled Students' Allowances, 2007/08 HE Student Finance*. Retrieved October 20, 2010, from http://www.asasa.org.uk/assessment/LA-DSA-2007.htm

DIUS. (2009). *Disabled Students and Higher Education, Research Report 09-06*, Retrieved October 20, 2010, from http://www.bis.gov.uk/assets/biscore/corporate/migratedD/publications/D/DIUS_RR_09_06

Donner, J. C. (2001). Using Q-sorts in participatory processes: An introduction to the methodology. In Krueger, R. A., Casey, M. A., Donner, J., Kirsch, S., & Maack, J. N. (Eds.), *Social Analysis, Selected Tools and Techniques, Social Development Papers, 36* (pp. 24–49). Washington: The World Bank.

DSA-QAG. (2010, March). SFE Recommendations – Standard Packages, *DSA-QAG Update*. Retrieved March 25, 2010, from http://www.dsa-qag.org.uk/assets/_managed/cms/files/MonthlyNewsletterMarch10.pdf

Dyson, A. (2005). Special needs education as the way to equity – An alternative approach? In Rix, J., Simmons, K., Nind, M., & Sheehy, K. (Eds.), *Policy and power in inclusive education: Values into practice* (pp. 121–129). London: Open University.

Elliot, J. (2009). *Evidence Check: Literacy Interventions*, Uncorrected Transcript of Oral Evidence given on 4 November 2009 before the House of Commons Science and Technology Sub-Committee. Reference HC 1080-i. Retrieved June 8, 2010, from http://www.publications.parliament.uk/pa/cm200809/cmselect/cmsctech/uc1081-i/uc108102.htm

Engeström, Y. (1993). Developmental studies of work as a testbench of activity theory: the case of primary care medical practice. In Chaiklin, S., & Lave, J. (Eds.), *Perspectives on Activity and Context* (pp. 64–103). Cambridge, UK: Cambridge University Press. doi:10.1017/CBO9780511625510.004

Engeström, Y. (1999). Activity theory and individual and social transformation. In Engeström, Y. (Eds.), *Perspectives on activity theory* (pp. 19–38). Cambridge, UK: Cambridge University Press.

Engeström, Y. (2000). Activity theory as a framework for analyzing and redesigning work. *Ergonomics*, *43*(7), 960–974. doi:10.1080/001401300409143

Fawcett, A. J. (2002). Dyslexia and Literacy: Key Issues for Research. In Reid, G., & Wearmouth, J. (Eds.), *Dyslexia and Literacy – theory and practice* (pp. 11–28). Chichester: John Wiley & Sons.

Foot, K. A. (2002). Pursuing an evolving object: a case study in object formation and identification. *Mind, Culture, and Activity*, *9*(2), 132–149. doi:10.1207/S15327884MCA0902_04

Guile, D., & Young, M. (1998). Apprenticeship as a conceptual basis for a social theory of learning. *Journal of Vocational Education and Training*, *50*(2), 173–192. doi:10.1080/13636829800200044

Hancock, R., & Mansfield, M. (2002). The Literacy Hour: a case for listening to children. *Curriculum Journal*, *13*(2), 183–200. doi:10.1080/09585170210136840

Hopkin, D. (2009). *Review of the delivery of financial support to students in England by the Student Loans Company for the academic year 2009/10 and plans for academic year 2010/11*, Retrieved February 24, 2010, from http://www.bis.gov.uk/assets/biscore/corporate/docs/d-09-1580-delivery-of-financial-support-to-students

Howe, K. R. & Welner, K.,G. (2005). School choice and the pressure to perform, In J. Rix, K. Simmons, M. Nind & K. Sheehy (Eds.), *Policy and power in inclusive education: Values into practice* (pp.36-46) London: Open University.

Jenlink, P. M. (2001). Activity Theory and the Design of Educational Systems: Examining the Mediational Importance of Conversation. *Systems Research and Behavioral Science*, *18*, 345–359. doi:10.1002/sres.429

Kangasoja, J. (2002). Complex design problems: an impetus for learning and knotworking, *Center for Activity Theory and Developmental Work Research*, Retrieved November 21, 2004, from http://www.edu.helsinki.fi/activity/publications/files/47/ICLS2002_Kangasoja.pdf

Kellett, M., & Nind, M. (2003). *Implementing Intensive Interaction in Schools: guidance for practitioners, managers and coordinators*. London: David Fulton.

La Paro, K. M., Siepak, K., & Scott-Little, C. (2009). Assessing Beliefs of Preservice Early Childhood Education Teachers Using Q-Sort Methodology. *Journal of Early Childhood Teacher Education*, *30*(1), 22–36. doi:10.1080/10901020802667805

Lammy, D. (2009). *Financial Support to Students*. Retrieved March 29, 2010, from http://www.bis.gov.uk/news/speeches/financial-support-students-lammy. London: House of Commons.

Lantolf, J. P., & Thorne, P. (2006). *Sociocultural Theory and the Genesis of Second Language Development*. Oxford: Oxford University Press.

Lave, J., & Wenger, E. (1991). *Situated Learning: Legitimate peripheral participation*. New York: Cambridge University Press.

Leontyev, A. N. (2009). *The Development of Mind*. Pacifica, CA: Marxists Internet Archive.

McKeown, B., & Thomas, D. (1988). *Q Methodology*. Thousand Oaks: Sage.

NADP. (2009a, November). *Report on Disabled Students Allowances [DSAs] situation from the National Association of Disability Practitioners [NADP]*, Retrieved March 29, 2010, from http:www.nadp-uk.org/docs/resources/nadp-dsa-report-nov2009.doc

NADP (2009b), *Evidence for Professor Sir Deian Hopkin's Review into Student Finance Delivery in England 2009*. Retrieved March 29, 2010, from http://www.nadp-uk.org/docs/resources/nadp-hopkins-review-submission.doc

National Audit Office. (2010). *The Customer First Programme: Delivery of Student Finance*. London: NAO / BIS.

National Working Party on Dyslexia in Higher Education. (1999). *Dyslexia in higher education: policy, provision and practice*. Hull: HEFCE.

News, B. B. C. (2010). *Student loan bosses stand down*. Retrieved May 25, 2010, from http://news.bbc.co.uk/1/hi/education/10157509.stm

Nicolson, R. I. (2002). The Dyslexia Ecosystem. *Dyslexia (Chichester, England)*, *8*(2), 55–66. doi:10.1002/dys.218

Oliver, M. (1992). Changing the social relations of research production? *Disability, Handicap & Society*, *7*(2), 101–114. doi:10.1080/02674649266780141

Osler, A., & Osler, C. (2005). Inclusion, exclusion and children's rights. In Rix, J. (Eds.), *Policy and power in inclusive education: Values into practice* (pp. 107–118). London: Open University.

Ott, P. (1997). *How to Detect and Manage Dyslexia*. Oxford: Heinemann.

Ozga, J. (2000). *Policy Research in Educational Settings*. Buckingham: Open University Press.

Paradice, R. (2001). An investigation into the Social Construction of Dyslexia. *Educational Psychology in Practice*, *17*(3), 213–225. doi:10.1080/02667360120072747

Pumfrey, P. D., & Reason, R. (1997). *Specific Learning Difficulties (Dyslexia), Challenges and Responses*. London: Routledge.

Quality Assurance Agency for Higher Education. (1999). *Code of practice for the assurance of academic quality and standards in higher education, Section 3: Students with disabilities*. Retrieved September 19, 2007, from http://www.qaa.ac.uk/academicinfrastructure/codeOfPractice/section3/default.asp#3

Rice, M., & Brooks, G. (2004). *Developmental dyslexia in adults: a research review*. London: NRDC.

Riddell, S., Wilson, A., Adler, M., & Mordaunt, E. (2005). Parents, professionals and special education needs policy frameworks in England and Scotland. In Rix, J. (Eds.), *Policy and power in inclusive education: Values into practice* (pp. 72–84). London: Open University.

Rix, J., & Simmons, K. (2005). A world of change. In Rix, J. (Eds.), *Policy and power in inclusive education: Values into practice* (pp. 1–9). London: Open University.

Robbins, P. (2005). Q Methodology. In Kempf-Leonard, K. (Ed.), *Encyclopedia of Social Measurement* (pp. 209–215). Elsevier Inc.doi:10.1016/B0-12-369398-5/00356-X

Rose, J. (2009). *Identifying and Teaching Children and Young People with Dyslexia and Literacy Difficulties, An independent report from Sir Jim Rose to the Secretary of State for Children, Schools and Families*. Nottingham: DCSF.

Roth, W.-M., & Lee, Y.-J. (2006). Contradictions in theorizing and implementing communities in education. *Educational Research Review*, *1*, 27–40. doi:10.1016/j.edurev.2006.01.002

Roth, W.-M., Tobin, K., Elmesky, R., Carambo, C., McKnight, Y.-M., & Beers, J. (2004). Re/Making Identities in the Praxis of Urban Schooling: A Cultural Historical Perspective. *Mind, Culture, and Activity, 11*(1), 48–69. doi:10.1207/s15327884mca1101_4

Salomon, G. (1997). *Distributed cognitions: Psychological and educational considerations.* Cambridge: Cambridge University Press.

Sawyer, R. K. (2002). Unresolved Tensions in Sociocultural Theory: Analogies with Contemporary Sociological Debates. *Culture and Psychology, 8*(3), 283–305.

Schmolck, P. (2010). *PQMethod Software.* Retrieved June 13, 2010, from http://www.lrz-muenchen.de/~schmolck/qmethod/

Skill: National Bureau for Students with Disabilities (2009). *Evidence for BIS / Professor Hopkin Review of Student Loans Company with specific reference to disabled students applying for Disabled Students' Allowance for entry October 2009 and onwards.* Retrieved March 29, 2010, from http://www.skill.org.uk/uploads/Skill_Hopkin%20Review_submission%20part%201.doc

Stake, R. E. (1995). *The Art of Case Study Research.* London: SAGE.

Stalker, K. (1998). Some ethical and methodological issues in research with people with learning difficulties. *Disability & Society, 13*(1), 5–19. doi:10.1080/09687599826885

Stephenson, W. (1935). Technique of factor analysis. *Nature, 136,* 297. doi:10.1038/136297b0

Stephenson, W. (1953). *The study of behaviour: Q-technique and its methodology.* Chicago: The University of Chicago Press.

Stetsenko, A. (2005). Activity as Object-Related: Resolving the Dichotomy of Individual and Collective Planes of Activity. *Mind, Culture, and Activity, 12*(1), 70–88. doi:10.1207/s15327884mca1201_6

Stringer, G. (2009, January 12). *Dyslexia is a myth.* Retrieved January 27, 2009, from www.manchesterconfidential.com

Student Loan Company (2008, October 21). *Letter of guidance from the Resolution Services Manager, Student Loan Company.* SLC: Doncaster.

Swain, J., & Cook, T. (2005). In the name of inclusion. In Rix, J. (Eds.), *Policy and power in inclusive education: Values into practice* (pp. 59–71). London: Open University.

Tabachnick, B., & Fidell, L. (2001). *Using multivariate statistics.* London: Allyn and Bacon.

Thomas, D. M., & Watson, R. T. (2002). Q-sorting and MIS research: A Primer. *Communications of the Association for Information Systems, 8,* 141–156.

Thomas, G. (2010). Doing Case Study: Abduction Not Induction, Phronesis Not Theory. *Qualitative Inquiry, 16*(7), 575–582. doi:10.1177/1077800410372601

Valsiner, J. (2008). Ornamented Worlds and Textures of Feeling: The Power of Abundance. *Critical Social Studies,* (*1*),67-78.

Van Eeten, M. J. G. (2001). Recasting Intractable Policy Issues: The Wider Implications of the Netherlands Civil Aviation Controversy. *Journal of Policy Analysis and Management, 20*(3), 391–414. doi:10.1002/pam.1000

Vincent, C., & Warren, S. (2005). 'This won't take long….': interviewing, ethics and diversity. In K. Sheehy et al,(ed) *Ethics and Research in Inclusive Education* (pp.102-118). Abingdon: Routledge-Falmer/OUP.

Wartofsky, M. (1979). *Models: Representation and scientific understanding.* Dordrecht: Reindel.

Watts, S., & Stenner, P. (2005). Doing Q methodology: theory, method and interpretation. *Qualitative Research in Psychology,* (2): 67–91. doi:10.1191/1478088705qp022oa

Wenger, E. (1998). *Communities of Practice – Learning, Meaning, and Identity*. Cambridge: Cambridge University Press.

Wigger, U., & Mrtek, R. (1994). Use of Q-technique to examine attitudes of entering pharmacy students toward their profession. *American Journal of Pharmaceutical Education, 58*, 8–15.

Williams, V. (2003). *User-led research with people with learning difficulties*. Exeter: University of Exeter Centre for Evidence-Based Social Services

ADDITIONAL READING

Brown, S. (2003). Comments on Watts & Stenner's 'Q Methodology, Quantum Theory, and Psychology'. *Operant Subjectivity, 26*(4), 176–183.

Brown, S. R. (1972). A fundamental incommensurability between objectivity and subjectivity. In Brown, S. R., & Brenner, D. J. (Eds.), *Science, psychology, and communication* (pp. 57–94). New York: Teachers College Press.

Brown, S. R. (1993-94). The structure and form of subjectivity in political theory and behaviour. *Operant Subjectivity, 17*, 30–48.

Brown, S. R. (1996). Q Methodology and Qualitative Research. *Qualitative Health Research, 6*(4), 561–567. doi:10.1177/104973239600600408

Brown, S. R. (1997). *The History and Principles of Q Methodology in Psychology and the Social Sciences*. Retrieved April 12, 2004, from http://facstaff.uww.edu/cottlec/QArchive/Bps.htm

Brown, S.R., & Robyn, R. (2003, October). *Reserving a key place for reality: Philosophical foundations of theoretical rotation*. Read at a meeting of the International Society for the Scientific Study of Subjectivity, Kent State University-Stark Campus.

Chaiklin, S., Hedegaard, M. & Jensen, U.J. (n.d.). *Activity Theory and Social Practices*. Aarhus: Aarhus University Press.

Chaiklin, S., & Lave, J. (1993). *Understanding Practice: Perspectives on activity and Context*. Cambridge: Cambridge University Press. doi:10.1017/CBO9780511625510

Cole, M., Engestrom, Y., & Vasquez, O. (1997). *Mind, Culture and Activity: seminal papers from the laboratory of comparative human cognition* Cambridge: Cambridge University Press.

Curt, B. (1994). *Textuality and tectonics: troubling social and psychological science*. Buckingham: Open University Press.

Dryzek, J. S. (1990). *Discursive Democracy*. Cambridge: Cambridge University Press.

Engeström, Y. (1990). *Learning, Working and Imagining: Twelve Studies in Activity Theory*. Helsinki: Orienta Konsultit Oy.

Engeström, Y. (1993). Developmental studies of work as a testbench of activity theory: the case of primary care medical practice. In Chaiklin, S., & Lave, J. (Eds.), *Perspectives on Activity and Context* (pp. 64–103). Cambridge: Cambridge University Press. doi:10.1017/CBO9780511625510.004

Engeström, Y. (1996). Interobjectivity, Ideality, and Dialectics. *Mind, Culture, and Activity, 3*(4), 259–265. doi:10.1207/s15327884mca0304_5

Engeström, Y. (2000). Comment on Blackler et al. - Activity Theory and the Social Construction of Knowledge: A Story of Four Umpires. *Organization, 7*(2), 301–310. doi:10.1177/135050840072006

Engeström, Y. (2001). *Expansive Learning at Work: Toward an Activity-Theoretical Reconceptualisation*. London: Institute of Education.

Engeström, Y. (2004). *Workplace Learning and Developmental transfer.* Retrieved April, 28, 2004 from http://www.edu.helsinki.fi/activity/pages/research/transfer

Engeström, Y., Engestrom, R., & Vahaaho, T. (1999). When the Center Does Not Hold: The Importance of Knotworking. In Chaiklin, S., Hedegaard, M., & Jensen, U. J. (Eds.), *Activity Theory and Social Practices.* Aarhus: Aarhus University Press.

Engeström, Y., Miettinen, R., & Punamaki, R.-L. (1999). *Perspectives on activity theory.* Cambridge: Cambridge University Press.

Engeström, Y., Puonti, A., & Seppanen, L. (2003). Spatial and temporal expansion of the object as a challenge for reorganizing work. In Nicolini, D., Gherardi, S., & Yanow, D. (Eds.), *Knowing in Organizations.* New York: M.E. Sharpe.

Good, J. M. M. (2003). William Stephenson, Quantum Theory, and Q Methodology. *Operant Subjectivity, 26*(4), 142–154.

Lave, J. (1988). *Cognition in practice: Mind, mathematics and culture in everyday life.* Cambridge, UK: Cambridge University Press. doi:10.1017/CBO9780511609268

Leontyev, A. N. (1978). *Activity, consciousness and personality.* Englewood Cliffs, NJ: Prentice Hall.

Rogoff, B., & Lave, J. (1988). *Everyday cognition: its development in social context.* Cambridge, MA: Harvard University Press.

Stainton Rogers, R. (1995). Q methodology. In Smith, J. A., Harré, R., & Van Langenhofe, L. (Eds.), *Rethinking methods in psychology* (pp. 178–192). London and Thousand Oaks, CA: Sage.

Stainton Rogers, R., & Stainton Rogers, W. (1990). What the Brits Got Out of Q: and Why Their Work May Not Line Up With the American Way of Getting Into It. *Electronic Journal of Communication, 1* (September) Retrieved October 5, 2010, from http://www.cios.org/www/ejc/v1n190.htm

Stainton Rogers, W. (1997/98). Using Q as a form of discourse analysis. *Operant Subjectivity, 21*(1/2).

Stephenson, W. (1977). Factors as operant subjectivity. *Operant Subjectivity, (1)*,3-16.

Stephenson, W. (1978). Concourse theory of communication. *Communication, 3,* 21–40.

Stephenson, W. (1980a). Consciring: a general theory for subjective communicability. In Nimmo, D. (Ed.), *Communication Yearbook 4* (pp. 7–36). New Brunswick, NJ: Transaction.

Stephenson, W. (1980b). Factor Analysis. *Operant Subjectivity, (3),*38-57.

Stephenson, W. (1983). Against Interpretation. *Operant Subjectivity, 6*(3), 73–103.

Stephenson, W. (1983). Against Interpretation. *Operant Subjectivity, 6*(4), 109–125.

Stephenson, W.(1986). Protoconcursus: The concourse theory of communication. *Operant Subjectivity, 9*(2),37-58 and *9*(3),73-96.

Thurstone, L. L. (1947). *Multiple-factor analysis: A development and expansion of The Vectors of Mind.* Chicago: University of Chicago Press.

Vygotsky, L. S. (1986). *Thought and language.* Cambridge, MA: MIT Press.

Watts, S., & Stenner, P. (2003). Q Methodology, Quantum Theory, and Psychology. *Operant Subjectivity, 26*(4), 157–175.

Wenger, E., McDermott, R., & Snyder, W. M. (2002). *Cultivating Communities of Practice: A Guide to Managing Knowledge*. Boston, MA: Harvard Business School Press.

KEY TERMS AND DEFINITIONS

Activity Theory: A framework for describing and analysing human activity. The motives, tools and relationships found within collective activity systems are examined in relation to their socio-cultural contexts. The nature of these dynamic relations is considered with regard to system development and transformation.

Dyslexia: A specific learning difficulty primarily affecting the development of literacy skills. The difficulties experienced can persist despite the provision of educational opportunities and dyslexia-specific interventions. Individuals with dyslexia can have cognitive profiles that appear inconsistent with their level of literacy.

Learning Support: That support provided to dyslexic students by their university to enable them to develop and achieve their potential as learners.

The support typically involves one-to-one study skills tutorials, workshops, and learning materials provided in a range of formats.

Q Methodology: A technique for investigating and modeling viewpoints on any given issue or topic. A Q study typically involves the ranking-ordering of items by individuals, followed by correlational and factor analysis by-person of those rankings. The procedure provides information on the variety of perspectives in relation to an issue including how these relate to each other in terms of areas of consensus and difference.

Sociocultural Theory: A perspective on learning which sees human development as arising out of social interaction and engagement in activity. Mediation is seen as a key aspect of the developmental process. Mediation involves the individual and collective use of physical and symbolic tools and artefacts in the construction and maintenance of relationships between individuals and in their relationships with the world around them.

Chapter 14

Inclusivity and Research:
Capturing the Lived Experiences of Young People with Disabilities

Hayley Fitzgerald
Leeds Metropolitan University, UK

Annette Stride
Leeds Metropolitan University, UK

Anne Jobling
University of Queensland, Australia

ABSTRACT

This chapter seeks to stimulate thinking and reflection by exploring the position and place of young people with disabilities in research. In doing this, the authors contextualize the chapter within the subject area of physical education. By mapping out the research terrain of young people with disabilities they find these young people have been marginalised and often precluded from research. More recent developments around 'inclusive research' do signal the possibilities for research and the benefits of actively engaging with young people with disabilities. They extend discussions in this chapter by highlighting how teaching and learning in Higher Education can draw on this kind of inclusive research in order to develop 'narratives'. These are stories based upon research data from young people with disabilities. In particular, the authors present two examples of research narratives and discuss how these can be used in teaching and learning to promote student thinking around the meaning and experiences of physical education for young people with disabilities.

DOI: 10.4018/978-1-61350-183-2.ch014

INTRODUCTION: 'A LIFE APART'

In 1972 Miller and Gwynne published *A Life Apart: A pilot study of residential institutions for the physically handicapped and the young chronic sick*. This book focused on case study research in five residential establishments in Britain. The research included observations of the day-to-day activities within these institutions and interviews with staff, volunteers and residents. At the time of publication, the research discussed in this book was the first that sought to capture the experiences of living and working in residential institutions. Although written nearly forty years ago we believe this text remains a compelling read as it draws attention to a number of issues which were significant then and remain equally important to contemporary debates and discourses around disability within society. In particular, *A Life Apart* offers powerful insights around: inclusion and exclusion; the challenges of engaging in disability research; and the importance of sharing the life stories of people with disabilities. Of course, a major shift in the UK since the publication of *A Life Apart* has been the deinstitutionalization of people with disabilities and a move towards independent living and inclusion within the community. To a large extent these changes have supported a shift in thinking in which people with disabilities are becoming increasingly recognised as legitimate members of society. This is in stark contrast to the conclusions made by Miller and Gwynne (1972, p. 80) about people with disabilities within the residential establishments they researched:

To lack any actual or potential role that confers a positive social status in the wider society is tantamount to being socially dead. To be admitted to one of these institutions is to enter a kind of limbo in which one has been written off as a member of society but is not yet physically dead. In these terms, the task that society assigns – behaviourally though never verbally – to these institutions is to cater for the socially dead during the interval between social death and physical death.

This rather poignant account portrays people with disabilities as possessing little value and having no meaningful purpose in life. In part, this analysis should serve as a powerful reminder of the ways in which people with disabilities have historically been marginalised within society. During the interim period since the publication of *A Life Apart*, the position of people with disabilities has continued to be (re)negotiated and to a large extent the catalyst has been the drive for a more inclusive society. Indeed, recent legislative and policy developments promoting inclusion and equity have gone some way to redressing inequalities (Slee, 2009). For example, the Equity Act (2010) requires public bodies to develop an equality scheme and action plan in order to demonstrate how people will be protected from discrimination and how equality and diversity will be promoted across the key equality strands, including disability. However, it should also be acknowledged that the legacy of discrimination remains ever present within contemporary society (Lakinski, 2008).

As well as providing a powerful reminder of a move from exclusionary and segregated living to more inclusive community contexts, *A Life Apart* also offers important insights into the processes and politics of doing research about the lives of people with disabilities. Indeed, since its publication, this book has provoked considerable debate about the role of researchers, power relations within research and inclusive approaches to data collection (Baker, Lynch, Cantillon, & Walsh, 2004; Mercer, 2002). Most notably, Hunt (1981) labelled the researchers, Miller and Gwynne, as 'parasite people', and claimed researchers were on the side of the oppressors, interested in their own research careers and consequently exploiting people with disabilities. These observations and discussions, stimulated through the *A Life Apart* research, also raise important questions about contemporary research focusing on disability. In particular, this has prompted us to continually reflect on research practices and ask critical questions about our research and that of our contemporaries. These questions revolve around the purpose of research, exploring who benefits and considering how people with disabilities are part of the research process. The *A Life Apart* research provides one means of re-presenting the lived experiences of people with disabilities and at the time of publication these people were largely represented in research through medical terms. This is in contrast to contemporary society where more diverse stories can now be found about the lives of people with disabilities in mediums such as biographies, poetry, film, drama, and other visual sources (see for example Cole, 2004; MacConville, 2007; Shah, 2008; Wilkinson, 2009). As educators, our ongoing challenge remains to ensure that the stories from the past, told in *A Life Apart,* and other contemporary tales are heard by our students and practitioners in order to help them better understand disability within society.

In this chapter we want to extend discussions, stimulated through *A Life Apart*, by focusing on research in relation to young people with disabilities, specifically in the context of physical education. We focus on physical education, as this is a subject where the physicality of pupils is explicitly exposed to others, such as teachers, classmates and support staff. Unlike other school subjects, physical education can magnify the visibility of some (in)abilities for young people with disabilities. Initially, we will map out the ways in which research has involved young people with disabilities in research. Following this we consider the notion of 'inclusive research' and the possibilities this brings to researching with young people with disabilities. Our discussions then move onto students in Higher Education and we focus on the research-teaching nexus by exploring how we can forge a greater connectedness with research in our teaching and learning. In particular we discuss how 'narratives', that is the stories of young people with disabilities, can be incorporated into curriculum design. We hope this chapter supports researchers to reflect on their engagement with people with disabilities within the research process and also promotes thinking around the use of narratives in teaching and learning.

BACKGROUND: RESEARCHING DISABILITY

Young People (with Disabilities) and Physical Education

Contemporary society has witnessed a radical shift in the way we understand young people. This re-articulation has resulted in an increasing recognition that we need to listen to the voices of young people, including young people with disabilities, to better understand their experiences. In this way, young people have become positioned as 'experts' in their own lives (Clark & Moss, 2001; Hill, Prout, & Tisdall, 2004) and not 'cultural dopes' (Prout & James, 1997, p. 23). This philosophy has extended to many spheres of life through the development of legislation (The Children's Act, 2004); policy (Department for Education and Skills, 2004); human rights (United Nations Convention of the Rights of Persons with Disabilities); and research in childhood studies (James, Jenks, & Prout, 1998; Save the Children, 2000). Importantly, according to Alderson (2008), these developments have extended the nature of legislative responsibility for young people, from protection and provision to 'participation rights'. For example, in the broader context of empowerment and self advocacy, a growing number of innovative examples exist within education of engaging pupils and involving them in decision-making (Barnardo's, 2002; Cruddas, 2001; Fielding, 2006; Harding, 2001; Weller, 2007). These examples serve to illustrate the immense abilities of young people to be 'agents of transformation' (Fielding, 2002).

Within this research context, there is also growing recognition that the views of young people are important and that they should be seen as positive contributors to understanding their lived experience(s). This recognition positions young people as active social agents who are able to articulate their experiences and express their own views (Christensen & Prout, 2002; Greig, Taylor, & MacKay, 2007; Smith, 2007). When specific consideration is given to young people with disabilities, it is evident that much research mirrors the way in which people with disabilities are perceived within society and is reflected through the insights found in *A Life Apart*. Typically, researchers listen to the views of carers or professionals and dismiss young people with disabilities as illegitimate sources of research information (Priestley, 1999; Smith, 2007). Without insights from young people with disabilities it is difficult to see how practitioners or researchers can effectively advance change within different dimensions of life, including schools and physical education. Indeed, the willingness and desire of young people with disabilities to engage in research was a striking feature highlighted in some recent research we conducted, "I want them to know how I get on in PE. I want them to know I like it. I want them to know I do it a lot. I'm glad my picture is like famous now" (Mary).

Mary was involved in focus group discussions and as part of this also generated a drawing of her physical education experiences. She was particularly keen to ensure that what she said was passed on to her physical education teachers, other school staff and her classmates. Although Mary's experience of being involved in research was positive, this is generally not the case. The position of young people with disabilities in research is rather ironic given that researchers advocate in findings for more inclusive practices. However, many researchers have yet to include young people with disabilities in 'inclusive' ways to enable them to contribute to the research process.

Within a physical education context, it is claimed that practitioners have "served well the talented, able-bodied, skilled, physically fit, educated, middle classes" (Macdonald, 2002, p. 184). Similarly, researchers within physical education have been preoccupied with specific groups of young people and largely ignored others, such as young people with disabilities (Flintoff, Fitzgerald, & Scraton, 2008). Moreover, when consideration has been given to disability, a medicalized imperative has dominated research concerned with physical education (DePauw, 2000). From this quantitative and medicalized perspective disability and 'the disabled body' have extensively been treated as an object to be tested, modified and retested. A number of writers have acknowledged that such data only provides a partial understanding of the experiences of disability, with DePauw (1997, p. 419) suggesting:

To most in our field ... The object of our study is the body or specific aspects of the performing body, but traditionally our study has not focused on the body as whole, the body in a social context, or the body in connection with self.

The re-articulation of young people as autonomous agents, and a recognition of people with disabilities as more than 'objects' to be researched on, means that new ways of approaching and undertaking research need to be developed and embraced. This has led some researchers to advocate for inclusive approaches to research and we next consider the possibilities this may bring.

Inclusive Research: It's More Than 'Smiley Face Syndrome'

Within contemporary society, working towards inclusion is seen as a solution to the many inadequacies of society that prevent people with disabilities from fully participating in social life.

Researchers have also begun to recognize the importance and need to develop inclusive approaches in research involving people with disabilities. Like broader understandings of inclusion (Armstrong & Barton, 2008; Barrow, 2001), researchers have differing conceptions of what this means and consequently how they go about researching. For example, some researchers have translated inclusive research into merely using 'smiley faces' on a Likert scale of a questionnaire. We have coined this kind of approach as 'smiley face syndrome'. It is not inclusive research, but rather ill-conceived attempts to make minimal changes in research that are uncritically perceived as inclusive. In this context, the change by a researcher is negligible and does not significantly question in any way current thinking and practices in research. On this matter, Henderson (2009, p. 104) recently talked about JUST research and, in part, advocated a need to "destabilize the presumed authority structure of research". This view represents a more radical shift in thinking that requires us to question the very foundations and essence of research. The need to work towards inclusive research becomes more apparent when considering some young people with disabilities. For example, a young person with a severe learning disability who does not verbally communicate may be excluded from a research project where the preferred method for data collection is interviews. This restricted view of listening and inflexibility in research design often means many people with disabilities, who communicate using Makaton (see: www.makaton.org) and other augmented forms, are presumed to be unable to make meaningful contributions to research. As we have found, engaging with young people with disabilities becomes far more productive when consideration is primarily given to the person's communication needs. From this standpoint, data collection strategies can be adapted in ways that reflect the research participants' preferred means of communication. Whilst this way of thinking may seem like a logical approach to researching with

people with disabilities, it is one that is not necessarily followed by the majority of researchers.

There are some examples of research that illustrate the ways in which people with disabilities can be involved and valued in research. Indeed, much of this work draws on participatory approaches found within childhood studies (Christensen & James, 2003) and disability studies (Barnes & Mercer, 1997). This research utilizes drawings and photography (Prosser & Loxley, 2007), drama and role-play (DIY Theatre Company & Goodley, 1999), narrative (Roets & Goedgeluck, 2007), augmented forms of communication (Germain, 2004) and working with young people as co-researchers (Fitzgerald & Jobling, 2004; Fitzgerald, Jobling, & Kirk, 2003; Johnson, 2009; Williams & Simons, 2005). Much of this research could be considered as inclusive because it is either participatory or emancipatory and in this way seeks to address a range of principles associated with inclusive research including:

1. The research question, problem or issue must be one that is owned (though not necessarily initiated) by people with disabilities.
2. It should further the interests of people with disabilities and non-disabled researchers should be on the side of people with disabilities.
3. It should be collaborative and people with disabilities should be involved in the process of doing the research.
4. People with disabilities should be able to exert some control over the process and outcomes.
5. The research question, process and reports must be accessible to people with disabilities.

(Adapted from Walmsley & Johnson, 2003, p. 64)

In different ways each of these principles disrupts the normative and traditional ideas associated with research. Importantly, these principles and the emerging body of research in this area show that we can engage with young people with profound and multiple disabilities but this requires researchers to think laterally and, as Henderson (2009) argues, destabilize what they know. Although we are involved in working towards inclusive research one of the overarching challenges we continue to face is how to embed the findings from this work into our teaching and learning in Higher Education. It is this research-teaching nexus that we now move on to consider and explore how narratives can enhance curriculum design and engage student learning in physical education and sport.

MOVING RESEARCH INTO THE CURRICULUM THROUGH A NARRATIVE APPROACH

It is widely acknowledged that students in Higher Education benefit from research informed teaching (Healey, 2005; Jenkins, Breen, & Lindsay, 2003). Whilst recognizing there are various ways to conceptualize the research-teaching nexus, we have been keen to ensure pedagogies incorporate research findings in ways that move beyond merely reading, reviewing, discussing and critiquing research papers. In seeking to develop student learning activities we have begun to use narratives as an alternative means of re-presenting research data. Like a number of scholars, we see the benefits of transgressing the boundaries of traditional writing genres by utilizing narrative approaches (Brown, Dodd, & Vetere, 2010; Connor, 2008; Owens, 2007). Narratives can be used in different ways in teaching and learning. For example, self-narrative offers opportunities for students to develop reflexively (Bailey, 2010), whilst research informed narratives provide a vantage point for students, and other practitioners, to learn through the story telling of others (Carless & Douglas, 2009; Douglas & Carless, 2008). As a way of illustrating the richness that narratives can bring to re-presenting data we next offer two narrative tales that were generated from research with young

people with disabilities and their encounters with physical education.

Our purpose in presenting these narratives is two-fold. Firstly, they signal the possibilities for research to move beyond traditional approaches to data generation and re-presentation. Indeed, it is widely acknowledged that researchers need to work harder to find accessible ways of presenting research findings. Within physical education and sport this is particularly important as policy makers, curriculum planners, PE teachers and coaches need to clearly understand what issues are at stake (such as what young people with disabilities think about physical education) before they begin to address the possibilities of change in their practices. We believe narratives offer the potential for practitioners to gain valuable insights about experiences without feeling overwhelmed by the theorizing and abstraction that sometimes dominates the content of scholarly journals.

Second, we present these narratives as an example of a teaching and learning tool that provides a means of more closely engaging students with empirically generated data. Like practitioners, our students also need to hear different stories and accounts of young people's physical education experiences. Through hearing these insights our students need to develop their abilities to review, problem solve and make connections with concepts and theories. We also want our students to be caring and compassionate practitioners and in this way develop empathy for young people who do not necessarily feel the same as they do about physical education and sport. Narrative stories seek to create conditions that appeal to the emotions, increasing sensitivity to others with whom we are not familiar (Denzin, 1989). Again, we believe narratives can be useful in teaching and learning to work towards the development and progression of our Physical Education students in this way.

Following Bruce (1998), the first non-fiction narrative, *'Dreaded PE'*, was melded together through the insights gained from the interviews, drawings and montages of a range of young people with disabilities. In this way, we have drawn on varied data sources to re-present a story about a central character called Dave who has a Cerebral palsy which affects movement on the right side of his body. The second narrative, *'Me and my helper in PE'*, tells the story of Mary who uses wheelchair after acquiring a disability, and this tale was woven together through insights from interviews and a drawing she produced.

Dreaded PE (Dave, Aged 13)

Oh no, I'm awake, the black cloud descends, is that Mum? 'Come on Dave, it's time to get up; you're going to be late. You need to get a move on, come on'. I don't want to wake up, I don't want to get up, I don't want to go there, I don't want to be me today. Quick close my eyes, maybe I'll fall back to sleep. Please let it be yesterday again, just not today. Today is the worst day, a terrible day, I hate today. I don't want to get out of bed. I don't want to go to school.

I feel ill. It's like my stomach is going around in circles, butterflies and all that. My toast sticks in my throat, a gluey lump. 'Hurry up, eat up' says Mum. Across the kitchen floor *the bag* stares at me. I could forget it and take the punishment – one hour detention is nothing. Yep, that's what I'll do. I move slowly to the front door, feeling lighter, feeling brighter, I'm sorted. Then Mum shouts 'Don't forget your PE kit, honestly you can be so forgetful at times. Go on, have a good day'. My heart sinks, how can I possibly enjoy school now? It's like my whole body is dreading school today. I don't want to go. I don't want to be there. I don't want to be me.

I can't remember getting to school, I don't know what we've just done in English but I know what's coming next, PE. I'm not a PE person. I hate PE. Why do they make me do PE? PE is for them, you know the ones. The sporty boys, the tough guys, the ones that have loads of mates, the ones the girls like, 'cause they're fit and fast, with muscles that'll get bigger and better. The guys that

can get into fights and come away battered and bruised and the winners. Yeah, that's what they are, winners. What does that make me?

So, here I am. The corridor stretching ahead of me with that lone door at the end, its peeling red paint like a warning sign. Enter at your own risk. Stay away, go away. As I slowly get closer that smell begins to hit me, assaults me. Like a stale sweaty smell of effort that separates the winners and losers. I don't sweat. Their noise of excitement gets louder and louder, chatter and laughing. What don't I see? When I get to the changing room I'm numb. I'm there but I'm not. I know what's coming and just don't want to be there. I move to the corner, to the safety of my locker. They can't see me here, can they? I am invisible. Mr. Evans gives a loud shout 'Boys it's ten past, you should be in the sports hall by now'. Oh no, he's looking for me, please don't pick on me. 'Dave, is that you hiding behind the coats. You can't stay there. Just what do you expect your school report to say if you don't bother with PE? Are you a man or a mouse'?

As I move into the sports hall eyes start staring. I feel like I'm in the middle of a big crowd of people and as they circle around me, like the lions I watched on last night's program, their wide open eyes are staring intensely at me and only me. I'm so hot, my fingers, hands and face are burning. This isn't a friendly place to be. Not for me, not for the mouse. Relief at last as Mr. Evans gets our attention. Their eyes move to him. I'm invisible again, but only for a short time. I watch and listen to what he's telling us to do. It's not that I don't want to try but I just know I won't be able to do it right, my body won't do it like that. My body moves in different ways. Why's it so crap. Why won't it work like it should, like the others?

Everyone's shuffling around 'Be with me', 'Tom, here quick', 'Let's go over there'. None of this is for me. No looks, no stares now. I am on my own, no one wants to be with me. When Josh is put with me, he's so not happy and lets everyone know, 'Why me? It's not fair'. Some of them look relieved and mock him 'Unlucky Josh, I told you not to stand so close'. With my unwilling partner and unruly body I have a go. I am like a clown, a spectacle to be watched and laughed at and the centre of attention for all the wrong reasons. All lions are staring at me again and there's nowhere to go and hide. I hate being me.

Me and My Helper in PE
(Mary, Aged 13)

There goes the bell, play time over. They all take off, like sprinters, running quickly to the end of the playground, pushing, shoving, screaming, shouting, surging towards the big blue doors for last lesson. I slowly wheel myself pass the bike stands, past Miss Clarke shouting at Paul McMahon and Andy Little, again. Keep on moving, don't stop or they'll stare and point. So, original! Detention for them, serves them right! Clare's sulking because I'm not with her next lesson. She kicks at the dust, head down, silent as we make our way slowly across the netball courts. I suppose I could be with her and the others next if I wanted to, but I like doing this class on my own, with my helper. It's more fun, I get stuff done. But I don't want her falling out with me. I look up and my eyes squint as the sun shines brightly as it bursts from behind a cloud. Then I spot them, out of the corner of my eye, the big netball posts, nets swaying in the breeze, too high for me. Can't get the ball to go anywhere near them, not that I get a chance. I'm always Goal Keeper and hardly ever touch the ball. I just sit there, cold and bored, wondering why I'm there. No one seems to notice me, not the teacher, not the others, it's like I'm invisible. They just play around me, until I get in the way. I mean how am I supposed to move so quickly in my chair? There's not enough room to wheel around and by the time I get to the ball someone else has picked it up. Can't they throw it at me? It's not so bad if Clare's near me. She always passes to me if no one is standing in front of me, blocking my view, or worse still, not marking me so that I get

to touch it. Should I be grateful or summat? We usually end up talking when the ball's down the other end, planning what we're gonna do after school. And then we get shouted at if we're not paying attention and the ball flies past us.

No, I'm going to do PE on my own today. I've made up my mind. I don't want to be just sat there, I want to do something. I want to play. Can't tell Clare that though, she wouldn't get it, she's not that bothered about PE. It'll be alright, she thinks I have to do this special lesson on my own. That's my little secret, mine and my helpers. She holds the door open for me and smiles, 'See you later then? I better run, or I'll be late again. Meet me outside the changing rooms when you're finished?' 'Sure' I reply. Phew, she's alright with me after all. She sprints off towards the changing rooms, gym bag bouncing on her back, footsteps echoing along the empty corridor, until she disappears through the swinging doors. Then, all that's left for me to see is the back of her head, bobbing up and down, red hair flying everywhere, seeing less and less until I hear the changing room door open and slam shut. It's alright, PE, with Clare and the others, but I wouldn't want to do it more than once a week. It depends what we do, I guess. I hate netball and hockey but I love badminton and fitness, and I'm never stuck with someone to work with. Clare is always my partner and Jenny and Sarah join with us. It doesn't matter if I miss the ball when I'm with them. I don't like doing stuff as a whole group though, like in a game. Then I just hide at the back and hope the ball doesn't come near me. But I get bored, I want to touch the ball but I daren't in case I miss it and some people groan, or laugh, or whisper. Most are OK though, but I'd hate it if I couldn't do some PE on my own.

I get close to the big red changing room door and it bursts open. They spill out, wearing bright green and blue bibs, throwing the balls at each other, yelling and laughing. They shout hello and smile and wave as they rush past and I wait patiently for them to file out. I look carefully,

Centre, Wing Attack, Goal Shooter, yep, all the best positions have gone. I wonder what's left? Goal Keeper? Well not today. I'm gonna do my own thing, I'm gonna do what I want to do. I get to choose. Netball, hockey, athletics, rounders, all briefly remembered and then gone, quickly forgotten for another week. I can do what I want! Peace descends as their voices get further away as they make their way to the courts. Excited, I begin to look at the equipment in the cupboards as I wait for Erin. She'll be late. She has to help someone else during break. Quickly move past the hockey sticks, stuffed into the metal bin, tape beginning to peel, past the shiny, new javelins, all lined up ready for next term. I reach for the tennis racket and fuzzy orange balls. What about the parachute, spilling out between the shot puts and the smelly kit people have forgotten? It tries to escape, begging to be played with, hardly ever used, unless the special needs kids come down to use it. A bag of balls, propped up in the corner, catches my eye. I could do some throwing and catching. Think that's what I'll do 'cause I've got tons better at that and that'll help me in the other lesson. I know, we can set a challenge like we did last week. Throw and catch ten in a row. And then when I've done that we can have another go at that target game. Yep, that was fun, I scored 50 points, could beat that easily. Yep, that's what we'll do. Now where's Erin? Let's get started!

Using These Narratives in Teaching and Learning

Through our experiences of supporting students enrolled on physical education courses, we recognize there are many similarities in their personal reflections on physical education. For example, our students are likely to have been successful in physical education, were probably in a school sports team and aspire to becoming a physical education teacher, sport development officer or coach. The challenge then is to open their eyes and alert them to alternative experiences to those dominant discourses and understandings. After all, when they have secured employment in teaching or coaching, they will not just be supporting young people who are carbon copies of themselves.

By adopting a narrative approach in teaching and learning, we believe our students will be better positioned to understand, at least to some degree, the physical education experiences of other young people including those with a disability. More broadly, counter-experiences to dominant discourses within physical education also encompass contextual issues concerned with policy and practice. Our students need to develop critical, reflective skills around these discourses in order that they are better equipped to recognize the 'slippage' that occurs between well-intended policy directives and actual practice in schools. For example, whilst policy underpinned by inclusive principles has increasingly dominated school and physical education policy this does not mean subsequent practices in schools have changed. Our students need to extend these kinds of understandings of policy discourses and be reflective upon the implications for their practice and young people's physical education experiences. In exploring issues such as these we recognize we are asking our students to reflect on complex issues. Like Douglas and Carless (2008, p. 36) we support the view that our students are "active *storytellers*" themselves, telling stories about particular days, lessons and pupils during their school placements, and because of this will be receptive to working with narratives in their teaching and learning in Higher Education.

The two narratives offered in this chapter capture the stories of two different young people with disabilities as they experience school physical education. We argue that, in combination, both tales provide a range of possibilities for reflective thinking around the meaning and experiences of physical education for young people with disabilities. We recognize each tale, like any form of text, can be read differently (Stanley & Wise, 1993; Weiner, 1994), and because of this, teaching and learning strategies need to be organized in a progressive and balanced way. This will enable different kinds of reflection to take place (self, other, subject and situational) and at the same time allow space for theoretical/conceptual thinking to be nurtured.

We next outline a number of learning tasks that could form the basis of a seminar session. In developing these tasks, we have adopted an approach that initially centralizes the student's individual reflective experiences of physical education. The tasks then move onto considering the experiences of other people (fellow students or young people with disabilities). In creating these tasks, we have attempted to ensure incremental developments in the way concepts or theories are introduced to the seminar content. As a guide to aid the progression of tasks within the seminar, we have drawn on the work of Douglas and Carless (2008), who found three main responses to narratives in Continuing Professional Development. First, a *summarizing* response that "is characterised by an analytical process that involves summarising the story in a relatively distanced, uninvolved, and unemotional fashion" (p. 40). Second, an *incorporating* response which occurs where "the listener incorporated the story within their own experience" (p. 41). Third, a *questioning* response to a narrative, suggesting "that [people] took the stories seriously and had begun to consider the possible implications of each story" (p. 38). In many ways parallels can be drawn with these three responses to Bloom's (1956) and Anderson and Krathwohl's (2001) taxonomy of learning, which both advocate progressive learning in which increasingly sophisticated thinking is encouraged. What follows is an overview of the seminar session and related learning tasks.

Table 1. Session Objective 1

Objective 1 Learning Tasks	Student activity	Organization of learning	Outcome
Learning Task 1 - 'Narrative of self' Having discussed the importance of being a reflective practitioner, students are asked to respond through a short narrative to the statement 'Your experiences of PE'.	Short self-reflective narrative such as a written paragraph or bullet points.	Individually working on narrative	Response (Bloom's taxonomy): Knowledge and comprehension Theory: Socialization into sport (Côté & Hay, 2002)
Learning Task 2 - Based upon the narratives from Learning Task 1, students are asked to discuss why they chose to write that particular narrative and the focus it has.	Identify key similarities or differences between experiences (e.g. activity, teacher relations, classmate relations, pedagogy, outcomes relating to skill development, winning or losing).	Paired or small group discussions	Response: Knowledge and comprehension Theory: Constructivist theories of learning (Rovegno & Dolly, 2006) Curriculum construction (Penney, Brooker, Hay, & Gillespie, 2009)
Learning Task 3 - Based upon the discussions from Learning Task 2, students are asked to consider why there were similarities and differences in their experiences.	Discuss the reasons for these similarities and differences.	Whole group discussion	Response: Comprehension and application Theory: Socialization into sport (Côté & Hay, 2002) Constructivist theories of learning (Rovegno & Dolly, 2006) Curriculum construction (Penney, et al., 2009)

Seminar Session Outline

Session Aim

Applying theoretical perspectives to narratives and counter-narratives of physical education to explore understandings of different pupil experiences.

Session Objectives

1. To reflect on personal experiences of physical education by developing a self-narrative.
2. To compare and contrast self-narratives with those of young people with disabilities and consider the reasons behind the differences and similarities in these stories.
3. To critically analyse the pedagogical implications of different pupils' physical education experiences.

Although these tables do not capture the detailed activities and exchanges that are likely to occur as a result of the various learning tasks, they offer

some insights into the possibilities for teaching and learning when narratives are incorporated into seminar sessions. On this occasion, we have presented the tasks and student activities associated with the session objectives in a basic teaching and learning structure. However, we recognize that there is a range of alternative possibilities that could be incorporated into a similar session, which would be dependent on the students' content knowledge of physical education, their practical experiences of teaching and the theoretical understandings they have already developed. Practically, the session could also be organized in different ways, for example, students could be divided into three groups and each group given a different learning task (one group writing their own narrative; another group reading Dave's narrative; and the final group reviewing Mary's narrative). Discussions could then take place within these groups similar to Learning Task 3. Following this, the students with different narratives could come together in small groups and share these in similar ways to tasks 4 to 8. This approach would enable students to hear about

Table 2. Session Objective 2

Objective 2 Learning Tasks	Student activity	Organization of learning	Outcome
Learning Task 4 - 'Pupil narratives', Students are asked to read the narrative of Dave or Mary and respond to the question 'How did this make you feel'?	Reading of narrative and high-lighting or noting key points.	Individual	Response (Bloom's taxonomy): Application and analysis Theory: Socialization into sport (Côté & Hay, 2002)
Learning Task 5 - Students are asked to consider the following question in relation to the pupil narrative and their response to Learning Task 4: 'Why did you feel like this'?	Discuss the reasons for these feelings.	Paired or small group discussions	Response: Application and analysis Theory: Socialization into sport (Côté & Hay, 2002)
Learning Task 6 - Students are asked to compare the narratives of Dave or Mary with the narrative written in Learning Task 1 and consider what the similarities and differences between these experiences are	Identify key similarities or differences between your experiences and those of Dave or Mary.	Paired or small group discussions	Response: Analysis and synthesis Theory: Socialization into sport (Côté & Hay, 2002) Inclusion (Slee, 2009)

Table 3. Session Objective 3

Objective 3 Learning Tasks	Student activity	Organization of learning	Outcome
Learning Task 7 - Students are asked to compare the narratives of Dave or Mary with the narrative written in Learning Task 1 and consider how they might use these insights to inform their teaching?	Discuss how you might use these insights to inform your teaching	Small group discussion and then whole group	Response (Bloom's taxonomy): Analysis and synthesis Theory: Socialization into sport (Côté & Hay, 2002) Medical /social models of disability and physical education (Barton, 2009) Inclusion (Slee, 2009)
Learning Task 0 Students are asked to compare the narratives of Dave or Mary with the narrative written in Learning Task 1 and discuss how they might use these insights to inform their understandings of disability?	Discuss how you might use these insights to inform your understanding of disability	Small group discussion and then whole group	Response: Application, analysis, synthesis and evaluation Theory: Medical /social models of disability and physical education (Barton, 2009) Inclusion (Slee, 2009)

these alternative stories through the lenses of fellow students and in doing so has the potential to evoke different kinds of responses, sharing and discussions from students.

CONCLUSION

As *A Life Apart* illustrates, people with disabilities were until very recently viewed as holding a tenuous position within society. In part, this situation has been exacerbated by narrow approaches to researching people with disabilities. Such approaches have continued to marginalize and objectify people with disabilities and in this way silence their voices within research. As a consequence, our historical insights and knowledge about people with disabilities have continued to be partial and tainted by notions that situate these people as 'socially dead' (Miller & Gwynne, 1972, p. 80). Contemporary developments associated with inclusive legislation and policies have gone some way to repositioning people with disabilities in society. Similarly, recent developments around inclusive research are also opening up possibilities for people with disabilities to take a legitimate and meaningful place in research. Like

Edwards (2002), we argue that more researchers need to become 'responsible researchers' and by doing this, take up the challenge to find ways of researching inclusively. As a way forward, we suggest researchers should reflect on these questions before they embark in research: Why am I doing this research? Who will benefit? How will I ensure people with disabilities are not excluded from my research? How will I disseminate my research to people with disabilities?

Our attention in this chapter has predominantly focused on the subject area of physical education and the experiences of young people with disabilities. However, we suggest that our later discussions around the use of narratives in teaching and learning are relevant to a range of academic staff and also those charged with supporting Continuing Professional Development activities across professions. Indeed, we believe that using narratives in teaching and learning lends itself well to exploring a range of issues focusing on the lived experiences of young people with disabilities. For example, within a broader school context, narrative stories would help to shed light on experiences of other school subjects, relations with teachers and support staff, decision making and choices about participating in after-school clubs and friendships at school. Beyond a school context, narrative tales could extend our understandings of young people with disabilities in relation to their leisure lives, friendships, relations with family and aspirations for the future. Although we have focused on disability in this chapter, it is also worth highlighting that other equity issues concerned with gender, ethnicity, class and sexuality could also be explored in similar ways. In research and teaching it is easy to lose sight of the participants involved. They are not just numbers, letters or pseudonyms. They are real living people, who are best positioned to tell us their stories about their lives. Adopting a narrative approach to re-present these insights enables these tales to reflect the whole person, the embodied self, and in this way authentically capture their lived experiences.

REFERENCES

Alderson, P. (2008). *Young Children's Rights: Exploring Beliefs, Principles and Practice*. London: Jessica Kingsley Publishers.

Anderson, L. W., & Krathwohl, D. R. (2001). *A Taxonomy for Learning, Teaching and Assessing: A Revision of Bloom's Taxonomy of Educational Objectives*. New York: Longman.

Armstrong, F., & Barton, L. (2008). Policy, Experience and Change and the Challenge of Inclusive Education: The Case of England. In Barton, L., & Armstrong, F. (Eds.), *Policy, Experience and Change: Cross Cultural Reflections on Inclusive Education* (pp. 5–18). Dordrecht: Springer.

Bailey, D. C. (2010). Engaging Family Studies Students: Using a Self-Narrative to Improve One's Teaching. *Family Science Review, 15*(1), 31–39.

Baker, J., Lynch, K., Cantillon, S., & Walsh, J. (2004). *Equality: From theory to action*. Basingstoke, UK: Palgrave.

Barnardo's. (2002). *The Spark Centre: Barnardo's Consultation with Children and Young People*. London: Barnardo's.

Barnes, C., & Mercer, G. (1997). Breaking the mould? An introduction to doing disability research. In Barnes, C., & Mercer, G. (Eds.), *Doing Disability Research* (pp. 1–14). Leeds: The Disability Press.

Barrow, R. (2001). Inclusion vs. Fairness. *Journal of Moral Education, 30*, 235–242. doi:10.1080/03057240120077237

Barton, L. (2009). Disability, physical education and sport: some critical observations and questions. In Fitzgerald, H. (Ed.), *Disability and Youth Sport* (pp. 39–50). London: Routledge.

Bloom, B. S. (Ed.). (1956). *Taxonomy of Educational Objectives - Handbook 1: The Cognitive Domain*. New York: David McKay Co Inc.

Brown, J., Dodd, K., & Vetere, A. (2010). 'I am a normal man': A narrative analysis of the account of older people with Down's syndrome who lived in institutionalised settings. *British Journal of Learning Disabilities, 38*(1). Retrieved from http://www3.interscience.wiley.com/cgi-bin/fulltext/123214615/PDFSTART. doi:doi:1111/j.468-3156.2009.00596.x

Bruce, T. (1998). Postmodernism and the Possibilities for Writing "Vital" Sports Texts. In Rail, G. (Ed.), *Sport and Postmodern Times*. Albany: State University of New York Press.

Carless, D., & Douglas, K. (2009). Stepping out of the box: How stories can inspire growth, development, and change. *Annual Review of High Performance Coaching and Consulting, 2009*, 175–185.

Christensen, P., & James, A. (2003). *Research with Children Perspectives and Practices*. London: Falmer Press.

Christensen, P., & Prout, A. (2002). Working in ethical symmetry in social research with children. *Childhood*, *9*(4), 467–477. doi:10.1177/0907568202009004007

Clark, A., & Moss, P. (2001). *Listening to young children: The mosaic approach*. London: National Children's Bureau and The Joseph Rowntree Foundation.

Cole, J. (2004). *Still Lives: Narratives of Spinal Cord Injury*. Boston: Massachusetts Institute of Technology.

Connor, D. J. (2008). (Manuscript submitted for publication). Urban Narratives [*Life at the Intersections of Learning Disability, Race and Social Class*. New York: Peter Lang.]. *Portraits*.

Côté, J., & Hay, J. (2002). Family influences on youth sport performance and participation. In Siva, J. M., & Stevens, D. (Eds.), *Psychological foundations of sport* (pp. 484–519). Boston: Allyn & Bacon.

Cruddas, L. (2001). Rehearsing for reality: Young women's voices and agendas for change. *Forum*, *43*(2), 62–66. doi:10.2304/forum.2001.43.2.7

Denzin, N. (1989). *Interpretive Interactionism*. Newbury Park, CA: Sage.

Department for Education and Skills. (2004). *Every Child Matters: Change for Children*. London: HMSO.

DePauw, K. P. (1997). Sport and physical activity in the life-cycle of girls and women with disabilities. *Women in sport and physical activity journal*, *6*(2), 225-238.

DePauw, K. P. (2000). Social-cultural context of disability: Implications for scientific inquiry and professional preparation. *Quest*, *52*(4), 358–368.

DIY Theatre Company, & Goodley, D. (1999). People with learning difficulties share views on their involvement in a performing arts group. *Community Work & Family*, *1*(3), 367–379.

Douglas, K., & Carless, D. (2008). Using Stories in Coach Education. *International Journal of Sports Science & Coaching*, *3*(1), 33–49. doi:10.1260/174795408784089342

Edwards, A. (2002). Responsible researcher: ways of being a researcher. *British Educational Research Journal*, *28*(2), 157–168. doi:10.1080/01411920120122121

Fielding, M. (2002). 'Beyond the rhetoric of student voice: New departures or new constraints in the transformation of 21ˢᵗ century schooling?' *International Symposium on Student Voice and Democracy in School*. Paper presented at the Annual Meeting of the American Educational Research Association.

Fielding, M. (2006). Leadership, radical student engagement and the necessity of person-centred education. *International Journal of Leadership in Education*, *9*(4), 299–313. doi:10.1080/13603120600895411

Fitzgerald, H., & Jobling, A. (2004). Student-centred research: Working with disabled students. In Wright, J., Macdonald, D., & Burrows, L. (Eds.), *Critical Inquiry and Problem-Solving in Physical Education* (pp. 74–92). London: Routledge.

Fitzgerald, H., Jobling, A., & Kirk, D. (2003). Valuing the Voices of Young Disabled People: Exploring Experiences of Physical Education and Sport. *European Journal of Physical Education*, *8*(2), 175–201.

Flintoff, A., Fitzgerald, H., & Scraton, S. (2008). The challenges of intersectionality: researching difference in physical education. *International Studies in Sociology of Education*, *18*(2), 73–85. doi:10.1080/09620210802351300

Germain, R. (2004). An exploratory study using cameras and Talking Mats to access the views of young people with learning disabilities on their out-of school activities. *British Journal of Learning Disabilities*, *32*, 157–204. doi:10.1111/j.1468-3156.2004.00317.x

Greig, A., Taylor, J., & MacKay, T. (2007). *Doing Research with Children*. London: Sage Publications Ltd.

Harding, C. (2001). Students as researchers is as important as the National Curriculum. *Forum, 43*(2), 56–57. doi:10.2304/forum.2001.43.2.5

Healey, M. (2005). Linking research and teaching: Exploring disciplinary spaces and the role of inquiry-based learning. In R. Barnett (Ed.), *Reshaping the University: New Relationships between Research, Scholarship and Teaching* (pp. 67-78). London: McGraw Hill / Open University Press. Henderson, K. (2009). Just Research and Physical Activity: Diversity Is More Than an Independent Variable. *Leisure Sciences, 31*(1), 100-105.

Hill, M., Prout, A., & Tisdall, K. (2004). Moving the participation agenda forward. *Children & Society, 18*(2), 77–96. doi:10.1002/chi.819

Hunt, P. (1981). Settling accounts with the parasite people: A critique of 'A Life Apart'. In E.J. Miller and G.V. Gwynne (eds). *Disability Challenge, May,* 37-50.

James, A., Jenks, C., & Prout, A. (1998). *Theorizing Childhood*. Cambridge: Polity Press.

Jenkins, A., Breen, R., & Lindsay, R. (2003). *Reshaping teaching in Higher Education, linking Teaching with Research*. London: Kogan Page Limited.

Johnson, K. (2009). 'No longer researching about us without us: a researcher's reflection on rights and inclusive research in Ireland'. *British Journal of Learning Disabilities, 37,* 250–256. doi:10.1111/ j.1468-3156.2009.00579.x

Lakinski, M. (2008). *Getting Away with Murder. Disabled people's experiences of hate crime in the UK*. London: Scope.

MacConville, R. (2007). *Looking at Inclusion: Listening to the Voices of Young People*. London: Paul Chapman Publishing.

Macdonald, D. (2002). Critical pedagogy: what might it look like and why does it matter. In Laker, A. (Ed.), *The Sociology of Sport and Physical Education*. London: Routledge/Falmer.

Mercer, G. (2002). Emancipatory Disability Research. In Barnes, C., Oliver, M., & Barton, L. (Eds.), *Disability Studies Today*. Cambridge: Polity Press.

Miller, E. J., & Gwynne, G. V. (1972). *A Life Apart. A pilot study of residential institutions for the physically handicapped and the young chronic sick*. London: Tavistock Publications.

Owens, J. (2007). Liberating voices through narrative methods: The case for an interpretive research approach. *Disability & Society, 22*(3), 299–313. doi:10.1080/09687590701259617

Penney, D., Brooker, R., Hay, P., & Gillespie, L. (2009). Curriculum, pedagogy and assessment: three message systems of schooling and dimensions of quality physical education. *Sport Education and Society, 14*(4), 421–442. doi:10.1080/13573320903217125

Priestley, M. (1999). Discourse and Identity: Disabled Children in Mainstream High Schools. In Corker, M., & French, S. (Eds.), *Disability Discourse* (pp. 92–102). Buckingham: Open University Press.

Prosser, J., & Loxley, A. (2007). Enhancing the contribution of visual methods to inclusive education. *Journal of Research in Special Educational Needs, 7*(1), 55–68. doi:10.1111/j.1471-3802.2007.00081.x

Prout, A., & James, A. (1997). A New Paradigm for the Sociology of Childhood? Provenance, Promise and Problems. In James, A., & Prout, A. (Eds.), *Constructing and Reconstructing Childhood*. London: Falmer Press.

Roets, G., & Goedgeluck, M. (2007). Daisies on the Road: Tracing the Political Potential of Our Postmodernist, Feminist Approach to Life Story Research. *Qualitative Inquiry, 13*(1), 85–112. doi:10.1177/1077800406295624

Rovegno, I., & Dolly, J. P. (2006). Constructivist perspectives on learning. In Kirk, D., Macdonald, D., & O'Sullivan, M. (Eds.), *The Handbook of Physical Education*. London: Sage Publications.

Save the Children. (2000). *Children and Participation: Research, monitoring and evaluation with children and young people*. Belfast: Save The Children.

Shah, S. (2008). *Young Disabled People: Aspirations, Choices and Constraints*. Surrey, UK: Ashgate Publishing Ltd.

Slee, R. (2009). The Inclusion Paradox: The Cultural Politics of Difference. In Apple, M. W., Au, W., & Gandin, L. A. (Eds.), *The Routledge International Handbook of Critical Education* (pp. 177–189). London: Routledge.

Smith, A. B. (2007). Children as Social Actors: An Introduction. *The International Journal of Children's Rights, 15*(1), 1–4. doi:10.1163/092755607X185537

Stanley, L., & Wise, S. (1993). *Breaking Out Again*. London: Routledge.

Walmsley, J., & Johnson, K. (2003). *Inclusive research with people with intellectual disabilities. Past, present and futures*. London: Jessica Kingsley Publishing.

Weiner, G. (1994). *Feminisms in Education: An Introduction*. Buckingham: Open University Press.

Weller, S. (2007). *Teenagers' citizenship: experiences and education*. London: Routledge.

Wilkinson, M. (2009). *Defying Disability: The Lives and Legacies of Nine Disabled Leaders*. London: Jessica Kingsley Publishers.

Williams, V., & Simons, K. (2005). More researching together: the role of nondisabled researchers in working with People First members. *British Journal of Learning Disabilities, 33*, 6–14. doi:10.1111/j.1468-3156.2004.00299.x

KEY TERMS AND DEFINITIONS

Inclusive Research: Refers to various principles of researching that enable a range of people (including people with disabilities) to be part of the research process. These principles of inclusive research influence the planning of a research project, data collection and dissemination.

Narratives: The tales people tell about their lives and can take the form of poems, drama or stories. Storied narratives can be fictional or non-fictional. If they are non-fictional they can be based on self narratives (the stories people write about themselves) or they can be threaded together by using research data.

Parasite Researchers: A phase that was coined by people with disabilities in the 1970s to describe the researchers they encountered. This term continues to be used today in relation to researchers who exploit people with disabilities.

Physical Education: : A practical and theoretical subject that is compulsory in England and in which like other school subjects a National Curriculum is followed by teachers in England. In the past ten years physical education has benefited from increased funding and this has resulted in the development of a more coherent infrastructure to support partnership working between schools and the community.

Research-Teaching Nexus: Concerns the relationship between teaching and research and in particular the ways in which research can be embedded within the curriculum in order to support student learning.

Chapter 15

Reflections on Personal Experiences of Staff Training and Continuing Professional Development for Academic Staff in the Development of High Quality Support for Disabled Students in Higher Education

Alan Hurst
National Bureau for Students with Disabilities, UK

ABSTRACT

Despite the progress made in the development of policy and provision for disabled students in Higher Education since the issue first received attention in the UK in 1974, there is still some way to go before a state of genuine inclusion is reached. The key to further improvement and enhancement of quality is seen to lie in training for staff. After presenting evidence showing the need for more and better training, a number of issues relating to initial training and continuing professional development are discussed. A number of sample tasks for inclusion in staff development sessions are described.

INTRODUCTION

Considerable progress has been made in developing high quality policy and provision for disabled students in higher education in the years since 1974 when the first study of the situation in the

UK was published (National Innovations Centre, 1974). Evidence for this assertion about progress can be found in number of sources such as Department for Industry, Universities and Skills (2009) and Higher Education Funding Council for England (2009a). At the start, much of the positive change was due to the activities of the newly created National Bureau for Handicapped Students

DOI: 10.4018/978-1-61350-183-2.ch015

which, as Skill: National Bureau for Students with Disabilities, continued to work effectively to support disabled students until its demise in 2011. Further progress came as a result of the actions of the national funding councils created following legislation in 1992 and also following the Dearing Report in 1996 (Hurst 1999). A third push for progress has been the introduction and spread of anti discrimination law since the first Disability Discrimination Act of 1995. However, whilst celebrating the progress, one must not become complacent.

Informal contacts with disability advisers suggest that most of the challenges they and the disabled students encounter are curriculum-related and classroom-based. Many issues stem from an unsatisfactory and/or an inadequate approach to staff training and continuing professional development (CPD) in higher education institutions. However, to build a case for change there is a need to collect and consider valid evidence about disabled students' experiences in higher education. This paper starts by outlining evidence indicating the need for more and better staff training and CPD. The following section discusses a range of issues associated with policy and provision of staff training and CPD. The final section provides some examples of activities which can be used in training sessions.

STAFF TRAINING AND CONTINUING PROFESSIONAL DEVELOPMENT: DOES MORE NEED TO BE DONE?

In recent years more evidence has accumulated indicating the need for improved staff training and CPD in relation to working with disabled students in higher education. The following section will focus on the most recent sources described in terms of three major themes: students' issues, staff concerns, and aspects of institutional policies.

Students' Issues

The example used here is the report on the outcome of the debates and discussions which resulted from meetings of the National Student Forum in 2009.

Within the National Student Forum's Annual Report (DBIS 2009) there is a specific chapter concerned with disabled students. Chapter Five is called "Improving the Experience of Disabled Students". It identifies five matters which warrant attention: a need for more tailored information prior to entry, a lack of adequate knowledge about sources of funding available, the existence of misconceptions and stigma in the higher education institutions which unwittingly contribute to the perpetuation of discrimination, academic disadvantages, and the non-academic challenges arising from insufficiently accessible features of the institutions. The report makes five recommendations in relation to each of the above: improve advice and guidance for prospective disabled students, review and revise induction and enrolment procedures to ensure that they are inclusive, raise awareness of disability issues amongst the wider student community in higher education, improve awareness of disability amongst all staff, and ensure that institutional feedback methods secure data from disabled students and are used to improve policy and provision.

The Report identifies factors associated with making good provision for disabled students and how students might recognize this high quality. It is suggested that good practices prevail if the disabled students can:

- Readily access information about the specialist support that is available at a particular university or college
- Freely access information about specialist funding
- See that expectations of their ability are based on performance – and not on preconceptions

- Access appropriate learning materials and facilities e.g. transcription and interpretation services, and electronic textbooks
- State that their lecturers vary their teaching methods for different learning styles and abilities
- Confirm that their development needs are recognised and supported, for example, through the use of personal development plans (PDPs)
- See that their needs are considered at each step of their education, from enrolment through to graduation

Changes cannot be accomplished alone and without support so it is interesting to note the government's responses to the National Student Forum. It referred a number of matters to the Equality Challenge Unit (ECU) but without any linked plan of action. These responses included: exploring the feasibility of creating an international association of disabled students, integrating disability awareness into the orientation programmes for all students, developing a bank of student ambassadors for disability, increasing the emphasis on disability matters in feedback mechanisms, establishing national guidelines to strengthen the use of Personal Development Plans (PDP), investigating the feasibility of a centralised electronic library for disabled students and commissioning research into the comparative progression rates of disabled students, and – most significantly for this paper - improving disability education for all staff.

Whilst not wishing to be critical of the above, for those of us working to promote inclusion and to move away from seeing disability as some kind of special case, it is also important to explore other sections of the NSF Report and to consider **their** implications for disabled students. For example Chapter One is called "Teaching and Learning – some issues faced by students". Points raised include: a lack of clarity and advance information about what learning is like in higher education,

insufficient emphasis on the development of pedagogical skills, inaccessibility of teaching staff, a lack of innovation in courses, a lack of choice in modes of study, the balancing of choice with coherence, and an over-emphasis on the assessment OF learning rather than FOR learning,

As with the chapter on disabled students, a list of recommendations follows. These include the need to:

- Pprofessionalise teaching and learning within all Higher Education Institutions(HEI),
- Personalise and differentiate approaches to take account of disabilities, learning difficulties and learning styles,
- Increase flexibility in course structures, to increase the range of modes of study,
- Develop a cross-institutional strategy to enable students to co-design and manage their learning,
- Undertake regular reviews of course content and material to ensure currency and relevance,
- Ensure a university-wide focus on assessment for, not just of, learning,
- Review the adequacy and accessibility of study resources for the number and range of students,
- Monitor and formally record students' broader learning,
- Incentivise HEI to achieve excellence in teaching and learning as well as research.

Arguably, much of the above could be addressed by improved staff training and CPD for teaching staff. For many disability support staff it is of fundamental importance to redress the imbalance of attention given to the two major dimensions of institutional activity: teaching and research in the UK at least. Some recent advertisements to recruit new teaching staff do not mention teaching as part of the job specification.

Academic Staff's Concerns

In 2009, a longitudinal study of the experiences of disabled students with a range of impairments in four higher education institutions in England and Scotland was published (Fuller et al 2009). It was funded by the Education and Science Research Council (ESRC) and was about enhancing the quality of disabled students' learning. Throughout the study, the need for staff training and development emerges but it is within Chapter Six that many of the issues are considered specifically. A number of themes emerged from the research indicating where students and staff felt the need for further training. These are grouped under four headings: curriculum design, learning and teaching, institutional policies and provision, and individual, personal concerns.

Curriculum Design

In recent times a lot of attention has been given to the idea of universal course design and the ways in which adopting this approach from the start should increase the accessibility of the programme and minimise the need for and number of "reasonable adjustments" as required by anti-discrimination law. It is also a way of meeting the other legal requirement to operate in an anticipatory way for instance by devising pedagogic strategies which do not disadvantage students with sensory impairments. Universal course design means that from the outset the curriculum structure, delivery and assessment should be created in such a way that there are few if any barriers to participation by students with a range of additional needs resulting from background, ethnic community, age, gender, disability, etc. Because this strategy of course design has only gathered greater momentum in recent years, much of the experience of the students and staff in Fuller et al's research (2009) pre-dated such developments.

Six topics for development in the area of curriculum were identified from the data collected in the investigation:

A. **Content of courses:** One way in which staff might become more familiar with aspects of disability is to ensure that it is included within the curriculum of as many subjects and courses as possible. One example from the research was of architecture students who were taught about making buildings accessible to comply with disability legislation.

B. **Flexibility of courses:** The experiences of some students indicated that their choice of study programme could be governed by their courses' non-negotiable requirements. In some examples disabled students were unable to avoid having to undertake aspects of courses which they found more challenging because of the nature of their impairment (e.g. fieldwork in geography courses).

C. **Requirements of professional bodies and fitness to practice:** Arguably the clearest example of the concerns relating to entry to a profession and fitness to practice involves initial teacher training courses. Some staff participants in the research mentioned the physicality of teaching as a barrier for physically disabled students and also sensory impairments as potential difficulties in terms of child safety in the classroom.

D. **Maintaining standards:** A concern for standards was cited by some and whether disabled students are able to meet them. Again, this was often linked to study programmes in which professional bodies had a significant involvement. There were debates about the distinction between competence standards (not subject to the legal requirement to make "reasonable adjustments" and which all must meet) and performance standards i.e. strategies of demonstrating that these standards have been met possibly by making "reasonable adjustments".

E.   **Placements and practical classes:** In some courses, an essential requirement is that students have to attend practical classes and/or undertake placements both in the UK and overseas. Clearly, if this is a non-negotiable aspect of the programme of studies, disabled students must fulfil it and appropriate arrangements need to be made.

F.   **IT based learning**: In the past, distance learning using study packs and telephone conversations was often seen as the answer to the access issues faced by many disabled people. Indeed, the successful record of the Open University in the UK provides evidence of the success of this approach when at one time the number of students who had disclosed a disability was greater than that resulting from combining the numbers in all other HEI. However, it must not be seen as the opportunity needed by all disabled learners. On the other hand, most institutions have developed e-learning policies and provision using a range of approaches and available technology. For example, in the research, there were often references to programmes such as WebCT, Blackboard, and Moodle.

Learning and Teaching

The matter which was the source of most comment was the provision of lecture notes in advance of classroom sessions. This is frequently seen as a simple "reasonable adjustment" for disabled students. Views on this from both staff and students were varied. Some saw advantages in providing materials in advance of classes, others had concerns for example about the impact on attendance at and participation in classes. A number of questions arose in the research about lectures as an effective learning strategy along the lines discussed by Bligh (1971). Some staff seemed aware of their shortcomings and tried to create

learning sessions which were more interactive and participative.

The Institutional Context

A.   **Internal organisation and administrative structures:** The four institutions involved in the research had all developed different internal structures and systems including those in place for supporting disabled students. Some aspects of these differing structures/systems appeared to be more helpful than others. For example, whilst all had a well-established central service for this group of students, the links between these and individual academic department/schools/faculties varied. In one, each faculty had a named co-ordinator who was a member of academic staff and within each faculty all departments had a named contact, preferably and usually again a member of the academic staff. Communication between these individuals was frequent and regular and covered a variety of matters ranging from information about the needs of individual students to the development of publicity and marketing materials. Others had not put in place such a clear structure and might be seen as lagging behind in moves towards shared responsibilities and a whole institution approach to the inclusion of disabled students.

B.   **Physical environment:** Each of the four institutions was located in a different local environment. Their sites presented a range of building styles, open spaces and overall layout. The result was that there were considerable variations in their accessibility to students with a range of impairments. When there is discussion of the physical environment, the focus turns immediately to the challenges posed for those with impaired mobility. However, it must not be forgotten that university sites might also be made more accessible and user-friendly to people with auditory and visual impairments. Improving access is more than the installation of ramps, elevators and adapted rest rooms. For example use of colour contrasts in the furnishing of buildings and of differing floor coverings can improve accessibility for blind and visually-impaired users whilst clear and unambiguous signage is of considerable help to users who are Deaf (note the use of the upper case D in order to comply with the preference of many members of the Deaf community who wish to emphasis that for them deafness is really a difference in culture, language, etc. rather than an impairment/disability) or hard-of-hearing.

C. **Health and safety:** Even before the greater attention paid to health and safety issues in the recent past, it was sometimes used as a first excuse to prevent disabled students being accepted on to a course rather than as a last resort. Under the terms of anti-discrimination law it is a valid reason to turn down an application from a disabled person but this should occur only after a properly undertaken risk assessment and the consideration of possible "reasonable adjustments". In one university the safe evacuation from fires of students who use wheelchairs had become the responsibility of university staff rather than the fire services. This had led to a new policy where mobility-impaired students were not allowed into rooms above ground level.

D. **Setting priorities:** Working to support disabled students emerged as low status work in most institutions. Academic staff in particular were seen to have other/conflicting priorities such as research. A colleague commented to Fuller et al:

We work in a research-intensive university which is RAE (Research Assessment Exercise) driven. And if you ask staff to spend a lot of time getting

materials ready for a handful of students, whereas they could be doing research, then that is difficult to manage... (Fuller et al, 2009 pp 85-86)

E. **Staff training and continuing professional development:** Many of the challenges faced by disabled students arise from a lack of training. There are two dimensions to this: basic training for life as a teacher in a university, and specialist training about disability and staff responsibilities following changes to the law. Probably, in the past twenty years, there has been some progress made in providing some basic training in teaching for staff new to the role. Part of this originated in the Dearing Report and the establishment of the Institute for Learning and Teaching in Higher Education which was intended to form the core of a professional association for those teaching in Higher Education. (Since its establishment the organization has been renamed the Higher Education Academy and operates in a different way to the original.) Tutors need to be aware that by adopting what are regarded as good classroom practices, all students benefit including those with disabilities.

Individual Factors

A. **Knowledge of impairments and their potential impact on study:** Given the level of general ignorance about disability in contemporary society, it should come as no surprise that there were considerable variations in the knowledge that staff in the institutions had about the range of impairments. For example some might need to be reminded of the distinction between visible and invisible impairments since the latter are often more misunderstood.

B. **Knowledge of appropriate assistive technology and "reasonable adjustments":**

Whilst it would be inappropriate to expect lecturers to be aware of the ways in which assistive technology has developed to support disabled students, arguably there are some basic points with which they should be familiar. For example changing the presentation of print based materials can be helpful in making them more accessible to some students (e.g. varying the colour contrast between print and background and/or using particular type fonts, usually those without serifs – see the chapter by Ball in this book).

C. **Lack of previous experience of working with students with a particular impairment:** When asked about the challenges they face in including disabled students in their classes, some staff commented on their lack of prior experience.

D. **Lack of time:** Making effective provision for disabled students was often viewed as a time-consuming activity. This additional demand occurred at a time when teaching staff were faced with many other demands, often seen by them as having greater priority. Some of the changes necessary to facilitate the inclusion of disabled students are relatively simple and can be made without too much additional effort. For example in one institution classes had been moved to a venue which was more accessible to wheelchair users.

Sometimes the inability to make appropriate provision is genuine and is linked to a lack of additional resources. However, one might retain some scepticism about this since, in the UK at least, the national funding councils do make available additional funds based on the number of disabled students who are enrolled at an institution and are in receipt of the Disabled Students Allowances (DSA). Further discussion of this could lead on to another interesting debate about what all in-stitutions should provide as part of their routine standard learning package for students and what individuals should purchase using their DSA. In 1998 the funding councils tried to address this matter by indicating what might be considered to be base-level provision. Since its publication (HEFCE 1999), a lot has changed especially following the Quality Assurance Agency's Code of Practice and the spreading coverage of anti discrimination legislation.

Institutional Policy-Based Themes

To investigate the extent of progress in policy and provision for disabled students in the ten years since the publication of the base-level circular in 1998 (HEFCE 1998), the English and the Welsh higher education funding councils jointly sponsored a research review. In addition to making available the full project report (HEFCE 2009a), both funding councils issued papers summarizing what was found and indicating to institutions what the funding councils working with the institutions might do to make further improvements (HEFE 2009b, HEFCW 2009).

Specific references to the importance of CPD in promoting inclusive practices for disabled students occur in Paragraphs 75 to 80 (HEFCE 2009b) and Paragraphs 24 to 28 and 49 in Annex A (HEFCW 2009). These note the desirability of ensuring that teaching staff are aware of a wide range of learning, teaching and assessment strategies which are needed to meet the entitlements of disabled students. The variety of existing approaches to CPD is recognized and also that different levels of experience and different staff responsibilities mean that CPD needs to be tailored to meet the needs of the potential participants. There is also the suggestion that initial classroom training and CPD relating to disability could be made compulsory although this does not appear to be given strong endorsement. Thus, following Paragraph 80 in the HEFCE document the good practice advice in relation to planning CPD states:

Keep CPD for staff under review and ensure it is appropriate; there are a variety of resources available and training should range from the general to the much more specific depending on the staff concerned.

CPD needs to take account of specific impairments within an inclusive context that acknowledges that everybody experiences disabilities differently. This will aid in planning and designing inclusive teach-ing and assessment, and in developing inclusive policies and practices, and will reduce barriers to learning. (HEFCE, 2009b page 14)

Similar versions of these statements are in-cluded in the Welsh Funding Council document (see page 16 in HEFCW 2009).

Whilst it is heartening to see comments such as these in documents published by such power-ful and influential bodies, one must also express disappointment with the handling of CPD. For example, following most sub-sections covering different aspects of policy and provision, there are short paragraphs indicating what the fund-ing councils can do to support institutions. The documents are strangely silent on their role in promoting CPD. Perhaps, too, it is equally puzzling and disappointing that having acknowledged the importance of CPD in the main text, there is no mention in the Executive Summary which opens the English document and which is the section most likely to be read by busy senior managers. Arguably, a valuable opportunity to further the cause of CPD has been lost here.

Moving on, it is time now to explore staff training in more detail. Before outlining some examples of activities which might be used to address some of the needs identified by staff, it is important to explore a number of general issues.

ISSUES IN POLICY AND PROVISION OF TRAINING AND CONTINUING PROFESSIONAL DEVELOPMENT

What Should Sessions Contain?

This is not an easy question to answer. Much de-pends on the participants and their interests, needs and responsibilities. However, using the research of Fuller et al (2009) it is possible to suggest four themes which seem to concern many of the staff and students interviewed for the project. All stem from a consideration of impairments which are not immediately obvious on first meetings between staff and students. These can be summarised as the four Ds:

A. **Definitions and models of disability:** The foundation for creating an inclusive institution is the social model of disability. (Oliver, 1990)This moves away from see-ing the challenges faced by disabled people as resulting from their own impairments and towards seeing them as a consequence of the ways in which we have chosen to build society. For example, in teaching a tutor might choose to use an audio-visual resource as an aid to learning. Unless this has been adapted for use with those who have sensory impairments, it will create a barrier to learning. It is important also to recognise that an impairment might not be immediately visible and that sometimes it might impact intermittently on the individual (e.g. epilepsy, m.e.). There is a natural lead here into a discussion of stereotyped images of disability and also about issues relating to disclosure for those whose impairment is not obvious on first meeting. It is not uncommon to find that people with impairments which are not immediately obvious choose not to disclose since they are anxious that it might result in negative responses for example to applications for places on courses such as school-teaching, social work and nursing. (See Stanley et al, 2007 for more details about this.)

B. **Dyslexia:** Many students and staff commented on several issues relating to dyslexia although it is interesting to note that all tended to see it as a form of specific learning difficulty (i.e. the application of an individual/medical deficit model of disability) rather than a learning difference (an educational model). By implementing the latter, responsibility shifts from learner to tutor whose professional knowledge, skills and experience should enable her/him to meet the needs of a diverse range of students whose preferred approach to learning differs from what tutors regard as the normal. It is clear that there is some lack of knowledge about the impact of dyslexia on study patterns. For example some viewed dyslexia as simply the inability to spell correctly.

C. **Disclosure of impairment:** The significance of disclosure for entry to some professions is evident from recent investigations by the UK Disability Rights Commission. Studies looked at the issue of disclosure of unseen impairments by staff employed in nursing, social work, and school teaching (Lin et al 2006; Stanley et al 2007). Disclosure is a cause of concern for students because they feel it might lead to discrimination of some kind. Once the information has been made known, there are additional concerns about confidentiality for the student. For members of the teaching staff, the issue is about getting the information in advance so that there is sufficient time to plan the required adjustments.

D. **Anti-discrimination laws:** If teaching staff make blanket assertions of the kind made by some staff they allow for the possibility of legal action to be taken against them. A lecturer in Chemistry in the research undertaken by Fuller et al (Fuller et al 2009)

commented that blind students cannot study Chemistry. If this position is adopted and becomes inflexible there is a risk of action under anti-discrimination law. To avoid this and to strengthen their position if challenged about refusing to offer places, teaching staff need to identify the core non-negotiable parts of the study programme and to show that even with reasonable adjustments it would be impossible for a student with a particular impairment to meet them.

In the research by Fuller et al there were indications that staff were aware of their duties to make "reasonable adjustments" and that disabled students were aware of their legal entitlements. What was less clear was staff's implementation of the anticipatory duties (i.e. universal curriculum design) and trying to ensure things are in place prior to the arrival of the student and the start of the course. This should be a major focus of CPD for teaching staff.

How Should Sessions Be Presented?

Given that the sessions are targeted towards teaching staff, it is essential that they are based on sound and proven pedagogic principles and practices. One strategy is to implement principles associated with effective learning. First and foremost they should be participative with those present being as actively involved as possible for as much of the time as possible. Given that people learn in different ways, there should be a variety of approaches used in the sessions – for example by using some visual materials in video or DVD format (but making sure that they are accessible to all who might be present!). The varied approaches also contribute to retaining interest. To secure and retain attention, the content should be perceived to be relevant. In this case, working with a clearly identified group of staff is helpful when planning the sessions. Last but not least, the range of activities should provide an enjoyable experience – learning can be fun. The cartoons of John Callahan use humour to stimulate thinking on a range of points some of which might indicate matters which are felt to be sensitive (Callahan 1998).

By implementing these principles, participants will have plenty of opportunities to interact with each other and with the presenters. It is this spontaneity and vibrancy that is of crucial importance. In the past few years a number of opportunities for training and continuing professional development in relation to disabilities have been made available on-line in many HEI (e.g. the DEMOS project at Manchester University first released in 2003 and the more recent DART project at Loughborough in 2006 – see the list of references for URL for these sources). Despite their quality and despite their usefulness, undertaking them as a solitary exercise loses a lot. At best they are a supplement to rather than substitute for face-to-face interaction and the liveliness and challenges these provide for both participant and presenter.

One approach used in the past was to include simulations. For example, materials are available to simulate a range of visual and auditory impairments or it might be possible to borrow wheelchairs for use by the participants. The approach was the subject of a paper by French (1992) where, as an individual with an impairment, she was very critical of simulations. She argued that they cannot represent the totality and permanence of having an impairment and hence they can be accused of trivialising disability. Since then others have suggested that the impact of simulations as learning experiences is questionable (Gosen and Washbush 2004).

Who is to be Involved?

There are two dimensions to this question. The first of these is about who should deliver the sessions. In a genuinely inclusive institution where disability is seen as a responsibility shared by all, organizing CPD is a mainstream activity

involving staff routinely and closely involved in training. This is especially true in relation to the professional development of teaching staff since what is really being promoted is good classroom practice. Given that there might be scope for some input of a specialist kind, ideally sessions should be a partnership of mainstreamers and specialists. One matter which is often raised is whether only those with disabilities are in the best position to conduct the sessions. Undoubtedly because of their personal experiences they have an important perspective. Working with disabled people in this context, especially if they came from outside the institution, could be seen as meeting the requirements of anti-discrimination laws. However, what they might lack is an appropriately detailed knowledge of learning, teaching and the general higher education context. Occasionally too the individual and personal can get in the way of objectivity and detachment. It would be dangerous too to assume that those involved do not themselves have impairments which are not immediately obvious and which they have chosen not to disclose. One aspect which has sometimes been useful is the involvement and participation of students with disabilities. If students are willing and have the confidence to participate and if the atmosphere in the sessions is supportive, opening themselves up to questioning can lead to staff gaining some useful insights. A recent commentary on student involvement has indicated that participation in staff development events is a strategy for ensuring the effective engagement of disabled students (ECU/HEA 2010).

The second dimension is about who should be the target for the sessions. There is an argument to be made for suggesting that disability education should be compulsory for all staff. This comes from adopting a position which could be more resistant to legal challenges under disability discrimination law than if attendance remains voluntary. Some institutions issue an open invitation to all staff; some identify particular units such as schools and departments and faculties; some organize sessions around a particular theme such as assessment or placement; some include sessions within existing training programmes, particularly those directed towards new and untrained staff. Only in the last case is there an element of compulsion. At many sessions, it comes as no surprise to those leading the event to find that those present are "the converted" and are already committed strongly to developing and improving their knowledge of disabilities. The concept of "compulsion" to some extent goes against the traditional culture of higher education in the UK at least where staff have been allowed to base their actions on their own professional judgments. However some staff do face compulsory professional development for example in relation to health and safety and equal opportunities.

In terms of the successful embedding of practice, perhaps the best answer is to ensure its inclusion in programmes directed to all new staff and which all must attend. This endorsed by the recommendations of the Quality Assurance Agency's Code of Practice which in effect is a collection of good practice guidelines:

Induction programmes for all staff, and accredited learning and teaching courses for new academic staff, should include information about the entitlements of disabled students and the support that staff can expect in contributing to the development of an institutional culture. (QAA, 2010 page 16)

One potential strategy to use when trying to attract staff already in post is to offer some incentive. For example some institutions use certificates of attendance; the gradual acquisition of these can count towards salary increments or promotion opportunities. Another powerful development is to try to organise sessions for senior managers of the institution. These set an example for all staff – after all if busy people like senior managers can attend, why not everyone else? It could also be very useful in terms of persuading this group

to reaffirm or enhance their commitment to high quality policy and provision for disabled students.

When Should Sessions Take Place and for How Long?

This is another challenging question. One could argue that it might be preferable to undertake some development prior to staff encountering disabled students on the grounds that they can be prepared before prejudices, stereotyping and expectations begin to grow - an additional reason to include disability in induction and training of new staff. In contrast, some of the content included in sessions could make use of previous experience of working with a range of students including those with impairments. Knowing a little of the background, experiences and any emerging concerns is helpful to those responsible for organizing and delivering the sessions.

It seems appropriate here too to consider the issue of time allocated to sessions. This is a real conundrum. When sessions have been organised to take half a day, in their evaluations many staff have said that they would have preferred more time. On the other hand, publicising sessions as taking a full day sometimes meets with the response that staff cannot afford to spend so much time. To return to the point made in the previous section, the matter could be resolved if decisions were made about its voluntary/compulsory status.

Before moving on, it should be noted that sometimes sessions are requested by colleagues anticipating future events. Perhaps the best example of this is the periodic Quality Assurance Agency's Institutional Visit when questions might be asked about the extent to which the various parts of the QAA Code of Practice (QAA, 2010) are being implemented. Equally significant might be when course validation and periodic review/evaluations are due to take place. Such events could include discussion of how the needs of a diverse range of students are addressed, thus creating another form of continuing professional development.

What's in a Name?

This question intends to prompt thinking about the terms used and their implications for the potential impact of sessions. This is an important consideration when devising publicity for sessions to attract participants. For example there is 'disability awareness', 'disability awareness training', and 'disability equality training'. The first of these implies a general effort to sensitise people to what it might mean for someone with an impairment to participate in society – in this case in life in higher education. The second suggests that participants will be given specific instructions on what to do and how to behave when meeting a person with a particular impairment. The third contains a focus on treating disabled people equally. All have weaknesses. 'Awareness' might mean knowing but not acting. 'Training' suggests ensuring particular actions occur irrespective of context and individual. 'Equality' with its inference on treating everybody in the same way ignores the old adage that equal treatment for all is unfair to some. Whilst not in common parlance, it might be preferable to promote the notion of 'disability education' since this recognizes not only that people have knowledge but that they can build on and adapt that knowledge to meet different situations. Perhaps the concept of disability education might embrace all aspects and would be congruent with views on professional development expressed by others (e.g. Craft 2000) who suggests that it is really an attempt to change culture. It might also be more appropriate to consider "equity" rather than "equality" since the heart of the matter is about securing fairness for everyone. In Australia, higher education institutions devise equity plans which are used by the federal government to allocate widening participation funding.

SOME SAMPLE TASKS FOR USE IN DISABILITY EDUCATION SESSIONS

The final section of this chapter provides an overview of the kinds of exercises and tasks which have been used successfully in disability education sessions for staff working in higher education. It is not possible to give step-by-step directions about how they can be used. (These can be found in Hurst 2006.) Also, it should be noted that creating a programe for a session from these exercises cannot be prescriptive; each session's plan will depend on the nature of the group with whom one is working. Some staff might be new to the context and have no knowledge or prior experience, some might seek a general overview rather than a specific focus, some might be from a clearly identified part of an institution and want a session with their unique situation in mind – for example work placements and study overseas, or admissions and the disclosure of impairment. It is also worth noting that the tasks described below are applicable to and have been used successfully by the author in countries outside the UK as well as within the UK.

Starting the Session

To open a session it is always useful to try to get the participants involved actively as soon as possible and to use tasks which can be run in a direct and lively style. Thus, if working with staff with little or no experience of disability, one can use pictures/ images to evoke responses, and this could lead later into a consideration of images used by HEI in their publicity. If appropriate an exercise might be used to make participants sensitive to their use of language and terminology. This too could lead on to an exploration of the language environment of the institution. Perhaps the fundamental point to convey and one which should lay the basis for everything that follows is to introduce models of disability since this is crucial to the need to make "reasonable adjustments" required by law. One approach is to use the work of Mike Oliver and ask participants to rewrite the set of questions used by the Office of Population Census and Surveys and which are rooted in an 'individual/medical/deficit model' into a form which demonstrates the application of the social model (Oliver 1990 pp7-8.). This approach could also be adapted to use the categories devised and used on many official application forms such as the standard application form used for most undergraduate courses in the UK and for which the University and Colleges Admissions Service (UCAS) has responsibility.

Word Association

This might be a useful and logical link to the next focus, namely students. Using a short word-association exercise, asking participants to respond to two different trigger words (e.g. "student" and "disabled student") often identifies hidden concerns of staff who often feel that they are open-minded. Moving on to detail about disabled students, using a list of factual statements which participants are asked to identify as "true" or "false" can prompt discussion on many items. For example the statement "Students must disclose their disability on the UCAS application form" can lead to a debate about issues around disclosure. The list of statements can be as short or as long as required. Depending on the nature of the participants and the time available, they could be asked to write their own statements and also to provide detailed reasons for their inclusion and for the responses they aim to elicit.

Case Studies

Another useful strategy to focus on students is to provide case studies. These can be of "real" students or they can be fictitious, created to prompt participants to think about specific issues. For instance the case history of a Deaf student seeking a place on a Film and Media course may well prompt thinking about whether coverage of

soundtracks in the syllabus is a core requirement and if so what "reasonable adjustments" might be made. (This is not to imply that "reasonable adjustments" are not necessary in situations where students pursue optional courses as part of their undergraduate program. Cases can be devised to encompass the special requirements of students with a range of impairments. Depending on the group, it may be more appropriate to use more complex examples for example students with multiple impairments. Again, the groups could be asked to devise their own cases and to justify their content.

Developing Inclusive Curricula

Having explored the situation from a student perspective, there is a need to address institutional aspects. If one is working with a group of academic staff the focus for the session might be on inclusive learning and teaching. The aim is to prompt staff to reflect on and review their current practices and so the starting point is to ask about the extent to which they consider that their courses are accessible. A lively opening might be to use an ideas inventory to collect suggestions about the barriers academic staff are likely to raise if asked to include disabled students in their classes. This could form a useful preliminary to the approach offered by the '*Teachability*' project in Scotland (SHEFC 2000). This began in the 1990s involving Higher Education Institutions (HEIs) in the west of Scotland and because of its success, was extended to include all Scottish HEI providers. The original focus was a set of questions guiding staff to think about the extent to which their modules/courses/programme are inclusive and meet the needs of students with a range of impairments. More recently this has been updated, revised and reissued as a series of shorter theme-based booklets on topics such as creating accessible information, lectures, tutorials and seminars, placements, assessment and e-learning. The ultimate aim of the original project working with Scottish HEI was to persuade course teams/ departments to provide a written report which provides an audit of existing practice. (For further details about inclusive learning and teaching see Hurst 2005.)

Returning to workshop activities, if time permits, sometimes a subsequent session can be arranged in which staff can discuss these written reports, perhaps as groups from the same section, perhaps with groups from other sections. The production of '*Teachability*' style reports in which barriers to learning are identified along with possible ways of overcoming them, has sometimes been undertaken in connection with quality assurance procedures both internal to the institution and also when external bodies have been involved.

Inclusive Academic Assessment

Additionally, other existing resources can also be used as the core for exercises/tasks working with academic staff - for instance the series of checklists devised by Waterfield and West (SWANDS 1997). As a short, sharp task to re-invigorate a flagging group, participants can be asked to list as many forms of academic assessment as they can think of in a restricted timed interval (e.g. two minutes). This can then be compared to the list taken from the SWANDS document (which lists over forty) and can prompt discussion about assessment and distinctions between modified and alternative formats and assessment for/of learning.

Sessions Focusing on a Specific Impairment

Some staff at workshops might have particular concerns about disability issues. As noted previously, many staff felt the need to know more about effective curriculum design and teaching students with dyslexia. To start this one might use an ideas inventory to collect views on what participants consider dyslexia to be. This might be followed up by discussion of definitions drawn from those

with expertise in dyslexia and their implications for teaching (e.g. from seeing dyslexia as a learning difference and not as a learning disability/ difficulty).

Seeing and Promoting Disability as a Shared Institutional Responsibility

If participants are from a range of backgrounds and include both teaching and non-teaching staff, it might be appropriate to approach inclusion in a different way. Starting from the principle that a genuinely inclusive institution involves everyone knowing both their rights and their responsibilities, one exercise to demonstrate this is to identify who should take what action at particular stages of a student's passage through higher education. This can be represented by a chart with roles listed across the horizontal axis and stages of progression in the vertical starting with initial enquiry and ending with graduation. A relevant anecdotal starting point could be the repetition of a frequently found experience when a call is made to the specialist disability services and the speaker begins, "Hello, I've got one of your students here...." The use of "your" indicates where responsibility is seen to lie.

Reviewing the Quality of Provision for Disabled Students

Another focus for tasks and exercises relates to quality assurance and the evaluation of policy and provision. At a simple level, participants could be given a list of the features identified by the Higher Education Funding Council for England (HEFCE) as constituting base level provision and asked to comment on how they view their own institution in terms of meeting these features (HEFCE 1999). It is possible also to list aspects of policy and provision associated with quality and ask that they be ranked in order of priority. Finally and more demandingly, certainly in terms of time, participants might be asked to devise their own evaluation tool,

A Word about Resources

Before ending, a word about workshop resources is needed. This links to the earlier point concerning the importance of variety of approach and of stimulus. There is a range of material available which can be used in disability education. Much is available free of charge. For example the video '*Talk*' produced by the former Disability Rights Commission is useful for setting the social context of disability in the United Kingdom. Using the version that is captioned, signed and has a voice over alongside the version without these features allows for a demonstration of what inclusive practice might look like when using visual materials and how this could circumvent issues such as disclosure, reasonable adjustments and anticipatory duties. It could also prompt a discussion of barriers which are intrinsic to the subject, barriers which are created as a result of decisions taken about how to deliver the course, and barriers which arise inadvertently. Also free of charge are promotional materials produced by many HEI both in the UK and overseas. The ways in which these can be used are many and varied and depend on the imagination of the organiser and the needs of the participants, but can prompt rich discussions about how HEIs promote themselves to students including those with disabilities. Other useful audio-visual resources are available for purchase. A good example of this is the DVD 'Making the Case' produced by the Learning and Skills Council in 2003 which explores issues stemming from the implementation of the UK SENDA legislation (access via www skill.org.uk). The DVD format plus the accompanying guidance notes present considerable flexibility in how this might be used to promote discussion on related issues. Equally useful and in the same style of presentation is the DVD and supporting materials produced in 2005 by the Open Rose Group (comprising academic

libraries in Yorkshire, UK) which can be used to explore issues about access to libraries for students with different impairments.

Finally one should not forget the possibilities offered by stories and features which are reported on television and radio and in the press, which can be accessed and used within workshop sessions. Their immediacy is often useful at the start of sessions – and of course they are usable free of charge or at minimal cost.

CONCLUSION

This chapter has set the context of provision for disabled students and has promoted improved initial training for staff and also their continuing professional development as the key to enhancing the quality of the students' experience especially in the learning and teaching context. After considering a range of evidence it moved to review aspects of training and development and provided some examples of exercises which might be included in sessions. What it has not done until now is to address the fundamental need for a change in institutional culture in many HEI. This is not easy to accomplish. Michael Fullan has outlined many of the relevant issues (Fullan 1993). He identified a number of basic aspects of approaches to change, all of which are relevant to staff training and professional development. These include the inability to force change on people (hence the often ineffective strategy of compelling staff to attend disability education sessions), the lack of a clear blueprint for what will happen (sometimes those attending are disappointed when they are not given "recipes" for the successful inclusion of every individual disabled student in their classes), and the fact that change cannot be implemented successfully without some linkages to the wider environment. Taking this final point, many have seen the implementation of anti-discrimination laws as the key catalyst for changing the situation of disabled students. However, it is not so simple.

In the words of the American disability activist, Mary Johnson, *"A law cannot guarantee what a culture will not give"* (Johnson 2003 frontis piece).

There is still much to be done to make a successful move away from seeing high quality policy and provision for disabled students as a source of additional expenditure and a time-consuming activity to something which is a value-added dimension, embedded within routine everyday procedures and practices of higher education institutions such as initial training for academic staff and in course design/validation/review systems. This chapter is intended to make a contribution to this

REFERENCES

Bligh, D. (1971). *What's the use of lectures?* Exeter, England: D.A. and B. Bligh.

Callahan, J. (1998). *Will the real John Callahan please stand up?* New York, USA: William Morrow and Co.

Craft, A. (2000). *Continuing professional development: A practical guide for teachers and schools* (2nd ed.). London, England: Routledge Falmer. doi:10.4324/9780203420041

DART. (n.d.). Retrieved from http://dart.lboro. ac.uk/tool/students.html accessed 25/09/2010

DEMOS. (n.d.). Retrieved from http://jarmin.com/demos/index.html accessed 25/09/2010

Department for Business. Innovation and Skills (DBIS) (2009). *National student forum annual report*. London, England: DBIS

Department for Innovation. Universities and Skills (DIUS)(2009) *Disabled students and higher education (DIUS Research Report 09 06)*. London, England: DIUS

Equality Challenge Unit (ECU)/Higher Education Academy. (HEA) (2010). *Strategic approaches to disabled student engagement*. London, England: ECU

French, S. (1992). Simulation exercises in disability awareness training. *Disability & Society, 7*, 257–266. doi:10.1080/02674649266780261

Fullan, M. (1993). *Change forces: Probing the depths of educational reform*. Lewes, England: The Falmer Press.

Fuller, M., Georgeson, J., Healy, M., Hurst, A., Kelly, K., & Riddell, S. (2009). *Improving disabled students' learning*. London, England: Routledge.

Gosen, J., & Washbush, J. (2004). A review of scholarship on assessing experiential learning effectiveness. *Simulation & Gaming, 35*(2), 270–293. doi:10.1177/1046878104263544

HEFCE. (2009b). *Report 2009/49 outcomes of HEFCE review of its policy as it relates to disabled students*. Bristol, England: HEFCE.

Higher Education Funding Council for England (HEFCE). (2009a). *Evaluation of provision and support for disabled students in higher education*. Bristol, England: HEFCE.

Higher Education Funding Council for Wales (HEFCW). (2009). *Outcomes of HEFCW review of support for disabled students*. Cardiff, Wales: HEFCW

Hurst, A. (1999). The Dearing Report and students with disabilities. *Disability & Society, 14*(1), 65–84. doi:10.1080/09687599926389

Hurst, A. (2005). Inclusive Learning in Higher Education: the impact of policy changes. In Hartley, P., Woods, A., & Pill, M. (Eds.), *Enhancing teaching in higher education: New approaches for improving student learning*. London, UK: Routledge Falmer.

Hurst, A. (2006). *Towards inclusive learning for disabled students in higher education – Staff development: a practical guide*. London, England: Skill/UClan/HEFCE.

Johnson, M. (2003). *Make them go away: Clint Eastwood, Christopher Reeve, and the case against disability rights.* Louisville, Ky: The Advocator Press.

Lin, C. H., Kreel, M., & Johnston, C. Thomas, A., & Fong, J. (2006*). Background to the Disability Rights Commission's formal investigation into fitness standards in social work, nursing and teaching professions.*

London, England: DRC National Innovations Centre (NIC) (1974). *Disabled students in higher education.*

London, England: NIC Oliver, M. (1990*). The politics of disablement.* London, England: Macmillan

Quality Assurance Agency for Higher Education (QAA). (2010). *Code of practice for the assurance of academic quality and standards in higher education Section3: Disabled Students.* Gloucester, England: QAA.

Scottish Higher Education Funding Council (SHEFC) (second edition 2004-5). *Teachability: Creating an accessible curriculum for students with disabilities.* Edinburgh, Scotland: SHEFC

South West Academic Network for Disability Support (SWANDS). (2002). *SENDA Compliance in higher education: An audit and guidance tool for accessible practice within the framework of teaching and learning.* Plymouth, England: University of Plymouth.

Stanley, N., Ridley, J., Manthorpe, J., Harris, J., & Hurst, A. (2007, June). Dangerous disclosures. *Mental Health Today (Brighton, England)*, 24–27.

ADDITIONAL READING

Rickinson, M. (2010). Disability equality in higher education: a synthesis of research. York, England: HEA (available at www.heacademy. ac.uk/evidence net)

KEY TERMS AND DEFINITIONS

Disabled Students Allowances (DSA): In the UK disabled students are entitled to claim additional financial support from government ; the fund has three dimensions to it: money to cover incidental costs incurred as a result of being a student with an impairment, money to cover the costs of buying non-medical personal assistance (e.g. sign language interpreters for Deaf students), both of which are available for each year of study, and an allowance for special equipment (e.g. laptop computer with appropriate software for students with dyslexia) which is available on a once only basis. The actual amounts vary between years and since their introduction in 1990 have usually increased to cope with inflation.

Disability Education, Staff Training, Continuing Professional Development: Different labels used to describe how staff are made aware of the ways in which the presence of disabled students in universities etc. can become part of the routine daily policies, procedures and practices of educational institutions.

Inclusion: The process by which participation and involvement is facilitated for disabled people – as distinct from integration where there is an implication that the opportunity to be present is sufficient and that no additional action is necessary.

Universal Course Design: Study programmes which are created with the possibility of easy access for disabled people considered at all stages of the design process and their involvement is recognised when learning, teaching and assessment strategies are decided; in the UK doing this implies being proactive and complies with the legal duty to fulfil anticipatory duties as opposed to being reactive and having to make reasonable adjustments subsequently.

Chapter 16
Reigniting the Voice of Disabled People in Higher Education

Michael Adams
Essex Coalition of Disabled People, UK

Sally Brown
Leeds Metropolitan University, UK

ABSTRACT

This concluding chapter brings together the key threads woven throughout the book. It provides an overall summary of the progress made by higher education across the UK in making inclusive learning, teaching and assessment practice a reality.

The analysis reinforces the complexity of the situation. It identifies clear momentum factors which have supported progressive approaches to inclusive practice, but also identifies key issues which have slowed down, and even limited the extent of expected achievements. This complex situation is overlaid with an exploration of the wider public policy changes which have taken place at the same time.

The second part of this chapter sets out the challenges for reigniting the voice of disabled people in higher education. Drawing on models of practice from other sectors, it sets out the key principles for putting choice and control back into the hands of individual disabled people.

INTRODUCTION

In the concluding chapter of our last key text we focused on disability issues in higher education (Adams & Brown, 2006), and we outlined a 'manifesto for change'. This manifesto acknowledged the tremendous developments which had already taken place: particularly the transformation of the higher education context to improve accessibility but equally important has been the development of organisational infrastructure. This is manifested most vividly through the creation of disability offices, now commonplace throughout the UK higher

DOI: 10.4018/978-1-61350-183-2.ch016

education sector, which take overall responsibility in many universities to promote inclusive practice for disabled students. The biggest challenge facing the sector at the time was in taking the next steps to change and embedding both the appropriate processes and required outcomes relating to inclusive assessment, learning, and teaching and their interface with disabled students.

Our manifesto was wide ranging in its scope and the following points reflect and develop selected key issues which we argued:

- It is essential to build credibility by further developing rigorous and evidence-based pedagogy which convinces both disability practitioners and those within the academic community that inclusive practice is not only appropriate but also highly effective. Inclusive pedagogic practice for disabled students usually represents highly effective pedagogy for all students since it focuses on what students can do rather than what they cannot, thus enabling students to maximise their potential.
- Those involved in learning and teaching need to continue to engage fully with research and scholarship and make best use of the range of international literature available. This will facilitate the adoption of action learning approaches, enabling the monitoring of the success of innovative initiatives, and prompting us to fine tune our practices, leading to wide disseminating of what we find works well.
- Practitioners need to think inclusively when designing assessment instruments, so alternative and reasonable adjustments to assignments for disabled students are built in from the outset enabling them to have equivalent if not identical learning experiences.
- It is essential to engage disabled students in all stages of curriculum design and review,

so that inclusive practices are informed by 'lived experience'.
- An awareness of disability matters needs to be embedded into the curriculum for all students, so that disability awareness is mainstreamed and fellow students engage in inclusive practices themselves, since it is acknowledged that fellow students can commonly be a source of discrimination.
- It is essential to draw on and adapt good practice that already exists in other institutions, learning from other sectors and other nations as appropriate.
- We need to promote pragmatic approaches and engage in academic/staff development to further raise awareness of inclusive practice.
- Staff in the sector need to continue regularly and thoroughly to reflect on our own practice to ensure continuous improvement and learning from the experience of others.
- We also need to avoid being risk averse, trying out different and innovative approaches while basing our practice on sound pedagogic research and maximising the involvement of others, especially disabled students and practitioners.

CONTEXT

Progress

The analysis of the extent to which universities and colleges have made demonstrable progress is mixed. In many ways the content of the chapters in this book crystallises the current position and provides a good barometer. On the one hand we recognise pockets of excellence both in terms of engaging with new technologies (see Ball's chapter as a good example) and advances in more specific subject areas (Moore's chapter on computer-based learning systems for people with autism excellently illustrates the subject focus) where a high degree of knowledge and expertise exists to promote inclusivity. On the other hand we lament the lack of systematic progress which has been made overall; the traction which existed over five years ago, prompted by legislative drivers has not translated into day-to-day policy and practice improvements. Improvements are continuing within silos rather than in a coherent fashion, and inclusive practice has not become mainstreamed to the extent previously expected.

This concluding chapter aims to achieve two things: firstly we offer some commentary on and further explanation of the developments in the intervening years, looking at both the 'momentum' factors and 'inhibitor' issues which have perhaps held progress back. But we will also look forward and outline a potential narrative for the future which puts disabled people at the heart of solutions.

'Momentum' and 'Inhibitor' Factors: A Fine Line

In the UK, the Special Educational Needs and Disability Act (2001) provided a real incentive for developments across the sector. In addition to the required legal framework, disability issues suddenly gained a degree of 'chutzpah'; partly because this was a hitherto relatively 'untouched' area of policy and practice, but also because it attracted developmental project funding. Universities and colleges simply could not ignore the issues since they risked serious penalties if they did so. Academic staff became interested in applying their subject knowledge and general pedagogic approach to finding solutions to questions that had rarely been raised in the mainstream arena. The fact that it was a less well developed area of study also provided a positive opportunity for academic staff to create a niche for themselves, and raise their research profile. From inclusive assessment instruments (Waterfield *et al*, 2006) to imaginative methods of bringing the fieldtrip to life for individual students (Healey *et al*, 2006),

the legislation and attendant development funding stimulated a wave of opportunities.

Developments in higher education also reflected the wider positive policy context across the UK. In 2005, the UK government produced a report, 'Improving the Life Chances of Disabled People' (2005), which was fully supported and endorsed by the Prime Minister at the time, Tony Blair. The overarching aim was to establish a framework to improve disabled people's opportunities, to improve their quality of life and thus strengthen society. The report set out an ambitious agenda and set out the aim that by 2025 disabled people would have full opportunities and choices to improve their quality of life and be included and respected as equal members of society.

The report concluded:

Disabled young people hope for the same things as other young people; to travel, get a good job, start a family and live independently. They want a voice, a leisure and social life, and to be involved as active, valued citizens ('Freedom to Live', 2010, p1).

The report provided the 'smoking gun' evidence that across a wide range of performance indicators, disabled people are disproportionately disadvantaged. For example:

- Incomes for disabled people are, on average, less than half that of non-disabled people (Prime Minister's Strategy Unit, 2005).

- Only one in two (50%) disabled people of working age are currently in employment compared to four out of five (80%) non-disabled people (Labour Force Survey, 2002. In Prime Minister's Strategy Unit, 2005).

- Among workless households with children, the majority has at least one disabled parent: children are more likely to experience poverty if there are disabled adults in their family (Stickland. 2003. In Prime Minister's Strategy Unit, 2005).

- A quarter of all children living in poverty have long term sick or disabled parents (Gordon *et al*, 2000. In Prime Minister's Strategy Unit, 2005).
- As many as three out of four families with disabled children live in unsuitable housing (Oldman & Beresford,1998. In Prime Minister's Strategy Unit, 2005).
- One in four disabled people have experienced hate crime or harassment (Disability Rights Commission, 2003. In Prime Minister's Strategy Unit, 2005,).

Further evidence of disadvantage is given in a recent survey (Equality and Human Rights Commission, 2009) looking at disabled people's class. The report highlighted the proportion of disabled people who have never worked, are long-term unemployed, full-time students or not classified is nearly double that of non-disabled people (31% compared to 17%). Within this the proportion who have never worked or are long-term unemployed declines with age for both disabled people and non-disabled people, but in all age groups the proportion of disabled people in this group is disproportionately high.

In education, the indicators also showed a mixed picture. In 2006, 26% of disabled people had no qualifications as opposed to 10% of non-disabled people (Papworth Trust, 2008). We also know that 20% of disabled young people said that they were actively discouraged from taking GCSEs (General Certificate of Secondary Education: the basic level of a subject taken in a UK school) because of their impairment (Prime Ministers Strategy Unit, 2005).

During the last decade, the overall number of disabled students participating in higher education has increased year on year. Recent higher education statistics (Higher Education Statistics Agency, 2009) have shown that in the UK the proportion of students known to have a disability within the

entire student population increased from 6.5% in 2004/05 to 8% in 2008/09. However, as the overall number of students in higher education increases the gap between disabled and non-disabled students has continued to widen.

But the figures above at best tell only part of the story, and at worst distort the picture. We would argue that the higher education sector has been a leading advocate for equality issues and taken the disability agenda to heart. A deep understanding of the Disability Equality Duty (2005) and its implementation showed higher education institutions were at the forefront of turning regulation into a reality, and making transparent their commitments and priorities (Disability Rights Commission, 2005).

National disability leadership at this time came from a strategic partnership comprising the Equality Challenge Unit (ECU), the Higher Education Academy (HEA) and Action on Access (the national Widening Participation team). These three non-governmental public bodies sphere of responsibility covered the higher education sector in England. The aim of the partnership was to drive disability issues into becoming an integral part of the fabric of universities' day to day work, rather than a bolt-on extra which sat at the periphery of their core business. This approach replaced the previous National Disability Team who operated as a discrete 'one issue' organisation, focussed on disability. The change of approach had both its supporters and critics, reflecting the existing policy debate taking place at the time across society more generally. This mainstreaming of disability is exemplified in two key examples: the bringing together of the Disability Rights Commission (DRC) and other single issues bodies into the Equality and Human Rights Commission, and in more recent times the introduction of the Equality Act 2010 (Government Equalities Office, 2010) which has superseded existing single 'strand' issues.

The DRC, with which the authors are well acquainted since one of us worked for them, had been established in 1999 to underpin the disability rights legislative framework which had been reawakened by the Disability Discrimination Act (1995), and to support future legislative amendments and attendant regulatory changes. The DRC's mission was to help create a society where all disabled people were treated as equal citizens, echoing the sentiments of the 'Improving the Life Chances of Disabled People' report (Prime Ministers Strategy Unit, 2005). In essence, the role of the DRC was to close the gap in opportunity between disabled and non-disabled people in the key areas of society. Education was acknowledged as one of the key drivers alongside employment, access to services and transport, health and independent living.

The approach adopted by the DRC was predicated on a wish to build change through working in partnerships with those organisations which set and monitored standards, developed the curriculum and regulated the education professions. The DRC worked with schools, post-16 education and higher education providers to promote and disseminate good practice.

However, by the middle of the decade the move towards a broader equalities and human rights narrative became the dominant ideological approach. The DRC became part of the Equalities and Human Rights Commission (EHRC), which brought together not only the hitherto separate disability, race and gender bodies but also encapsulated age, sexuality and religion and belief strands of work. This was overlaid with a strong and powerful human rights narrative.

At the time of writing (Autumn 2010) it is too early to determine whether the approach adopted by the EHRC has been a success. However critics would argue (Green, 2009) that the focus on the individual equality strand has been diluted as a result of the new organisation.

Perhaps it was inevitable that a consolidation in equality legislation would follow. The Equality Act 2010 became law in the UK on 1 October 2010 and has brought together current equality law. Alongside harmonising extant coverage, the Act also introduced other provisions, including a new concept of 'dual discrimination', putting a prohibition on age discrimination, and toughening up the existing duty on public sector organisations not to discriminate on the grounds of age, gender, sexual orientation, race, religion and belief and disability. In terms of disability coverage the duty retains the key principles mandated under the now subsumed Disability Equality Duty: the need to eliminate discrimination; the promotion of equality of opportunity between disabled people and other people; the elimination of harassment related to the individual's impairment; a need to promote positive attitudes; the encouragement of active participation of disabled people in public life; and steps to meet the needs of disabled people, even if this requires more favourable treatment (Disability Rights Commission, 2005).

To qualify for protection from discrimination, a disabled person no longer has to show that his or her impairment affects a particular capacity, such as mobility or speech. However, there are drawbacks. Although not perfect by any means the Disability Equality Duty did provide a direct focus on disability issues. For example, in higher education some institutions had started to produce more overarching generic equality plans but in the main, where this did occur, disability issues were easily identifiable throughout the plans, and how the particular issue manifested itself to different impairment groups was generally well articulated. The current duty is underpinned by a much more 'light touch' regulatory approach to monitoring, with self-assessment by organisations a key plank of review. We fear, although this is currently untested, that this will lead to an overall weakening of the ability of the legislative framework to be a powerful 'force for change'.

Again, it is far too early to analyse the impact of the change in legislation. However, with both the Equality and Human Rights Commission, and wider legislation it is easy to construct arguments for both a contribution to a 'momentum' factor or an 'inhibitor'. The reality is however a change to both the context and landscape in which inclusive policy and practice operates within higher education institutions. The examples also provide a backdrop to the development of a renewed narrative to put disability issues at the heart of decision-making and therefore make such issues an integral element of the solution.

Addressing the Challenge

In many ways, addressing disability issues for higher education institutions and the needs of individual disabled students are both about being able to understand and implement inclusive practice. Universal design is an excellent example of how the higher education sector has directly addressed inclusion within its teaching and learning framework.

Universal design is a concept which sets out a detailed guide for educators about how to innovate and facilitate the broadest learning opportunities for an increasingly diverse student population – not just for disabled students. The concept of universal design (Wolfgang and Ostroff, 2001) is predicated on:

- Course content being delivered via a range of different formats.
- The student being able to demonstrate their application and knowledge through a range of assessment methods.
- Students being enabled to engage with a wide range of other networks to learn from peers and swap knowledge and ideas, drawing on online technologies to achieve this.

The premise of recognising that students learn best in a variety of different ways, and therefore those designing curricula need to consider this difference, requires a rejection of the 'one size fits all' approach to the collection of curriculum materials and to assessment, teaching and learning methodologies. This indiscriminate approach

has inadvertently provided the basis for many of the unintended barriers which currently exist for disabled students today.

Traditionally disabled students with differing impairments would have little choice but to integrate and adapt themselves to meet the structure and delivery of the curriculum as presented to them, with individual adaptations being made, only where requested and reasonable. With universal design approaches, the curriculum should be flexible enough to meet each learner's unique needs. With the increasing availability of powerful digital technologies, this provides the possibility to create personalised, flexible, and customised learning environments for diverse learners. Central to the success of universal design is the aim that an individual's impairment should not be seen as a barrier but rather that the focus of how best that individual learns becomes the central concern.

Nevertheless, addressing the overall disability challenge involves more than tweaking approaches to teaching and learning. There needs to be a further investment in disability research, in relation to academic subjects, individual impairment and the interface with pedagogy. Elsewhere in this book there are detailed examples of case studies of institutions undertaking such activities as the chapter by Reaney *et al* clearly demonstrates.

CASE STUDY: THE LEEDS MET RESEARCH CONFERENCE

In terms of research, the development of a disability research network at Leeds Metropolitan University provides a powerful vignette to the challenges threaded through this chapter. The original catalyst for the network came from several academics involved in disability related research looking for peer support. An open invitation to get involved, via an email on the internal intranet, flushed out the well kept secret: there was an 'army' of more than 70 academics working throughout the organisation on disability-related activity, largely unbeknown to one another. Small sums of money were found internally to seed the network, and substantial numbers of individual researchers became involved following their personal interests, to reveal a web of unique and varied activity which was being undertaken. After meeting, the group agreed to host a small event to promote awareness and understanding of the different activity, and to establish a visible focus to encourage other people to get engaged. The disability research conference has run for the last four years and has become a key conference date within the institution's calendar. Its reputation quickly attracted both interest and participation from individuals in other institutions across the UK who had not previously found a platform for their work. The conference topics are diverse including appraisals of technology driven products to support individuals with high level autism through to debates on the relevance of the social model to higher education. In recent years the conference has been oversubscribed both by participants eager to attend and for those wanting to disseminate their research and emerging findings. A concrete outcome of the emergent network has been this book, which brings together a collection of the ideas and presentations from the last four years. However, there is a sense of irony that as this book goes to print, the future of the research network remains uncertain.

Finding the Voice

The creation of the disability movement within the UK was a proactive response to the 'nothing about us, nothing without us' mandate by and for disabled people which gained prominence in the early 1980s. While this remains, there is an acknowledgement that with control comes responsibility and that future solutions lie directly in the hands of disabled people themselves and not simply at the behest of policy makers and other significant stakeholders.

Applying these principles to higher education puts disabled students at the forefront of finding solutions to the complex problems that create disadvantage and therefore different (and generally poorer) learning experiences than their peers.

There are lessons to be learned from other sectors, notably Social Care, where models have been adopted which provide leadership by disabled people. The introduction of the concept of User-Led Organisations (ULOs) was founded on the principle that end users (disabled people) should be involved in the creation and development of services, and that by doing so it adds value to the overall product and services delivered (Morris, 2006).

The creation of ULOs has been perceived in some quarters as simply re-branding existing Disabled People's Organisations (DPOs); but they are nevertheless providing a powerful and credible voice for disabled people. Each ULO is run and controlled by disabled people with at least 75% of its governing board being comprised of individuals with a self-declared impairment; in many cases these make up a full 100% of the board. ULOs actively seek the day-to-day 'lived experiences' of individual disabled people, focussing on how their impairment plays into everyday living, and translates these issues into a coherent and collective voice – fully acknowledging difference but melding together broad themes and issues which are generic and consistent. A good example might be an individual's experience of taking a personal budget to meet their care needs, where the detail might manifest itself in different ways but general issues remain, for example, how to access high quality and cost effective personal support.

As a membership organisation disabled people can coalesce around a ULO infrastructure which articulates a collective voice, which in turn reflects and mirrors their own personal experiences.

Coming together in such a way has led to a number of distinct advantages. Firstly, ULOs seek to provide the voice of disabled people in their localities; they do not pretend to represent every disabled person across the country although it is undoubtedly true that some issues will have a high degree of resonance nationally. Being 'locality' based translates nicely into a higher education institution's community and higher education institutions could usefully explore how the concept of ULOs could be adapted and used within their own organisational systems.

ULOs provide explicit opportunities for users to directly shape the services provided. The learning and teaching challenges in Higher Education Institutions (HEIs), including the thorny issue of assessment (and attendant quality assurance matters), are seen by many to be a principal site of poor practice in relation to inclusivity (Waterfield *et al*, 2006). These are increasingly being considered by a combination of academic staff (who best know their academic subject and learning/teaching methods), individual students who best understand their own impairment, and a range of other support staff within and external to the institution who understand the legal and financial environments in which decision making has to operate. The advances in the application of universal design approaches and the information technologies to support them more generally have opened up a panoply of opportunities which hitherto did not exist.

In Social Care, ULOs work across more than one policy area and are more easily able to 'join up the dots' on the ground, responding to the needs of an individual rather than seeing the solution as merely implementation of the policy, by the letter of the law. In higher education the need to consider academic and welfare issues, all within a quality assured paradigm, means this type of approach has the potential to be highly productive.

ULOs pride themselves on being more nimble than statutory agencies and are predicated on the 'what works' dynamic, meaning they are able to adjust quickly to a changing environment. What better than to have a repository of ideas and practice drawn from disabled students - real experiences to inform challenges going forward? Although every

individual's experience is different regardless of impairment, being able to learn from peers can be both powerful and informative. Facilitating peer support to enable pooled creativity, knowledge and experience to find solutions is the essence of higher education.

Emerging evidence (Department of Health, 2009; Department of Health, 2009) is supporting the view that ULOs are uniquely positioned to enhance overall outcomes. They provide a high level of legitimacy to work related to disabled people, based on their ability to articulate a voice and contribute to shaping the nature of the delivery of services required. The fact that they imbue a values base which encompasses the social model of disability and the principles of independent living further adds to their credibility. Finally, and perhaps most importantly, their work is directly leading to better outcomes for the people they are there to represent, enabling individuals to achieve their goals and increase their own social capital (ECDP, personal communication, May 2009) more generally.

Higher education already has a relatively strong track record in enabling the voice of individual students to be heard. Experienced organisations such as SKILL (www.skill.org.uk) provide a strong voice for disabled students in post -16 education, (including higher education). Many individual institutions have invested both time and money to promulgate the use of student voices and peer-led approaches, both with disabled students and the wider student community more generally.

Aligning Models

The ULO model does not and cannot entirely translate neatly into higher education although, as shown above, the principles are ones which chime and align with wider ambitions for inclusivity. For example, the principle that higher education is about more than an academic qualification but equally about social development and broader learning means that this approach is highly relevant since it is also about providing equality of opportunity for all those passing through their doors to graduation.

But in higher education this cycle of students 'passing through' also provides a challenge in trying to establish a ULO model. First and foremost, disabled students are students, spending time in an institution for a specified number of years depending on the qualification, from Foundation Degree to PhD. The members of any 'higher education ULO' will be constantly changing, as new students arrive, and others move on. How can the lived experience of individuals be captured and the people concerned involved in a meaningful way, and without hampering all the other opportunities available to students? Contributing to disability issues, although important and practically beneficial must remain a subset of an individual's overall higher education experience.

Information and communication technologies open up opportunities for innovation and creative solutions. These days, face to face meetings at which issues of inclusivity are raised which can require a substantial time commitment only need to be a part of the solution, if at all. Texting, Twitter and blogging have provided real time access to the issues facing disabled people. A well established ULO (www.ecdp.org.uk), recently responding to a Government announcement of a proposal to close an independent living funding stream, used Survey Monkey (ECDP, 2010) to seek the views of its members. Through the power of Twitter, the message reached over 22,000 people in 48 hours and elicited over 150 detailed responses. In previous consultations using more traditional methods, the ULO had only ever captured a handful of thoughts and feedback. The feedback from the survey, triangulated with other evidence sourced, provided a quick, but accurate picture of the issues which then informed discussions with relevant civil servants. Students in universities are similarly likely to be willing to use a range of innovative media to share their thoughts on matters of inclusivity.

Technology on its own will not deliver a coherent student voice but it is clearly a major part of the solution. Ultimately, it will require the active engagement of individuals who see the benefits to themselves and to their wider community of students of getting involved and providing their views.

THE VOICE REIGNITED

This chapter and the book as a whole represents a microcosm of the situation in which higher education finds itself when addressing disability issues. Progress has been made and patches of innovation and creativity exist, however this is still fragmented and has not transferred effectively into the mainstream world.

Our original manifesto set out a series of challenges which would support the development of teaching, learning and assessment approaches for disabled students. Progress has certainly been achieved and where inhibiting factors still exist, they need to be redressed or removed.

However, the transformation required lies substantially in the hands and voice of disabled students. Indeed, higher education must utilise existing models of practice, from within both higher education and other sectors, and adapting them to make choice and control for disabled students a reality. In the meantime this book provides a positive contribution to how the learning, teaching and assessment environment can be transformed to enable an equality of opportunity for all students.

REFERENCES

Adams, M., & Brown, S. (Eds.). (2006). *Towards Inclusive Higher Learning in Higher Education – Developing Curricula for disabled students. Abingdon.* Routledge.

Department of Health. (2009). *Putting People First – Working Together with user-led Organisations*. Retrieved June 3rd, 2010, from Department of Health Website: http://www.dh.gov.uk/ prod_consum_dh/groups/dh_digitalassets/documents/digitalass et/dh_096659.pdf

Department of Health. (2010). *Sharing the learning: user-led organisations action and learning sites 2008–2010*. Retrieved June 9th, 2010, from: http://www.dh.gov.uk/prod_consum_dh/groups/ dh_digitalassets/@dh/@en/@ps/docu ments/ digitalasset/dh_114152.pdf

Disability Rights Commission. (2005). *The Duty to Promote Disability Equality - Statutory Code of Practice England and Wales*. Retrieved from Do the Duty Website: http://www.dotheduty.org/ files/Code_of_practice_england_and_wales.pdf

Equality and Human Rights Commission. (2010). *How fair is Britain? Equality, Human Rights and Good Relations 2010 – The First Triennial Review*. Retrieved September 9th, 2010 from: http:// www. equalityhumanrights. com/uploaded_files/ triennial_review/ how_fair_is_britain_-_complete_report.pdf

Essex Coalition of Disabled People. (2010). *Changes to DLA and ILF: An ECDP survey on disabled people's views*. Retrieved August 13th, 2010, from: http://www. ecdp.org.uk/ storage/ ECDP%20DLA%20and%20ILF%20survey%20 results% 20 and%20 analysis%20-- %20 FINAL%20July%202010.doc

Freedom to Live. (2010). Retrieved August 26th, 2010, from Livability website: http://www.livability.org.uk/case.asp?id=1343

Government Equalities Office. (2010). *Equality Act 2010*. Retrieved September 13th, 2010, from Government Equalities Office Website: http:// www.legislation.gov.uk /ukpga/ 2010/ 15/pdfs/ ukpga_20100015_en.pdf

Green, D. (2009). Equality loses out in the battle of victim groups. *The Telegraph*. Retrieved August 13, 2010, from: http://www.telegraph.co.uk/ comment/ personal-view/5906926/Equality-loses-out-in-the-battles-of-victim-groups.html

Healey, M., et al. (2006).Listening to Students: the experiences of disabled students of learning at university. In M, Adams & S, Brown (Eds.), *Towards Inclusive Higher Learning in Higher Education – Developing Curricula for disabled students* (pp. 32-43). Abingdon: Routledge.

Higher Education Statistics Agency. (2009). *Performance Indicators 2008/09: Summary tables and charts*. Retrieved September 3rd, 2010, from: http://www.hesa.ac.uk/ index.php?option=com _content&task= view&id= 1706& Itemid= 141

Morris, J. (2006). *Centres for Independent Living/ Local user-led organisations: A discussion paper*. London: Department of Health.

Papworth Trust. (2008). *Key facts about disability*. Retrieved August 20th, 2010, from: www. papworth.org.uk/.../keyfactsaboutdisabilitynew _081103143956.pdf

Prime Minister's Strategy Unit. (2005). *Improving the Life Chances of Disabled People*. Retrieved September 1st, 2010, from the Department of Health Website: http://www.cabinetoffice.gov.uk/ media/cabinetoffice/strategy/assets/disability.pdf

Waterfield, J., et al. (2006). Support inclusive practice: developing an assessment toolkit. In M, Adams & S, Brown (Eds.), *Towards Inclusive Higher Learning in Higher Education – Developing Curricula for disabled students* (pp 79-94). Abingdon: Routledge.

Wolfgang, P., & Ostroff, E. (Eds.). (2001). *Universal Design Handbook*. New York: McGraw-Hill.

KEY TERMS AND DEFINITIONS

Action Learning Approaches: Approaches which have been informed by the lived experience of individuals – this provides the evidence to the approaches undertaken.

Dual Discrimination: Dual discrimination enables people to bring claims where they have experienced less favourable treatment because of a combination of two protected characteristics.

Inclusive Assessment Instruments: Instruments which are able to adapt to the needs of different individuals and ensure the required outcomes are assessed.

Inclusive Practice: Teaching, learning and assessment practice which takes at its starting point, the needs of the individual student.

Reasonable Adjustments: Under the UK Disability Discrimination legislation there is a duty to make reasonable adjustments. This duty aims to remove barriers that prevent disabled persons from integrating fully into the workplace. Employers are required to make reasonable adjustments to any of their provisions, criteria or practices that place a disabled person at a particular disadvantage compare to non-disabled persons. This is an onerous duty that can require an employer to do things for a disabled person that it would not have to do for others.

Social Model of Disability: The social model of disability identifies systemic barriers, negative attitudes and exclusion by society (purposely or inadvertently) that mean society is the main contributory factor in disabling people. While some people have physical, sensory, intellectual, or psychological variations, which may sometimes cause individual functional limitation or impairments, these do not have to lead to disability, unless society fails to take account of and include people regardless of their individual differences. See Penson's chapter for further information on the social model of disability.

Compilation of References

A guide to communicating with people with PMLD (n.d). *A guide to communicating with people with PMLD*. Retrieved May 1, 2010, from http://www.mencap.org.uk/guides.asp?id=459

Aarons, M., & Gittens, T. (1998). *Autism: A Social Skills Approach for Children and Adolescents*. Oxford: Winslow Press Limited.

ADA. Americans With Disabilities Act (1990). Retrieved January 19, 2010, from http://www.usdoj.gov/crt/ada/adahom1.htm

Adams, M., & Brown, S. (Eds.). (2006). *Towards Inclusive Learning in Higher Education: developing curricula for disabled students. Abingdon*. Routledge.

Adams, M., & Holland, S. (2006). Improving access to higher education. In Adams, M., & Brown, S. (Eds.), *Towards Inclusive Learning in Higher Education: developing curricula for disabled students. Abingdon* (p. 15). Routledge.

ADSHE. (2009). *Guidelines for Quality Assurance in Specialist Support for Students with SpLDs in Higher Education*. Retrieved September 29, 2010, from http://adshe.org.uk/wp-content/uploads/ADSHE-Guidelines-June-20091.pdf

AFB AccessWorld. (2005). From Optacon to Oblivion. Vol 6 (4). Retrieved 19th November, 2010, from http://www.afb.org/afbpress/pub.asp?DocID=aw060403

Alderson, P. (2008). *Young Children's Rights: Exploring Beliefs, Principles and Practice*. London: Jessica Kingsley Publishers.

Allen, B. (2009). Foucault's Nominalism. In Tremain, S. (Ed.), *Foucault and the Government of Disability*. Michigan: The University of Michigan Press.

ALT. (2010). *Assessment, Learning and Teaching Strategy 2008-12 Leeds Metropolitan University*. Retrieved July 03, 2010, from http://www.leedsmet.ac.uk/ALT_Strategy_2008-12.pdf

Anderson, L. W., & Krathwohl, D. R. (2001). *A Taxonomy for Learning, Teaching and Assessing: A Revision of Bloom's Taxonomy of Educational Objectives*. New York: Longman.

Anthony, A. (1992). Non-Oral Language Approaches for Autistic-Like Students. In H. J. Murphy (ed.), *Proceedings of the Seventh Annual Conference Technology and Persons with Disabilities*, (pp. 27-31). Office of Disabled Student Services: Los Angeles.

Armstrong, F., & Barton, L. (2008). Policy, Experience and Change and the Challenge of Inclusive Education: The Case of England. In Barton, L., & Armstrong, F. (Eds.), *Policy, Experience and Change: Cross Cultural Reflections on Inclusive Education* (pp. 5–18). Dordrecht: Springer.

Armstrong, D. (1994). Bodies of Knowledge/knowledge of bodies. In Jones, C., & Porter, R. (Eds.), *Reassessing Foucault: Power, Medicine and the Body*. London: Routledge.

Asamura, N., Tomori, N., & Shinoda, H. (1998). Selectively stimulating skin receptors for tactile display. *Computer Graphics and Applications*, *18*(6), 32–37. doi:10.1109/38.734977

Asamura, N., Yokoyama, N., & Shinoda, H. (1999). *A Method of Selective Stimulation to Epidermal Skin Receptors for Realistic Touch Feedback*. Paper presented at the IEEE Virtual Reality '99 Conference.

Aslaksen, F., Bergh, S., Bringa, O. R., & Heggem, E. K. (1997). *Universal Design: Planning and Design for All. The Norwegian State Council on Disability*. Retrieved from http://home.online.no/~bringa/universal.htm

Asperger, H. (1991). 'Autistic psychopathy' in childhood. In *Frith, U. (1991). Autism and Asperger Syndrome*. Cambridge, UK: Cambridge University Press. doi:10.1017/CBO9780511526770.002

Aspy, D. (1972). *Towards a Technology for Humanising Education. Champaign, IL*. Illinois: Research Press.

Atkinson, P., Coffey, A., Delamont, S., Lofland, J., & Lofland, L. (2001). *Handbook of Ethnography* (2nd ed.). London: Sage.

Attwood, T. (1986). Do Autistic Children Have Unique Learning Problems? *Communication, 20*, 9–11.

Attwood, T. (1998). *Asperger Syndrome, A Guide for Parents and Professionals*. London: Jessica Kingsley.

Attwood, T. (2007). *The Complete Guide to Asperger's Syndrome*. London: Jessica Kingsley.

Augmentative Communication in Practice. An Introduction. (1998). *Augmentative Communication in Practice: An Introduction*. Retrieved May 1, 2010, from http://callcentre.education.ed.ac.uk/SCN/Intro_SCA/IntroIN_SCB/introin_scb.html

Bahiss, K., Cunningham, S. J., & Smith, T. (2010). *Investigating the usability of social networking sites for teenagers with autism*. In H. Ryu (Ed.) *CHINZ 2010: Proceedings of the 11th International Conference NZ Chapter of the ACM Special Interest Group on Human-Computer Interaction (SIGCHI-NZ)* (pp. 5-8). New York: ACM.

Bailey, D. C. (2010). Engaging Family Studies Students: Using a Self-Narrative to Improve One's Teaching. *Family Science Review, 15*(1), 31–39.

Baillie, S., Shore, H., Gill, D., & May, S. (2009). Introducing Peer Assisted Learning into a Veterinary Curriculum: A Trial with a Simulator. *Journal of Veterinary Medical Education, 36*(2), 174–179. doi:10.3138/jvme.36.2.174

Baker, J., Lynch, K., Cantillon, S., & Walsh, J. (2004). *Equality: From theory to action*. Basingstoke, UK: Palgrave.

Ball, S., & McNaught, A. (2008). Round Peg, Square Hole: Supporting Via the Web Staff and Learners Who Do Not Fit into Traditional Learner-Teacher-Institution Scenarios. In *Proceedings of the International Conference on Computers Helping People with Special Needs. Lecture Notes in Computer Science, 5105*, 215–218. doi:10.1007/978-3-540-70540-6_31

Ball, S., & Sewell, J. (2008). Accessibility Standards are not always enough: the development of the Accessibility Passport. In *Proceedings of the International Conference on Computers Helping People With Special Needs. Lecture Notes in Computer Science, 5105*, 264–267. doi:10.1007/978-3-540-70540-6_39

Ball, S. (2009). 12 Steps Towards Embedding Inclusive Use of Technology as a Whole Institution Culture. *JISC TechDis*. Retrieved from www.jisctechdis.ac.uk/12steps

Baptista, P. M., Mercadante, M. T., Macedo, E. C., & Schwartzman, J. S. (2006). Cognitive performance in Rett syndrome girls: a pilot study using eyetracking technology. *Journal of Intellectual Disability Research, 50*(2), 662–666. doi:10.1111/j.1365-2788.2006.00818.x

Barker, J. H. (2008). Q-methodology: An alternative approach to research in nurse education. *Nurse Education Today, 28*(8), 917–925. doi:10.1016/j.nedt.2008.05.010

Barnardo's. (2002). *The Spark Centre: Barnardo's Consultation with Children and Young People*. London: Barnardo's.

Barnes, C., & Mercer, G. (1997). Breaking the mould? An introduction to doing disability research. In Barnes, C., & Mercer, G. (Eds.), *Doing Disability Research* (pp. 1–14). Leeds: The Disability Press.

Baron-Cohen, S. (2001). Theory of mind in normal development and autism. *Prisme, 34*, 174–183.

Baron-Cohen, S. (2008). *Autism and Asperger syndrome: the facts; all the information you need, straight from the experts*. UK: Oxford University.

Baron-Cohen, S., Scott, F. J., Allison, C., Williams, J., Bolton, P., Matthews, F. E., & Brayne, C. (2009). Prevalence of autism-spectrum conditions: UK school-based population study. *The British Journal of Psychiatry, 194*, 500–509. doi:10.1192/bjp.bp.108.059345

Baron-Cohen, S., Hill, J., Golan, O., & Wheelwright, S. (2002). Emotions: an interactive electronic guide. *Communication*, Autumn 2002, 31-32.

Barriers, B., & Blog, B. (2010). Retrieved January 19, 2010, from http://bbandbohmy.blogspot.com/2010/01/disability-simulation-exercises-promote.html

Barrow, R. (2001). Inclusion vs. Fairness. *Journal of Moral Education*, 30, 235–242. doi:10.1080/03057240120077237

Barry, J.ᵃ & Proops, J. (1999). Seeking sustainability discourses with Q methodology. [b,*]. *Ecological Economics*, 28(3), 337–345. doi:10.1016/S0921-8009(98)00053-6

Barry, M., & Pitt, I. (2006). Interaction design: a multidimensional approach for learners with autism. In K. Raiha & J. Hoysniemi (Eds.) *Proceedings of the 2006 conference on Interaction design and children* (pp. 33-36). New York: ACM.

Barton, L. (2009). Disability, physical education and sport: some critical observations and questions. In Fitzgerald, H. (Ed.), *Disability and Youth Sport* (pp. 39–50). London: Routledge.

Bassey, M. (1999). *Case Study Research in Educational Settings*. Buckingham: The Open University Press.

Batten, A., Corbett, C., Rosenblatt, M., Withers, L., & Yuille, R. (2006). *Make school make sense. Autism and education: the reality for families today*. The National Autistic Society. Retrieved October 5, 2010 from http://www.autism.org.uk/About-autism/Autism-library/Magazines-articles-and-reports/Reports/Our-reports/Make-school-make-sense.aspx.

Bauer, H. J. (1952). Discrimination of tactual stimuli. *Journal of Experimental Psychology*, 44(6), 455–459. doi:10.1037/h0056532

Beardon, L., Parsons, S., & Neale, H. (2001). An interdisciplinary approach to investigating the use of virtual reality environments for people with Asperger syndrome. *Educational and Child Psychology*, 18(2), 53–62.

Beardon, L., & Edmonds, G. (2007). *The Needs of Adults with Asperger Syndrome*. Uk: National ASPECT Consultancy. Retrieved October 30, 2010, from http://www.aspectaction.org.uk/ASPECT%20Consultancy%20report.pdf.

Behler, G. T. (1993). Disability Simulations as a Teaching Tool: Some Ethical Implications and Issues. *Journal on Postsecondary Education and Disability*, 10(2), 1993.

Benali-Khoudja, M., & Hafez, M. (2004). *VITAL: A Vibrotactile Interface with Thermal Feedback*. Paper presented at the IRCICA International Scientific Workshop.

Benjamin, S. (2005). Valuing diversity' – a cliché for the twenty-first century? In Rix, J. (Eds.), *Policy and power in inclusive education: Values into practice* (pp. 175–190). London: Open University.

Bentall, R. P. (2009). *Doctoring the Mind: Why psychiatric treatments fail*. London: Penguin.

Berger, P., & Luckman, T. (1966;1991). *The Social Construction of Reality: A Treatise in the Sociology of Knowledge*. London: Penguin.

Bernard-Opitz, V., Ross, K., & Tuttas, M. L. (1990). Computer Assisted Instruction for Autistic Children. *Annals of the Academy of Medicine*, 19(5), 611–616.

Bernard-Opitz, V., Sriram, N., & Nakhoda-Sapuan, S. (2001). Enhancing Social Problem Solving in Children with Autism and Normal Children Through Computer-Assisted Instruction. *Journal of Autism and Developmental Disorders*, 31(4), 377–384. doi:10.1023/A:1010660502130

Bertelson, P. (1984). *A Study of Braille Reading: 2. Patterns of Hand Activity in One-Handed and Two-Handed Reading*. Université libre de Bruxelles, Brussels, Belgium.

Beukelman, D., & Mirenda, P. (2005). *Augmentative and alternative communication: Supporting children and adults with complex communication needs* (3rd ed.). Baltimore: Paul H. Brookes.

Bhabha, H. (1994). *The Location of Culture*. London: Routledge.

Biederman, I. (1987). Recognition-by-components: A theory of human image understanding. *Psychological Review*, 94(2), 115–117. doi:10.1037/0033-295X.94.2.115

Biggs, J. (1996). Enhancing teaching through constructive alignment. *Higher Education*, 32, 347–364. doi:10.1007/BF00138871

Billett, S. (2006). Work, Subjectivity and Learning. In Billett, S., Fenwick, T., & Somerville, M. (Eds.), *Work, Subjectivity and Learning* (pp. 1–20). Dordrecht: Springer. doi:10.1007/1-4020-5360-6_1

Bishop, J. (2003). The Internet for educating individuals with social impairments. *Journal of Computer Assisted Learning*, *19*, 546–556. doi:10.1046/j.0266-4909.2003.00057.x

Bissa, E. (2009). Providing digital resources in Classics. *JISC TechDis HEAT Scheme*. Retrieved from http://www.jisctechdis.ac.uk/techdis/resources/detail/HEAT/HEAT_Round3_HCA301

Bligh, D. (1971). *What's the use of lectures?* Exeter, England: D.A. and B. Bligh.

Block, J. (1956). A comparison of the forced and unforced Q sorting procedures. *Educational and Psychological Measurement*, *16*(4), 481–493. doi:10.1177/001316445601600406

Bloom, B. S. (Ed.). (1956). *Taxonomy of Educational Objectives - Handbook 1: The Cognitive Domain*. New York: David McKay Co Inc.

Boehmer, E. (2005). *Colonial and Postcolonial Literature: Migrant Metaphors*. Oxford, UK: Oxford University Press.

Bondy, A., & Frost, L. (1994). The Picture Exchange Communication system. *Focus on Autistic Behavior*, *9*, 1–19.

Boraston, Z., & Blakemore, S. (2007). The application of eye-tracking technology in the study of autism. Topical Review. *The Journal of Physiology*, *581*(3), 893–898. doi:10.1113/jphysiol.2007.133587

Bosseler, A., & Massaro, D. W. (2003). Development and Evaluation of a Computer-Animated Tutor for Vocabulary and Language Learning in Children with Autism. *Journal of Autism and Developmental Disorders*, *33*(6), 653–672. doi:10.1023/B:JADD.0000006002.82367.4f

Bottery, M. (2006). Education and globalization: redefining the role of the educational professional. *Educational Review*, *58*(1), 95–113. doi:10.1080/00131910500352804

Boulos, M. N. K., Hetherington, L., & Wheeler, S. (2007). Second Life: an overview of the potential of 3-D virtual worlds in medical and health education. *Health Information and Libraries Journal*, *24*(4), 233–245. doi:10.1111/j.1471-1842.2007.00733.x

Boyle, M. (1990). *Schizophrenia: A Scientific Delusion*. London: Routledge.

Breakey, C. (2006). *The Autism Spectrum and Further Education: a Guide to Good Practice*. London, UK: Jessica Kingsley.

Brenner, W., Mitic, S., Vujanic, A., & Popovic, G. (2001). *Micro-actuation Principles for High-resolution Graphic Tactile Displays*. Paper presented at the Eurohaptics 2001, Birmingham, UK.

Bridging the gap (2010). *A guide to Disabled Students' Allowances (DSAs) in higher education*. Retrieved August 03, 2010, from http://www.direct.gov.uk/prod_consum_dg/groups/dg_digitalassets/@dg/@en/@educ/documents/digitalasset/dg_183900.pdf

Broadhead, P. (2006, Apr). Developing an understanding of young children's learning through play: the place of observation, interaction and reflection. *British Educational Research Journal*, *32*(2), 191–207. doi:10.1080/01411920600568976

Brooker, A., & Bryan-Kinns, N. (2003). Computer Based Support for Learning Facial Expressions. In *Proceedings of HCI 2003: Designing for Society* (Volume 2 pp 1-4). Bristol, UK: Research Press International.

Brown, W. (1993). What is a good school for this child? In *Children with Asperger Syndrome, A Collection of Papers from Two Study Weekends run by the Inge Wakehurst Trust, 1992-1993*. London: The Inge Wakehurst Trust.

Brown, S. R. (1971). The forced-free distinction in Q-technique. *Journal of Educational Measurement*, *8*(4), 283–287. doi:10.1111/j.1745-3984.1971.tb00939.x

Brown, S. R. (1980). *Political Subjectivity – Applications of Q Methodology in Political Science*. New Haven, London: Yale University Press.

Brown, J., Dodd, K., & Vetere, A. (2010). 'I am a normal man': A narrative analysis of the account of older people with Down's syndrome who lived in institutionalised settings. *British Journal of Learning Disabilities, 38*(1). Retrieved from http://www3.interscience.wiley.com/cgi-bin/fulltext/123214615/PDFSTART. doi:doi:1111/j.468-3156.2009.00596.x

Brown, S. (2005). How can we make the Higher Education Learning Experience Inclusive? The role of Staff and Educational Development. *Proceeding of TechDis Higher Education Conference* (2005).

Brown, S. R. (1997). *The History and Principles of Q Methodology in Psychology and the Social Sciences.* Retrieved April 12, 2004, from http://facstaff.uww.edu/cottlec/QArchive/Bps.htm

Bruce, T. (1998). Postmodernism and the Possibilities for Writing "Vital" Sports Texts. In Rail, G. (Ed.), *Sport and Postmodern Times.* Albany: State University of New York Press.

Bruce, I., McKennell, A., & Walker, E. (1991). *Blind and partially-sighted adults in Britain: the RNIB survey.* London.

Bruner, J. (1990). *Acts of meaning.* Cambridge, MA: Harvard University Press.

Bunning, K., Heath, B., & Minnion, A. (2009, Jul). Communication and Empowerment: A Place for Rich and Multiple Media? *Journal of Applied Research in Intellectual Disabilities, 22*(4), 370–379. doi:10.1111/j.1468-3148.2008.00472.x

Bunning, K., Heath, B., & Minnion, A. (2010). Interaction between teachers and students with intellectual disability during computer-based activities: The role of human mediation. *Technology and Disability, 22*(1/2), 61–71.

Burgstahler, S., & Doe, T. (2004). Disability-related simulations: If, when, and how to use them. *Review of Disability Studies: An International Journal, 1*(2), 4-17. Retrieved January 19, 2010, from http://staff.washington.edu/sherylb/RDSissue022004.html

Calder, I. (2001). Dyslexia across the curriculum. In Peer, L., & Reid, G. (Eds.), *Dyslexia – Successful Inclusion in the Secondary School* (pp. 174–181). London: David Fulton Publishers / BDA.

Callahan, J. (1998). *Will the real John Callahan please stand up?* New York, USA: William Morrow and Co.

Cameron, A. (1897). The Imagery of One Early Made Blind. *Psychological Review, 4*(4), 391–392. doi:10.1037/h0063985

Campbell, F. K. (2009). 'Legislating Disability: Negative Ontologies and the Government of Legal Identities'. In S. Tremain, S. (Ed.) *Foucault and the Government of Disability.* Michigan: The University of Michigan Press.

Carless, D., & Douglas, K. (2009). Stepping out of the box: How stories can inspire growth, development, and change. *Annual Review of High Performance Coaching and Consulting, 2009,* 175–185.

Carlton, S. (1993). *The Other Side of Autism.* Worcester: Self Publishing Association Ltd.

Carrington, S., & Elkins, J. (2005). Comparison of a traditional and an inclusive secondary school culture. In Rix, J., Simmons, K., Nind, M., & Sheehy, K. (Eds.), *Policy and power in inclusive education: Values into practice* (pp. 85–95). London: Open University.

Challis, B. P., & Edwards, A. D. N. (2000). *Design principles for tactile interaction.* Paper presented at the Workshop on Haptic Human-Computer Interaction.

Channel 4 (2005). *The Dyslexia Myth.* Broadcast September 8, 2005, Dispatches series. London: Channel 4.

Charlop-Christy, M. H., Carpenter, M., LE, L., Leblanc, L. A., & Kellet, K., (2002). Using The Picture Exchange Communication System (PECS) with Children with Autism: Assessment of PECS Acquisition, Speech, Social-Communicative Behavior, and Problem Behavior. *Journal of Applied Behavior Analysis, 35,* 213-231 Number 3 (fall 2002).

Chen, S. H., A., & Bernard-Opitz, V. (1993). Comparison of Personal and Computer-Assisted Instruction for Children with Autism. *Mental Retardation, 31*(6), 368–376.

Cheng, Y., & Ye, J. (2010). Exploring the social competence of students with autism spectrum conditions in a collaborative virtual learning environment – the pilot study. *Computers & Education, 54,* 1068–1077. doi:10.1016/j.compedu.2009.10.011

Cheng, Y. (2005). *An avatar representation of emotion in Collaborative Virtual Environments (CVE) technology for people with autism,* PhD thesis, Leeds Metropolitan University.

Christensen, P., & James, A. (2003). *Research with Children Perspectives and Practices.* London: Falmer Press.

Christensen, P., & Prout, A. (2002). Working in ethical symmetry in social research with children. *Childhood, 9*(4), 467–477. doi:10.1177/0907568202009004007

Clark, A., & Moss, P. (2001). *Listening to young children: The mosaic approach*. London: National Children's Bureau and The Joseph Rowntree Foundation.

Clegg, S., & McNulty, K. (2005). The creation of learner identities as part of social inclusion. In Rix, J. (Eds.), *Policy and power in inclusive education: Values into practice* (pp. 213–222). London: Open University.

Cobb, S., Parsons, S., Millen, L., Eastgate, R., & Glover, T. (2010). Design and Development of Collaborative Technology for Children with Autism: Cospatial. In *Proceedings of INTED2010 (International Technology, Education and Development Conference)* – to appear.

Cohen, S. (1998). *Targeting Autism: What We Know, Don't Know, and Can Do to Help Young Children with Autism and Related Disorders*. Los Angeles: University of California Press.

Cohen, R. F., Fairley, A. V., Gerry, D., & Lima, G. R. (2005). *Accessibility in Introductory Computer Science*. In Proceedings of the 36th SIGCSE Technical symposium on Computer science education, St. Louis, Missouri USA, February 23-27 (pp. 17-21). New York: ACM Press.

Cole, J. (2004). *Still Lives: Narratives of Spinal Cord Injury*. Boston: Massachusetts Institute of Technology.

Colella, V. (2000). Participatory Simulations: Building Collaborative Understanding Through Immersive Dynamic Modeling. *Journal of the Learning Sciences, 9*(4), 471–500. doi:10.1207/S15327809JLS0904_4

Collins, J., Harkin, J., & Nind, M. (2002). *Manifesto for Learning*. London: Continuum.

Comrey, A. L., & Lee, H. B. (1992). *A first course in factor analysis*. Hillsdale, NJ: Lawrence Erlbaum.

Connor, D. J. (2008). (Manuscript submitted for publication). Urban Narratives [*Life at the Intersections of Learning Disability, Race and Social Class*. New York: Peter Lang.]. *Portraits*.

Cooper, B. (2004). Empathy, interaction and caring; teachers' roles in a constrained environment. *Pastoral Care in Education, 22*(3), 12–21. doi:10.1111/j.0264-3944.2004.00299.x

Cooper, B., & Brna, P. (2002). Supporting high quality interaction and motivation in the NIMIS in the classroom using ICT: the social and emotional learning in the NIMIS project. *Education Communication and Information, 2*(2/3), 109–138.

Cooper, B. (2003, June). Emotion and relationships at the heart of learning with ICT - for children and teachers: The Ripple Project. Invited speaker at *BECTA Annual conference*, London.

Cooper, B. (2005, April). *Learning to love ICT: emotion and esteem in learning for teachers and children*. American Educational Research Association, April 11th-15th 2005, Montreal.

Cooper, B. (2006) *The Significance of Emotion and Empathy in Learning with MC3*, ICALT 2006 Kerkrade, Holland July 4th- 7th.

Cooper, B. (2008). *Embedding the Person in Personalised Learning: Findings from a Study in Empathy in Learning Relationships*. British Education Research Association Conference, Herriot-Watt University Sept 3rd-6th.

CoP. (2007). *Code of Practice: Post-16 Education*. DRC, 2007. London: The Stationery Office. Retrieved August 03, 2010, from http://www.opsi.gov.uk/si/si2007/uksi_20071496_en_1.

Copeland, D., & Finlay, J. E. (2008). *A Specification for a Haptic Graphic Display*. Paper presented at the Third International IASTED Conference on Human-Computer Interaction, Innsbruck, Austria.

Cornbleth, C. (1990). *Curriculum in Context*. Basingstoke, UK: Falmer Press.

Côté, J., & Hay, J. (2002). Family influences on youth sport performance and participation. In Siva, J. M., & Stevens, D. (Eds.), *Psychological foundations of sport* (pp. 484–519). Boston: Allyn & Bacon.

Craft, A. (2000). *Continuing professional development: A practical guide for teachers and schools* (2nd ed.). London, England: Routledge Falmer. doi:10.4324/9780203420041

Cruddas, L. (2001). Rehearsing for reality: Young women's voices and agendas for change. *Forum, 43*(2), 62–66. doi:10.2304/forum.2001.43.2.7

Cumine, V., Leach, J., & Stevenson, G. (1998). *Asperger Syndrome: A Practical Guide for Teachers*. London: David Fulton.

Damasio, A. (1999). *The feeling of what happens: body, emotion and the making of consciousness*. London: Heinemann.

Damasio, A. R. (2003). *Looking for Spinoza: Joy, sorrow and the feeling brain*. London: Heinemann.

DART. (n.d.). Retrieved from http://dart.lboro.ac.uk/tool/students.html accessed 25/09/2010

Dautenhahn, K. (1999). Embodiment and Interaction in Socially Intelligent Life-Like Agents. In Nehaniv, C. L. (Ed.), *Computation for Metaphors, Analogy and Agents* (pp. 102–142). New York: Springer-Verlag. doi:10.1007/3-540-48834-0_7

Davidson, P. W., & Whitson, T. T. (1974). Haptic Equivalence Matching of Curvature by Blind and Sighted Humans. *Journal of Experimental Psychology, 102*(4), 687–690. doi:10.1037/h0036245

Davis, L. (1995). *Enforcing Normalcy: Disability, Deafness and the Body*. London: Verso.

Davis, M., Dautenhahn, K., Nehaniv, C., & Powell, S. (2006). Towards an interactive system eliciting narrative comprehension in children with autism: A longitudinal study. In Clarkson, J., Langdon, P., & Robinson, P. (Eds.), *Designing Accessible Technology* (pp. 101–114). London: Springer-Verlag. doi:10.1007/1-84628-365-5_11

Davis, L. (2006). Constructing Normalcy: The Bell Curve, the Novel, and the Invention of the Disabled Body in the Nineteenth Century. In Davis, L. (Ed.), *The Disability Studies Reader* (2nd ed.). London: Routledge.

DDA. (1995). *Disability Discrimination Act*. Retrieved July 03, 2010, from http://www.opsi.gov.uk/acts/acts1995/ukpga_19950050_en_1

Deignan, T. (2009). Enquiry-based learning: Perspectives on practice. *Teaching in Higher Education, 14*(1), 13–28. doi:10.1080/13562510802602467

Deignan, T. (2005). (2005, September). *Transferable People: reframing the object in UK post-compulsory education and training*. Paper presented at the University of Manchester conference on Sociocultural Theory in Educational Research and Practice, Manchester, UK.

DEL. (2006). *FE Means Business - A programme for Implementation 2006*, Retrieved October 10 2010, from www.del.gov.uk.

DEMOS. (n.d.). Retrieved from http://jarmin.com/demos/index.html accessed 25/09/2010

Denzin, N. K., & Lincoln, Y. S. (1994). *Handbook of Qualitative Research*. London: Sage.

Denzin, N. (1989). *Interpretive Interactionism*. Newbury Park, CA: Sage.

Department for Business. Innovation and Skills (DBIS) (2009). *National student forum annual report*. London, England: DBIS

Department for Education and Skills (DfES) (2002). *Special Educational Needs Code of Practice*.

Department for Education and Skills (DfES) (2004). *Removing Barriers to Achievement: The Government's Strategy for SEN*.

Department for Education and Skills. (2004). *Every Child Matters: Change for Children*. London: HMSO.

Department for Innovation. Universities and Skills (DIUS) (2009) *Disabled students and higher education (DIUS Research Report 09 06)*. London, England: DIUS

Department of Health. Valuing People: a new strategy for learning disability for the 21st Century. (2001). Retrieved May 1, 2010, from http://valuingpeople.gov.uk/dynamic/valuingpeople4.jsp

Department of Health. (2009). *Putting People First – Working Together with user-led Organisations*. Retrieved June 3rd, 2010, from Department of Health Website: http://www.dh.gov.uk/prod_consum_dh/groups/dh_digitalassets/documents/digitalass et/dh_096659.pdf

Department of Health. (2010). *Sharing the learning: user-led organisations action and learning sites 2008–2010*. Retrieved June 9th, 2010, from: http://www.dh.gov.uk/prod_consum_dh/groups/dh_digitalassets/@dh/@en/@ps/docu ments/digitalasset/dh_114152.pdf

DePauw, K. P. (2000). Social-cultural context of disability: Implications for scientific inquiry and professional preparation. *Quest, 52*(4), 358–368.

DePauw, K. P. (1997). Sport and physical activity in the life-cycle of girls and women with disabilities. *Women in sport and physical activity journal, 6*(2), 225-238.

DETI. (2003). *Department of Enterprise, Trade & Investment; Northern Ireland Labour Force Survey (LFS) Autumn 2003*. Retrieved June 10, 2010 from www.deti.gov.uk.

DfEE. (2001). *Code of Practice on the Identification and Assessment of Special Educational Needs. Department for Education*. London: Central Office of Information.

DfES - Department for Education and Skills Great Britain. (2006). *Report of the Review of Higher Education Student Finance Delivery in England*. London: DfES.

Directgov, (2010). *Disability support in higher education*. Retrieved October 25, 2010, from http://www.direct.gov.uk/en/DisabledPeople/EducationAndTraining/HigherEducation/DG_4000917

Disability Rights Commission. (2006). *Publicly Available Specification 78: Guide to good practice in commissioning accessible websites*. Retrieved from http://www.equality-humanrights.com/uploaded_files/pas78.pdf

Disability Rights Commission. (2010). *Accessibility Simulation*. Retrieved January 19, 2010, from www.drc-gb.org/employers_and_service_provider/services_and_transport/inaccessible_website_demo/start_page.aspx

Disability Rights Commission. (2007). *Understanding the Disability Discrimination Act: A Guide for colleges, universities and adult community learning providers in Great Britain*. UK: Skill.

Disability Rights Commission. (2010). *Disability equality duty*. Retrieved December 9, 2010 from http://www.dotheduty.org/.

Disability Rights Commission. (2005). *The Duty to Promote Disability Equality - Statutory Code of Practice England and Wales*. Retrieved from Do the Duty Website: http://www.dotheduty.org/files/Code_of_practice_england_and_wales.pdf

Disabled World. (2010). *Cognitive Disabilities*. Retrieved from http://www.disabled-world.com/disability/types/cognitive/

DIUS. (2007, March). *Disabled Students' Allowances, 2007/08 HE Student Finance*. Retrieved October 20, 2010, from http://www.asasa.org.uk/assessment/LA-DSA-2007.htm

DIUS. (2009). *Disabled Students and Higher Education, Research Report 09-06*, Retrieved October 20, 2010, from http://www.bis.gov.uk/assets/biscore/corporate/migratedD/publications/D/DIUS_RR_09_06

Dix, A., Finlay, J., Abowd, G., & Beale, R. (1998). *Human-Computer Interaction* (3rd ed.). Pearson Education Limited.

DIY Theatre Company, & Goodley, D. (1999). People with learning difficulties share views on their involvement in a performing arts group. *Community Work & Family, 1*(3), 367–379.

Donner, J. C. (2001). Using Q-sorts in participatory processes: An introduction to the methodology. In Krueger, R. A., Casey, M. A., Donner, J., Kirsch, S., & Maack, J. N. (Eds.), *Social Analysis, Selected Tools and Techniques, Social Development Papers, 36* (pp. 24–49). Washington: The World Bank.

Douglas, K., & Carless, D. (2008). Using Stories in Coach Education. *International Journal of Sports Science & Coaching, 3*(1), 33–49. doi:10.1260/174795408784089342

DRC - Disability Rights Commission. (2005). *The Duty to Promote Disability Equality: Statutory Code of Practice*. London: DRC.

DRC - Disability Rights Commission. (2009). *Involving Disabled People*. Retrieved February 26, 2009, from http://www.dotheduty.org/. London: DRC.

Driver, F. (1994). Bodies in Space: Foucault's account of disciplinary power. C. Jones, & R. Porter, (Eds.). *Reassessing Foucault: Power, Medicine and the Body*. London: Routledge.

DSA-QAG. (2010, March). SFE Recommendations – Standard Packages, *DSA-QAG Update*. Retrieved March 25, 2010, from http://www.dsa-qag.org.uk/assets/_managed/cms/files/MonthlyNewsletterMarch10.pdf

Duchowski, A. (2007). *Eye Tracking Methodology Theory and Practice* (2nd ed.). London: Springer-Verlag.

Durham University. (2006). *Active Learning in Computing.* Retrieved January 19, 2010, from http://www.dur.ac.uk/alic/

DynaVox Mayer-Johnson EyeMax - Eye Gaze & Eye Tracking Augmentative & Alternative Communication Device. (n.d.). Retrieved May 1, 2010, from http://uk.dynavoxtech.com/products/eyemax/

Dyson, A. (2005). Special needs education as the way to equity – An alternative approach? In Rix, J., Simmons, K., Nind, M., & Sheehy, K. (Eds.), *Policy and power in inclusive education: Values into practice* (pp. 121–129). London: Open University.

ECU. (2010). *Equality Challenge Unit Briefing, May 2010: Equality Act 2010, Implications for higher education institutions.* Retrieved December 9, 2010 from http://www.leedsmet.ac.uk/rso/downloads/ECU_EqualityAct2010-Briefing.pdf.

EDF - European Disability Forum. (2007). *Promoting Equality and Combating Disability Discrimination: The Need for a Disability Specific Non-Discrimination Directive Going Beyond Employment.* Retrieved January 19, 2010, from http://cms.horus.be/files/99909 / MediaArchive/Top5Campaigns/Microsoft%20Word%20 -%20The%20need%20for%20a%20Disability%20Specific%20Directive_October%202007_FINAL.pdf

Education and Skills Committee. (2006). *Clarification of inclusion policy.* London, HMSO. Retrieved August 03, 2010, from http://www.publications.parliament.uk/pa/cm200506/cmselect/cmeduski/478/47807.htm

Education and Training Inspectorate. (2004). *Survey of Provision for Students with Learning Difficulties and/or Disabilities (SLDD) in Colleges of Further Education in Northern Ireland.* Retrieved November 28, 2010, from http://www.etini.gov.uk/report-of-a-survey-of-provision-for-students-with-learning-difficulties-and-or-disabilities-in-colleges-of-further-education-in-northern-ireland.pdf

Edwards, A. (2002). Responsible researcher: ways of being a researcher. *British Educational Research Journal, 28*(2), 157–168. doi:10.1080/01411920120122121

Ekman, P. (1975). *Unmasking the face: a guide to recognizing emotions from facial clues.* London: Prentice-Hall.

Elliot, J. (2009). *Evidence Check: Literacy Interventions,* Uncorrected Transcript of Oral Evidence given on 4 November 2009 before the House of Commons Science and Technology Sub-Committee. Reference HC 1080-i. Retrieved June 8, 2010, from http://www.publications.parliament.uk/pa/cm200809/cmselect/cmsctech/uc1081-i/uc108102.htm

Elliott, T., & Wilson, C. (2007). *Targeting and recruitment of disabled learners.* Aimhigher.

Elzouki, S., Fabri, M., & Moore, D. (2007). Teaching severely autistic children to recognise emotions: Finding a methodology. *Proceedings of the 21st BCS HCI Group Conference. HCI 2007 Volume 2* pp. 137-140. London: BCS.

Engeström, Y. (2000). Activity theory as a framework for analyzing and redesigning work. *Ergonomics, 43*(7), 960–974. doi:10.1080/001401300409143

Engeström, Y. (1993). Developmental studies of work as a testbench of activity theory: the case of primary care medical practice. In Chaiklin, S., & Lave, J. (Eds.), *Perspectives on Activity and Context* (pp. 64–103). Cambridge, UK: Cambridge University Press. doi:10.1017/CBO9780511625510.004

Engeström, Y. (1999). Activity theory and individual and social transformation. In Engeström, Y. (Eds.), *Perspectives on activity theory* (pp. 19–38). Cambridge, UK: Cambridge University Press.

Equality and Human Rights Commission. (2010). *How fair is Britain? Equality, Human Rights and Good Relations 2010 – The First Triennial Review.* Retrieved September 9th, 2010 from: http:// www. equalityhumanrights. com/ uploaded_files/ triennial_review/ how_fair_is_britain_-_complete_report.pdf

Equality Challenge Unit. (2010). Retrieved August 03, 2010, from http://www.ecu.ac.uk/

Equality Challenge Unit (ECU)/Higher Education Academy. (HEA) (2010). *Strategic approaches to disabled student engagement.* London, England: ECU

Essex Coalition of Disabled People. (2010). *Changes to DLA and ILF: An ECDP survey on disabled people's views.* Retrieved August 13th, 2010, from: http://www.ecdp.org.uk/storage/ECDP%20DLA%20and%20ILF%20survey%20results%20 20 and%20 analysis%20-- %20FINAL%20 July%202010.doc

European Commission. (n.d.)) Design for All. Europe's Information Society Thematic Portal. Retrieved from http://ec.europa.eu/information_society/activities/einclusion/policy/accessibility/dfa/index_en.htm

Evans, R. Moore, D. J. (2007). *A Computer-Based Story Builder Shell*. Internal paper, Leeds Metropolitan University. Available by email from d.moore@leedsmet.ac.uk.

Fabri, M., Moore, D. J., & Hobbs, D. J. (2004). Mediating the expression of emotion in educational collaborative virtual environments: an experimental study. *International Journal of Virtual Reality*, 7(2), 66–81. doi:10.1007/s10055-003-0116-7

Fabri (2006). *Emotionally Expressive Avatars for Collaborative Virtual Environments*. PhD Thesis. Leeds Metropolitan University.

Fawcett, A. J. (2002). Dyslexia and Literacy: Key Issues for Research. In Reid, G., & Wearmouth, J. (Eds.), *Dyslexia and Literacy – theory and practice* (pp. 11–28). Chichester: John Wiley & Sons.

Fell, B., & Wray, J. (2006). Supporting disabled students on placement. In Adams, M., & Brown, S. (Eds.), *Towards Inclusive Higher Learning in Higher Education – Developing Curricula for disabled students. Abingdon*. Routledge.

Fenwick, H. (2009). Virtual field trips for archaeology. *JISC TechDis HEAT Scheme*. Retrieved from http://www.jisctechdis.ac.uk/techdis/resources/detail/HEAT/HEAT_Round3_HCA304

Fielding, M. (2006). Leadership, radical student engagement and the necessity of person-centred education. *International Journal of Leadership in Education*, 9(4), 299–313. doi:10.1080/13603120600895411

Fielding, M. (2002). *'Beyond the rhetoric of student voice: New departures or new constraints in the transformation of 21ˢᵗ century schooling?' International Symposium on Student Voice and Democracy in School*. Paper presented at the Annual Meeting of the American Educational Research Association.

Fitzgerald, H., Jobling, A., & Kirk, D. (2003). Valuing the Voices of Young Disabled People: Exploring Experiences of Physical Education and Sport. *European Journal of Physical Education*, 8(2), 175–201.

Fitzgerald, H., & Jobling, A. (2004). Student-centred research: Working with disabled students. In Wright, J., Macdonald, D., & Burrows, L. (Eds.), *Critical Inquiry and Problem-Solving in Physical Education* (pp. 74–92). London: Routledge.

Flintoff, A., Fitzgerald, H., & Scraton, S. (2008). The challenges of intersectionality: researching difference in physical education. *International Studies in Sociology of Education*, 18(2), 73–85. doi:10.1080/09620210802351300

Foot, K. A. (2002). Pursuing an evolving object: a case study in object formation and identification. *Mind, Culture, and Activity*, 9(2), 132–149. doi:10.1207/S15327884MCA0902_04

Foucault, M. (1979). *The History of Sexuality 1: the will to knowledge*. London: Penguin.

Foucault, M. (2000). Interview with Michel Foucault. In Faubion, J. D. (Ed.), *Power: essential works of Foucault 1954-1984 (Vol. 3)*. London: Penguin.

Foucault, M. (1980). Body/power. In Gordon, C. (Ed.), *Michel Foucault: Power/Knowledge- Selected Interviews and Other Writings 1972-1977*. London: Harvester Wheatsheaf.

Foucault, (1971;1984). 'Neitzsche, Genealogy, History'. In P.Rabinow,(Ed). *The Foucault Reader*. London: Penguin.

Foucault, M. (1961, 1987). *Madness and Civilization: A History of Insanity in the Age of Reason*. London: Tavistock/Routledge.

Foucault, M. (1963:2010). *The Birth of the Clinic*. London: Routledge.

Foucault, M. (1975:1991). *Discipline and Punish: The Birth of the Prison*. London: Penguin.

Foucault, M. (1976: 2004). *Society Must Be Defended*. London: Penguin.

Fraenkel, J. R., & Wallen, N. E. (2006). *How to Design and Evaluate Research in Education*. New York: McGraw–Hill.

Francioni, J. M., & Smith, A. C. (2005). *Computer Science Accessibility for Students with Visual Disabilities*. In Proceedings of the 36th SIGCSE Technical symposium on Computer science education, St. Louis, Missouri USA, February 23-27 (pp. 91-95). New York: ACM Press.

Freedom to Live. (2010). Retrieved August 26th, 2010, from Livability website: http://www.livability.org.uk/case.asp?id=1343

French, S. (1992). Simulation exercises in disability awareness training. *Disability & Society, 7,* 257–266. doi:10.1080/02674649266780261

Frith, U. (1989). *Autism, Explaining the Enigma.* UK: Basil Blackwell.

Fullan, M. (1993). *Change forces: Probing the depths of educational reform.* Lewes, England: The Falmer Press.

Fuller, M., Healey, M., Bradley, A., & Hall, T. (2004). Barriers to learning: a systematic study of the experience of disabled students in one university. *Studies in Higher Education, 29*(3), 303–318. doi:10.1080/03075070410001682592

Fuller, M., Georgeson, J., Healy, M., Hurst, A., Kelly, K., & Riddell, S. (2009). *Improving disabled students' learning.* London, England: Routledge.

Garrett, S. A. (2004). *Speech and Language Therapy in Rett syndrome.* Rett Syndrome Association UK.

Genessse, F. (1994). *Educating second language children: the whole child, the whole curriculum.* Cambridge, UK: Cambridge University Press.

Gerhard, M., Moore, D. J., & Hobbs, D. (2004). Embodiment and copresence in collaborative interfaces. *International Journal of Human-Computer Studies, 61*(4), 453–480. doi:10.1016/j.ijhcs.2003.12.014

Germain, R. (2004). An exploratory study using cameras and Talking Mats to access the views of young people with learning disabilities on their out-of school activities. *British Journal of Learning Disabilities, 32,* 157–204. doi:10.1111/j.1468-3156.2004.00317.x

Getzel, E., Briel, L., & McManus, S. (2003). Strategies for Implementing Professional Development Activities on College Campuses: Findings from the OPE-Funded Project Sites (1999-2002). *Journal of Postsecondary Education and Disability, 17*(1), 59–78.

Gibbs, C. (2006). *To be a teacher: journeys towards authenticity.* New Zealand: Pearson Education.

Golan, O., & Baron-Cohen, S. (2006). Systemizing empathy: Teaching adults with Asperger Syndrome and High Functioning Autism to recognize complex emotions using interactive multimedia. *Development and Psychopathology, 18*(2), 589–615. doi:10.1017/S0954579406060305

Goode, J. (2007). Managing disability: early experiences of university students with disabilities. *Disability & Society, 22*(1), 35–48. doi:10.1080/09687590601056204

Gosen, J., & Washbush, J. (2004). A review of scholarship on assessing experiential learning effectiveness. *Simulation & Gaming, 35*(2), 270–293. doi:10.1177/1046878104263544

Government Equalities Office. (2010). *Equality Act 2010.* Retrieved September 13th, 2010, from Government Equalities Office Website: http:// www.legislation.gov.uk /ukpga/ 2010/ 15/pdfs/ukpga_20100015_en.pdf

Graham, D., Benest, I., & Nicholl, P. (2007). *Interaction design for teaching visually impaired students.* Paper presented at the IASK International Conference on E-Activity and Leading Technologies.

Grandin, T. (2006) *THINKING IN PICTURES with 2006 Updates from the Expanded Edition.* Retrieved October 21, 2010, from http://www.grandin.com/inc/visual.thinking.html

Gray, C. (2000). *The new social story book: illustrated edition.* Arlington, TX: Future Horizons.

Green, D. (2009). Equality loses out in the battle of victim groups. *The Telegraph.* Retrieved August 13, 2010, from: http://www.telegraph.co.uk/ comment/ personal-view/5906926/Equality-loses-out-in-the-battles-of-victim-groups.html

Green, S. J. (1990). *A Study of the Application of Microcomputers to Aid Language Development in Children with Autism and Related Communication Difficulties.* PhD Thesis, Sunderland Polytechnic.

Green, S. J. (1993). Computer-Based Simulations in the Education and Assessment of Autistic Children. In *Rethinking the Roles of Technology in Education, Tenth International Conference on Technology and Education,* (Volume 1 pp 334-336).

Green, S., Sinclair, F., & Pearson, E. (1995). From special needs to neural nets. In *Leadership for Creating Educational Change: Integrating the Power of Technology, Twelfth International Conference on Technology and Education* (Volume 2, pp. 740–2).

Greig, A., Taylor, J., & MacKay, T. (2007). *Doing Research with Children.* London: Sage Publications Ltd.

Grynszpan, O., Martin, J., & Nadel, J. (2005). Designing educational software dedicated to people with autism. In Pruski, A., & Knops, H. (Eds.), *Assistive Technology: From Virtuality to Reality, AAATE 2005, Assistive Technology Research Series 16* (pp. 456–460). Amsterdam: IOS Press.

Grynszpan, O. (2005). *Multimedia human computer interfaces: designing educational applications adapted to high functioning autism.* PhD thesis, Paris XI University, Doctoral School of Computing, LIMSI-CNRS.

Guile, D., & Young, M. (1998). Apprenticeship as a conceptual basis for a social theory of learning. *Journal of Vocational Education and Training, 50*(2), 173–192. doi:10.1080/13636829800200044

Hagiwara, T., & Myles, B. (1999). A Multimedia Social Story Intervention: Teaching Skills to Children with Autism. *Focus on Autism and Other Developmental Disabilities, 14*(2), 82–95. doi:10.1177/108835769901400203

Hancock, R., & Mansfield, M. (2002). The Literacy Hour: a case for listening to children. *Curriculum Journal, 13*(2), 183–200. doi:10.1080/09585170210136840

Hanner, S., Tomkinson, C., Byrne, J., Boadle, H., Lashley, N., & Stampone, S. (2003). Results after one year of facilitating autism friendly socialisation (FAFS) using laptops to network young people with autistic spectrum disorder. In *Lisboa 2003 – International-Autism-Europe Congress* (p. P31).

Harding, C. (2001). Students as researchers is as important as the National Curriculum. *Forum, 43*(2), 56–57. doi:10.2304/forum.2001.43.2.5

Hardy, C., Ogden, J., Newman, J., & Cooper, S. (2002). *Autism and ICT, A guide for teachers and parents.* London: David Fulton Books.

Harrison, G., & Gray, J. (2006). *A Computer-Assisted test for Accessible Computer-assisted Assessment.* In Proceedings of the 10th CAA International Computer Assisted Assessment Conference, Loughborough, UK, July 4-5 (pp. 205-209). Loughborough: Professional Development Loughborough University.

Harrison, G., & Gray, J. (2007). *An Improved Computer-Assisted test for Accessible Computer-assisted Assessment.* In Proceedings of the 11th CAA International Computer Assisted Assessment Conference, Loughborough, UK, July 10-11 (pp. 253-265). Loughborough: Professional Development Loughborough University.

Harrison, S. M. (2005). *Opening the Eyes of Those Who Can See to the World of Those Who Can't: A Case Study.* In Proceedings of the 36th SIGCSE technical symposium on Computer science education, St. Louis, Missouri USA, February 23-27 (pp. 22-26). New York: ACM Press.

Hart, J. (2010). *The emerging Top 100 Tools for Learning 2010.* Retrieved from http://www.c4lpt.co.uk/recommended/top100-2010.html

Healey, M. (2005). Linking research and teaching: Exploring disciplinary spaces and the role of inquiry-based learning. In R. Barnett (Ed.), *Reshaping the University: New Relationships between Research, Scholarship and Teaching* (pp. 67-78). London: McGraw Hill / Open University Press. Henderson, K. (2009). Just Research and Physical Activity: Diversity Is More Than an Independent Variable. *Leisure Sciences, 31*(1), 100-105.

Healey, M., et al. (2006). Listening to Students: the experiences of disabled students of learning at university. In M, Adams & S, Brown (Eds.), *Towards Inclusive Higher Learning in Higher Education – Developing Curricula for disabled students* (pp. 32-43). Abingdon: Routledge.

HEFCE. (2009b). *Report 2009/49 outcomes of HEFCE review of its policy as it relates to disabled students.* Bristol, England: HEFCE.

HEFCE. (2008). *Widening participation indicators for higher education are improving.* Retrieved January 13, 2009, from http://www.hefce.ac.uk/news/hefce/2008/wp.htm#note1

HEFCE. Higher Education Funding Council for England (2005). *Centres for Excellence in Teaching and Learning.* Retrieved January 19, 2010, from http://www.hefce.ac.uk/learning/TInits/cetl/

Heimann, M., Nelson, K., Tjus, T., & Gilberg, C. (1995). Increasing Reading and Communication Skills in Children with Autism Through an Interactive Multimedia Computer Program. *Journal of Autism and Developmental Disorders,* *25*(5), 459–480. doi:10.1007/BF02178294

Hejmadi, M., Bullock, K., & Lock, G. (2009). Creating video resources for students on placement. *JISC TechDis HEAT Scheme.* Retrieved from http://www.jisctechdis.ac.uk/techdis/resources/detail/HEAT/HEAT_Round3_BIO303

Herrera, G., & Vera, L. (2005). Abstract Concept and Imagination Teaching through Virtual Reality in People with Autism Spectrum Disorder. In Pruski, A., & Knops, H. (Eds.), *Assistive Technology: From Virtuality to Reality, AAATE 2005, Assistive Technology Research Series 16* (pp. 449–455). Amsterdam: IOS Press.

Herskowitz, V. (2009). *Autism and Computers: Maximizing Independence Through Technology.* Bloomington, IN: AuthorHouse.

HESA - Higher Education Statistics Agency. (2009). *Students and Qualifiers Data Tables.* Retrieved July 01, 2010, from http://www.hesa.ac.uk/index.php?option=com_datatables&Itemid=121&task=show_category&catdex=3#disab

HESA. Higher Education Statistics Agency (2006). *First year UK domiciled HE students by qualification aim, mode of study, gender and disability 2005/06.* Retrieved January 19, 2010, from http://www.hesa.ac.uk/dox/dataTables/studentsAndQualifiers/download/disab0708.xls

Hetzroni, O. E., & Tannous, J. (2004). Effects of a Computer-Based Intervention Program on the Communicative Functions of Children with Autism. *Journal of Autism and Developmental Disorders, 34*(2), 95–113. doi:10.1023/B:JADD.0000022602.40506.bf

Hewett, D., & Nind, M. (1998). *Interaction in Action, Reflections on the Use of Intensive Interaction.* London: David Fulton.

Higgins, K., & Boone, R. (1996). Creating Individualised Computer-Assisted Instruction for Students with Autism Using Multimedia Authoring Software. *Focus on Autism and Other Developmental Disabilities, 11*(2), 69–78. doi:10.1177/108835769601100202

Higgins, K., & Boone, R. (1996). Creating Individualised Computer-Assisted Instruction for Students with Autism Using Multimedia Authoring Software. *Focus on Autism and Other Developmental Disabilities, 11*(2), 69–78. doi:10.1177/108835769601100202

Higher Education Academy. (2010). Retrieved July 01, 2010, from http://www.heacademy.ac.uk/

Higher Education Funding Council for England (HEFCE) (2007). *Higher education outreach: targeting disadvantaged learners, Guidance for Aimhigher partnerships and higher education providers*

Higher Education Funding Council for England (HEFCE). (2009). *Strategic Plan 2006-11, Widening Participation and Fair Access.* Updated June 2009. Retrieved November 26, 2010, from http://195.194.167.100/Pubs/hefce/2009/09_21/09_21.pdf

Higher Education Funding Council for England (HEFCE). (1996). Specification for Disability Statements required from Institutions. *HEFCE Ref 1996/8.* Retrieved July 01, 2010, from http://www.hefce.ac.uk/pubs/hefce/1996/c8_96.htm

Higher Education Funding Council for England (HEFCE). (2009). Outcomes of HEFCE review of its policy as it relates to disabled students. *HEFCE Ref 2009/49.* Retrieved July 01, 2010, from http://www.hefce.ac.uk/widen/sldd/allocat.asp.

Higher Education Funding Council for England (HEFCE) and the Higher Education Funding Council for Wales. (HEFCW) (1999). Guidance on base-level provision for disabled students in higher education institutions. *HEFCE Ref 99/04.* Retrieved November 18, 2010, from http://www.hefce.ac.uk/pubs/hefce/1999/99_04.htm.

Higher Education Funding Council for England (HEFCE). (2009a). *Evaluation of provision and support for disabled students in higher education.* Bristol, England: HEFCE.

Higher Education Funding Council for Wales (HEFCW). (2009*). Outcomes of HEFCW review of support for disabled students*. Cardiff, Wales: HEFCW

Higher Education Statistics Agency. (2009). *Performance Indicators 2008/09: Summary tables and charts*. Retrieved December 10, 2010, from: http://www.hesa. ac.uk/index.php?option=com_content&task=view&id= 1706&Itemid=141

Hill, E. L. (2004). Executive dysfunction in autism. *Trends in Cognitive Sciences, 8*(1), 26–32. doi:10.1016/j. tics.2003.11.003

Hill, M., Prout, A., & Tisdall, K. (2004). Moving the participation agenda forward. *Children & Society, 18*(2), 77–96. doi:10.1002/chi.819

HMSO. (1995). *Disability Discrimination Act 1995 (c. 50)*. Retrieved January 19, 2010, from http://www.opsi. gov.uk/acts/acts1995/1995050.htm

HMSO. (2001). *Special Educational Needs and Disability Act 2001*. Retrieved January 19, 2010, from http://www. opsi.gov.uk/acts/acts2001/20010010.htm

Hobbs, D. J., & Moore, D. J. (1998). *Human Computer Interaction*. London: FTK Publishing.

Hopkin, D. (2009). *Review of the delivery of financial support to students in England by the Student Loans Company for the academic year 2009/10 and plans for academic year 2010/11*, Retrieved February 24, 2010, from http://www.bis.gov.uk/assets/biscore/corporate/ docs/d/09-1580-delivery-of-financial-support-to-students

Howe, K. R. & Welner, K.,G. (2005). School choice and the pressure to perform, In J. Rix, K. Simmons, M. Nind & K. Sheehy (Eds.), *Policy and power in inclusive education: Values into practice* (pp.36-46) London: Open University.

Howlin, P., Baron-Cohen, S., & Hadwin, J. (1999). *Teaching Children with Autism to Mind-Read, A Practical Guide for Teachers and Parents. London: John Wiley and Sons Irish Autism Society (1995). A Story of Autism*. Ireland: Irish Autism Society.

Hughes, B. (2004). Disability and the body. In Swain, J., French, S., Barnes, C., & Thomas, C. (Eds.), *Disabling barriers- Enabling Environments*. London: SAGE.

Hughs, B. (2009). What Can a Foucauldian Analysis Contribute to Disability Theory? In Tremain, S. (Ed.), *Foucault and the Government of Disability*. Michigan: The University of Michigan Press.

Hunt, P. (1981). Settling accounts with the parasite people: A critique of 'A Life Apart'. In E.J. Miller and G.V. Gwynne (eds). *Disability Challenge, May*, 37-50.

Hurst, A. (1999). The Dearing Report and students with disabilities. *Disability & Society, 14*(1), 65–84. doi:10.1080/09687599926389

Hurst, A. (2005). Inclusive Learning in Higher Education: the impact of policy changes. In Hartley, P., Woods, A., & Pill, M. (Eds.), *Enhancing teaching in higher education: New approaches for improving student learning*. London, UK: Routledge Falmer.

Hurst, A. (2006). *Towards inclusive learning for disabled students in higher education – Staff development: a practical guide*. London, England: Skill/UClan/HEFCE.

Iacono, T. A., & Miller, J. F. (1989). Can Microcomputers be used to Teach Communication Skills to Students with Mental Retardation? *Education and Training of the Mentally Retarded, 22*(1), 32–44.

Ikei, Y., Wakamatsu, K., & Fukuda, S. (1997). *Texture Display for Tactile Sensation*. Paper presented at the 7th International Conference on Human-Computer Interaction.

Immersion Corporation. (2007). *Engaging the Sense of Touch*. Retrieved 19th November, 2010, from http://www. immersion.com/

Ino, S., Shimizu, S., Odagawa, T., Sato, M., Takahashi, M., Izumi, T., & Ifukube, T. (1993). *A tactile display for presenting quality of materials by changing the temperature of skin surface*. Paper presented at the 2nd IEEE International Workshop on Robot and Human Communication.

Jacklin, A., Robinson, C., O'Meara, L., & Harris, A. (2007). *Improving the experiences of disabled students in higher education* (pp. 22–23). Higher Education Academy.

Jacklin, A., & Farr, W. (2005). The computer in the classroom: a medium for enhancing social interaction with young people with autistic spectrum disorders? *British Journal of Special Education, 32*(4), 202–210. doi:10.1111/j.1467-8578.2005.00398.x

James, A., Jenks, C., & Prout, A. (1998). *Theorizing Childhood*. Cambridge: Polity Press.

Jenkins, A., Breen, R., & Lindsay, R. (2003). *Reshaping teaching in Higher Education, linking Teaching with Research*. London: Kogan Page Limited.

Jenlink, P. M. (2001). Activity Theory and the Design of Educational Systems: Examining the Mediational Importance of Conversation. *Systems Research and Behavioral Science*, *18*, 345–359. doi:10.1002/sres.429

JISC TechDis. (2009) Accessibility Essentials: The Complete Series. Retrieved from http://www.jisctechdis.ac.uk/accessibilityessentials

JISC TechDis. (n.d.) The HEAT Scheme. Retrieved from http://www.jisctechdis.ac.uk/heat Kelly, B., Phipps, L., & Swift, E. (2004). Developing a holistic approach for e-learning accessibility. *Canadian Journal of Learning and Technology 30*(3).

JISC TechDis. (n.d.) Upwardly Mobile: A Guide to Getting Started with Inclusive Mobile Learning. Retrieved from http://www.jisctechdis.ac.uk/upwardlymobile

JISCMail. (2010). *Discussion list for disabled students and their support staff*. Retrieved July 03, 2010, from www.jiscmail.ac.uk/lists/dis-forum.html.

Johnson, K. (2009). 'No longer researching about us without us: a researcher's reflection on rights and inclusive research in Ireland'. *British Journal of Learning Disabilities*, *37*, 250–256. doi:10.1111/j.1468-3156.2009.00579.x

Johnson, M. (2003). *Make them go away: Clint Eastwood, Christopher Reeve, and the case against disability rights*. Louisville, Ky: The Advocator Press.

Johnson, S., Hennessy, E., Smith, R., Trikic, R., Wolke, D., & Marlow, N. N.(2005). Academic attainment and special educational needs in extremely preterm children at 11 years of age: The EPICure Study. *Archives of Disease Fetal neonatal Edition* 2009; 94, 283-289.

Jordan, R. R. (1991a). *The National Curriculum: Access for Children with Autism. 1. The Special Educational Needs of Pupils with Autism*. Bristol, UK: The Inge Wakehurst Trust.

Jordan, R. R. (1991b). *The National Curriculum: Access for Children with Autism. 2. English*. Bristol, UK: The Inge Wakehurst Trust.

Jordan, R. R. (1992a). *The National Curriculum: Access for Children with Autism. 3. Mathematics*. Bristol, UK: The Inge Wakehurst Trust.

Jordan, R. R. (1992b). *The National Curriculum: Access for Children with Autism. 4. Science*. Bristol, UK: The Inge Wakehurst Trust.

Jordan, R. R. (1991). *The National Curriculum: Access for Children with Autism. 1. The Special Educational Needs of Pupils with Autism*. Bristol, UK: The Inge Wakehurst Trust.

Jordan, R., & Jones, G. (1999). Review of research into educational interventions for children with autism in the UK. *Autism*, *3*(1), 101–110. doi:10.1177/1362361399003001009

Jordan, R. (2007). A rose by any other name? In *Communication*, winter 2007 pp 10-12.

Jordan, R. R. (2001). *Autism with Severe Learning Difficulties, A Guide for Parents and Professionals*. London: Souvenir Press (Educational & Academic) Ltd.

Jordan, R. R., & Powell, S. (1995). Factors Affecting School Choice for Parents of a Child with Autism. *Communication*, Winter 1995, 5-9.

Kangasoja, J. (2002). Complex design problems: an impetus for learning and knotworking, *Center for Activity Theory and Developmental Work Research*, Retrieved November 21, 2004, from http://www.edu.helsinki.fi/activity/publications/files/47/ICLS2002_Kangasoja.pdf

Kellett, M., & Nind, M. (2003). *Implementing Intensive Interaction in Schools: guidance for practitioners, managers and coordinators*. London: David Fulton.

Kelly, B., Sloan, D., Brown, S., Seale, J., Petrie, H., Lauke, P., & Ball, S. (2007). Accessibility 2.0: People, Policies and Processes. ACM International Conference Proceeding Series; Vol. 225 In *Proceedings of the 2007 international cross-disciplinary conference on Web accessibility* (W4A).

Kennedy, J. M., Gabias, P., & Heller, M. A. (1992). Space, Haptics and the Blind. *Geoforum, 23*(2), 175–189. doi:10.1016/0016-7185(92)90015-V

Kerr, A. M., McCulloch, D., Oliver, K., McLean, B., Coleman, E., & Law, T. (2003). Assessment of medical needs. *Journal of Intellectual Disability Research, 134.* doi:10.1046/j.1365-2788.2003.00453.x

KGS-America LLC. (2010). *KGS Corporation.* Retrieved 19th November, 2010, from http://www.kgs-america.com/

Kincaid, N. (2009). The Visual Scribe: podcasting for dance students with dyslexia. *JISC TechDis HEAT Scheme.* Retrieved from http://www.jisctechdis.ac.uk/techdis/resources/detail/HEAT/HEAT_Round3_PAL301

Kirkpatrick, A. E., & Douglas, S. A. (2001). *A Shape Recognition Benchmark for Evaluating Usability of a Haptic Environment.* Paper presented at the First International Workshop on Haptic Human-Computer Interaction.

Klatzky, R. L., Lederman, S. J., & Reed, C. (1987). There's More to Touch Than Meets the Eye: The Salience of Object Attributes for Haptics With and Without Vision. *Journal of Experimental Psychology. General, 116*(4), 356–369. doi:10.1037/0096-3445.116.4.356

Klein, M. (1961). *Narrative of a Child Analysis: The Conduct of the Psycho-analysis of children as seen in the treatment of a ten-year-old boy.* London: Virago Press Limited.

La Paro, K. M., Siepak, K., & Scott-Little, C. (2009). Assessing Beliefs of Preservice Early Childhood Education Teachers Using Q-Sort Methodology. *Journal of Early Childhood Teacher Education, 30*(1), 22–36. doi:10.1080/10901020802667805

Lakinski, M. (2008). *Getting Away with Murder. Disabled people's experiences of hate crime in the UK.* London: Scope.

Lammy, D. (2009). *Financial Support to Students.* Retrieved March 29, 2010, from http://www.bis.gov.uk/news/speeches/financial-support-students-lammy. London: House of Commons.

Lang, C. (2008). Caring and touch as factors in effective teaching. *Annual Conference of the Scottish Educational Research Association [SERA] Royal George Hotel, Perth, Scotland, 27-29 November 2008.*

Lantolf, J. P., & Thorne, P. (2006). *Sociocultural Theory and the Genesis of Second Language Development.* Oxford: Oxford University Press.

Lave, J., & Wenger, E. (1991). *Situated Learning: Legitimate peripheral participation.* New York: Cambridge University Press.

Laycock, D. (1996). *Surveys into the Operation of the Disabled Students' Allowances.* London: University of Westminster Press.

Lederman, S. J., & Abbott, S. G. (1981). Texture Perception: Studies of Intersensory Organization Using a Discrepancy Paradigm, and Visual Versus Tactual Psychophysics. *Journal of Experimental Psychology, 7*(4), 902–915.

Lederman, S. J., & Taylor, M. M. (1972). Fingertip force, surface geometry and the perception of roughness by active touch. *Perception & Psychophysics, 5*(12), 401–408. doi:10.3758/BF03205850

Leeds Met. (2009). *Leeds Metropolitan University Equality Scheme.* Retrieved December 9, 2010 from http://www.leedsmet.ac.uk/rso/downloads/LM_EqDiv_SES_Disability.pdf.

Leeds Metropolitan University. (2005). *Assessment, Learning and Teaching at Leeds Metropolitan University: an Education Strategy.* Retrieved January 19, 2010, from http://www.leedsmet.ac.uk/about/keydocuments/Version-32AssesmentTeachingLearningStrategy1.pdf

Leeds Metropolitan University. (2007). *Active Learning in Computing.* Retrieved January 19, 2010, from http://www.leedsmet.ac.uk/inn/alic

Leeds Metropolitan University. (2010). *About Leeds Metropolitan University.* Retrieved July 03, 2010, from http://www.leedsmet.ac.uk/vco/index_about.htm

Leontyev, A. N. (2009). *The Development of Mind.* Pacifica, CA: Marxists Internet Archive.

Lewis, B. (2006). *Moving Beyond Prozac, DSM, and the New Psychiatry: The Birth of Postpsychiatry.* Michigan: The University of Michigan Press.

LexDis – Ideas for e-learning (2007). *JISC project 2007 – Feb 2009.* Retrieved Feb 1, 2010, from http://www.lexdis.org.uk/

Lichtman, M. (2006). *Qualitative Research in Education: A User's Guide*. London: Sage.

Lin, C. H., Kreel, M., & Johnston, C. Thomas, A., & Fong, J. (2006). *Background to the Disability Rights Commission's formal investigation into fitness standards in social work, nursing and teaching professions.*

Lockhead, G. R. (2004). Absolute Judgments Are Relative: A Reinterpretation of Some Psychophysical Ideas. *Review of General Psychology, 8*(4), 265–272. doi:10.1037/1089-2680.8.4.265

London, England: DRC National Innovations Centre (NIC) (1974). *Disabled students in higher education.*

London, England: NIC Oliver, M. (1990). *The politics of disablement*. London, England: Macmillan

Lotter, V. (1978). Childhood Autism in Africa. *Journal of psychology and psychiatry, 19*(3), pp 231-244.

LSIS. (n.d.). *Excellence Gateway: Accessibility In Learning*. Retrieved from http://www.excellencegateway.org.uk/page.aspx?o=jisctechdis

MacConville, R. (2007). *Looking at Inclusion: Listening to the Voices of Young People*. London: Paul Chapman Publishing.

Macdonald, D. (2002). Critical pedagogy: what might it look like and why does it matter. In Laker, A. (Ed.), *The Sociology of Sport and Physical Education*. London: Routledge/Falmer.

Macdonald, A. (1994). Symbol Systems. In S.Millar and A.Wilson (Eds.), *Augmentative Communication in Practice: An Introduction* (pp 19-26).CALL Centre: University of Edinburgh.

Mack, C. (1994). *Symposium on High-Resolution Tactile Graphics*. Retrieved 21st November, 2010, from http://www.trace.wisc.edu.

Madriaga, M. (2007). Enduring disabilism: students with dyslexia and their pathways into UK higher education and beyond. *Disability & Society, 22*(4), 399–412. doi:10.1080/09687590701337942

Madriaga, M., Goodley, D., Hodge, N., & Martin, N. (2007). *Enabling transition into higher education for students with Asperger Syndrome*. Retrieved January 12, 2009, from http://www.heacademy.ac.uk/assets/York/documents/manuel_madriaga_report.pdf

Mancil, G. R., Haydon, T., & Whitby, P. (2009). Differentiated Effects of Paper and Computer-Assisted Social Stories™ on Inappropriate Behavior in Children With Autism. *Focus on Autism and Other Developmental Disorders, 24*(4), 205–215. doi:10.1177/1088357609347324

Marsden, P. (1993). Asperger Syndrome: A Parent's View. In *Children with Asperger Syndrome, A Collection of Papers from Two Study Weekends run by the Inge Wakehurst Trust, 1992-1993*. London: The Inge Wakehurst Trust.

McCormack, C., & Jones, D. (1998). *Building a web-based education system*. New York, NY: Wiley.

McFadden, D. (1995) AAC in the community - A Personal Viewpoint, In S.Millar and A.Wilson (Eds.), *Augmentative Communication in Practice: An Introduction* (pp 90-91). CALL Centre: University of Edinburgh.

McKeown, B., & Thomas, D. (1988). *Q Methodology*. Thousand Oaks: Sage.

McLean, S., & Hagan, P. (2009). Creating reflective videos during practical classes. *JISC TechDis HEAT Scheme* Retrieved from http://www.jisctechdis.ac.uk/techdis/resources/detail/HEAT/HEAT_Round3_BIO301

Mercer, G. (2002). Emancipatory Disability Research. In Barnes, C., Oliver, M., & Barton, L. (Eds.), *Disability Studies Today*. Cambridge: Polity Press.

Miles, M. B., & Huberman, A. M. (1994). *Qualitative Data Analysis*. London: Sage.

Miller, E. J., & Gwynne, G. V. (1972). *A Life Apart. A pilot study of residential institutions for the physically handicapped and the young chronic sick*. London: Tavistock Publications.

Mindful Employer. (2010). *Charter for Employers*. Retrieved December 17, 2010, from: http://www.mindfulemployer.net/charter.html

Minogue, J., & Jones, M. G. (2006). Haptics in Education: Exploring an Untapped Sensory Modality. *Review of Educational Research, 76*(3), 317–348. doi:10.3102/00346543076003317

Moon Literacy. (2006). *What is Moon?* Retrieved 21st November, 2010, from http://www.moonliteracy.org.uk/whatis.htm

Moore, D., Cheng, Y., McGrath, P., & Powell, N. J. (2005). Collaborative virtual environment technology for people with autism. *Focus on Autism and Other Developmental Disorders, 20*, 231–243. doi:10.1177/10883576050200040501

Moore, D. J., McGrath, P., & Thorpe, J. (2000). Computer Aided Learning for people with autism - a framework for research and development. *Innovations in Education and Training International, 37*(3), 218–228. doi:10.1080/13558000050138452

Moore, D. J., & Taylor, J. (2000). Interactive multimedia systems for people with autism. *Journal of Educational Media, 25*(3), 169–177. doi:10.1080/1358165000250302

Moore, M., & Calvert, S. (2000). Brief report: vocabulary acquisition for children with autism: teacher or computer instruction. *Journal of Autism and Developmental Disorders, 30*(4), 359–362. doi:10.1023/A:1005535602064

Moore, D., Cheng, Y., McGrath, P., & Powell, N. J. (2005). Collaborative virtual environment technology for people with autism'. *Focus on Autism and Other Developmental Disorders, 20*, 231–243. doi:10.1177/10883576050200040501

Moore, D. J., & Taylor, J. (2000). Interactive multimedia systems for people with autism. *Journal of Educational Media, 25*(3), 169–177. doi:10.1080/1358165000250302

Moore, D. (2005, November). *Collaborative virtual environment technology for people with autism.* Paper presented at the Scottish Autism Research Group Seminar on the Integrated View of Research on Autism: From Theory to Practice, seminar 3: From Socio-cognitive research to information technology for autism spectrum disorders, University of Edinburgh.

Moore, D. J. (1998) Computers and People with Autism/Asperger Syndrome; *Communication*, Summer 1998, 20-21.

Moore, D. J. (2009) IT and Autism. Keynote speech, The 2009 *International Conference on the Current Trends in Information Technology*, December 15-16 2009, Dubai, United Arab Emirates.

Morris, J. (2006). *Centres for Independent Living/Local user-led organisations: A discussion paper*. London: Department of Health.

Moy, G., Singh, U., Tan, E. & Fearing, R. S. (2000). Human psychophysics for teletaction system design. *The Electronic Journal of Haptics Research, 1*(3).

Moyles, J. (2005). *The Excellence of Play*. Berkshire, UK: Open University Press.

Murray, S., & Gillham, M. (2003). *Investigating the use of a computer-based, interactive timetable designed for primary school children with Asperger's Syndrome* (p. P9). Lisboa: International-Autism-Europe Congress.

Murray, D. K. C. (1997). Autism and information technology: therapy with computers. In Powell, S., & Jordan, R. (Eds.), *Autism and Learning: A Guide to Good Practice* (pp. 100–115). London: David Fulton.

Murray, S. (2007). *An Interactive Classroom Timetable for Children with High-functioning Autism: Development and Qualitative Evaluation of a Computer-Based Timetable*. PhD Thesis. Queen Margaret University, UK.

NADP. (2009a, November). *Report on Disabled Students Allowances [DSAs] situation from the National Association of Disability Practitioners [NADP]*, Retrieved March 29, 2010, from http:www.nadp-uk.org/docs/resources/nadp-dsa-report-nov2009.doc

NADP. (2009b). *Evidence for Professor Sir Deian Hopkin's Review into Student Finance Delivery in England 2009*. Retrieved March 29, 2010, from http://www.nadp-uk.org/docs/resources/nadp-hopkins-review-submission.doc

Najafi, L., Friday, M., & Robertson, Z. (2008). Two case studies describing assessment and provision of eye gaze technology for people with servere physical disabilities. *Journal of Assistive Technologies, 2*(2), 6–12. doi:10.1108/17549450200800013

NAO - National Audit Office. (2007). *Staying the course: the retention of students in higher education*. Retrieved July 03, 2010, from http://www.nao.org.uk/publications/0607/student_retention_in_higher_ed.aspx

NAO National Audit Office (2002). *Widening Participation in Higher Education in England.*

NAO National Audit Office (2008). *Widening Participation in Higher Education.*

NAS (1999). Software for children with autism/Asperger Syndrome. *Communication*, Spring 1999, 13-16.

NAS. (1995). *Fact Sheet – Computers and people with Autism*. London: National Autistic Society.

NAS. (2001). *Ignored or ineligible? The reality for adults with autism spectrum disorders*. Retrieved October 15, 2010 from http://www.nas.org.uk/content/1/c4/28/61/ignored.pdf

NAS. (2005). *What is autism?* Retrieved November 1, 2005 from http://www.nas.org.uk/nas/jsp/polopoly.jsp?d=211.

NAS. (2008). *I Exist: The Message from Adults with Autism in England*. Retrieved November 12, 2010, from http://www.autism.org.uk/global/content/search%20results.aspx?q=I%20exist

NAS. (2010). *Computers: applications for people with autism*. Retrieved June 30, 2010 from http://www.autism.org.uk/en-gb/working-with/education/educational-professionals-in-schools/resources-for-teachers/computers-applications-for-people-with-autism.aspx.

NAS. (2010a). *What is autism?* Retrieved September 13, 2010 from http://www.autism.org.uk/About-autism/Autism-and-Asperger-syndrome-an-introduction/What-is-autism.aspx.

NAS. (2010a). What is Asperger syndrome? Retrieved September 15, 2010, fromhttp://www.autism.org.uk/en-gb/about-autism/autism-and-asperger-syndrome-an-introduction/what-is-asperger-syndrome.aspx

NAS. (2010b). *Computers: applications for people with autism*. Retrieved June 22, 2010 from http://www.autism.org.uk/en-gb/working-with/education/educational-professionals-in-schools/resources-for-teachers/computers-applications-for-people-with-autism.aspx.

NAS. (2010b). Statistics: how many people have autistic spectrum disorders? Retrieved October 30, 2010, fromhttp://www.autism.org.uk/About-autism/Some-facts-and-statistics/Statistics-how-many-people-have-autism-spectrum-disorders.aspx

NAS. (2010c). *Employment*. Retrieved November 1st, 2010, from http://www.autism.org.uk/living-with-autism/employment.aspx

NAS. Scotland (2010). *We Exist A Bill for Autism, A Bill for Scotland: Accept difference. Not indifference*. Retrieved October 14, 2010, from www.autism.org.uk/scotland

National Audit Office. (2010). *The Customer First Programme: Delivery of Student Finance*. London: NAO / BIS.

National Collaborating Centre for Mental Health. (2009). *Schizophrenia Core interventions in the treatment and management of schizophrenia in primary and secondary care*. London: The British Psychological Society /The Royal College of Psychiatrists.

National Disability Team (NDT) and Skill: National Bureau for Students with Disabilities (2004). *Aspiration raising and transition of disabled students from Further Education to Higher Education*.

National Working Party on Dyslexia in Higher Education. (1999). *Dyslexia in higher education: policy, provision and practice*. Hull: HEFCE.

Newell, A., & Gregor, P. (2000). "User sensitive inclusive design" – in search of a new paradigm. ACM Conference on Universal Usability, In *Proceedings of the 2000 conference on Universal Usability*, pp39-44. Retrieved from http://portal.acm.org/citation.cfm?id=355470

News, B. B. C. (2010). *Student loan bosses stand down*. Retrieved May 25, 2010, from http://news.bbc.co.uk/1/hi/education/10157509.stm

NHS. (2010). *Diabetic Retinopathy*. Retrieved 21st November, 2010, from http://www.cks.nhs.uk/patient_information_leaflet/diabetic_retinopathy#-461960

Nicolson, R. I. (2002). The Dyslexia Ecosystem. *Dyslexia (Chichester, England)*, *8*(2), 55–66. doi:10.1002/dys.218

Nielsen, J., & Mack, R. L. (1994). *Usability Inspection methods*. New York: Wiley.

NIMH. (2010). *Autism Spectrum Disorders (Prevalence Developmental Disorders)*. Retrieved November 20, 2010, from http://www.nimh.nih.gov/health/publications/autism/complete-index.shtml

Nimmo, C. (1994). Autism and Computers. *Communication*, *28*(2), 8–9.

Noffke, S. (1997). Professional, personal and political dimensions of action research. *Review of Research in Education, 22*(1), 305–343. doi:10.3102/0091732X022001305

Northumbria University. (2006). *Human Resources, Evaluation of Staff Training and Development: Guidance Notes*. Retrieved January 19, 2010, from http://northumbria.ac.uk/sd/central/hr/std/td_eval/

Oakley, I., McGee, M. R., Brewster, S., & Gray, P. (2000). *Putting the Feel in 'Look and Feel'*. Paper presented at the CHI 2000 Conference on Human Factors in Computing Systems, The Hague, Netherlands.

Oberleitner, R., Ball, J., Gillette, D., Naseef, R., & Hudnall Stamm, D. (2006). Technologies to lessen the distress of autism. *Journal of Aggression, Maltreatment & Trauma, 12*(1/2), 221–242. doi:10.1300/J146v12n01_12

ODI. (2010). *The social model of disability*. Retrieved December 10, 2010 from: http://www.officefordisability.gov.uk/about-the-odi/the-social-model.php.

Office of Public Sector Information. (2005). *Disability Discrimination Act (2005)*. Accessed at http://www.opsi.gov.uk/acts/acts1995., 1431, 19th March, 2010.

Office of Public Sector Information. (2007). *Mental Health Act (Amended) (2007)* Accessed http://www.opsi.gov.uk/acts/acts2007/ukpga 1435, 19th March, 2010.

Oliver, M. (1983). *Social Work and Disabled People*. Basingstoke: Macmillan.

Oliver, M. (1992). Changing the social relations of research production? *Disability, Handicap & Society, 7*(2), 101–114. doi:10.1080/02674649266780141

Osbourne, T. (1994). On Anti-medicine and clinical reason. In Jones, C., & Porter, R. (Eds.), *Reassessing Foucault: Power, Medicine and the Body*. London: Routledge.

Osler, A., & Osler, C. (2005). Inclusion, exclusion and children's rights. In Rix, J. (Eds.), *Policy and power in inclusive education: Values into practice* (pp. 107–118). London: Open University.

Ott, P. (1997). *How to Detect and Manage Dyslexia*. Oxford: Heinemann.

Owens, J. (2007). Liberating voices through narrative methods: The case for an interpretive research approach. *Disability & Society, 22*(3), 299–313. doi:10.1080/09687590701259617

Ozga, J. (2000). *Policy Research in Educational Settings*. Buckingham: Open University Press.

Page, T. (2009). *Text justification – issues and techniques*. Retrieved from http://www.pws-ltd.com/sections/articles/2009/justified_text.html

Papadopoulos, G., & Pearson, E., (2007). *Accessibility awareness raising and continuing professional development – The use of simulations as a motivational tool*. ALT online newsletter, Issue 7, January 2007.

Papworth Trust. (2008). *Key facts about disability*. Retrieved August 20th, 2010, from: www. papworth.org.uk/.../keyfactsaboutdisabilitynew_081103143956.pdf

Paradice, R. (2001). An investigation into the Social Construction of Dyslexia. *Educational Psychology in Practice, 17*(3), 213–225. doi:10.1080/02667360120072747

Parkes, D. (1988). *Nomad: an Audio-Tactile Tool for the Acquisition, Use and Management of Spatially Distributed Information by Partially Sighted and Blind Persons*. Paper presented at the Second International Symposium on Maps and Graphics for Visually Handicapped People, King's College, University of London.

Penn, P., Petrie, H., Colwell, C., Kornbrot, D., Furner, S. & Hardwick, A. (2001). *The Haptic Perception of Texture in Virtual Environments: An Investigation with Two Devices*. Paper presented at the First International Workshop on Haptic Human-Computer Interaction, Glasgow, UK.

Parsons, S., & Mitchell, P. (2002). The potential of virtual reality in social skills training for people with autistic spectrum disorders. *Journal of Intellectual Disability Research, 46*(5), 430–443. doi:10.1046/j.1365-2788.2002.00425.x

Parsons, S., Mitchell, P., & Leonard, A. (2004). The use and understanding of virtual environments by adolescents with autistic spectrum disorders. *Journal of Autism and Developmental Disorders, 34*(4), 449–466. doi:10.1023/B:JADD.0000037421.98517.8d

Parsons, S., & Wallace, S. (2006, October). *Inclusive design and development of Virtual Environments for social understanding of children with Autistic Spectrum Disorders: the 'Your World' project.* Paper presented at the Technology and Autism Conference Coventry University, UK.

Pearson, E. J., & Koppi, A. J. (2006). Supporting staff in developing inclusive online learning. In Adams, M., & Brown, S. (Eds.), *Towards Inclusive Learning in Higher Education* (pp. 56–66). London, New York: Routledge.

Peeters, T. (1995). The Best Treatment for Behaviour Problems is Prevention. *Communication,* Winter 1995 29-30.

Penney, D., Brooker, R., Hay, P., & Gillespie, L. (2009). Curriculum, pedagogy and assessment: three message systems of schooling and dimensions of quality physical education. *Sport Education and Society, 14*(4), 421–442. doi:10.1080/13573320903217125

Pennington R. C. (2010).*Computer-Assisted Instruction for Teaching Academic Skills to Students With Autism Spectrum Disorders: A Review of Literature.* In press for Focus on Autism and Other Developmental Disabilities.

Pick, D. (1989). *Faces of Degeneration: A European Disorder, c.1848-c1918.* Cambridge: Cambridge University Press. doi:10.1017/CBO9780511558573

Plymouth University. (2010). *Twenty-one things you need to know about current assessment practice for disabled students when considering inclusiveness.* Retrieved November 15, 2010, from http://www.plymouth.ac.uk/files/extranet/docs/SWA/3.%20Twenty-one%20things%20you%20need%20to%20know%20about%20current%20assessment%20practice%20for%20disabled%20students%20when%20considering%20inclusiveness.pdf

Poole, A. (2005). *Which are more legible: serif or sans serif typefaces?* Retrieved from http://www.alexpoole.info/academic/literaturereview.html

Potter, C., & Whittaker, C. (2001). *Enabling Communication in Children with Autism.* London, Philadelphia: Jessica Kingsley Publishers.

Powell, S., & Jordan, R. (1997). Rationale for the approach. In Powell, S., & Jordan, R. (Eds.), *Autism and Learning - A Guide to Good Practice* (pp. 1–14). London: David Fulton.

Powell, J. (1997). *Derrida for Beginners.* Danbury: For Beginners LLC.

Powell, N., Moore, D., Gray, J., Finlay, J., & Reaney, J. (2003). *Dyslexia and Learning Computer Programming.* In Proceedings of the 4th Annual Conference of the LTSN Centre for Information and Computer Sciences, Galway, Ireland, August 26-28. (pp. 11-16). Newtownabbey: LTSN-ICS.

Price, G., Upton, S., & Lewis, G. (2009). Providing lecture recordings for language students. *JISC TechDis HEAT Scheme.* Retrieved from http://www.jisctechdis.ac.uk/techdis/resources/detail/HEAT/HEAT_Round3_ABER301

Priestley, M. (1999). Discourse and Identity: Disabled Children in Mainstream High Schools. In Corker, M., & French, S. (Eds.), *Disability Discourse* (pp. 92–102). Buckingham: Open University Press.

Priestly, M. (2003). *Disability.* Cambridge, UK: Polity Press.

Prime Minister's Strategy Unit. (2005). *Improving the Life Chances of Disabled People.* Retrieved September 1st, 2010, from the Department of Health Website: http://www.cabinetoffice.gov.uk/media/cabinetoffice/strategy/assets/disability.pdf

Prosser, J., & Loxley, A. (2007). Enhancing the contribution of visual methods to inclusive education. *Journal of Research in Special Educational Needs, 7*(1), 55–68. doi:10.1111/j.1471-3802.2007.00081.x

Prout, A., & James, A. (1997). A New Paradign for the Sociology of Childhood? Provenance, Promise and Problems. In James, A., & Prout, A. (Eds.), *Constructing and Reconstructing Childhood.* London: Falmer Press.

Pumfrey, P. D., & Reason, R. (1997). *Specific Learning Difficulties (Dyslexia), Challenges and Responses.* London: Routledge.

Purkey, W. W. (1970). *Self-Concept and School Achievement.* New York: Prentice-Hall.

QAA. (2010). *Code of practice for the assurance of academic quality and standards in higher education.* Retrieved December 9, 2010 from http://www.admin.cam.ac.uk/univ/disability/practice/pdf/qaa.pdf

Quality Assurance Agency for Higher Education. second edition (2010*). Code of Practice for the Assurance of Academic Quality and Standards in Higher Education. Section 3: students with disabilities*. Gloucester: QAA.

Quality Assurance Agency for Higher Education. (1999). *Code of practice for the assurance of academic quality and standards in higher education, Section 3: Students with disabilities*. Retrieved September 19, 2007, from http://www.qaa.ac.uk/academicinfrastructure/codeOfPractice/section3/default.asp#3

Quality Enhancement Committee. (2010). *A report on the quality enhancement audit on the experiences of disabled students*. Academic Board Leeds Metropolitan University.

Quantock, P., Atlay, T., & Curtin, J. R. (2003). *work with me* (p. C54). Lisboa: International-Autism-Europe Congress.

Rajendran, G., & Mitchell, P. (2000). Computer mediated interaction in Asperger's syndrome: the Bubble Dialogue program. *Computers & Education, 35*, 187–207. doi:10.1016/S0360-1315(00)00031-2

Ranfelt, A. M., Wigram, T., & Øhrstrøm, P. (2009). Towards a Handy Interactive Persuasive Diary for Teenagers with a Diagnosis of Autism. In S. Chatterjee & P. Dev (Eds.) *Proceedings of the 4th International Conference on Persuasive Technology*. New York: ACM.

Read, J., & Masson, J. (2004). Genetics, eugenics and mass murder. In Read, J., Mosher, L., & Bentall, R. P. (Eds.), *Models of Madness: Psychological, Social and Biological Approaches to Schizophrenia*. Hove: Brunner Routledge. doi:10.4324/9780203420393_chapter_4

Red Cross. (2010). *The social model of disability*. Retrieved November 28, 2010 from http://www.redcross.org.uk/What-we-do/Teaching-resources/Teacher-briefings/Disability.

Reicher, S. (2001). Studying Psychology Studying Racism. In Augoustinos, M., & Reynolds, K. J. (Eds.), *Understanding Prejudice, Racism, and Social Conflict*. London: SAGE.

Renshaw, J. A. (2006). *Educational Assessment of Children and Adults with Profound Multiple Learning Difficulties using Eye Tracking Technology*. Private communication.

Report, T. 14-19 Curriculum and Qualifications Reform (2004). *DfES Publications*. Retrieved May 1, 2010, from http://www.dcsf.gov.uk/14-19/documents/Final%20Report.pdf

Rice, M., & Brooks, G. (2004). *Developmental dyslexia in adults: a research review*. London: NRDC.

Riddell, S., Tinklin, T., & Wilson, A. (2005). *Disabled Students in Higher Education; Perspective on widening access and changing policy*. London, New York: Routledge.

Riddell, S., Wilson, A., Adler, M., & Mordaunt, E. (2005). Parents, professionals and special education needs policy frameworks in England and Scotland. In Rix, J. (Eds.), *Policy and power in inclusive education: Values into practice* (pp. 72–84). London: Open University.

Rix, J., & Simmons, K. (2005). A world of change. In Rix, J. (Eds.), *Policy and power in inclusive education: Values into practice* (pp. 1–9). London: Open University.

RNIB. (2010). *National Centre for Tactile Diagrams*. Retrieved 21st November, 2010, from http://www.nctd.org.uk/

RNIB. (2010). *Prevalence Statistics*. Retrieved 3rd October, 2010, from http://www.rnib.org.uk/aboutus/Research/statistics/prevalence/Documents/2008_3_Revised-Prevalence_Stats_PDF.PDF

RNIB. (2010). *Reading Braille*. Retrieved 21st November, 2010, from http://www.rnib.org.uk/livingwithsightloss/readingwriting/braille/Pages/reading_braille.aspx

RNIB. (2010). *Supporting Tactile Graphics: Navigation*. Retrieved 21st November, 2010, from http://www.rnib.org.uk/professionals/accessibleinformation/accessible-formats/accessibleimages/tactilegraphics/supporting/Pages/navigation_strategies.aspx

Robbins, P. (2005). Q Methodology. In Kempf-Leonard, K. (Ed.), *Encyclopedia of Social Measurement* (pp. 209–215). Elsevier Inc. doi:10.1016/B0-12-369398-5/00356-X

Robins, B., Dautenhahn, K., te Boekhorst, R., & Billard, A. (2004). Effects of repeated exposure to a humanoid robot on children with autism. In Keates, S., Clarkson, J., Langdon, P., & Robinson, P. (Eds.), *Designing a More Inclusive World* (pp. 225–236). London: Springer-Verlag. doi:10.1007/978-0-85729-372-5_23

Robson, C. (1993). *Real World Research: A Resource for Social Scientists and Practitioner Researchers*. London: Blackwell.

Robson, C. (2007). *How to Do a Research Project a Guide for Undergraduate Students*. London: Blackwell.

Rock, P. (2001). Symbolic Interactionism and Ethnography. In Atkinson, P. (Eds.), *Handbook of Ethnography* (pp. 26–37). London: Sage.

Roets, G., & Goedgeluck, M. (2007). Daisies on the Road: Tracing the Political Potential of Our Postmodernist, Feminist Approach to Life Story Research. *Qualitative Inquiry*, *13*(1), 85–112. doi:10.1177/1077800406295624

Rogers, C. R. (1975). Empathic: An Unappreciated Way of Being. *The Counseling Psychologist*, *5*(2), 2–10. doi:10.1177/001100007500500202

Roschelle, J., Patton, C., & Tatar, D. (2007). Designing networked handheld devices to enhance school learning. In M. Zelkowitz (Ed.) *Advances in Computers, 70*, 1-60.

Rose, J. (2009). *Identifying and Teaching Children and Young People with Dyslexia and Literacy Difficulties, An independent report from Sir Jim Rose to the Secretary of State for Children, Schools and Families*. Nottingham: DCSF.

Roth, W.-M., & Lee, Y.-J. (2006). Contradictions in theorizing and implementing communities in education. *Educational Research Review*, *1*, 27–40. doi:10.1016/j.edurev.2006.01.002

Roth, W.-M., Tobin, K., Elmesky, R., Carambo, C., McKnight, Y.-M., & Beers, J. (2004). Re/Making Identities in the Praxis of Urban Schooling: A Cultural Historical Perspective. *Mind, Culture, and Activity*, *11*(1), 48–69. doi:10.1207/s15327884mca1101_4

Rovegno, I., & Dolly, J. P. (2006). Constructivist perspectives on learning. In Kirk, D., Macdonald, D., & O'Sullivan, M. (Eds.), *The Handbook of Physical Education*. London: Sage Publications.

Ryan, S., Scott, B., Freeman, H., & Patel, D. (2000). *The Virtual University: The Internet and resource-based learning*. Philadelphia, PA: Kogan Page.

Safran, S. P. (2008). Why Youngsters With Autistic Spectrum Disorders Remain Underrepresented in Special Education. *Remedial and Special Education*, *29*(2), 90–95. doi:10.1177/0741932507311637

Salomon, G. (1997). *Distributed cognitions: Psychological and educational considerations*. Cambridge: Cambridge University Press.

Salzberg, C. (2002). Opinions of disability service directors on faculty training: The need, content, issues, formats, media, and activities. *Journal of Postsecondary Education and Disability*, *15*(2), 101–114.

Salzberg, C. (2003). *Preparing Higher Education Faculty for Students with Disabilities: It's right; it's smart; and it should be mandatory*. Retrieved January 19, 2010, from http://asd.usu.edu/resources/files/preparing_faculty.pdf

Save the Children. (2000). *Children and Participation: Research, monitoring and evaluation with children and young people*. Belfast: Save The Children.

Sawyer, R. K. (2002). Unresolved Tensions in Sociocultural Theory: Analogies with Contemporary Sociological Debates. *Culture and Psychology*, *8*(3), 283–305.

Schlosser, R. W., & Sigafoos, J. (2006). Augmentative and alternative communication interventions for persons with developmental disabilities: Narrative review of comparative single-subject experimental studies. *Research in Developmental Disabilities*, *27*, 1–29. doi:10.1016/j.ridd.2004.04.004

Schlosser, R. W., & Blischak, D. M. (2001). Is there a role for speech output in interventions for persons with autism? *Focus on Autism and Other Developmental Disabilities*, *16*, 170–178. doi:10.1177/108835760101600305

Schmolck, P. (2010). *PQMethod Software*. Retrieved June 13, 2010, from http://www.lrz-muenchen.de/~schmolck/qmethod/

SCOTENS. (2010). *The Development of Education for Children with Special Educational Needs (NI)*. Retrieved November 28, 2010 from http://scotens.org/sen/articles/develofspecialedni.pdf

Scottish Higher Education Funding Council (SHEFC) (second edition 2004-5). *Teachability: Creating an accessible curriculum for students with disabilities*. Edinburgh, Scotland: SHEFC

Self, J. (1990). Bypassing the Intractable Problem of Student Modelling. In Frasson, F., & Gauthier, G. (Eds.), *Intelligent Tutoring Systems - at the Crossroads of AI and Education* (pp. 107–123). Norwood, New Jersey: Ablex Publishing Corporation.

Senda Special Educational Needs and Disability Act 2001 (2001). Retrieved November 01, 2010, from http://www.legislation.gov.uk/ukpga/2001/10/contents

SensAble Technologies. (2010). *PHANToM Haptic Devices*. Retrieved 30th March, 2010, from http://www.sensable.com/products-freeform-systems.htm

Shah, S. (2008). *Young Disabled People: Aspirations, Choices and Constraints*. Surrey, UK: Ashgate Publishing Ltd.

Shakespeare, T. (1997). Reviewing the Past, Developing the Future. *Skill Journal, 58*, 8–10.

Shakespeare, T. (2004). The social model of disability. In Davis, L. (Ed.), *The Disability Studies Reader* (2nd ed.). London: Routledge.

Siebers, T. (2006). Disability in Theory: From Social Constructionism to the New Realism of the Body. In Davis, L. (Ed.), *The Disability Studies Reader* (2nd ed.). London: Routledge.

Silver, M., & Oakes, P. (2001). Evaluation of a new computer intervention to teach people with autism or Asperger Syndrome to recognise and predict emotions in others. *Autism, 5*(3), 299–316. doi:10.1177/1362361301005003007

Silver, M. (2000) *Can people with autistic spectrum disorders be taught emotional understanding? The development and randomised controlled trial of a computer training package*. PhD thesis, University of Hull, UK.

Simmonds, C. (1993). The Asperger Student in a Mainstream Setting. In *Children with Asperger Syndrome, A Collection of Papers from Two Study Weekends run by the Inge Wakehurst Trust, 1992-1993*. London: The Inge Wakehurst Trust.

Sinclair, F., & Green, S. J. (1995). Assessing Autism Using Neural Nets - Subdividing the Autistic Continuum Using neural network Technology. In *Leadership for Creating Educational Change: Integrating the Power of Technology, Twelfth International Conference on Technology and Education* (Volume 2 pp 743-745).

Skill (1997). *The Coordinator's Handbook*. London, Skill: National Bureau for Students with Disabilities.

Skill: National Bureau for Students with Disabilities (2009). *Evidence for BIS / Professor Hopkin Review of Student Loans Company with specific reference to disabled students applying for Disabled Students' Allowance for entry October 2009 and onwards*. Retrieved March 29, 2010, from http://www.skill.org.uk/uploads/Skill_Hopkin%20Review_submission%20part%201.doc

Slee, R. (2009). The Inclusion Paradox: The Cultural Politics of Difference. In Apple, M. W., Au, W., & Gandin, L. A. (Eds.), *The Routledge International Handbook of Critical Education* (pp. 177–189). London: Routledge.

Smedley, J. (2009). Using podcasts and vodcasts in assessment and feedback practices in Law and Economics. *JISC TechDis HEAT Scheme*. Retrieved from http://www.jisctechdis.ac.uk/techdis/resources/detail/HEAT/HEAT_Round3_ECONLAW301

Smith, A. B. (2007). Children as Social Actors: An Introduction. *The International Journal of Children's Rights, 15*(1), 1–4. doi:10.1163/092755607X185537

Snyder, S. L., & Mitchell, D. T. (2006). *Cultural Locations of Disability*. Chicago: The University of Chicago Press.

South West Academic Network for Disability Support (SWANDS). (2002). *SENDA Compliance in higher education: An audit and guidance tool for accessible practice within the framework of teaching and learning*. Plymouth, England: University of Plymouth.

Stake, R. E. (1995). *The Art of Case Study Research*. London: SAGE.

Stalker, K. (1998). Some ethical and methodological issues in research with people with learning difficulties. *Disability & Society, 13*(1), 5–19. doi:10.1080/09687599826885

Stanley, L., & Wise, S. (1993). *Breaking Out Again*. London: Routledge.

Stanley, N., Ridley, J., Manthorpe, J., Harris, J., & Hurst, A. (2007, June). Dangerous disclosures. *Mental Health Today (Brighton, England)*, 24–27.

Stein, D. K. (2007). *Louis Braille: The Father of Literacy for the Blind*. Retrieved 19th November, 2010, from http://www.nfb.org/images/nfb/Publications/fr/fr28/fr280105.htm

Stephenson, W. (1935). Technique of factor analysis. *Nature, 136*, 297. doi:10.1038/136297b0

Stephenson, W. (1953). *The study of behaviour: Q-technique and its methodology*. Chicago: The University of Chicago Press.

Stetsenko, A. (2005). Activity as Object-Related: Resolving the Dichotomy of Individual and Collective Planes of Activity. *Mind, Culture, and Activity, 12*(1), 70–88. doi:10.1207/s15327884mca1201_6

Stevens, J. C. (1996). Tactile Acuity, Aging, and Braille Reading in Long Term Blindness. *Journal of Experimental Psychology. Applied, 2*(2), 91–106. doi:10.1037/1076-898X.2.2.91

Stevens, S. S. (1957). On the Psychophysical Law. *Psychological Review, 64*, 153–181. doi:10.1037/h0046162

Stokes, E. (2006b). *Teaching and Research into Multimedia Games for Pupils on the Autistic Spectrum*. Proceedings of the Autism and Technology Conference, Coventry University, 6th October 2006.

Stokes, S. (2006a). *Assistive technology for children with autism*. Retrieved October 3, 2006, from http://www.cesa7.k12.wi.us/sped/autism/assist/asst10.htm

Stringer, G. (2009, January 12). *Dyslexia is a myth*. Retrieved January 27, 2009, from www.manchesterconfidential.com

Student Loan Company (2008, October 21). *Letter of guidance from the Resolution Services Manager, Student Loan Company*. SLC: Doncaster.

Swain, J., & Cook, T. (2005). In the name of inclusion. In Rix, J. (Eds.), *Policy and power in inclusive education: Values into practice* (pp. 59–71). London: Open University.

Swettenham, J. (1996). Can Children with Autism be Taught to Understand False Belief Using Computers? *Journal of Child Psychology and Psychiatry, and Allied Disciplines, 37*(2), 157–165. doi:10.1111/j.1469-7610.1996.tb01387.x

Tabachnick, B., & Fidell, L. (2001). *Using multivariate statistics*. London: Allyn and Bacon.

Tanaka, J. W., Wolf, J. M., Klaiman, C., Kocning, K., Cockburn, J., & Herlihy, L. (2010). Using computerized games to teach face recognition skills to children with autism spectrum disorder: the Let's Face It! *Program. Journal of Child Psychology & Psychiatry, 51*(8), 944–952. doi:10.1111/j.1469-7610.2010.02258.x

Tantam, D. (1993). *A Mind of One's Own*. London: National Autistic Society.

TechDis. (2006a). *TechDis*. Retrieved January 19, 2010, from http://www.techdis.ac.uk/

TechDis. (2006b). *Sim-dis: A view into the unknown*. Retrieved January 19, 2010, from http://www.techdis.ac.uk/resources/sites/2/simdis/index.htm

TechDis. (2006c). *TechDis Staff Packs*. Retrieved January 19, 2010, from http://www.techdis.ac.uk/index.php?p=3_3

The Scottish Government. (2007). *Review of disabled students allowance project*. Retrieved August 03, 2010, from http://www.scotland.gov.uk/Resource/Doc/82254/0054157.pdf

Thomas, D. M., & Watson, R. T. (2002). Q-sorting and MIS research: A Primer. *Communications of the Association for Information Systems, 8*, 141–156.

Thomas, G. (2010). Doing Case Study: Abduction Not Induction, Phronesis Not Theory. *Qualitative Inquiry, 16*(7), 575–582. doi:10.1177/1077800410372601

Thompson, L. J., Chronicle, E. P., & Collins, A, F. (2006). Enhancing 2-D Tactile Picture Design from Knowledge of 3-D Haptic Object Recognition. *European Psychologist, 11*(2), 110–118. doi:10.1027/1016-9040.11.2.110

Tinklin, T., & Hall, J. (1999). Getting round obstacles: Disabled students' experiences in higher education in Scotland. *Studies in Higher Education, 2*(24), 183–194. doi:10.1080/03075079912331379878

Tjus, T., Heimann, M., & Lundalv, M. (2003). *Multimedia enhancement of language and reading skills* (p. C14). Lisboa: International-Autism-Europe Congress.

Tjus, T., Heimann, M., & Nelson, K. E. (2001). Interaction patterns between children and their teachers when using a specific multimedia and communication strategy: observations from children with autism and mixed intellectual disabilities. *Autism*, *5*(2), 175–187. doi:10.1177/1362361301005002007

Tjus, T., & Heimann, M. (2000). Language, multimedia and communication for children with autism– searching for the right combination. In Powell, S. (Ed.), *Helping children with autism to learn* (pp. 78–93). London: David Fulton publishers.

Tobii: Assistive Technology, Communication Solutions, Eye Control.(n.d.) Retrieved May 1, 2010, from http://www.tobii.com/assistive_technology.aspx.

Tomlinson, J. (1996). *Inclusive Learning: principles and recommendations*. Coventry: The Further Education Funding Council.

Tomlinson, J. (1996). *Inclusive FE, Report of the Learning Difficulties and/or Disabilities Committee, FEFC*. Retrieved November 28, 2010 from http://www.csie.org.uk/publications/tomlinson-96.pdf

Touch Graphics. (2010). *Talking Tactile Tablet*. Retrieved 30th March, 2010, from http://touchgraphics.com/OnlineStore/index.php/featured-products/talking-tactile-tablet-2-ttt.html

Trehin, P. (1996) *Computer Technology and Autism*. Retrieved November 26, 2010 from http://www.autism-resources.com/papers/LINK.htm

Tremain, S. (Ed.). (2009). *Foucault and the Government of Disability*. Michigan: The University of Michigan Press.

Tremain, S. (2006). On the Government of Disability: Foucault, Power, and the Subject of Impairment. In Davis, L. (Ed.), *The Disability Studies Reader* (2nd ed.). London: Routledge.

Tuceryan, M., & Jain, A. K. (1998). *Texture Analysis. The* (2nd ed., pp. 207–248). Handbook of Pattern Recognition and Computer Vision.

U.S. Department of Education, National Center for Education Statistics. (2006). *Question: What proportion of students enrolled in postsecondary education have a disability?* Retrieved January 19, 2010, from http://nces.ed.gov/fastfacts/display.asp?id=60

UK Government. (1995). *Disability Discrimination Act*. Retrieved from http://www.legislation.gov.uk/ukpga/1995/50/contents

UMUC. University of Maryland University College (2005). *Accessibility in Distance Education A Resource for Faculty in Online Teaching*. Retrieved January 19, 2010, from http://www.umuc.edu/ade/

UNESCO. The General Conference of the United Nations Educational Scientific and Cultural Organization (1960). *Convention against Discrimination in Education*. Retrieved January 19, 2010, from http://www.unhchr.ch/html/menu3/b/d_c_educ.htm

United Nations Article 13 (n.d.) Retrieved May 1, 2010, from http://www.unicef.org/cbsc/files/Articles12-13-17.pdf

University of Bradford. (n.d.). *IT Services Documentation*. Retrieved from http://www.brad.ac.uk/lss/documentation/

University of Exeter. (n.d.). *Personal Tutoring: Supporting Students with Disabilities*. Retrieved from http://as.exeter.ac.uk/support/staffdevelopment/aspectsofacademicpractice/personaltutoring/supportingstudentswithdisabilities/

University of York. (2005). *Touchy Feely Map Makes Life Easier on York Campus*. Retrieved 21st November, 2010, from http://www.york.ac.uk/admin/presspr/pressreleases/tactilemaps.htm

University of York. (2010). *Centre for Tactile Images*. Retrieved 21st November, 2010, from http://www.cs.york.ac.uk/tactileimages/

Valsiner, J. (2008). Ornamented Worlds and Textures of Feeling: The Power of Abundance. *Critical Social Studies*, (*1*),67-78.

Van Eeten, M. J. G. (2001). Recasting Intractable Policy Issues: The Wider Implications of the Netherlands Civil Aviation Controversy. *Journal of Policy Analysis and Management*, *20*(3), 391–414. doi:10.1002/pam.1000

Van Scoy, F., Kawai, T., Darrah, M., & Rash, C. (2000). Haptic display of mathematical functions for teaching mathematics to students with vision disabilities: design and proof of concept. *Haptic Human-Computer Interaction*, *2058*, 31–40. doi:10.1007/3-540-44589-7_4

Van Scoy, F., McLaughlin, D., & Fullmer, A. (2005). *Auditory Augmentation of Haptic Graphs: Developing a Graphic Tool for Teaching Precalculus Skill to Blind Students.* Paper presented at the Eleventh Meeting of the International Conference on Auditory Display (ICAD 05).

Vincent, C., & Warren, S. (2005). 'This won't take long….': interviewing, ethics and diversity. In K. Sheehy et al,(ed) *Ethics and Research in Inclusive Education* (pp.102-118). Abingdon: RoutledgeFalmer/OUP.

WAI-AGE Project. (2010). *European Commission IST Specific Support Action.* Apr 2007 – September 2010. Retrieved January 19, 2010, from http://www.w3.org/WAI/WAI-AGE/deliverables.html

Walmsley, J., & Johnson, K. (2003). *Inclusive research with people with intellectual disabilities. Past, present and futures.* London: Jessica Kingsley Publishing.

Warner, R. (1985: 2004). Recovery of Schizophrenia: Psychiatry and Political Economy. Hove: Brunner Routledge.

Warnock, M. (1978). *The Warnock Report: Special Educational Needs: Report of the Committee of Enquiry into the Education of Handicapped Children and Young People.* London: HMSO.

Wartofsky, M. (1979). *Models: Representation and scientific understanding.* Dordrecht: Reindel.

Waterfield, J., et al. (2006). Support inclusive practice: developing an assessment toolkit. In M, Adams & S, Brown (Eds.), *Towards Inclusive Higher Learning in Higher Education – Developing Curricula for disabled students* (pp 79-94). Abingdon: Routledge.

Waters, B. (2002). *Inclusion, Independence and Choice*, Address to the Universities UK Policy Conference, London 2002.

Watts, S., & Stenner, P. (2005). Doing Q methodology: theory, method and interpretation. *Qualitative Research in Psychology*, (2): 67–91. doi:10.1191/1478088705qp022oa

WebAIM – Center for Disabled Persons, Utah University. (2010a). Retrieved February 10, 2010, from http://www.webaim.org

WebAIM – Center for Disabled Persons, Utah University. (2010b). Retrieved February 10, 2010, from http://www.webaim.org/standards/wcag/checklist

Webb, N., & Renshaw, J. A. (2008). Eyetracking in HCI. In Cains, P., & Cox, A. L. (Eds.), *Research Methods for human-computer interaction* (pp. 35–69). Cambridge, UK: Cambridge University Press.

Weiner, G. (1994). *Feminisms in Education: An Introduction.* Buckingham: Open University Press.

Weller, S. (2007). *Teenagers' citizenship: experiences and education.* London: Routledge.

Wenger, E. (1998). *Communities of Practice – Learning, Meaning, and Identity.* Cambridge: Cambridge University Press.

Whitehead, M. (1990). *The concepts and principles Equity and Health.* Copenhagen: World Health Organisation. Retrieved August 03, 2010, from http://www.dhsspsni.gov.uk/ehr-introduction.pdf

Wies E. F., G. J. A., Sile O'Modhrain M., Hasser C. J. & Bulatov V. L. (2001). Web-based Touch Display for Accessible Science Education. *Haptic Human-Computer Interaction*, 52-60.

Wigger, U., & Mrtek, R. (1994). Use of Q-technique to examine attitudes of entering pharmacy students toward their profession. *American Journal of Pharmaceutical Education, 58*, 8–15.

Wilkinson, M. (2009). *Defying Disability: The Lives and Legacies of Nine Disabled Leaders.* London: Jessica Kingsley Publishers.

Williams, J. H. G., Massaro, D. W., Peel, N. J., & Bosseler, A. (2004). Visual-auditory integration during speech imitation in autism. *Research in Developmental Disabilities, 25*, 559–575. doi:10.1016/j.ridd.2004.01.008

Williams, D. (1996). *Autism An Inside – Out Approach: An innovative look at the mechanics of autism and its developmental cousins.* London and Bristol, UK: Jessica Kingsley.

Williams, V., & Simons, K. (2005). More researching together: the role of nondisabled researchers in working with People First members. *British Journal of Learning Disabilities, 33*, 6–14. doi:10.1111/j.1468-3156.2004.00299.x

Williams, V. (2003). *User-led research with people with learning difficulties.* Exeter: University of Exeter Centre for Evidence-Based Social Services

Wing, L. (1996). *Autism Spectrum Disorders*. London: Constable.

Wing, L. (1996). *The Autism Spectrum: A Guide for Parents and Professionals*. London: Constable.

Wolfgang, P., & Ostroff, E. (Eds.). (2001). *Universal Design Handbook*. New York: McGraw-Hill.

Wolman, D. (2010). The autie advantage. *New Scientist, 1*(May), 33–35.

Yates, P. (1993). Social Skills Training. In *Children with Asperger Syndrome, A Collection of Papers from Two Study Weekends run by the Inge Wakehurst Trust, 1992-1993*, London: The Inge Wakehurst Trust.

Yu, W., & Brewster, S. A. (2002). *Multimodal Virtual Reality Versus Printed Medium in Visualization for Blind People*. ACM ASSETS.

Yu, W., & Kangas, K. (2003). *Web-based haptic applications for blind people to create virtual graphs.* Paper presented at the 11th Symposium on Haptic Interfaces for Virtual Environment and Teleoperator Systems, Los Angeles, California.

Yu, W., Ramloll, R., & Brewster, S. A. (2000). *Haptic graphs for blind computer users*. Paper presented at the First Workshop on Haptic Human-Computer Interaction.

Zimler, J., & Keenan, J. M. (1983). Imagery in the Congenitally Blind: How Visual are Visual Images? *Journal of Experimental Psychology. Learning, Memory, and Cognition, 9*(2), 269–282. doi:10.1037/0278-7393.9.2.269

About the Contributors

David Moore is a principal lecturer in the Computing and Information Systems department of the Faculty of Arts, Environment and Technology, Leeds Metropolitan University. He has published widely in the field of computer technology for people with autism. He set up and now chairs Leeds Metropolitan University's Disability Research Group, the annual conferences of which generated much of the material for this book.

Andrea Gorra is a lecturer in the Business School at Leeds Metropolitan University (UK) in the Business Analysis and Strategy group. As part of her work for the Centre for Excellence in Teaching and Learning - Active Learning in Computing, she has been involved in disability related research projects that provide advice and guidance to university teaching staff on how they may best cater for the needs of students with disabilities. Andrea's primary research interests include disability, grounded theory methodology and the use of social software and mobile devices for assessment, learning and teaching. Andrea holds a Ph.D. from Leeds Metropolitan University in the area of mobile communications and privacy, an MSc in E-Commerce, as well as a degree in Business-Computing from the University of Applied Sciences Dortmund, Germany.

Mike Adams is Chief Executive of ECDP, an Essex based user-led disabled people's organization. ECDP delivers a range of support services and provides a representative voice of disabled people across the county. Mike's previous working track record includes being one of the senior management team at the Disability Rights Commission, Director of the National Disability Team for Higher Education, co-director of a research centre and a disability officer at Coventry University. He recently completed a three year visiting professorship in Inclusive Learning at Leeds Metropolitan University. Mike is a widely recognized international thought leader in disability issues with a strong publication record.

John Reaney is Disability Services Manager at Leeds Metropolitan University. He has many years experience working with disabled people and also of management roles in both industry and education. He has worked in a specialist college for deaf people and has a hearing impairment himself. His interests include cultural identity and language and in particular the idea of 'thirdspace' which was the topic of his MA dissertation.

Helen Smith has been the co-ordinator of a collaborative partnership of West Yorkshire Higher Education Institutions known as Higher Education Aspiration Raising – West Yorkshire (HEAR WY) for the past eight years. The partnership has as its aim to share best practice and work together to develop and deliver 'widening participation' projects. Helen is also the West Yorkshire Aimhigher Disability Co-ordinator, seeking to actively encourage disabled young people to make informed choices about higher education.

***

Chris Adams is a graduate of the University of Sheffield, now residing in Leeds, UK. With over ten years experience of working in the area of Disability Support within Higher Education, the author has been a Learning Facilitator for seven years. He has gained considerable experience in assisting students with autism spectrum condition, both socially and academically. Furthermore, he is employed by Stat-northern (UK) as a specialist Disability-Related Information and Communication Technology trainer.

Simon Ball leads the work of the JISC TechDis Service in Higher Education, in addition to leading on E-Assessment across the sectors. Simon has recently launched the research paper *12 Steps Towards Embedding Inclusive Practice with Technology as a Whole Institution Culture* (see www.jisctechdis. ac.uk/techdis/resources/detail/goingdigital/TCI_Report). This paper is accompanied by a briefing aimed at senior managers in HE institutions setting out clear steps they can take to achieve a more inclusive use of technology across their institution. Simon has also managed the JISC TechDis HEAT Scheme (www. jisctechdis.ac.uk/techdis/pages/detail/workinginpartnership/The_HEAT_Scheme) and co-developed an online self-evaluation and benchmarking tool for accessible and inclusive practice (www.jisctechdis. ac.uk/techdis/userneeds/auditing/onlineassessmentservices). He has co-authored material on the accessibility benefits and barriers of virtual worlds, the development of an accessible e-portfolio for students with learning disabilities, and the accessibility of e-book platforms.

Brian Boullier is Head of Information, Communication and Assistive Technology at the Hollybank Trust. He has a broad range of experience, commencing his career in biomedical research and academia before expanding into the rapidly advancing fields of educational technology and 'new media'. He has travelled widely as a consultant and currently specialises in media production and corporate IT management.

Sally Brown is Emeritus Professor of Higher Education Diversity in Teaching and Learning at Leeds Metropolitan University and was until July 2010 Pro Vice Chancellor (Academic). Sally is a champion of diversity in education and is at the forefront of the University's work in this area. She was for 5 years Director of Membership Services for the Institute for Learning and Teaching, prior to which she worked at the University of Northumbria at Newcastle for almost 20 years as a lecturer, educational developer and Head of Quality Enhancement. She is a National Teaching Fellow and was awarded a £200,000 NTFS (National Teacher Fellow Scheme) grant for three years to research Innovative Assessment at Masters level. She is widely published, largely in the field of teaching, learning and assessment and has recently collaborated on a number of publications on best practice in relation to inclusive learning and internationalisation in the education context. Sally is also a workshop facilitator and keynote speaker at conferences and events in the UK and internationally.

Ian Clarke is Equality and Diversity manager at Leeds Metropolitan University. He has an M.Ed. from Leeds University and is a trained teacher, trainer and mediator. Previously Ian has worked in Student Services and led on disability support in a further education college. Ian has also led on curriculum development in a further education context to support young people and adults with disabilities into post-compulsory education and training.

Bridget Cooper is currently Professor of Education in the Centre for Pedagogy at the University of Sunderland and before that worked at Leeds Metropolitan University, Leeds University and the Open University in teacher education and research. Previously she worked in primary, secondary and adult education in various capacities for 15 years. She has a variety of research interests including affective issues and human relationships in education, moral education, ICT in education, artificial intelligence, special educational needs, literacy and language and teacher education and has authored a range of publications and projects.

Damian Copeland is a development manager and interface analyst for a software company specialising in automated systems. His professional background is in the field of e-learning and speech recognition and he has been working in interaction design for over 20 years. He was awarded a PhD from Leeds Metropolitan University in 2008 for his research into haptic graphic displays. He has spoken at a number of conferences and symposia on the subject of haptic graphics and has published papers on the subject in international journals. In addition to his professional life, Dr Copeland remains an active researcher within the field of human computer interaction and he is an associate lecturer with the Open University's Faculty of Mathematics, Computing and Technology.

Tim Deignan is an independent researcher, consultant and trainer. He worked as a lecturer and manager in the post-compulsory education and training sector for ten years before going freelance in 2000. Tim acts as a consultant for a range of clients in the public and private sectors, working on projects at local, regional, national, and international level. His work typically involves modeling different values and perspectives on complex issues in order to improve system performance. His interests include sociocultural theory, learning support and education reform.

Pauline Dowd was the first research manager in the Further Education Sector in Northern Ireland and has managed the Centre for Applied Research & Development in the Belfast Metropolitan College (previously Belfast Institute) for almost nine years. Pauline has been the lead researcher on a range of student research projects examining areas such as disability and the workplace, supported learning, key skills and entrepreneurship. She has managed research activities for external organisations including the Department for Employment & Leaning (DEL), the British Council, LSDA, Queen's University Belfast and the University of Ulster and she has worked collaboratively with a range of other organisations. Pauline has written and published reports based on the research she has managed and has had articles published in the local press including the *Belfast Telegraph*, the *Irish News,* the *Tatler* and the *Ulster Business Magazine*. The findings of her work have been used by a number of organisations including the Northern Ireland Colleges and Universities and the Scottish Parliament Inclusive Learning Inquiry.

Salima Y. Awad Elzouki gained her first degree in Industrial Engineering in Libya where she developed her interest in human interaction with machines. After obtaining a Master's degree from City University, Dublin, in Engineering Education, she commenced a PhD at Leeds Metropolitan University

(Leeds Met) in the area of Human Computer Interaction (HCI) and education. Currently she is completing her thesis, which evaluates the success of students with severe autism in learning how to recognise facial expressions via computers. As part of her PhD she worked for a year as a volunteer in a unit for children with severe autism and learning difficulties, where she gained considerable experience in this area. During her study at Leeds Met she also worked as a researcher on a project concerning students with autism in Higher Education and acted as research assistant to a member of staff with autism.

Hayley Fitzgerald is a Senior Lecturer in Sociological aspects of Sport at the Carnegie Faculty, Leeds Metropolitan University, England. Prior to taking this position Hayley worked as a researcher at Loughborough University and managed the evaluation of a range of national and regional projects focusing on disability and youth sport. She has also worked for a number of disability sport organisations in England. Hayley has extensive experience of developing accessible and participatory research strategies. Theoretically, Hayley's work draws on disability studies, the sociology of physical education and sport and the work of Pierre Bourdieu. Hayley recently edited a book called *Disability and Youth Sport*.

Stewart Geddes is currently the Enrichment Manager, Hollybank Trust, England with responsibility for managing the adult services provision at Hollybank including post 19 education, activities, work based and creative arts projects in West Yorkshire. Previous appointments include: Special Needs PMLD Teacher in Hollybank School (2001- 2006) teaching music, art and drama, Course Tutor SLD/PLMD Barnsley FE College (1998-2001) where he established arts group with Corridor Arts on relationships and sexuality using music and film making for people with learning difficulties, Resource Centre Manager for Delos Community managing services for adults with learning difficulties (1996- 1998), Provision Leader PMLD/SLD Huddersfield FE College (1994-1996), Creative Director - No Limits Experimental Theatre Company -adults with learning difficulties (1994), Freelance Community Artist, running drama, music and art workshops for children and adults with learning difficulties (1990-1994).

John Gray has held lecturing posts at a number of universities in the North West of England since 1990. His last post was Associate Dean at the Innovation North Faculty of Leeds Metropolitan University in 2007. Currently he is a self employed educational consultant who has been involved in supporting and project managing a variety of JISC funded projects focused on technology enhanced learning together with the use of coaching to support personalised learning. His particular interests include staff development, computer –assisted assessment and the impact of disability on the student learning experience.

Elizabeth Guest is a Reader in the Faculty of Arts, Environment and Technology at Leeds Metropolitan University. She obtained her PhD at Edinburgh University in 1995 in the area of Image Processing. The methods she developed as part of this PhD are still state of the art. Past funded projects include signal processing for identifying concealed weapons or explosives without having to search them and automatic marking of short free text answers. She has invented solutions for non-linear image registration, 3D surface matching, finding robust correspondences on 2 and 3D images, a method for parsing sentences for languages with varying degrees of word order flexibility, a new framework for semantics, and a new method for identifying keywords in text.

Gill Harrison has been a Senior Lecturer in the Computing and Information Technologies group within the Faculty of Arts, Environment and Technology at Leeds Metropolitan University since 1998.

She is a Teacher Fellow and a member of the University's Technology Enhanced Learning Team, with interests in staff development, disability, peer observation and computer-assisted assessment. Her experience outside Leeds Metropolitan University includes many years with the Open University as well as commercial experience in software development.

Hanim Hassan is pursuing her studies at the Leeds Metropolitan University. Her doctoral thesis investigates the support for students with specific learning difficulties in higher education. Previously attached to a number of leading government agencies in Malaysia, she has developed strong interests in issues related to diversity and equality especially in the areas of teaching and learning.

Alan Hurst, formerly Professor in the Department of Education, University of Central Lancashire, Preston, England is a trustee of Skill: National Bureau for Students with Disabilities and chairs its Higher Education Working Party. Alan has degrees from the universities of Hull, Manchester and Lancaster. He has published books and articles and been invited to lecture and lead workshops on disability in higher education in many countries. He was awarded an honorary doctorate by the Open University in June 2005 for his contribution to developing policy and provision for disabled students. His most recent publication is a handbook for mainstream staff developers on supporting disabled students. Having retired from his full time post in 2007 he is currently working with many organisations and institutions in both the UK and abroad on developing high quality inclusive policies and provision. He was a member of the group established by the Higher Education Funding Council for England to review its policies on disabled students since 1997 and of the group set up by the Quality Assurance Agency to devise an updated version of the Code of Practice. In 2007 he was the recipient of the Myriam Van Acker Prize, an award made every three years by staff working worldwide in disability support in higher education in recognition of his work over many years.

Anne Jobling is an Adjunct Professor at the University of Queensland, Australia. Until recently Anne was the Co-Director of the Down Syndrome Research Programme and managed a Literacy and Technology Course – Hands On (LATCH-ON). This course offers continuing education for individuals experiencing intellectual disability. Anne's major research covers lifelong aspects of development related to motor development and health as well as education and self regulation. Other interests include inclusive education, play, leisure and recreation for people with disabilities and transdisciplinary teamwork in education environments. She is a member of the Editorial Board of a number of journals including the *International Journal of Disability, Development and Education*.

Ailsa Moore is Deputy Headteacher at Hollybank Trust. She is qualified in early years education but has worked in special needs for most of her career, teaching across all key stages. Her current research interest is learner autonomy and pupil voice for students with PMLD and complex needs.

William, J. Penson is a University Teacher Fellow and Senior Lecturer in Mental Health at Leeds Metropolitan University and a Fencing Coach at Bradford University. He worked in mental health practice for eleven years mainly in social care and the charitable sector. He has an interest in developing a cross fertilisation of ideas between humanities and human sciences.

Tony Renshaw is a senior lecturer at Leeds Metropolitan University. His specialist discipline is human computer interaction and his research interests include how people interact with computers, films and games and how these interactions might be captured. He has been responsible for the development of new and improved eye tracking metrics which have greatly enhanced the analysis techniques available for the interpretation of eye movements and human computer interactions. Tony graduated from Loughborough University of Technology in Chemistry and Management Studies and has held a variety of senior positions as a Financial Manager on the board of REACT Centre Ltd, the Prison Service and in the Services Division of Internal Computers Limited. His interests include science, photography, walking and DIY.

Jakki Sheridan-Ross is a Learning Technologist working cross-institution for the Assessment, Learning and Teaching service at Leeds Metropolitan University. As a Research Fellow for CETL ALiC, the Centre for Excellence in Teaching and Learning, Active Learning in Computing, she was involved in the research, development and construction of a computer assisted assessment tool to raise awareness of the types of challenges faced by people with certain disabilities when using computers. Prior to completing her first degree at Leeds Metropolitan University in 2004, Jakki was a principal local government officer managing an innovative One Stop Enquiry Centre. The One Stop Centre handled face-to-face enquiries from over 1000 customers each day, many of whom had disability or accessibility problems and had faced barriers in their ability to access crucial services. Jakki's research currently includes the use of social media tools, student group-work, and appropriate tools to enhance the student learning experience in creative and engaging ways.

Annette Stride is a Lecturer in Sport Business Management at the Carnegie Faculty, Leeds Metropolitan University, England. Prior to this Annette taught on sport, leisure and physical education courses at a number of educational institutions and most recently was the Curriculum Leader for Sport and Public Services at Bradford College, Yorkshire, England. Here she initiated a successful partnership between non-disabled sports students and the Personal and Community Skills course (supporting students with physical and learning disabilities). Annette's research interests focus on equity in physical education and sport and she is working on a PhD focusing on issues concerned with gender and ethnicity.

Index